GUIZOT

STUDIES IN POLITICAL HISTORY

Editor : Michael Hurst

Fellow of St John's College, Oxford

GUIZOT

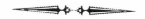

Aspects of French History
1787-1874

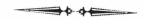

by
DOUGLAS JOHNSON

GREENWOOD PRESS, PUBLISHERS
WESTPORT, CONNECTICUT

Library of Congress Cataloging in Publication Data

Johnson, Douglas W   J
    Guizot : aspects of French history, 1787-1874.

    Reprint of the ed. published by Routledge &
K. Paul, London, in series: Studies in political
history.
    Bibliography: p.
    Includes index.
    1. Guizot, François Pierre Guillaume, 1787-1874.
DC255.G8J6 1975   944.06'092'4 [B]   75-35335
ISBN 0-8371-8566-1

Originally published in 1963 by Routledge & Kegan Paul Ltd, London

Reprinted with the permission of Routledge & Kegan Paul, Ltd.

Reprinted in 1975 by Greenwood Press,
a division of Williamhouse-Regency Inc.

Library of Congress Catalog Card Number 75-35335

ISBN 0-8371-8566-1

Printed in the United States of America

EDITOR'S NOTE

UNLIKE so many history series this one will not attempt a complete coverage of a specific span of time, with a division of labour for the contributors based on a neat parcelling out of centuries. Nor will it, in the main, be a collection of political monographs. Rather, the aim is to bring out books based on new, or thoroughly reinterpreted material ranging over quite a wide field of chronology and geography. Some will be more general than others, as is to be expected when biography is included alongside of detailed treatment of some comparatively short period of crisis like the appeasement of the Axis Powers. Nevertheless, whatever mode of presentation may have been appropriate, each work should provide an exposition of its subject in context and thus enable the reader to acquire new knowledge amidst things he knows, or could have known.

MICHAEL HURST

St. John's College,
Oxford.

CONTENTS

PLATES

ACKNOWLEDGEMENTS

I WISH to thank Monsieur Jean Schlumberger for all the help he has given towards this book, for his courtesy in allowing me access to the papers of Guizot and for his hospitality at the Val-Richer.

My thanks too to Monsieur de Félice for his assistance when I consulted material belonging to the Société de l'Histoire du Protestantisme Français in Paris, and to the General Editor of this series, Mr. Michael Hurst of St. John's College, Oxford, for his help in preparing the manuscript for publication. I am grateful to many of my colleagues for their advice and encouragement, amongst whom I would like to mention Professor H. A. Cronne, Professor H. S. Ferns, Professor J. A. Hawgood, Professor T. J. B. Spencer and Miss Margaret Tillett. I also wish to thank Mrs. Anne Hutton for having typed the manuscript.

Lastly I would like to say that I had the good fortune to be a pupil of Professor Charles Pouthas of the University of Paris, and that I owe much to his knowledge of all things connected with Guizot.

DOUGLAS JOHNSON

Birmingham; Saint-Servan-sur-mer.

'Un homme considérable dont il y a tant à dire'

SAINTE-BEUVE

I
INTRODUCTION

'Je suis de ceux que l'élan de 1789 a élévés et qui ne con-
sentiront point à descendre.'   GUIZOT

GUIZOT once said that he had had three lives: one literary,
one political and one religious; he hoped that people would
be able to see the connection between them.[1]

Guizot was a proud man, but he was not given to boasting. Had
he wanted, he could have shown that he had had a great many
different types of activity. He had started to earn a living as a
journalist, from 1807 onwards contributing regularly to reviews, and
producing work on language, literature and art, before turning more
decidedly in the direction of politics and becoming a successful
pamphleteer. From 1812 Guizot was a Professor of History in the
University of Paris; some years later his lectures on the history of
civilization in Europe and in France were an outstanding success;
they represented a work of analysis, but Guizot also made a study of
the English Revolution during the seventeenth century which was a
work of narrative and of detail, and his final historical production
was a history of France written especially for his grandchildren.
After 1814 he entered politics as an official of the Ministry of the
Interior; after 1830 he was a deputy and was minister in a number of
different cabinets, eventually becoming Prime Minister. During the
Restoration he was associated with liberalism and was a severe critic
of several administrations; during the July Monarchy he was
associated with conservatism and was a defender of the established
order. Early in his career he had interested himself in problems of
child psychology and pedagogy, and in 1832 he became Minister for

---

[1] Guizot: Mme Lenormant, October 1st, 1865, *Lettres à M. et Mme Lenormant.*
Les Années de Retraite de Monsieur Guizot, Paris 1902, p. 245. Mme Lenormant
was a niece of Mme Récamier; Lenormant was an archaeologist who became
director of the Catholic review *Le Correspondant.*

1

Public Instruction, founding by legislation the system of primary education in France. Brought up as a Protestant, he passed through a phase of scepticism, and then went on to become one of the most prominent administrators of the French Protestant Church and one of the acknowledged spokesmen of its orthodox theology. Whether in the Chamber of Deputies or in the Académie Française, Guizot was accepted as one of the greatest orators of France; whether in his innumerable publications or in his private correspondence, he wrote in a style which was outstanding for its clarity and force; in political or religious societies, or in international diplomacy, which he knew both as French ambassador in London and as minister for foreign affairs, Guizot was a capable administrator and statesman. His career was thus varied; stretching from the Empire to the years following the Franco-Prussian War, this career was also long. Even in the nineteenth century, and even in France, it was rare to achieve distinction in so many different ways.

François-Pierre-Guillaume Guizot was born in Nîmes on October 4th, 1787. He was the first child of André Guizot and his wife (née Sophie-Élisabeth Bonicel), both of whom were Protestants. André Guizot was a moderately prosperous lawyer, who seems to have been growing in wealth and power about this time. As an intellectual and as a 'bourgeois' he welcomed the Revolution (there is possibly some significance in the name Jean-Jacques which he gave to his second son, born in October 1789). He became a prominent member of the local *Club des Amis de la Constitution*, whilst his father-in-law, Bonicel, had contacts with the democratic party. He was, however, soon caught up in the Federalist movement which represented the opposition of much of provincial France to events in Paris, to the overthrow of the Gironde and to the seizure of power by the Commune and the Mountain. After the failure of this movement he returned to Nîmes, apparently protected by the influence of Bonicel. This protection seemed to be sufficient, for when in October 1793 an order was made for his arrest, André Guizot merely hid in his own house. But in January 1794 a new warrant was issued and this time he took to the hills. In April he was caught, rapidly tried, and executed. His estates were confiscated, and until they were restored, towards the end of 1795, Madame Guizot was without any resources of her own. In 1799 she moved to Geneva with her two sons, and it was in this town that François Guizot was educated at the Collège and at the Academy.

In 1805 Guizot came to Paris, intending to study law, but he rapidly became involved in the literary life of the capital. Through a friend from Nîmes, Mira Chabaud, whom at one time he had wanted to marry in spite of her being fourteen years his senior, he was introduced into the household of Paul-Albert Stapfer, a former minister of the Helvetic Republic who was then living in Paris and who was looking for a tutor for his two sons. Until 1810 Guizot occupied this post, and through Stapfer he was presented to a wide circle of acquaintances, amongst whom was notably Suard, the perpetual secretary of the Académie Française, who gave Guizot the opportunity of contributing to certain reviews. Through this and other openings Guizot began to enlarge the possibility of his work. In 1809 he published a Dictionary of Synonyms; in 1810 his account of the Salon; in 1811 a translation of a book by Rehfues on Spain, whilst from 1808 he was engaged in editing and translating Gibbon's *Decline and Fall*.

In his work on Gibbon Guizot was helped by Pauline de Meulan, who was also in Suard's circle of friends. The circumstances of their meeting are well known. Because of illness, Pauline de Meulan found difficulty in writing her articles for *Le Publiciste*, and since it was by her writing that she supported her family, this was a particularly difficult situation for her. Guizot offered his services anonymously, and wrote articles which were published in her name. He later presented himself to her and they began to collaborate together. From 1811 to 1814 they edited the review *Annales de l'Éducation*, which they had jointly founded. In 1812 they were married.

But Guizot did not only have literary ambitions. He had tried to get a post in the Ministry of Foreign Affairs, through the influence of Madame de Rémusat, the cousin of Pasquier, Prefect of Police. This attempt was not successful, but when the Grand Maître de l'Université, Fontanes, was looking for someone to teach modern history, Suard recommended Guizot and he was appointed in December 1812. At the University, Guizot became the colleague of the Professor of Philosophy, Royer-Collard, who became one of his closest friends. Guizot had already met certain of the philosophers who were prominent in the movement which was criticizing eighteenth-century materialism; he had met Maine de Biran and de Gérando at Stapfer's, and during 1814 Guizot, along with Royer-Collard, Gérando, Victor Cousin, Ampère and the Cuviers, used to attend meetings organized by Maine de Biran, which Sainte-Beuve called 'un laboratoire de psychologie'.[1] In this way Guizot became associated with 'l'opposition idéologique', an opposition which was both restrained and restricted, being intellectual rather than political.

Guizot's friendship with Royer-Collard was to have further consequences. In 1814, when the signs of Napoleon's downfall were increasingly evident, Imperial officials entered into a series of negoti-

[1] *Sainte-Beuve, Causeries du lundi*, Paris (3rd ed.), vol. xiii, p. 318.

ations which they hoped would enable them to keep their posts under a new government. They favoured the moderate brand of royalism, and the abbé de Montesquiou, who became a member of the provisional government, was acceptable to them. With the Restoration proper he was made Minister of the Interior, and he called on his friend and political associate Royer-Collard, to assist him in his ministry. Royer-Collard took over the Librairie, or Publications, section of the Ministry and brought with him two other friends. One was Becquey, who became Director of the Agricultural section, and the other was Guizot, who became Secretary-General of the Ministry.

Thus Guizot, who had arrived in Paris without friends and without wealth, had at the age of twenty-six reached an important post at a crucial moment in French history. It is worth while pausing a moment to see exactly how it was that Guizot had made such rapid progress. One must immediately say that up till 1814, none of his publications had had any notable success. None of the articles, on a variety of subjects, scattered through several periodicals, was of much importance. Many of them, particularly those in *Le Publiciste*, were little more than summaries of books, with the addition of a few general remarks. Reading them now, it is disappointing to find that Guizot was so chary of giving his own opinion, or that a young man should be so hesitant at praising some great work, such as *Werther*, or so insistent upon the 'dangers' of certain types of writing. The books and editions for which he was responsible were works of reference or erudition, rather than works of original creation; Guizot himself said of some of them that they were not very brilliant.[1] Nor is any explanation for Guizot's success to be found in his political ideas. He does not seem to have evolved any definite system of politics; he was not part of any clearly defined political group, the success of which he could share. He later claimed that, at this time, he was not particularly interested in politics.

To understand Guizot's success one must try to understand the society in which he found himself. In an article written in 1829, he recalled the salons which he had known, the salon of the Suards which was held on Tuesdays and Saturdays, of the Countess d'Houdetot which took place on Wednesdays, of the abbé Morellet on Thursdays. He recalled these ruins of another age with some affection, but when he criticized this intellectual, philosophical society as being weak and isolated, existing without precise intentions or determined objects, he described French society towards the end

---

[1] *Le Publiciste*, April 1st, 1809; Guizot: Prévost (undated, possibly January 1809), *Prévost MSS.* Bibliothèque Publique et Universitaire, Geneva. There is a typescript copy of this correspondence in the Library of the Société de l'Histoire du Protestantisme Français in Paris.

of the Empire.[1] There was a small and restricted 'élite' which was separated from the world of affairs and commerce, cut off from the bulk of the population, without any contact with the army, and yet this society played a great part in the appointment and recruitment of officials. At a time when there was no great movement of opinions and no established principles or maxims of conduct, advancement was dependent upon personal recommendation. People were observant, critical, cynical; but they were tolerant, inactive, simply expectant. This was not a time for gestures; it was rather a time for a young man to make influential friends and to make himself generally acceptable.

This is precisely what Guizot did. He afterwards spoke of himself as having lived, during the Empire, in 'la société de l'opposition'.[2] But this was hardly the word for it. The only real opposition was that of conspirators, such as Semallé, or adventurers, such as General Malet, and Guizot never had anything to do with them. The opposition with which Guizot was associated was one of conversation; even Suard's salon has been described as 'neutral'.[3] Not only was Guizot a successful candidate for a post in the Imperial hierarchy, but when he wished to found the *Annales de l'Éducation* the police reported favourably on him.[4] In a sense, even his luke-warm Protestantism was a help. It separated him from the Catholics and from the worst reactionaries, since no Protestant could look back to the Ancien Régime with any enthusiasm; it distinguished him from the rationalism which had supposedly led to the excesses of revolutionary impiety. Guizot knew how to make himself affable and was a skilful and impressive talker.[5] He was self-confident and bold; he did not hesitate, for example, to present himself to Madame de Staël at Ouchy, near to Lausanne (unwittingly arriving at a moment when relations between her and Benjamin Constant were particularly difficult). Above all he was learned and industrious; through these qualities he could make himself indispensable. Chateaubriand prefaced the first edition of *L'Itinéraire de Jerusalem* with an acknowledgement of Guizot's help and there were many other eminent men who were similarly indebted. Montesquiou, who was not himself very energetic and who had little experience of administration, must have found Guizot an extremely useful acquisition.

[1] *Revue Française*, 1829, pp. 214 ff.

[2] *Mémoires*, vol. i, p. 5.

[3] 'neutre et bienveillant', according to *Sainte-Beuve, Portraits de Femmes*, Paris 1884, p. 134.

[4] *Archives Nationales*, F⁷ 3459.

[5] Henry Reeve later said that Guizot's conversation was better than that of any other man he had known. *Life and Letters of Henry Reeve* (ed. Laughton), vol. i, p. 116.

During the first Restoration Guizot served Montesquiou; during the Hundred Days Guizot returned to his university teaching and on behalf of the moderate royalists undertook a mission to the fugitive Louis XVIII which was frequently to be remembered by his opponents; during the second Restoration he served successive ministers, holding minor posts in the Ministry of Justice and the Conseil d'État, but by writing ministers' speeches, drafting laws and publishing articles, he greatly increased his influence. It was in 1818 (which Sainte-Beuve called 'le beau moment de la Restauration') and in the following year that this influence was most considerable, but the successes of a more violent liberalism and the assassination of the Duc de Berry in 1820 brought an end to this period. Guizot was dismissed from the Conseil d'État and from other administrative posts. He returned to his university teaching. When his lectures were stopped in 1822, he devoted all his energies to journalism and writing.

He was living at this time in the Rue St. Dominique. He and his wife were constantly in need of money. It seems that there was no type of work which they were not prepared to undertake. In 1821, for example, Guizot published a translation of Shakespeare with a long introductory article. He demonstrated clearly a quality which he was always to possess, that when one form of activity was forbidden to him, he did not hesitate to start on another. Pauline de Meulan helped him in all his work, and when she died in 1827, and Guizot later married her niece, Élisa Dillon, his second wife helped him in exactly the same way. This industry and activity was turned to more practical ends with the political society, *Aide-toi, le ciel t'aidera*, which prepared the elections, with the resumption of Guizot's university lectures in 1828, and with his own election to the Chamber in 1830. On the eve of the Revolution of 1830, both as an intellectual and as a practical politician, Guizot was one of the most prominent of the moderate liberals. The Revolution was to start him on his ministerial career.

But during the Revolution Guizot was hesitant. It is true that this hesitancy was shared by many politicians and journalists, who waited on events rather than controlled them. Nevertheless, in some ways both Guizot and Thiers acquired reputations during the July Days which were to stay with them. Guizot, who had learned of Charles X's ordinances on his way back to Paris from Nîmes, returned to the capital to share with other deputies an impression of powerlessness before the actions of the people. His greatest efforts were aimed at limiting the Revolution and at integrating it to his own intellectual system. He therefore appeared ineffective. This was not the same with Thiers. A younger man than Guizot, who had come to Paris even poorer and who had an even more rapid rise to power and fortune (so that in later years he was to say 'je ne suis pas un bourgeois, je suis un rien'), he behaved during the July Days as an activist rather than as a spectator. When Thiers saw a political movement his instinct was to seize it, to take it over, rather than to analyse it. Therefore he gained a reputation for adventure, even for conspiracy, and for some people he was always somewhat untrustworthy and dangerous.

In the first years of the July Monarchy Guizot was rather effaced. He was Minister of the Interior for only a few months whilst the atmosphere was still one of a provisional government. Then he was excluded from the next two governments, that of Laffitte and that of Casimir Périer. His exclusion from the latter was all the more noticeable since Périer was the exponent of the conservative policy which Guizot himself was advocating. Guizot was not always very insistent in his claims for office and for several years he was content with the Ministry of Public Instruction. This was a time of great personal sadness for him. His wife Élisa died in March 1833; his elder son François (the only child by his marriage with Pauline de Meulan) died in 1837, at the age of twenty-two; his own health was bad. Yet in spite of all this, his reputation increased. His speeches made a great impression on the Chamber; he was one of the few politicians who had the gift of expressing the ideas and the ideology behind a policy. He could not be ignored; once again he was indispensable.

Once again, too, he was adaptable. By 1840 the internal political situation had become inextricably involved. It was thought that a solution would be more easily found if one of the two political leaders, Guizot or Thiers, would at least temporarily withdraw from the scene. It was Guizot who accepted to withdraw, and whilst it is true that by this time certain aspects of his policy had earned him many enemies and that such a withdrawal seemed advisable, nevertheless he was not only willing to become ambassador in London, he was also capable of filling the post. No one suggested that Thiers was fitted to lead an embassy to the Court of St. James.

When the new ambassador came to London there was general astonishment at the English court that this was his first visit to England. It was strange that Guizot, who had for a long time been particularly interested in English history and in English institutions, did not follow the example of his Restoration associates, Auguste de Staël and Charles de Rémusat for example, and visit England. It is true that Guizot had, during the Restoration period, been frequently short of money, but Élisa Dillon had brought him some resources, and his failure to travel reveals rather the predominantly literary approach which was his. In the same way, it was not until 1850 that he visited Germany.

When he came to recall his stay in England as ambassador, he showed how he took with him his French preoccupations. He recalled the world of Holland House and of Lansdowne House, the talk of Sidney Smith and of Francis Jeffrey, the monologues of Lord Macaulay. When he met, at one of Lord Palmerston's receptions, members of the aristocracy, and representatives of the Whig, Tory and Radical parties, he saw in this gathering an example of England's social equilibrium which had been established by events of the seventeenth century. He did not show the same curiosity as Michelet, who visited England some years earlier, and who had seen England as the scene of a great struggle, where the Englishman, armed with fire and iron, was engaged in subjugating nature, and who could write of the area between Birmingham and Wolverhampton, that it was 'breathless from the fight'. Guizot tended to present things didactically: thus the crowd which had watched him embark at Calais was scattered and talkative, lookers-on in search of amusement; but at Dover the people who watched him disembark were busy, silent and attentively observant. Like Madame de Staël, he thought of society in terms of conversation and intelligence, and he wrote privately back to France, lamenting that 'thought in the true sense of the word, free and disinterested thought, is a pleasure which one must give up when one crosses the Channel', and writing of Englishmen, 'they act, they govern, and for them, that is enough'.[1]

However, in 1840 Guizot's principal attention was still fixed on Paris. The liquidation of Thiers's ministry in October meant that Guizot returned as the obvious leader of the right and right centre groups, so that his stay in England was only a prelude to his greatest political opportunity. The means by which he was the effective leader of the government from 1840 to 1848 require to be studied in some detail, but there can be little doubt that this period of the 1840s is a contrast to the preceding decade.

The Revolution of February 1848 made Guizot an exile in London. Once again he had to change the nature of his activity. His property and his income in France were confiscated; in order to support his children who had accompanied him to England, he had

---

[1] Guizot: Michel Chevalier, July 12th, 1840; Guizot: Vitet, March 5th, 1840. *Val-Richer MSS*. For Guizot's account of England and English society see *Mémoires*, vol. v, particularly Chapters XXVII and XXX. For Michelet's visit to England see his *Journal* (ed. Paul Villaneix), vol. i, Paris 1959. The version published in *Sur les Chemins de l'Europe*, Paris 1893, is imperfect (see *J. M. Carré* in the *Revue de Littérature Comparée*, 1924). In 1858, when talking to Nassau Senior about England, Guizot said that when he stayed in an English country neighbourhood, in every house he ate the same dinner and heard the same conversation. *Nassau William Senior, Conversations with M. Thiers, M. Guizot and other distinguished persons.* . . . 1878, vol. ii, p. 194.

to write and publish. Therefore he returned to journalism, and to seventeenth-century English history. Although he had to give up any hope of returning to the French political scene in 1849, he always intended to return to France as soon as he could. For this reason he refused offers which suggested that he was going to settle permanently in England, such as the offer of a chair at Oxford. In periods of violence memories are short and when Guizot returned to France, apart from a half-hearted manifestation at Le Havre, fifty or sixty 'polissons' stirred up, as he put it, 'par quelques coquins', this return was hardly noticed. Guizot spent much of his time in the Val-Richer, the country house near to Lisieux which he had acquired in 1836, and which was in the electoral circonscription which he represented from 1830 to 1848. He spent his time writing. It was during these years that he completed his study of the English Revolution, that he wrote his *Mémoires*, and that he composed his religious works. Surrounded only by his children and grandchildren, Guizot was 'l'illustre solitaire' of the Val-Richer, whose resignation and calm impressed all his visitors. In Paris Guizot devoted a great deal of his time to Protestant affairs and to the Académie Française (to which he had been elected, unopposed, in 1836). It has often been said that Frenchmen who have been disappointed in politics console themselves with literature. If ever this was true it was true of the Second Empire when the Académie was both a nucleus of opposition to Napoleon III, and a consolation whereby men such as Guizot could demonstrate their superiority to the shocks of fate. Rival politicians and revolutionaries might have exulted at Guizot's fall from power in 1848; but he went on to write the history of the English Revolution and to act as the chief spokesman of the Académie; this was his revenge and his final victory.

He never had any great opinion of Napoleon III, whom he thought of as a man whose ambitions were tempered by idleness as well as by a taste for pleasurable distractions. He had no need to modify his judgement, made in 1849, that Napoleon would found nothing but that nevertheless he would last a long time. This did not prevent him from regarding the 'coup d'état' as a humiliation for France, which encouraged him to stand aside from any collaboration with the government, at least until the liberalization of the régime with Émile Ollivier, when he accepted to sit on a commission studying higher education.[1] Apart from a desire to bring about a fusion of the

---

[1] Guizot: Aberdeen, July 28th, 1849, December 21st, 1851. *Aberdeen Papers* B.M. Add. MSS. 43134. Guizot and Aberdeen maintained the friendship which had been formed when they were Foreign Ministers and their correspondence continued until Aberdeen's death in 1860. In 1848 Aberdeen invited Guizot to Scotland, but Guizot did not have the money to make the journey.

royal houses, Orleanist and Bourbon, and apart from a particular interest in diplomatic questions, Guizot accepted the rôle of spectator. It was only by literary means that he sought to influence opinion. The Franco-Prussian War aroused his indignation; he wrote to Gladstone and to Wilberforce, the Bishop of Winchester, condemning the Prussian annexation as an outrage, but he did not emerge from his retirement except for Protestant business. The rumours that he would return to London as ambassador once again were never confirmed. Chateaubriand, after 1830, was rumoured to live with the secret hope that he would be called upon to return to the political stage. 'Si l'on faisait appel à un vieux pilote?' he was reported as saying. But Guizot was more resigned. 'Je ne reproche rien et ne demande rien', he said when he returned home in 1849. 'Je me suis résigné à vivre avec mes blessures', he repeated in 1865.[1]

Meanwhile he was growing old. He found a day's writing more tiring; he found it more difficult to leave his narrow bedroom in the Val-Richer with the early morning light. His friends, his former colleagues, his former rivals, were dying. 'Que de grandes morts j'ai vues', he commented. The Princess Lieven, Lord Aberdeen, Victor de Broglie, Prosper de Barante, Ludovic Vitet were his closest friends. Molé, Duchâtel, Piscatory, Villemain, Montalembert, Lamartine, Berryer, Sainte-Beuve were others with whom he had been associated one way or another. 'L'année est mauvaise pour les grands hommes', wrote Prosper Merimée in 1869, and the following year he followed them. Thiers had said that no one would be left to mourn for Guizot and himself. But in fact Guizot was not the last of his political generation to disappear. Thiers, Charles de Rémusat, Duvergier de Hauranne, Léonce de Lavergne (who had served in the Ministry of Foreign Affairs under Guizot) all survived him when he died on September 12th, 1874. But even when they died it was not the end of an epoch. The men of the Third Republic continued in the tradition of the July Monarchy. The government of France is always carried on.

Perhaps Guizot, more than most of his contemporaries, realized this. He never accepted to be placed in what Chateaubriand called 'la progression descendante'. He refused to share the mania of old age which exalted the past and abused the present. 'I do not despair of my country's future', he wrote, shortly before his death, 'and I am as much concerned with it as if I was going to take part in it.'[2] Countries only exist by having a future, and statesmen can only be respected if they have a sense of that future.

[1] Guizot: Aberdeen, July 28th, 1849, ibid; Guizot: Mollien, June 12th, 1865. De Witt (ed.), *Guizot, Lettres à sa famille et à ses amis*, Paris 1884, p. 401.
[2] Guizot: Vitet, *Val-Richer MSS.* (undated).

Yet historians have not been kind to Guizot. It is not merely that the changing perspective of historical and religious enquiry has undermined his work, as it has that of most nineteenth-century intellectuals. More particularly, historians have liked to suppose that there lay behind this austere character a fundamental incapacity, even a certain dishonesty. If his historical work has been remembered, and if his theological work is sometimes recalled, these intellectual preoccupations are usually thought of as irrelevant to his career as a statesman, and it is customary to think of Guizot essentially as an unsuccessful politician. At best he is a superior mediocrity, a dull dog, someone whose importance is only grudgingly admitted, so that an English historian has chosen to write of 'the strange preponderance of Monsieur Guizot'. At worst he typifies class oppression, bourgeois democracy, corruption, and the perversion, or in the words of a modern French historian, 'l'asphyxiation' of liberal, parliamentary institutions. It is typical of a rather unthinking approach to Guizot that an American historian should refer to him as 'ageing and reactionary' although he was only fifty-three when the government of October 29th, 1840, was formed, and it is typical of a prejudiced approach when an English historian, doubtless unable to forgive anyone who had scored a diplomatic victory over Lord Palmerston, should seek to contrast the 'realist' Guizot, to the more noble and 'idealist' Lord Aberdeen.[1] Nor has history been any kinder. Most French towns, whatever their size, have a Boulevard or a 'Place' named after Thiers; but it is rare to find any street or square named after Guizot.

Both historians and history are following in the tradition of most of Guizot's contemporaries, who were continually hostile to him. They sought to denigrate him in every way possible. It was suggested for example that he did not really exist as an independent personality, that he was a mere figure of cardboard, 'un télégraphe' worked by others, such as Louis-Philippe or the Duc de Broglie. His personal character was attacked. He was made out to be 'une nature maigre, jaune, soucieuse, ratatinée, étrangère à tous les côtés riants et gracieux de l'existence', clinging to power out of an arid love of power.[2] It is a fact that Guizot was never popular. There were occasions when he aroused enthusiasm, as when he lectured on the history of civilization. There were occasions when 'Monsieur Guizot'

---

[1] See *Mrs. Irene Collins* in *History*, February 1961, p. 20; *Sherman Kent, Electoral Procedure under Louis Philippe*, 1937, p. 110; *E. Jones Parry, The Spanish Marriages*, 1936.

[2] *Hippolyte Castille, Les Hommes et les Moeurs en France sous le Régime de Louis Philippe*, Paris 1853, p. 33; *A. J. de Marnay, D'Une Chute à l'Autre 1830-1898*, Paris 1880 ed., p. 281; *Lord Morley, Life of Richard Cobden*, vol. i, p. 445.

was a name to be treated with respect, as when he spoke at some grand occasion at the Académie or when he contributed to the Protestant Synod of 1872. But this was not popularity, and towards the end of his life, this was one of Guizot's rare complaints. 'On n'a jamais voulu me rendre cette justice que j'étais bon', he told Jules Pédézert.[1]

A new insight into this unpopularity has recently been given by the publication of the Memoirs of Charles de Rémusat[2]; in the early volumes at least Guizot is one of the dominant characters. He is presented as difficult, ambitious and egotistical. Any attractive or generous gesture made by him was, according to Rémusat, carefully calculated; he thought of everything which would effect his career. Rémusat's picture of a man with a pompous and displeasing manner, with exaggerated pretentions and only limited abilities, is extremely hard. At times Rémusat regrets his own 'severity', although hostility would be a more appropriate word. But the most striking feature of the Guizot who emerges from these pages is his unpopularity. Rémusat shows Guizot as disliked by everyone. Louis-Philippe distrusted 'sa société', Casimir Périer referred scornfully to 'sa côterie', Talleyrand thought of him as a 'Genevois' reminiscent of Necker whom he hated, Duchâtel found his manner hard and displeasing, and even de Broglie, in his distinguished way, is shown as having some reserves concerning him. The centre groups in the Chamber supposedly found him 'detestable', and so great was his unpopularity, according to Rémusat, that some people (including Thiers) thought that at his reception to the Académie he ran the risk of being booed. All this recalls Sainte-Beuve's remark that there were some people who were naturally likeable, and he gave Lamartine as an example, whilst there were others who were naturally dislikeable, and Guizot was his example of this.[3]

These judgements have to be considered critically, with particular regard to their authors. The case of Sainte-Beuve is the more simple. His own character has been the subject of much controversy, and it does not seem that he can be treated as a reliable authority concerning personalities. *Mes Poisons* is a very particular compilation, the accumulation of secret spites. Even less attention can be attached to his comments on Guizot since Sainte-Beuve, with his extreme susceptibility, was over-eager to consider himself insulted by Guizot. When, for example, he published an article on Pauline de Meulan, Guizot wrote to thank him; but the letter was thought by Sainte-

[1] *J. Pédézert, Guizot*, Paris 1874, p. 11.

[2] *Charles de Rémusat, Mémoires de Ma Vie* (edited by Ch. Pouthas), Paris, vol. i, 1958, vol. ii, 1959, vol. iii, 1960.

[3] *Sainte-Beuve, Mes Poisons*, Paris 1926, p. 67.

Beuve to be offensive. When Guizot was Minister of Public Instruction he was ready to enter into a complicated arrangement whereby Sainte-Beuve would succeed Ampère at the École Normale. This did not, in fact, take place and Sainte-Beuve might well have harboured resentment against the Minister. Guizot tried to make amends by appointing him to the Comité des Travaux Historiques in 1834, but he tired of this work and gradually abandoned it. After 1848 Sainte-Beuve shared, in a rather unthinking way, the popular opinion that it was Guizot's stupidity which had been the cause of the revolution, and this 'plus bête que Polignac' idea was present in his thoughts for some time. Furthermore, Sainte-Beuve was determined to demonstrate that he had never benefited from the patronage of the July Monarchy, and with this intention he was perhaps anxious to show his scorn for the leading politician of the overthrown régime. However, one has to notice that as time went by Sainte-Beuve became markedly less hostile, and began to show open respect and admiration, and to point to the unity of Guizot's achievement, as well as to its courage and dignity. It is noticeable too that Guizot, who had always treated Sainte-Beuve with respect, and who seems to have voted for his election to the Académie in 1844, responded to this consideration. He wrote to Sainte-Beuve that he regretted they did not share the same opinion, for between them, as he put it, they could cause it to triumph, 'nous serions bien forts à nous deux pour le faire prévaloir'.[1]

The case of Rémusat is more complicated. His *Mémoires* are written elegantly and easily, with an attention to detail and circumstance which gives an impression of complete reliability. It is certain too that Rémusat knew Guizot extremely well, having for several years been his closest companion. Yet one has to ask whether it is possible that Guizot was, in fact, so unpopular as Rémusat suggests, whether it is likely that Guizot could be so universally detested, but yet persist as an important and successful public figure. One also has to remember what Rémusat himself was at this time. He was a journalist who was often without a newspaper, a thinker without any positive ideas, a deputy without any real following in the Chamber. He had made himself into a sort of 'éminence jeune', the friend of many important people, a negotiator and a go-between, a would-be constructor of governments. It is natural that he should exaggerate the importance of his own activities and his picture of Guizot emphasizes his own indispensable qualities since he appears almost as Guizot's only friend. The descriptions of Guizot's unpopularity

[1] Guizot: Sainte-Beuve, November 16th, 1864, *Nouveaux Lundis*, Paris 1884, vol. ix, p. 109 n. See also Sainte-Beuve's remark 'les écrits de Monsieur Guizot forment tout un enchaînement, on ne peut toucher à un anneau sans remuer, sans ébranler tout le reste', *Causeries du Lundi*, op. cit. vol. i, p. 312.

suggest that Guizot's success was due largely to the interventions and loyalty of this one unique supporter. It should also be recalled that Rémusat had no illusions about his political future under the July Monarchy, if he were associated exclusively with Guizot. As all ministries were coalitions, Guizot would not be able to bring an unlimited number of friends with him into the cabinet. Once places had been found for Guizot himself, de Broglie and Duchâtel, then there was not much likelihood of there being a place for Rémusat. He therefore cultivated other centres of political power, Casimir Périer, Thiers, Broglie and was sometimes ostentatious in demonstrating that he could act independently from Guizot. At the same time Rémusat was always something of a dilettante. It is difficult to see how Guizot and he could have remained constant friends. Guizot was serious; he had, like most of his contemporaries been plunged from his earliest youth into dangerous controversies; he had neither the temperament, nor the wealth, nor the family connections, which would permit him to treat affairs lightly or carelessly.

When viewed in this light, Rémusat's portrait of Guizot is less reliable than it at first appears. Yet one cannot altogether reject what Rémusat and other contemporaries thought about Guizot. There is one anecdote told by Rémusat which is particularly striking. It concerns the day on which Pauline de Meulan died. Rémusat was in Guizot's house, whilst Guizot was at his wife's bedside. When Guizot joined the members of the family and Rémusat, to announce that death had taken place, he stayed for only a few minutes, and then turning to his two nieces he said, 'Allons-nous habiller', meaning that they should put on their mourning. Rémusat never doubted, indeed he knew better than anyone, that there was no reason to doubt the real affection that had united the Guizots. There was therefore no hypocrisy in this anxiety to be seen in mourning; it was rather the affectation of what was true, and it reveals a 'gaucherie' in human relations, which one must appreciate if one is to understand Guizot. He was always particularly susceptible to the opinion of others, and for that reason was anxious to compose a public countenance which was correct, severe and absolute. It is this public countenance which was disliked, and which is difficult to penetrate.

Guizot wrote a great deal. His great-grandson, Jean Schlumberger, has described 'the passion to publish' as endemic in his family,[1] but in any bibliography of his family's productions it is still Guizot himself who fills most pages. Yet most of this writing is descriptive, analytical or argumentative. Very little of it was creative or imaginative, and apart from impressing one with Guizot's belief in reason and in a logical exposition of the facts being the way to a

[1] *Jean Schlumberger, Éveils,* Paris 1950, pp. 113-14.

solution of almost any problem, one learns little about Guizot himself from this mass of writing. At times Guizot was deliberately impersonal. He called his Memoirs, *Mémoires pour servir à l'histoire de mon temps* (a title which, quite unjustifiably, annoyed Sainte-Beuve). The eight volumes which were published are everything which the title indicated. Memoirs are usually produced by French politicians either because this is the only way in which they can give some significance to their unimportant existences, or because they are obsessed by a sinister interpretation of history, the belief that things had happened in a particular way because of some secret force or arrangement which they could now reveal. In both cases the writing of Memoirs is a sign of impotence. But Guizot's *Mémoires* are very different. They are not 'pour servir à l'histoire de Guizot'. They represent essentially a collection of documents to which is added a gallery of portraits. They form, for certain years, a fairly complete diplomatic and parliamentary history, from which almost everything that is personal, and a great deal that is anecdotal, is rigorously suppressed. Guizot deliberately did not say all that he could have done; he was anxious, when writing these volumes not only to avoid controversy but also to avoid offending former associates, such as Thiers.[1] It is typical of Guizot that whilst he considered writing a more personal collection of souvenirs it would have been for his family only, and not for publication. It is typical too that he told his family of how, when staying in Windsor, he had one night lost his way and inadvertently wandered into the Queen's bedroom. He claimed to have told Queen Victoria of this and asked her, if ever he wrote his Memoirs, whether she would mind if he recounted this incident. Although he supposedly got her permission, this anecdote does not appear in the *Mémoires*.[2]

[1] Guizot: Léonce de Lavergne. July 4th, 1861, *Correspondance de Guizot avec Léonce de Lavergne* (ed. Ernest Cartier), Paris 1910, p. 117. See also Guizot's correspondence with Thiers regarding the *Mémoires* in *Papiers Thiers*, Bibliothèque Nationale, Paris, Nouvelles Acquisitions 20619. Guizot was not free from errors and exaggerations in his *Mémoires*. On his visit to Louis XVIII at Ghent it is interesting to compare the account which he sent to his wife in 1815, quoted in *Pouthas, Guizot Pendant la Restauration*, Paris 1923, pp. 84 ff., with the account in the *Mémoires*, vol. i, pp. 83 ff. The latter makes Guizot far bolder. Guizot occasionally makes small mistakes in the documents which he quotes, either by running one letter into another, or by failing to indicate omissions.

[2] Guizot: Pauline Guizot, June 22nd, 1840, *Mme de Witt* (*née* Guizot), *Monsieur Guizot dans sa famille et avec ses amis*, Paris 1880, pp. 221-224. One must not however exaggerate Guizot's neglect of small personal details. E. L. Woodward, for example, finds it typical of Guizot that he should not mention his cook at the London Embassy, who was one of the causes of the Embassy dinners being successful (*Three Studies in European Conservatism*, 1929, p. 112 n. 4), but in fact Guizot does mention this 'excellent cuisinier' and quotes Lady Holland as explaining part of his success in exactly this way (*Mémoires*, vol. v, p. 138).

INTRODUCTION

It is in his private correspondence that Guizot reveals himself most. In his letters to his mother, in letters to Pauline de Meulan, in letters also to Madame Lenormant, to Madame Laure de Gasparin and to the Princess Lieven, one discovers a man completely different from the austere Huguenot who was so unpalatable to his contemporaries.[1] In these letters Guizot seems to be sincere and unaffected, sensitive and affectionate. The fact that he should have found the need to write these letters, and the fact that they are written to women, are interesting characteristics of the man. They show a need for affection, a desire for friendship and support which is a contrast to the intellectual absolutism which is to be found elsewhere in Guizot. He was unable to take pleasure in things when alone; writing was often a refuge from loneliness. Victor Hugo had noticed that Guizot seemed to be attracted towards women older than himself (as was the case with Mira Chabaud, Pauline de Meulan and the Princess Lieven), and this too probably reflects his need for affection and companionship. Without these private letters Guizot would be a shadowy figure, endlessly at work, endlessly covering sheets of small format paper with his neat writing, but only showing his official countenance. Perhaps too these private letters took the place of a 'Journal', which is always a sign of the uncertain writer, the man who, despite appearances, is lacking in confidence.

It is worth considering in some detail the light that Guizot's friendship with the Princess Lieven throws on his personality. At first sight it seems extraordinary that Guizot, who was serious, intellectual and bourgeois, should have formed this long and sentimental friendship with a woman who had been associated with several men (including Metternich), who was completely unintellectual and who carried consciousness of her aristocracy to considerable lengths. It can of course be suggested that the Princess was a most assiduous cultivator of friendships with those who were near to the sources of power, and that Guizot's interest in her was

[1] *Monsieur Guizot dans sa famille et avec ses amis* (op. cit.); *Lettres de Monsieur Guizot à sa famille et à ses amis* (op. cit.); *Lettres de Guizot à Pauline de Meulan*, edited by Edouard Dolléans in *Revue de Deux Mondes*, Sept.-October, 1954; *Lettres à M. et Mme Lenormant* (op. cit.); *François Guizot et Madame Laure de Gasparin* (ed. Andre Gayot), Paris 1934 (Laure de Gasparin, *née* Daunant, was from a Nîmes family, and her brother Achille was one of Guizot's oldest friends. Her husband Auguste was for a time a deputy; her brother-in-law Adrien became Prefect of the Isère department after the Lyons rising in 1831 and later became a minister. Adrien's son Agénor was a prominent Protestant and his daughter-in-law Mme Agénor de Gasparin was the author of many moralizing novels); Jean Schlumberger and Jacques Naville are publishing, in six volumes, Guizot's correspondence with the Princess Lieven, to whom for a time he used to write every day; some of these letters are quoted by *Ernest Daudet, Une Vie d'Ambassadrice au Siècle Dernier*, Paris 1903.

16

part of his ambition, what Edgar Quinet called his 'allures de Gascon'. But such an explanation does not withstand any examination of this affair.

Guizot and the Princess Lieven first met in the winter of 1836 at the Duc de Broglie's, but it was from June 1837, from the time of a dinner at the Comtesse de Boigne's at Chatenay, that their close association seems to date. Guizot was then a widower for the second time, and the Princess was living separated from her husband, who died in January 1839. Guizot quickly established for himself a particular place in her salon, which was held in Talleyrand's old house in the Rue St. Florentin. It was soon understood that he and the Princess wished to be alone at certain hours, and visitors who came at the wrong time were discomfited by their reception. This friendship continued until the death of the Princess in 1857. It was rumoured many times that they were secretly married, and this association attracted a good deal of attention. Obviously an 'affaire' between two middle-aged people is easily rendered ridiculous. Sir Charles Webster tells us that when the Princess was with Guizot in London, during 1840, 'the love-sick ambassador' was a great joke in the diplomatic corps; Chateaubriand refers slightingly in his *Mémoires* to the 'grave doctrinaire' who had fallen at the feet of Omphalis, and Prosper Merimée, who was 'mauvaise langue', claimed that if Guizot was ill it was because he tired himself 'à causer avec la Princesse de Lieven depuis minuit jusqu'à trois heures du matin'.[1] Daudet has suggested that this friendship inspired Balzac in his composition of *Les Secrets de la Princesse de Cadignan*, that Madame de Cadignan was really Madame de Lieven, and that d'Arthez was Guizot. Modern Balzac specialists however prefer other identifications for d'Arthez, if they find it necessary to trace any real identity at all, and the suggestion is weakened by Daudet's belief that the Princess Lieven was like many Balzacian heroines.[2] But what most of these observers failed to appreciate was the note of sadness which persisted throughout this friendship. A common sense of tragedy and of bereavement served as a bond between them. For all her activity, the Princess Lieven was an unhappy woman,

[1] *Sir Charles Webster, The Foreign Policy of Palmerston*, 1951, vol. ii, p. 688; *Chateaubriand, Mémoires d'Outre-Tombe* (Ed. Garnier), vol. iv, p. 180; Merimée: Mme de Montijo, November 23rd, 1844, *Correspondance Générale* (ed. Maurice Parturier), vol. iv, 210-211.

[2] See *Ernest Daudet* (op. cit.) and in *Le Temps* January 10th, 1898. His suggestions have not received support from modern critics. For recent studies of Balzac's characters and their origins see *H. J. Hunt*, Portraits in La Comédie Humaine, *The Romanic Review*, vol. xlix 1958 and *Bruce Tolley*, The 'Cénacle' of Balzac's Illusions perdues, *French Studies* vol. xv 1961. I am grateful for the advice given me in this matter by Dr. Charles Gould of Bristol University.

particularly so after the death of her son Constantine in 1838, and all the more so since she only learnt of his death when a letter which she had written to him in America came back with the word 'dead' scrawled across the envelope. Guizot told Lady Alice Peel that it was with the death of his son François that his friendship with the Princess started. There was therefore a mutual need for consolation.

Guizot's letters to her are not all as magnificent as Ernest Daudet suggests. But there is something impressive in his patience when he regrets some of the characteristics of the society in which the Princess has been accustomed to live, when he regrets that she is sometimes violent and when he wishes that she would turn to some serious occupation. And the Guizot who could write 'When I saw you suffer, I felt and I still feel like an old soldier covered with wounds who sees the exhaustion, the weariness and the pain of a young man whom he loves and looks after', was as unlike 'the austere intriguer' as the Princess was unlike the shallow 'Doyenne des salons' so frequently depicted. This friendship was covered with pools of sadness, and when the Princess died Guizot wrote,'j'ai perdu my social home', and described himself wandering from salon to salon in search of conversation like any romantic lover. With Guizot moments of revelation were rare, and as with many sentimentalists, it is in his relations with women that they occur most frequently.[1]

A recent biographer of Ernest Renan begins his book with the words that there is nothing surprising in Renan having been born at Tréguier, it was the birthplace which suited him best.[2] Much the same could be said of Guizot and Nîmes. It has often been said that to understand Guizot one must understand Nîmes and its surrounding country. This town was outstanding, not only because of its large Protestant population, over one-third of its forty or fifty thousands belonging to the reformed religion, but also because the area of the Cévennes and of the Bas-Languedoc was the area of the most heroic Huguenot resistance and martyrdom. This was the region of the Camisards, whom Gibbon had compared to the Circumcellions, the fiercest and most fanatical of the African sects; this was the region of the 'Inspirés' and of the great Church of the Desert. For these reasons, as well as for reasons of climate and environment, the Nîmois is in many ways exceptional. He is surrounded by one of the most desolate

[1] Guizot: Lady Alice Peel, March 26th, 1859. This correspondence has been published in the *Revue de Paris*, June 1st and 15th, 1925. Monsieur André Maurois told me that were he to write a biography of Guizot he would devote a lot of attention to the subject 'Guizot et les femmes'. This subject has been discussed by the *Baron Seillière, François Guizot: Psychologue du Sentiment*, Paris 1944, but not very satisfactorily.

[2] *François Millepierres, La Vie d'Ernest Renan*, Paris 1961.

regions of France. A succession of wild hills and gorges form a silent wilderness where only the hardiest vegetation can survive; the climate moves from one extreme to another; even where villages are numerous, they still appear solitary, and the same can be said for people. For the Nîmois the whole of the area is associated with suffering, and for all that Protestantism survived, it is associated with defeat. The Protestant from Nîmes is pursued by the memory that he was from the smaller and the weaker of 'the two Frances' which were in conflict. Thus the Nîmois is on the defensive, is extreme in his reactions, serious in his beliefs. Other inhabitants of the Midi are supposed to be gay, cynical and nonchalant, but the Nîmois is obstinate rather than volatile, taciturn rather than expansive. He is sectarian and partisan, and has none of the superficial generosity which characterises other southerners. Thus, under the July Monarchy, when people liked to contrast Guizot and Thiers, the 'méridional grave' and the 'méridional gai', they were furthering the traditional contrast between Nîmes and Marseilles.

Guizot was more involved in Nîmes, and in the tradition of the Desert, than many. In the first place there was his grandfather, Jean Guizot, who had been a pastor at a time when, as has been said, if one needed to be courageous to be a Protestant, one had to be heroic to be a pastor. Little is known of him, other than that he became a pastor in 1756 at the age of twenty-seven, and that he died ten years later, shortly before the birth of his second son, André, who was to be the father of François Guizot. Apparently he led the wandering, unsettled life of the Protestant minister during a period when there were still brutal repressions and when the hunt for those who ministered to the Huguenots was particularly well organized.

Then there was the Revolution, which in a town such as Nîmes had particular aspects. Political and social conflicts were edged by religious quarrels. The period of the constitutional, or 'bourgeois', revolution meant the rise of the Protestants. Whilst only a short time previously Protestant services had been held in a sewer, after the Revolution Protestants were buying churches and converting them into temples. It may be that there were many people who opposed these Protestants as Protestants, and it is certain that in the atmosphere of conspiracy which characterized these years of Revolution there was a genuine fear of Protestantism; but whoever was opposed to the new governing classes, for whatever reason, could attack them on the grounds of their religion. If, as sometimes happened, the employers were Protestant and the employees mainly Catholic, then a social conflict could assume the appearance of religious strife. There were therefore at least two Revolutions in Nîmes: the one was the reflection of the national revolution, the other was an affair of

INTRODUCTION

local rivalries, jealousies and personalities. By the time of the Thermidorean reaction, both revolutions seemed to have led Nîmes towards ruin. Its population was greatly reduced, the prosperity of its silk industry had disappeared, its Academy and literary societies had been suppressed. Thousands of its inhabitants were living a threadbare existence. Everywhere there was mourning and bitterness. Protestants and Catholics, Federalists and Democrats, employers and employees, everyone had suffered and was suffering; each group thought of another group as being responsible for the deaths that affected them most. The Guizot family resembled many others in their mourning and in the disappearance of their property. They never recovered any position in the town or any happiness in being there, and because of André Guizot's links with Federalism and Bonicel's connections with the democrats, they were particularly open to hostility and to 'malveillance'.

Guizot never forgot that he was a southerner, although he settled in Paris and in Normandy. He told his son in 1852 that after nearly fifty years in the north he had only to close his eyes and it was the sky and the sun of the Midi that he saw. He did not forget his early experiences in Nîmes either. He remembered visiting his father in prison; he remembered seeing his mother kneel down and give thanks when she learned of the death of Robespierre; he remembered a great deal which suggested that he could not trust his fellow-men. These experiences helped to make him a solitary figure, who once said that he felt sympathy for men in general, but individually for very few men.[1]

There was also his mother. Madame Guizot Mère is now best remembered by the portrait Ary Scheffer did of her. She is painted in deep mourning, against a purple background, an open Bible by her side. She seems to have been a woman dominated by three passions: by her grief at the death of her husband (she told Élisa Dillon that she had wept for thirty-five years); by a possessive attachment to her son, whose career she watched with a mixture of anxiety and pride until she followed him into exile in 1848, dying in London on March 31 and being buried at Kensal Green; by her religion, which was one of the more pessimistic versions of Calvinism. Madame Guizot Mère thought of man as born to be unhappy, in order that through suffering he should recognize God; success was a danger for the unwary; man's natural tendency towards evil could only be overcome by discipline and constraint. Although she has been placed in a collection of 'Illustrious Mothers', she was not ambitious for her son's worldly success. Every advance that Guizot

[1] Guizot: Guillaume Guizot, April 12th, 1852, *Monsieur Guizot dans sa famille* (op. cit.), pp. 294-295. Guizot: Léonce de Lavergne, September 22nd, 1838, *Correspondance de Guizot avec Léonce de Lavergne* (op. cit.), p. 4.

20

made in his political and social career was for her a reason for worry and for uneasiness.

Guizot was an attentive and devoted son. But with this jealous and plaintive mother he needed all his deference and all his patience. Yet at the same time one cannot help noticing that like his mother he distrusted any natural and spontaneous movement within himself; he feared any relaxation of principle, he was suspicious both of impulse and of inspiration; everywhere he looked for controls and safeguards. When, as a young man, he wrote of the passions as an enemy which had to be resisted, or when, as an old man, he attacked religions which seemed to worship man rather than God, he showed himself to be in the same mould as his mother. Perhaps one should recognize both in Madame Guizot Mère and in François Guizot the influence of what Michelet called the 'Judea' of Nîmes and the influence of what was for them a catastrophic revolution.

The move from Nîmes to Geneva is also significant. By 1799 this small town with a population of some twenty thousand had hardly had time to accept the fact that it had been annexed by France. If only by the hostility which the inhabitants showed to this annexation and the degree of independence which they attempted to maintain, Geneva was an unusual French town, and Napoleon was to accuse it of being a foyer of liberalism and of pro-English sentiment. But for a young boy at this time the outstanding feature of an education in Geneva was the possibility of learning foreign languages and of learning about foreign literature and thought. In particular, Geneva was one of the few places on the Continent where one could become acquainted with English literature. The *Bibliothèque Britannique*, even when shorn of its political articles, remained a source of information about England and about publications in England which must have appeared exciting within the sterility of the Empire. Guizot's teacher Pierre Prévost, who introduced him to philosophy, was the translator of Adam Smith and was to become the translator of Malthus. One of Guizot's first literary efforts was a translation of Gray's famous elegy, and when Guizot began to write in *Le Publiciste* and other reviews, he took upon himself the task of acquainting his readers with English and German books. In 1808 he wrote to his old teacher Prévost, showing that he had understood the advantages of his Genevan education, '. . . there is nothing more advantageous than forcing the French to go and find amongst foreigners what they vainly look for amongst themselves, and the English, a most eminently sensible nation, are a rich mine to work'.[1]

Yet if the intellectual awakening which accompanied the discovery of foreign languages and literatures is to be thought of as one of the

[1] Guizot: Prévost, July 3rd, 1808, *Prévost MSS.*, op. cit.

advantages of Geneva, there was a corresponding drawback. The Genevan education tended to emphasize what already existed in the Nîmes side to Guizot's make-up, namely, something particularly un-French. He tended to look at affairs through the eyes of a foreigner, and if he possessed qualities remote from those of the French amongst whom he was living, he tended also to be out of touch and out of sympathy with many of the dominant trends of French society. It may well be that much of Guizot's celebrated unpopularity is to be explained by Nîmes and Geneva.

Guizot was a small man. He was slightly built, but in middle age became more thickset. As if to combat this lack of inches, he used to hold both his head and his shoulders extremely high, so that in Rémusat's words he was like 'a hunchback who has no hump'. When he spoke in the Chamber or in the Académie, however, his stature was forgotten. As with Chateaubriand, the tribune concealed his smallness and emphasized the piercing fineness of his eyes. His gestures were carefully studied and his eloquence measured. As he sought to impose his ideas, so he sought to make his appearance imposing. His features were sensitive and expressive, though somewhat drawn, and his profile had a severe and sombre dignity. His face was pale, with the complexion of a southerner. Sometimes his expression was disdainful, even petulant, and this was probably emphasized by the high collar which was fashionable under Louis-Philippe, as well as by his habit, when displeased, of making a scornful 'moue'. His portraits, by Delaroche and G. F. Watts, suggest a lined and weary face which one can hardly imagine young, although Guizot's daughters claimed that the Revolution of 1848 made him younger by ten years (a remark to which he replied that he would willingly have given up these ten years if he could have avoided the Revolution).

Some contemporaries thought that they saw a resemblance between Guizot and Lord John Russell, particularly in their attitude when in Parliament. Possibly one can now see some similarity in the alleged coldness of both statesmen. Certainly if one recalls the lines about Russell,

> How formed to lead if not too proud to please,
> His fame would fire you but his manners freeze.
> Like or dislike he does not care a jot:
> He wants your votes but your affections not.

they could be applied to Guizot, as could the reference to the way in which oratory seemed to transform the man.

> But see our statesman when the steam is on,
> And languid Johnny glows to glorious John.

Victor Hugo said that when Guizot mounted the tribune, then his head touched the heavens. One could also compare Guizot to other English statesmen. To the younger Pitt for the concentration of his character, to Sir Robert Peel for a certain hankering after unpopularity, to Sir James Graham for fear of any movement which originated with 'the people'. Such comparisons are not altogether idle. They suggest how in many ways Guizot was 'Victorian'. But in other respects he was decidedly more at home in France, and not least in his love of conversation and of the 'salon', which went with his passion for general ideas and his delight in a pointed phrase. His sense of humour was also French in the sense that it was never gratuitous. Thus, when during his illness in 1845, he was asked if he was feeling better, 'Much better' replied Guizot, holding up a copy of Thiers's *History of the Consulate and of the Empire*, 'as you can see, I'm now reading novels'.

The life of a scholar-statesman is apt to appear somewhat monotonous. One is not so much interested in what they have done as in the issues and the subjects which they have encountered. The pages which follow are not therefore a biography, not even an intellectual biography. They seek to study Guizot and the items of the history of France which surround his career. They should be free from what Macaulay called the 'lues Boswelliana', the disease of admiration; they do not seek either to justify or to condemn, they only try to understand. Although it is true that after one has spent much time reading a man's private papers and published works, one comes to have affection for him, all authors necessarily aspire to say of their subject, as Sainte-Beuve said of Talleyrand, 'Je ne hais ni aime Talleyrand; je l'étudie et l'analyse.'

2

POLITICAL THOUGHT

When we come to the Chamber and ask it to decide in favour of one system or another, we are not asking for the Chamber to give us a diploma, to adopt in advance certain formulae from which one can deduce certain principles. That would be, if I may say so, scholastics rather than politics. A policy starts off from certain general ideas and proceeds within their sphere, loosely and freely. It realizes that all the consequences cannot be rigorously deduced; it knows how to adapt itself to circumstances and to events; it knows how to wait. That is politics, and it is that which we are discussing, not any schoolboy system.

GUIZOT IN THE CHAMBER OF DEPUTIES, DECEMBER 5TH 1834

THE story has often been told of how the opera by Beaumarchais and Salieri, 'Tarare', underwent significant modifications between its first Paris production in June 1787 and its later performances. When it was first written, liberal ideas were very fashionable, especially when they had an infusion of scientific knowledge; thus in this work, Nature (or the Genius of Reproduction) and the Genius of Heat sang a duet together about the laws of gravitation, and successively manufactured the different characters of the opera, notably Tarare, who is a virtuous and intelligent soldier, and Atar, King of Ormuz, who is a despot endowed only with the advantages of birth. In the 1787 version Atar steals Tarare's wife, but in the ensuing struggle he is defeated and kills himself: Tarare is then proclaimed king in his place. In 1790, when 'Tarare' was next produced, Louis XVI was a constitutional monarch, and the opera was remodelled so that Tarare could be elected a constitutional king, so that national sovereignty and the power of the laws could be proclaimed. In the production of 1795 Tarare was not allowed to become a king at all and indignantly refused the crown. Under Bonaparte the

24

opera had to have further changes, and in 1819 much of it was entirely rewritten. In this last version Tarare had become more fervently monarchist than ever before; he displays his loyalty by defending the King of Ormuz from a popular insurrection, and then falls with emotion at the feet of the King, who shows the magnanimous reasonableness of the new monarchy by restoring Tarare's wife and by appointing Tarare commander of his forces. This story of the strange destiny of a fairly mediocre work resembles the development of much French political thought; there is a continual adaptation of doctrines as the actual political situation changes. It is curious that French thought should so frequently have been accused of being aggressively systematic, of trying to reset the range of the Alps on the line of St. Peter's Colonnade; more frequently French writers and thinkers were merely trying to establish some order out of immediate circumstances, or simply commenting on the course of events. French political thought follows closely the declivities of French politics.

The outstanding feature of the ending of Napoleonic government in France was the ease and speed with which the whole system collapsed. Within little more than a week, in the absence of any important movement of opinion in favour either of Napoleon's family or of the Bourbons, private negotiations and individual intrigues succeeded in bringing about the restoration. Louis XVIII thought that he owed his throne to the will of Providence and to his fellow-monarch George IV, but Talleyrand knew better, although Lord Holland suggested that Talleyrand himself had been surprised by events.[1] With Napoleon's escape from Elba the following year, the fate of the Bourbons became uncertain once again. Even when Napoleon's success was seen to be only temporary, the allies were reluctant to attach themselves openly to Louis XVIII's sad little court in Ghent, and many diplomats and politicians looked favourably on the Duke of Orleans. Wellington afterwards said that had he not bargained with Fouché, then Orleans would have been proclaimed the next day.[2]

Thus the French royal house was twice restored in doubtful conditions; the constitutional circumstances of both restorations were scarcely less fortuitous and inconclusive. On March 31st, 1814, the Czar had issued a declaration on behalf of the Allies, declaring that they would respect and guarantee the constitution which the French nation would choose; he thus accepted a constitution which had not yet been worked out. From April 3rd to April 6th the Senate,

---

[1] See *Mémoires du Prince de Talleyrand*, ed. Albert de Broglie, Paris, 1891-1892, vol. ii, p. 146; *Lord Holland, Foreign Reminiscences*, 1850, p. 299.
[2] See C. K. Webster, *The Foreign Policy of Castlereagh, 1812-1815*, 1931, p. 456.

either directly or through a special committee, worked out a Constitution, based upon the principle of a compact between sovereign and people, and suggesting that the prince who was called to the throne by the Constitutional Act was no more than a private person until he had accepted this act.[1] On April 14th the Comte d'Artois, whilst declaring that he could not commit his brother Louis (who was still in England), gave assurances that he accepted the basis of this Constitution. Louis XVIII only left England on April 20th, but during his leisurely journey from Boulogne to Paris he received many visits and deputations, which stressed the fact that he was King by right, independent of any negotiations with the Senate. On May 2nd, as the King arrived at Saint Ouen, practically at the gates of Paris, a declaration was hurriedly drawn up (the final draft was supposedly made whilst the King slept) which rejected the senatorial constitution, but which promised to establish a commission charged with the task of working out the form of government. This was the basis of the charter, and of the idea that it had been granted by a generous king to his people. In 1815, after the abdication of Napoleon in favour of his son on June 22nd, it was the Legislative Chamber this time which tried to impose a constitution and choose a monarch who would fit it; a Commission was appointed on June 28th, which produced the sketch of a constitution the next day. Events moved too swiftly, however, and on July 5th the Chamber had to confine itself to a declaration. This stated that a monarch could only give any real guarantees as to his conduct if he swore to observe a constitution drawn up by the representatives of the nation and approved of by the people. The reticence of the Declaration of St. Ouen in 1814 had its counterpart in the declaration of good intentions which Louis issued at Cambrai. Thus both in 1814 and in 1815 there was no certainty as to the type of institutions with which France was to be equipped or as to the aims or mentality of the new governments.

These uncertainties were prolonged long after the restoration had been completed, and became characteristic of French public life. Just as the adroitness of Talleyrand and of Fouché had been of vital importance during both restorations, so the King's predilection for a reactionary émigré such as Blacas and then for a moderate reformer such as Decazes, and his egoistic readiness to abandon both, was revealed as equally important during the following years. When the extreme right wing thought that it commanded general support in the country, then it found itself anxious to make a more national

[1] On this Constitution and its history, see the article by *J. P. T. Bury* on 'The End of the Napoleonic Senate' in the *Cambridge Historical Journal*, 1948, vol. ix, pp. 165-189.

appeal and resist the King's prerogative; more liberal politicians found themselves relying on the throne and the distribution of royal favour. An observer such as Montlosier found that he could not understand events, and for none of the parties, nor for the King and his government, could he say what they wanted or what they were trying to do.[1] Personal quarrels and animosities were always important even within the main political groupings. The Villèle government, formed in December 1821, appeared to have completely eliminated the liberals from the Chamber with their victories in the elections of 1824. Yet disagreements amongst Villèle's party caused new and powerful oppositions to be formed. An opposition party arose from the personal feud between Villèle and Chateaubriand; an opposition party of right-wing extremists, led by De La Bourdonnaye was disappointed that Villèle did not use his opportunities for counter-revolutionary revenge; Gallicans, whose spokesmen were Montlosier and Dumesnil, attacked the influence of the Jesuits. In such a situation it became tactically advantageous for oppositions to combine in electoral or parliamentary matters, even although such alliances were doctrinally absurd. The action of the extreme royalists at Grenoble in 1819, when they voted for the abbé Grégoire, a priest who had accepted the civil constitution of the clergy during the Revolution, and who had approved of the execution of Louis XVI, became a precedent for many similar manœuvres, both in elections and in the Chamber of Deputies. It is obvious that doctrines were bound to appear of little importance in the face of such contrivings. In a situation which was often paradoxical, it was only fitting that many of the leading politicians were themselves paradoxical personalities. Chateaubriand and Benjamin Constant are obvious and well-explored examples, their idealism and their genius contrasting with their egoism and their pettiness; but people such as Talleyrand and Molé were in their own ways no less paradoxical, their ambition and their abilities being frequently nullified by indolence and indifference; Thiers himself could be amazingly careless and unpredictable, and Lord Aberdeen commented, after an interview with him, 'He is a queer fellow to have been twice the Minister of a great country.'[2] The historian of France from 1814 to 1848 recalls Clarendon, and is tempted to see this period in terms of 'the pride of this man and the popularity of that; the levity of one and the moroseness of another; the spirit of craft and subtlety in some and the rude, unpolished integrity of others'. It could hardly be a great age of political thought; almost every French politician could have said

---

[1] *De la Monarchie Française au premier janvier 1821*, Paris, 1821, vol. i, p. v.
[2] Lord Aberdeen: Peel, October 21st, 1845, *Aberdeen Papers*, B.M. Add. MSS. 43065.

with Madame de Staël, 'My political opinions consist of proper names.'

One of the most influential political thinkers of the Restoration period was Royer-Collard; on one occasion he was elected deputy by seven different electoral colleges; he was President of the Chamber of Deputies at the time of the 1830 Revolution. Yet, for all this importance, it is noticeable that he never published any important political work; he told Tocqueville that he despised both the quality of author and the life of deputy.[1] His political ideas were expressed in speeches; each speech was called forth by some occasion or by some problem. His political ideas therefore appear rather as responses to a series of crises, or circumstances, rather than as a compact doctrine. For all that they have an appearance of logic and unchanging principle, each speech had an element of *ad hoc* thinking about it. As the situation developed, so the principles evolved in consequence. Faguet, who admired Royer-Collard, comments ironically on this 'versatility', but other observers were less indulgent.[2]

Sympathetic observers in England, if not in France, remembered Fox's saying that a Restoration was the most pernicious of all revolutions; Frenchmen, such as Constant or Sainte-Beuve, frequently spoke of 'the revolution of 1814' or 'the revolution of 1815'. However much affairs resembled a comedy, with 'Vive la République', 'Vive l'Empereur', 'Vive le Roi', 'Vive l'Empereur', 'Vive le Roi' and 'Vive le Roi quand-même' exhausting the enthusiastic, yet tragedy was always just around the corner. Albert de Broglie claimed that even when France was most prosperous the recollection of the year '1793' had the effect of the ghost in 'Macbeth'. Thus the confrontation of political ideas was the conflict of possible systems of government; it was a period of policies rather than philosophies, theories of government rather than theories of politics, considerations of power rather than considerations of humanity. Even as dogmatic a thinker as de Maistre remarked that politics was like physics, an experimental science; the first need of the political scientist was for an almanack, so that he knew in what year he was writing. Madame de Staël, in one of her earliest publications, had dismissed *The Social Contract* as unpractical and abstract, and Guizot, in one of his early political pamphlets, was frequently scornful of the theories of government as contrasted to the political habits

---

[1] See *Lanzac de Laborie*, 'L'amitié de Tocqueville et de Royer-Collard', *Revue des Deux Mondes*, August 15th, 1930, p. 884, p. 897.

[2] *Emile Faguet, Politiques et Moralistes du Dix-Neuvième Siècle*, Première Série, Paris 1891, pp. 257-306. See also *Jean Bordas-Demoulin, Lettres sur l'éclectisme et le doctrinarisme . . .* , Paris 1834.

which he hoped would grow in time.[1] Guizot was to be typical of several generations of French political thinkers when he spoke almost as a key-word of 'la nécessité, sévère, inflexible, inexorable'.[2] It is obvious therefore that from the start much of French political thought was to be essentially conservative, since it was concerned with France as it was in 1814 and afterwards, not in terms of France as it ought to have been. These thinkers were not trying to describe the ideal state; they were trying to justify the one they had.

In his early career Guizot played an important part in the process of trying to understand the France which existed in 1814. He was the author of what was perhaps the most important document of the first Restoration, the report on the condition of the country, which was presented to the Chamber of Deputies by Montesquiou on July 12th, 1814.[3] This report, which was largely statistical, was a condemnation of the Empire, whilst in certain respects it was a justification of the Revolution. The expenditure of the Empire on the army and on the wars, its wastage of men, its falsification of accounts, its suppression of liberty, had been disastrous for the moral and material welfare of France. Some of the acts of the Revolution, however, such as the distribution of land, had had a stimulating effect upon the French economy. This attempt to appraise the situation objectively, rather than by applying any system of beliefs or prejudices, was not well received everywhere, but it was necessary if France was to be governed. A more tendentious report might well have had the worst of effects, either within France or amongst the allied governments. In the routine administration of his department, Guizot had to deal with similar problems. There was a problem of personnel. Should those men who owed their position to the Emperor be maintained in office, or should their posts be redistributed amongst the loyal subjects of the King who had returned with him from exile? In reality, the greater part of the administrative personnel was retained in its functions; the changes that were effected were often made necessary by the revision of the French frontiers and the necessity of reintegrating officials from departments which had been removed from France. Of 43 new prefects, only 7 had been émigrés and only

[1] *Madame de Staël, Lettres sur les ouvrages et le caractère de Jean-Jacques Rousseau*, Paris 1789. The pamphlet by Guizot is *Du Gouvernement Représentatif en 1816*, Paris 1816.

[2] *Guizot, Du Gouvernement de la France depuis la Restauration*, Paris 1820, p. 23.

[3] The report was published in *Le Moniteur*, July 13th, 1814. *The Times* published long extracts from it on July 18th.

2 were pronounced royalists.[1] In a mémoire written in May 1814, and which Montesquiou submitted to the King, Guizot urged the government to have nothing to do with the political parties, which he described as 'Bonapartists', 'aristocrats' and 'republicans'. He urged the government to act energetically and clearly so as to dispel uneasiness; he saw France as wanting only leisure and peace.[2] This was a purely administrative, and a-political, piece of advice. The law on the press of July 5th, 1814, had been drafted by Royer-Collard, with the assistance of Guizot, and Guizot published two pamphlets to justify the law. The one was published before July 5th and the other was reproduced in the official newspaper, Le Moniteur.[3] He stressed the advantages of the liberty of the press, and showed the civic disadvantages which had resulted from the servility of the press under the Empire; yet he nevertheless concluded that in view of the circumstances he was in favour of a limited and provisional censorship. Benjamin Constant records in his Journal that he met Guizot in August 1814, and that he had quarrelled with him; it is certain from the context that the subject of the dispute was the press law, and it is with reference to Guizot's abandonment of principles that he comments, 'The smallest bit of power is a great corrupter.'[4]

With the return of Napoleon, Guizot left the Ministry of the Interior and returned to his university teaching. His political activity was restricted to a small circle, consisting of some of his former colleagues, such as Royer-Collard and Becquey, and others whose careers had been made in the Imperial bureaucracy, such as Prosper de Barante, Pasquier, Portalis; in this group too was Camille Jordan, the friend of the constitutionalist Mounier, and of Madame de Staël, who had represented Lyons under the Directory. When this group had become convinced that the return of Napoleon represented only a temporary success, then they concerned themselves actively with the second restoration of the Bourbons. It would be necessary to avoid the mistakes which had discredited Louis XVIII's government and which had facilitated the return of Napoleon; these mistakes were seen as mistakes of detail and of personalities. When Guizot was sent by this group to Ghent, to see the refugee King, it was largely to advise the King on the people whom he should employ; the group wanted the dismissal of Blacas and the nomination of Talleyrand. They were pursuing the course which had been suggested

[1] *Pouthas, Guizot Pendant le Restauration*, op. cit., pp. 55-58. (Two of the new nominations were personal friends of Guizot, one being his brother-in-law and another being a Protestant from Nîmes.)

[2] *Val-Richer* MSS. See *Pouthas*, op. cit., pp. 40-44.

[3] *Quelques idées sur la liberté de la presse*, Paris 1814; *Sur le nouveau projet de loi relatif à la presse*, Paris 1814; *Le Moniteur*, July 27th, 1814.

[4] *Benjamin Constant, Œuvres*, Bibliothèque de la Pléiade, Paris, 1957, p. 737.

by Montesquiou in the council of ministers, on March 16th when the Emperor was only five days from Paris, that the King should appoint as ministers men such as Lally-Tollendal, Lainé, and Voyer d'Argenson.[1] These suggestions were simply that the monarchy should surround itself with men who were popular rather than with courtiers who inspired distrust. Guizot's mission to Ghent was not successful, and it was because of other promptings that Louis XVIII sent Blacas away and turned to Talleyrand and Fouché, but it seems doubtful whether Guizot himself could have wished for more.

With the second Restoration Guizot became Secretary-General at the Ministry of Justice, when the minister was Pasquier until September 1815; with the formation of the Duc de Richelieu's first government, Guizot remained as Secretary-General to the new minister, Barbé-Marbois, but in May 1816 Richelieu made a number of cabinet changes and both Barbé-Marbois and Guizot lost their posts. Although it was not until April 1817 that Guizot was appointed a full member of the Conseil d'État, he remained extremely influential. All his major preoccupations were with direct political action. During the Talleyrand ministry, Pasquier, who was said to be 'le ministre dirigeant',[2] surrounded himself with an unofficial commission of advisers. Guizot, Royer-Collard, Becquey and Prosper de Barante (who had Guizot's former post at the Interior) are together again. Beugnot (who had been secretary to the commission which had drawn up the Charter) and Molé also appear. The group developed after September 1815. Several other personalities, mainly lawyers (amongst whom one must notice de Serre), join what Pasquier calls 'une petite réunion' where the questions which were to be raised in the Chamber were discussed in advance, and where tactics and procedure were agreed upon.[3] By July 1816, the Minister of Police in Richelieu's government had decided that faced with a violently hostile right-wing majority in the Chamber of Deputies, the situation of the ministry was impossible, both in France and in Europe. One way out of the impasse was by proclaiming the dissolution of this 'Chambre Introuvable', but Decazes had a long and difficult task in convincing firstly his colleagues, especially Richelieu and Lainé (the Minister of the Interior), and secondly the King, that such a move was wise. At the same time these negotiations had to take place in absolute secrecy. Decazes took Pasquier into his confidence, and through him, Guizot and Barante. During August three

---

[1] *De Vitrolles, Mémoires et Relations Politiques* (ed. Forgues), Paris 1884, vol. ii, pp. 327-328.

[2] *Barante, La Vie de M. Royer-Collard*, Paris 1863, vol. i, p. 162.

[3] *Pasquier, Histoire de mon temps. Mémoires publiés par d'Audiffret-Pasquier*, Paris 1893-1895, vol. iv, p. 15.

successive memoranda were submitted to the King with the object of deciding him. They were written by Decazes, Pasquier and Guizot. It is impossible to say which of these notes most influenced the King: Guizot himself does not speak of his own contribution as being of outstanding importance, and he almost certainly ante-dates the decision of the King to dissolve by placing it as early as August 14th, which is actually before the date of his own note, which was presented on August 18th. It would seem that the King finally made up his mind immediately after hearing the arguments of Guizot, but it seems also likely that more personal considerations weighed with him, and that he was as much influenced by annoyance at the language and tenure of the ultras as by the political arguments of his advisers.[1]

After the decree of dissolution had been decided upon, it was to Guizot that the government turned for advice on the form the elections should take in 1816. Guizot helped to prepare the electoral law of February 1817, and when it was ready, Lainé confessed to certain 'perplexités' and asked Guizot to write the speech with which he would have to present it to the Chamber.[2] He prepared speeches both for Decazes and for Pasquier, and was notably the author of the speech made by Gouvion-Saint-Cyr, then Minister for War, on January 26th, 1818. This speech was one of the most successful made by a minister during the Restoration, justifying the law on recruitment and promotion in the army which was promulgated on March 12th, 1818, one of the most important laws which was passed by a Restoration government. The resignation of Richelieu at the end of 1818, led to the formation of a ministry which was effectively directed by Decazes. With Decazes in power, the direct influence of Guizot and his friends in the preparing of various projects of law was to be even more considerable.

Guizot appears therefore as a man whose talents enabled him to achieve a real and effective power; he had succeeded in impressing a number of very different men, Royer-Collard, the abbé de Montesquiou, Pasquier, de Serre and Decazes, but he might well have become indistinguishable from the many able Conseillers d'État or from the many politicians whose actions were determined by events and by the circumstances of personal relationships. However, in the course of 1817 people began to speak of the 'doctrinaires'. The term seems to have been applied to Royer-Collard by *Le Nain Jaune*

[1] See *Guizot, Mémoires*, vol. i, pp. 147-153. *Duvergier de Hauranne, Histoire du Gouvernement Parlementaire en France*, Paris 1859, vol. iii, p. 480. *Pouthas*, op. cit., pp. 134-138. The King seems to have accepted the principle of dissolution on August 18th. The vital conseil des ministres was on August 20th.

[2] *Guizot, Mémoires*, vol. i, p. 165. The speech was made at the end of November 1816. Guizot also wrote two articles in *Le Moniteur* on December 31st, 1816, and on January 22nd-23rd, 1817, defending the law.

Réfugié, a Bonapartist paper published in Brussells, in 1816, but even by December 1817 the term was not widely known.[1] The word seems to refer to the Pères de la Doctrine de l'Oratoire, at whose school at Saint-Omer Royer-Collard had been educated, but it was invariably used as a form of abuse. Some people said that the word was coined by a 'huissier' of the Chamber of Deputies, who, tired by the length of a speech by Royer-Collard, asked 'Est-ce qu'il n'a pas fini de doctriner? Quel fichu doctrinaire.' The 'doctrinaires' first emerged as an effective group towards the end of 1817 and the beginning of 1818. By this time the Richelieu ministry was divided into two tendencies. Richelieu, Lainé and Pasquier were concerned at the increase of liberal strength in the country; on the other hand Decazes, Gouvion-Saint-Cyr and Molé opposed what they considered to be reactionary tendencies on the part of their colleagues. The group which had been formed around Pasquier could no longer exist, and the dissentient portion formed itself into the 'doctrinaires'. They were not numerous enough to form a party, or to have any voting strength in the Chamber. Many people were therefore witty at their expense; it was said that they could all sit on the same sofa as it had been said that the Foxite Whigs could get to the House in two coaches. The 'doctrinaires' were ordinarily thought of as being four in number, Royer-Collard, Camille Jordan and de Serre, who were deputies, and Guizot, who was still too young to be eligible for election. It was said that sometimes the doctrinaires could not believe that it was possible for there to be four people on earth with such intelligence as theirs and they then claimed to be only three, dropping Jordan or de Serre. It was said also that when they wished to frighten their enemies, they pretended to be five, Prosper de Barante (who was also excluded from the Chamber by the age limit) being originally the candidate for the fifth place. Beugnot, Mounier and the prefect Germain were associated with the doctrinaires at the beginning; the Duc de Broglie was to join them later, as was the young Charles de Rémusat, whose review of Madame de Staël's *Considérations sur la Révolution Française* was published by Guizot in the *Archives Philosophiques, Politiques et Littéraires* for December 1818. Other young men whose names were linked with the doctrinaires were Charles Villemain, who held a chair at the Sorbonne, de Mirbel, a botanist with political ambitions, and Auguste de Staël.

So far as the leaders were concerned they were men of different ages, varied backgrounds and contrasting temperaments. They were far from being agreed amongst themselves, and they were not always on good terms with each other. Royer-Collard fled responsibility.

[1] See *Duvergier de Hauranne*, op. cit., vol. iii, p. 534. *Rémusat, Mémoires de Ma Vie*, op. cit., vol. i, p. 332.

Whilst he had no desire to hold office, his disdain for those who achieved advancement in this way was accompanied by some jealousy; he was a notoriously difficult person to get on with, critical, destructive and at the same time indecisive. Camille Jordan was an elegant thinker and orator, but he had little patience with the details of public business; he had been reluctant to return to politics with the elections of 1816, and there were only certain subjects which interested him. He had a passionate hatred of injustice (as he showed by his attitude to the repression of the Lyons disturbance in June 1817) and a secret liking for popularity. De Serre was the least intellectual of the group; for a time he was completely dominated by Guizot and de Broglie, but he had an independent, obstinate character. He had been a young officer in the pre-Revolutionary army, and he always preferred action to discussion. One of his aims was the formation of a new aristocracy. A magistrate under the Empire, he was easily frightened by any illegality. He became the most considerable amongst the 'doctrinaires', becoming President of the Chamber of Deputies in 1818, and Garde des Sceaux with the Dessolles-Decazes ministry at the end of the year. It was de Serre who broke away most decidedly from Royer-Collard, Camille Jordan and Guizot and put an end to their collaboration. One-fifth of the Chamber of Deputies had to be elected each year, and the elections of September 1819 were a big defeat both for the right wing and for the government, being a great victory for the left. Some thirty-five new deputies came to the Chamber, including General Foy, the regicide conventional Grégoire, and several who had accepted posts during the Hundred Days. De Serre agreed with Decazes on the necessity of changing the electoral law so as to prevent a repetition of this, and it was then that doctrinaire agreement openly disappeared. Victor de Broglie was courageous, as his solitary vote in the Chamber of Peers against the sentence of death passed on Marshal Ney had shown in 1815: he was learned in his understanding of the English and American systems of government. Although he had known Royer-Collard and Guizot in the salon of his mother-in-law, Madame de Staël, he had at first collaborated with the politics of his step-father, the liberal Voyer d'Argenson and with liberals in his own department such as Dupont (de l'Eure), Bignon and Dumeilet; yet in spite of this tendency to the left he was the one doctrinaire to agree with de Serre in October 1819.

It is natural therefore that historians, in writing about the 'doctrinaires', should have emphasized their lack of doctrine. Yet in so doing they have undoubtedly missed the significance of this group, which was an original phenomenon in Restoration France. They are not to be compared to the groups and reunions which met at

Laffitte's or at Ternaux's amongst the left wing, or at Piet's or around Cardinal Bausset amongst the right. The 'doctrinaires' were not simply a tactical pressure-group; they tried to be a doctrinal pressure-group. Their attitude towards government and society was a sharp contrast to that of their contemporaries; whereas others were traditionalist, or emotional, or purely speculative, it was the intention of the 'doctrinaires' to elucidate principles as a guide to action. Long before the fall of Napoleon, French politics had fallen into a routine of historical memories, naive ambitions, and *ad hoc* reasoning. Those who did not wish to reopen the Revolution had no hope other than to close the Revolution; the 'doctrinaires' were more ambitious, they thought in terms of regeneration, and they realised that to do so, it was necessary to give to politics a sound philosophy.[1]

It was Guizot who most clearly realized the necessity of aligning practical considerations to theory. Of all the doctrinaires, he was the most faithful to this belief. After the movement towards the right began, following upon the assassination of the Duc de Berry in February 1820, Guizot was in July of that year dismissed from his post at the Conseil d'État; in October 1822 he was forbidden to lecture at the University. Thus he was forcibly provided with the leisure with which to pursue more intellectual and abstract studies than the drafting of laws and the preparation of speeches. But as early as June 1816, in the edited translation that he then published of Frederick Ancillon's study of sovereignty, he had spoken of the need for politicians to work out a theory of society, a theory of institutions and a theory of morality. To do this it was necessary to understand the principles and laws on which a society was based; if one did not have this understanding, then government would be at the mercy of events, and statesmen would not realize what was happening. In France especially, where Bonaparte had concealed all ideas of liberty and constitutional government, it was necessary to examine the doctrines which were current, rejecting those which were false and dangerous and substituting those that were wiser, in order to prevent France from wandering again in devious paths.[2] From July 1817 to December 1818 Guizot edited a monthly review, the *Archives Philosophiques, Politiques et Littéraires*. This review, as its name suggests, was not merely political; it tried to put within its scope the intellectual topics which were prominent in Europe, invariably from a

---

[1] *Guizot, Mémoires*, vol. i, pp. 158-159.

[2] *Frederick Ancillon, De la Souveraineté et des formes de gouvernement*, Paris 1816. See pp. 142-145, p. 9. Guizot accompanied the translation of this work by a number of critical notes. Ancillon, who was of French origin, was Professor in the Royal Military Academy at Berlin, and acted as a tutor in the Prussian royal family.

philosophical viewpoint (Cousin published some of his first writings in the *Archives*). Guizot himself frequently referred to the poverty of political thought in France. People, he said, could observe political phenomena; they could see the way things were going; they could analyse national interests, they showed a certain political tact. But that was all. Everyone agreed that the principles of representative government had been misunderstood and misapplied, but no one was trying to make that understanding better. The study of power in France had become a matter of pure observation; power was considered a plague which had either to be fled or resisted. In reality power was an instrument which had to be studied and mastered.[1] Guizot was to criticize statesmen who had no 'credo', who possessed only negative opinions, and who were frightened of any general idea. The science of such men consisted in doubting that there was any truth, in giving way to necessity, avoiding difficulties, running from commitments and putting off any solution. In 1821 he gave Pasquier as an example of 'this numerous class of men'; he had only one belief, and that was to beware of all beliefs.[2] Later, when writing his *Mémoires*, he was to criticize statesmen whom he admired but who considered questions only in terms of circumstances and not in terms of philosophical principles; both Casimir Périer and Louis-Philippe himself were criticized for these reasons.[3]

Guizot believed that it was in the nature of men that they had to have a theory with which to support their beliefs. There was a time when it was possible simply to appraise facts; but now they had to be put in line with theory. Politics, like political history, could not avoid being philosophical.[4] It is because he realized this that Guizot became important rather than merely useful. But one thing must always be borne in mind. The doctrinaire dialectic, as Rémusat called it, was constructed in conscious opposition to certain existing ways of thinking. The Counter-Revolution was always a reality; the remnants of revolutionary theories still existed as principles or as prejudices. Guizot deliberately set out to attack their doctrines. The doctrine of absolute power according to Bonald, of infallibility according to de Maistre, of passive obedience as it was then expressed by Lamennais, or any of the theories of equality, or of the rule of the

[1] *Archives P.P.L.*, vol. iv, July 1818, p. 37.
[2] *Guizot, Des Moyens du Gouvernement et d'Opposition*, Paris 1821, p. 45. Pasquier was very hurt by this criticism.
[3] *Guizot, Mémoires*, vol. ii, pp. 237-238.
[4] *Guizot, Histoire de la Civilisation en Europe* (1848 ed.), pp. 91-94. The first edition of this work was published in Paris in 1828. *Histoire des Origines du Gouvernement Représentatif* (1880 ed.), vol. ii, p. 130. The first edition was published in Paris in 1851. Both publications were based on Guizot's lectures at the University during 1828 and 1820-1822 respectively.

numerical majority, which had been dominant during the Revolution, all these were unacceptable. Guizot's thought therefore had all the characteristics of the method by which it developed; it was a counter-system rather than a system.

The first problem was that of sovereignty. No one could be blind to the nature of the Bourbon return. As Guizot wrote in his memorandum of May 1814, a fortnight before the Restoration, such an event would have appeared as 'an absurd fable'. In the same way the Charter itself appeared to be, at best, a happy accident. If these sources of authority had been only accidentally established, then how could their authority be accepted? A theory of sovereignty had to be worked out.

There were two rival doctrines. There were those who saw authority as lying in God; the word of God was revealed to man through religion and through monarchy. In practical terms this theory was expressed by Louis XVIII at Hartwell in 1814, when he was told that he had been proclaimed king. 'Have I ever ceased to be King?' was his supposed reply. One must notice that this doctrine was not always as metaphysical as one might expect; Lamennais framed this theory as a result of observation. He claimed that all societies in the past which had been successful were based upon religious principles; that is to say, authority had to be based upon some principle which was uncontested. Whereas one could criticize or resist a human power, once one had admitted the existence of God, then one could not resist his power.[1] The rival theory placed sovereignty in the people. The doctrine could also claim to have a divine origin, since it claimed to represent the omnipotence of God in human terms, and the superiority of selflessness over egoism which was to be found in a people rather than in an individual.[2]

The conflict between these theories was the conflict between Louis XVIII, who was returning to France because he was the rightful King, and the Napoleonic Senate, who were inviting him to accept or to refuse the constitution. This conflict had been removed rather than resolved. Some theoretical solution had to be found if it was not going to recur in some other form. Guizot, like Royer-Collard, chose to reject both theories, and presented a third. This stated that sovereignty existed nowhere on earth. To assert that

[1] These ideas are most clearly expressed in the first volume of *L'Essai sur l'Indifférence*, Paris 1817.
[2] See an article by *Lerminier* in the *Revue des Deux Mondes*, vol. i, 1834. Jean-Louis Lerminier (1803-1857) was Professor of Comparative Legislation at the Collège de France. A Saint-Simonien, he had collaborated with *Le Globe* during the Restoration.

sovereignty existed wholly in some human institution was to establish arbitrary despotism. If anyone even asks, believed Royer-Collard, where sovereignty lies, then he proclaims himself a supporter of arbitrary government.[1]

Guizot devoted part of his enforced leisure, after he had been dismissed from the Conseil d'État and from his university teaching, to the compilation of a work of political theory which was to be a refutation of Rousseau. This work was never completed, but the portion of it to be published was devoted to the question of sovereignty. He had earlier discussed this question in his edition of Ancillon and in his 1820-1822 lectures on representative government.

When he takes the individual as his starting-point, Guizot shows first of all man's need for God. He is unable to see God in a purely terrestial form, but he is equally unable to abandon all hope of ever seeing God. Therefore to escape the dilemma he is for ever investing somebody or something with power and treating them as his master, as if they were God. Sometimes such power would be given to a man, sometimes to a family, sometimes to a group or caste of people, even to the people altogether. But no sooner has man attributed this power than he feels the need to contest it, that is to say, to withdraw it. However, in spite of this oscillation and uncertainty, man never abandons the idea that one day he will find his real sovereign. Hence men fear despotism but are anxious to instal a despot somewhere; even in his most superb moments man was ready to humiliate himself before some idol. It was a sign of pride that man should think himself capable of finding and recognizing the true God; it was a sign of his weakness that he felt the need to take rest within such a faith.

By a familiar process of reasoning, Guizot went on from this description to see this perpetual idolatry as a proof of the real existence of God. God is not the idol, but it is God that man searches for within the idol; if God did not exist, then idols would not receive such adoration. Therefore God exists, and human society has a sovereign. From this sovereign comes reason, justice and truth. In any human society, in any family or in any state, whenever a dispute arises men recognize that there is a truth which will settle the dispute; this is a recognition of the sovereign. It is obvious that no man can claim to have a monopoly of this truth or reason; if a man does claim this infallibility, he may take away from other men all guarantee of the sovereign law. 'Whether governments oppress or whether philosophers reason, whether the would-be sovereign is the people or Caesar, the same result is imposed on men.' Therefore there is no

---

[1] Quoted in G. Rémond, *Royer-Collard: Son Essai d'un Système Politique*, Paris 1933, p. 39.

force on earth which possesses the rightful sovereignty or which can command the right to be fully and everlastingly obeyed.[1]

When Guizot took society as his starting-point, he carried the argument a stage further. He adopted the principle that in each society there must be a government which establishes the law. The idea of society therefore implies the idea of government (and any contract theory is unacceptable). But the question is, what is the nature of the law which is part of society? The answer can only be that it is a law which is based on justice; any law which is based on force only will always be contested—as history proves. It is necessary to distinguish between two different types of sovereignty, the 'souveraineté de droit' or lawful, rightful sovereignty, the sovereignty of justice, and the 'souveraineté de fait' or the effective sovereignty of ordinary governments. It had been the vice of governments that they had tried to combine both sovereignties in themselves. They had pretended that rightful sovereignty existed in some portion of society, in one man, in several, or in all. Some had believed in divine right and had said there is one God, therefore there is one King and he is the representative of God; some had believed in the sovereignty of the people and had said there is one people, therefore there should be one Legislative Assembly. Such arguments led to government by force, to despotism. The only rightful sovereignty comes from God; God exists nowhere on earth; no man and no people can claim perfect knowledge of God or can claim to obey his laws only. God exists and his will exists in man's conscience; government results from the realization that man wishes to try to obey the will of God. The task of government, of 'souveraineté de fait', is to govern as nearly as possible to the precepts of rightful sovereignty, of 'souveraineté de droit'. The task of political science is to try and discover which form of government is best suited to discovering rightful sovereignty, that is to say, of ruling according to justice, truth and reason.[2]

This idea of the sovereignty of reason was expressed by a number of Guizot's associates. Rémusat, for example, in a number of articles on Lamennais in *Le Globe* during 1829, repeats the main theme of Guizot's argument. No human infallibility is possible. The only infallible law is divine wisdom. Yet this law can be revealed in this world; this sovereign wisdom can communicate with certain human intelligences. It provides a rule for human reason, a law for human justice, a type for human wisdom. Whenever one says 'this is true', 'this is right', 'this is reasonable', then one is appealing to the

[1] *Le Globe*, November 25th, 1826.
[2] *Histoire des Origines du Gouvernement Représentatif,* op. cit., vol. i, pp. 88 ff.; vol. ii, pp. 142 ff.

sovereign law.[1] Victor Cousin spoke of 'the sovereign power of reason which is in humanity as God is in the Universe'.[2] Royer-Collard never ceased to proclaim the sovereignty of reason.[3] To Guizot, as to his colleagues, it would have appeared strange to have asked for more particulars about the law of reason, how it was to be recognized and understood. They might well have replied with Burke, that 'although no man can draw a stroke between the confines of day and night, yet light and darkness are upon the whole tolerably distinguishable'. In a pamphlet which attacked the government's policy of executing those who were found guilty of conspiracy, after the wave of republican and Bonapartist plots of 1821 and 1822, Guizot gave an example of a law of justice which conflicted with a law of government. When in 1793 Engrand d'Alleray was asked by the President of the Revolutionary Tribunal whether he did not know that there was a law which forbade the sending of money to 'émigrés', he replied that he knew that law, but that he also knew an older law which obliged him to support his children.[4] Morality was not always determined by the text of a law. Providence did not allow force to make and unmake what was a crime or what was a virtue. If there was not a justice superior to legal justice, then there would be no justice. Guizot quotes Montesquieu, 'To say that there is nothing just or unjust but what is ordered or forbidden by positive laws, is to say that before the circle was drawn the radii were not equal.'[5]

Political interpretations of the sovereignty of reason could vary. Guizot believed that the form of government best suited to discovering reason and truth was representative government, only the government had to be in the hands of those who had the capacity to seek for and discover truth. Lerminier, and even Lamartine, on the other hand, spoke of reason as being found in the whole of the people, in society altogether. Other people saw in the appeal to human reason an example of a Socratic method, which was essentially democratic. But the main political implications of the theory are clear. The doctrines of sovereignty which Guizot denied were in practice doctrines of supremacy; Guizot has therefore rejected the supremacy

[1] The articles were collected by *Rémusat* in *Études Critiques et Littéraires, Passé et Présent*, Paris 1859, vol. i, pp. 365-401.

[2] *Victor Cousin, Cours d'Histoire de la Philosophie Morale*, Brussels 1841. See the Eighth Lecture.

[3] See, for example, his speech in 1831 on the heredity of the peerage. '. . . Une autre souveraineté, la seule qui mérite ce nom, souveraineté supérieure aux peuples comme aux rois, souveraineté immuable et immortelle comme son auteur, je veux dire la souveraineté de la raison, seul législateur véritable de l'humanité.' *Barante, Royer-Collard*, op. cit., vol. ii, p. 459.

[4] *De la Peine de Mort en Matière Politique*, Paris 1822. See p. 289 in *Mélanges Politiques et Historiques*, Paris 1869.

[5] Ibid., p. 342. The quotation is from the first chapter of *L'Esprit des Lois*.

of any single power in the state. The state should be a multiplicity of different powers working in harmony rather than the entrenchment of any one particular power.

The fear of supremacy was the fear of arbitrary rule, of the Convention or of the Empire. To the 'doctrinaires' as to Tocqueville, once one felt the hand of power, it little mattered whether it came from one man or from a million. But this fear of supremacy forms a contrast between France and England, and helps to explain some of the differences between French and English statesmen. Guizot's view of sovereignty conflicts with what was taking place in England at about this time, and which was to be theoretically expressed by Austin. The England of the Reform Act believed in the summary omnipotence of Parliament, that social utility was the basis for the law, and that the state was justified by social well-being. It was possible to separate law from morals and to adopt a conception of sovereignty which was essentially legislative. Guizot's theory of sovereignty resembled in some respects the beliefs of the English opponents of the Bentham school, who insisted upon the importance of custom and of the old unwritten common law. It also recalls the rôle of the French 'Parlements' in the eighteenth century; these were neither popular institutions, nor were they supposed to participate actively in the work of government. They existed in order to discipline the rule of the King, and to verify that he willed only that which was just and reasonable. Guizot was not consciously working in this tradition (indeed, he gives the Parlements as a practical example of the bad effect of combining two separate functions, the political and the judicial, since the former often invaded the latter),[1] but the theoretical assumption of both was the same, namely that the power of an institution was limited by both moral and rational imperatives. Both these comparisons, however, suggest that such a theory of sovereignty can lead to a view of politics which can fairly be described as 'conservative'.

Why did Guizot put forward this theory? One can suggest personal reasons. It is in many ways Protestant, and resembles the strictures of Théodore de Bèze that obedience to princes is subject to the condition that their commands are not contrary to religion or to morals. Benjamin Constant, another Protestant, in his Commentary on Filangieri, approaches the same theory of sovereignty, whilst Royer-Collard was steeped in the Jansenist tradition of Troyes and of Sompuis. One might also recall that all the leading 'doctrinaires' had

[1] *Des Conspirations et de la Justice Politique*, Paris 1821. See p. 140 in *Mélanges Politiques et Historiques*. This pamphlet was written after the discovery of a Bonapartist plot in August 1820 and is one of the best examples of the doctrinaire method of treating a particular incident in terms of general principles.

suffered, either directly or indirectly, from the Revolution; to deny the sovereignty of the people was one way of ensuring that there would not be another Convention. But one must not make too much of personal memories. One cannot suppose that important movements of thought result from Guizot's recollection of his mother, on her knees, giving thanks for the death of Robespierre, or of Joseph de Maistre remembering how his mother told him that he must not be so gay because a great misfortune had happened, the Parlement of Paris had expelled the Jesuits. Nor is it enough to say that this was a period when men were undergoing the influence of the Kantian discussion of reason and of innate understanding. There were practical reasons why such a theory was relevant to the affairs of France. It was a means of neutralizing the positions of two rival groups. It was meant to appeal to the bourgeoisie, as a theory which was beyond persons and classes, which recognized their victory over absolutism and feudalism, and which by denying the sovereignty of the people denied that there was any further class conflict. The contract theory had served its purpose; it was now full of dangerous consequences for the victorious class. Guizot could not believe that the bourgeoisie could prefer a compressive régime to one that gave them freedom. Therefore, in order to attack absolutism he had to fall back on the moral law which is not made by man, in much the same way as Montesquieu had done in the attack on Hobbes. Lastly, such a theory arose from a realistic appraisal of the French situation; even without being a Protestant, a pluralist view of the state must have come naturally to a Frenchman who based his principles on observation. French society was too complex for there to be any simple fixing of one point of authority; no power was absolute in practice, groups had power and retained loyalties. The unity of a state existed in terms of real forces, not merely in legal unity; the effectiveness of a law depended not so much on its formal declaration but upon its coincidence with social forces. Sovereignty could not therefore be placed in any one part of the state. It is only fair to add that there is in this ethical conception of government a strong element of idealism. It is this that attracted Lord Acton to the 'doctrinaires', and to Guizot in particular.[1]

With the theory of sovereignty, one must consider the theory of monarchy and of representative government.

Hortense Allart, the friend of the Comtesse d'Agoult, of Chateaubriand and of Bulwer Lytton, once wondered why it was that men

---

[1] *G. E. Fasnacht, Acton's Political Philosophy*, 1952, pp. 42 ff. Acton's notes however, in the Cambridge University Library, have surprisingly few references to Guizot.

respected the monarchy; in order to find out, she took to reading Hume. Many of her contemporaries were continually to ask the same question and, like Hortense Allart, they sought the answer theoretically and historically; it is characteristic of Guizot and his associates that they placed in the forefront of the discussion the fact that the monarchy already existed. Guizot was later to say that Louis XVIII in 1814 formed 'a constituent power'. During his lifetime he said that he had known three such constituent powers, the other two being Napoleon in the year VIII and the Chamber of Deputies in 1830. There was no lesson to be drawn from these powers; they could not be explained, it was destiny which had arranged for them to be there.[1] This was similar to the Duc de Broglie's statement that to be 'legitimate', government had to be effective; thus during the Revolution and the Empire, legitimate government was in Paris, and not in an émigré court, whilst with the first Restoration, legitimate government remained in Paris with the king and was in no way transferred to Elba.[2] Thus we find the doctrinaire argument of acceptance applied to the monarchy.

But the argument could not stay there. Guizot believed that monarchy was necessary to France, and that the events of the Revolution and of the Empire had demonstrated this. This was why Joseph de Maistre had, with his sense of fatalism, thought of Bonaparte as being destined to bring about the return of the Bourbons. 'Let Napoleon alone', he had written shortly after Bonaparte had become Consul for life. 'Let him rule France with his rod of iron . . . let him make a majesty and imperial highness, marshals, hereditary senators and knights of his orders; let him replace the lilies on his empty escutcheon etc. etc. and then, Madame, how can you doubt that the people, however silly they will be, will not have sense enough to say: it is true then, it seems, that a great nation cannot be governed by a Republic, it is true then, that we must necessarily fall under the rule of a sceptre of some kind, and obey some man or other, it is true then that equality is a chimera.'[3] Royer-Collard was probably not a royalist when he was accused of being one on the 18th Fructidor, yet he shortly became one. The necessity of royalism for him came from the overwhelming evidence of human weakness and uncertainty; men wanted the strength and conviction which would be provided by tradition. The symbol of

[1] Chambre des Députés, August 18th, 1842. *Histoire Parlementaire*, vol. iii, p. 681.
[2] Chambre des Pairs, October 14th, 1831. *Duc de Broglie, Écrits et Discours*, Paris 1863, vol. ii, pp. 351 ff.
[3] Joseph de Maistre: Madame la Baronne de P . . . , July 1802, *Lettres et Opuscules*, Paris 1851, vol. i, pp. 12-18.

tradition and of the past was to be found in the monarchy. Here, then, were immediate justifications of royalism. But it is noticeable that Guizot, in his lectures, gave a much wider interpretation of the rôle of monarchy. He emphasized the importance of royalty in the history of Europe and of the world; royalty as an institution penetrated everywhere; it adapted itself to the most varied situations of civilization and barbarism, and to the most diverse forms of society. That such an institution was so widespread could not be explained in terms of chance or of coincidence. It was certain that there must be some analogy between royalty, considered as an institution, and individual man, or between royalty and human society. Guizot suggested as an explanation that royalty should not be considered as the rule of one man, or the expression of his will, even although it was usually under that form that it appeared; in the minds of people who gave their allegiance to a king, he personified the sovereignty of law, a will which was enlightened, just and impartial; the royal will rose above all individual wills and for that reason was entitled to rule them. The theocrat saw in the king the image of God on earth; the lawyers saw in the king the living law; others saw in the king the personification of the state, of the general interest of society. A king is unique, as there is only one justice; he is permanent, above the vicissitudes and hazards of the world; he is both spectator and judge. A monarchy is adaptable to all varieties of circumstances, and creates or maintains the unity of societies. Hence monarchy is justified both historically and philosophically.[1]

But, as Rémusat was to put it when addressing the Academy, when one looks for kings one cannot invent them, one finds them, and one finds them not in theory but in history. That is to say that although monarchy is justified because it fulfils a function, the function can only be performed if the monarch is a true one; the principle of legitimacy is essential to the principle of monarchy. Guizot admitted this principle during the Hundred Days, since he was never attracted to the cause of the Duke of Orleans (unlike de Broglie), for all that the Duke possessed many advantages as a conciliator of the different parties in France, as he was, according to a current 'mot', both of Bourbon blood and covered with it. One could only make a king in two ways, said Guizot. Either, like Napoleon, one made oneself king by military means and this was not an example of permanence; or one was born a prince, one was 'of the wood of which princes are made'. It was not possible even for thirty-two million men to take the first comer from amongst them and make him king.[2] Guizot, like

[1] *Histoire de la Civilisation en Europe* (op. cit.), 9th lecture.
[2] Chambre des Députés, January 3rd, 1834. *Histoire Parlementaire*, vol. ii, p. 189.

Benjamin Constant in *De l'Esprit de Conquête et de l'Usurpation*, is not far from de Maistre's belief that what one said to royalty was 'Who are you?' rather than 'What can you do?'

The theory of legitimacy was obviously shaken by the events of 1830. If one supported the Revolution, accepted the new dynasty, and became minister in the new government, then how could one maintain the principle of hereditary as opposed to elective monarchy? Yet Guizot constantly maintained both his monarchical beliefs and his belief in the Revolution of 1830; after 1848, in the negotiations which took place between the Bourbon and Orleanist branches of the French royal house, with a view to effecting their 'fusion', Guizot insisted that the Comte de Chambord should recognize that the Revolution of 1830 was both 'national and legal'; even in extreme old age he would not tolerate any disparagement of these events.[1] The solution of this apparent contradiction lies in the fact that while Guizot saw the monarchy as an institution performing a function in the state, yet he never lost sight of the fact that the monarch was a man. In this he differs from moderate royalists both of the Restoration and of the July Monarchy period. Ballanche, for example, denied that the sovereign was a man; the sovereign was a thing. Fonfrède said that the king was transfigured by his office, no longer had any particular interest as a man, and therefore was no longer a man, but 'an animated institution, which neither lives nor dies, but which last'.[2] For Guizot, the monarch was a man who was doing his job, and he was doing it well or he was doing it badly, according to his capacity, or according to his advisers. One must, he wrote in 1828, distinguish between the king as an abstraction, and as a reality. When the king comes to the throne, he does not cease to be a man; he cannot rid himself of everything which he has personally thought, or felt, or experienced. His political councillors have to say many things which astonish him, or ask him for things which displease him.[3] In 1846 he said that there sat on the throne someone who was intelligent and free, who had his own ideas, sentiments, desires and wishes, as had any other person.[4] Charles X failed in his duty because

[1] See *Claude-Noel Desjoyeaux, La Fusion Monarchique*, Paris 1913, p. 17. One of the reasons why Guizot refused to accept the projected version of Émile Ollivier's speech to the Academy in 1874 was because it implied that the revolution was a 'coup d'état'. See *Émile Ollivier, Lamartine*, Paris 1874.

[2] *Ballanche, Le Vieillard et le Jeune Homme*, Paris 1819, in *Oeuvres*, Paris 1830, vol. ii, p. 415. *Henri Fonfrède, De la Société, du Gouvernement, et de l'Administration* [1839] in *Œuvres* (edited by Ch.-Al. Campan), Bordeaux 1844-1846, vol. i, p. 232. Fonfrède, a journalist from the south-west, was a writer very hostile to the 'doctrino-conservateurs'.

[3] *Revue Française*, September 1828. See *Mélanges Politiques*, op. cit., pp. 488-489.

[4] Chambre des Députés, May 29th, 1846. *Histoire Parlementaire*, vol. v, p. 228.

he failed to govern with the accord of the powers which the constitution had established; in 1830 the dynasty was shown as being incapable of governing; France was forced to choose between the ruin of her institutions or a revolution.[1]

Even as the throne of Charles X trembled, Frenchmen instinctively knew, according to Guizot, that France was a monarchy, and could not hope for salvation without that institution; but France could not elect a king. It was foolishness to pretend, as some did, that Louis-Philippe was 'the king of our choice'; Louis-Philippe was unique and necessary. The wishes of the people are not sufficient to make kings, 'he who becomes king must carry within him and bring as his "dot" to the country which weds him, some of the natural and independent characteristics of royalty'.[2] The declaration of the Chambers, which was drawn up by Guizot, therefore registered the fact that the throne was vacant, and called in the younger branch of the royal family. Louis-Philippe was king because of his Bourbon blood, even although some said that he was king in spite of his Bourbon connections. The Duc de Broglie was one of those who would have liked to emphasize royal continuity by calling the monarch Philip VII; enthusiastic Orleanists had to content themselves, however, with referring to him as Louis-Philippe the First. Some people thought that the situation of the Orleans monarch fairly deserved the description of 'quasi-legitimate'. Guizot was not one of them. He denied using this word (which he said had been attributed to him by Le Figaro) since he regarded the new monarchy as fully legitimate.

On July 13th, 1842, the Duke of Orleans, heir to the throne, was killed in an accident. His son, the Comte de Paris, was still a child; his father, the King, was ageing. It was therefore necessary to make arrangements for a Regency, since no provision for such a situation had been made by the Charter. The whole affair was rendered particularly complicated since it followed closely upon the elections, which had been disappointing for the government of Guizot, since they had not increased his majority. Therefore two questions were at stake when the Regency Bill was presented; in the first place the institution of monarchy and its principles were being debated; in the second place the future of the Guizot government, which certain people thought would have to resign, was being tested. Three solutions were put forward. One was that the Duke's widow would assume the regency if ever her son was called upon to rule whilst still a minor; this was a solution which attracted many who claimed that

---

[1] Chambre des Députés, January 6th, 1834, August 9th, 1834. Ibid., vol. ii, p. 195, p. 277.

[2] Chambre des Députés, January 3rd, 1834. Ibid., p. 189. Mémoires, vol. ii, pp. 236-237.

the Duchess, as the prince's mother, was the natural regent, and who were also influenced by the belief that she had liberal inclinations. Another solution was that the Chamber of Deputies should elect a regent, and should do so each time a similar situation existed; this, it was said, would ensure that only an able man would become regent, and by this argument the principle of an elective monarchy was obviously being suggested; the election of a regent would also have been a good ground on which to combat the Guizot ministry. The solution put forward by the government was the natural sequence to the monarchical principle, namely, that the regency should go to the next in the line of succession who was of age. In this case, the Duke of Nemours would be designated, a prince whose supposed reactionary tendencies provided an additional reason why many members of the opposition wished to oppose the government plan. The debate, which ended in a government victory, was noticeable for two things; for the action of Thiers, who did not associate himself with the opposition of Odilon Barrot, Tocqueville and Lamartine, but whose desire to see the monarchy strengthened caused him to support the government, and for the speech in which Guizot explained his conception of a monarchy. The royal power represented action in the state, as the king was head of the executive; it represented fixity, since by its hereditary character it was a perpetual power. In a democracy, and Guizot believed that France was the greatest modern democratic society, the mission of the monarchy was particularly to counter-balance the weakness and mobility of the individual wills which made up democratic society. In social affairs a democracy gave great liberty to individual wills; but in government a democracy particularly tries to restrain these same individuals. To introduce the elective element into the monarchy would therefore not only upset the distribution of power in the state by giving more power and responsibility to the Chamber of Deputies, but also would weaken that part of the government which was supposed to combat the imperfections of democracy. Royalty was no longer a family patrimony; it was a public power, and as such Guizot did not believe that it could be represented by a woman. A female ruler or a female regent increased the possibility of an influential court, which Guizot obviously distrusted; the power of a woman could be considerable within a château or a palace, but he did think that it could be powerful in a democratic society.[1]

This is monarchy by expediency as well as monarchy by right. In its conception of society it recalls some of Benjamin Constant's ideas on the difference between liberty in the ancient world and liberty

[1] Chambre des Députés, August 18th, 1842. *Histoire Parlementaire*, vol. iii, pp. 677 ff. For the Regency question see below, pp. 194-196.

amongst the moderns. In the ancient world individuals were consulted on many public questions, they had the right to deliberate in public places on war, peace, treaties and other matters of public policy; but in their private existences they were not free and did not have the right to control their private actions, such as their religion or their occupation, as they wished. In modern societies, on the contrary, the individual is free in his private life, but in practice he is excluded from exercising any control over public affairs; if, on certain fixed but rare occasions, the individual can exercise this control, then it is only so that he can immediately abdicate it.[1] Both for Guizot and for Constant there is implied a separation between government and society; government is limited, it does not extend to all activities of society, but at the same time the separation is not unlike a distinction between conquerors and conquered, the rulers and the ruled. For Guizot, the ordinary individuals of society are weak, uncertain and dangerous; for Constant they have little interest in public affairs, they lack convictions and they are attracted to liberty only because of the material enjoyments which it permits. When Guizot associates this theory of society to his theory of monarchy, then the latter takes on a further significance; the monarchy becomes a hereditary principle of exclusion; it serves as a bulwark for the politically privileged classes, and is therefore both a weapon with which to attack those who wish for change and a necessary target for the reformers. Such a theory of monarchy could have been produced in reply to those who wished for a more political democracy, but such a theory helped to create a corresponding theory of republicanism. The monarchy ceased to be a compromise or a means to a compromise; it became a source of dispute. It was not monarchy as seen by Montesquieu, who had said that in a state which was governed by a prince divisions were easily resolved since there existed a coercive power which could settle them, whereas in a republic it was the very power capable of applying the remedy which was attacked.[2]

Since the monarchy was an essential piece of political machinery it could never be restricted to what Guizot once called a 'pompous impotence', and the monarchy played an important rôle in his conception of parliamentary government. In practice he did everything

[1] *Benjamin Constant*, Conférence à l'Athenée de Paris, 1819, in *Collection Complète des Ouvrages publiés sur le Gouvernement Représentatif . . .* (ed. Laboulaye), Paris 1861, vol. ii, pp. 539-560. See also the same idea in De l'Esprit de Conquête et de l'Usurpation, Paris 1814, in *Œuvres* (Bibliothèque de La Pléiade), Paris 1957, pp. 1044-1048.

[2] *Considérations sur les Causes de la Grandeur des Romains et de leur Décadence*, chapter 4. In the *Archives P.P.L.* for September 1817 Guizot had referred to *L'Esprit des Lois* as the best book for proving the excellence of monarchy. See vol. i, p. 294.

that he could to increase the prestige of monarchy. He took a great interest in protocol, and on two occasions he protested that letters from the Prince Consort to Louis-Philippe were incorrectly phrased.[1] In another letter to Sainte-Aulaire enquiring about a question of precedence between ambassadors and princes, he showed that it was he who was preoccupied with this kind of question, not merely the French court. To favour ambassadors rather than princes was 'carrying water to the river, since these days it is only the princes who need to be supported; public authorities have and are gaining ground over the rights of birth; one must look after the sovereign races which are already weakened; if one puts oneself above the ideas, passions and customs of our times . . . one sees that in the midst of aristocratic decadence, the sovereign races are a necessary part of social order and an indispensable part of government. What would happen to us without them? We would fall into the difficulties of the radical democracies, such as America or Switzerland, who do not know with what they can construct power, since they no longer find the elements of power within themselves. We must therefore take care of the sovereign races, their privileges and their honours.'[2] In 1842 an important difficulty arose between the French and the Spanish governments, as the French ambassador Salvandy wished to present his credentials to the Queen of Spain, Isabella, rather than to the Regent, General Espartero, and the Spanish government decided that this was not acceptable. This affair was complicated since Guizot's source of information in Madrid (who was Roths-child's agent) claimed that the British representative, Aston, had encouraged the Spanish government in their attitude; however, the French conception was clear, an ambassador was sent from one royal family to another, rather than from one country to another. Guizot never spoke ill of any of the monarchs he had known, even although he had often had no illusions as to their qualities. Even for Otto, King of Greece, he showed great forbearance, and whilst Piscatory, the ambassador in Athens, would lament the King's stupidity and obstinacy ('But the King!! The King!! Wherever did providence go to find him?'), even in his private correspondence Guizot contented himself with saying that the King would save more trouble than he would make.[3] Guizot never ceased to urge that people should over-look the personal failings of a monarch, in view of his intrinsic value. He recalled that during the eighteenth century England had had two

[1] Guizot: Sainte-Aulaire (ambassador in London), November 16th, 1841, and May 16th, 1843. *Archives Nationales*, 42 A.P. 8. The exchange of letters followed upon the birth of children to Queen Victoria.

[2] Ibid., March 30th, 1843.

[3] Piscatory: Guizot, April 28th, 1845. *Archives Nationales*, 42 A.P. 7. See *Mémoires*, vol. vii, pp. 312-314, for Guizot's defence of the King.

kings who did not know a word of English, who were personally disagreeable, and whose one idea was to leave the country; but in England it was realized that neither George I nor George II had been called to the throne because of their merits or their charm, but because they were necessary to the country. England had therefore to put up with their royal fantasies in things which were unimportant. France should similarly subordinate her tastes to her interests. For Guizot the monarchy was necessary, however disagreeable the monarch.[1]

The weakness of all theories of monarchy is that they are easy to attack, and after 1830 it was particularly easy to criticize Guizot's theory of Orleanist legitimacy. It was said that after 1830 such a theory was only a foolishness, and that a dogma could not recognize an 'à peu près'; it was said that in 1830 the bourgeoisie had simply changed their dynasty as if they were transferring credit from one bank to another; Guizot's insistence upon legitimacy, it was alleged, was simply a manœuvre in answer to theories of popular sovereignty.[2] There was probably a great deal in Louis Blanc's remark that the French monarchy was something which was new, and had no analogies with monarchies at other times or in other places, except that it was showing the secret desire of all royalties to attach themselves to the chain of tradition.[3] Another source of weakness in Guizot's conception of monarchy undoubtedly lay in the personality of Louis-Philippe. He has probably never been better described than by Guizot himself in his *Mémoires*; the King appears with all his qualities and most of his defects; but in spite of all his kindness, wisdom and concern, it is difficult to see him as a royal character. He was not the first 'gentilhomme' of his kingdom; he was merely the first bourgeois; he had forgotten none of his experiences and he had learnt only that he dared not consider his royalty as permanent. He told Queen Victoria that ever since his days of exile and poverty, he had always carried a knife in his pocket with which to eat; such a habit appealed to Guizot in its simplicity (although in Charles Bovary it had shocked and disgusted Emma), but it does not appear appropriate in a man who is king by right of birth. It was easier to criticise the King than to venerate him. Talleyrand, who had disliked Louis XVIII, was probably more typical of Frenchmen when he recorded his distrust of Louis-Philippe ('I dislike these ogres who think that they increase their own reputation by devouring the reputations of

[1] Guizot: Léonce de Lavergne, October 11th, 1848. *Correspondance* (op. cit.), pp. 43-45.

[2] *F. Malebouche, Le Système des Doctrinaires*, Paris 1831; Eugène Pelletan in the *Revue Indépendante*, February 1st, 1842, p. 506; *Revue des Deux Mondes*, Chronique Politique, January 15th, 1834, pp. 229-230.

[3] *Revue du Progrès Social*, March 1st, 1839, p. 219.

others'),[1] but in speaking in this way Talleyrand was illustrating what Guizot meant when he said that Talleyrand was not fitted to the circumstances of the times. Monarchy was necessary, therefore a theory of monarchy was necessary; epigrams at the expense of the monarchs were unnecessary. Frenchmen were working *a posteriori*, trying to reassemble the series of causes and effects which had come undone.

The idea of representative, or parliamentary, government was in the nature of things by 1814. Talleyrand saw that it had become characteristic of society to govern with a certain amount of consent; Chateaubriand believed that the Bourbons could not possibly get themselves up as an absolute monarchy based on military support. The Charter of 1814 was therefore a practical realization of what was obvious; yet it was expressed in very general terms. Within a short period of the second Restoration it became obvious that interpretation of the Charter was going to become the key to much political activity. It became necessary to understand the way this type of government should work.

Guizot believed that representative government was the system whereby the sovereignty of reason might most effectively be attained; yet he was particularly concerned with representative government as a system which would fit the needs of France. Guizot's approach to this problem was in many ways that of a theoretical rationalist. He thought of government as discussion, as the critical appraisal of institutions and ideas. He never doubted the power of reason which he thought of as being common to all men of good will. But he was not a complete rationalist. He could not be classified amongst those liberals whom Renan criticized because they sought to found institutions by reflexion alone, without reference to historical roots. He was not a rationalist like Benjamin Constant trying to find formulae sufficiently abstract to be accepted by everyone. Unlike Voltaire, he did not believe that the only way of having good laws was to destroy all existing laws and to start afresh. He believed that the greatest of modern plagues was an incurable impatience with what already existed, and an insatiable desire for change. He thought historically. In his 1820 lectures he said that a thorough acquaintance with history was not merely the accomplishment of a cultivated mind, but that it was a necessity to every citizen who wanted to take part in the affairs of his country or who needed to appreciate them correctly. After 1848 he put it more succinctly. 'When history speaks, it is well for politics to listen.' He believed that if one was to understand some characteristic of a social state, then it needed to have

[1] Quoted by *Sainte-Beuve, Nouveaux Lundis*, op. cit., vol. xii, p. 95 note 2.

existed for a long time, 'that ages should have studied it whilst under its effects'. He believed that societies were like sick people who could only be cured with their own consent and assistance; the time for strait-jackets was over; democratic societies in particular would not recognize that something was harmful until they had suffered from it a great deal. It was not only when considering religious sentiment that Guizot urged his readers to learn from their experience, and commented, 'We have more good sense than enlightenment.'[1]

Many more examples could be given to show the consistency of his manner. When he was a younger man he may have been bolder in his outlook; he was less afraid of revolutionary figures such as Grégoire or Manuel or Lafayette, more confident in the desire of the multitude for peace and order, readier to adopt reforms and to campaign that they should become law. But in so far as conservatism is a way of thinking rather than a series of detailed decisions, there is no evidence that he thought in any other way. It might have been Guizot and not de Maistre who asked that although a man might see sixty generations of roses, yet who has seen the life of an oak? It might have been Guizot, and not Lord Acton, who said that political science is the one science which is deposited by the stream of history like grains of gold in the sand of a river. It is only the style which makes it impossible for Guizot to have said these things; he would have avoided such imagery.

One must not exaggerate the influence of England on Guizot's political thought. Like everyone else he compared the English and the French constitutions; such a comparison was inevitable, even the uneasy legislature of 1814 found itself quoting Blackstone and Delolme. But whilst England was later to be held up by Guizot as a model to France, it was principally in the sense that England had succeeded in avoiding revolution. Guizot himself wrote that in 1815 he knew little about English institutions and governmental practice, and although he was later to study in detail the development of representative government in England, at the same time he studied the development of French society, being convinced that revolutionary reformers had been wrong to neglect the traditions of 'l'ancienne France'.[2] Sometimes French politicians saw themselves as playing a rôle which had English counterparts. The *Revue Française*, which Guizot founded and edited from 1828 to 1830 and which was the

[1] *Histoire des Origines du Gouvernement Représentatif* (op. cit.), vol. ii, p. 10; Guizot: M. Lenormant, November 5th, 1848, *Lettres à M. et Mme Lenormant* (op. cit.), p. 14; La Démocratie dans les Sociétés Modernes, *Revue Française*, November 1838; Guizot: de Broglie, July 5th, 1847, *Archives Nationales*, 42 A.P. 8; Guizot: Jarnac, October 29th, 1846, 42 A.P. 7; De l'État des Ames [1838] in *Méditations et Études Morales*, Paris 1852, p. 15.

[2] *Mémoires*, vol. i, p. 111, p. 321.

predecessor and in many ways the prototype of the most important French review of the nineteenth century, the *Revue des Deux Mondes*, was thought of by its supporters as being the French equivalent of the *Edinburgh Review*; 'nous étions des Whigs de notre pays', remarked de Broglie. Guizot was to use many English analogies in his writings as in his speeches, but they are illustrations rather than objectives, such as George III's calling on Pitt to form a government and his dissolution of the House of Commons being an example of the rôle of the Crown in a parliamentary system; frequently, too, they are shown as contrasts to the French situation, the English system of local responsibility of justices of the peace, of sheriffs and juries, being compared to French centralization. The general arguments concerning England were in any case varied in value; that the suspension of the 'Habeas Corpus' Act in England was not accompanied by any suspension of the liberty of the press may have been significant for France; that armed rebellion ceased in England only when literary opposition became possible (as Benjamin Constant claimed) may have been plausible; but the deputy who argued that the Great Charter of 1215 made no mention of the liberty of the press and Louis Blanc's belief that the English reverence for authority and love of liberty came from the mixture of Norman and Saxon blood, show how barren such a type of discussion could become. It is true that occasionally there was an English institution or method which attracted a genuine admiration and which, it was thought, could be adopted in France. Duvergier de Hauranne, for example, admired the English judicial procedure which was used to discuss disputed elections (after the 1770 Act) and the use of commissions of enquiry. But generally what men such as Guizot, Tocqueville or Thiers found excellent was a system of government which was a product of experiment rather than the outcome of some political logic; with this attitude there was no possibility of grafting a foreign system on to the French 'corps social'.

Therefore Guizot's theory of representative government started neither from the desire to plan rationally nor from imitation of any other country. Nor did it start from any conception of rights, natural or otherwise. The right to govern, or the right to be represented, were not considered to be part of man's natural heritage. Guizot thought that a right attached to birth was characteristic either of democracy or aristocracy; whereas in a state organized so as to establish the effective sovereignty of reason and law, the right to govern was a question of capacity. This meant that a system of government ought not to be an arithmetical machine counting the number of individual wills. There existed in society a certain number of ideas and wills which were just: the task of government was to discover these ideas and wills; the sovereignty 'de fait', the effective government, should therefore be given to those most capable of discerning justice. But since the sovereignty 'de fait' was distinct from the sovereignty 'de droit', or in other words since government was not the same as sovereignty, certain precautions had to be taken against government. It was these precautions which established what was called representative government. In the first place power in the state should be divided, in order to prevent any one man or any one assembly of men from coming to regard each other as infallible; the different powers in the state should together search for the truth, limiting and restraining each other reciprocally. In the second place, if the government stayed continuously in the same hands, it would degenerate into a despotism, and therefore it was necessary to have an elective element which would enable the government to vary and to follow the evolution of society. Thirdly, publicity in government affairs was necessary, it was the link between a society and its government.[1]

This is a theory of government and not a theory of representation. After the Revolution it seemed that the cult of individual liberty and rights, and the idealization of the individual as an end in himself, could go no further. Guizot does not attack the Declaration of Rights as did Bentham, but when he does consider individual rights, he describes them as being civil and moral, and he distinguishes them from political rights. The universal rights for Guizot were the right to justice, the right to be protected by public authority against injustice, and the right to dispose of one's individual existence according to one's desires and one's interest, provided one does not harm someone else in their individual existence. Political rights were of another nature. A political right was a social power, a portion of government; whoever possessed political rights decided not only his personal affairs but also the affairs of society. Therefore political rights could not be given to everyone and experience showed that in practice they were not distributed evenly, many classes of individuals were everywhere without political rights.[2] The ideas of Rousseau on the sovereignty of the individual will which could not be alienated were for Guizot destructive of all government and of all society.

[1] *Histoire des Origines du Gouvernement Représentatif* (op. cit.), vol. i, pp. 109 ff., vol. ii, pp. 309 ff.

[2] Chambre des Députés, October 5th, 1831. *Histoire Parlementaire*, vol. i, p. 308. Guizot had said much the same thing in an article in the *Archives P.P.L.* in June 1818. 'Il s'agit simplement d'empêcher que l'individu, seul être réel et sensible, ne subisse dans la famille, dans la cité, dans la commune, à raison de sa pauvreté et de son obscurité, une injustice qui le dépouille de son existence positive, de quelqu'un des droits qui découlent de sa nature morale.' Vol. iii, p. 406. Elsewhere he spoke of liberty of conscience as a right.

If Rousseau's ideas were put into practice, they would cause to be established either a government which had no power at all over individual wills, which was anarchy, or a government over which individuals had no effective control, which was tyranny. The source of such error lay in the elevation of the individual will. This had led to bad government and it ought therefore to be rejected as a doctrine. It was wrong to believe that man had to be represented or that there was no law and no assembly which could overrule the representatives of the people. There was nothing sacrosanct about a representative, or deputy. In a system of government he had to be treated as an official like any other, he was a 'chargé d'affaires', chosen for a particular reason. One man could not think of himself as the passive and mechanical instrument of another's will and opinions; still less of the will and opinions of a numerous body of men. The deputy was an official who existed in order to take part in government.[1]

One can see how the Revolution is constantly present in this approach to politics. Montlosier believed that on every church door there should be written the words 'There has been a Revolution!' One feels that this phrase actually does occur on every page which Guizot wrote after 1815. He was in the forefront of the generations which attempted to understand the Revolution, which tried to approach the subject with understanding and interpret the facts with intelligence. Madame de Staël was the most famous example of such methods. The Revolution was no longer to be seen as a plot or as an accident, nor was it the accomplishment of certain personalities. It was the outcome of a change in the nature of society. It was useless to pretend that there had been nothing wrong with the Ancien Régime; death, said Guizot, was a reliable symptom of illness.[2] It was useless simply to criticize the Revolution; one should not study its gestures, but its principles. 'When those who were poor, obscure, ignorant and without influence, had become rich, respected, enlightened and powerful, then they needed to occupy in law the place which they occupied in reality. Certain superiorities, which lacked strength since they had ceased to serve a purpose, claimed to maintain their position because they were old. They were completely defeated by the two powers which rule this world, by facts and by reason; they tried to defend themselves with dates and with parchment.'[3] However, the Revolution did not remain a movement for

[1] *Histoire des Origines du Gouvernement Représentatif* (op. cit.), vol. ii, pp. 129 ff. *Ancillon* (op. cit.), pp. 123 ff.
[2] *Archives P.P.L.*, June 1818, vol. iii, p. 402.
[3] Ibid., August 1817, vol. i, p. 139. Madame de Staël's book was published in 1818 after her death; it was her son Auguste de Staël and her son-in-law de Broglie who arranged the manuscript for publication.

justice; it became a mixture of truth and falsehood, a chaos of principles, many of which had nothing to do with the real principles of 1789. The idea of equality, hatred of the past, the sovereignty of the people and of the numerical majority, these ideas often served a purpose; they helped to destroy the old system, they helped to assemble great forces and overcome absolutism. In the same way, the idea of despotism served its purpose, since it could violently reassemble a society which was breaking up. Thus both Jacobinism and Bonapartism had their moments of historical necessity. Bonapartism, according to Guizot, was 'a violent method of getting out of the Revolution, as the Revolution had been a violent method of getting out of the Ancien Régime'.[1] But by 1814 the principles of 1789 had been accomplished; justice and legal equality existed; the two things which had been asked for in 1789, the Monarchy and the Charter, were present in 1814. The Revolution had been a war, and the war was over.

However, there remained remnants of the various groups which had been fighting; not all of them were ready to accept peace or to admit that their victory could not be more complete. In an article in the *Archives Philosophiques, Politiques et Littéraires* which can probably be attributed to Guizot (although not with absolute certainty) it was said that there were four main groups of opinion in France. There were those who wished that the Revolution had not taken place and who were opposed to its achievements; there were those who believed in the fundamental principles of the Revolution and who believed that its essential results were embodied in the 1814 Charter; there were those who were simply tired of incessant struggle and who wanted only rest; and there were those who, out of habit or belief or personal interest, remained revolutionaries. Of these four groups, Guizot believed that the first and fourth were parties; the second and third he believed were France.[2] It would therefore be directly contrary to the interests of France, and contrary to reason, if those parties which wished to start the revolutionary struggle all over again should become powerful. Hence their very existence prevented institutions from functioning freely and without control. In other words, in order that there should be co-operation or discussion amongst different groups in France, it was necessary that there should be a basic common agreement that the Revolution was concluded and that its results were acceptable. It was because such an agreement was difficult to obtain that believers in parliamentary government such as Guizot adopted particular views of the rôle of executive government and administration, of governmental influence, of the

---

[1] *Archives P.P.L.*, vol. iii, p. 396.
[2] Ibid., vol. ii, pp. 275-277.

position of the parliamentary majority, and of many 'liberties', such as the right to vote, the liberty of the press and the right of association. It is for this reason too that French statesmen were less flexible in their approach to their opponents than were their English counterparts. The English Conservatives could be opportunist, and could govern by means of timely concessions; they could talk of proved abuses and real grievances, and they could accept legislation which had been passed by another party and other statesmen. They could do all this because they were working within the framework of general agreement on institutions. A society which is cohesive can regulate itself by discussion; disagreement is only peripheral. But a society which has experienced a deep social schism, such as post-Revolutionary France, must rely to some extent on compulsion. Within the English system a concession could be a timely adjustment which would render the future easier; within the French system a concession was a confession of weakness to an opponent who sought to destroy the system itself. 'In England', wrote Guizot, 'the deputies arrive in Parliament, having only committed themselves for or against the ministry; there is no question of changing institutions or of supporting interests which are contrary to the national interest; no one fears and no one wishes for such things. In France the quarrel is deeper; it is not only between rival ambitions and different opinions that there is debate; it is between the most hostile interests, the most violent passions, the most contrary intentions. The deputies come, wanting or apprehending, not the triumph of a particular policy or the keeping of changing of the ministry, but a real revolution.'[1]

After 1830 such differences grew deeper. Those who wanted the Revolution to be more than a mere change of dynasty were not prepared to accept the confiscation of the July movement. Guizot described the riots and disturbances of 1831 as representing more than mere anarchy, they were the preparation for civil war. After 1815 there had been the counter-revolutionaries and the remnants of the Jacobins; after 1830 there were 'three great political parties', the republican, the legitimists and the bonapartists.[2] Their existence could not but vitiate theories of government as their existence threatened to convulse France. Their existence, too, necessarily affected individual Frenchmen. Once violence and conspiracy entered politics then the population became afraid and uncertain. Guizot reminded Lord Aberdeen in 1852 that on numerous occasions in the recent past Frenchmen had paid for their votes with their heads.[3]

[1] *Du Gouvernement Représentatif,* in *Mélanges Politiques* (op. cit.), p. 62.
[2] *Mémoires,* vol. ii, p. 200.
[3] Guizot: Aberdeen, April 26th, 1852. I have published this letter in the *Revue d'Histoire Moderne et Contemporaine,* January-March 1958, vol. v, pp. 62-69.

One could not put too great a strain on people, individuals had to be protected; behind whatever devices one might use for protection (such as the secret ballot) there had obviously to be an effective and strong government.

The idea of a powerful executive was long-standing in France. It was associated with the defence of French territory; Louis XVIII had believed that France, not being an island but a continental power with an extensive frontier, needed a large army and a strong authority to direct it.[1] It was above all present in the administrative system both of the Revolution and of the Empire. The Charter of 1814 had not manufactured a state, as its critics such as de Maistre and Lamennais had said; it had rather inherited a state. Pierre Leroux claimed that from 1814 onwards France was a mixture of Napoleonic government and of an English monarchy 'à la Montesquieu'. It would have been surprising if political theorists, who were also practising politicians, had sought to give up this heritage. It would have been particularly surprising had Guizot disowned the principle that government should have extensive power. He differed considerably in this respect from Royer-Collard and from Benjamin Constant; they distrusted all power and believed that the best government was that which governed least; Guizot believed that the best government was that which governed most justly. This belief can be explained by the exigencies of the French situation, as has been explained; but also by the exigencies of theory.

The law of reason is in many respects like Rousseau's general will. It existed within man, in his conscience, perceived by his intelligence. It also had a positive existence of its own, beyond the individual and independent of the human mind, as it came from God. But like the general will, whilst it always has an objective reality, in order that it should become a political reality, it must be willed. Guizot believed that man was always aware of his conscience; he believed that most people wanted their own well-being, wanted peace, order and justice. But he did not believe that man was naturally good. He did not believe that society was responsible for man's defects; as he once put it, it was not the 'garde-champêtre' who was responsible for infringements of the forest laws.[2] Because men were weak and tended towards error and sin, the question had to be asked, what should be done if people did not recognize the law of reason, or if recognizing it, they nevertheless would not will it? Obviously they had to be persuaded to

[1] See the discussions between Macartney and Louis XVIII in 1795. *Public Record Office*, F.O. 27/45.

[2] See the article 'Nos mécomptes et nos espérances' in the *Revue Contemporaine*, vol. xviii, 1855. Republished in *L'Église et La Société Chrétiennes en 1861*, Paris 1861, pp. 212 ff.

recognize it; in other words, when the government was right and the multitude of the people was wrong, then the system of government should be such that the government should not have to give way. Guizot did not hesitate to give examples of popular errors. In August 1830 four of the ministers who had served in the last government of Charles X were arrested, the others having succeeded in leaving the country. Polignac, Peyronnet, Chantelauze and Guernon de Ranville were tried on a charge of treason before the Chamber of Peers. Popular opinion, if it can be judged by the conduct of the populace and the Garde Nationale, was clearly in favour of the death sentence; the government and the Chambers wished to avoid what would have been a useless blood-letting, based on very shaky judicial foundations. According to Guizot, they were right and public opinion was wrong, and after the event they were proved right. Similarly in 1831 there appeared to be a feeling in the country that France should go to war with Russia in order to rescue Poland; according to Guizot, it was not long before it was generally realized that such a war would have been contrary to French interests. The government (of Casimir Périer) was therefore proved right in refusing to give way to pressure.[1] Guizot's apparent disdain for opinion outside the Chambers, which he described as 'impressions, which are so mobile, so diverse, so slight, so unconsidered',[2] does not arise from personal pride but from the belief that the government was less likely to be mistaken than the public, and that it was the government's duty to lead rather than to follow.

The power of government was not an evil. He wrote in 1818 that society only existed through its government. When the government was weak, then society was ready to break up; it held society together, and 'the social interest' was not that government should be feeble, but that its strength should be regulated. There was no reason to think that representative government should be weak government; on the contrary, it should bring into existence the strongest governments ever seen, since they would dispose of a wider social force than any absolute government.[3]

[1] Chambre des Députés, October 5th, 1831. *Histoire Parlementaire*, vol. i, pp. 319-320. Whilst no one could disagree with Guizot in his appreciation of these two incidents, one should nevertheless note that from a purely legal point of view the sentences passed on the ex-ministers could not be justified. It was obviously better that they should be simply imprisoned (and amnestied in 1837) than that they should be executed; but the government in passing any sentence at all was satisfying popular prejudice at the expense of legality. See the article by Paul Bastid on this subject in the *Revue d'Histoire Moderne et Contemporaine*, July-September 1957, vol. iv, pp. 171-211.

[2] Ibid., January 22nd, 1844, vol. iv, p. 198.

[3] *Archives P.P.L.*, April 1818, vol. iii.

Thus once again Guizot chooses to start from the principle of government rather than from the principle of representation. His concern is to find a device which will avoid both anarchy and absolutism and which will establish a just and effective form of government. The idea of representation was antipathetic to the idea of a state; the principle of representation rendered difficult even the formulation of policy. Given Guizot's own position and given the situation of France, his choice was not surprising. The danger of this choice has been illustrated, not by Guizot's own personal failure so much as by a century and a half of French history. Politics was reserved for a class of experts (whether chosen from a limited social class or not). This belief that society and government were distinct from one another has undoubtedly contributed to prevent the development of a French political community.

When critics of Guizot have accused him of adapting his political principles to suit his momentary convenience, and when they have even denied him any 'first principle' in politics at all, they have invariably been thinking of his attitude to parliamentary government. Both in theory and in practice they consider Guizot to have been an opportunist.[1] Such a view is not supported by the evidence, but it needs to be explained. The explanation probably lies in two considerations. In the first place Guizot did not express his ideas on parliamentary government in any one concise work. His ideas developed over a period of years, frequently in the form of contradictions of some opponent. Thus *Du Gouvernement Représentatif et de l'état actuel de la France* was published in 1816 in reply to a pamphlet by the royalist Vitrolles, *Du ministère dans le gouvernement représentatif. Du Gouvernement de la France depuis la Restauration et du ministère actuel* was written in 1820 after the break-up of the Decazes ministry and after Guizot had been dismissed from the Conseil d'État. If we are to believe Rémusat, Guizot thought that this pamphlet would facilitate his return to power and it was supposedly written with this intention; although its success rescued Guizot from a difficult financial position (as it did the publisher Ladvocat, who went on to become one of the most famous of romantic publishers, producing editions of Shakespeare, Byron and Schiller), it did not restore him to office, and the 1821 pamphlet *Des moyens de gouvernement et d'opposition dans l'état actuel de la France* is both bolder and more bitter. The articles in the *Revue*

[1] Many examples of this attitude could be given. See, for example, *P. H. Soltau, French Political Thought in the Nineteenth Century*, 1931, pp. 41 ff.; see also the gay but rather superficial treatment of the early Guizot in *Dominique Bagge, Les Idées Politiques sous la Restauration*, Paris 1952.

Française in 1828 and in 1829, the articles in the same review when it was revived in 1838, the 1849 pamphlet *De la Démocratie en France*, all were written with particular intentions and all were influenced by particular circumstances. It is therefore normal that a scattered collection of publications should show some variation in the treatment of the theme of parliamentary government. What is surprising is that these variations should consist primarily in changes of emphasis rather than in deviations of doctrine. It would be an exaggeration to use Dr. Johnson's expression and say that Guizot had started life with his faggot of opinions made up, and that to draw out a single stick would weaken the whole; but the constancy of his political belief is remarkable.

Secondly, many of the critics of Guizot have their own view of parliamentary government, which is particularly restricted. They assume that this form of government necessarily implies both universal suffrage (that is to say popular sovereignty) and the complete supremacy of the elected assembly. This is the 'Reform Association' interpretation of history. When applied to French history it is natural that a statesman such as Guizot, who professed his attachment to the idea of representative government but who denied both universal suffrage and the 'régime d'assemblée', should appear as a man with neither principle nor understanding. Yet this interpretation of parliamentary government was never the only permissible interpretation. Sir Ernest Barker has shown how some people think of authority as descending in a series of cascades; all power is supposedly in the hands of the electorate, which appoints a subordinate parliament, which in turn appoints a still more subordinate cabinet. Such a conception is far from real; there can be few desirable examples of a legislature dominated by the electorate and a cabinet dominated by the legislature.[1] It was not obligatory upon Guizot or upon anyone else to think in such a way. The system of parliamentary government, as Guizot understood it and practised it, has often been compared unfavourably to that of England. Yet frequently assumptions are made about English parliamentary life, about the working of the two-party system, the functioning of majority rule, the rôle of the Crown and the Executive, which are not justified by the facts. Between the first and the second Reform Acts, English parliamentary life has many resemblances to French parliamentary life as Guizot knew it. As a system of government it presented problems which both countries found difficult to solve. In France the system had no traditions and scarcely any precedents. There was no reason, as Guizot said, why one should consider the nature of representative government as being 'evident and impera-

Sir Ernest Barker, *Reflections on Government*, 1942, pp. 50-51.

tive'.[1] This belief was certainly applicable to France; some people might have thought that it applied equally to nineteenth-century England. Furthermore, whilst the prestige of Victorian parliamentarianism is so great, one must not forget that the success of this mode of government must partly be explained by the privileged economic position then held by England in the world.

Guizot was a great 'Chamber of Deputies man'. He became a deputy in 1830, not long after he had reached the necessary age of forty. Having unsuccessfully tried to become a candidate in the Côte d'Or, he became a successful candidate in the Lisieux division of Calvados, one of the richest of the agricultural regions, and he remained deputy until 1848.[2] From 1830 onwards Guizot was forced to devote a great part of his time to speaking in one or other of the two Chambers, since a French minister had the right to speak in either Chamber, and since he was minister in eight of the seventeen different ministries which existed under Louis-Philippe, being in office for about thirteen years. It was said of him by one of his critics that his ideal government was the one which made the finest speeches to the most compact majority.[3] He thought of Parliament as a place for debate, for discussion, for the exchange of views. He was obliged to think of it as a place where the government explained its policy and argued with its critics. If government by dialogue is a characteristic of the parliamentary system, then we must notice that whilst leading ministers such as Talleyrand or Polignac had hardly bothered to attend the Chambers, no minister was more punctilious in his attendance or more regular in his intervention than Guizot. During the period when he was the effective chief minister, from 1840 to 1848, the demands of the Chambers on his time and energy became a considerable physical strain. 'I like the Chamber', he wrote to Sainte-Aulaire, 'but I am rather blasé about the pleasure which it now gives me.'[4] Parliament was for Guizot 'an arena in which the whole of society shows itself, with all its interests, ideas and passions'.

[1] *Du Gouvernement Représentatif* (op. cit.), in *Mélanges Politiques* (op. cit.), p. 63.

[2] On this subject see *Pouthas, Les élections de Guizot dans le Calvados*, Mémoires de l'Académie de Sciences, Arts et Belles-Lettres de Caen, Caen 1920. Guizot's own *Mémoires*, vol. i, pp. 342-343, are rather unreliable on the subject of how he became a deputy. He suggests that the offer came to him spontaneously and to his surprise. In reality he had been looking for a means of getting into the Chamber ever since he had fulfilled the age qualification and he had good contacts in the department through the electoral society '*Aide-toi—le ciel t'aidera*', as well as through de Broglie and Dupont de l'Eure. It was in 1836 that he bought the Val-Richer, a few miles west of Lisieux, which became his home until his death.

[3] *Edmond Scherer, Études Critiques sur la Littérature Contemporaine*, Paris 1863, p. 89.

[4] Guizot: Sainte-Aulaire, May 25th, 1842, *Archives Nationales*, 42 A.P. 8.

He saw it as the confrontation of the most diverse elements, different temperaments, different attitudes towards power and liberty, those who were anxious to acquire conflicting with those who were anxious to conserve, hopes and fears contrasting with each other. It was a theatre in which the fermentation of society was concentrated most usefully and least dangerously; from the debate of all these forces, thought Guizot, should emerge a realization of public well-being.[1] His belief that parliamentary life should unite together 'all interests, all influences and all opinions',[2] recalls Parliament as thought of by Sir Robert Inglis, the opponent of the Reform Bill, who described it as a 'concordia discors', opening 'the door to the admission here of all the talents, of all classes, and of all interests'. Parliament should not represent merely individuals, or certain interests, or a certain collection of interests. It ought to represent everything.[3] Such an opinion of Parliament influenced Guizot's solution of the problems connected with parliamentary government. These problems are primarily two: there is the problem of the relations between Parliament and government, since Parliament being an 'arena' and a 'theatre' is obviously not a government; and there is the problem of the relations between Parliament and the rest of the population.

One has always to remember that Guizot was trying to solve the problem of French government by establishing a government which would be successful because it was just and reasonable. He was working in the tradition of Montesquieu in that he believed that such a government was necessarily a moderate government; that is to say he was not trying to organize power so much as a control of power. His theory of the sovereignty of reason and his distinction between sovereignty and government was in some ways a theoretical justification for Montesquieu's theory of the separation of powers. In practice this means the separation of the executive and of the legislative powers, and the refusal to accept that either of them was supreme in the state; such a supremacy would have meant that one of them would have regarded itself as sovereign and as infallible, and would have established government by force. But whilst the executive power, the king and the ministry, existed separate from the legislative power, Guizot's theory did not imply that they should be rivals. There should be no conflict between these powers; on the contrary there should be co-operation. The real sense of moderate government was that the powers in the state should be forced to establish a political

---

[1] *Des Conspirations et de la Justice Politique* (op. cit.), in *Mélanges Politiques* (op. cit.), p. 176.

[2] Chambre des Députés, May 2nd, 1833, *Histoire Parlementaire*, vol. ii, p. 56.

[3] Sir Robert Inglis in the House of Commons, March 1st, 1831, *Hansard*, 3rd series, vol. ii, c. 1108-1109.

unity between themselves, and that whilst maintaining their separate
characters they should amalgamate together. If Guizot reached these
conclusions by an interpretation of Montesquieu, he was well in
advance of modern commentators, who have only recently seen in
the famous Chapter XI of *L'Esprit des Lois* a programme for the
effective political fusion of the three powers of king, nobility and
people. He certainly saw these conclusions demonstrated in English
history; under the Stuarts the rivalry between the monarchy and the
House of Commons had led to conflict, but when the Hanoverians
had accepted the fusion of royal authority and parliamentary
authority, then the conflict ceased, government became united and
strong and the English nation was free.[1] Guizot anticipated Bagehot
in pointing out that the successful working of the British Constitution
depended upon the co-operation of the executive and the legislature.
But how was this co-operation to be established? What should be the
rôle of the king? Who should choose the ministers?

The answer to all these questions turns on the conception of the
parliamentary majority. On this question there appears an apparent
contradiction between theory and practice. As a minister, and
particularly as chief minister, no one gave a better demonstration
than Guizot of the constitutional need to possess a majority in the
Chamber of Deputies. He clearly stated that government could not
exist without the confidence and co-operation of the Chambers; he
claimed that the Molé governments, which he opposed in 1838 and
1839, were weak because of their weakness in Parliament, and it was
the parliamentary impotence of the government which condemned
successive Parliaments to death twice in eighteen months.[2] From
1840 to 1848 each vote was a battle to maintain the majority; when
in January 1845 an amendment to the address which the Chamber
annually voted in reply to the king's speech was defeated by only
eight, with about a dozen deputies abstaining, Guizot seriously considered resigning (and was apparently advised to do so by his closest
advisers, the Princess Lieven, de Broglie and Duchâtel). Yet in theory
he continued to deny the principle of majority rule in the state, and
he never abjured his early condemnation of majority rule when it
implied the principle of numerical superiority, that is to say the
sovereignty of the people. Even in an assembly where each member
was of proved capacity, it was not certain that the majority necessarily
saw what was just and reasonable, and therefore the minority had

[1] *Du Gouvernement représentatif* (op. cit.), in *Mélanges Politiques* (op. cit.),
pp. 28 ff.
[2] Chambre des Députés, December 6th, 1834, *Histoire Parlementaire*, vol. ii,
p. 308; Monsieur Guizot à ses commettants, February 6th, 1839, *Revue Française*,
vol. x, pp. 169 ff.

to be given the chance of proving their point of view. In that same assembly, because the majority had once been right, there was no reason to suppose that they should continue to be right simply because of their numerical superiority.[1] His attitude is similar to that of Burke, namely, that there is no right, as there is no policy or utility, to suppose that 'a majority of men, told by the head' should be able to will the law. 'Numbers in a state', wrote Burke, '. . . are always of consideration, but they are not the whole consideration.'[2]

The explanation of this apparent contradiction is to be found partly in terms of Guizot's conception of sovereignty and partly in terms of French political experience. If sovereignty was to be distinct from government and no one power was to be supreme, then the principle of majority rule was unacceptable since it would make the executive, the Crown and the ministers subordinate institutions. Therefore the Crown had complete freedom to choose whatever minister or councillor it wished; the Crown was not even obliged to take its ministers from the Chamber of Deputies. If the Chamber intervened directly, so as to influence the choice of ministers and the composition of the Cabinet, that would be an infringement upon the prerogative of the Crown, and would create a considerable upset in the relations between public institutions. But in practice the Crown would (and did) choose its ministers from amongst 'les hommes considérables' of the Chambers, not in order to strengthen the Chambers, but in order to strengthen itself. The influence of the Chambers on the government was thus indirect and far from diminishing the executive, this influence rather fortified it.[3]

In 1816 Guizot described the reality of the parliamentary majority as it existed in France. It was not an invariable quantity, it was uncertain and mobile, something which the government won, then lost, then won again. Against a hostile majority the government had two resources, the power of dissolution, and the influence which could be exercised in elections.[4] This view was expressed when a reactionary ultra majority dominated the Chamber of Deputies, but Guizot never ceased to believe in its truth. Although he believed it possible that one day a homogeneous majority would emerge which would facilitate the formation of the government, such a day always

[1] *Histoire des Origines du Gouvernement Représentatif* (op. cit.), vol. i, p. 110.
[2] *An Appeal from the New to the Old Whigs. Works* (Bohn Edition), vol. iii, p. 85.
[3] See the *Archives P.P.L.*, April 1818, vol. iii, pp. 138 ff., and speeches to the Chamber of Deputies, March 11th, 1835, *Histoire Parlementaire*, vol. ii, pp. 349-350, and January 19th, 1839, ibid, vol. iii, pp. 242-243.
[4] *Du Gouvernement Représentatif* (op. cit.), in *Mélanges Politiques* (op. cit.), pp. 44-45.

seemed a long way off.[1] The majorities which he knew were always unstable and occasional; they were made up of various groups which might vote together on one issue and then might never vote together again. Ideas, interests, personalities or day-to-day happenings might draw such groups together momentarily, whilst changing circumstances and personal defections inevitably caused their disintegration. In 1815 one writer listed seven main political groups.[2] Until the Act of 1824 one-fifth of the Chamber was elected annually, so that majorities were perpetually changing as new deputies arrived who did not know each other and whose political commitments did not necessarily fit in with the political patterns of the existing Chamber. Even when integral renewal replaced partial renewal, the break-up of Villèle's party showed the difficulties of organizing a majority. 'Newcomers to the Chamber', wrote Bonald in 1828, 'know neither each other nor those whom they are replacing. Each brings his own mind, his own opinions, his own interests and views, and the parties organize themselves differently.'[3] After 1830 the disaggregation of the majority became more apparent. Although 221 members had voted their protestation to Charles X and had in the main been re-elected in 1830, once the new dynasty had been installed this majority began to disintegrate. Some people believed that the situation became worse under Louis-Philippe because the Chamber was given greater powers of amendment and individual members were thus given greater scope for legislative efforts which prevented any internal discipline.[4] Some people believed that the struggle of the Restoration had been one between the aristocracy and the bourgeoisie —'on top the nobility and power; down below commerce and money', according to Balzac—and that after 1830, once the bourgeoisie had won, then the only struggle left was of the 'ins' and 'outs' variety, the 'satisfaits' and the 'insatisfaits'; competition for the spoils of office necessarily leads to shifting allegiances. The social divergences natural to France were being intensified by uneven industrial and urban development, so that one can see how within a particular group one must make distinctions based upon geography; amongst the supporters of the Bourbons, for example, one has to distinguish between the legitimists who come from the South, have the backing of the Church, and whose intransigence made them a Jacobite-type party, and the legitimists from the industrial regions of the north

[1] *Archives P.P.L.*, December 1817, vol. ii, pp. 186-187. Chambre des Députés, March 14th, 1835. *Histoire Parlementaire*, vol. ii, p. 366.

[2] *Julien Maréchal, Considérations sur l'état politique de la France*, Paris 1815.

[3] *Bonald, De l'Esprit de Corps et de l'Esprit de Parti*, Paris 1828.

[4] *Louis de Carné, Commentaire sur la Charte Constitutionnelle*, Paris 1836, p. 138.

and east, who tended towards some form of co-operation with Orleanist institutions. Although it was noticed in 1837 that it was becoming more and more the rule for candidates in elections to make a statement of political belief, a 'profession de foi', it was estimated that nearly one-third of the Chamber was made up of new deputies whose opinions were uncertain.[1] In 1842 Duvergier de Hauranne estimated that twenty of the newly elected deputies would set out for Paris not knowing whether they would vote for or against the government.[2] In the elections of 1846 it was far from rare that a candidate had to be considered as a government supporter who intended to vote at least occasionally against the government.[3]

It is difficult not to believe that if an elective assembly was left to itself, in France at least, it would never produce a majority. In these circumstances, the only possible doctrine was that the starting-point in parliamentary government was the government and not the parliamentary majority. The majority ought to belong to the government, not the government to the majority. The majority only became a positive force when it was organized by the government. 'Waters which do not have any limits spread out, divide and stay stagnant,' wrote Guizot in 1817. 'But if one constructs a bed out of which they cannot escape, then they stay together and follow the same direction.'[4] Guizot had a greater constitutional sense than most of his contemporaries, since although he believed that majorities could be mistaken, he never believed that government should do without the majority, as was sometimes suggested.[5] He welcomed reforms which would facilitate the formation of the majority, such as the renewal of the whole of the Chamber rather than the annual renewal of one-fifth, which he had advocated as early as 1819. He realized that the working of the majority system depended upon two things, upon the existence of a homogeneous ministry, and upon the organization of political parties.

[1] *Le National*, November 2nd, 1837; *Revue des Deux Mondes*, December 15th, 1837, vol. xxviii, p. 770.

[2] Duvergier de Hauranne: Thiers, July 16th, 1842, *Papiers Thiers*, Bibliothèque Nationale Manuscrits, Nouvelles Acquisitions 20616.

[3] For example, Casimir Royer who was elected at Grenoble, or General de Bellonnet elected at Colmar. See the discussion of their views in *Archives Nationales*, BB[17] A 146.

[4] *Archives P.P.L.*, December 1817, vol. ii, p. 198.

[5] Royer-Collard did not believe that the government should be at the discretion of the parliamentary majority and he claimed that the absence of a fixed and invariable majority was to the honour of the French Chamber. See his speech on the Electoral Law of 1817 in *Barante, La Vie de M. Royer-Collard* (op. cit.), vol. i, pp. 207 ff. When the majority proved over-elusive it was suggested that the government would be obliged to dispense with it. See *Journal des Débats*, January 29th, 1839.

One of the differences between Guizot and Molé was their different appreciations of the nature of the ministry. Molé believed that the ministry ought to reflect the parliamentary majority, and ought there-fore to be a varied combination; Guizot believed that a ministry should be homogeneous and that it would only be effective if it was composed of men agreed on principles of action.[1] Although, in opposition to Molé, Guizot had joined with Thiers and Odilon Barrot in the famous 'coalition', this alliance was only parliamentary, and Guizot did not believe that there was sufficient agreement between Odilon Barrot and himself for them to serve in the same government. Guizot's ministry of October 29th was an example of this insistence upon homogeneity. He himself took Foreign Affairs, and gave the other main posts to close associates. Duchâtel, who had attended Guizot's lectures when a young man, and who had been listed amongst the 'doctrinaires' of the 1830's, became Minister of the Interior; Villemain, who after a brilliant academic career had been associated with the 'doctrinaires' under Decazes, and who had lectured with Guizot and Victor Cousin at the Collège de France, was Minister for Public Instruction; Humann, whose Alsatian accent was supposedly a guarantee for his honesty, became Minister of Finance. Although the last-named was more of a technician than a politician, he was a determined and authoritarian figure, who resembled Guizot not only in his ideas, but also in his gift of making himself unpopular. The remaining posts were given to technicians, who sat in the centre or right-centre. Although there were repeated rumours that Guizot was attempting to persuade either Dufaure or Passy, leaders of one of the central groups, to enter his government, this did not take place, and group leaders are quite absent from this government. It formed the most unified ministry of the July Monarchy, and even when changes had to be made, the principle of unity was maintained. Its only constitutional failing was that the Presidency of the Council was given to Marshal Soult. One of the characteristics of French constitutional government had been the absence of a 'Prime Minister', or the filling of the post by some figure-head. Political nonentities, who were usually soldiers, filled the rôle of 'busts' or 'glorious swords', and Dessolles, Gérard, Mortier and Soult are obvious examples of this type of President. That Guizot accepted the fiction that Soult should be chief minister (for the third time) suggests that he had not fully realized the significance of this office in a parliamentary system. He had no high opinion of the ability of Soult; the marshal spoilt the unity of the government by speaking against his colleagues in the debate on the fortification of

[1] See the exchange between Guizot and Molé in the Chamber of Deputies, May 3rd, 1837. *Histoire Parlementaire*, vol. iii, pp. 66-92.

Paris in 1841; it was because of his insistence that the Ministry of Public Works was held by Teste for three years, an appointment which did the government much harm when Teste was later convicted of corruption. The only advantage of Soult's fictive presidency was that it suited Guizot, for parliamentary and national reasons, to have a renowned military name presiding over a government dedicated to peace. Doubtless, too, this arrangement suited the King. However, it was a constitutional anomaly which was only removed by the Ordonnance of September 19th, 1847, which appointed Guizot President of the Council on the withdrawal of the aged Soult.

Guizot was also one of the first French constitutionalists to recognize the importance of organized political parties. They had generally been thought of as factions, as the outward signs of the corrupt and the unpatriotic. Even Madame de Staël and Benjamin Constant, usually so prescient in constitutional matters, had thought of the régime of parties as being a régime of political passions and violence. After 1815 it was only the revolutionary parties which organized themselves to a practical end, republicans, carbonari, legitimists or bonapartists. The word 'party' was suspect; Chateaubriand's review *Le Conservateur* apologized to the royalists for suggesting that they were a party, and as late as 1839 when Guizot used the word, he felt obliged to assure his listeners in the Chamber that he was using it in its innocent sense.

It was probably after 1848 that Guizot fully realized the importance of parties in a constitutional régime; when he wrote his *Mémoires* he stated that it was only by coherent parties, whether based on interests, or ideas or on passions, that continuity could be assured. He claimed that in 1840 he had felt this instinctively rather than rationally, but in a speech of 1846 he said that representative government could only function regularly and effectively through the formation of big political parties.[1] His whole policy was to divide the Chamber into two distinct groups of government and opposition, and put an end to the oscillation of power between the groups of the centre and of the left. He tried to abolish the tendency of the majority to maintain its old allegiances, to Molé, to Dufaure and Passy, or to the device of a central government which excluded Guizot, Thiers and Molé, such as the combination which Soult led on May 12th, 1839. He tried to organize a conservative party which could present itself at elections and ask to be judged on the government's record. With such a conservative party there should be no more hidden struggles amongst parties none of which really aspired to govern. Such a party

[1] *Mémoires*, vol. viii, pp. 7 ff. Chambre des Députés, August 31st, 1846. *Histoire Parlementaire*, vol. v, p. 294.

was to be the means of clarifying the political issues.[1] By 1846 this policy had been largely successful. The voting habits of the Chamber had become more regular, and after the 1846 elections the government seemed to be assured of a certain majority of over 100.

Yet one must beware of comparing Guizot to Sir Robert Peel as the creator of a Conservative party (with Duchâtel and Guizot's chief assistant, Génie, playing the rôles of Graham and Bonham). He was not working within the framework of a great political tradition or of long-standing family connections; nor was he the sponsor of a detailed programme of reforms and adjustments around which a party could collect. Although he recognized that the development of parties was natural in a representative system, he did not, like Erskine May, exalt them into being 'the very life-blood of freedom'. He was too realistic not to see that he could never hope to achieve the mechanical party voting that had at times existed in England, and which he thought of, in any case, as the negation of the parliamentary system. In a country where constitutional government was recent and still hazardous, there could be only one desirable party, 'le parti de gouvernement', which supported the existing régime. Outside this party were factions, intrigues and conspiracies. Therefore Guizot's work of reconstructing the government party was more a work of clarification than anything else. This government party existed with both liberal and conservative tendencies; it spread over three of the five main groups into which every Chamber of the July Monarchy was composed, covering the left centre, the centre and the right centre, but never going into the extreme left or extreme right. A government which was formed from the left centre, with the support of the extreme left, would split the governmental party, part of which in the centre and right centre would be abandoned. This was what took place when Thiers was in power. Molé, by personal manœuvres and by his subservience to the King, had equally split the government party; and Guizot had found it necessary to distinguish between a 'parti conservateur' which remained with Molé, and a 'parti parlementaire' which opposed Molé's methods. Thus, as Guizot saw it, the government party had been split since 1836 and there had resulted the confusions and dangers of the period from 1836 to 1840. Therefore he sought to put an end to the indecisive conflict of the party groups by concentrating the constitutional idea into a single party. This is the party of those who wish to preserve the national institutions. It is necessarily conservative and based upon a conviction of danger. 'When bad men combine,'

[1] Guizot: Barante, December 12th, 1840, *Archives Nationales*, 42 A.P. 9. Guizot: Sainte-Aulaire, June 18th, 1842, Ibid., 42 A.P. 8. Guizot: Duchâtel, August 6th, 1846, Ibid.

wrote Burke, 'the good must associate; else they will fall, one by one, an unpitied sacrifice in a contemptible struggle.'[1]

Such a conception of the rôle of party had its disadvantages, and must be borne in mind when one considers Guizot's responsibility for the Revolution of 1848. It undoubtedly caused him to consider opposition as either revolutionary or as personal. Thus Guizot's explanation for the opposition of Tocqueville was too simple, that Tocqueville wished to be in his place. It was also his desire to maintain the unity of the governmental party which made him regard issues of reform with suspicion. He wrote to Bresson, then in Berlin, at the beginning of 1842 that the Chamber was divided into two, and that in the debate on the King's speech 'the third party' had ceased to exist; but he feared that this party might reappear in the discussion on electoral reform, and this was the chief danger of such a discussion.[2] But whatever the practical weaknesses of this conception of party politics, it was far and away more suitable for a parliamentary system than was the irresponsible attitude of many of Guizot's contemporaries. Thiers, for example, changed his associates in a way which is often bewildering; he tried to gain the support of deputies by a mixture of argument, temporizing, bravado and individual seduction which was invariably aimed at the destruction of old allegiances rather than at the construction of new ones. Molé thought essentially in terms of a personal clientèle. Most irresponsible of all, perhaps, was the attitude of Dupin, who made it an article of faith that 'the third party' would not definitively commit itself to any policy or to any cabinet, and who regarded the setting up of conservative party machinery as if such an act was antagonistic to a representative system.[3] Guizot's attempt to establish a homogeneous ministry and an organized party was the only noteworthy attempt to introduce coherence to the French parliamentary régime. The only other man who seemed to share Guizot's understanding in this respect was his former associate, Duvergier de Hauranne, who after 1840 was the chief organizer of the opposition.[4]

[1] *Thoughts on the Causes of the Present Discontents. Works* (Bohn Edition) vol. i, p. 372.

[2] *Correspondence and Conversations of Alexis de Tocqueville with Nassau William Senior*, 2nd ed., 1872, vol. ii, p. 261. Guizot: Bresson, February 5th, 1842, *Archives Nationales*, 42 A.P. 8.

[3] On 'the third party' see *Dupin, Mémoires*, Paris 1860, vol. iii, pp. 40 ff., pp. 111 ff. On the meeting of 190 deputies, January 29th, 1845, when a Bureau and a permanent commission of the conservative party were established, see vol. iv, pp. 253-255.

[4] Duvergier de Hauranne's letters to Thiers of June 11th and 17th, 1841, *Papiers Thiers*, op. cit., 20616, are examples of his attempts to persuade Thiers to become a leader of the opposition in the English sense, who should be ready to speak on any important issue. He had little success, as Thiers was irregular in

71

When one turns from Guizot's consideration of the relations between government and Parliament to the second main problem of representative government, the relations between Parliament and the rest of the population, one sees that for him the issue was simple. Once again he was not definitively attached to any system of rights; an electoral law was a law which could be changed, like any other law, in the light of circumstances. Thus in September 1819, when the partial elections brought strong liberal successes which threatened the majority of the Dessolles-Decazes ministry, Guizot, like the other doctrinaires, thought it natural to change the mode of election. He approved of the extension of the franchise which took place in 1831, and for all that he opposed the proposals for parliamentary and electoral reform which were put forward by Ganneron and Ducos in 1842, he later claimed that he had no fixed objections to either of these reforms, and that he envisaged the right to vote as being extended progressively to a greater number of voters.[1] His objections were of a strategical nature. He did not believe that there was any real movement in the country in favour of reform. Just as Lord North had taunted reformers with 'the horrid sound of silence' which came from Manchester and Birmingham and which failed to support their claims, so Guizot claimed that nowhere in the country was there any sense of injustice or any genuine movement for reform. Hence the so-called reformers were merely opponents of the government, attempting by this particular means either to overthrow it, or at least to weaken its authority. In 1847, when the campaign of the banquets suggested that there was a more widespread desire for electoral change, Guizot still suspected a manœuvre rather than a sense of grievance. Furthermore, in 1847 another strategical principle was at stake. Guizot always believed that it was unwise to give way to pressure from outside parliament; to do so was a concession to popular force, that is to say, to revolutionary force.[2]

In terms of doctrine Guizot believed two things. Firstly, that elections should be direct, and secondly, that the right to vote should be associated with political capacity. He had stated the first as early as 1814 when in a note of May 19th he had criticized Montesquiou's suggestion that the King should nominate the deputies. Clausel de Coussergues had proposed that there should be a primary assembly

his contributions to debates. In the 1843 session he did not speak at all, and in 1847 only once.

[1] *Mémoires*, vol. vi, p. 369.

[2] Rémusat believed that the real objection which both Guizot and de Broglie had to abolishing the hereditary peerage was because it was a concession, rather than because they believed in the efficacity of the Chamber of Peers. See *Rémusat, Mémoires*, vol. ii, p. 358.

composed of the three hundred largest tax-payers of the arrondissement, which would elect candidates, from whom a secondary
assembly, composed of the three hundred largest tax-payers of the
department would nominate the deputies. Barbé-Marbois proposed a
similar system, based on the canton rather than on the arrondissement.[1] The object of these suggestions was to find a method of
election which would ensure a reliable and moderate Chamber.
However, Destutt de Tracy favoured indirect election as being the
only means whereby all the population could participate in government, and Louis de Carné evolved a complicated system whereby the
largest tax-payers should elect the municipal councils, which elect
in their turn the arrondissement councils, which elect departmental
councils, and the last-named elect the deputies. For Guizot all these
systems were unacceptable, in the first place because they were based
upon a misconception; the elector had to be able to choose a good
deputy; but in a system of indirect election people who were thought
incapable of choosing a good deputy were nevertheless thought
capable of choosing a good elector. Secondly, indirect election
opened up great possibilities of intrigue. Thirdly, it eliminated the
minority. Fourthly, the system of indirect election was a distortion of
universal suffrage, and was essentially an attempt to disinterest the
electors.[2]

That the right to vote was a question of capacity, was obviously
part of the belief in the sovereignty of reason, but it was necessary to
find the external signs which were indicative of this capacity. These
signs could vary. Guizot, in 1826, warned his readers that one must
not fall into the error of England, which had a system of franchise
incapable of changing as conditions changed; he also believed that
political capacity, and electoral rights would be more extensive in a
small society than in a large one. But essentially society was divided
into three classes: those who owned land or capital and who lived
on these possessions; those who worked in industry or in some other
form of activity, either with their own or with borrowed capital, who
worked for profit, and who paid the individuals whom they employed;
and those who had little or no capital, or few possibilities of borrow-
ing, and who were obliged to support their families and themselves
by their everyday work. These three classes could be described in
another way. Those whose leisure permitted them to cultivate their
intelligence; those whose occupation obliged them to reach a
superior standard of knowledge and intelligence; and those whose
work prevented them from leaving the narrow circle of individual

[1] See *Beugnot, Mémoires*, Paris, 1866, vol. ii, pp. 191-195.
[2] See the article by Guizot, 'Élections' in the *Encyclopédie Progressive*,
September 1826.

interests and the day-to-day satisfaction of immediate needs. Whilst such a 'schema' might mean a certain amount of injustice towards individuals, Guizot, like the Whigs who were discussing reform in the years following 1832, was unable to find any means of discerning capacity in society other than by this material method. In France it was only by according the vote to those who paid a certain sum in direct taxation that one was able to link the possession of the franchise with the possession of the qualities needed for its exercise.

For Guizot the idea that the representative system was essentially the representation of classes was an idea that was no longer applicable. Society had been divided into classes which were not so much diverse as hostile one to another; the nobility and the bourgeoisie, the urban and the rural populations, the landowners and the industrialists, had been in a perpetual struggle against one another. In such circumstances political rights were weapons which the class possessing them used against the class deprived of them. Hence had arisen the desire for a more equitable distribution of political rights. But for Guizot such a situation was in the past. French society was united; there were no longer any class struggles, there was no longer any diversity of interests. What interests, asked Guizot, separated the man who paid 300 francs in direct taxation from the man who paid 250 francs, or 150 francs? They had the same interests, they lived in the same civil condition, under the same laws. Thus the elector, who paid 300 francs in direct taxation, represented perfectly the man who paid 200 or 100 francs. 'All classes,' he claimed, 'all social forces, amalgamate, combine, and live in peace within the great moral unity of French society.'[1]

It is interesting that Guizot did not here see the inadequacy of his analysis. Both in the 1820s and in *De la Démocratie en France*, which he published in 1849, Guizot insisted that what characterized individuals was their position in the social order, whether they possessed or did not possess land or capital. 'The political order', he wrote, 'is necessarily the expression and the reflection of the social order.'[2] Yet he did not believe, in the 1840s, that inequalities in the social order led to any divergence of interests in the political order. The *Revue Indépendante* asked if in the question of the importation of cattle into France, as in the question of corn importation into England, the interests of the whole population could be legitimately represented by landowners. Was it blindness, they asked, or deceit,

[1] Chambre des Députés, February 15th, 1842. *Histoire Parlementaire*, vol. iii, pp. 555-558.

[2] *Histoire des Origines du Gouvernement Représentatif* (op. cit.), vol. ii, p. 296.

or ignorance, which caused Guizot to make such statements?[1] The answer lies in Guizot's conception of the middle class and of its rôle in the state. Ultimately all his views of parliamentary government are dependent upon this view of society.

In nineteenth-century England it was a commonplace for men to suggest that the true aim of government was the protection of property and that the natural governing class was the property-owning class. For Macaulay it was not by numbers that a country should be governed but by wealth and intelligence; for Brougham it was the middle classes which were 'the genuine depositaries of sober, rational, intelligent and honest English feeling'. It is not surprising that similar sentiments were even more widespread in France. From 1789 onwards it was apparent that if government was to be secure, then it had to be founded upon something stronger than abstract rights or public opinion. This could only be property. 'The government of crime', according to Madame de Staël, existed when the government was in the hands of the propertyless. Such a belief was not merely a matter of logic. It was the recognition of apparent facts. Certainly as Guizot saw these facts, the Revolution of 1789 which had successfully created a new society, had as its principle the bourgeois slogan of equality before the law, and as its fundamental element, the middle classes.[2] Successive governments had followed the reasoning of Barnave in 1791, that they should look for electors amongst the middle classes. The Revolution of 1830 made this even more of a practical necessity. Guizot told Reeve in 1858 that having been forced to make or accept revolution, and wishing to found the constitutional system, 'before us were the Legitimist party which would not accept the monarch of 1830, and the masses of the people of both towns and country, who neither cared nor understood anything about the constitutional system. They proved this clearly in 1848, and again at the present time. We had no support but the middle classes; they alone were really with us in wishing to restore the younger branch of the Bourbons and free institutions. It was necessary for us to keep in line with our only true and intelligent friends. The moment we advanced beyond it we got in amongst revolutionary longings, Bonapartist memories, or the constitutional ignorance and indifference. In this lay the real difficulty. I should not have had the least objection to our extending the suffrage, if it had been likely to strengthen our cause, but it promised us nothing but danger or embarrassment. . . .'[3]

[1] *Revue Indépendante*, March 1st, 1842, vol. ii, p. 847.

[2] *Mémoires*, vol. i, p. 296.

[3] Guizot: Reeve, November 4th, 1858, *Life and Letters of Henry Reeve*, (ed. Laughton), vol. i, pp. 396-397.

Guizot had earlier, in March 1840, in a similar way explained to Lord Palmerston that as the government of Louis-Philippe was not supported by a portion of the landowning class, it was bound to be particularly attentive to the manufacturing and financial classes which had always given it loyal support.[1]

When it came to defining what one meant by 'middle class', Guizot always sought a definition in political and historical terms, rather than a definition of economic function. In an article for a political dictionary published in 1865, Guizot summed up and repeated much of what he had often been saying. The middle classes were the most important part of French history. The Third Estate had been the most active and decisive element in the Old Régime; their movement against the feudal aristocracy had been more extensive in France than in any other country and had culminated in the greatest of the European revolutions. The middle classes, who were the successors to the Third Estate, were the truest representatives of the general interests of society. Their mission was to oppose both retrograde attempts to restore privilege and the pretensions of those who wished to establish social equality by means of a levelling-down process. It was because of this mission that the middle classes would continue to have a predominant influence in the state. They are thus defined partly in terms of the past, as those who had attacked the system of privilege, and partly in terms of the future, as a force which would protect society from further upsets.[2] Guizot had the same conception of the middle classes as had Royer-Collard, who believed that all the interests of society were wrapped up with the middle class, and that if ever the influence of this class was compromised then its very security was disturbed. Similarly, Benjamin Constant believed that whilst everyone needed the middle class, it was independent and needed no one, and that by looking after its own interests this class was looking after the interests of all.[3] Such definitions, which attribute an historical vocation to a class are necessarily inclusive, whilst definition in terms of economic function is necessarily more limitative and exclusive. As there was no legal barrier between the middle class and any other, Guizot suggested that definitions which tended to separate classes were impossible. 'Who can say where the middle classes begin and where they leave off?' he asked, in the article on the *Tiers État*. Thus the middle class, in Guizot's mind, was large. It occupied a vast space in the heart of society, to which the doors

[1] *Mémoires*, vol. v, pp. 31-32.

[2] See article 'Tiers-État' in *Maurice Block, Dictionnaire Générale de la Politique*, 2 vols., Paris 1864-1865.

[3] See *Barante, Royer-Collard*, op. cit., vol. i, p. 456. *Constant, Cours de Politique Constitutionnelle*, ed. Laboulaye, Paris 1861, vol. ii, pp. 254, 393-394.

were always open and where there was always room for anyone who was capable and willing to enter.[1] Writers such as Pierre Leroux or Louis Blanc, on the other hand, sought by economic definition to show that the middle class was in reality a small and exclusive section of society, infinitely more powerful and infinitely less numerous than a suffering and underprivileged proletariat. The fact that there was no absolute barrier between bourgeoisie and proletariat did not prevent them from being separate from one another, any more than the existence of half-castes in a colonial territory did not rule out the existence of black and white.[2]

One must therefore wonder why it was that since Guizot attributed to the middle classes such a vital political rôle, and since he obviously saw them as a large and growing section of the population, he could theoretically justify the restriction of political rights to a very small group. He frequently gave one explanation of this. From the time of the electoral law of 1817, political power had been placed in the most independent, enlightened and capable part of society. This power had descended as far down as possible, 'to the limit at which political capacity stops'. Obviously this limit would vary as wealth increased and enlightenment spread, but the principle remained that political rights were attached to capacity, in accordance with the sovereignty of reason.[3] But a more vital reason why Guizot thought in terms of restrictive political rights, and one which has often been ignored, was because he thought of an 'élite' as being natural to society. He did not believe that the Revolution had destroyed all the elements of aristocracy in France, although it might have changed its nature. He thought that if the Revolution could settle down, then it would produce its own aristocracy.[4] Modern democracy was a contrast to the democracies of the ancient republics; in the modern democracies (he was referring to France in 1831) there was no seeking after power, no desire to take part in government, no preoccupation with political passions. He thought that essentially people were concerned with their own private and domestic affairs and only wanted guarantees of liberty and security. Hence it was more than ever necessary in a

[1] *Mémoires*, vol. vi, pp. 348-349.

[2] See *Jean Reybaud, Revue Encyclopédique*, April 1832. Adolphe Granier de Cassagnac sought, in his *Histoire des Classes Ouvrières et des Classes Bourgeoises*, Paris 1837, to extend the ranks of the bourgeoisie by economic definition. Since the proletariat was the class which had no property or fortune whatsoever, then it was composed of only four groups, workers, beggars, thieves and prostitutes. Granier de Cassignac was at this time an admirer of Guizot. He declared in the preface to this volume that there were only two historians in France, Guizot and Victor Hugo.

[3] Chambre des Députés, May 5th, 1837. *Histoire Parlementaire*, vol. iii, pp. 104-106.

[4] *Du Gouvernement de la France depuis la Restauration*, op. cit., p. 108.

modern society to find men who by birth and situation were able to devote themselves to public affairs and political life. Such an aristocracy was a condition of modern society and a necessary consequence of modern democracy. In fact, since within each class there were inequalities of wealth as there were diversities of talents, then there was not merely an aristocracy, but aristocracies. The fact that they were not barricaded behind exclusive legal privileges removed any objection from Guizot's mind.[1] He approved of these aristocracies, and after 1848 he more than once returned to this theme. He wrote to Lenormant that France could not be governed by or with the middle classes. The government should fix its lever and choose its instruments higher in the social scale.[2] The middle classes were apt to be attracted towards new ideas, contrary to their interests; they were also inclined to become disgusted with politics. They needed some counterbalancing influence and Guizot believed that such an influence could be found amongst those classes whose fortune was already made, who were stable and less absorbed by private interests.[3] It was for this reason that he so much admired the English aristocracy; it was for this reason that he approved of the way in which industrialists often invested their profits in land (although economically it would have been more advantageous had they invested their money in industrial expansion and improvement). 'Je suis grand partisan de la race des country-gentlemen,' he told Sainte-Aulaire.[4] Doubtless it was for this reason too that he was never prepared to make any effective reduction in the powers of the centralized administration. He approved of a system which distributed the personnel of this aristocracy throughout France and animated them with the same principles.

The objection to such theories is obvious. Guizot's view of the bourgeoisie links together as a class a number of different groups. The basis of their union is their political and civic virtues. They are thought of as being the most effective supporters of stability, of liberty and of progress. Yet if these groups cannot be classified together in terms of some economic function, then their union can hardly be effective. Guizot's critic from Bordeaux, the irritable Fonfrède, wrote of 'an alleged middle class, which is not a class at all, which has no collective being, which possesses neither direction nor stability. This alleged middle class, a pêle mêle confusion of

[1] Chambre des Députés, October 5th, 1831, January 3rd, 1834. *Histoire Parlementaire*, vol. i, pp. 316-317, vol. ii, pp. 190-191.

[2] Guizot: Lenormant, January 11th, 1849, *Lettres à M. et Mme Lenormant* (op. cit.), p. 23. Lenormant was advising Guizot at this time on his book *De la Démocratie en France*.

[3] Nos mécomptes et nos espérances, *Revue Contemporaine*, vol. 18, 1855.

[4] Guizot: Sainte-Aulaire, March 11th, 1842. *Archives Nationales*, 42 A.P. 8.

twenty, fifty or a hundred different classes, each having moral and industrial interests which are often different and sometimes contradictory, and having no principle other than personal motives or local intrigues. It cannot have any general view of affairs, any political opinions, any governmental system, any general knowledge of this country or of relations with other countries.'[1] The *Revue Indépendante* claimed that the egoism of the bourgeoisie prevented it from founding anything which was real and solid. Soon it would be necessary to reverse Sieyès and say 'Qu'est-ce que le Tiers État? Rien.'[2] In this respect the middle classes did not live up to Guizot's optimism. It was their divergences, more than anything else, which rendered parliamentary government impossible. But equally it was representatives of this same middle class who objected to Guizot's attempt to govern through an élite, even although this élite was composed of the upper bourgeoisie rather than being a totally distinct nobility. A host of French political observers have commented on the Frenchman's dislike of any form of aristocracy. From General Foy, who considered that the rule of one man was thought preferable to the rule of 'superior classes', to Tocqueville, who claimed that 'l'esprit français' would not admit of any superiors, whilst 'l'esprit anglais' wished rather for inferiors, it would be possible to amass a considerable collection of quotations. When *Le Charivari* wrote, 'All that we have gained is to have substituted for the old Oeil de Boeuf the aristocracy of the Vatouts, the Barthes, the Testes, the d'Argouts, the Persils, the Decazes, the Lacave-Laplagnes', it almost certainly expressed a widespread sentiment.[3]

Most people today seem to agree with those critics of Guizot who considered that the most objectionable feature of his system was the political and economic predominance of one class. France was divided into a small 'pays légal' which had the effective power, and a large 'pays réel' which contained millions who were suffering, yet whose interests were officially ignored. 'The domination of an exclusive interest,' wrote Louis Blanc, 'whether it be of a man or of a caste has always been the affliction of humanity.'[4] This division of France into the 'mangeurs' and the 'mangés' (as it was sometimes called) was considered to be both unjust and unwise. Unjust, when one of the intellectual characteristics of this period was the conviction that the suffering of individuals could be prevented, and that to do so was the task of governments and the responsibility of society. Unwise, because of the strength which the radical parties were able

[1] *Henri Fonfrède, Œuvres* (op. cit.), vol. vi, p. 62.
[2] *Revue Indépendante*, July 1842, p. 216.
[3] *Le Charivari*, December 19th, 1843.
[4] *Louis Blanc, Histoire de Dix Ans* (9th ed.), vol. i, p. 134, Paris 1849.

to draw from their attack on the new feudalism, and because of the explosive nature of the bourgeoisie-proletariat relationship. Guizot was undoubtedly aware of these arguments. Whereas some of the bourgeoisie (for example, in the newspaper *Le Constitutionnel*) denied the existence of hardship amongst the French working classes and claimed that France was better off in this respect than England, Guizot was always aware of this social problem. In 1831 he said that distress and suffering amongst the French labouring population was even greater than appeared.[1] He realized that revolutionary doctrines concerning the organization of society and the distribution of property were widely diffused amongst these classes. The essential check to this type of revolutionary disposition was, he thought, a moral one, which should exist within the individual, in terms of his beliefs. In 1837 this check was absent, and the only effective restraint, apart from force, was the need to work. But one day, Guizot believed, even this check would be missing.[2]

Nevertheless, whilst realizing some of the drawbacks and dangers of the situation, he rejected completely all the socialist doctrines which were current at this time. He put them all together, and treated them as prolongations of the moral, social and political crisis which had existed from the end of the eighteenth century onwards. Saint-Simonism and Fourierism he thought of as containing some realization of political truth. They understood the necessity of authority, of discipline and of hierarchy. But supporters of these doctrines had placed themselves in an impossible position; at the same time as they defended state power, they let loose all the forces of anarchy by fomenting amongst the masses a jealous urge for material welfare.[3] Politically, Guizot's objection to socialism was the same as his objection to any form of political democracy, that it could not produce any form of good or stable government. 'The melancholy condition of democratic governments', he wrote, 'is that while charged as they must be with the repression of disorder, they are required to be complaisant and indulgent to the causes of disorder. They are expected to arrest the evil when it breaks out and yet they are asked to foster it whilst it is hatching.' He had the same criticisms to make of democracy as had Mallet du Pan (an earlier and in many ways similar exile in England). Anarchy could never become order, since there were some who had an interest in prolonging disorder and laws were passed only in order that illegalities might be committed.[4]

---

[1] Chambre des Députés, October 20th, 1831. *Histoire Parlementaire*, vol. i, p. 324.
[2] Ibid., May 3rd, 1837, vol. iii, pp. 78-79.
[3] *Mémoires*, vol. ii, pp. 206-207.
[4] *De la Démocratie en France* (op. cit.), pp. 24 ff.

Philosophically Guizot's objection to socialism is that it contains an essential contradiction. Whilst exalting human nature and the individual, at the same time it depresses humanity with an equal lack of proportion. With the wildest enthusiasm, socialists attacked the natural inequalities which existed amongst men; in order to further these attacks they found themselves obliged to attack both property and religion, which Guizot considered to be the distinguishing characteristics of man. The philosophical implication of the views of a writer such as Proudhon (whom Guizot thought of, in 1849, as the best of the socialist writers) was that human society was made up of a mere collection of individuals, without contact between the various generations and without any higher wants than those of animals.

Guizot saw no reason why the existence of suffering should modify the Revolutionary settlement. There were no longer any legal barriers to the movement of men or of goods and it was always possible for a man to rise in the world. 'The movement of ascension is nowhere stopped. With work, good sense, good conduct, one rises, one can rise as high as it is possible to rise in the social hierarchy.' Those who did not rise were the stupid or lazy, or dissolute, and they remained in the restricted and precarious existence of the wage-earner.[1] Men had come into the world with unequal opportunities, this was the natural order of things. To pretend that this could be changed was but pride or fantasy. The most one could hope for was that the possessing classes would not be egoistic, and that the poorer classes would not be envious. Guizot here has nothing to offer except warnings about pride, and nothing to recommend except the paintings of Hogarth, 'The good and the bad apprentice', 'The good and the bad employer'. Only at extraordinary moments was it possible to intervene and to modify this natural order. At moments of crisis, then, the property-owners should help the working class, as the government should, on similar occasions, help a languishing industry. But such help should be given only on condition that it was temporary and that it was limited. Any form of a Poor Law would be iniquitous, a tax on the rich in order to maintain the poor; such a measure would be harmful to liberty.[2]

For all that Guizot had the reputation of being more humane than many of his contemporaries, and he certainly lacked the brutal

[1] Chambre des Députés, March 12th, 1834. *Histoire Parlementaire*, vol. ii, p. 224. *De la Démocratie* (op. cit.), p. 76.
[2] See the speeches at the *Société Protestante de Secours Mutuel et de Patronage de Nîmes*, April 22nd, 1860, reprinted in *Guizot, Discours Académiques* etc., Paris 1861, and in the Chambre des Députés, October 20th, 1831. *Histoire Parlementaire*, vol. i, pp. 327-328.

cynicism of Thiers, nevertheless one is struck by his failure to contribute anything to social thought, as his ministry contributed little to social legislation. In seeking an explanation of this failure, one is again obliged to consider personal reasons as well as more general reasons of class and situation. Personally he showed a tendency which has often been associated with Geneva, to regard pauperism and misery as a reflection on an individual rather than a reflection on society. He saw the labouring populations essentially as artisans, as peasant landowners, as peasant-cum-artisan. In the prevailing conditions of the eighteenth-century economy it was possible for an artisan to acquire wealth and property. Yet in the nineteenth century many of the artisan class were giving way to the machine; the industrial worker, or the independent craftsman within an industrialized system, had little hope of changing their condition. 'Always, always, always is the everlasting word drummed into your ear by the mechanical roaring which sets the floors trembling', wrote Michelet of the industrial worker.[1] Guizot never had the imagination to write like this. Sismondi said of Madame de Staël that she could never put herself in the place of others; Guizot shared this defect with her. The historian of civilization could write of socialism as a mere 'phase of human nature that reappears at epochs when society is like a boiling cauldron, in which every ingredient is thrown to the surface and exposed to view'. But he had not therefore understood nineteenth-century socialism, nor had he disposed of it.

Yet beyond the intellectual failings of Guizot there are other reasons why his appreciation of socialism was imperfect. One of the explanations for the rise of socialist thought in the nineteenth century is that once it was appreciated that new techniques existed for the production of wealth, then it appeared that poverty was unnatural rather than natural, the result of imperfect organization rather than the inevitable condition of man. But in Guizot's France this argument was less convincing than elsewhere. A large-scale redistribution of property had taken place before the process of industrialization had effectively started; furthermore, once the process of industrialization did get under way in France, it was slow and uneven. There was no dramatic renewal of the productive apparatus, changing the structure of French society. Still less was there any complete change in the 'ideological super-structures'. Inequalities still appeared inevitable; where there were inequalities there was incomprehension; where there was incomprehension there was fear and apprehension. In these circumstances Guizot sometimes forgot about the moral nature and purpose of the state, and its need to satisfy the interests of men only when their ideas were satisfied.

[1] *Michelet, Le Peuple*, Paris 1847, p. 83.

The issue of government became a choice between the intimidation of the 'honnêtes gens' and the intimidation of the 'malhonnêtes gens'[1]. In this respect Guizot, like all other French statesmen, showed that he too could not keep from extremes.

After this survey it is clear that Guizot was not a great political thinker. He was not original, nor was he particularly acute. But for reasons which have been explained, it was not a great age of political thought. Many people even denied the existence of political philosophy. The foremost critics of Guizot at times confessed their own bankruptcy in this respect. Auguste Comte believed in 1824 that there was no alternative to governing from day to day in a purely provisional manner, until the spiritual reorganization of society had been effected. Pierre Leroux, as late as 1842, still considered political philosophy to be an 'ignotum', and Tocqueville described his contemporaries as centring their thoughts and their actions on themselves 'faute de mieux'.[2] It would be foolish therefore to underestimate Guizot. His contribution is considerable when compared to the various types of nostalgia which masqueraded as idealism, or when compared to the various resentments which inspired successive oppositions. Lerminier in a series of articles in the *Revue des Deux Mondes* in 1832 surveyed the current political ideas and their representatives. He found much to condemn, and here and there found men whom he was glad to praise, but it is significant that he reserved most praise of all for Lafayette, a man who for most of his life chose to appear as an obstinate and irrelevant revolutionary, around whom there lay the myth of a man of action, but who never laid claim to be a man of thought. Lamennais and Lamartine, for all that their theories could be as lucid as they were dramatic, were dominated by their belief in the necessity of occasional, if not successive, revolutions. If society was progressive by nature, it was also revolutionary by nature; such a doctrine was not meant to be reassuring, but neither was it helpful. The description of the people as a 'child-king' shows Lamartine's political skill, but did not help anyone to understand the nature of government. Constant and Royer-Collard, for all their incisiveness, did not take their conception of the state beyond the old conceit that the end of government was liberty. Michelet merely exalted popular instinct and inspiration over 'their aristocratic sister', reflection and reason.

[1] Chambre des Députés, August 20th, 1835. *Histoire Parlementaire*, vol. ii, p. 433. See also *Mémoires*, vol. vi, p. 345.
[2] Comte: Valat, December 25th, 1824, *Lettres d'Auguste Comte à Monsieur Valat*, 1815-1848, Paris 1870, pp. 156-157; Pierre Leroux, *Revue Indépendante*, July 1842, p. 17; Tocqueville: Royer-Collard, September 8th, 1842, *Revue des Deux Mondes*, August 15th, 1930, p. 909.

Everywhere there were assumptions rather than theories. It was assumed that the voice of the people, like the voice of God, could only find expression in a Republic. It was assumed that the Church was an enemy of progress. Some assumed that the best government was the cheapest, whilst others assumed that any institutions created by men were bound to prove inadequate. In certain of these thinkers there is what Carlyle called in Voltaire 'an entire want of Earnestness'. At least Guizot cannot be criticized for this. He and Tocqueville were probably the most earnest thinkers of the nineteenth century.

There are other similarities between Guizot and Tocqueville besides this earnestness. They were both opponents of the equalizing process which they called democracy; they thought that democracy would mean the destruction of the kind of society that they valued; the disappearance of any governing 'élite' would mean government by a crowd which had no motives but 'self-interest', and would lead inevitably to the most ruthless of all despotisms. They both thought that there were occasions when universal suffrage could be useful, even valuable, but in general they thought it (in Tocqueville's words) 'a challenge to reason'. Neither of them was prepared to consider government by a numerical majority as being the same thing as good government. Tocqueville, like Guizot, disapproved of socialist theories, and was horrified at the 'maladies des esprits' whereby men believed that the state could not only save them from suffering but that it could also provide them with luxury and well-being. Again like Guizot, he thought historically. He could not talk of a nation without considering what it had been fifty years earlier. Above all, to understand the France of his own time it was necessary to understand the Revolution. Tocqueville made the more determined and effective effort to do this, but both of them were anxious to demonstrate the forces that had been at work, rather than to be distracted by personalities or narrative. Although they were analytical historians, they both admitted divine intervention in world affairs. Tocqueville probably despised the 1848 Revolution even more than did Guizot. He compared it to 1789, which, he said, had emerged from the brain and heart of the nation, whilst 1848 had partly come from the stomach.[1] For both of them property was a barrier, perhaps the last, against democracy and all the radical changes which that would bring. Often their vocabulary was as similar as their ideas, and the objective, 'to restrain and to sustain power', is present in the writings of both. They even shared many of the same faults. They generalized

---

[1] Tocqueville: Bouchitté, May 1st, 1848. *Œuvres Complètes*, Paris 1866, vol. vii, pp. 235-236. Sainte-Beuve commented on this that there was nothing more respectable than the stomach. 'Il n'y a pas de cri qui parle plus haut que celui de la misère.' *Nouveaux Lundis*, vol. x, p. 317.

from flimsy and isolated evidence, they showed a lack of insight regarding the significance of industrialization, they were both over-preoccupied with the middle classes. Their writings and speeches were sometimes characterized by a sententious intellectualism, and they were both parodied on the Paris stage, Guizot in *Le Fils de Giboyer* by Émile Augier, and Tocqueville in Edouard Pailleron's *Le Monde où l'on s'ennuie*.

Obviously there were differences between the two. Tocqueville, by his attacks upon the alleged corruption of political life, was one of the chief critics of the Guizot administration. He regretted the absence of any social policy, and was probably right in thinking that a Poor Law might advantageously have been introduced into France before 1848. Above all he looked down on the French middle classes with all the scorn of an aristocrat. Where Guizot saw civic virtues and a sense of progress, Tocqueville saw timidity, dishonesty, egoism and, above all, mediocrity. Yet the essential difference between Guizot and Tocqueville is not to be found in any of these details. Guizot was a practical statesman whose political theory was aligned to the necessities of policy and government. Tocqueville was a prophet, and invariably a prophet of gloom. He saw many of the evils and possible dangers of the future, but he did little to combat them. Guizot was undoubtedly justified when he wrote to Tocqueville in 1835, after the first volume of *Democracy in America*, 'You judge Democracy like an aristocrat who has been defeated but who is convinced that his victorious opponent is right.'[1] Tocqueville claimed that a new political science was needed for a completely new world, but he did not provide one. He was an observer, a fatalist, and at most put forward some pious hopes, that elections would be less corrupt, that the opposition would be less revolutionary, that the possessing classes would be less complacent. He did nothing to defend or to further a parliamentary system; his fastidious intellect was bored by the realities of government. Guizot did not possess his vision or his penetration. The writings of Guizot do not hold the same interest for the twentieth century as do those of 'the Prophet of the Mass Age'. Yet in terms of nineteenth-century French politics it was Guizot's which was the more notable contribution.

In many respects too it was Guizot who was right. The French middle classes eventually proved their resilience. The history of the nineteenth century as a whole shows that the French Revolution did produce social stability, and the French possessive classes were never deprived of their economic and social power. The period of the liberal Empire and the Third Republic gave the lie to Tocqueville,

[1] Quoted in *Pierre Marcel, Essai Politique sur Alexis de Tocqueville,* Paris 1910, p. 69.

as they did to all extremists of both the Left and the Right. One might add that if Louis Napoleon were the people's choice, then this too confirms Guizot's judgement. As Macaulay remarked, the constancy of the people in its choice of favourites constitutes a vice and not a virtue.

Some of the defects of Guizot's thought have already been mentioned. He was too fond of repeating himself; he was too oblivious of new developments; he often used terms imprecisely; his *De la Démocratie en France* for example, although Croker thought it the finest defence of property since Burke, suffers from the absence of any definition of the word 'democracy'. His political theory contains four major weaknesses. In the first place, his system of government required intelligence upon the part of those who had to work it. A wiser man, especially in France, would have tried to devise a well-oiled machine which stupid and harmless people would be able to run. He took too little account of irrational aspirations. He did not understand why the doctrine of the sovereignty of the people should be so powerful. Secondly, he did not locate any one theoretical centre of power in the state. It was argued by some deputies that the Chamber could make the law, any law. The doctrine of the sovereignty of reason did not allow any constitutional body to possess the constituent power. Guizot considered that when the Chamber had wielded that power, as in 1830, then this was accidental. Thus whilst trying to institute a form of parliamentary government, by refusing to establish any body in the state as supreme, Guizot was effectively reducing the value of the Chamber of Deputies. Thirdly, for all that he was a pluralist, he never tried to analyse the various groups to which French people owed their loyalties. He never tried to understand the nature of the conflict between the middle and the lower classes which overthrew his government. On the contrary, he refused to acknowledge the true strength of the disruptive forces within France, and he even created a retrospective myth of the unity of all classes in 1789, in contradiction to his many earlier statements about the aristocratic opposition to the Revolution. Fourthly, too much of his thought, like all conservative thought, was a reaction to some other form of thought. It was a reaction rather than a response. The liberal economists, such as Say and Bastiat, were said to have reasoned on economic matters with side glances at socialist doctrines, and therefore to have confused their theories of wealth with the quite separate issue of defending particular institutions. So Guizot was more concerned with strengthening a system of government against its enemies rather than with devising an ideal system. The need to justify was stronger than the need to understand, and this is regrettable in any thinker.

86

In July 1842 the church of La Madeleine was consecrated. It looked on to the Place de la Concorde where the revolutionary guillotine had stood, which was bordered by the Chamber, the royal palace of the Tuileries and the Champs Élysées, at the head of which stood the recently completed Arc de Triomphe. 'The whole of France', said the Dominican Lacordaire, 'is here. Royalty, armed glory, liberty, religion, revolution.' (A few months later another part of France was nearly added, as it was proposed to build a railway station next to the church, but this project was abandoned.) The French were always conscious of the complexity of their past and the complications of their present. Sometimes they were proud of this diversity, sometimes they were sorrowful over the difficulties which this created. Their very self-consciousness becomes part of the problem to be studied. One therefore studies not only the theory and manner of politics but also more concrete ways in which this involved society developed. One is led to the history of education, and here too the part played by Guizot is important.

3

EDUCATION
AND PUBLIC INSTRUCTION

Everywhere I found Monsieur Guizot's name held in
honour for the justice and wisdom of his direction of
popular education when it was in fashion, for his fidelity to
it now that it is no longer talked of.

MATTHEW ARNOLD

THOSE who have drunk deeply of the small beer of educational
theory have often thought that the differences between English
and French societies are to be explained by differences of educational
method. In England, the aim of education has supposedly been to
develop character; in France, a complex series of educational programmes has sought to impart knowledge. In England, order and
method were sacrificed in order to produce a community with a sense
of duty and a spirit of toleration. Within such a community there
could be compromise and understanding; differences could be
adjusted, disputes could be confined to discussion, and anomalies
could persist without danger. In France, however, there has been a
uniform system. The imposition of this system has made Frenchmen
increasingly aware of their differences without making them more
understanding or tolerant. Individual exertions and initiative have
been stifled by the action of the state in conferring education upon
the people. Not only have French governments prevented any natural
or spontaneous development in educational matters, but by their
interference they have contributed to their own deconsideration. If
ever a government is to be accused of governing too much, then it is
in education that the fault is most visible. Villages became conscious
of their government when they were given a school and a schoolmaster. Hostility to the one or to the other meant hostility to the

government. The whole could be said to serve as an illustration of what Burke meant when he wrote, 'Statesmen who know themselves will proceed in the superior orb of their duty, steadily, vigilantly, severely, courageously: . . . but if they descend from the state to a province, from a province to a parish, from a parish to a private house, they go on accelerated in their fall. They cannot do the lower duty; and in proportion as they try they will certainly fail in the higher.'[1]

This suggestion, that it was the educational system which made English society eminently governable and which rendered modern French society difficult to govern, cannot be accepted as it stands. Apart from the confused thinking about English education which it contains, it supposes that educational institutions help to form the political customs of the country. Yet more often than not it is the political issues which affect the educational. Educational institutions are part of the political institutions of any society. In a country which is politically disturbed, then education is invariably a controversial subject. All questions concerning the methods, extent and nature of education become part of the more general political and social dissent. Thus the crisis of French society in the eighteenth century is illustrated by the discussions which took place about education. It can doubtless be shown that these discussions owed their intellectual origins to a number of writers, such as the German Comenius, such as Rabelais or Locke, or perhaps to the ideas of certain pedagogues such as the great Oratorian teacher Lamy. But these discussions owed their importance to the social crisis of the eighteenth century. Educational matters became vital as the bourgeoisie grew more actively hostile to aristocratic privilege. If it was believed that men should be equal before the law, then it was assumed that there were no inherent superiorities. Men came from nature with an equality and sameness of minds. A child's mind was thought of as being a blank sheet at birth, and hence there could be no presumption of hereditary superiority. Education was the only differentiating force, and by praising its power one was attacking privilege.

But if education was to be effective, it had to be practical, and this meant that it had to be reformed. It could no longer be abstract and ideal; it could no longer be based upon a stereotyped classical culture, or on an artificial humanism. Hence the existing educational establishments of the Ancien Régime were found unsatisfactory. Education had to be linked to society if it was to be useful, and when it was entirely in the hands of the Church, with the catechism serving

[1] *Edmund Burke, Thoughts and Details on Scarcity. Originally presented to William Pitt . . . Works* (Bohn Edition), 1855, vol. v, p. 108.

as the generally accepted textbook, then it was not fulfilling its necessary function. Condillac was not alone in complaining that Frenchmen wearied themselves throughout their childhood in learning things that were useless; not until they became adults did they begin to receive any real form of 'instruction'.

One can therefore see that the preoccupation with education and the movement for educational reform fit in to the different crises of the Ancien Régime. They are part of the crisis of authority, of the clash between different powers, particularly between the ecclesiastical and the civil powers. Education thus becomes one of the great critical exercises of the eighteenth century. 'All the literary pirouettes are turned towards education,' wrote one observer. 'There is no author slender enough not to have his say upon this interesting subject, but it is to be feared that they will do as did the good grandmother of Henry IV, who caressed her children to the point of smothering them.'[1]

The course of events also contributed to bring educational matters to the fore. The expulsion of the Jesuits, for example, brought about a crisis, owing to the large number of schools which they possessed. It was said that within the area governed by the Parlement of Paris alone they had forty colleges, and when they disappeared teaching arrangements had to be improvised and other religious orders had to take over in order to prevent the colleges from closing. The Oratorians moved in to several colleges in this way and thereby imposed a heavy strain on their organization. The economic depression which coincided with the reign of Louis XVI reduced their resources, and prior to the Revolution a number of their colleges had to be abandoned. Such incidents served to confirm that this unco-ordinated complex of education was unsuitable, even for the crumbling social system of eighteenth-century France.

This being so, there were two ways of approaching reform. The one was to see it as a question of organization. The physiocrats wanted some form of state system, usually with a Council for National Instruction, whilst the 'parlementaires' wanted some system of regional universities, where each university would take over responsibility for education within its own area. The other way of approaching reform was itself derived from the new belief in education. Once education had ceased to be a formalism and had become a process, then it had become something which could be studied. Education became a science; the study of childhood and of teaching became significant. When Rousseau showed that the nature of a child was something different from that of an adult, and that the

---

[1] *Essai sur les moeurs du temps*, Londres 1768, p. 85. This was published anonymously but is thought to have been written by the *Abbé Reboul*.

identity of a child was separate from that of an adult, then an important advance was made in educational possibility. The personality of the child was recognized as being quite as complex as that of the man and education had to be accommodated so as to fit in to the various stages of the child's development. This awareness of the special characteristics of the child was the starting-point for a whole series of educationalists, who doubtless did not share all Rousseau's principles, yet who owed their inspiration to *Émile*. People such as Basedow, Kant, Campe and Froebel in Germany, Pestalozzi in Switzerland, Edgeworth and Day in England, all followed Rousseau in their conception of education as a science based upon the observation and understanding of children. It is not suggested that Guizot was a great educationalist whose name deserves to be placed alongside those who have just been mentioned (although his first wife, Pauline de Meulan, might have some such claim). However, as will be shown, he did combine in his work both approaches to educational reform. As an official and as a politician he was concerned with organization; as an editor, writer and teacher, he was concerned with pedagogy and child psychology.

With the Revolution the need for reform became more urgent. The suppression of feudal dues, the abolition of municipal excise and the confiscation of Church wealth were sufficient to destroy the financial framework of the existing scholastic system. The rise of prices and the devaluation of the currency made this destruction complete. The Civil Constitution of the clergy, which led to a cleavage between those who accepted to take an oath of loyalty and those who refused to take such an oath, not only scattered the teaching population but made the schools question vital in the struggle between revolution and counter-revolution. Who controlled the schools became a matter of public policy, and, for some of public safety. For both the Revolutionary and the Imperial governments, a great deal of legislation arose from this controversy, and much of it was improvised *ad hoc*. One scheme led to another, the laws were ineffective and there was no agreement on new laws.

Yet if the Revolution had achieved nothing in practice, 'a flood of words and nothing more' as Guizot was later to put it to Matthew Arnold,[1] it had put forward principles which were difficult to reject. Article 22 of the 1793 Declaration of the Rights of Man stated, 'Instruction is the need of all men'; such a principle, once advanced, could not lightly be abandoned. The Empire, on the other hand, had offered little in the way of principles, yet it had created a body of men who were specialists on educational matters. Towards the end of the imperial period there were several instances of how this corps of

[1] *Matthew Arnold, The Popular Education of France*, 1861, p. 29.

specialists was preparing some type of reform. The inspector-general of the University, Ambroise Rendu, seems to have prepared several projects. There was an enquiry into the state of the schools in 1810, in 1811 a committee was formed under the chairmanship of Frédéric Cuvier to consider what reforms were necessary, and in the same year Georges Cuvier, his elder brother, published a report on the schools of the Low Countries and of Germany. It was in this situation that in 1811 Guizot and Pauline de Meulan began to publish the *Annales de l'Éducation*.[1]

Guizot had certain qualifications for the job of editing an educational journal. Anyone from a Protestant region was likely to be aware of educational problems, since one of the ways in which the Catholic Church had tried to stamp out heresy was by the installation of Catholic schools in the Protestant regions. The Protestant communities had replied with their own schools and with teachers of their own choice. This rivalry had led to a relatively high degree of instruction being given, even in poor regions. The Protestants were fully conscious of the importance of schools, and the importance of an education which was moral and religious, not merely instructional. Guizot had avoided the mediocrity of the Napoleonic lycée by being educated at the Collège and at the Academy of Geneva. Whilst the lycée at Marseilles had given Thiers his first stirrings of militarism, the Genevan establishments had introduced Guizot to German and to British thought which at the time was often preoccupied with pedagogical problems. One of the professors at Geneva, Marc-Auguste Pictet, was the friend and, with his brother, translator of the Edgeworths, whose *Practical Education* appeared in 1798.

But Guizot's real preparation for editing the *Annales de l'Éducation* came from his association with Stapfer. Stapfer had held the Chair of Humanities and Philosophy at Berne, and from 1798 to 1800 he was Minister for Arts and Science in the Helvetic Republic. This Ministry was responsible for educational matters and Stapfer had prepared a considerable educational reform. He had been particularly interested

[1] *Ambroise Rendu* (1778-1860) was a friend of Chateaubriand and a collaborator of Fontanes on the *Mercure*. He was Inspector General of the University and from 1820 to 1850 was a member of the Commission for Public Instruction. *Frédéric Cuvier* (1773-1838), although less famous than his brother, was an inspector of the Paris Academy. He was the author in 1815 of *Projet d'organisation des écoles primaires*. *Georges Cuvier* (1769-1832) was the leading French naturalist and anatomist, who had a distinguished career in the University of Paris. Royer-Collard called him the greatest mind of the century. Napoleon entrusted him with a number of administrative tasks and intended him to be his son's tutor. Cuvier became a Conseiller d'État with the first Restoration in 1814 and in 1815 he became one of the five members of the Commission for Public Instruction; he later became President. Both the Cuviers were Protestants.

in teaching methods and had followed closely the work of Campe, Fellenberg and Pestalozzi.[1] Stapfer had materially helped Pestalozzi. He had offered him the directorship of a teachers' training college which Stapfer intended to set up; on Pestalozzi's refusal he made him director of a newspaper, the *Helvetische Volksblatt*. In 1798 he put Pestalozzi in charge of an orphanage in Staaz, and when this venture failed, he stood by him very loyally. In 1799 he gave Pestalozzi an official grant to help his establishment at Burgdorff. Stapfer was particularly interested in primary education. What we now call 'secondary education' was established long before primary education, and it was only in the nineteenth century that primary education came to be considered seriously and even to be treated as fundamental. Thus Guizot's association with Stapfer is very important. From 1805 onwards Guizot was tutor to Stapfer's two sons, and was obliged to familiarise himself with the work of educationalists who were not well known in France; one of the aims of the *Annales de l'Éducation* was to introduce French readers to the methods and beliefs of these reformers.

Through Stapfer Guizot met others who had a similar interest in education; Charles de Villers, who introduced Kant into France and who published in 1808 a study of the universities and the method of instruction of Protestant Germany; Maine de Biran, who had been influenced by Pestalozzi and whose psychological work had important pedagogical implications; de Gérando, who had been one of the founders, in 1802, of the *Société d'Encouragement pour l'Éducation Industrielle*, and who had advised Napoleon's minister Champagny on educational matters. Gérando was to be one of the most prominent educationalists in France until his death in 1842, and his work on the education of deaf-mutes was to become a classic. Guizot also went to the Saturday receptions of his co-religionist Georges Cuvier, whom he must also have seen at the Friday receptions of Madame de Rumford. Guizot knew the philanthropists, such as La Rochefoucauld-Liancourt, who were greatly concerned with education and who used to meet in the house of another Protestant, Benjamin Delessert, the banker.

The six volumes of the *Annales de l'Éducation* were published in monthly instalments from 1811 to 1814; publication ceased when

[1] *Joachim-Henry Campe* (1746-1818) was born in Brunswick. He created several famous teaching establishments and was a prolific composer of books for the use of children. He was a follower of Locke, Rousseau and Basedow. *Philip Emmanuel de Fellenberg* (1771-1844) was from Berne. In 1799 he set up at Hofwyl, near Berne, an establishment which was intended to teach both agricultural and educational science. Lord Brougham was a great admirer of his work. *Henry Pestalozzi* (1746-1827) has been most recently studied by *Kate Silber, Pestalozzi. The Man and his Work*, 1960.

Guizot's entry into the Ministry of the Interior caused him to abandon the review. The greater part of these volumes was written by Guizot himself and by Pauline de Meulan (who of course became his wife in 1812). Each published a major series of articles. Guizot had a series 'Conseils d'un Père', as well as a series devoted to great educationalists of the past, Rabelais, Montaigne, Kant and Tasso; Pauline de Meulan published thirty-five instalments of a 'Journal adressé par une femme à son mari sur l'éducation de ses deux filles' as well as a series of the 'contes' for which she was later to be famous. Their most distinguished collaborator was Dupont de Nemours, who wrote several articles on the educational system of the United States, which were later published in book form. Friedlander, a German from Koenigsmark who had settled in France, wrote some long articles on Physical Education. Their insistence on the development of the will seems to give them wider implications than is at first apparent, and these articles are all the more noticeable since physical education was continuously ignored in France in spite of the interest shown by the Prefect of the Seine, Chabrol, in 1820, and in spite of the intervention of two of the ministers of the Second Empire, Fortoul and Victor Duruy, this subject was not seriously studied until the end of the century. The *Annales* contained several articles on natural history, and a good deal of space was given up to translations. There are stories by Maria Edgeworth and John-Paul Richter, articles by Niemeyer and from the *Edinburgh Review*. There are many references to foreign methods and experiences. Pestalozzi, Betty Gleim, Fellenberg, Campe, Kant, Elisabeth Hamilton, Bell and Lancaster are all discussed. An insistence upon what is happening abroad seems to be one of the characteristics of all the contributions. Friedlander, for example, refers to the work of Gutsmuths in Germany, Nachtegal in Denmark and Strutt in England. Such cosmopolitanism was to become one of the characteristics of the nineteenth-century educationalists. They would back their demands for greater efforts by showing how some foreign country had a higher ratio of school attendance or was reaching a higher standard of instruction. Nationalism in educational matters seems to have been curiously inverted.[1]

[1] *Maria Edgeworth* (1770-1849) seems to have been widely read in France. *Practical Education*, which contains criticisms of a number of French educationalists, first appeared in a mutilated form in the *Bibliothèque Britannique* in Geneva; Pictet's translation was published in Paris and Geneva in 1801. Her works were also translated by Madame Swanton Belloc, the grandmother of the poet, with some inaccuracy. *John-Paul Richter* (1763-1825) was a Bavarian writer who hoped that the names John-Paul would become as significant as the names Jean-Jacques. *Hermann Augustus Niemeyer* (1754-1828) was a German critic of Pestalozzi. *Betty Gleim* (1781-1827) was from Bremen. She was an admirer of

The ideas of the *Annales de l'Éducation* can conveniently be summarized under four main headings. The first concerns the nature of childhood. Guizot is careful to discourage dogmatism in educational matters; one of the dangers to which both parents and educationalists are liable is the acceptance of absolute truths and precepts without reference to circumstances or to details. 'It is not simply a matter of saying that every rule has its exception,' he writes. 'One should rather say that every individual has his rule. . . . Our tailor measures us so that we can have clothes which fit, how can parents do without measuring their children in order that they can be formed and directed?'[1] Hence children must be observed and studied in a scientific manner. The way in which one child differs from another will provide an indication of how he should be treated. Parents and teachers should study the moral tendencies of children. One boy will lie because he is trying to avoid punishment or reproach; another boy will lie because he refuses to be contraried. The one lies out of timidity, the other out of self-assurance. In order to cure them of lying, totally different methods must be used. Children must be studied when they are with other children. It is then that their spontaneous activity reveals their character. Guizot quotes Montaigne's words, 'The games of children are not games, they should be regarded as their most serious occupations', a quotation of which Froebel was to approve. Parents and teachers can study their children's intellectual tendencies more easily than their moral inclinations. These appear more naturally without any attempt at concealment, but it is just as important to realize how one child is different from another. One child may be naturally imaginative,

---

Pestalozzi and applied his methods in her own school. In 1810 she published a two-volume work on the education and instruction of girls. Guizot reviewed the first volume in the *Annales de l'Éducation*, vol. iv, pp. 204 ff. *Elisabeth Hamilton* (1758-1816) was born in Ireland, and was best known for her *Elementary Principles of Education*. *Bell* (1753-1832) and *Lancaster* (1778-1838) were the rival English 'inventors' of the method of mutual instruction. *John-Christopher Frederick Gutsmuths* (1759-1839) is often considered to be the creator of the teaching of physical education in Germany. *Franz Nachtegal* (1777-1847) was one of the pioneers of physical education in Denmark. *Joseph Strutt* (1749-1802) was an engraver and antiquary, but he became well known through his book, *Sports and Pastimes of the People of England*, 1801. Guizot's discussion of Kant's Pedagogy is in vol. iv, pp. 65 ff., of Campe in vol. i, p. 105. Pauline de Meulan's account and criticisms of Pestalozzi are in vol. v, pp. 8 ff., pp. 72 ff., pp. 142 ff. and pp. 193 ff.

[1] See the article 'Des Modifications que doit apporter dans l'Éducation la Variété des Caractères'. This was published in the *Annales de l'Éducation*, vol. i, pp. 65 ff., but it can be more conveniently consulted in the *Méditations et Études Morales*, op. cit., pp. 213 ff., which collects together a number of articles on education. See p. 215.

another naturally observant. It is necessary to know what is natural in a child's make-up before education can usefully proceed. One must discover what disposition predominates, and then this disposition should become the central point of education and care; and this disposition should not be fought, it should be seconded and cultivated.[1]

One of Guizot's frequently repeated principles in matters of education is that every natural disposition of childhood has both its good and its bad side. It is from the good side that the bad will be fought successfully. In other words, education must follow the natural tendencies of the child. It is easy to force the logic of children, because they are inexperienced. It is easy to capture their will, because they are weak. For Guizot, to do either was bad.[2] Both he and Pauline de Meulan used to say that because grown-ups were naturally the stronger they should not think that they were the owners of the children with which they had to deal. They wanted education to be based on observation of the individual child and on respect for the complexity of childhood.

The second subject discussed by the *Annales* was that of how children should be taught. For Guizot, as for Rousseau, the most necessary feature of a child's activity was the activity itself. It was a pedagogical necessity, because it revealed things about the child which both parents and teachers needed to know, and because children needed the impression of activity during the process of learning. Thus a child would quickly learn a foreign language if he were obliged to speak it; he would quickly learn something if he had to teach it to children younger than himself (as in the monitorial system of the Lancastrian schools); he would learn to read more quickly if he was learning to write at the same time (as in the method of Campe). 'One must try in one's method of teaching', wrote Guizot, 'to make the child an active being who can exercise his growing forces on what he is learning, rather than a passive being placed so as to receive what people want to confer on his memory or thought.'[3] He praised Rabelais, whose Ponocrates had seen that for education to be interesting and profitable it should be active and present in the ordinary circumstances of everyday life.

Guizot follows Dugald Stewart and Reid in pointing out that early education should encourage observation, but discourage reflection. The child's curiosity and need for action leads him naturally towards observation and this is the source of his experience. Reflection leads to precocity, to sentiments that are entirely unsuited to a child's age

---

[1] Op. cit., p. 236.
[2] *Annales de l'Éducation*, vol. i, pp. 105 ff.
[3] Ibid., vol. i, p. 106.

and situation. That he should meditate over his own ideas, sentiments and emotions, or that he should try to understand those of grown-ups, is not only useless but positively harmful. The education must concentrate upon observation, attention and memory, and avoid anything which would encourage premature meditation. Thus, for Pauline de Meulan, a good form of history to teach to young children is natural history since it contains no moral.[1]

If one is seeking to develop powers of observation, then one must teach children how to observe, since they only enjoy doing what they are able to do well. The object of their attention should be in itself a source of activity, and interest, without being simply a source of pleasure. For children to develop their powers of observation they must have self-discipline and perseverance. ('To reach children whilst amusing them is something about which there has been a lot of talk but which has hardly ever been done' was Pauline de Meulan's comment.[2]) But the teacher can assist the child by arranging the lessons in a logical way. Subjects should be associated whenever possible, not simply added one to another. Each subject should be presented in an orderly way so that the child could assimilate its general principles. Contrary to the ideas which had recently been put forward by Haffner, Guizot claimed that one cannot learn Latin by speaking it, one must learn the principles of grammar. History, without reference to the synchronization of time and place, would become a chaos of names and incidents. Geography, without the natural divisions of continent and climate, would be a string of details which no child could remember. But once the subjects had been ordered and arranged, then one could expect children to extend their knowledge. Pauline de Meulan later wrote of the education of her own son 'when the central point of education is fixed and certain, then the more varied radii there are which go back to it, the better'.[3]

Guizot considers in some detail the different ways in which children could be encouraged to work and to learn. As in the government of men, he wrote, so in the government of children, one usually rules by reference to what is bad rather than by reference to what is good. When one wants children to obey, one exploits their weakness, and when one wants them to do something, one appeals to their self-interest. But the problem of persuading children that they should work and strive to acquire knowledge and instruction is real and acute. Guizot compares the position of children in the world to that of a young man who is born into an easy and comfortable life. He has

[1] See Guizot's essay 'De l'Inégalité des Facultés' in *Méditations*, op. cit., pp. 229 ff. See also *Annales de l'Éducation*, vol. i, p. 62.
[2] Ibid.
[3] Pauline de Meulan: Guizot, June 19th, 1822, *Val-Richer MSS*.

no difficulties and no responsibilities. Why should he become hard-working and serious? No one requires him to do this, and nothing suggests that it is necessary. In exactly the same way children are looked after and have no sense of future difficulties. Neither for their parents nor for themselves is it indispensable that they should become studious and zealous in their work. How then can they be persuaded to work? Not by force, since whilst authority is necessary, no child will work well simply because he is obliged to. If authority and force are applied to small details, then the same authority will soon lose its efficacy. Nor is it wise to appeal to the sensibility of children by suggesting that they should work in order to please their parents. The affections of children are too feeble and uneven to become a principle of action. Children who depend completely upon their parents are not likely to believe that their parents' happiness is so easily created and so easily destroyed. If they do believe this, then the authority of the parents will be severely shaken. The sentiment of duty is weak in children as in men. If one appeals to it, and then rewards the child who has responded, the child has not acted through this feeble sense of duty, but through the strong desire for reward. Guizot is also critical of the Lancastrian method which deployed excessive use of emulation, as well as of mutual punishment and of stimulating a young person through the ridicule of his fellow-pupils. The sentiment to which Guizot turns is one which is most powerful in children, namely the need for approbation. The conscience of children is formed by the approval and disapproval of others. This is the sentiment which parent or teacher must exploit. This is an appeal in terms of virtue rather than in terms of vanity. The child is pleased to have worked well because the fact of working well has met with general approval. Out of this pleasure a sense of duty can be acquired; from the combination of the two a powerful means of stimulating the activities of children is at the disposal of parents and teachers.[1]

We can see how Guizot envisages education as something like an experimental science and how he writes in the tradition of those who place observation of the pupil at the centre of the educational scheme. Like Pestalozzi he does not seek for material outside the child, but only in the faculties, sentiments and nature of the person who is to be educated. Yet one subject which could with difficulty be adapted was that of religion. If there were absolute truths, then they had to be taught as such. For Guizot, as for most men of his time, one of the fundamental purposes of education was to teach religious and moral truths. This could be said to be the third of the main preoccupations of the *Annales de l'Éducation*.

[1] See the article 'Des Moyens d'Émulation' in *Méditations*, op. cit., pp. 281 ff.

Both Guizot and Pauline de Meulan found themselves in disagreement with certain of their contemporaries on this subject. Guizot contradicted Betty Gleim who had put forward the view that man was innately corrupted, and Pauline de Meulan was highly critical of Hannah More, whose 'Strictures on Modern Education' had described children not as innocents with certain weaknesses, but as examples of corrupted nature.[1] Guizot did not agree with those who were excessively preoccupied with the mysterious origins of things, or who were too anxious to distinguish between man's nature and his tendencies or leanings. He believed rather that these tendencies could form their nature. If a man had some leaning towards good, then education could encourage this, so that some day the good part would overcome all the others. Hence it was impossible to talk of man as a corrupt being. 'I have known men who did not deserve my esteem,' he wrote, 'but I have never seen anyone of whom it could not be said that with care, patience and perseverance he could be made a good man.' Moral education was like all other education: it was necessary to find out what was good and then fortify it.

There were three general forms which moral education, according to the *Annales*, should take. The first was religious education. Pauline de Meulan disagreed with those who, like Elisabeth Hamilton, thought that religious education should not begin too soon. Like Pestalozzi she thought that religious sentiment and religious instruction should be linked, and she disagreed with his critics who claimed that in the Pestalozzi schools the children were given the Bible too soon and dogma too late.[2] Guizot and Pauline de Meulan thought that religious instruction should begin with a study of the Bible, in a special edition.[3] Secondly, moral discussions should be shown as direct issues in life. A simple story would allow a child to grasp a moral issue, and in the *Annales* Guizot himself wrote the sort of story or 'conte' which was à la mode at this time. He wrote about a number of people travelling by coach; amongst them is a woman who tells her companions that she has hidden all her fortune in her shoe. Shortly afterwards the coach is held up by bandits. They demand money, but the money that comes to them from the purses of their victims does not satisfy them, and they threaten to break open all the luggage unless they are given more. At this point a man amongst the travellers tells the bandits about the money hidden in the woman's shoe. With this money they are satisfied and they allow the travellers to proceed without further interference. The woman concerned is naturally broken-hearted at her loss and overcome by the wickedness

[1] *Annales de l'Éducation*, vol. iv, pp. 204 ff., vol. ii, p. 140.
[2] Ibid., vol. i, pp. 292 ff., vol. v, pp. 142 ff.
[3] Ibid., vol. iv, p. 242.

of the man who had revealed her secret. When the travellers spend the night in a town she is unable to sleep or rest. The next morning, however, she receives a letter from the man who had betrayed her. He explains that he had just returned from America with a fortune hidden in his luggage. Had the bandits carried out their threat of breaking open all the boxes and cases, then this fortune would certainly have been lost. He had therefore directed their attention to the woman's hidden money in order to preserve his own, more considerable, hoard. Out of this he was able to pay the woman the money she had lost, and more, so as to compensate her for her temporary unhappiness. The problem was, was the man's action justified? Was his behaviour morally correct? In the story as Guizot wrote it the children discuss these questions. From the story and from the discussion of this and similar predicaments certain moral precepts were stressed as part of everyday life. One is unable to foresee the result of one's actions, one can never foresee the workings of Providence, wrong arises when one acts out of sentiment rather than out of principle, one should never deliberately cause suffering, and so on.[1] The third form which moral education took was one whereby man was belittled. This was done in order that vanity and egoism could be attacked. Guizot wanted to stress the unimportance of individual man, when there were, he said, a thousand million men on earth. What was the importance of one man's affairs when there were a multitude of other people who did not even know of his existence? In the street thousands of individuals could be seen, they knew nothing and they could not care about particular ambitions. If, thought Guizot, a child could indirectly, in this way, understand man's insignificance, then his vanity might become more hesitant and his moral education be furthered.[2]

This moral education is obviously restrained, for all that it is important. Guizot does not specify at what age the children have these discussions. Presumably they are old enough to have passed the stage at which reflection is considered dangerous. There is little or nothing said about catechism, Church, priest or pastor; considerations of dogma are entirely absent; the *Annales* have no apparent contact with those who thought of education as a preparation for eternity. Like most educational reformers, Guizot and Pauline de Meulan were concentrating on what was rational, and it is in this way that educational reformers come into conflict with the Church. The story is told that once somebody criticized Pestalozzi by claiming that he spent too much teaching-time on mathematics. Pestalozzi

[1] *Annales de l'Éducation*, vol. iv, pp. 306 ff. Questions de morale proposées par un père à ses enfants.
[2] 'Des Moyens d'Émulation' in *Méditations*, op. cit., pp. 311 ff.

replied that he would never tell his pupils anything which he could not prove. The religious implications of this attitude would obviously appear unsatisfactory to many. Whilst the Guizots were never so downright as this, and Pauline de Meulan did find the Pestalozzian system too rigid, yet they did think of education as a rational process. The logic of children, according to Guizot, was more rigorous than was generally thought. One should never teach anything which had later to be 'untaught'.[1]

The *Annales* were not concerned with beliefs but with behaviour. Here the rôle of education seemed to vary. Sometimes Guizot described it as elevated, aiming at the perfection of human nature; sometimes more modestly, it is to teach man to look after himself when others have ceased looking after him.[2] But nowhere is education described as an all-powerful force capable of transforming man. With the Scottish philosophers, whom Royer-Collard had just started to popularize, Guizot never accepted the 'tabula rasa' theory of Locke, that the mind of a new-born infant is a blank to be compared to a sheet of white paper and on which nothing had so far been written. If one accepted this theory, then there were no limits to the ways in which an organized, rational education could develop the mind and form the character. Guizot thought of education as being more limited. It only worked on something which already existed, it was not creative. 'Education does not give us a character,' he wrote, 'all that it can do is to turn in a good direction the character which God has given us.'[3]

The way in which this education could be organized in society is the fourth and final of the headings under which the *Annales de l'Éducation* have been considered. In the very first number Guizot assumes that a national system of education should exist. The problem was how could uniformity be made at that time, when there was a conflict of confused ideas and a bizarre assembling of new ideas and old prejudices? In the last number of the *Annales*, when Guizot took leave of his public, he comments that France has never had a national system. The Ancien Régime had had a number of learned men who formed a race apart, and who had thought of education as something to be exploited for the benefit of knowledge itself, and not as something which had to fit in to the needs of the century or accommodate itself to the tendencies of society. But érudition in itself was disagreeable and useless. When young men left school, if they wanted to be good at something, then they had to forget all

---

[1] *Annales de l'Éducation*, vol. i, p. 105, p. 53.

[2] Ibid., vol. iv, p. 71. 'De l'Éducation qu'on se donne soi-même' in *Méditations*, op. cit., p. 327.

[3] *Méditations* (op. cit.), p. 215.

that they had learned. The classical education they had received had taught them a patriotism which was inapplicable to their times, and it was in this way, according to Guizot, that classical studies had effected the Revolution, rather than by creating revolutionaries who took the name of Brutus or Scevola. After the Ancien Régime, the Revolution did nothing more to create a national system. It simply substituted for the idolatry of old prejudice, a fanaticism for innovation.[1]

It remained therefore a necessary task to combine ideas which although old were still useful, with ideas which although enlightened were still untried. It was necessary to create something both from the ruins of the old institutions and from the germs of the new. It was not possible to leave things to themselves. In a century of doubt and confusion a new impulse had to be given to society, a fixed point had to be found from which it could develop. An educational system was thus a social necessity. This is of great significance, since this desire for some form of 'étatisme' becomes one of the controversies of the nineteenth century. As Matthew Arnold was later to put it, 'Theocracy in France, with Monsieur de Bonald for its organ, may desire to entrust education to a clerical corporation; Modern Society in France, with the first Napoleon as its organ, may desire to entrust it to a lay corporation; but both are agreed not to entrust it to itself.'[2]

Guizot does not say much about the type of organization he would favour. The circumstances were hardly propitious for this type of pronouncement. But his assumption, both in 1811 and 1814, that no adequate system of education yet existed, suggests that he might have been thinking of primary education, in which Napoleon had shown little interest. This seems to be confirmed by his comments upon Bell. He joins with those who reproach Bell with restricting education amongst the poor to reading only, and he approves of the Lancastrian method because it would enable increasing numbers of children to be taught without requiring a great increase in the number of teachers.[3]

The concluding article in the *Annales* points the direction that Guizot was to take. He moved away from pedagogy towards a more administrative view of education. This was partly personal. His career as a tutor had ceased, his career as a lecturer was interrupted. Henceforward he was a politician and an administrator. But as so frequently happens with Guizot, his personal evolution corresponds

---

[1] *Annales de l'Éducation*, vol. i, pp. 6-7; vol. vi, pp. 317 ff. [In some copies of the *Annales* there is a mistake in pagination, what should be p. 312 appearing as p. 412.]

[2] *Matthew Arnold*, op. cit., p. 10.

[3] *Annales de l'Éducation*, vol. iii, pp. 318 ff.

to a great extent to a national evolution. Taine was later to lament the decline that had taken place in French pedagogical science. In 1892 he complained that 'la belle science' which had flourished in eighteenth-century France with Rousseau, Condillac, Valentin Haüy, the Abbé de l'Épée and others, no longer existed in France. It still lived in Germany and Switzerland, but in what Taine called its native country there was no research, no experiment, no theory, and one notices that he adds no 'Revue'. Another writer had earlier said that France produced more books on silkworm-breeding than on the management of schools.[1] There is a great deal of truth in this criticism. Educational reform became more administrative and people dropped the notion of education as an experimental science. Literature on education became rare. M. A. Jullien's book on Pestalozzi, which Pauline de Meulan had found ill-informed and unsatisfactory when published in 1812, was republished by Hachette in 1842 and was virtually the only source of information about the Swiss reformer; both publishers and reading public were out of touch with this branch of knowledge. Yet at the same time one must beware of exaggeration. There were certain lessons of the *Annales* which Guizot at least never forgot; one of them was the importance of the teacher. As Minister, Guizot was always concerned that teachers should be trained as well as being conscious of the responsibility and complexity of their task. He founded an official review devoted to primary instruction, and by circulars, textbooks and inspectors, as well as by certain personalities whom he directly encouraged, he was far from neglecting this subject. Before one dismisses the nineteenth century in France as being pedagogically barren, one should consider all these aspects of the work of Guizot.

With the downfall of Napoleon the movement for educational reform, which had already animated certain of his officials, became more open and optimistic. In 1814 there was a continuity of personnel. Fontanes, the Grand Master of the University since 1808, remained in his post,[2] together with Ambroise Rendu and Guéneau de Mussy,

---

[1] *Taine*, La Reconstruction de la France en 1800. *Revue des Deux Mondes*, June 15th, 1892, p. 767 (Haüy, 1745-1822, was the founder of the Blind Institute in Paris, and the Abbé de l'Épée, 1712-1789, was the inventor of a method for the instruction of deaf-mutes); *Michel Bréal, Quelques mots sur l'instruction publique*, Paris 1872, p. 300.

[2] *Louis-Marachin de Fontanes*, 1757-1821, had achieved some celebrity as a poet and journalist, and he had been exiled by both the Convention and the Directory, before he became one of Napoleon's close advisers. Although he helped to draw up the law which created the University, his nomination as Grand Master was a surprise to many as it was thought that Fourcroy, the chemist, would have this post. It seems likely that Napoleon preferred to nominate a Catholic.

whom he had described as the eyes and the arms without which the machine would not work. Georges Cuvier became a member of the Conseil d'État, and if Royer-Collard and Guizot left their professorial chairs for the Ministry of the Interior, educational matters remained their direct concern. However, it is not the continuity of personnel only which explains the attitude towards education. There were two closely associated movements of thought which became relevant to educational matters. There was a realization of the political importance of education, and there was resentment against the activity of the state in educational affairs.

It was natural that after so many years of revolution Frenchmen should philosophise about the causes of these varied upsets. It was natural too that there was disagreement about these causes. For some, the calamities of the Revolution which they deplored had been brought about by too great a diffusion of knowledge amongst the lower classes. For others it was precisely the contrary. It was through ignorance that people had been led to excesses and had been ready to follow Robespierre or Bonaparte, or other disturbing influences. Had not Adam Smith written of the advantages which the state derived from the education of the 'inferior ranks of the people'? 'The more they are instructed', he wrote, 'the less liable they are to the delusions of enthusiasm and superstition, which amongst ignorant nations frequently occasion the most dreadful disorders. An instructed and intelligent people . . . are always more decent and orderly than an ignorant and stupid one . . . they are more disposed to examine and more capable of seeing through, the interested complaints of faction and sedition; and they are, upon that account, less apt to be misled into any wanton or unnecessary opposition to the measures of government.'[1] A teacher at Clermont-Ferrand, at the annual prize-giving, referred to the moral malady which had been tormenting the nation. This malady was carried in the blood, handed on from father to son. Against such an evil even the Church had often been ineffective. It was the function of education to combat this malady.[2]

Nor did people consider the political necessity of education as a matter of idle speculation. The Imperial lycées were foyers of bonapartism and jacobinism, their education had to be hurriedly seen to, as events of 1814 were to prove.[3] White cockades were hurriedly distributed, religious services were made to include prayers for the King, the uniforms were modified and many of the military

---

[1] *The Wealth of Nations*, Book V, Chapter I, Article 2.

[2] August 27th, 1814. *Archives Nationales*, F17 3119.

[3] See *J. Poirier*, Lycéens Impériaux, 1814-1815, *Revue de Paris*, May 15th, 1921, pp. 380 ff.

traditions changed, a bell, for example, replaced the drum as the signal for the end of a teaching period. But these measures led to violent incidents. The white cockades were given the most insulting treatments that the minds of young boys could devise; at Orleans the bell was broken, at Rennes the attendance in chapel sang 'Domine salvum fac imperatorem', and some lycées such as Versailles had extensive revolts. Urgent measures of 're-education' had to be taken. Pupils in the lycées were isolated, as far as possible, from the outside world; their excursions outside the lycée were stopped, their correspondence read; contact between boarders and day-boys prevented. Discipline and supervision were tightened up, as could be expected. Every effort was made to generate affection for the new régime. The subjects of composition were chosen so as to inculcate enthusiasm for the Bourbons and for their miraculous return. Attendance at mass and observation of religious duties were enforced on all the teaching personnel; morning and evening prayers and regular confession were compulsory for all pupils. The principle was thus established that if the régime of 1814 was to have any stability, the ten thousand pupils of the lycées had to be made loyal.

The political nature of the new régime confirmed that education was a political necessity. Rights and functions in the working of the constitution were conferred on a number of people. They were chosen by virtue of their wealth, and it was suggested that many of them were totally uneducated or illiterate. It seems likely that this was true. The fact that men had been able to amass a large amount of money without being able to read or write was even used as an argument against education. Whilst in 1820 the *Edinburgh Review* asked, 'Can anyone say, in England, that among his acquaintance there is a single proprietor of £600 per annum who cannot read, unless he won it in the lottery or by some other lucky chance?'[1], nevertheless in France such a situation seems to have existed. Whatever this proved about the economic value of education, if the new constitution was to be successful, especially in the provinces, the illiteracy of the parents should not be handed on to their children.

For many, the violence and disorder which occurred in certain of the lycées, many of which reaffirmed their loyalty to Napoleon during the Hundred Days, illuminated the sinister character of the University. The University had established a monopoly of all education in the country. It was exclusively charged with public instruction and education throughout the Empire. From March 17th, 1808, no school and no educational establishment of any kind could be formed out of the University without authorization. No one could open a school or teach publicly without being a member of the

---

[1] *Edinburgh Review*, May 1820, p. 507.

University and without having graduated in one of its Faculties. All schools and establishments were subject to inspection and control by a minister who was closely associated with the University. The Grand-Master of the University was dressed by Napoleon in a violet silk symer, gold lace and ermine. He was one of the most distinguished of the Imperial dignitaries, and for many the University was one of the most detestable of the Imperial institutions. 'It was not enough to fetter the fathers,' wrote Chateaubriand, 'the children too had to be dealt with. . . . They were placed in schools where, to the sound of the drum, they were taught ungodliness, debauchery, scorn for all the domestic virtues and blind obedience to the sovereign. The authority of a father, which was respected by the most atrocious tyrannies of antiquity, was treated by Bonaparte as an abuse and a prejudice.'[1]

The University was attacked by both Catholics and Liberals as an instrument of despotism. 'Is it not astonishing', asked one priest, hypothetically, 'that I can take my son to the temple of Luther or to the synagogue of the Jew? Should I so desire, I can make him hear the preaching of Calvin, the sermon of the Catholic or the Rabbi's Sabbath. But to make him learn Tricot's Latin grammar I am not allowed to choose the man who is worthy of my confidence, were he a Plato or an Aristotle.'[2] The Liberal Dunoyer thought that the government had no right to prevent people from opening schools or to prevent people from sending their children to the school of their choice. Freedom to teach, like other freedoms, was a public right.[3]

Thus there were various reasons why there should be changes in the organization of French education. In this situation Guizot's action was important on at least three occasions. The first was in the Report on the Situation of the Kingdom, presented to the Chamber on July 12th, 1814. As has been shown, it was Guizot who both inspired and wrote this account. It appears that the actual wording of the passage which concerned the University was a revised version of Guizot's draft, but the sentiments expressed were undoubtedly unchanged. 'Public instruction', read Montesquiou, 'has not been able to respond to the efforts of the respectable body which directs it. These efforts have continually been thwarted by a despotism which

[1] *Chateaubriand, De Bonaparte et des Bourbons*, 1st ed., Paris 1814, pp. 16-17. This sentence was modified after the first edition, doubtless on account of Chateaubriand's friendship for Fontanes. On this subject *Louis Grimaud, Histoire de la Liberté d'Enseignement en France*, vol. v, *La Restauration*, Paris (undated), makes an invaluable bibliographical survey.
[2] *Abbé Girod, La Fille Légitime de Buonaparte*, Paris 1814, p. 14, quoted in *Grimaud*, op. cit., p. 24.
[3] *Le Censeur*, vol. vii, pp. 115-183, quoted in *Grimaud*, op. cit., pp. 32-36.

sought to dominate all minds and to possess every existence. National education must return to a more liberal tendency....'[1] This announcement, whilst promising reform, does not attack the University. It followed upon the decree of June 22nd, which had provisionally maintained the University, and upon the invitation to Fontanes to continue in his office. That the University should be maintained at all, and that it should be praised by a Minister, led to a series of pamphlets and writings attacking this institution.[2]

The second occasion on which Guizot intervened in University matters was when the reform was being prepared. Two projects were in process of elaboration during the first Restoration. Ambroise Rendu and Guéneau de Mussy worked within a commission which Fontanes set up in June 1814; Royer-Collard and Guizot were working secretly at the Ministry of the Interior. The first prepared a reform which fully maintained the University in its monopoly of teaching, and which only revised details. The second tried to bring about more fundamental changes.

The suggestions of Royer-Collard and Guizot were sent to the King in the form of a memorandum, written by Guizot. This memorandum made two points. The educational system of the Ancien Régime could not be resuscitated; the Napoleonic system had led to the degradation of the University. Therefore a new system would have to be created. Meanwhile Guizot praised the personnel of the University, which had tried to use its authority to restore academic standards, which had by-passed and diluted many decrees, and which had collected together many of the opponents of the Imperial Régime.[3]

The outcome of this procedure was the ordonnance of February 17th, 1815. The Preamble to this ordonnance (which was also written by Guizot) defined the aim of education as being 'the propagation of sound doctrines, the maintenance of morality, and the formation of men who by their knowledge and by their quality will be useful to society'. The system of a single authority in charge of all education was incompatible with such intentions as it was incompatible with the liberal spirit of the government. Such a system, furthermore, was inefficient. It was bound to overlook details and could better be replaced by some local authority which would be more familiar with the local situation and more concerned with being successful. If

---

[1] *Le Moniteur*, July 13th, 1814. See *Pouthas, Guizot pendant la Restauration*, op. cit., p. 46.

[2] See *Jean Poirier*, L'opinion publique et l'Université pendant la Première Restauration, *Révolution Française*, 1909, pp. 234-270.

[3] Memorandum of January 1st, 1815. *Val-Richer MSS*. See *Pouthas*, op. cit., pp. 62-64.

all appointments were made by one man, then the teaching profession was too dependent upon him, their situation was too unstable, there was too much room for error and favour. Thus the decree which followed was an attempt at decentralization.

The decree abolished the Imperial University and established in its place seventeen provincial universities. Each of these universities was to take its name from the town where it was situated. It was to be governed by a Rector and by a University Council on which the Prefect and the Bishop were *ex-officio* members. Each university was responsible not only for its own faculties but for secondary education. This meant that the University supervised the lycées (which were to be called royal colleges) and the communal colleges, that is secondary schools supported by the commune. This meant too that no one could open a school or boarding school, or become director of such an institution, without having been examined and approved by the relevant University Council. If any private secondary school existed in a town where there was a royal college or a communal college, then its pupils had to attend the lessons at the college. Each University Council employed two inspectors who could visit any secondary school within the region. The teachers to royal and communal colleges were chosen and appointed by the Rector except for the higher grades; for them the University Council was the appointing body.

This system of provincial universities was unified by two central institutions, the Royal Council for Public Instruction, and the École Normale. The Royal Council had a President and eleven members, all of whom were appointed by the King. Two of these eleven had to be clergy, and another two Conseillers d'État; the remainder were to be chosen on nothing more specific than their talents and their services to public instruction. The body regulated the teaching and the discipline in all the universities. It had the right of inspection and it appointed the Deans and Faculties from candidates whose names were put forward by the provincial universities themselves. The Royal Council for Public Instruction controlled the École Normale, which was to fulfil its unifying function by supplying the provincial universities with teachers who had attended a three-year course.

This scheme had many interesting features. For one thing it revived an idea which Napoleon had considered when Fourcroy had suggested that a number of regional universities would stimulate competition and thus raise standards. But what is most noticeable is that the decentralizing clauses of this ordonnance were very unusual at this time. Even before the Revolution, according to Tocqueville, Paris had been the sole preceptor of France, and its power and prestige had grown considerably since 1789. To challenge this intellectual predominance was thus extremely bold. However, as Guizot himself was later to admit, it was too ambitious to try and create as many as seventeen centres of intellectual activity outside Paris. It would have been wiser to have started with four or five.[1]

Another feature of the ordonnance was that as it broke the power of the Imperial University, it brought Royer-Collard and Guizot into conflict with the University leaders, and it is noticeable that the University was defended on practical rather than on doctrinal considerations. Ambroise Rendu simply criticized the authors of the ordonnance of destroying when they were unable to create.[2] Fontanes was dismissed with the Légion d'Honneur as compensation (which Guizot later admitted to have been shabby treatment) and he was significantly replaced by de Bausset, Bishop of Alais. Thus if the control over secondary education was being maintained, an effort was made to attract Catholic opinion. It did not have much success, however, amongst many of the Catholic spokesmen. 'Cursed be the mother and the daughter,' wrote Lamennais to his brother, 'the old and the new Universities.'[3]

The underlying conception of this ordonnance is that the nature of the educational system should coincide with the political system. Royer-Collard and Guizot seek to do away with a University which existed at a time of personal despotism. But equally they resist a system of complete educational freedom, and they maintain a modified control which they doubtless thought of as corresponding to the moderate form of government which they believed in. No one could more clearly demonstrate that education was part of politics. Their ordonnance was strikingly modern in both conception and language. It might have had some important effects had it been put into practice, but within a few days of its publication Louis XVIII was once more a refugee, and Napoleon restored the University according to his law of 1808.

The third occasion in this period of anticipated reform when Guizot intervened to some effect in educational policy was after Waterloo. No attempt had been made, with the second Restoration, to revive the ordonnance of February 17th, and the ordonnance of August 15th, 1815, simply maintained Napoleon's University,

---

[1] *Mémoires*, vol. i, p. 52. The text of the ordonnance is published as Pièce Historique VI in this volume, pp. 416-430. For the secrecy of its preparation, see *Pasquier, Mémoires* (op. cit.), vol. iii, p. 64.

[2] *Ambroise Rendu, Quelques Observations sur l'Ordonnance royale du 17 février 1815 concernant l'Instruction publique*, Paris 1815. For his own project see his *Système de l'Université en France ou Plan d'une éducation nationale essentiellement monarchique*, Paris 1816.

[3] *A. Blaize, Œuvres Inédites de Lamennais*, Paris 1866, p. 201.

although it stated that this was provisional. The only significant changes were the abolition of certain offices, the Grand Master, the Chancellor, the Treasurer, as well as the Council of the University. They were replaced by a simple commission of five with the more modest title of Commission for Public Instruction. The reasons given for maintaining the Napoleonic system were shortage of money (the creation of seventeen provincial universities would have required a considerable expenditure) and the political situation.[1] The ultras, who held the majority in the Chamber (the Chambre Introuvable), were not willing to return to the 1814 policy of compromise. Theirs was a policy at worst of vengeance, at best of purifying France of the remnants of revolutionary infection. The University was therefore attacked more vigorously than before.

A government that is threatened looks everywhere for support. The government of the second Restoration considered that it had a valuable source of support in a centralized and disciplined University. It is said that by maintaining an institution which seemed destined to disappear, they gained the support of some 22,000 primary school teachers as well as the adhesion of many thousands of influential people who either served or supported the University.[2] Furthermore, as the attack on the University was part of a general attack on the institutions of modern France, so the defence of existing institutions became the defence of the University. To maintain the Charter it appeared necessary to maintain the University.

In January 1816 the deputy Murard de Saint Romain proposed a reform of the system of public instruction. This proposal, which he made to the Chamber, wanted to establish religion as the basis of all education. Schools and boarding schools would be placed under the supervision of the hierarchy; the bishops could dismiss any teacher if they thought him unsuitable; they could create religious seminaries as they thought fit. The Commission for Public Instruction was abolished and the Minister for the Interior was made responsible for the universities, it being expressly stated that he would seek to find ways of introducing religious habits into his charge. Murard de Saint Romain was not a well-known deputy; he was from the Ain department, and had doubtless been chosen because this department had neither faculty nor lycée. He was supposed to have been prepared for his speech by the Abbé Liautard and he was supported in the

[1] Preamble to the Ordonnance of August 15th, 1815: '. . . voulant surseoir à toute innovation importante dans le régime de l'instruction publique jusqu'au moment où des circonstances plus heureuses que nous espérons n'être pas éloignées nous permettront d'établir par une loi les bases d'un système définitif. . . .'

[2] A. Basset, Coup d'œil général sur l'Éducation et l'Instruction Publique en France, Paris 1816, p. 21.

Chamber by Bonald, two of the most prominent of the Catholic opponents of the University. This proposal, for all that it was carried no further because of the summer recess, therefore called forth a number of replies. Ambroise Rendu, Taillefer of the Paris Collège Louis-le-Grand, de Sèze, Rector of the Academy of Bordeaux, wrote defending the University. But the most important of these replies was written by Guizot at the direct request of Royer-Collard, who had become the first President of the Commission. He was helped by Cuvier, who supplied him with material. It has been suggested that this *Essai sur l'histoire et l'état actuel de l'Instruction Publique en France* owed as much as four of its six chapters to Cuvier, and that this may well be the reason why Guizot made no mention of it in his *Mémoires*.[1]

This pamphlet was written for a particular reason. Like so many of Guizot's writings, and conservative thought in general, it seeks to justify an existing system. Yet it is not simply 'une thèse de fait' as has been suggested.[2] It is a closely argued piece of writing which is based upon a coherent body of doctrine, and it represents an advance in Guizot's thought. It states two principles which have not before appeared in his work. First, education is put forward as a necessity, something which is necessary for all classes of society. It is noticeably necessary for the lower classes. Doubtless were it possible to condemn a class to irrevocable ignorance, then there would be people who would do so, in order to ensure their own superiority. But such a policy is impossible and is positively dangerous. It is ignorance which makes a population turbulent and fierce, and which permits it to be an instrument at the disposal of factions. Instruction gives the lower classes the means whereby they can extend their activity and better their conditions; in this way instruction enriches the state. Secondly, if education exists for all classes, it can serve one of two functions. Either it is a means of upsetting class barriers or it is a means of maintaining them. Guizot believed that it fulfilled the second of these two. He divided education into different grades, primary, secondary and special. Each grade was appropriate to a particular social class. This meant, in practice, that secondary education should not be given without 'discernment', otherwise young people become discontented and eager to quit 'their obscure and laborious existences'. They would be misled by a deceptive superiority in school work into thinking that they should have a real superiority in society. Thus far from education being a means of social change, education should rather reflect social

---

[1] This suggestion is made by *Poirier* in his article 'L'Université provisoire 1814-1821' in the *Revue d'Histoire Moderne*, January and February 1927, p. 5.
[2] *Grimaud*, op. cit., p. 279.

distinctions and should accept to be limited by the divisions of society. Destutt de Tracy had earlier divided society into two classes, those who worked by labouring and those for whom the work of the mind had a greater share than that of the body. He called the two classes, the working class and the intellectual class. These divisions of society were paralleled by divisions of education into primary and secondary.[1] Such a view of education and society had obvious implications. Education would be a means of checking social development. It was not a continuous progress, since secondary education was not allowed to be a continuation of primary education. In order that this separation should be maintained either primary education would have to be deliberately restrained (and Guizot had joined in the criticism of Bell for supposedly wanting this) or secondary education would have to be made increasingly aristocratic. Victor Cousin later told of a similar situation arising in Holland, where the schools for the poor, which were run by the towns, became much better than the private schools. This was, in Cousin's words, 'a serious derangement in the right order of things, for the children of the middle ranks were worse educated than the children of the poor, an inconsistence which, in the long run, might have led to social disorder. The necessity of averting such a danger was felt and the towns established public intermediate schools.'[2]

Guizot repeated the views which he had earlier expressed concerning the political functions of educational institutions. Their rôle was not limited to instruction, they also had to form men suitable for the state's stability and attached to both the laws and the sovereign. Such a rôle could only be fulfilled when there was concordance of public doctrine, national custom and political institutions. In France, in particular, the influence of the state in education was necessary to prevent children from being divided as their fathers had been. Those opinions which were 'national' should be sorted out, so that they could be concentrated and arranged in such a way that they could be treated as precepts suitable for schools. A uniform education could establish the unity of the nation in much the same way as Jeanbon St. André, an earlier Protestant, had hoped it would establish a uniform standard of morality.

It was evident to every reasonable man, thought Guizot, that Public Instruction was within the domain of the state, all the more when the government had to struggle against prejudices and threaten-

[1] *Destutt de Tracy, Observations sur le système actuel d'instruction publique*, Paris An IX.

[2] *Victor Cousin, On the State of Education in Holland as regards schools for the Working Classes and for the Poor.* Translated with Preliminary Observations by Leonard Horner, 1838, p. 109.

ing theories, as was the case in 1816. Freedom in education was not practicable and could be harmful; the state could not abandon education to independent local authorities or to private individuals as they then existed. For all these various reasons Guizot found the University necessary. What had been wrong with the University had been Napoleon. This had partly been the fault of Napoleon himself, 'that incoherent and gigantic mind where a multitude of bizarre ideas were for ever fermenting; he thought they were sublime inventions and he sought to make them the laws of the world'.[1] This was partly the fault of the situation, since when the interests of an individual are associated with the interests of society, then there is bound to be corruption. It may be that Guizot exaggerated the extent of this corruption when he assumed that the system of scholarships in secondary education existed as a means of buying support. It was not so much that Bonaparte was creating what Guizot called 'an immense adopted family' as that the only way of popularizing the lycées and encouraging parents to entrust their children to this new institution was by offering financial inducements.[2] The Napoleonic University without Napoleon, thought Guizot, would be a corps within the state. It would be independent, homogeneous (thus excluding those who owed allegiance to other bodies, such as the Dominicans) and capable of forming its own members through the École Normale.

It is difficult to agree with Professor Pouthas when he describes this publication as a political advance, but a doctrinal retreat. Royer-Collard asserted doctrine when he said that the University had a monopoly of education as the tribunals had a monopoly of justice. But such a statement is the doctrine of *obiter dicta*, and was based upon exasperation rather than upon analysis. Guizot, on the other hand, founds his assessment of actuality upon doctrine. There were only two systems of education possible, either a system of freedom whereby education is abandoned to independent corporations, municipal authorities and individuals; or a system of control, where the state directs, supervises and provides. Most modern states possessed a mixture of the two, but where the institutions necessary to the system of freedom had ceased to exist, it was impossible to re-create them. 'One cannot re-produce by laws what was not the product of laws.'[3] This is not just a riposte to the Chambre Introuvable. It is the doctrine of conservatism.

[1] *Guizot, Essai sur l'histoire et l'état actuel de l'Instruction Publique*, Paris 1816, pp. 54-55.

[2] *Guizot*, ibid., p. 59. In the Year X, both Fourcroy and Siméon had admitted that the only way of filling the lycées was by being generous with scholarships. See *de Lanzac de Laborie*, L'Instruction Secondaire et Napoléon, *Revue de Paris*, November 15th, 1924, pp. 317-318.

[3] *Guizot*, ibid., p. 127.

In March 1815 the *Société d'Encouragement pour l'Industrie Nationale*, with de Gérando as Secretary-General, held a special meeting to discuss the possibilities of extending education to the poorer classes. It was decided to create a new society which was called the *Société pour l'amélioration de l'enseignement élémentaire*. Its first meeting was held on June 16th, 1815, and lasted over three days, coinciding with Waterloo. Guizot did not attend any of these inaugural meetings as he was then on his mission to Ghent, but by the end of the year his name was listed amongst the members of the new society. One of the aims of this society was to introduce into France the method of mutual instruction, that is to say teaching in large numbers with a single teacher, helped by older pupils or monitors. This system had been developing in England, and in 1815 it was associated with the names of Bell and Lancaster, although French supporters of this system found it easy to suggest that the abbé de la Salle under Louis XIV, or Paulet in his orphanage at Vincennes under Louis XVI, were the real founders of the method. At all events it was in 1814, when a number of Frenchmen visited England, that 'l'enseignement mutuel' as it was called, first began to attract attention in France. Before then, although a number of writers had drawn attention to it, such as Guizot in the *Annales de l'Éducation* or Cuvier in his report on education in Holland, it had been mentioned mainly with reference to the divisions it had engendered in England, when the Church of England adopted the Anglican parson Bell, and the Dissenters the Quaker Lancaster, as their respective champions in a sharp religious controversy. With peace, the Egyptologist Jomard, the economist Say, the philanthropist de Laborde, all visited England for various purposes and returned as protagonists of this method which they had admired in a number of English industrial towns. In 1814 the French ambassador in London, de Lachastre, wrote a long memorandum to Montesquiou on the subject. Guizot, then working with Montesquiou, encouraged this interest.[1]

By 1816 'l'enseignement mutuel' was having a great vogue. Private philanthropists founded schools which were to practise the method, municipal councils voted funds for 'l'école mutuelle', the Minister of the Interior circularised prefects concerning the advantages of this system. It became a fashionable diversion, with ladies of fashion attending classes; in 1818 the Académie Française was asked to give a prize to the best poem on the subject.[2] It is easy to see some of the reasons for its success. It was cheap, and its supporters claimed that

[1] *Maurice Gontard, L'Enseignement Primaire en France de la Révolution à la loi Guizot (1789-1833)*, Annales de l'Université de Lyon, Paris 1959, p. 275.

[2] Victor Hugo, then aged sixteen, entered for this competition. Part of his poem is quoted by *Gontard* (op. cit.), p. 295.

to educate the children of Paris alone by this method would be an economy of over two million francs. It was a means of getting round the shortage of teachers and it opened up the possibility of educating the masses. It spared the teacher the fatigue of incessant teaching, it avoided wasting the children's time, and when well organized it was attractively mechanical and simple. But these were not the only reasons. Victor Cousin, who by the 1830s was an opponent of the system, explained its success by reference to the political and religious circumstances of these years. It was when both the Charter and the University were being attacked, and when the Church in particular was showing its hostility to these modern institutions, that people saw the possibilities of mutual instruction. 'Seeing people thus governed by children, they found a species of self-government which they thought would be a useful preparation for the infusion of the democratic principle; and it is obvious that a Christian education is impossible under such a system, for what monitor, even of twelve years of age, can give instruction in religion or morals? They saw that the religious education amounted to nothing, unless the dry repetition of a catechism . . . can be called by that name; and this they viewed as a triumph over the clergy . . . thus one extreme produces another. . . .'[1]

Cousin undoubtedly exaggerated, and was seeking to decry 'l'enseignement mutuel', which had by the 1830s considerably declined in prestige. But essentially he was right. The quarrel over mutual instruction was an aspect of the political and religious struggle of the Restoration. It was Madame Guizot who said in 1817 that mutual instruction was the introduction of constitutional government into education and mutual instruction was the Charter which assured the child that he would have his say in the law which he obeyed.[2] Some of the supporters of mutual instruction even thought that this principle should be extended to the administration of justice.[3] The opponents of mutual instruction were not mistaken in opposing it. It was an attack upon authority, and it was an attack upon religion in the sense that its method could only deal with relations between man and man, rather than relations between man and God. It did attract many Protestants, freemasons and liberals, and the deputy Cornet d'Incourt understandably cried in1820, 'Show me one enemy of religion and of the monarchy who is not a fanatical partisan of mutual instruction.'[4]

[1] *Victor Cousin, On the State of Education in Holland* (op. cit.), pp. 33-34.
[2] Quoted by *Rousselot*, Une épisode de l'histoire de l'enseignement primaire. Les écoles mutuelles et la Restauration. *Revue Pédagogique*, 1887, vol. ii, p. 360.
[3] *Alexandre de Laborde, Plan d'éducation pour les enfants pauvres*, Paris 1815, chapter xi.
[4] Quoted in *O. Gréard, Éducation et Instruction*, Paris 1887, p. 38.

Guizot supported the method but without the wild enthusiasm which marked some of his contemporaries, such as Jomard or Boulay de la Meurthe. He played a part in establishing a mutual instruction school which owed its existence to the generosity of Benjamin Delessert. In 1816 Guizot was one of a committee of three who supervised the installation of the school in the Rue Coq-Saint-Jean; at this time it was one of six mutual instruction schools in Paris. Guizot's brother Jean-Jacques translated a book by Hamel, who had been sent to England by the Czar in 1813 in order to gather information about Bell and Lancaster.[1] But apart from his official support in 1814 and in the first years of the second Restoration, Guizot did not write or speak on the subject. When he became minister he did not seek to extend this system, since he did not consider it to be generally applicable, and since he did not wish to revive the quarrels with the Church. It would probably be true to say that Guizot had supported mutual instruction for political rather than pedagogical reasons, and as a means of extending education in the absence of government action.

During the 1820s Guizot's interventions in educational matters were rather isolated. The ordonnance of February 27th, 1821, decreed that the basis of education in the 'collèges' should be religious and the necessary supervision was conferred on the bishops. The Protestants were alarmed that no mention was made of their rights and Guizot was chosen by the Consistory of Paris to be their spokesman. The same ordonnance also laid down that certain private secondary schools should be allowed to attain the same rank as the royal and communal colleges whilst retaining their private character. Guizot attacked this as representing a reduction of the state's power to the benefit of a particular political party.[2] He also returned to the subject of childhood education in the review he wrote of Madame Necker de Saussure's first volume, *De l'Éducation Progressive Pendant le Cours de la Vie*.[3] But it was as a lecturer in the University that Guizot was most active at this time.

[1] *Joseph Hamel, L'enseignement mutuel ou l'histoire de l'introduction et de la propagation de cette méthode par les soins de Docteur Bell, de Lancaster, et d'autres*, Paris 1818. Some authorities wrongly attribute the translation to François Guizot, e.g. *Buisson, Dictionnaire de Pédagogie et d'Instruction Primaire*, part i, vol. i, p. 213.

[2] *Guizot, Des Moyens de Gouvernement et d'Opposition dans l'État actuel de la France* (op. cit.), pp. 95 and 96.

[3] *Revue Française*, No. 5, September 1828. Republished in *Méditations et Études Morales*, op. cit., pp. 179 ff. *Adrienne-Albertine Necker de Saussure*, 1766-1841, was the daughter of a distinguished Genevan scientist who married Jacques Necker, the botanist and nephew of the financier. She had been a great admirer of the *Annales de l'Éducation* (see *E. Causse, Madame Necker de Saussere*, Paris 1930, vol. ii, p. 11) and was a friend of the Duchesse de Broglie.

The University of Paris under Napoleon was far from being a centre of learning. It was not even a centre of intellectual activity. It was said of the Emperor that powerful and victorious as he was, there was only one thing in the world that made him uneasy, people who spoke, or failing that, people who thought.[1] The University was not erudition or learning teaching, it was the state authority teaching. Education was professional instruction, the organized distribution of certificates and grades. Those who studied medicine had no general curriculum of science, they were rapidly pushed into the dissecting rooms and hospitals. Those who studied law did not have the opportunity of studying history or the development of societies, they were obliged to study Roman law and the Napoleonic code without having any sense of the centuries which separated them. Napoleon wanted practical lawyers, he did not want critics. Nor did he want the École Normale to produce fine minds or 'littérateurs', he required schoolmasters. Although Fontanes, the Grand Master, tried to modify the system in practice, and was allowed to because of the protection which he owed to Madame Baccioli, Napoleon's sister, the standard of scholarship remained low. Dacier, the secretary of the Institute, reported to Napoleon in 1808 that Greek scholarship was almost extinct in the provinces, and Latin literature was little cultivated.[2] The Rector of the Academy of Nîmes reported in 1811 that a Chair of History was pointless in a Faculty of Arts and urged that it should be abolished.[3] The only exception to the generally low standard was to be found in the Paris Faculty of Science, where there was a number of distinguished names, such as Thénard, Professor of Chemistry; Gay-Lussac, Professor of Physics; Biot, Professor of Astronomy; Poisson, who was a mathematician. By the end of the Empire the Faculty of Letters had delivered 31 licentiates and 17 doctorates; the Faculty of Science had delivered 79 licentiates and 5 doctorates.

The installations of these institutions were lamentably poor. The Faculty of Theology was lodged in an outhouse of what is now the Rue de la Sorbonne; the Law Faculty had its own building, but it was much too small; the École de Médecine had what is now the Institut de Langues Vivantes (in the Rue de l'École de Médecine), and both Arts and Science were lodged in the Collège Duplessis in the Rue Saint Jacques. The École Normale had to put up with the attics of the Lycée Impérial (later Louis-le-Grand).

[1] *Villemain, Souvenirs Contemporains*, Paris 1853, vol. i, p. 145.

[2] *Dacier, Rapport sur les progrès de l'histoire et de la littérature ancienne depuis 1789* . . ., Paris 1810. Re-edited by *Silvestre de Sacy* as *Tableau Historique de l'Érudition Française depuis 1789*, Paris 1862.

[3] *Louis Liard, L'Enseignement Supérieure en France*, Paris 1888-1894, vol. ii, p. 137.

It was hardly to be expected that the teaching personnel of the Imperial University, largely dependent upon examining for its salary and dependent upon the general public to fill the empty benches of their University courses, would form a centre of independent activity. This was a time when the Emperor could threaten to dissolve the Institute itself 'comme un mauvais club'. Chateaubriand was not able to publish what he desired, and Corneille and Racine had to be edited before being performed at the Comédie Française. The University was thus in a poor way at the time of the Restoration.

It was in 1821 that Richelieu was persuaded to do something for the University, and he signed the order handing over the Sorbonne building (then occupied by artists) to Public Instruction. The Faculties of Theology, Science and Letters moved there, but even before this transfer the revival and recovery of the University had started. This revival, in the Faculty of Letters at all events, is associated with the names of Guizot, Victor Cousin and Villemain.

Cousin and Villemain had been lecturing since the beginning of the Restoration. In 1812 Cousin had become an instructor at the École Normale and this work always formed the most important part of his teaching activity. It was there that he formed a nucleus of pupils and disciples who afterwards became influential, and sometimes famous, teachers.[1] It was in December 1815 that he first began to lecture at the Sorbonne, having been made 'suppléant' or deputy to Royer-Collard, whose official duties prevented him from lecturing. Cousin laid great stress on the history of philosophy; he presented philosophy not as an activity for those with leisure and culture, but like law and medicine a subject which required training if it was to be mastered, and like law and medicine, too, a subject which conferred a professional status on those who succeeded in it. Thus it was that little by little Cousin began to make a great impression upon the young men of the time. Villemain had had an outstandingly brilliant career; as a student he had won all the prizes; when he became a Professor at the age of twenty-five (in November 1815) and a member of the Académie five years later, it was difficult to think of comparable success. His lectures on French literature began to draw big audiences. Guizot had been appointed to his Chair in 1812 (at the age of twenty-five), and it was in December 1812 that he had started his first course of lectures on the Barbarians and the decline of Rome. His University career was interrupted by his work in the different ministries, but according to French custom he did not resign his Chair and he was replaced by a 'suppléant' (who for a short time was Villemain).

[1] *R. R. Bolgar*, 'Victor Cousin and Nineteenth Century Education', *Cambridge Journal*, 1948-1949, vol. ii, pp. 357 ff. Cousin (1792-1867) continued to teach at the École Normale until his retirement in 1852.

1. Guizot (about 1837), a painting by Couder or Ary Scheffer.

2. Madame Guizot Mère. By Couder.

Hence when he was dismissed from the Conseil d'État in the reaction that followed on the assassination of the Duc de Berry, he was able to return to his professorial lectures, and in December 1820 he began a course on the History of Representative Government. These lectures (still held in the Collège Duplessis) became highly successful. They were famous enough to attract the attention of a visitor to Paris like Thomas Moore, who went to hear one of these lectures in 1822, and who commented that there were many young men present taking notes. Guizot himself described his audience as being young and much less numerous than it was later to become. He recalled that his lectures were not immediately successful and that he had to overcome both the listeners' prejudices and their lack of knowledge. However, he believed that the audience was gradually converted to an 'equitable' view of history and of his ideas.[1]

The popularity of these lectures was paralleled by the popularity of scientific lectures and demonstrations, given by scientists such as Thénard, Biot and Gay-Lussac,[2] but in the case of Guizot, there were political reasons for the success of his lectures. This was the period when University students, both in Paris and the provinces, began to take a prominent part in political life, and when the University attempted to show its political independence. In June 1819 a deputy Professor in the Faculty of Law, Bavoux, lecturing upon civil and criminal procedure, took the opportunity to refer to the Rights of Man, the Revolution, the émigrés and other delicate subjects, which caused some of his audience to applaud, and some to show their disapproval. Although warned by the Dean of his Faculty that he should refrain from these references, he persisted, and his lecture on June 29th led to actual violence. The Dean suspended Bavoux's lectures, but on July 1st students turned up in force in the expectation of hearing him lecture and there was a riot of quite considerable proportions. The École de Droit was then temporarily shut, but the students supporting Bavoux petitioned the Chamber of Deputies, and many critics of the Commission of Public Instruction saw this as an opportunity to attack it and its president, Royer-Collard. Although some observers regarded all this with cynicism, and one of them commented that soon the Chamber would be receiving a petition from children whose parents were thinking of changing their

[1] *Memoirs, Journal and Correspondence of Thomas Moore*, Edited by Lord John Russell, vol. iii, pp. 337-338. *Mémoires*, vol. i, pp. 314-316. In 1819 Augustin Thierry spoke of eight hundred young men attending the lectures of Cousin. See *Dix Ans d'Études Historiques*, Paris 1883 edition, p. 221.

[2] *Thénard* (1777-1857); *Biot* (1774-1862); *Gay-Lussac* (1778-1850). Charles de Rémusat attended their lectures rather than those of Cousin or Villemain. They were all held in the same building, but he thought of literature and philosophy as a mere 'divertissement'. *Mémoires de Ma Vie* (op. cit.), vol. i, pp. 241-243.

servants,[1] the whole affair caused great excitement. After the death of the Duc de Berry the students closely followed the attempts of the government to change the electoral law. On one occasion, on a procedural issue, the opposition won a division by one vote; this winning vote was attributed to de Chauvelin, who was unwell and who had been carried into the Chamber in a sedan-chair. Chauvelin was treated as a hero and his chair was everywhere escorted by enthusiastic students. These manifestations of enthusiasm brought about further demonstrations, which led to clashes with the troops, and on June 3rd a law student, Lallemand, was killed. This led to widespread disorder which undoubtedly owed its impulse to the student area of the capital.

There were similar movements in Montpellier, Grenoble, Toulouse and Poitiers, and they were to be repeated in the following years. The 'jeunesse des écoles' became a subject of praise or of blame, and the direction of the University became increasingly authoritarian. Royer-Collard resigned as President of the Commission for Public Instruction in August 1819, probably for personal reasons. He was replaced by Georges Cuvier, but on November 1st, 1820, the Commission was abolished and replaced by the University Council, which Villèle's friend and Minister of the Interior, Corbière, presided over. On June 21st, 1822, the office of Grand-Master was revived and the post was given to Frayssinous, Bishop (in partibus) of Hermopolis. On August 26th, 1824, a new ministry was formed for Ecclesiastical Affairs and for Public Instruction. Frayssinous became the first minister. Although Frayssinous was probably not as reactionary as was often thought, his nomination as Minister represented the climax of the movement to control the University and to put in under Catholic influence.[2]

The ordonnance of February 27th, 1821, restored the University to something approaching its position under Napoleon. 'Youth requires a direction which is religious and monarchical,' read the ordonnance, '. . . the teaching corps will take as the basis of its teaching religion, monarchy, legitimacy and the charter.' Napoleon had enumerated 'the Catholic religion, the Napoleonic dynasty and liberal ideas'. The supervision exercised by Corbière and Frayssinous was more effective than that of Fontanes, as events were to show. Shortly after the resignation of Royer-Collard, Tissot of the Collège

[1] The 'mot' is from Fiévée, quoted in *Duvergier de Hauranne, Histoire du Gouvernement Parlementaire*, op. cit., vol. v, p. 183.

[2] *Frayssinous*, 1765-1841, has been studied in a thesis of the University of Grenoble by *Garnier, Frayssinous, Son Rôle dans l'Université sous la Restauration, 1822-1828*, Paris 1925. Frayssinous is one of the many Catholics who were protected by Fontanes during the Empire. He became Inspector of the Academy of Paris in 1809.

de France (one of the constituent bodies of the University, created in 1530) was dismissed because a textbook that he had written praised the Convention for having saved the country. In 1821 Victor Cousin's 'suppléance' was not renewed. Shortly afterwards the Collège de France suggested that Cousin should be appointed to a Chair, but the government ignored this recommendation and appointed a Monsieur de Portets, who was unknown. In 1821, too, the government closed down the Faculty of Law at Grenoble, and the Minister of Justice wrote a memorandum in which he said that disturbances would only cease when all Law Faculties everywhere were disbanded, and all law students studied in their homes. In February 1822 two law students and two medical students were excluded from the University in Paris because they had supposedly taken part in anti-religious disturbances. Protesting law students attacked de Portets, who had let it be known that he approved of their exclusion. The Faculty of Law was closed for six months. In September 1822 the École Normale was closed down and its library confiscated. In October 1822 it was the turn of Guizot. His lectures were suspended and he was replaced by a certain Durosoir. In November 1822 the Faculty of Medicine was closed and only reopened after its best-known and most capable professors had been eliminated. Doubtless Benjamin Constant exaggerated in his protestations of 1827 against the general invasion of the University by priests, but there seem to have been a large number of ecclesiastical appointments. By 1824 seven of the rectors were priests, and in 1827, when de Boisgiraud was candidate for the Chair of Physics at Toulouse he was asked to abjure his Protestantism.

Yet, ironically enough, it was at this time that the University established itself most firmly in the state. Once the idea of capturing the University replaced the idea of abolishing it, then the University was secure. As Guizot pointed out, the creation of a Ministry of Public Instruction officially classified this subject as one of the great public affairs,[1] and when the liberal revival of 1827 replaced Villèle by Martignac the Ministry of Public Instruction was freed from its connection with Ecclesiastical Affairs and the University was freed from the oppression of the last few years. Guizot and Cousin were permitted to lecture again, and in 1828 the University of Paris started on one of its most distinguished phases.

Few lectures can have excited so much enthusiasm and attention as those delivered at this time by Guizot, Cousin and Villemain. Guizot lectured on the History of Civilization, first in Europe and then in France, Cousin renewed his attack on the philosophy of the eighteenth century, and Villemain continued his survey of French

[1] *Mémoires*, vol. iii, pp. 31-32.

literature, being mainly concerned with the eighteenth century. These lectures became public events. The amphitheatres of the Sorbonne were crowded, and the public fought for places as if each lecture were a reception day at the Academy. People queued up in order to applaud the lecturers as they left the building, and some even went so far as to throw laurel leaves. Thureau-Dangin wrote that it was an incomparable audience such as has not existed since, for added to the youth of the individuals present was the youth of the century itself.[1] The lectures were reproduced and were widely discussed both at home and abroad. They established a tradition that a University event was part of the national life, and the excitement which surrounded Jouffroy's inaugural lecture on the Philosophy of Antiquity in 1829, or Michelet's inaugural in 1834, followed on the precedents of 1828.

Sainte-Beuve and others have described the lectures of these 'trois merveilleux talents', 'the regents of the age'.[2] Guizot was thirty-nine, Villemain thirty-eight and Cousin thirty-six. It would seem that Guizot was the most austere and probably the most erudite. His manner was severe and he made no concessions to the size and variety of his audience; but each lecture was meticulously planned and emphatically delivered. He was undoubtedly the most original. Whilst Villemain could claim Fontanes as his master, and Cousin claimed Royer-Collard as his, no one had ever lectured on history in Guizot's manner before. Villemain was perhaps the most eloquent and the most successful; his audiences forgot his unprepossessing appearance as they listened to his graceful and subtle improvizations. Cousin was sometimes the most impressive and brilliant. Royer-Collard said that of the seven days of the week there were three when Cousin was absurd, three when he was mediocre, but one when he was sublime.

One can find no clearer illustration of the way in which the University was part of politics, and politics part of the University, than that these three 'chefs de file' should each, after 1830, have become Minister of Public Instruction.

Revolutions engender enthusiasm and it is at times of enthusiasm that education becomes a popular subject. The revolution of 1830 had particular characteristics which affected education. It was liberal, national and anti-clerical. There were some who considered that it was also a social revolution.

The anti-clerical movement arose largely because of the apparent identification of the Catholic Church with the government of

[1] *Thureau-Dangin, Histoire de la Monarchie de Juillet,* Paris 1884-1892, vol. iii, p. 38.
[2] Sainte-Beuve: Juste and Caroline Olivier, August 27th, 1843, *Correspondance de Sainte-Beuve,* (ed. J. Bonnerot) Paris 1935-1962, vol. v, p. 244.

Charles X and Polignac. For a long time after July 1830 popular disturbances were to be associated with anti-religious demonstrations; the Revolution was thought to have been partly caused by 'the exaggeration of the priests'; and treason to the government of Louis-Philippe was thought to be organized by the priests, and the necessary correspondence went 'from presbytery to presbytery' until it reached the exiled Charles X.[1] In these circumstances it is hardly surprising that all educational institutions which were bound up with the Church suffered. Sometimes there were popular demonstrations against the friars' schools, municipal councils reduced their allowances, or government officials sought to reduce the power and influence of bishops and priests.

Politically speaking, there were some who thought that the Revolution had affirmed the rightful power of the people. Their conclusion was simple, 'If the people are sovereign they must be educated,' wrote Lerminier.[2] Others did not accept this doctrine. But they were all the more fearful of the power of the people, and for them after 1830, like their English counterparts after 1832, fear became a powerful auxiliary to benevolence in pleading the cause of the uneducated poor. They contemplated the vast numbers of manufacturing populations congregated in towns and they thought 'they have learned the secret of their own power without the knowledge of how to use it right'.[3]

This was a time for statistics on educational matters. They showed that France was in a bad position in relation to other countries, and was in a bad position as a nation. It was said in 1828 that about one-third of the population was unable to read or write, and that of five and a half million children between the ages of six and fifteen, four millions did not attend any school.[4] In 1830, out of 294,975 young men reporting for military service, 153,635 could neither read nor write, and 12,801 could only read. In some departments over 80 per cent. of the children were totally uneducated. Another calculation stated that in the United States of America one child out of every four inhabitants was educated, in Prussia it was one out of six, in England one out of eleven, in France one out of twenty.[5]

[1] *Archives Nationales*, F19 5561 and BB18 1319-1320: Letter from the Procureur-Général at Toulouse, September 1830, BB18 1188; letter from Procureur-Général at Rennes, January 31st, 1831, BB18 1319-1320.

[2] *Revue des Deux Mondes*, 1834, vol. i, p. 270.

[3] *Edinburgh Review*, October 1833, vol. 58, pp. 1-2.

[4] Jomard, *Tableaux Sommaires faisant connaître l'état et les besoins de l'Instruction Primaire dans le département de la Seine*, Paris 1828.

[5] These figures, taken from French sources, are quoted in the *Quarterly Journal of Education*, 1831, vol. ii, p. 382, and 1833, vol. v, p. 173. The Prefect of Corrèze, de Bondy, opening a teachers' training college at Tulle, said that Prussia

For those who thought in terms of the wealth and economic situation of the country, the education of the working classes was vital for 'the advancement of industry and of agriculture which . . . are still backward in many ways'.[1] Some of those who helped to make the Revolution of 1830 had long thought that the content of education needed to be corrected. One of them had asked whether it was wise to persist in a form of education which was no longer appropriate to either social needs or social interests, and had suggested that it was time to consider what was useful for the mass of the people.[2]

Thus it could easily be said, after 1830, that there was not a voice raised against the principle of popular education.[3] A promise to create a new law concerning public instruction was one of the first promises to be made in August 1830. But when it came to incorporating this enthusiasm into a law and implementing this promise in a text, considerable difficulty arose. For one thing the controversy of 1814 reappeared with particular bitterness. Many Catholics became partisans of freedom in teaching and opponents of state control and supervision, especially when their schools were suffering from the post-revolutionary anti-clericalism. Many liberals continued their opposition to state interference with private interests and only a few weeks before his death Benjamin Constant, in November 1830, repeated what he had always believed about freedom in educational institutions. The supporters of the state wanted the maintenance of their rights as a precaution against counter-revolution, as a security against seditious ecclesiastics and legitimists. They believed that the necessary impulse for educational progress could only be given by the state, and that only through the government could the material condition of the teachers be improved. Those who were in the administrative service knew only too well the sometimes desperate conditions prevailing, of schoolmasters depending for their livelihood upon what was sometimes called 'le casuel', the odd jobs of the church and the mayoral services.

But this disagreement was not alone in making governmental decision about public instruction difficult. The political instability

---

had for long enjoyed the benefits of popular education and had not suffered from the revolutions which had shaken her neighbours. *Journal Général de l'Instruction Publique, 1832-1833*, vol. i, p. 281. It was pointed out that Prussia, with a population of 13 millions to France with 32 millions, sent more children to school. Ibid., pp. 203-204.

[1] *Jomard*, op. cit., p. 18.

[2] *Ternaux (l'aîné), Discours prononcé à la séance du mardi 23 juin à la Chambre des députés*, Paris 1829.

[3] *Jomard, Rapport fait à la Société pour l'instruction élémentaire*, Paris 1832, p. 1.

made legislation almost impossible. In the first ministry of Louis-Philippe, founded in August 1830, de Broglie was Minister for Public Instruction and for Religious Affairs. With the collaboration of Ambroise Rendu he set about preparing a comprehensive law, but in November 1830 a new government under Laffitte was formed, and both de Broglie and Guizot (who had been Minister of the Interior) went into opposition. Merilhou, who had the reputation of being one of the most advanced members of the Cabinet, took over Public Instruction and announced that a reform was in preparation. But in December he became Minister of Justice in a cabinet reshuffle, and Barthe became the new Minister for Public Instruction. In January 1831 Barthe presented a Bill to the Chamber of Peers; fearing that the Deputies would give the project a rough passage, he preferred to start in what he hoped was the calmer atmosphere of the Upper House. But the Peers were themselves awaiting a settlement of their own future, a decision had yet to be taken whether membership of the Upper House was to be hereditary or not. They did not want to be concerned in some other controversial matter, possibly in a conflict with the Deputies. It was therefore for tactical reasons that a committee of the Peers suggested that legislation of this sort should be started in the elected chamber, and they handed back the doubtful chalice to the Minister. Meanwhile in February, riots in Paris around the Church of Saint-Germain l'Auxerrois and the archbishop's Palace revealed the ineffectiveness of Laffitte's government. After lengthy negotiations on March 13th Casimir Périer formed his ministry, and no more was heard of Barthe's proposed law. The new Minister for Public Instruction was Montalivet. It was really a matter of convenience only that he should have taken this post; he had been Minister of the Interior under Laffitte, but Casimir Périer had decided to take this position himself, on account of the dangerous situation. Périer, like many who had been educated by the Jesuits, had no particular love of Catholicism, and Montalivet, the son of an Imperial minister and a product of the Lycée Napoléon, was not a man of deep religious convictions. But by this time both were concerned at the extent of the anti-clerical movement and of its social implications. Therefore in their educational and religious policy they aimed at ending the struggle with the Church and at establishing clearly what were the divisions between Church and state activity.[1] But the government was slow in producing a law and on October 21st a deputy, Emmanuel Las Cases, who had long been interested in the subject, initiated a Bill in his own name. Three days later Montalivet and Cuvier tabled the government's project. A commission was formed to examine the two texts and it concluded by

[1] *Montalivet, Fragments et Souvenirs*, Paris 1899, vol. i, pp. 369 ff.

recommending substantial changes in Montalivet's proposal. The simplest way out of the difficulty was to let both projects drop, and this was done. On April 1st Casimir Périer was taken ill, and shortly afterwards Montalivet replaced him at the Ministry of the Interior. When a new Minister was appointed to Public Instruction it was Girod de l'Ain, who had been President of the Assembly, but who had been most unsuccessful in this position. A post had to be found for him, and it was not the sort of appointment from which legislative accomplishments could be expected. The whole political situation was uncertain, and it was not until the formation of the Ministry of October 11th, 1832, that any further progress could take place. In this 'ministry of all the talents', so-called because de Broglie, Thiers and Guizot were together, Guizot became Minister for Public Instruction. This appointment was made a condition of de Broglie's accepting a post at all; at the same time neither the King nor Thiers wanted him to have a more influential post. But according to Guizot, it was the most popular of all ministerial departments which he was given, and he was to direct it for the next four years, apparently satisfied with his own power and prestige, and accepting that he was considered to be 'une specialité' for this ministry.[1]

First of all Guizot settled the internal order of his ministry, which at the time of his taking office was still precarious and unsettled, reflecting the way in which this ministry had emerged under Frayssinous. He felt that, as a Protestant, religious affairs should not be within his province, and they were transferred to the Ministry of Justice. This simply repeated what Vatismesnil had done, and what Polignac had undone; more important was to gather to his department various functions which had been dispersed elsewhere, and to arrange them in two main sections. Firstly, the administration of public instruction, all the schools, primary, secondary and superior, which were regarded as forming the University of France. Secondly, the administration of a number of establishments and activities which were connected with learning, such as the Collège de France, the Jardin des Plantes or the École des Chartes. This section also contained the scientific and literary societies which received money from the government, such as the Institute, the Academy of Medicine and the learned societies which existed in the provinces. The Ministry encouraged science and letters by publishing works directly or by helping individuals in their publications, as well as by maintaining public libraries in Paris and elsewhere. Although some schools remained under the control of other ministries, such as the Polytechnique, which was under the War Ministry, or schools for the deaf

[1] *Mémoires*, vol. iii, p. 11; Mémoire sur le Duc Victor de Broglie, *Revue des Deux Mondes*, November 1st, 1871, p. 622.

and dumb, which were under the Ministry of the Interior, and although Guizot himself regretted that his Ministry did not have more positive control of the arts, yet this reorganization was effective and rational. The ministry ceased to be an expedient and became a regular part of the machinery of government.[1]

Having settled this internal organization, Guizot turned to the question of primary education. As has been shown, it was in this subject that there was the greatest confusion and controversy, it was here that the most had been promised and the least done, and it was here too that there was the most urgent need for creative legislation. The preparation of the proposed law was delayed some time by illness, Guizot falling ill the day that the new government faced the Chamber for the first time, in November 1832. For six weeks Guizot was laid up with bronchitis and it was widely rumoured that he might not recover. However, the Bill was tabled on January 2nd, 1833. On January 11th Madame Guizot (née Élisa Dillon) gave birth to a son, but she never recovered her strength, and she died on March 11th. The debate on the proposed law began on April 29th.

Guizot prepared this law in the Royal Council for Public Instruction. Cuvier had died in May 1832, three days before Casimir Périer, but the Council still contained Ambroise Rendu and Guéneau de Mussy, whose experience and knowledge were considerable; it contained two eminent scientists, the mathematician Poisson (whom the anti-clericalism of 1830 had accused of being a Jesuit) and the chemist Thénard, as well as Guizot's former colleagues at the Sorbonne, Villemain and Cousin. The last named had been sent to Germany in May 1831 in order to study the state of primary education there, particularly in Prussia. His report had aroused wide interest. It was natural that many of the discussions in the Council centred around Cousin's report, and Cousin afterwards claimed that he was the author of the law. This was however an exaggeration, as so frequently occurred in Cousin's language. The law of 1833 drew its inspiration from many sources other than Cousin's report, such as the various projects which Rendu and others had worked on and which had never come to anything, such as the laws of 1816 and of 1828, not to mention Guizot's own ideas on the subject, which date back to Stapfer and the *Annales de l'Éducation*.[2]

[1] *Mémoires*, ibid., pp. 34-35.

[2] *Victor Cousin, De l'Instruction Publique dans quelque pays de l'Allemagne particulièrement en Prusse*, Paris 1833. English translation by *Mrs. Sarah Austin, Report on the State of Public Instruction in Prussia*, London 1834. For Cousin's claim to be the author of the law, see *Barthélémy de Saint-Hilaire, Monsieur Victor Cousin, Sa Vie et Sa Correspondance*, Paris 1895, vol. i, pp. 378 ff., vol. iii, p. 228.

Guizot denied that his law sought to impose a system on primary education. He refused to accept any of the 'principles' of primary education which had existed in the past, by which it was made the exclusive domain of the state, or the commune, or the Church, or by which it was absolutely free and organized upon a commercial basis. It was fatal for primary instruction when any one of these principles was allowed to dominate. Guizot's law claimed to be practical and in true eclectic fashion it took what was good from the various past systems and thus called upon the resources of the various elements of society. As Guizot explained it to the Chamber, the law had three main sections. First of all it was necessary to define the nature of primary instruction; secondly to establish the procedure for the creation of schools; thirdly to determine the supervisory authorities.[1]

In defining the scope of instruction, the proposed law made an interesting innovation. Primary education was divided into two classes, elementary and higher. In the first the necessary rudiments of knowledge were taught, reading, writing, arithmetic, the French language, weights and measures, together with religious and moral instruction. In the second a number of additional subjects were taught, drawing, geometry, physical science, natural history and some history and geography. It was laid down that every commune which had a population of over six thousand should have a superior primary school, and it was also stated that the master in charge of such a school was to receive a minimum salary which was exactly double the minimum salary accorded to a teacher in an ordinary (or elementary) primary school.

Guizot believed that there were two dangers in education. On the one hand there was the danger of instruction which was badly understood, badly assimilated, which he later called 'le mauvais petit savoir populaire'[2]; on the other hand there was instruction which was too limited and which did not allow for any development. The danger of inappropriate instruction and the danger of insufficient instruction could combine when parents, realizing the inadequacy of primary education, sent their children to the colleges, where they were given an education which was not only above their heads but which, according to Guizot, also gave them ambitions incompatible with their place in society. Therefore there was need for some form of intermediary education, and for the creation of the superior primary school which could develop according to the local needs and desires of those classes who were between the working class and the rich bourgeoisie.

[1] Chambre des Députés, January 2nd, 1833. *Histoire Parlementaire*, vol. ii, pp. 3-20.
[2] *Mémoires*, vol. iii, pp. 64-65.

This was one of the solutions which Cousin had recommended after having seen the Prussian Bürgerschule. He had recommended it as a means of preventing the richer lower classes from entering the colleges; it was an instrument of social restriction as well as a help to social ascension. The government ought not, he wrote, 'to furnish facilities for everybody to quit the track in which his fathers have trod'.[1] But it was also in line with Guizot's ideas. In 1832 a teacher at the Collège Charlemagne in Paris recalled how Guizot's 1816 pamphlet had warned against an imprudent distribution of secondary education,[2] and when Charles Renouard became reporter of the commission which examined the proposed law in the Deputies, it was remembered that he had once won a literary competition which had been set by Guizot. In January 1823 an opposition paper called *Les Tablettes Universelles*, at the instigation of Guizot, asked for contributions in answer to the following questions. 'Is there not in our system of public instruction a gap between the primary schools and the colleges preoccupied with classical studies? Should not this gap be filled by establishments of a special nature? What would be the advantages of these establishments? What should be the organization and what should be the course of study?' Guizot made his report on this competition in September 1824, to the *Société de la morale chrétienne*, as the *Tablettes Universelles* had ceased to exist. Nine years later he and Renouard were putting their ideas into law.[3]

Moral and religious instruction was included amongst the subjects which were to be taught in primary schools; in the projected law it was this subject which was placed first on the list. In a later article it was stated that the wishes of fathers would be followed in this matter, but it was not clear whether this meant that a child need not attend any form of religious instruction at all, or that a father could only opt between different possibilities, being obliged to choose one. At all events to place religious instruction amongst the subjects to be taught in the primary school was contrary to the early theories of the *Société pour l'enseignement élémentaire*, which had assumed that the greater part of religious instruction was the privilege of the priest or pastor, that is to say that it was to be separate from the school and the schoolmaster. Without this separation mutual instruction was difficult, particularly amongst Catholics. However, Guizot denied that religion was a subject like any other, which could simply have its

[1] *Victor Cousin, Report on the State of Public Instruction in Prussia*, op. cit., pp. 114-121.

[2] See Bouillet in the *Journal Officiel de l'Instruction Publique*, December 27th, 1832, and February 3rd, 1833.

[3] *Les Tablettes Universelles*, January 28th, 1823; *Pouthas, Guizot Pendant la Restauration* (op. cit.), pp. 356-357; *Charles Renouard, Considérations sur les lacunes de l'éducation secondaire en France*, Paris [1824].

hour; he thought of it as being present in all the teaching. Doubtless here the question of supervision and of subject matter are allied, and the makers of the law agreed with Cousin's advice, 'The less we desire our schools to be ecclesiastical, the more ought they to be Christian.'[1]

The second section of the proposed law restored liberty of teaching. It was plainly stated that there were two types of primary education, public and private. It was no longer necessary to have a special authorization in order to open a primary school and the list of prosecutions against teachers who opened schools without the permission of the University authorities came to an end. The only conditions laid down for teachers in private schools were those of age (they had to be over eighteen), capacity (they had to have a certificate appropriate to the kind of primary education they proposed to give), and morality (they had to have certificates attesting their moral character and conduct, from the communal authorities where they had lived for the last three years). Infraction of these conditions would be dealt with by the civil authorities in the usual way. Guizot welcomed the competition of independent private schools. He believed that there could never be enough schools, and in particular he believed in the friars' schools, such as those founded by Jean de Lamennais (the brother of Félicité) in Brittany. He would have been glad to exempt these friars from the obligation to produce a certificate of capacity, but he knew that such an exemption would arouse resentment and that it might well have been defeated in the Chamber.[2]

However, private education was open to many hazards. Private schools were like volunteers to the army. One made use of them but one could not count upon them. Therefore every commune was obliged to have a school, either to itself or shared with one or more neighbouring communes. The proposed law insisted upon a building where a teacher could be lodged, and a minimum annual salary to a teacher of two hundred francs. The cost of this would be met from three sources, the commune, the department and the state, the first two by local taxation, and the third by a subsidy. Having arranged for the provision of schools and teachers, the question then arose whether attendance at school should be compulsory or not, and whether these public schools should be free or not. Guizot decided against both possibilities. Compulsory education was thought to be out of place amongst a people which valued liberty; free education for all was nothing but a chimera. Yet these suggestions were not

[1] *Victor Cousin*, ibid., p. 290.
[2] *Mémoires*, ibid., p. 68. Guizot asked Jean de Lamennais to form one of his friars' schools in the commune of Saint-Ouen-le-Pin, near to the Val-Richer, but this project never came to anything. See also *A. Merlaud, Jean-Marie de Lamennais*, Paris 1960, p. 241.

completely ruled out, since parents were invited to send their children regularly to school, and lists were to be drawn up of those children in the commune who did not attend school. Lists were also to be made of those children whose parents were considered too poor to pay, and those children were to be admitted gratuitously.

It was accepted that for the schools to function successfully, then the teachers should be properly trained. The method proposed was that of the Écoles Normales, or teachers' training college. The term 'école normale' is said to have been first used by Lakanal, although the first teacher's training establishment in the modern sense owed its existence to Franks and Gesner in Germany. When Guizot became minister there were twenty-nine Écoles Normales. He immediately set about encouraging the establishment of more; his order of December 14th, 1832, made them the responsibility both of the state and of the department, and it was thus at a time when many new Écoles Normales were in process of being formed that the projected law made it obligatory for each department to have a training college for primary school teachers. The government was well aware that the value of these Écoles Normales was not confined to pedagogical affairs alone. The teacher who had been through the training college could return to his village where he would exercise a profound influence on the rest of the population, an influence which it was expected to be all the more salutary, since generally the power of the government was expressed only through the tax collectors and the police. The government hoped that in creating this educational system it was reinforcing the régime.[1]

This political preoccupation is to be seen in the third section of the law, which established the authorities which would control and supervise primary education. These authorities were to be three: the state, through the Minister, the University, and the Prefects; the local authorities, usually through the mayor and other notabilities; and the Church, through the local clergy. In each commune there was to be a committee, consisting of the mayor, the priest or pastor, and three municipal councillors. This committee was responsible for the salubrity and discipline of its school, and it was supposed to arrange for the free instruction of those who could not afford to pay. At times of crisis it could temporarily dismiss a teacher, but for more important matters it had to turn to its superior committee, the 'comité d'arrondissement', consisting of the Prefect or Sub-prefect, various officials of the administration of justice and representatives of the Churches, the 'conseil général', and the 'conseil d'arrondissement'. It was this 'comité d'arrondissement' which reported to the minister, which made the appointments in the commune (receiving

[1] Ibid., p. 66.

recommendations from the lower, local committee and having their nominations signed by the minister) and which wielded the main disciplinary power. In each department there were special commissions whose job it was to issue diplomas certifying the qualifications of teachers, and to examine those who applied for such certificates. These commissions were appointed directly by the minister.

This was the bill which was presented to the Chamber by Guizot (who was in fact still unwell) in January; it was discussed by a commission which by their spokesman Renouard, presented their report in March. There then followed procedural difficulties, since a number of members claimed that a bill which had earlier been presented by Eschasseriaux should have priority, whilst the government, worried by other legislative matters, was anxious to avoid discussing Eschasseriaux's project but at the same time wanted to postpone their own bill. In these procedural wrangles it was obvious that the government did not always have much support, and when the debate eventually opened at the end of April, the fate of the bill was not easily foreseeable.

There was a number of important provisions which passed virtually without comment. The obligation on each commune to create a school, the obligation to create more Écoles Normales, the minimum wage for teachers and the possibility that those who were too poor to pay could receive free instruction, were all provisions which implied an increase in local spending. Nevertheless, they were accepted. The nature of primary instruction and the creation of higher primary schools, occasioned little discussion, other than the fear of some members that the increase of schools would lead to social instability, or the suggestion of other members that primary instruction should contain a political education and should emphasize the need for loyalty to the dynasty. The clauses which were most controversial, and over which the government had the greatest difficulty, were those which concerned the authorities. The rôle of the minister was attacked; it was thought wrong that he should sign the nomination of communal teachers, and wrong that he should appoint the commissions which issued certificates. This was thought incompatible with the freedom of teaching. The importance given to the priest in the local committees was also strongly criticized. It was said that the Catholic clergy, which was thought to be hostile to the régime established in 1830, and which in any case represented a power which was hostile to Gallican principles and to liberty, was given too much power over both schools and schoolmasters.

The government was highly embarrassed by the strength of the opposition on these two matters; it was also divided, since Barthe, who was then Minister of the Interior, was known to oppose the presence *de jure* of the priest on the local committee. Without going into the details of the debates in both Chambers,[1] it should be noted that whereas the government was able to salvage most of its project, it was forced to compromise over the rôle of the clergy. The compromise consisted of separating the local functions. The school was to be supervised by the committee, of which the priest was automatically a member; the municipal council would receive applications for the job of communal teacher, and would make recommendations; the power of temporarily suspending the teacher would belong to the mayor, who could use it if the local committee requested him to do so. Finally, an additional guarantee against the local clergy was sought in a provision which gave the minister power to dissolve a local committee, and to replace it by one in which no one had *de jure* membership.

The law received the royal sanction on June 28th, 1833, and was published in *Le Moniteur* on July 2nd. It has always been known as 'la loi Guizot', and although it has been suggested that it is wrong to speak of this law as if it was his exclusive creation, in its attempt to resolve differences and to organize progress, it faithfully represents his political and social philosophy.

Guizot had had a short experience of administering educational matters when he had collaborated with Royer-Collard at the Ministry of the Interior in 1814. Otherwise his activities had been entirely those of writer and teacher. But with the law of 1833 he once again became an administrator, and one of the differences which distinguishes Guizot's law from those which had preceded it was the care with which it was enforced. A whole series of decisions, decrees, circulars and letters shows the minister's determination to examine the conditions of primary education and to supervise the way in which the new regulations were to be enforced and interpreted. He particularly asked that all the letters which indicated defects and omissions in the law should be carefully collected and classified.[2] Consequently Guizot was one of the best informed of ministers, and he created a tradition whereby the Minister of Public Instruction concerned himself with the slightest detail of the smallest school. One way in which he found out about the schools, the masters and

[1] For a summary of the debates see *Gontard*, op. cit., pp. 505-529.
[2] See Guizot's note on a letter from the Rector of the Academy of Aix, April 4th, 1835. *Archives Nationales*, F[17] 9109. A collection of ministerial communications is to be found in *O. Gréard, La Législation de l'Instruction Primaire*, Paris 1874, vols. i and ii. Many of the decrees and circulars were published in the *Bulletin Universitaire* and the *Journal Général de l'Instruction Primaire*.

the pupils was when, in 1833, he sent some 490 improvised inspectors to visit every commune and to report on what they had seen. A summary of their reports was made by one of them, Paul Lorain, and published in 1837.[1] This forms a valuable guide to the new material with which Guizot was working.

When one considers how the local authorities entrusted with the working of the law responded to their mission, then one is struck with the wisdom of a writer calling himself 'Le Régent Picard'. Writing in the review *Journal Officiel de l'Instruction Publique* in 1833, he said, 'Messieurs de Paris, you do not know the countryside.'[2] It was a long way from Paris to the small towns and villages. Only in Paris apparently did people believe that to build a school was to destroy a prison; in the provinces many thought that to build a school was to create an unnecessary burden. Only in Paris could a Victor Hugo envisage society as a ladder, with the Chamber of Deputies at the top, and with the primary school as the first rung; in the countryside it was pointed out that the sun shone alike on those who could read and those who could not. The landowners asked where they would find their labourers once all the children of the village could read and write; the notaries wondered how many procurations would be entrusted to them once everybody could sign his own name; those who claimed to want only peace and order and the protection of property dreaded the time when popular education would permit everyone to read the newspapers. It is not only the reports assembled by Lorain which show the hostility of the mayors and the local notables to the advancement of education. The archives abound with documents which illustrate how municipal councils refused to bring the benefits of education to their communes, or at best their slowness in appointing teachers and making the necessary arrangements for

---

[1] *P. Lorain, Tableau de l'Instruction Primaire en France*, Paris 1837. Lorain, 1799-1861, had been Professor of Latin Eloquence at the University of Paris; in 1833 he became editor of the *Journal Général de l'Instruction Primaire*. His *Tableau* has been widely used by all those who have written on French primary schools at this time. See for example *E. Fournière's* chapter on 'L'Organisation et la Défense de l'École Primaire sous Louis-Philippe' in *La Lutte Scolaire en France*, Paris 1912, or *George d'Avenel's* article 'Le Goût de l'Instruction et son Prix depuis Trois Siècles' in the *Revue des Deux Mondes*, August 15th, 1929, pp. 827-859. The *Tableau* was also used by *Eugène Sue* for his novel *Martin l'Enfant Trouvé*.

[2] *Journal Officiel de l'Instruction Publique*, January 17th, 1833, p. 86. This review, edited by Boutmy and later by Paul Dupont, is not to be confused with the *Journal Général* (sometimes called *Manuel Général*) *de l'Instruction Primaire*. already referred to and edited first by Matter, and then by Lorain. The latter was an official review under the supervision of the Minister and the Conseil Royal, as explained by Guizot when this periodical was launched. *Rapport au Roi . . .*, October 19th, 1832, published in *Mémoires*, vol. iii, p. 341.

teaching to start.[1] There are many examples of mayors who tried to turn the situation to their own advantage. At Villeneuve in the south-west, for example, a mayor tried to have his son appointed school-master; this would have been a source of income and it would not have interfered with his normal occupations since the mayor intended to see to it that there would be no pupils. When this plan failed, the mayor refused to have anyone else appointed.[2] It was not uncommon for the post to be regarded as a sinecure which would augment a man's income, especially if he were a peasant farmer. It was not infrequent for mayors to try to use the money which ought to have been spent on education for other, more popular, purposes. They tried to reduce the number of pupils, so as to avoid providing a new schoolroom,[3] or they tried to recover the money spent on the teacher by making him do other work in the commune for which he was not paid anything extra.[4] It was not only the poor and ignorant mayors such as Balzac wrote about in *Les Paysans* who were guilty of such deceptions. The inspector who visited Cognac, in the Haute-Vienne, was told by the municipal council that there was no point in establish-ing a school there since there were no children who would attend it. Yet according to the inspector there were 128 children between the ages of eight and fourteen in this commune. The council which made this surprising statement contained a former minister and deputy, by name Bourdreau (who had been Garde des Sceaux in 1829).[5] Even prosperous towns, such as Amiens or Montauban, often showed great reluctance to spend money on education, either through parsimony or through the force of inertia and routine which hampered all kinds of progress.

Naturally there were both explanations and excuses for this indifference. Amongst those populations where children could find work, to send them to school was to reduce the family income. Even when it was recognized that a family was poor and when the school was therefore free, children had to provide their own pencils, paper, slates and pens.[6] It was unrealistic to expect that these children would attend school. There was a general rule in the countryside that the

---

[1] See for example the Prefect of the Sarthe to the Minister, October 27th, 1833; the Conseiller de Préfecture of the Hautes-Alpes to the Minister, January 3rd, 1834. *Archives Nationales*, F[17] 9109.

[2] The Rector of Toulouse: The Minister, June 22nd, 1837, Ibid.

[3] Mayor of Verberie, Oise: The Minister, September 17th, 1835, Ibid.

[4] The Minister forbade this on November 12th, 1833. Gréard, *Législation* . . ., op. cit., vol. i, pp. 276-277, but there is a lot of evidence which suggests that this abuse continued, e.g. The Minister: Monsieur Charbonne, schoolteacher in the Marne, January 11th, 1834, *Archives Nationales*, Ibid.

[5] *Lorain* (op. cit.), p. 181.

[6] *Gréard, Législation*, op. cit., vol. i, pp. 336-337.

school would only function during the winter months, 'from All Saints Day to Easter' was the common phrase, since at other times everyone was required to work on the land. Geographical conditions often determined the level of instruction. The Rector of Aix wrote that in the rural communes of Provence there were less children attending school because agricultural work was continuous. He explained that 'often, a father who is determined to see to it that his children should receive an elementary education, fails to persist in his good intentions once it is time to gather the mulberry leaves, the almonds, the figs or the olives, once it is time for gleaning or for the wine harvest or for any other kind of harvest, since he is reminded that he needs his children for these various tasks. In Upper Provence, it is not the same. There, the cold season is long, the summers are short, and there is little cultivation. For this reason, one finds that ability to read and write is more widespread as one goes up towards the Hautes-Alpes. At Barcelonnette all the children can read, because for four or five months in the year every stable is used as a warming room and as a schoolroom.'[1] In addition to these questions of geography, there were often difficulties in finding the school buildings required by the law. It was expensive to build, and it was not always easy to buy property.

However, whilst one must not overlook these inevitable obstacles, they cannot alter the fact that the greater part of the notables to whom Guizot looked in order to make his law effective failed to live up to ministerial expectations. When the scholastic actions of the mayors has been studied in detail it has been found either ill-intentioned or sterile, and the mayors themselves appear to have been thoroughly inept.[2] The inspector who toured Calvados in 1838 (and in whose report Guizot was particularly interested) wrote: 'You need to attend one of these meetings in a café, besides a jug of cider, if you are ever to understand how far the deepest ignorance and the coarsest egotism is capable of going. How can they ever grant a favour to their schools, these men who think that a teacher is a good-for-nothing whose idleness they nourish with 200 francs a year? Too far removed from instruction to appreciate what they are missing and too satisfied with their present condition, they recall what school was like in their day, and they ask themselves whether

---

[1] Recteur d'Aix: The Minister, April 4th, 1835, *Archives Nationales*, Ibid.

[2] *René Lemoine, La Loi Guizot. Son Application dans le département de la Somme*. (Thèse de l'Université de Lille) Abbeville 1933, p. 55. On the supremacy of these country mayors Lemoine quotes (p. 61) *La Sentinelle Picarde* for May 3rd, 1829, which wrote, 'It is sad to see that there in the rural districts the mayors of the communes have as their deputies or councillors no-one but their own tenants, their woodsmen, their harvesters or even their servants.'

their children have any need to be more educated than they were.'[1]

The 'comité d'arrondissement' was undoubtedly better intentioned than the local committees, but it proved to be ineffective. It was quickly pointed out that when the 'comité d'arrondissement' found itself in conflict with the local committee, then it had no organization to which it could turn, no immediate or practical remedy, but only the laborious process of appealing either directly or via the Prefect, to Paris; furthermore, since certain members of the 'comité d'arrondissement' were preoccupied with their elections to departmental offices, such as the 'conseil général', then they took care to show the greatest tenderness to 'the tiny local passions' of the communes.[2] The hope expressed by Renouard and by Guizot that 'l'esprit départemental' would prove valuable to the educational law was largely unfounded. As Matthew Arnold put it, 'a due supply of zealous and respectable persons, both able and willing to superintend primary schools is wanting in the country districts of France'. Guizot created inspectors and urged them to visit even the most remote districts in the hope of encouraging the local populations to take an interest in their schools. It was hoped that when they saw that 'neither distance, nor hardship of season, nor difficulty of access, prevented the government from bestowing active care on them', then they would appreciate the value of their schools. But whereas in England, according to Arnold, such interest and appreciation existed, in France a minister had to work to try and create it.[3] This was disappointing.

There were further disappointments when the minister came to consider the 'instituteurs', the school-teachers. Guizot had wished them to be extremely important. The letter which he had sent to every schoolmaster of France in July 1833 sought to explain the new law and to stress the importance of the teacher in the new system. In this letter the teacher was described as being one of the authorities of the 'commune', and whilst he was expected to show deference to the mayor, it was clearly stated that he was not expected to humiliate himself before the priest, and that, as equals they should collaborate.[4]

[1] Rapport de l'Inspecteur des écoles de Calvados [no date]. *Archives Nationales*, 42 A.P. 21.

[2] *Journal Officiel de l'Instruction Publique*, January 27th, 1833, p. 97; Recteur de Toulouse: Monsieur le Ministre, June 27th, 1837, *Archives Nationales*, F17 9109.

[3] *Matthew Arnold, The Popular Education of France* (op. cit.), pp. 58-59. Arnold was quoting from Guizot's circular to inspectors of August 13th, 1835, which is published in 'Pièces Historiques' of the *Mémoires*, vol. iii, pp. 352-370.

[4] This letter of July 18th, 1833, is published in the 'Pièces Historiques' of the *Mémoires*, vol. iii, pp. 344-351. The first draft of this letter was written by Rémusat.

However, the reality was very different. All the evidence agrees to show that the teacher was the least respected official of the commune: all the evidence agrees that the principal reason for this was his poverty. The minimum salary of 200 francs a year seems to have been just sufficient to have kept him from starvation. Some would go and beg for bread; others would accept payment in bread (which for a time at least was illegal) and would then try to sell what they did not need at the church door on Sundays; others would trundle a barrow through the streets in search of whatever food or drink would be given them. Almost every teacher sought some additional form of employment which would supplement his meagre income, and the most usual, and traditional, was that he would help the local priest. It was so customary for the schoolmaster to be sexton or custodian that in the north-west the word 'cuistre', which was a corrupted form of 'coustre' meaning 'custodian', had come to mean 'pedant', and this meaning, with strong pejorative implications, had become fairly general in France before 1833. The new law in many cases increased the dependence of the schoolmaster on the church, since the most economical way of finding a schoolroom was often to take over part of the presbytery. The new law for some teachers meant increased poverty, since many of the richer communes which had been paying the schoolmaster over 200 francs a year, decided to treat the legal minimum as if it was a maximum and they economized by reducing the teacher's salary.[1] In the greater part of France the schoolmaster was nothing more than 'le très humble valet' of either the mayor or the priest or both.

The poverty of the schoolmaster was hardly likely to attract people of merit. Lorain's *Tableau* presents a depressing procession of drunkards, cripples, idlers and incompetents who have turned to school-teaching because no other profession is open to them. Their standard of learning and their knowledge of teaching was low. In many cases they hardly knew French, but only the 'patois'. When they did speak French they spoke it as badly as their pupils, and Balzac's story of the teacher correcting the little boy who had talked of 'le chevau' with the words 'On dit cheval, animau!' was very likely taken from direct observation. It was said that in the towns there were many teachers who were supposed to use the Lancastrian or 'mutual' method, who had neither studied it nor seen it practised. In the country districts the books in use were usually ancient and were sometimes quite unsuitable books of theology and devotion. The teacher made no effort to introduce the books recommended by the

---

[1] There is a lot of evidence for this. See for example the memorandum by *Léon de Bussierre*, Notes sur quelques réformes et innovations à introduire dans les Écoles Normales primaires de France, *Archives Nationales*, 42 A.P. 21.

government, possibly because he knew he would be unable to understand them himself. Sometimes a teacher would allow the children to bring any books they could find, and it is not surprising that with this confusion the teaching was ineffective. It is not surprising either that communes frequently complained of the mediocrity of the teachers or that Guizot himself recognised that in a large part of France teaching was in the hands of men whose knowledge was quite inadequate.[1]

The government was hampered in its desire to improve the standard of teaching by the shortage of teachers. It advised certain departments to allow the teachers who had been appointed before 1833 to go on teaching, even if they had no qualifications, since they were not likely to find any others. It abandoned any attempt to exact qualifications from the 'instituteurs ambulants', who went from hamlet to hamlet in the more inaccessible parts of the country. Even in those areas where a commune was both rich and enlightened the shortage was felt; the town of Louviers, for example, in January 1834, advertised for a teacher in several newspapers, with a salary well above the minimum, but they only had one applicant.[2] The government accepted a great many combinations of different jobs in order to ease the material difficulties. Often these must have detracted from the efficiency of the teacher, and there were frequent complaints of the 'instituteur' abandoning his class in order to accompany the priest on some mission, to ring the church bells or to sing in the church. There were complaints too that teachers were often chosen for the quality of their voices and not for their pedagogical ability, since their position as 'chanteur' in the church was thought to be more important than their teaching. Perhaps the strangest combination of different jobs was accepted by Guizot's successor Victor Cousin in 1840, when he allowed the rural postman of Manosque to be at the same time schoolmaster of Saint Martin de Renacas. The postman, 'in this way doubly a man of letters', would visit his class and carry out his teaching, whilst on his morning round.[3]

Yet, although this shortage made their task difficult, the government was very much to blame for the failure of the teachers to live up to expectations. Guizot, in particular, contributed to this in three different ways. Firstly, there was ample evidence to show that the minimum of 200 francs was too low, and that it should have been increased. To have increased the minimum salary would, of course,

[1] The Minister: Président du Comité d'instruction primaire de Méréville, Seine-et-Oise, January 11th, 1834, *Archives Nationales*, F[17] 9109.

[2] *Archives Nationales*, F[17] 9240.

[3] Recteur de l'Academie d'Aix: The Minister, June 20th, 1840. The Minister replied on August 25th. *Archives Nationales*, F[17] 9109.

have necessitated much more direct governmental aid, since even 200 francs a year was more than the total budget of some rural communes. But even without a general increase, it should have been possible to have improved the situation by laying down some ruling whereby the teacher was not dependent on the paying pupils to increase his salary and he should have been certain of getting more from the commune or from departmental funds for the indigent pupils whose schooling was free. Thus the teacher whose class was empty was no worse off than the teacher whose class was filled with non-paying pupils. Yet four years after the law, the minister was still repeating that it would be 'only just' to increase the salary of a teacher who had a large number of non-paying pupils, but that there was no machinery for ensuring that this was done.[1] The law was weak because it avoided compulsion and relied too much on persuading the local notabilities.

Secondly, Guizot was too frightened of instruction and learning going beyond certain fixed limits. Whilst he lamented the ignorance of the teachers, he was always worried in case the schoolmasters should receive a training which took them beyond the village level, when as he saw it, they could become promoters of disquiet. He deliberately tried to restrict the programmes of the Écoles Normales primaires in order to avoid cultivating in the teacher any knowledge, erudition or skill which would make him discontented with his humble station and humble material conditions. Simplicity, modesty and frugality were to be the rules of the teacher's life.[2] Nor did Guizot make it easy for a teacher who was already appointed and who through professional pride or ambition wanted to learn his craft at the École Normale primaire. It was only possible for him to do this if he had not undertaken to teach for a period of ten years, a contract which earned him exemption from military service. Even if the teacher had not given any such undertaking, he was obliged to find a fully qualified teacher to replace him, and in the event of this teacher moving away, then he had to leave the École Normale and return to his school.[3] Under these conditions the opening of the new Écoles Normales were of little value to those already teaching, and both teachers and pupils continued to suffer.

[1] Gréard, Législation (op. cit.), vol. i, pp. 468-469. This circular was signed on June 2nd, 1837, Guizot having ceased to be minister on April 15th. The policy, however, was as much his as it was that of his successors, Salvandy, Villemain and Cousin.
[2] See his circular of October 11th, 1834. Gréard, Législation . . . (op. cit.), vol. ii, pp. 165-166. In spite of official policy the scope of the work done in the Écoles Normales primaires continued to grow, and in 1840, in a report to the Académie des Sciences Morales et Politiques, Théodore Jouffroy claimed that the education given was too elevated.
[3] Gréard, Législation (op. cit.), vol. i, p. 368.

Thirdly, Guizot refused to give any responsibility to the teachers. Nothing is more striking than to see so much power granted to local committees and to the 'comités d'arrondissement', that is to people who knew little or nothing about education, when the one person who might have known something about the subject in question, namely the teacher, was deliberately excluded from these committees. He was excluded on the grounds of administrative logic. The teacher could not become mayor, nor could he become a municipal councillor, nor could he be a priest. The mayor, the municipal council and the priest were by law on the committee which supervised the school and the schoolteacher. The teacher could not therefore be on the committee which supervised himself, he could not be both 'surveillant' and 'surveillé'. That this was logical does not alter the fact that the teacher's status was still further depressed by this kind of restriction.

In all these ways, and at the critical moment when the law was being put into operation, Guizot failed to give the school-teachers of France the support that they might have expected from him, since he had attributed so much importance to their actions. It is not surprising that those periodicals which were concerned with the wretched state of the teachers, such as *L'Écho des Instituteurs*, bitterly and repeatedly attacked Guizot. But it was only one of their two chief complaints against him. The other complaint was that education was once again falling into the hands of the Church, both by the ease with which independent or Church schools could be founded, and by the way in which the teaching in the communal schools was necessarily religious and therefore linked to the priest or pastor, who was in any case one of the supervising authorities. 'We recall with terror', wrote a petitioner, 'those times when one did not know whether the hand which governed France held the sceptre or the cross, whether the seat of established authority was the throne or the altar . . . there are deplorable signs, each day more numerous and more noticeable, which seem to presage an early return to this odious régime.'[1] The satirical 'Régent Picard', when he had learnt the terms of the new law, wrote, 'Rejoice, sextons and vergers, husbands and fiancés of the presbytery's servants, you will live again that brilliant epoch from 1824 to 1828, when in order to find jobs for you the good teachers were eliminated.'[2]

It was suggested that this policy of conciliation towards the Church could be explained politically. Since the 1830 Revolution, the hostility of the Church to the Orleanist dynasty was a constant weakness of the régime. Even if emnity was not openly declared, many

[1] *Archives Nationales*, C 2778.
[2] *Journal Officiel de l'Instruction Publique*, January 17th, 1833, p. 86.

141

people thought that the dynasty would only be secure when the Church rallied to its support. The law of 1833 was supposed to have created an organization whereby the government could put pressure on the Church. A former director of an École Normale Primaire, Arsène Meunier, the founder and editor of *L'Écho des Instituteurs*, was responsible for many rumours about Guizot's policy in this respect. In private, Guizot was supposed to have outlined his policy in these terms. If the Church rallied to the Orleanist monarchy, or if it continued in its sulky isolation, then the 'instituteur' would stay in his existing situation. However, should the Church start to oppose the dynasty, openly and positively, then the instituteur was to be elevated, so that he would counter-balance the influence of the priest. From this reported conversation Meunier and his associates concluded that since the Church had in fact, by the 1840s at least, abandoned the cause of the fallen royal family and had rallied to the support of the Orleans family, then Guizot had lost interest in the 'instituteur', and was in fact ready to depress his position still further.[1] It must be remembered that this interpretation of Guizot's policy comes from people who were, in the main, republican and anti-clerical. Their hostility to the system of government which Guizot represented was only equalled by their hostility to his advisers at the Ministry of Public Instruction, particularly to 'the bigotted Monsieur Rendu'.[2]

It is certain that Guizot did see in the 'instituteurs' a source of moral power which would be at the government's disposal; it has already been shown that he envisaged the Écoles Normales as peopling the countryside with such influences. It is likely too that Guizot would have been prepared to protect the régime against the Church by means of the 'instituteurs' had it been necessary. However, it is most unlikely that Guizot was expecting such a crisis to arise. He did not anticipate any ecclesiastical offensive against the dynasty, as he was convinced that the Church of the Ancien Régime had disappeared and that the existing Church was prepared to co-operate with the new institutions.

It is more appropriate to realize that for Guizot, as for most promoters of primary instruction, religious and moral instruction

[1] *L.-Arsène Meunier, La Lutte du principe clérical et du principe laïque dans l'enseignement*, Paris 1861, pp. 223-224. This book is a collection of articles which had appeared in *L'Écho des Instituteurs* during the 1840s. Meunier claimed to have been told of Guizot's conversation by the Prefect of the Eure. *Gontard, L'enseignement primaire en France* (op. cit.), p. 493, and H. Dubief, Arsène Meunier, instituteur et militant républicain in *Études. Bibliothèque de la Révolution de 1848*, vol. xvi, pp. 38-39, repeat Meunier's allegation as if it were true.

[2] *Meunier*, ibid., p. 242.

142

was a necessary part of all education and it was therefore natural that it should be made compulsory in all communal primary schools. He specifically associated religious instruction and the intervention of the Church with 'the instinct for order, the desire for honesty, the state of moral respect and inner peace which are the sweet guarantees of social tranquility as well as of individual dignity'.[1] Such was the value of this religious instruction that Guizot was never convinced by the protests of those who complained that a knowledge of the catechism was treated by the Church as being more important than a knowledge of writing and ciphering.[2]

Undoubtedly, too, there were practical considerations. If primary education was to be largely in the hands of the local notabilities, then the priest was one of the more desirable. The lower the abilities of mayors and municipal councillors, then the more necessary was it that at least one man of education should attend the committee meetings. It does seem that in certain communes the uncertain enthusiasm of the responsible inhabitants for their school was sustained and encouraged by the priests. Even critics of the 1833 law admitted that the nature of the local committees, and their choice of teachers, would have been worse without the priests.[3] Ecclesiastical representatives were also expected to play an important rôle on the examining bodies, and once again their presence was valuable since many of the departmental notabilities were reluctant to assume such duties, if only because they were frightened of revealing their ignorance.[4]

It would obviously have been unwise to have ignored the Church when the system of primary education was being worked out. It was justly observed that had the priest been excluded from all relations with the official schools, then he would have believed that such education was deliberately directed against the Church and against religion, and it would then have become a matter of duty for

---

[1] Circular of November 12th, 1835. *Gréard*, vol. ii, p. 210. A handbook recommended by the Minister of Public Instruction and destined for primary school teachers stressed the importance of religious teaching in making the teaching of all subjects successful. 'Vainement les maîtres les plus habiles travailleraient-ils avec le secours des meilleures méthodes à développer les intelligences, si la religion ne venait en même temps former les coeurs, calmer les passions et plier les volontés à l'accomplissement des devoirs de toute nature. L'enseignement religieux et l'enseignement humain doivent se prêtre un mutuel secours; dans un bon système d'éducation ils sont inséparables.' *Guide Des Écoles Primaires Par un Recteur d'Académie*, Paris 1836. *Archives Nationales*, AD XIX[H] 36.

[2] See for example L.-P. *Desabes, Critique du projet de loi sur l'Instruction Primaire*, Laon 1833.

[3] *Journal Officiel de l'Instruction Publique*, January 27th, 1833, p. 97.

[4] Circular of August 5th, 1833. *Bulletin Universitaire*, vol. ii, p. 323.

him to have opposed such schools. In the French countryside the priest was powerful. It was impossible to abolish his power arbitrarily. Hence it was advisable to co-operate with him.[1] And if one co-operated with him, then it was possible to hope for great things, even for national unity. When children came from families which professed different religions and opinions, then Guizot hoped that if, from an early age, they were together in the same establishments, then they would develop habits of mutual tolerance and goodwill, which amongst adults, could become habits of justice and harmony.[2] This was a political calculation; but it is very different from the sort of calculation which people, such as Meunier, attributed to Guizot.

However, the harmony which was hoped for did not always exist, and as the years passed there was an increasing number of conflicts between the Church and the school authorities. The makers of the law underestimated the difficulties of putting in the same commune a teacher, often fresh from one of the new, or at all events, recent Écoles Normales, and a priest, formed by one of the traditional seminaries. In spite of ministerial attempts to restrict it, the syllabus of the Écoles Normales continued to grow. Its education was scientific and rational, and even allowing for biassed evidence, it seems likely that religious instruction in the Écoles Normales declined.[3] The priest received an education which stressed matters of belief and questions of ritual; it was otherwise very inadequate as the greater part of the Church remained outside the intellectual movements of the nineteenth century. Priests knew nothing of Cuvier or of geology, and they believed in the six days of creation: they knew no Biblical criticism, and to the indignation of Montalembert they rarely knew any Church history. Many of the books published by priests in the 1830s could just as easily have been published in the 1770s; they went little beyond a conventional attack on Voltaire and Rousseau. Thus there were many communes where the confrontation of priest and 'instituteur' became the conflict of two cultures, all the more intense because in both cases the culture was imperfectly

[1] *Journal Général de l'Instruction Primaire*, vol. i, pp. 41-43.

[2] Circular of July 24th, 1833. *Bulletin Universitaire*, vol. ii, pp. 293 ff.

[3] See for example in *De l'Éducation Morale de la Jeunesse*, Paris 1840, the criticisms of *Théodore-Henri Barrau*, who was one of the winners of the prize essay set by the Académie des Sciences Morales et Politiques in 1840. It was this competition, the subject being 'Quels perfectionnements pourrait recevoir l'institution des écoles normales primaires?', which occasioned a famous report by Jouffroy attacking the Écoles Normales. Barrau (1794-1865), who was a Protestant, directed the collège at Chaumont until 1845, when he became editor of the *Manuel Général de l'Instruction Primaire*, and wrote many widely read books on educational matters.

assimilated. It was a conflict too which was all the more bitter because the 'instituteur' resented the supervisory powers of the priest, and resented even more his economic subservience.

Various movements within the Church tended to make it more difficult for the ecclesiastical authorities to co-operate with the 'instituteur' unless they could control him. The financial situation of many of the priests was extremely bad, and after 1830 there were many attempts to have it improved[1]; it was a time when priests were anxious to show their zeal, to win the respect of their parishioners, and to encourage the generosity of the wealthier landowners. One way was by interfering in the communal school. But even without a great desire to demonstrate devotion, the importance which the Church at this time attached to the teaching of the catechism was such that all priests necessarily had a great deal to do with the children in the commune. Furthermore, in the 1830s the disciplinary control of the bishops became more effective, their diocesan reunions more frequent, and individual priests found it more difficult to follow individual policies of conciliation. In many cases they found themselves equipped with an independent school, or 'école libre', which was invariably a school run directly or indirectly by the Church authorities. One of the effects of the 1833 law was to make it easier to found such schools, and it was often impossible for the priests not to show disfavour to the communal school as they approved of the independent school. In all these ways, relations between 'instituteur' and priest were difficult.

Undoubtedly Guizot had underestimated these difficulties. Perhaps as a Protestant he found it hard to realize all the implications of the question, since in departments with large Protestant populations, it seems that the pastor and the schoolmaster worked together with enthusiasm and success.[2] One should notice too that the École Normale which Guizot had thought of as a model establishment was at Strasbourg, again in a Protestant region.[3] Perhaps Guizot's fear of revolutionary movements, which grew progressively more intense in the 1830s, caused him deliberately to ignore these difficulties since he was turning increasingly to the Church as a conservative influence. As important, however, was his determination, once the 1833 law was passed, not to reopen the controversy over primary education. He was already in difficulties over the relations between Church and State in secondary education.

[1] *Archives Nationales*, F[19] 1948.
[2] Rapport Général de l'Inspecteur primaire du Département du Doubs, May 7th, 1837. *Archives Nationales*, 42 A.P. 21.
[3] *L'Huillier, Eckert, Schneider, Terrisse, Woerz, L'École Normale a Cent Cinquante Ans*, Strasbourg 1960.

Secondary education presented a particular problem in most European countries during the nineteenth century. It had existed long before primary education had become a national preoccupation, but whereas in the eighteenth century it had been largely unchanging, from the time of the Revolution onwards people became uncertain about its true purpose. Some believed that education ought to move away from abstract considerations and concentrate upon everyday reality, centring its activities upon the materials of nature and on science. Others believed that if primary education was spreading to the masses, then secondary education should become more aristocratic, and should exist for the benefit of a restricted élite. Their opinions expressed themselves in terms of disagreement over the content of secondary education, whether it should consist of the study of classical languages and civilizations, or the study of modern languages and scientific subjects. But when the astronomer Arago disputed with the poet Lamartine in the Chamber of Deputies over the importance of languages which the first defined as 'dead' but which the second described as 'immortal', in reality this discussion of the time-table was only an aspect of the greater problem, the attempt to understand the real aim and nature of secondary education.[1] In the same way, the disagreement over who should control the secondary schools was really disagreement about the purpose of these schools.

In France the control of the University over secondary education was nearly complete. Apart from the royal colleges (formerly the lycées) and the communal colleges, which were completely under University supervision, the private institutions existed by grace of the University. There were two private equivalents to the royal colleges (both in Paris, the colleges Saint Barbe and Stanislaus), and a great many private speculations or ecclesiastical foundations. Their directors had to have certain University qualifications, their teachers had to have the approval of the Rector, they had to pay about one-twentieth of their pupils' fees to the University and few of them could prepare their pupils beyond the age of sixteen (they were not allowed to have rhetoric or philosophy classes). Candidates for the 'baccalauréat', with few exceptions, had to produce a certificate stating that they had prepared for the examination in a royal or communal college. The University thus had a virtual control over the channel that led to higher education, to the higher posts of the administration and to the professions. The only exception to this rule was the 'little seminaries', the ecclesiastical schools where boys destined for the

---

[1] On this subject see E. Durkheim, L'Évolution Pédagogique en France, Paris 1938, vol. ii, pp. 152 ff., pp. 190 ff. Clément Falcucci, L'Humanisme dans l'enseignement secondaire en France au dix-neuvième siècle, Paris 1939.

priesthood might receive secondary education (the 'big seminaries' were the schools of theology). By a law of 1814, each bishop was authorized to have one or more of these schools in his diocese, which were free from any form of University control and which were exempt from the University retribution. Subsequent laws had tried to limit the number of pupils in these 'little seminaries' to 20,000, and had tried to impose certain obligations, such as the wearing of priest's robes after the first year. Nevertheless, an enquiry in 1835 revealed that these seminaries were in reality a disguised form of secondary school, receiving both boarders and day-boys, and administering a non-scientific education which was invariably of poor quality.[1]

For some this system of University control was tyrannical and excessive; for others, the 'little seminaries' made it incomplete. If secondary education was thought of as a matter for the individual, or for the family, then they should have the right to select a purely religious education, and the control of the University should be removed. If secondary education existed for the benefit of a small élite, then the University was too democratic. The aristocracy and part of the upper bourgeoisie was traditionally in favour of religious education, particularly that of the Jesuits. If secondary education was a means of bringing about a general social ascension, then the University was too restrictive. In this way both Catholics and liberals claimed the liberty of teaching, which had rather accidentally found its way into the revised Charter of 1830.[2] But if, on the other hand, the purpose of education was to bring about national unity, then in both primary and secondary education alike, the existence of independent private schools, whether they were speculative or confessional, created misunderstandings, hatreds and separatism, and the University was a national institution which needed to be extended.[3]

Thus it can be seen that the problem of secondary education was particularly difficult. Some ministers, such as Cousin and Salvandy, avoided the problem of University authority, and concentrated on time-table adjustments.[4] Guizot, however, preferred to deal with the

[1] *Archives Nationales*, F¹⁹ 3955.

[2] On this subject see *Louis-Grimaud, Histoire de la Liberté D'Enseignement en France*, vol. vi, La Monarchie de Juillet, Paris no date.

[3] One of the proposed laws for primary education, put forward in the name of Eschassériaux, Salverte etc. in 1832, included the teaching of 'political duties'. See *Gréard*, op. cit., vol. i, pp. 223 ff. The opponents of the religious schools always stressed national unity both in primary and secondary education, e.g. Edgar Quinet. See *Buisson*, 'Edgar Quinet et l'Enseignement Primaire' in *Revue Bleue*, February 4th, 1888.

[4] Narcisse-Achille de *Salvandy* (1795-1856), author of a *History of Poland* (1827), became minister in April 1837 for a short time, and returned to the same ministry from 1845 until February 1848. He may have considered his position

147

first aspect of the subject. Whilst he concerned himself with this legislation, he was particularly hampered by the instability of the governments in which he was serving. His projected law was tabled in the Chamber on February 1st, 1836, and the government, led by the Duc de Broglie, resigned four days later. Guizot did not serve in the government of Thiers which succeeded, and his place at the Ministry was taken by Pelet de la Lozère,[1] who simply continued a number of enquiries on this particular matter. Guizot returned to the Ministry on September 6th, 1836, in the government of Molé, but it was not until March 1837 that the debate on the original Bill was able to start; just as the debate on the law concerning primary education had been postponed because of the death of the second Madame Guizot, so this time it was the illness and death of Guizot's elder son which delayed proceedings. By March, there were certain disagreements evident in the government which were already presaging its dissolution. Guizot resigned on April 15th and the law was abandoned. It would therefore be true to say that this prolonged affair did not have Guizot's undivided attention. It may even be true that he grew weary of it, certainly by the end of the debate.

Guizot saw secondary education as being designed to fill the ranks of the administration and of the professions. Socially, it was by secondary education that the middle classes would affirm their victory and their superiority. There could not therefore be any restriction, beyond certain elementary guarantees, to the meeting of the middle classes' demands. In a society where there was freedom of discussion, and of conscience, it appeared to Guizot wrong that there should not also be freedom in educational matters. Therefore he thought that one simple principle should preside over the reform of secondary education, namely abolition of the University monopoly, and that whilst University-controlled schools should continue to exist, he thought that they should do so in competition with the independent and private schools. The only obligations upon a Frenchman, aged twenty-five or over, who wished to open and direct a school would be that he should give proof of his capacity and of his

---

difficult because of his marriage to a Protestant, a Mlle Feray, niece of the industrialist Oberkampf. Cousin had in fact prepared a project, but he makes little mention of this in his own account of 'Huit Mois au Ministère de l'Instruction Publique', *Revue des Deux Mondes*, March 15th, 1841.

[1] *Pelet de la Lozère* (1759-1842) had been associated with Guizot in the Ministry of the Interior under the Restoration. His appointment was because of his position in the 'third party' which was responsible for de Broglie's downfall. In at least some circles it was considered a ridiculous choice. See *Journal de Viennet* (ed. Duc de la Force), Paris 1955, pp. 180-181, where he is called 'un carafon d'eau tiède'.

morality. There was no similar obligation on assistant masters. The University had the right to inspect all schools and to express its opinion concerning the teaching and organization, but it had no special sanctions, and no particular judicial tribunal by which it could effect compliance to its opinions. The projected law made no mention of the 'little seminaries', which presumably were expected to continue unchanged.

During the 1840s, when the same subject was causing particular bitterness, Catholics looked back on the law of 1836 with regret, and claimed that the clergy had unanimously welcomed this law.[1] The same, however, could not be said of the politicians, or of some educationalists. J. P. Gasc was one of this last class; himself a director of a private educational institution, he claimed that the project did not go far enough; the University, according to Gasc, remained in a privileged position, and still continued to exercise control and supervision over private schools and teachers. Auguste Anot, of the collège of Bordeaux, attacked the law for different reasons, and lengthily defended the principle by which the University should control all education.[2] But it was above all the politicians who feared that liberty of teaching would lead to Catholic, and more particularly Jesuit, successes. This danger appeared all the more probable because of the government's silence over the 'little seminaries' and their continued exemption from the ordinary law. The strength of this fear was demonstrated during the debate on the law. On March 16th a deputy, Schauenbourg, successfully proposed an amendment by which anyone wishing to open or to direct a school would be obliged to take an oath of allegiance to the King and declare that he did not belong to any unauthorized association. This anti-Jesuit amendment was strongly backed by a number of deputies, including Vatout, who was sometimes thought of as expressing the views of the King, but it was not supported by any of the political leaders of the Chamber. It was curious that Guizot did not himself speak in opposition to this amendment. He did intervene later, when he opposed an amendment which had been put forward by several members of the University and which sought to bring the 'little seminaries' in line with the law, and this amendment was narrowly defeated. Had he intervened in the debate on Schauenbourg's motion he might have been equally successful. One can only suppose, as he hints in his *Mémoires*, that he was ready to abandon a law which had envenomed the issue which

[1] See for example *Dupanloup, De la Pacification Réligieuse*, Paris 1845, p. 36. Guizot gives his own account of the projected law in *Mémoires*, vol. iii, pp. 87 ff.
[2] *J.-P. Gasc, Examen critique du projet de loi sur l'instruction secondaire . . .,* Paris 1836; *A. Anot, De l'instruction et de l'éducation dans une monarchie constitutionelle*, Bordeaux [1836]. See *Grimaud*, vol. vi, op. cit., pp. 249 ff.

it had been intended to solve. The law was approved by the Chamber of Deputies on March 29th, its majority being twenty-nine, but it never went any further.

This episode demonstrated one thing very clearly. Educational matters had always been part of politics; nevertheless, it had been possible for Guizot to confine himself within the Ministry of Public Instruction as a speciality; after 1837, this was no longer possible. He moved away from the technicalities of education to the larger issues of politics and foreign affairs, and from 1840 to 1848 he became the effective Prime Minister.

England and France experienced many of the same educational problems. In England, as in France, there was the complaint of insufficient education. In 1837 it was claimed that England needed to double the number of existing schools, since only half the population up to the age of fourteen was receiving any education.[1] In England, too, religious differences were liable to be exacerbated by attempts at reform. From the eighteenth century, when Dr. John Brown's scheme of organizing a national educational system according to the principles of the Church of England aroused the wrath of the Nonconformists as expressed by Joseph Priestley, to the 1830s and 1840s, when each denomination tried to make its own position unassailable by becoming increasingly theological, and when Matthew Arnold claimed that he saw more religious intolerance in English schools than in the French, the religious question always hung over English education. Many English educationalists, too, tended to take for granted the vocational devotion of school-teachers, and whilst accepting the fact that their emoluments would never be high, supposed that they would be satisfied with their rank in society. 'Many a curate', remarked one such writer, 'has not the income of a cotton spinner',[2] and the assumption that this sort of comparison was valid, and that teachers did not need to be paid much, was common to many people in both England and France.

However, there are certain significant differences between England and France in this part of their educational history, and it is interesting to see that Guizot helped to form the particularly French method of organizing instruction and education. In England, schools of all sorts grew piece-meal in a number of separate, distinct ways, according to private initiatives and local needs, as well as to general economic movements, such as the development of railways. When reforming movements took place, particularly in secondary education,

---

[1] *Edinburgh Review*, April 1837, vol. 65, p. 251.
[2] *Leonard Horner, Translation with Preliminary Observations of Victor Cousin's On the State of Education in Holland* . . . 1838, p. liii.

3(b). Élisa Dillon.

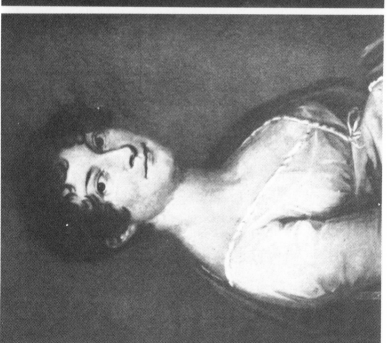

3(a). Pauline De Meulan.

4(a). Guizot at work. From a contemporary engraving in the possession of Trinity College, Cambridge.

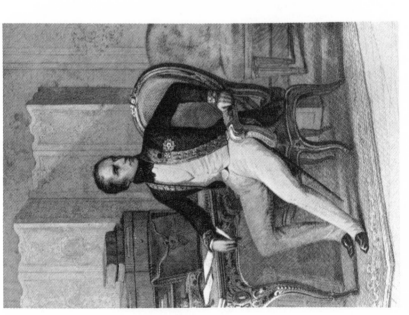

4(b). Guizot as seen by Daumier (1833).

they were individual in character, reforming from within the system rather than changing the system, and often associated with particular headmasters. Sometimes attempted changes were prevented by purely local considerations, as when, in 1805, Leeds Grammar School found itself legally unable to substitute modern subjects for classics, because this had not been the intention of their founder. This variety and independence of English educational establishments was for some a cause for pride, for others a cause for despair, but at all events it was a contrast to the more uniform French system. Guizot, from the days of his writing in the *Annales de l'Éducation*, had believed in the necessity of having a national system, because the destruction of the Revolution had made it necessary to create afresh. Instruction was organized like any other administrative service, and even in secondary education, as has been shown, the removal of the University monopoly did not imply the abandonment of a national system. In this sense the educational leaders of the Third Republic were right to see Guizot as the first of a line of Ministers which for them culminated in Jules Ferry.[1] Guizot was never in the position of his successor under Napoleon III, Hippolyte Fortoul, who would pull out his watch and proudly say to a visitor, 'I know the very thing that they are doing at this moment in all the lycées of France'; but minute legislation, detailed pedagogical advice, consultation with the Ministry on everything to do with schools, all received a new importance from the time of Guizot's period as Minister.

This organized and national system aroused the admiration of people such as the Whig Roebuck, Lord Brougham, or Matthew Arnold. But other observers pointed out how it emphasized another important difference already apparent between England and France. Whenever education is highly organized, it is inevitable that it should be organized in terms of subjects and examinations, that is to say in terms of scholastic achievement. Furthermore, a system of education in a country where there was a coherent system of administration tended to concentrate upon the tangible ends of schooling, the acquisition of a grade whereby the professions and civil and military positions would become accessible. Therefore it was said in England that all French education was merely a species of instruction, whereas the great principle of the British teacher was to pay more attention to the formation of the character of his scholars, rather than to their successes in any of the branches of learning taught. It was proudly claimed of the English public school man that 'many a fine fellow who would fail lamentably in extracting a cube root, will in after-life

[1] *Felix Pécaut*, Deux Ministres Pédagogues. Monsieur Guizot et Monsieur Ferry. *Musée Pédagogique*, fascicule 33, Paris 1887.

face an enemy's square and break it effectually', and a sense of pity was aroused for 'the over-taught pupil of the French Polytechnique' and for 'those pale, bright-eyed lads in the képi and embroidered uniform'.[1]

Guizot as minister probably helped to emphasize the importance of acquiring and imparting knowledge. Although the pedagogical advice that was ministerially inspired always stressed religious and moral instruction, yet its most useful rôle was in giving practical information on teaching methods or simply in providing information which could be passed on. The effect of the conferences of 'instituteurs' within a department seems to have been similar. Furthermore, Guizot thought that part of his duties as Minister was to encourage and organize learning and erudition. It has been shown that he tried to restrict the educational ambitions of the 'instituteurs'. The same reasoning led him to try and stimulate the intellectual activities of the bourgeoisie. He was one of those who believed that in proportion as elementary instruction became general so 'the higher orders of society' should advance their study and their science. He therefore gave an atmosphere of social competition to the acquisition of knowledge, as he gave ministerial encouragement and support to libraries and museums, created and organized the *Société d'Histoire de France* and launched its great series of publications. It was difficult to distinguish between the minister who was alarmed at learning becoming too elevated for its rural, poverty-ridden milieu, and the minister who put himself at the head of all the learned societies of the provinces. The minister who advised teachers not to beat their pupils, who fixed the order of lessons in primary schools, and who laid down that each pupil should occupy a space of eight decimetres square, was the same minister who sent Francisque Michel to England to study historical monuments, who entrusted Charles Weiss with the archives at Besançon, or who helped Arcisse de Caumont's *Bulletin Monumental*.

The pedagogical writings of this time tended to be of a very general nature, directed towards the teachers and the subjects taught rather than towards the pupils. One recalls the principles put forward by Guizot, and Pauline de Meulan in the *Annales de l'Éducation*, that every individual had his particular rule, and that education must

---

[1] See for example the *Manual of the System of Primary Instruction pursued in the Model Schools of the British and Foreign School Society*, 1834, p. 8; *Quarterly Review*, December 1848, pp. 238 ff. (Guizot helped in the writing of this article); October 1857, p. 334; April 1865, p. 405; October 1868, p. 486. Certain French visitors admired the British system, because they claimed that it did not sacrifice the individual as did the French system. See *Eugène Rendu, De l'Instruction Primaire à Londres* . . ., Paris 1853.

be adapted to the pupil. It is interesting to see that those who held similar opinions were to become opponents of Guizot, and of his successors, in educational matters.[1]

Both in England and in France the educational systems tended to intensify class separatism. The lycées and the public schools served the upper bourgeoisie and the aristocracy, and removed them still further from the poor. But it is in France that this attitude was systematized, rather than in England. Guizot created an 'ensemble' of primary education consisting of the primary school, the higher primary school and the École Normale Primaire; he endeavoured to create an 'ensemble' of secondary schools; but he never considered any system where the two would be joined. In this respect the primary school system was closed; it was not intended to be a means of social promotion. Secondary education was a bulwark for the exclusive use of the bourgeoisie, and the system established by Guizot was an attempt to impose a fixed pattern on society. The educational system reflected and reinforced the dualism of bourgeoisie and poor, it did not try to change it. An English review commented that it was easier for a poor but able English boy to get into some of the public schools (if the religious test did not exclude him), or for a Prussian boy to win a grant, than it was for a French boy to break out from a constrictive system.[2] It is noticeable too that Guizot did very little for the education of girls, which could have brought about considerable social change.

One should not think that this is simply a conservative policy applied to educational matters. Guizot found in his ministerial dossiers much which confirmed his political ideas. If the notables of the commune were so unenlightened in their approach to their local school, should they be given the vote, and entrusted with the choice of a deputy? If the administration of the schools aroused so many local rivalries and routine hatreds, was it advisable to place national issues in such a milieu? There were communes who claimed that they did not need a school, as they did not need a post office or any postal services. But as time went on they came to realize the value of the latter; still later, they came to appreciate the necessity of the school. The administrator had to wait on progress as well as to impel it forward. The history of French education shows the longevity of many issues. All the Republics have failed to solve the religious question as it affects schools, and they can hardly be said to have filled the gap between primary and secondary education or found the ideal syllabus. The difficulties of the 'instituteur' in a hostile community, the problem of the single class in the village school, the

[1] For example *J.-P. Gasc, Des méthodes d'enseignement* . . ., Paris 1830.
[2] *Quarterly Journal of Education,* vol. viii, p. 27.

problem of the 'normalien' adjusting himself to rural life, though less frequently evoked these days, have still not disappeared.

The slowness of French development represents yet another contrast between England and France. Yet for many Englishmen the biggest contrast between England and France in the 1830s was that a distinguished scholar and prominent politician could in France occupy a ministerial post for the purpose of promoting Public Instruction. That he could, by legislation, increase the number of communal primary schools by one-third in fourteen years, and that his legislation could give the impulse which led to the creation of a still greater number of private schools, seemed a highly enviable state of affairs. It was impressive, too, that when he addressed the students of the great École Normale in Paris, he could not only tell them that one day they would teach what they had been learning, but he could say that they would be teaching in the name of the French state. It seemed to be particularly fitting that one whose lectures, with their carefully constructed arguments and sense of synthesis, were memorable in the history of the University, should himself help to shape the educational future of his country.

Englishmen, impressed by this phase of Guizot's career, wondered for how long they would have to wait before such a post would be created in England and entrusted to someone of similar distinction.

4

THE SOULT-GUIZOT GOVERNMENT

Le gouvernement représentatif est comme Louis XI: il fait
beaucoup de fautes, puis il les répare.
                              GUIZOT TO PROSPER DE BARANTE
On trouve que je dis beaucoup, si on savait tout ce que je
ravale.   GUIZOT TO SAINTE-AULAIRE

Guizot resigned from the Ministry of Public Instruction on
April 15th, 1837, and for nearly three years he was without
any official post. During this time he actively opposed the government presided over by Molé which was in power until May 1839,
and he inactively supported the government presided over by Soult
which followed and which appointed him ambassador in London at
the beginning of 1840. Guizot had hardly arrived in London when
the Soult government was defeated and resigned, but Guizot continued to serve as ambassador when Thiers formed his ministry on
March 1st, and in this way Guizot became one of the principal actors
in the Mehemet Ali crisis. By October 1840, Louis-Philippe had
decided to break with Thiers, since Thiers seemed determined to
maintain his threatening and warlike attitude, even if it provoked a
European conflict. When Thiers read his draft of the speech which
the King was to make to the Chambers in November, the King
produced his own proposals. Thiers offered his resignation, which
was accepted, and the King then called upon Guizot to return to
Paris and to help him form a government. The ministry of October
29th, formed by Guizot behind the façade of Soult's presidency, was
thus the result of a crisis in international relations, the consequence of
different views on the nature of French foreign policy.

But October 1840 was also a crisis in domestic affairs. Whenever
there was a resignation it was difficult to say when the new govern-

ment would be formed, who would lead it, or for how long it would be in office. This type of political crisis was not merely recurrent, it seemed to be a natural part of the régime, a permanent feature of French political life. The parliamentary system, for this reason, appeared to be a failure, and this was all the more serious since its weaknesses communicated itself to all types of governmental activity. It could be said, for example, that Thiers would never have adopted such bellicose attitudes had he not been anxious to create support for his government. At all events, the ministry of October 29th did not only have to resolve a diplomatic crisis, it also had to try to arrest the progressive decline of French parliamentary government.

Many people considered that Guizot was not the right person to carry out these tasks. As ambassador, he had collaborated with Thiers and he was in some way responsible for the diplomatic crisis; as one of the most ubiquitous politicians of the régime, he had served in several administrations, and was one of the 'orchestrators' of the ministerial confusion which had reigned over the last ten years. Nor were the accusations against Guizot the politician of a purely general nature. It was pointed out by contemporaries, and it has been repeated by historians, that one of the greatest distortions of the parliamentary system, and one of the episodes which most debased political morality, was the 'coalition' formed by Guizot, Thiers and Odilon Barrot in 1839, in order to overthrow Molé. In this coalition, it was said, Guizot completely abandoned his principles. In attacking Molé he attacked the King, the policy of conservatism at home and the policy of peace abroad. He associated himself with Odilon Barrot, the leader of the so-called 'dynastic left', who had been in opposition to all the governments since 1831, and who had advocated more adventurous social and diplomatic policies than Guizot had ever been prepared to accept. Guizot had started his oratorical duels with Barrot immediately after the 1830 Revolution, and he had always claimed that Barrot essentially represented a revolutionary party. As he is once supposed to have put it, 'the art of Barrot is to put "culottes" on ideas which are naturally without them'. Guizot was not alone in this opinion. When Royer-Collard was introduced to Barrot, he remarked 'I have known you for fifty years: you used to call yourself Pétion.'[1] Guizot was even less in sympathy with the legitimists, led by Berryer, or with the radicals, led by Garnier-Pagès, who voted with the coalition. It seemed therefore that Guizot was inspired only by the idea of ousting a personal rival and of taking his place. It was the spectacle of the 'coalition' which gave Sainte-Beuve

[1] *Pétion* (1756-1794) was mayor of Paris in 1791 and President of the Convention.

the idea of writing a novel which would be a sequel to *Volupté* and which he wanted to call *Ambition*.

The 'coalition' was very heavily criticized. The *Revue de Paris* could not understand that there could be an agreement between 'the most ardent enemies of the July Monarchy' and those statesmen who had sworn to defend the monarchy; the *Journal des Débats* referred to the coalition as having created 'anarchy'; Royer-Collard denounced the coalition as representing 'the spirit of revolution', which he claimed to recognize 'by the hypocrisy of its words, by the folly of its pride and by its profound immorality'.[1] The excitements and excesses of the coalition both alarmed and disgusted Metternich, and led him to comment sadly, 'And all because Monsieur Thiers and Monsieur Guizot wish at all costs to be ministers.' The fact that the coalition, once it had succeeded in making Molé's government impossible, was unable to form a government itself because of its disagreements, was called by Sainte-Beuve 'the most bitter of jokes against representative government'.[2] It was only natural that Guizot should be particularly singled out for disapproval. Molé always claimed that it was Guizot who was the bitterest and most impatient of the coalition, whilst the *Journal des Débats* claimed to see something pathetic in 'this old athlete of the majority' as they called him, now obliged to wound all the sentiments of this same majority.[3] Amongst Guizot's close friends there were many, Prosper de Barante and Laure de Gasparin to name only two, who disapproved of his attitude. Guizot himself in his *Mémoires* comes near to confessing that the coalition was a mistake. He admits that the personal element, that is his dislike of Molé, was probably greater than he had realised at the time; he admits too that certain of the criticisms levelled against Molé's conduct of foreign affairs were unjustified; looking back, he considered that he had been unwise in taking such a prominent part in it.[4] It is not surprising, therefore, in view of this chorus of disapproval and these admissions of regret, that even a historian as favourable to Guizot as Thureau-Dangin should have regarded the episode of the coalition as singularly unfortunate.[5]

[1] *Revue de Paris*, March 10th, 1839; *Journal des Débats*, February 7th, 1839; *Prosper de Barante, Royer-Collard* (op. cit.), vol. ii, pp. 524-525.

[2] Metternich: Apponyi, January 25th, 1839; Metternich: Sainte-Aulaire, February 9th, 1839. *Mémoires laissés par le Prince de Metternich*, Paris 1883, vol. vi, p. 353, p. 358. Sainte-Beuve: Mme Juste Olivier, April 5th, 1839. *Sainte-Beuve, Correspondance*, op. cit., vol. iii, pp. 84-85.

[3] *Marquis de Noailles, Le Comte Molé 1781-1855. Sa vie, ses mémoires*, Paris 1922-1930, vol. vi, p. 168; *Journal des Débats*, January 10th, 1839.

[4] *Mémoires*, vol. iv, pp. 286-287, p. 292, p. 311.

[5] Thureau-Dangin, *Histoire de la Monarchie de Juillet*, op. cit., vol. iii, chapters v to viii.

Yet the implications of this judgment are extremely wide. Everyone knows that the domestic crisis of the July Monarchy persisted, and that the Revolution of 1848 marks the failure of the Orleanist politicians to find any solution. So sudden was the departure of Louis-Philippe, so successful were the revolutionaries in the absence of any real defence of the monarchy, that some simple explanation had to be found. It was asked how it was that the July Monarchy had gained so little hold on people's affections, how it was that both the men and the institutions were disliked and distrusted? Many, when offering an answer, went back to the coalition of 1839. They claimed that it was then that the real separation was felt between the politicians and the rest of France, when the egoism of individuals was revealed, and when the public was openly encouraged to attack its institutions and its monarchy. This was the expressed opinion of Lamartine, Montalembert, Tocqueville, Proudhon and others. For them, therefore, Guizot, as the most significant creator of the coalition, bears responsibility for the Revolution. To this must be added a further consideration. It was often said, and it has often been repeated by historians, that from 1840 to 1848 Guizot maintained himself in power by corruption, that is to say by the deliberate misuse of the machinery of government, by the 'asphyxiation' of parliamentary rule. It is therefore important to examine these years in Guizot's career, and to consider these allegations which would make him the evil genius of French political life.

The coalition of 1839 cannot be considered in isolation. The wider the period of French history considered, the more frequent are such alliances 'contre-nature'. Coalitions between the extreme left and the extreme right existed at the time of the Restoration, both in electoral and in parliamentary matters; they were also used against Guizot in the 1840s. Agreements amongst individuals and groups who differ widely about many issues, although they may be agreed upon one issue, can be a normal part of parliamentary life. In this sense it was a 'coalition' which precipitated the crisis of 1830, since the 221 who voted the address in July were only agreed on their fear of Charles X; one could say that political history after 1830 is the story of the break-up of the 'coalition' of the 221. Such examples are not confined to France. It was a 'coalition' which voted Sir Robert Peel out of office, as it was a coalition which repealed the Corn Laws.

Nor should one pay too much attention to contemporary con-demnation of the coalition. Most of its critics were constant in their criticism of French politics or politicians. 1839 was not an outright exception. Metternich chose to appear scandalized because he seized any opportunity of attacking a system of government which was both the product of a popular revolution and possessed representative institutions. He may have been particularly concerned because events were otherwise calm, and because he found Molé an easy minister to work with. Royer-Collard was extremely jealous of Guizot, and took every opportunity of attacking him. His dislike was also shared by Molé, who wrote scores of letters with the express aim of turning people against Guizot, accusing him of ambition, egoism and pride. This sort of defence was one of the few weapons at Molé's disposal since the coalition had great superiority over his government in both talent and oratory. He was helped by the King and the whole court, as well as by many of the leading newspapers and reviews which were susceptible to government persuasions. When Guizot came to write about the coalition in his *Mémoires* he was anxious not to awaken old animosities. He had become reconciled with Molé after 1848, he was on quite friendly terms with Thiers and was cultivating this friendship. He wanted the 'Orleanists' to work together, he did not want to fight the battles of 1839 all over again, and therefore he deliberately avoided saying all that he could have said.[1] In so far as he admits errors, he admits to errors of tactics rather than of principle. He was undoubtedly right to consider that he had played too prominent a part in the struggle. It made his relations with the conservative right (the former supporters of Molé, who had in a vote numbered 221 and were called that) difficult; when the coalition could not continue after the election of March 1839, and could not go on to form a government, Guizot found himself in difficulties with some of his own supporters, who found it hard to get over their disappointment. But whilst acknowledging that he would have been wiser to have left it to someone else to have been chief spokesman for the coalition, Guizot never believed that he had betrayed parliamentary government. Quite the contrary, as he saw it, the coalition of 1839 had been successful in one respect, namely, that it had emphasized the importance of the Chamber in the parliamentary system.[2]

The episode of the coalition has to be studied against a background of political uncertainty. In the ten years between July 1830 and October 1840 there were fifteen different governments. One of these ministries lasted for eight days (that headed by Maret, Duc de Bassano, in November 1834). The longest ministry was Molé's second ministry, which lasted from April 15th, 1837, to March 31st, 1839, some 715 days (that is, if one does not accept February 2nd, 1839, as marking the beginning of his third government, as some people do). There were only two other governments, apart from Molé's

[1] His remark to Léonce de Lavergne has already been quoted above, p. 15.
[2] *Mémoires*, vol. iv, pp. 310-311.

second ministry, which lasted for more than a year, the Casimir-Périer ministry, from March 13th, 1831, until his death on May 16th, 1832, and Soult's first ministry of October 11th, 1832, which lasted until his resignation in July 1834. Six of the governments (including Bassano's) lasted less than three months. The effective existence of many governments was preceded or followed by long periods of negotiation, when various personalities and groups either tried to form a government or discussed the possibility of creating one. The ministry of October 11th was only formed after three weeks' discussion, as was Molé's second ministry. The longest crisis of all occurred after Molé's resignation of March 8th, 1839, when, being faced by a political impasse, the king created on March 31st a government which was officially described as temporary, and which was made up of 'technicians'. It was not until May 12th, 1839, that is after six weeks of crisis, that Soult succeeded in forming his second administration. Some years were particularly bad. Both in 1834 and in 1835 there were four different governments; in 1836, 1839 and 1840 there were three different governments. Governments were identified not so much by the names of their leaders, since sometimes they had no leader and since frequently their leader was a figurehead, as by the dates of their formation, the date given being the month and not the year. This was a custom which delighted journalists since it often gave them scope for satirical writing, exploiting the confusion which it created.[1]

Not only were the governments unstable, they invariably functioned badly. Since each administration was the result of negotiation and bargaining, agreement was usually short-lived. It was difficult to find a cabinet which was homogeneous, in spite of their smallness, with only seven or eight posts. It was equally difficult to find a cabinet with an effective leader, and before 1840 only the ministry of April 15th, 1837, had been assembled by its leader Molé. The King had called upon both Molé and Guizot to present lists of possible ministers; having seen the lists he preferred Molé's, and in this way, Molé chose

[1] 'Si le 12 mai, qui a amené le 6 juin, s'était souvenu qu'au 11 août a succédé le 2 novembre; si les doctrines du 13 mars et du 10 octobre ne lui avaient pas fermé les yeux sur une péripétie nécessaire et semblable à celle du 27 octobre succédant au 4 février, il n'aurait pas si promptement rompu avec le 6 septembre et le 22 février.

'En vain le 12 mai cherche un appui dans le 11 octobre, il tombera, comme le 15 avril, sous le 22 février et le 6 septembre, qui se réuniront jusqu'à défaite du 12 mai, après quoi on verra se renouveler le 4 novembre ou le 9 août.' January 1840, *Alphonse Karr, Les Guêpes*, Paris 1859, vol. i, p. 78. Karr has here deliberately confused the dates of administrations, such as February 22nd for Thiers, with the dates of other events, June 6th, 1832, being the date of a riot. The second ministry of Thiers, the ministry of March 1st, was called, on account of its warlike spirit, Mars Premier.

160

his own ministry. It is noticeable that his government, which was in this way unique, was made up of rather insignificant people.[1]

Instability was not confined to the ministries. No Parliament ever lasted its full time (which was reduced from seven to five years in 1830), and the political history of the July Monarchy is studded with elections. There were some 135 elections held in October 1830 to fill vacancies, most of which had been caused by the Revolution, and after these widely spread partial elections, there were general elections in 1831 (the first to be held under the law of April 1831), 1834, 1837 and 1839. These frequent electoral consultations were held without there being any highly organized political parties. There were rather groups and 'reunions' which met at a particular deputy's house. In the divisions and subdivisions of the Chamber it required a practised eye to be able to distinguish between those who were 'ministériels' and those who were 'ministériels quand même', between those members of the so-called 'third party' who were 'formalists', voting according to the wording of the texts, those who wanted to postpone all issues until next year, and those who attacked the government but who then voted in its favour. Observers were only sure about the 'députés flottants', about whose votes they could never be certain since their attitude was determined entirely by their electoral position. The life of these men was one of perpetual anguish, since a tax-collector could not be transferred or a village mayor suspended but what they were held responsible. 'There is not, in all Paris, a door bell more worn-out than theirs, nor a door more besieged by petitioners. Should they succeed in obtaining what is asked of them, then their chances of re-election are strengthened. Should they fail, then by God! what complaints, what storms! Yet they have the best of intentions: to remain deputies, that is all they ask.'[2]

The group which, by common consent, had the most discipline and homogeneity, and according to Prosper Merimée the most loyalty, was the 'doctrinaires'. This was the name given to the group which surrounded de Broglie and Guizot, and which referred back to the 'canapé' of the Restoration. The name was sometimes used as a term of abuse, but essentially in the 1830s as in 1818, it referred to an ideology, to an attempt to find the doctrinal basis for political action. Therefore this 'nuance of political science' was linked together by

[1] The best political history of the July Monarchy remains the seven volumes of *Thureau-Dangin* (op. cit.). For a brief survey of the successive ministries see *Pierre Deslandres, Histoire Constitutionnelle de la France*, Paris 1933, vol. ii, pp. 161-213. For a discussion of the ministerial problems see *Ch. Pouthas*, Les Ministères de Louis-Philippe, *Revue d'Histoire Moderne et Contemporaine*, vol. i, April-June 1954, pp. 102-130; *Raymond Hayem, Le Conseil des Ministres pendant la Monarchie de Juillet*, Paris 1939.

[2] La Chambre de 1837, *Revue des Deux Mondes*, vol. 25, 1837, p. 101.

both principles and ideas.[1] Guizot and de Broglie were the accepted leaders of the party, they could divide their activities conveniently between the Peers and the Deputies, and they were united by close friendship. But this party was never very numerous, probably never going above fifty (in a Chamber of 459). Furthermore, even in this comparatively well-organized group one can see rivalries and differences. This probably explains why, after the death of Casimir Périer, Guizot and Royer-Collard seem to have supported Charles de Rémusat's plan of persuading Talleyrand to become 'Président du Conseil'. He would have been a House of Lords figure-head whose superior eminence would have prevented 'doctrinaire' squabbles and jockeying for positions. Royer-Collard disliked Guizot; both Guizot and his wife looked with coolness upon Rémusat's close association with Casimir Périer, and Rémusat wrote in his *Mémoires* of 'mes amis et moi' and 'cette brigade' as if he had had his own group[2]; some deputies used occasionally to support the 'doctrinaires', such as François and Benjamin Delessert; then someone like Saint-Marc Girardin would normally vote with 'doctrinaires' but would occasionally separate from them, being more anti-Catholic in educational matters than Guizot, for example; people such as the philosopher Jouffroy or the Inspector-General of the University, Dubois, were often classed as 'doctrinaires' but in reality they were individuals who reserved their liberty of action and who always showed a good deal of hesitation; after 1835 de Broglie seems to have been on better terms with Thiers than was Guizot. Thus political commentators tried to distinguish between the different 'nuances' of the 'doctrinaires' by referring to the 'doctrinaires persecuteux, réactionnaires' and the 'doctrinaires sérieux', the 'école pratique' and the 'école philosophique', or 'more simply, the 'doctrinaires' and the 'sous-doctrinaires'. By April 1839 Merimée described the thirty-six doctrinaires as being divided into four main groups.[3]

Thus it is clear that the political system was functioning badly, and that in the course of the 1830s it was getting progressively worse. The instability of governments, the difficulty of forming new administrations, the fragmentation of parties and the confusion of ideas, were the constant symptoms of a chronic illness, they were not the creation of the coalition of 1839. Together they form a condition which requires explaining.

From 1830 onwards it was customary to distinguish between those political parties and personalities who were said to form the 'mouve-

[1] *Charles de Forster, Quinze Ans à Paris*, Paris 1849, vol. ii, p. 30.
[2] *Charles de Rémusat, Mémoires de Ma Vie* (op. cit.), vol. ii, pp. 526-527.
[3] Prosper Merimée: Mme de Montijo, April 6th, 1839, *Correspondance* (op. cit.), vol. ii, pp. 213 ff.

ment', and those who were said to make up the 'résistance'. The
former recognized and accepted the fact of revolution and sought to
realize all its implications and to resist all attempts at 'confiscating'
the revolutionary impulse and ideology. The latter accepted the
Revolution as an accident rendered necessary by events, notably the
folly of Charles X, and wished to limit it to a change of government
rather than to a change of régime. For modern historians this
dichotomy of 'mouvement' and 'résistance' has been expressed in
terms of the conflict between the revolutionary principle, representing
change and progress, and the monarchical principle, representing
conservation, continuity and immobilism, or as an episode in the
struggle of 'les deux Frances', the struggle between the 'left' and the
'right'.[1] Behind the apparent confusion it is suggested that there is a
simple struggle between two principles, which were both part of the
1830 Revolution, but which were nevertheless mutually antipathetic.

Yet this explanation is not wholly unsatisfactory. Historians who
support it give only one example of the 'mouvement' coming to
power, namely the ministry of the banker Jacques Laffitte from
November 2nd, 1830, to March 13th, 1831. Yet it seems strange to
consider this government as one of the 'left' or as representing the
implications of revolution, since its president was a long-standing and
close friend of the King. 'St. Philip and St. James', Louis-Philippe
used to say, alluding to their Christian names, "are not more closely
united in heaven than they are here on earth." It was possibly in
order to prove this that the King rescued Laffitte from an embarrassing financial position. Two of the most important ministries were
occupied by men who were so closely associated with the palace as
to be thought of as royal nominees; they were Foreign Affairs, with
Sébastiani as minister, and the Interior, with Montalivet. Those who
describe Laffitte as representing the 'mouvement' like to contrast him
to his successor Casimir Périer, who is always said to be the apothe-
osis of the 'résistance'. Yet Périer inherited most of his ministers from
his predecessor and fellow-banker (Sébastiani, Montalivet, Soult,
Barthe and d'Argout) as well as projected laws which he adopted. It
is absurd to imagine that Laffitte, with little political ability or ideas,
and with even less energy, was exceptional amongst French
'présidents du conseil'. His speeches were like those of other
politicians; indeed, most of them were written by Thiers. So that all
the governments and all the ministers were of the 'résistance'. Why
then was their continual disagreement?

Another explanation begins by dividing the first ten years of the
reign into two periods. The dividing-line is somewhere about 1834

[1] *Deslandres* (op. cit.), vol. ii, p. 249; *François Goguel, La Vie Politique de la
Société Française Contemporaine*, Paris (Cours de Droit) 1948-1949, pp. 56-57.

and 1835. Up to 1834, it is said that the régime is in constant danger. There is the danger of European war, the possibility of legitimist counter-revolution, the likelihood of popular uprisings. Therefore it is claimed that a rough unity persisted amongst the French politicians. This unity in the face of danger was particularly obvious in the governments of Casimir Périer and of October 11th; in the latter 'all the talents', Guizot, de Broglie and Thiers, served under Soult. But with the failure of the republican movements in Paris, Lyons, Saint-Étienne and elsewhere, and with the passing of repressive legislation in 1834 and September 1835, the danger of social revolution seemed to recede, whilst by this time the return of the legitimists or the outbreak of war had become highly improbable. Therefore the need for unity and political co-operation had passed, and the two branches of the majority began to split up. Guizot and Thiers quarrelled with Soult over Algeria in July 1834 and provoked his resignation, as Louis-Philippe intrigued against de Broglie in March 1834 and in January 1836. Eventually the change was consummated when Thiers formed his ministry of February 22nd, 1836, excluding both Guizot and de Broglie. Long before this the Chamber, elected in June 1834, had shown its aversion to any systematic line of politics and came to represent as many different fractions of party as there were men of distinction, and 'combinations of imperceptible minorities composed a majority without fixed principles or fixed direction.'[1] Thus the very success of the monarchy in overcoming its difficulties provoked the ending of alliances and allowed the development of dissidence.

This interpretation is to some extent supported by Guizot and by Rémusat. They believed that when the impression was given of the danger being passed, then the sense of urgency was lost and deputies felt themselves free to follow their prejudices and personal interests. It was at this time that the so-called 'third party', composed of these unfixed and uncertain elements, began to attract attention, and it was at this time, too, according to Guizot, that Thiers began to show dissatisfaction with his own influence and power and began to believe that if he was to assert himself then he needed to break with the 'doctrinaires'.[2] Yet this interpretation is far from being complete. In fact, it is in the first months after July 1830 when the dangers from foreign powers, political clubs and counter-revolutionaries were most real that the greatest disagreement existed amongst the ministers, and when the Cabinet could not even preserve the secret of its delibera-

[1] *The British and Foreign Review*, vol. vi, January-April 1838. *Georges Lefevbre, La Monarchie de Juillet*, Paris (no date), p. 134. Duvergier de Hauranne put the dividing line in 1836.
[2] *Guizot, Mémoires*, vol. iii, pp. 250-252, pp. 289-291.

tions. It is probably true to say that these disagreements were obscured by the strong personality of Périer rather than abolished by him, and it is certainly true to say that ministerial instability persisted throughout the period of mutualist and republican insurrection. From October 11th, 1832, to March 12th, 1835, there were five different governments, headed by Soult, Gérard, Bassano, Mortier and de Broglie. Nor is it true to say that the dangers to the régime had disappeared or had even seemed to disappear after 1835. There was always the possibility of war when Thiers was in power, whether through intervention in Spain (1836) or through defending Egypt on the Rhine and the Alps (1840). There was always the danger of republican movements and attacks on the life of the King were so frequent that people used to say that attempted assassination was part of the ceremonial of the opening of Parliament. (When a deputy asked in 1836 whether he should congratulate the King, who had just escaped being shot, the King's son Joinville replied, 'Certainly. We always do it.'[1]) In 1836 and in 1840 there were the two Bonapartist attempts, and however farcical they may appear to the historian, at least the first of them, at Strasbourg, aroused anxiety. Guizot himself describes how the telegraph message, dated October 30th, 1836, arrived in the evening, stating that Louis Napoleon, with the help of an artillery colonel, had appeared in the streets of Strasbourg, and then the message ended. The ministers spent the greater part of the night at the Tuileries, with the royal family, discussing and preparing for all eventualities. 'Weariness made us sleep and impatience woke us up. I was struck by the sadness of the King; not that he appeared uneasy or depressed; but he was preoccupied by his uncertainty as to the gravity of this event; and the repetition of these conspiracies, these attempts at creating civil war which came from the republicans, legitimists, bonapartists, and the continued need to fight, repress and punish, all weighed heavily upon him, like a detestable burden.'[2] The Parisian uprising of May 12th, 1839, led by Barbès, Blanqui and their companions, revealed again the possibility of revolution. It seemed that there was part of the population of Paris which was always ready to start shooting, and that there were people who regarded the revolutions of 1789 and 1830 as mere trifles compared to the revolution which they were preparing. This population could always succeed in agitating the

---

[1] *Prince de Joinville, Mémoires*, quoted in *M.D.R. Leys, Between two Empires*, p. 212. *Viennet, Journal* (op. cit.), pp. 172-174, reports Thiers's account of the boldness of some would-be assassins and the difficulties which the police had in discovering their organization. This conversation took place in August 1835.

[2] *Mémoires*, vol. vi, pp. 198-199.

country, and could always hold it at bay.[1] It hardly seems accurate therefore to divide the 1830s into periods of danger and periods of calm, and to suppose that it was in the latter period that the politicians could offer themselves the diversion of instability.

A more helpful interpretation emphasizes the restricted nature of the political world. To record the instability of ministries is to forget the continuity of policies, and above all the permanence of a certain personnel. Within a few weeks of July 1830, the personalities of the reign had emerged and staked their claims, and they were hardly to have any significant additions until the next revolution. In fact, although from 1830 to 1848 seventeen different governments provided ministerial and under-secretary posts for 154 different men, there were only 60 different office-holders. Of these a good many were 'Monsieur le Ministre' for only a fleeting moment, but in contrast there are the 'professionels de Ministère'. Guizot and Duchâtel were in eight different administrations, Thiers and Persil in six, Humann, de Rigny and Soult in five, Sébastiani, Montalivet, d'Argout, Barthe, Molé, Salvandy, de Broglie, Passy and others in at least three or four.[2] This meant that the political life of the country tended to become a continuous reshuffle. It was said that when a government was defeated it gave way to a government that had already been defeated and which it would proceed to defeat again. What a deputy voted against today could only be replaced by what he had voted against yesterday. In such a game of 'chasse-chasse', it is useless to look for principles or for parties based on principles. All that one can find in a Chamber composed of a single social class, according to this theory, is a war of 'ins' and 'outs'. A struggle between those who have power and those who are seeking power. It was a game for a reserved number of players in which the outsiders (Odilon Barrot, Mauguin, Garnier-Pagès on the left, Berryer and Lamartine on the right) were kept outside. Seen in this light, the coalition of 1839 was only one example, although a particularly shameless one, of the reigning immorality.

It would be foolish to deny that there is some truth in this analysis. The July Monarchy did suffer both from instability and from immobilism. Politicians in France were ambitious and did compete for office. But does this explain all the political history of the reign? Such ambition and such competition were also known in England. If it was sometimes difficult to distinguish between an English government which was 'without a principle' and an opposition which was 'without a cry', it was always easier to distinguish between the parties in terms of rival personalities. The Carlton and the Reform Clubs

[1] Prosper Merimée: Mme de Montijo, May 25th and June 15th, 1839, *Correspondance* (op. cit.), vol. ii, pp. 228 ff., 242 ff.
[2] See *Pouthas, Les Ministères de Louis-Philippe* (op. cit.), p. 108.

were each mirrored in the windows of the other; only the members were different. Furthermore, in England electioneering was still an aristocratic pastime. What sport was there finer than that of fighting a county election, and winning or losing by a handful of votes? It is true that in France there was a greater rivalry of personalities, because there was no aristocratic predominance. In England it was taken for granted that the young Lord Stanley would become Prime Minister, but no one was taken for granted in France. Guizot, Thiers, de Broglie, Molé, who was to give way to the other? Each could lay claim to great ability, and whilst the first two could stress their oratorical talents, the third could point to the respect in which he was everywhere held and the fourth could recall that his experience in administration went back to the days when Napoleon had discerned his quality. And if one was going back to Napoleon, then Marshal Soult could stake his claim, for should not his experience and patriotism qualify him for the highest position? It can therefore be argued that the very ability of these politicians and their equality of opportunity explained the political strife.

Yet this cannot be the whole explanation. The struggle of 'ins' against 'outs', unperturbed by any unegoistical consideration, can only take place in the 'flat' periods of history, when there are no issues, no controversies, no sense of urgency. When a government is not expected to do anything, then there are no two ways of doing it and then politics becomes a simple question of who is to do it. But no one can say that the 1830s was such a period. On the contrary, it was a period when the most important issues were raised. The rapid succession of régimes which had followed upon 1789 was not conducive to indifference; 1830 had merely sharpened the need for some sort of political certainty. The discordant politicians of the 1830s realized that they were working against a background of doom; much of their egoism and play-acting is to be explained by different attitudes of mind, different temperaments testing a situation in a different way. The Orleanists, like the later Hapsburgs, suffered from a 'dissolution complex', as one can see in Louis-Philippe's paternal anxiety that his children would go hungry, in the bitter jokes of the Duke of Orleans who use to say that there was no point in his saving money, or in the silly parlour games of the legitimists. (These last used to say that the figures 1789 added up to 25, and the Revolution had ended in 1814, 25 years after it had begun; the figures 1815 added up to 15, and 15 years added to 1815 made 1830; 1830 they would point out added up to 12, and they prophesied that the July Monarchy would end in 1842.) It was said of each of the governments of Molé, Soult and Thiers after 1837, that 'this is the Martignac ministry of the July Monarchy', the prelude to disaster.

Therefore it would be strange if the political history of the 1830s does not contain within itself trends of opinion and principle. It remains to try and find them, and it seems likely that there were at least three different principles whereby the politicians grouped themselves. The first was pointed out by one of the most able commentators of the *Revue des Deux Mondes*, Louis de Carné. It was with particular reference to the ministry of October 11th, 1832 (Soult's first), that de Carné made his analysis, but he obviously intended it to be of wider application. He found two equivalent forces in French politics, 'l'élément bourgeois' and 'l'élément doctrinaire', which roughly balanced one another in the Chamber. This doctrinaire element must not be confused with the doctrinaire party. The party was small, but the doctrinaire element was composed of several different groups and parties, which shared a similar attitude towards the problems of government. They represented government by ideas, a theoretical and rational approach. They thought that France required certain institutions, such as a strong second Chamber and a highly developed royalty, and they made these requirements into principles. This intellectual, administrative or 'official' view was best represented by Guizot, although once again it must be emphasized that there were many men in the doctrinaire element who were never included in the doctrinaire party. This element supposedly owed its strength to the force of its ideas, to the talent with which these ideas were expressed, and to the probity and reputation of its supporters. The 'élément bourgeois' represented government by interests, government according to what suited industrialists, landed proprietors and 'rentiers'. It meant a less systematic approach to politics, a day-to-day policy, long periods of indifference followed by moments of intense activity and concern over particular issues. It was this 'élément bourgeois' which thus provided majorities for every cabinet but a majority for none. Its leader was Thiers, who represented most clearly that section of the population which had profited directly from the Revolution of 1830.[1]

This division into 'doctrinaires' and 'bourgeois', as explained by Carné, might, of course, have led to a regularization of political relations. But if one accepts it, and there are undoubtedly times when it is correct, one has to realize how it was vitiated by three further factors. The most important of these was that the two sections were split on the question of foreign policy. For Guizot, the great task of government was to consolidate its position in the interior; his policy was therefore one of peace and caution. But for others amongst the doctrinaires, one way of strengthening the monarchy, one way of

[1] *Louis de Carné's* article is in the *Revue des Deux Mondes*, vol. 28, 1837, pp. 158-165.

arousing the affectionate loyalty of the population, was through a vigorous and successful foreign policy. In this, people such as Rémusat and Duvergier de Hauranne, or even Tocqueville (whose approach to politics was 'doctrinaire' even although he never accepted to associate himself with Guizot), joined up with Thiers who held similar beliefs. But the greater part of the 'élément bourgeois' was opposed to foreign adventures if they threatened to jeopardize their interests. Most of their economic activity was purely internal and therefore on this question they were prepared to join Guizot. In this way the question of France's foreign relations acted as a solvent, upsetting the party divisions. The same could be said of the religious question, and the importance which was attributed to the Catholic Church. Finally there was the unpredictable and unstable character of Thiers, about which more will have to be said later on. Thus, by taking this division of 'doctrinaire' and 'bourgeois' one can see not only a principle of separation, but also how the principle could become complicated.

A second principle whereby the politicians grouped themselves arose from the fact that the 'bourgeoisie', whose 'golden hour' was allegedly the reign of Louis-Philippe, was in fact a divided social class. One gets the impression that this class was united, if one over-emphasizes the significance of 1830. It is true that the appointment of the bankers Laffitte and Casimir Périer as chief ministers in 1830 and 1831 was significant; they now played a dominant rôle whereas before they had been confined to opposition. All 'présidents du conseil' under the Restoration were noblemen, apart from Decazes, who was a royal favourite and who was ennobled. Yet the social significance of 1830 must not be overstressed. Before 1830 many of the bourgeoisie had achieved what they wanted in so far as they had a system of protection; after 1830 the landowning class was still the most important section of the electorate. The 1831 electoral law gave the vote to those who paid 200 francs a year in direct taxation, but the nature of taxation gave greater prominence to those who paid the land tax. It is not true to suppose that after 1830 there was one political class, one bourgeoisie. Although industrialists bought land, there is a fundamental cleavage between agriculture and industry, in so far as capital did not move out of agriculture into industry as it did in other countries which were becoming industrialized. If one thinks in terms of the electors, then it is clear that there can be little similarity between the poor departments, such as the Manche, Mayenne, or Finistère, and the rich agricultural departments such as the Marne, Oise or Aisne. In the latter it was the wealthy culti-vators, working their own lands, who voted; in the former, the votes were scattered, even isolated. In Finistère one man in every 297 had the right to vote, and Tocqueville, who became deputy for Valognes in the Manche, said that he knew no other area where the main condition of public life, that men should meet together and exchange ideas, was so strikingly absent. (He believed that in 1840 few of the inhabitants of the Manche knew that Thiers was 'Prime Minister'.[1]) There could be little similarity between the electors of either of these types of department, and the electors of the Parisian arrondissements, where one man in 30 had the vote, and where the small tax-paying class (not landowning) predominated. When one analyses the electoral lists of a single department, one is struck by the extreme diversity of social classes which one finds there, going from a rich landowner, paying 11,000 francs, to master-craftsmen, owning a field, and just surmounting the barrier of the 'sens'. A list of the twenty 'richest' men in a department (richest, that is, from the tax-paying point of view) reveals nobles and 'bourgeois', landowners and industrialists, men who are known for their legitimist ideas and men who are from Orleanist families. The complexity is extreme and should make one chary of generalizations which see a landowner-legitimist combination facing an industrialist-Orleanist alliance. One must also realize that a similar complexity appears in the Chamber. This does not appear only in those questions where personal interests, or where a particularly geographical interest, are concerned. These obviously arise on many occasions, when the wine-growing districts, for example, hope for freedom of trade, whilst the textile-producing areas cling to protection. Such conflicts and alliances of interest are part of any representative assembly. Peel, for example, was concerned that the House of Commons elected in 1841 would be too sharply divided between the agricultural and the industrial interest. It was said by the *Edinburgh Review* that Peel's income tax proposals only got through Parliament in 1842 because they were supported by a combination between the country gentlemen who thought that they were securing the Corn Laws, the planters who thought that they were maintaining sugar preference, and those members whose constituencies thought that the income tax was a blow to the aristocracy.[2] It is true that these combinations were more important in France, both because of the unevenness of French development and because of the absence of traditional political parties. However, the social diversity of the electorate and of the Chamber made for extreme differences of attitude amongst the deputies. A question of foreign policy would be viewed differently according to whether one

[1] Tocqueville: Royer-Collard, August 15th, 1840, in *Revue des Deux Mondes*, August 15th, 1930, pp. 902-904.
[2] Peel: Ripon, July 17th, 1841. *Ripon Papers*, B.M. Add. MSS., 40, 863; *Edinburgh Review*, vol. 75, p. 217.

was a banker, with large foreign interests, the representative of some small family firm, a military official or a journalist. Some of the deputies made a fetish of their independence, such as Tocqueville, and were always anxious to demonstrate it; others, such as Dupin, were determined to show that they were not only independent but also indispensable. Others were moved by purely religious considerations: it was these, rather than social situation, which were the strongest promoters of legitimism. This variety of individual attitudes and personal ideologies, unchecked and undisciplined, goes a long way towards explaining that a coherent, permanent majority could not be formed.[1]

The third explanation of why French politicians behaved as they did during the 1830s was that one constitutional question did remain outstanding; namely, what was to be the rôle of the King? If, as Casimir Périer had said, there had not been a revolution, but simply a change in the person of the head of state, then one would expect that the King would behave like his predecessors, and would play the dominant rôle in the choice of chief minister. On the other hand, if the revolution had wider implications, then it would be the Chamber, or some group in the Chamber, which would have the power to make and un-make governments. In reality, Louis-Philippe firmly believed in the first, and both by ability and by temperament he was well suited to become the chief negotiator of all the groups. Seeing the politicians singly or in twos or threes, showing favour here, flattering there, passing on rumours, announcing his decided hostility to some political leader whom he would afterwards treat with great affability, accepting or refusing advice, Louis-Philippe undoubtedly tried to minimize the power of parties and tried to prevent the emergence of a permanent majority or of a strong Prime Minister. Presumably he thought that by making himself indispensable in political affairs, he was demonstrating the necessity of monarchy and thus consolidating his dynasty. It would seem that he impressed many who saw him by his wisdom, and by his insistence upon peace and upon domestic calm. It used to be said that Frenchmen would not mind Thiers becoming king, provided that he made Louis-Philippe his Prime Minister. However, this does not alter the fact that the political struggles and ministerial changes of the 1830s can be interpreted in terms of the insistence of royal influence and the resistance to it.

The negotiations which followed upon the death of Casimir

[1] On electoral lists, see two articles by *A.-J. Tudesq*, 'La bourgeoisie du Nord au milieu de la Monarchie de Juillet', *Revue du Nord*, October-December 1959, pp. 277-285; 'Les listes électorales de la Monarchie Censitaire', *Annales* (Économies, Sociétés, Civilisations), 1958, vol. 13, pp. 277-288.

Périer ('Monsieur Périer est mort, est-ce un bien, est-ce un mal?' was the King's reputed comment when he heard the news) are the first real example of this. The King tried to persuade Dupin to form a ministry, but refused to accept the idea that the 'présidence du conseil' should be effective; he then tried to create a ministry in which Thiers would be the most important minister, but in which he would have someone else as ineffective leader. From June until October it is the King, with his conditions and his exclusions, who prolonged the uncertainty. The formation of the ministry of October 11th, 1832, represented the failure of the King's insistence, and was a parliamentary victory in the sense that its leaders drew their strength from their position in Parliament. But the King proceeded to intrigue against de Broglie in order that he might more directly have his say in foreign affairs. Once de Broglie had resigned (over the American treaty in April 1834) and was succeeded by a man of less calibre, de Rigny, the King's position was stronger. Other ministerial changes, the resignations of Barthe, d'Argout and Soult, were meant to strengthen the hand of Parliament, and when Marshal Gérard, the 'président du conseil' who had succeeded Soult, resigned because of disagreement with Guizot and Thiers over a proposed amnesty bill, the parliamentary forces prepared their revenge by proposing that the Duc de Broglie should return as 'président'. When this was refused, Guizot and Thiers resigned. After an unsuccessful attempt to persuade Thiers to separate from Guizot, the King then tried, with the help of Dupin and the third party, to create his own ministry. Headed by Maret, duc de Bassano, whose nomination on November 10th, 1834, astonished his numerous creditors as much as it delighted them, this manœuvre appointed two ministers without first consulting them. Dupin was too skilful to allow himself to be drawn into this weak combination, but he allowed his younger brother to become Minister of the Marine. The King realized the impossibility of this government which was killed by ridicule. After the so-called 'ministry of three days', sometimes called the 'journée des Dupins', the King recalled Guizot and Thiers, and for all that they accepted the compromise of having yet another marshal as president, this time Mortier, yet there was no doubt that this was a parliamentary victory. When Mortier, a military innocent lost in the wilderness of a spiteful Chamber, decided to give up the presidency, the parliamentarians followed victory with victory, and the King was forced to accept the return of the duc de Broglie in February 1835. Once again de Broglie, Guizot and Thiers were together, 'Casimir Périer in three persons' as the King was supposed to call them, and this time de Broglie held the presidency.

But the King was not finished. In February 1836 the Chamber

172

gave him the opportunity he was looking for by defeating the government over the question of the conversion of the 'rentes'. This was a question where the parliamentary forces were completely split. There were those who advocated it for technical reasons, arguing sound finance; there were those who opposed it because they felt they would suffer financially; there were those who supported it as a means of attacking Paris interests and of lightening the budget. The King undoubtedly delighted in this situation, and allowed his entourage to criticize de Broglie. Shortly after he had accepted de Broglie's resignation, he succeeded in doing what he had frequently tried to do, he separated Thiers from his two colleagues. It is ironical that the statesman who had proclaimed that the King reigned and did not govern accepted to be chief minister simply as a gift from the King. Thiers worked directly with the King, the 'conseil des ministres' or Cabinet meetings fell into disuse, and were replaced by meetings at the King's residence in Neuilly, when Louis-Philippe, the Duc d'Orleans and Thiers transacted business. Other business was carried out by the Minister of the Interior, Montalivet, another royal nominee. It was true that Thiers was as unrealiable for the King as he was for the parliamentary forces, and his Spanish policy brought about disagreement. But the King dismissed him as easily as he had appointed him, and turned to a man who was isolated from the main parliamentary groups, Molé. After the Guizot-Molé interval, Molé's ministry of April 15th, 1837, was a complete victory for the King.

Thus the struggle between the parliamentary forces and 'le King' as Prosper Merimée called him, is a recurrent theme in politics. Everyone was conscious of this conflict, if only through Roederer's pamphlet of 1834, *Adresse d'un constitutionnel aux constitutionnels*, or through Louis-Philippe's unceasing commentaries in the royal salons and consultations in the royal billiard rooms. When a choice had had to be made between Guizot and Molé, the King had chosen Molé who had no position in the Chamber and whose policies had already failed. Against Molé were all the talents of the Chamber. For him was the King. When the government was weak in Parliament it was not the government which was dissolved, but it was Parliament which was dissolved twice in eighteen months. In order to stay in power the government followed the line of least resistance. Although the King was advised on all accounts to strengthen his ministry by adding to it more parliamentary forces, he did not do so. Although Guizot made some of his greatest speeches, and although the government was expected to fall, it did not do so. Parliament seemed impotent against the King. Thiers let it be known that during his ministry much had passed in foreign affairs of which he had not been informed, and the most sinister rumours began to circulate. Thus

Parliament was becoming useless, the government was ineffective, and the Crown was dangerously exposed to criticism and to opposition.

It was in these circumstances that the coalition was born. It did not create a crisis; it arose out of a crisis. It was part of the constant struggle between royal and parliamentary forces, an attempt to emerge from a dangerous deadlock, an answer to the provocations of Molé who was trying to destroy the parliamentary groups by winning over individuals with his influence and patronage. Although de Broglie did not actively join in the coalition, he agreed with it to a large extent, and he claimed that the complaints against the King's predominance and against the ineffectiveness of the government were justified.[1] There can be no doubt that the final resignation of Molé was a victory for the parliamentary forces and a defeat for the King. But the failure of any government to emerge between March and May 1839 represented a victory for the King, and Soult's ministry of May 12th, hurriedly formed at the news of the Parisian insurrection of the same date, was acceptable only because it deliberately excluded the main political leaders. The defeat of Soult in February 1840 over the dotation to be voted to the King's son, the duc de Nemours, was clearly a defeat for the King. The majority was supposedly assembled against the King by Thiers, but as it had no spokesman this was difficult to prove. Villemain, who had been Minister for Public Instruction, said that they had been strangled by mutes. 'That is the usual fate of eunuchs' was supposedly the comment of an 'homme d'esprit'.

The arrival of the Thiers ministry on March 1st was undoubtedly a defeat for the King, but not necessarily a victory for the parliamentary party. Ever since 1836 Thiers had obviously been an uncertain ally. His attitude to Parliament began to resemble that of Molé. Since he had not the support of the various groups he would try to destroy them; he tried to attract individuals by a series of promises, flattery, cajolery and material gifts. He would try to appear for as long as possible to be going in the direction demanded by each of the different groups of the Cabinet, which meant that the wording of his speeches became a perpetual 'tour de force' and that the appearance of legislation on controversial matters had to be indefinitely postponed. It was for all these reasons that he tried to turn the attention of the country towards the return of Napoleon's remains and it was perhaps for this reason too that he welcomed the atmosphere of crisis which grew up over the Eastern Question. It was commented at the time that a minister who had attacked his pre-

[1] This is reported by his son. See *Revue des Deux Mondes*, January 15th, 1925, p. 330.

decessors because they had not been sufficiently parliamentary, was by September proceeding to spend millions and to threaten war, without consulting parliament. Once again the King decided that Thiers had gone too far, and that he had placed himself in a position where he could safely be dismissed. Was the dismissal of Thiers and the summoning of Guizot to be just another incident in this long rivalry of King and Parliament?[1]

It has been shown that the political history of France in the 1830s revolved around four main principles. The first, a question simply of personalities, 'ins' against 'outs'. The second, the division of the Chamber into 'doctrinaire' and 'bourgeois' elements, a division which was complicated by several factors, the main one being the differing attitudes to foreign policy. The third, the divisions within the society which elected and which made up the Chamber. The fourth, the rivalry between King and Chamber. By October 29th, 1840, Guizot was in the unique position of being able to control all of these factors. From the personal point of view he had the best claim. Thiers had been discredited; he had gambled too obviously on Mehemet Ali's strength, and by October everyone could see that this strength was non-existent. Molé was discredited in many circles; he was at a disadvantage since he was a member of the Chamber of Peers, and he could not hope to assemble a government strong enough to meet the crisis. For the same reason a re-edition of Soult's May 12th ministry was also impossible. De Broglie, still saddened by the death of his wife in 1838, had no intention of taking office. The only 'outsider' who was mentioned was Lamartine, and nobody really considered that he had a chance. Guizot was therefore the only serious candidate. The war-scare had succeeded in effacing the differences between most of the 'bourgeois' and the 'doctrinaire' elements. In 1840 the Bourse was called 'The Temple of Fear', and those who were frightened by the dangers of war joined with those who were angered by the folly of such a war. Fear tended to efface many of the differences amongst the deputies and to lessen their tendency towards fragmentation. Finally, Guizot hoped to be able to establish a better arrangement with the King than had hitherto been possible. He was too important to be a Molé or a Montalivet; he was more reliable than Thiers, more supple than de Broglie. The King, by dismissing Thiers, had exposed

---

[1] Apart from the volumes of *Thureau-Dangin* (op. cit.), the *Mémoires de Monsieur Dupin*, Paris 1860, 4 vols., are an interesting source of information about these political events, as are the recollections of Thiers's mother-in-law, *Madame Dosne, Mémoires* (ed. Henri Malo), Paris 1928, 2 vols. For Guizot's explanation of his attitude in the coalition see 'Monsieur Guizot à ses commettants', February 6th, 1839, in the *Revue Française*, vol. x, pp. 169 ff., reprinted in the *Mémoires*, vol. iv, p. 452; *Monsieur Guizot à Monsieur Leroy-Beaulieu, Maire de Lisieux*, Paris 1839, reprinted in the *Mémoires*, ibid., p. 463.

himself to severe criticism. In the excitement of October attacks on the King's action were attacks on his patriotism and on the dynasty. He was therefore dependent upon Guizot to extricate him from a position of danger and he was not in a position to be exacting. Guizot therefore represented the possibility of being a minister who would work with the King, rather than for him or against him, who would give satisfaction to the King and at the same time draw his strength from Parliament.

When Guizot left for England, in February 1840, political commentators were talking gloomily about the political situation, and about representative government being within a shade of its disappearance; after the formation of the Thiers government they were still gloomy and it was claimed that since 1830 the situation had never been graver, the peril more real, the remedy more uncertain and hazardous.[1] It was therefore natural that Guizot should take care to keep himself well informed about political affairs in Paris, and that the pressure of diplomatic events never obscured for him this essential preoccupation. As he was later to say, he was always a deputy before he was an ambassador.[2] He wrote frequently to de Broglie, who remained one of his closest friends, and who was able to keep him informed about events since he had accepted to be the distant, and rapidly disapproving, 'patron' of the Thiers government, and to speak in its favour in the Chamber of Peers. Guizot also was in correspondence with Rémusat, who had become Minister of the Interior (after much hesitation, and after having been persuaded by de Broglie), and with Jaubert, who had also accepted a post from Thiers. Duvergier de Hauranne had refused Thiers's offer of a ministry (and had suggested his brother-in-law Jaubert instead), but he began to abandon Guizot, never really getting over his disappointment that the coalition had not succeeded in forming a ministry. However, at least in the beginning he wrote quite often to Guizot. The most important correspondent, however, after de Broglie, was undoubtedly Duchâtel, who wrote detailed and acute appreciations of the situation, and who frequently received from the King allusions and messages which he passed on. The King also corresponded with Guizot, through General Baudrand, an aide-de-camp of the royal household, whilst other doctrinaires who had refused to co-operate with Thiers were Villemain and Dumon.

Guizot had posed two conditions before accepting to continue as ambassador when Thiers became 'président du conseil'. One was that

---

[1] *Revue des Deux Mondes*, January 15th, 1840, p. 142; March 15th, 1840, p. 676.

[2] Guizot: de Broglie, October 20th, 1840. *Mémoires*, vol. v, p. 399.

there should be no dissolution; if the government did not have a majority, then an obvious remedy would be to try and seek one in fresh elections, but many people felt that a third set of elections in three years, at a time of great uncertainty, could only clarify the situation by giving greater influence to the extremists. Guizot's second condition was that there should be no reform, either electoral or parliamentary. He therefore watched Thiers's relations with the left very closely. It looked as if Thiers could stay in power only for as long as he could persuade Odilon Barrot and others on the left to vote for him; this seemed to lead him towards accepting some sort of reform. Otherwise, if Thiers was to break with the left, it looked as if he would have to ask the King for a dissolution. Shortly after the formation of the government Guizot had warned Rémusat of the dangers of this policy. 'Believe me,' he wrote, 'there are times when one can derive strength from the left, but one can never make it a permanent support . . . the left disturbs and excites instead of con-solidating the two bases of social order, which are ordinary interests and moral beliefs.'[1]

He was not alone in looking anxiously at this reliance on the left. De Broglie wondered if the government could last through the parliamentary session, but he felt certain that it would need to seek reinforcement before confronting the Chamber again. This he did not think Thiers could arrange. Towards the end of April the King dropped a hint via Duchâtel that he might be calling on Guizot in the near future. Molé too was watching the situation closely and was impressed by Thiers's dependence upon the left, and commented, 'Monsieur Barrot is from now on more the leader of the left than Monsieur Thiers, and Monsieur Garnier-Pagès is more the leader of the left than Monsieur Barrot.'[2]

Guizot therefore, whilst ambassador in London, was patiently awaiting events, and without actively intriguing against Thiers, was preparing for his accession to power. He was worried lest the summons from the King should come too soon, and the King's hint in April was not fully to his liking. He knew that he would have to count on the main conservative forces in the Chamber if he was to be successful, and he recalled that on two occasions in the recent past, in 1837 and in 1839, the conservative party had failed to support him. If this was not to happen a third time, then he should return to power only when called by some evident and obvious necessity. The situation needed to be one of danger, so that the conservative party would be prepared to commit itself along with Guizot and Duchâtel.

[1] Guizot: Rémusat, March 5th, 1840. *Val-Richer MSS.*
[2] Molé: Prosper de Barante, April 25th, 1840, *Barante, Souvenirs*, vol. vi, p. 443.

A few days later, Guizot wrote again to Duchâtel, 'I know nothing worse than those remedies which are administered too soon: they do not cure the patient and they get rid of the doctor.'[1] He therefore wanted to wait until the situation made him necessary. Furthermore, if he was to lead the conservatives, then there had to be no confusion about his relations with Molé. From London he announced that he intended to have nothing to do with Molé, and that if Molé became minister for foreign affairs then he would resign. He believed that Molé's direction of policy would be impossible, and he claimed that he could still see in England the bad effects of Molé's earlier handling of foreign affairs. Guizot wanted to attract those deputies who had supported Molé, but he wanted to do so by himself, and not through any patched-up and slender reconciliation with him.[2] This was all the more significant since it was suggested, as the Eastern crisis became more obvious, that Molé would be a good person to solve it since he had avoided committing himself on this question.

Guizot was also careful to strengthen his hand in another way. The treaty of July 15th, 1840, brought together England, Russia, Prussia and Austria in a collective attempt to bring pressure on to Egypt; France was isolated. The July 15th treaty had come as a surprise to Guizot in so far as he had not expected it to be signed so soon. He had thought (acting probably on information supplied by Princess Lieven) that the Prussian delegate would have to await an authorization, and that the matter could not be concluded at once. He also thought that the French government would be given one last chance to join with the other powers. But although he had not expected the convention of July 15th to be arranged so rapidly, he had undoubtedly expected some such move to be made, and he had warned Thiers of the possibility of France finding herself isolated. He had not shared the easy optimism of the King, who was always reported as being convinced that England would never be party to a four-power arrangement.[3] He was therefore very anxious to emphasize, once the treaty had been signed, that he had given full warning of this possibility, and he wrote a good many letters, quoting his correspondence with Thiers, in order to dissociate himself from a diplomacy which was proving unsuccessful. He thus confirmed what had been suggested in certain circles, that Thiers was not a good

[1] Guizot: Duchâtel, April 29th, 1840; May 9th, 1840, *Papiers Duchâtel, Archives Nationales*, 2 A.P. 8.

[2] Guizot: Duchâtel, April 29th, ibid.; Guizot: Villemain, March 8th, 1840, *Val-Richer MSS.* Guizot in 1838 wrote, 'M. Molé est avant tout, par dessus tout, un poltron, qui veut le pouvoir sans ses charges, les affaires sans leur danger.' *Guizot et Madame Laure de Gasparin* (op. cit.), p. 154.

[3] The King's belief was reported in General Baudrand: Guizot, March 30th, 1840; de Rémusat: Guizot, April 1st, 1840. *Val-Richer MSS.*

diplomatist. Sainte Aulaire, then ambassador in Vienna, wrote to Barante, his colleague in St. Petersburg, that Thiers had 'de mauvaises formes diplomatiques', and he expected that 'through ignorance or through disdain' Thiers would increase the difficulties and complications of the situation.[1]

By September and October the air was heavy with rumours. Duvergier de Hauranne, now advising Thiers, was reporting that Montalivet, always extremely close to the King, had said that the Cabinet was being allowed to continue in office, but that if a moment of great decision was reached, then it would be dismissed. Léon Faucher the journalist told Thiers that the King was counting on the Chamber to defeat the government.[2] At the same time the talk of war, the threats of war in the ministerial press, along with the threats of social violence made in the radical press and confirmed by a series of strikes and disorders in early September, were causing wide uneasiness and the suggestion was being made that France was living again the situation of 1831. The analogy of 1831 turned to Guizot's advantage. Thiers was given the rôle of Laffitte, and Guizot the rôle of Casimir Périer. Duchâtel and Villemain, together with certain newspapers, launched an attack on the 'dictatorship' exercised by Thiers. On October 1st, Duchâtel reported to Guizot on the extent of the crisis, stressing the fluctuations of the Bourse and the weakness of credit. The next day brought the news of Napier's action at Beyrouth and a clear indication of Mehemet's weakness. On October 10th, Duchâtel wrote again to Guizot, expressing his conviction that the greater part of the country did not want war, and that it was necessary for Guizot to return and lead those who wished to oppose their veto to war. On October 13th, Guizot asked the government's permission to return to Paris and take part in the opening debates of the Chambers, which were convoked for October 28th.[3] The situation which he had foreseen in April, and for which he had patiently waited, had come about. As he put it to de Broglie, it was the interior rather than the diplomatic crisis which rendered him most uneasy. France was faced with the possibility of revolution, when such a revolution had nothing to offer either to France or to Europe.[4]

When on October 15th Darmès attempted to assassinate the King, this act seemed to symbolize the progress of anarchy. To those who were seeking for an opportunity to withdraw from the 'tambourinage' organized by Thiers and Le Constitutionnel, this was a good

[1] Sainte-Aulaire: Prosper de Barante, June 27th, 1840, Barante, Souvenirs (op. cit.), vol. vi, p. 454.
[2] Duvergier de Hauranne: Thiers, September 23rd, 1840; Faucher: Thiers, October 11th, 1840, Papiers Thiers, Bibliothèque National, Nouv. acq. 20609.
[3] Guizot, Mémoires, vol. v, pp. 387-390.
[4] Guizot: de Broglie, October 13th, 1840, Ibid., pp. 390-395.

opportunity. Three days later, when Duchâtel saw the King at Saint-Cloud, the King told him that all the conservatives, including Molé, were convinced of the dangers of the situation and were ready to support a Soult-Guizot ministry.[1] The ministers themselves were divided. The ministers for war and for the marine had never joined in the irresponsible view that a war against the rest of Europe would be easy; it was said that another minister told the King that he must dismiss them.[2] There was little response from the remaining ministers and their supporters. They waited to be dismissed, and were witty at the expense of the King. 'Give us this day our daily platitude' was reported to be the King's morning prayer, and on the eve of the rupture Duvergier de Hauranne wrote, 'In a certain place an immense platitude is being prepared.'[3]

Thus when Guizot returned to France his government was rapidly formed. Guizot himself (Foreign Affairs and the chief spokesman of the government in the Chambers), Duchâtel (Interior) and Villemain (Instruction) represented the doctrinaire party, the right-centre group of the Chamber. Humann (Finance) was a technician, but he had been associated with this same group. Martin du Nord (Justice), Cunin-Gridaine (Commerce) and Duperré (Marine) represented the conservatives who had supported Molé: the first-named had been a member of Molé's government of April 15th, 1837. The whole was presided over by the war-worn profile of Soult, whose presence was to protect them against the allegations of wanting 'peace at any price' and who was also expected to bring them votes from the right-centre and even from the left-centre. Soult brought into the Cabinet his spokesman Teste (Public Works), representative of a small group in the Chamber, sometimes maliciously referred to as the 'fournisseurs' since they looked to the government for contracts. A post was offered to Lamartine, which would have increased the support from the Molé group, but he did not consider it important enough to accept. The important group in the left-centre, led by Dufaure and Passy, had also been approached. They had definitely broken with Thiers, and relations between him and Dufaure were very bad. But whilst they were prepared to support the government, at least for the time being, they did not feel ready to enter a government in which the 'doctrinaires' controlled the important ministries.[4] Hippolyte Passy's brother Antoine became under-secretary at the Interior.

[1] Duchâtel: Guizot, October 19th, 1840, Ibid., pp. 402-404.
[2] *Dupin, Mémoires* (op. cit.), vol. iv, p. 100. It is thought that this minister was Victor Cousin.
[3] Duvergier de Hauranne: Thiers, October 21st, 1840, *Papiers Thiers*, ibid.
[4] This was stated by the British ambassador Lord Cowley in a despatch to Palmerston, October 30th, 1840. *P.R.O.* F.O. 27/606.

In the same way as there was little difficulty in forming the government, so there was never any real question that the government would be given the necessary number of votes to liquidate the Middle East crisis. It is of course true that in a French assembly nothing is ever certain, and the influence of both court and government had to be carefully deployed, Guizot had to word his speeches with great care. But when the discussion of the address was begun in the Chamber of Peers on November 17th, and in the Deputies on November 25th (the original convocation for October 28th having been countermanded), the drama of the situation was to some extent false. On October 11th, Duvergier de Hauranne had calculated that if Thiers proposed Odilon Barrot for the Presidency of the Chamber, he would be defeated since he would have had against him the conservative followers of Molé and the April 15th government, the supporters of Soult's May 12th government from the centre (and these two groups according to Duvergier composed nearly half of the Chamber) and all those who were partisans of 'peace at any price'; these last, it was said, were to be found in all the groups.[1] The majority which rendered Odilon Barrot's candidature impossible was the majority which was already committed to support Guizot. The only questions that remained were how in fact would the debate develop, and what sort of an impression would Guizot make, in his first important appearance before the Chambers since the collapse of the coalition.

Guizot was helped in this by Thiers. In fact it is remarkable at this point to notice the lack of political skill which Thiers was demonstrating. Duvergier was right when he urged Thiers to take some decisive step of policy, to reply to the British bombardment of Beyrouth by the occupation of some Middle Eastern port in the same way that Casimir Périer had sent the French Navy to Ancona in 1831, counterbalancing Austrian action in the Papal States. If Thiers was to fall, then he should 'fall well'. But Thiers did not do this. He stayed in power waiting to be dismissed, when it would have been wiser to have resigned, three weeks earlier, either just before or just after the news from Beyrouth.[2] To these mistakes Thiers now added another tactical error. He decided to attack Guizot both as ambassador and as minister, and to defend his policy to the limit, both in the past and in the present. Thus began the great oratorical duel between the two, when for the first four days of the debate they appeared to follow each other at the tribune to the exclusion of other speakers, before an attentive and excited assembly. Within a short time, both speakers

[1] Duvergier de Hauranne: Thiers, October 11th, 1840, *Papiers Thiers*, Ibid.

[2] Duvergier de Hauranne: Thiers, October 11th, 1840; November 19th, 1840, *Papiers Thiers*, ibid.

were producing documents from the ministerial files in order to demonstrate each other's mistakes, and were revealing the confidence of conversations and despatches. Such a debate could only turn to the disadvantage of Thiers. It was always Guizot's 'forte' to give a grand tone to a debate; it was always part of his professorial eloquence to turn to texts in order to substantiate his elevated phrases. He had no difficulty in showing that Thiers had never responded to the British government's suggestions, that he had ignored warnings of possible French isolation, that he had, in short, allowed the situation to deteriorate without taking any action at all. Guizot was able to show, perhaps more than was justifiable, that under the ministry of March 1st, war was certain, and that it was to be a war against the remainder of Europe in support of an ally who had already been defeated and whom Thiers had allowed to be defeated. There was no ministerial file which Thiers could call upon which could conceal these defeats. It was suggested that the ministry of October 29th needed these defeats in order to prove its case.[1] If this was the case, then it was well served. Guizot was also able to suggest that one reason for Lord Palmerston's suspicion, and for the decision to conclude the Convention of July 15th, was the rumour that Thiers was trying to arrange a direct agreement between Alexandria and Constantinople which would constitute a rebuff to the 'Concert of Europe' and would greatly enhance French influence. This suggestion was denied by Thiers, but it did not appear so unreasonable at the time (and it has not appeared unreasonable to subsequent historians); it came after rumours that Thiers had been speculating on the Bourse, and it drew a lot of attention to the unconventional friends with whom Thiers chose to surround himself. As Heine wrote, on October 7th, 'He who sleeps with dogs, gets up with fleas.'[2] It became widely believed that there was something untrustworthy about Thiers.

Thus Thiers drew attention to his own shortcomings in order to win a handful of votes when the result of the debate was obvious. He had no reply at all when Guizot pointed to the revolutionary dangers which his policies had sustained. It was to this rather than to the details of diplomatic exchanges that the Chamber listened most attentively. As Louis de Carné put it, 'The Eastern Question has not been debated by itself; it has been dominated by internal considerations.'[3] In this way Thiers enabled the new government to distinguish itself most clearly from its predecessor, to strike an attitude and to suggest that they were the saviours of France. If Guizot was to have any hope of staying in power and of governing

---

[1] *Revue des Deux Mondes*, December 15th, 1840, p. 624.
[2] *H. Heine, Lutèce*, Paris 1878 edition, p. 130.
[3] *Revue des Deux Mondes*, January 15th, 1841, p. 716.

effectively, then his greatest need was to divide the Chamber, with revolution and war on the one side, stability and peace on the other. It was the policy of Thiers when minister and his attitude when in opposition that enabled him to do this. The government's majority in the debate was 86, and although this was unnaturally high, Guizot calculated that he could count on a certain majority of from 50 to 60. Guizot hoped that he would be able to organize, with this, a real government party which would be 'as compact and as loyal as the state of our society permits'. To Prosper de Barante he proclaimed the end of the system which had prevailed since 1836, whereby the government had no certain support. 'The Chamber', he wrote, 'is split into two. The government has emerged from the oscillation between the centre and the left which has been the ruin of everything for the last four years . . . but all that is only a beginning.'[1]

Yet questions could occur which would falsify this successful division, and one of them had to be settled which was more dangerous for the government than the debate on foreign policy. This was the question of the fortifications of Paris. Thiers had by a simple ordonnance decreed that work should be started on the construction of a fortified wall surrounding Paris. The government of Guizot had to decide what it should do about this project. If it was not to be abandoned, then it had to be paid for. The continued uncertainties of the diplomatic situation were such that Guizot decided to maintain the programme of armaments started by Thiers. This was the complement to French isolation, it was the riposte to suggestions that France was weak and governed by a weak Cabinet. Therefore in December a Bill was tabled which would open a special credit of 140 million francs. This Bill was to be discussed in January.

The difficulty arose because this project was not at all agreeable to the right and right-centre conservatives who had supported the government. Lamartine was opposed to the Bill, but more important than Lamartine, Molé was reported to have seized this occasion as a means of challenging Guizot's leadership. He alleged that Guizot had not the courage to pursue the policy of peace to its logical conclusion and that the fortifications of Paris were a concession to the warlike policies of Thiers. As Dufaure and Passy, in the left-centre, were also known to be hostile to the proposition, it seemed likely that a Molé-Dufaure combination could wreck the government. On the left, the radicals and some of the supporters of Odilon Barrot opposed the fortifications, claiming that these were not being constructed against any invader but against possible risings or popular movements within Paris. The fortifications were a device to

[1] Guizot: Sainte-Aulaire, December 10th, 1840, *Archives Nationales*, 42 A.P. 8; Guizot: Prosper de Barante, December 12th, 1840, Ibid., 42 A.P. 9.

ensure that July 1830 would not be repeated. Thus the government was surrounded by opposition and its situation was not made easier by its own disagreements on this matter. Humann disliked the expense and the former supporters of Molé were concerned at their own position. But the real complication came from Soult himself, who did not agree with the proposed plan, since he preferred a system of separate forts to a fortified wall. Soult and Guizot had never been very close friends. Guizot had no high opinion of Soult's political rôle, and does not seem to have had much real esteem for him as a man. On one occasion when Soult came into the room he was supposed to have said, 'Here comes Soult. Put your hands over your pockets.' The two quarrelled over Algerian affairs in 1834 and were not on speaking terms for three years. Therefore it seemed that the government was in danger both of parliamentary defeat and of internal disrupture.

However, once again it was Thiers who saved Guizot. This time by direct and deliberate action. As this plan for the fortification had been his, he decided that he was honour bound to defend it and to play a prominent part in its passage. He brought with him Rémusat and Odilon Barrot and the greater part of the left. But even this did not avoid the government's embarrassment when Soult, speaking in favour of the project, revealed his criticism of this method and showed his preference for the amendments which had been put forward, some of them by his close associates. It required an intervention by Guizot before the situation could be straightened out. He had, as diplomatically as possible, to point out that the marshal did not show the same skill in parliamentary debate that he had shown on the field of battle. That being so, he had revealed his own opinion on the fortifications, but in reality he had accepted the opinion of the Cabinet on this question, and he supported the proposed plan, or at least Guizot said that he did. After these difficult negotiations, the law was passed by a majority of 75, and Soult, in true Wellingtonian fashion, decided that he had not heard Guizot's explanation of his position. The government had therefore emerged from its second crisis. Guizot wrote to Bourqueney, the chargé d'affaires in London, that the confusion of Constantinople was clarity itself compared to the sort of confusion with which he had had to deal.[1] But the voting was ominous; Thiers brought to the support of the project the greater part of the left; large numbers of the right and right-centre had opposed it. The government therefore had had two successive majorities; it did not yet seem as if it had a majority.

These difficulties were prolonged by the delay in sending the Bill on the fortifications to the Chamber of Peers, and by a series of

[1] Guizot: Bourqueney, January 28th, 1841, *Archives Nationales*, 42 A.P. 9.

disagreements which centred around Marshal Soult. It became known, for example, that Soult considered that his son should be given a high diplomatic post, and was annoyed that Guizot should consider other possibilities. Soult continued to disagree with the Duke of Orleans on military matters, and it began to appear that the ministry might disappear with Soult's resignation, or that it might be killed thanks to Soult's ineptitude. The 'mot' that went round the salons was that Soult was not so much 'an illustrious Sword' as 'an illustrious Scabbard'.

This attack on Soult was an example of a more subtle attack upon the existence of the ministry which became particularly dangerous in February 1841. It was suggested that Guizot's policy of dividing the Chamber into two was both unnatural and dangerous. From the start of his ministry it had been claimed that the real majority of the Chamber lay in the union of the conservatives and what was 'gouvernemental' in the constitutionally-minded left-wing. Without this union the Chamber would move to extremes, and would eventually be divided into an ultra-conservative party and a revolutionary party. It was said that the union of Guizot and Thiers was the natural expression of the real majority in the Chamber. 'They are two halves of a political whole', wrote one commentator, and it was not believed that one of them in isolation could produce a powerful government.[1] After the debates of November the idea of a Guizot-Thiers ministry had to be dropped, but the idea of a ministry drawing its support more from the left was not abandoned. A good opportunity for putting this case came when Jouffroy, reporter of the commission which examined the government's demand for secret funds, advocated a domestic policy of immobilism mixed with repression. This speech, of February 18th, was obviously one which could be expected to render many of the left-centre uneasy. Dufaure and Passy found their differences with the right illuminated by this sort of talk, and Thiers was quick to take advantage of it. On February 25th he made a skilful political speech. Moving a long way from his speeches of 1840, he suggested that in reality there was by this time little difference between the government's policy and his own. What he particularly stressed was the danger of having a majority placed in one of the extremities in the Chamber; what he wanted was to place it in the true middle of parliament. The implication was obvious, and it had all the force of its vagueness; Guizot's majority would disintegrate, and Thiers would help to reform it amongst those who were in favour of moderate reforms and less uniform immobilism. This was not simply an attempt to found a Thiers-Dufaure-Passy government. It was an attempt to rally a new

[1] *Revue des Deux Mondes*, October 31st, 1840, pp. 240 ff.

majority around a principle of activity, and to demonstrate the disagreements of the existing majority.

The same idea was put forward by the *Revue des Deux Mondes*,
whose director, Buloz, was always more favourably inclined to either
Thiers or Molé than to Guizot, and who was opening his review at
this time to Duvergier de Hauranne and to other critics of the government. At the end of March 1841 an article attacked those men who
had been eminent under previous régimes and whose experience was
precious, but who neither understood nor appreciated the type of
régime which had been introduced in 1830. The same article also
attacked those who sought only to ensure the government's existence,
who had been fatigued rather than enlightened by events, and who
tended towards a stationary form of politics. Amongst them
'philosophers' erected this practical conservatism into a system. In
this way Soult, Guizot and much of the majority were attacked; it
was suggested that if the régime was to prosper, a majority capable
only of expediting day-to-day affairs would have to be replaced by
one capable of enterprise and action. The episode of the fortifications
had demonstrated the incapacity of certain individuals (Soult) and
had shown that when something energetic and original was being
attempted, then it was to a different majority that the government
had to turn. It was thus in the name of 'une politique d'action' that
Guizot's government was attacked.[1]

Guizot's reply to such an attack was helped by circumstances.
There was not one attack but two, the Thiers attempt to reform a
government around the majority which had passed the Paris
fortifications law, and the Molé intrigue, notably in the Chamber of
Peers, implicating the legitimists and the Chancellor Pasquier, to
get the law rejected. The differences between Molé and Thiers were
as obvious as those between Molé and Guizot. When Molé was
received at the Académie Française on December 30th, 1840, neither
Guizot nor Thiers were present and absences on such an occasion
were particularly noticed.[2] It was widely felt that a Dufaure-Passy
ministry would be a simple re-edition of the May 12th government
and would not be any more viable. To have such a ministry when
international negotiations were continuing on the Eastern Question
seemed all the more unwise since there were rumours (which were
sedulously encouraged by the Princess Lieven both in her salon and
in her extensive correspondence, as well as by the Tuileries) that
France's diplomatic position was getting stronger every day. This

[1] De La Force du Gouvernement Actuel, *Revue des Deux Mondes*, March 30th,
1841, pp. 304-316.
[2] When Guizot was received at the Academy on December 22nd, 1836, the
absence of Thiers was interpreted as a sign of the rift between them.

seemed to be confirmed by the policy of Palmerston, who with his ambassador at Constantinople, Ponsonby, appeared to be putting as many obstacles as possible in the way of an agreement over Turkish and Egyptian affairs. The obvious disintegration of the Whigs also seemed to herald the coming of a new minister to the Foreign Office; this would be a diplomatic change which a new, uncertain ministerial combination could hardly meet.

Guizot's principal reply to Thiers was to deny the suggestion that the differences between the majority and the opposition were slight. His answer was to remind the Chamber that when the ministry of March 1st was in power, war was certain. 'You can try your best,' he said. 'You can force yourselves to attenuate and to reduce the question; you can try your hardest to make yourselves small today, to try to make yourselves agreeable to the majority which rejected you, you will not deceive them.' It was essential to Guizot to demonstrate that the majority was united in its opposition to the policy of March 1st. If there were, as he admitted, dissensions amongst them on other questions, these were questions which could be left in abeyance for the time being. The Chamber had to remember that it was divided in two, it had to remember the dangers and excitements of the last year.

When Thiers returned to the attack in April Guizot was again able to meet him by insisting upon his past failures. Thiers had hinted that the Middle East agreement, then being negotiated, was disadvantageous, even humiliating for France. Guizot refused to discuss the negotiations. He took up the attitude that it would be incorrect to debate a matter which was then the subject of delicate diplomacy, but he had no hesitation in saying that Thiers was mistaken in his allegations. 'Whatever he may have said,' he commented, 'he is very badly informed and he is lightly skating over a great many things.' He went on to say that he would prove, when the time came, the inexactitude of Thiers's remarks.[1]

These speeches of Guizot were extremely skilful. He was showing himself a master of parliamentary management. Thiers could not oblige the government to say what they thought about Jouffroy's report, nor could he oblige them to divulge the details of their negotiations in London. But Guizot could remind the Chamber of Thiers's past mistakes, and by suggesting that Thiers was continuing to act with a similar jaunty irresponsibility he could further depreciate his reputation. It was all the easier for the Chamber to remember past adventures since they were in process of paying the bills which those incipient adventures had run up. Guizot too was strengthening his

[1] For Guizot's speeches of February 25th, February 27th and April 13th see *Histoire Parlementaire*, vol. iii, pp. 425 ff., pp. 449 ff.

position in the Chamber. One of the doctrinaires. Piscatory, who had split with Guizot in 1840, accepted to go on a mission to Greece. Other deputies began to show interest in the diplomatic movement which Guizot was preparing, and the very slowness of the preparation was valuable in this respect. Eventually de Flahault was removed from the orbit of Thiers and sent to Vienna, Salvandy was removed from Molé and sent to Madrid. A reconciliation with Royer-Collard, whilst only superficial, helped to lessen at least one centre of personal animosity. Dufaure and Passy maintained their hostility to Thiers and waited for others to join their group rather than for their group to commit itself to any of the opposition leaders. The rumours of impending dissolution caused a general reflection amongst deputies, and reflection in the French Chamber was invariably the promoter of inactivity.

'Let the impression of danger be maintained and our success will be maintained also . . . I will do my best to see to it that as peril becomes more distant it is not lost sight of completely.'[1] So wrote Guizot in December 1840. He had succeeded in reminding the Chamber of this, with Thiers's unwitting assistance, but in the summer and autumn of 1841 a wave of popular disturbances and disorders served his purpose even more effectively. The Finance Minister Humann, worried by the size of the deficit and by the inadequacy of the receipts, decided to apply the provisions of a law passed in 1838 by carrying out a national survey of built-up property and of personal taxation, with a view both to increasing the revenue and to making the distribution of tax-payments amongst departments more equitable. He announced this plan by a circular to the prefects on February 25th, 1841, and by a circular to all agents of the Treasury on the next day. In April the minister was criticized for this action in the Chamber, and he defended himself with a number of unfortunate phrases. These were taken up by the opposition press with alacrity. His remark that if one was to protect oneself against the rest of Europe then one had to have a dictatorship, was taken as an attack against representative government. The investigation of personal properties and situations was seen as an attack on liberty and as a brake on progress. Humann was said to be a minister without ideas, who would fail to meet the deficit with such trifling methods. His honesty was called into question, and it was fortunate for the opposition that amongst the latest appointments to Treasury jobs which he had just announced were those of his own nephew, a nephew of Guizot's and a nephew of Duperré's (the Minister of the Marine). Stimulated by this newspaper hostility, local committees

---

[1] Guizot: Bresson (Ambassador in Berlin), December 12th, 1840, *Archives Nationales*, 42 A.P. 8.

and organizations began to be set up and resistance was organized.

The disorders lasted from July until October. They did not affect the whole of the country, being mainly concentrated around the four centres of Toulouse, Bordeaux, Clermont and Lille. They varied from place to place. Usually barricades were erected, peasants came from outlying villages, with firearms and other weapons, and the investigating officials were met with cries of 'down with the government!' or more musically with the 'Marseillaise' or the 'Parisienne'; Humann and Guizot were hung in effigy, and it was proudly proclaimed that the tax-collector 'would not get through'. But whereas in some places, such as Toulouse, the municipality and even some of the government officials showed sympathy for this movement, in other places it was the legitimist and republican newspapers, the secret societies and anti-bourgeois sentiments which seemed to inspire a nineteenth-century form of 'jacquerie'. Today one is struck by the anti-centralization and anti-Paris sentiment of this movement. It represented a form of federalism, and it looked forward to later provincial protestations against taxation.[1]

An attempt to assassinate the Duc d'Aumale in September appeared as the dramatic symbol of this movement. The opposition could claim that the government had created it by their ineptitude; but the sentiment of danger was more widespread, the fragility of the régime more evident. Although Duvergier de Hauranne was to repeat the idea of a transaction amongst the different groups so as to create a new majority, this idea had by the end of 1841 made little progress. Guizot, in December, wrote that he would try to bring issues before the Chamber in the form of battles, rather than allow them to proceed as intrigues. The form of a parliamentary battle was favourable to the administration, and Guizot therefore looked forward to a series of dramatic parliamentary demonstrations of strength. He realized that there was one disadvantage of such tactics, that he was at the mercy of accidents and of all 'l'imprévu parlementaire'.[2] But he did not seem aware of the other danger: whilst to emphasize the revolutionary character of the opposition might succeed in immediately discrediting the opposition, it might also make the idea of revolution more widespread, more inevitable and even more respectable.

By the end of 1841 and the beginning of 1842 the Chamber of

[1] See *Roubaud*, 'Les troubles du rencensement sous la monarchie de Juillet', *Bulletin mensuel de la Société d'Histoire Moderne*, June 1914, pp. 331 ff.; *Ponteil*, 'Le Ministre des Finances Georges Humann et les émeutes antifiscales en 1841', *Revue Historique*, January-June 1937, vol. 179, pp. 311 ff.

[2] Guizot: Sainte-Aulaire, December 16th, 1841, Ibid., 42 A.P. 8.

Deputies was divided into two in the sense that there were only two possible leaders, Guizot or Thiers. De Tocqueville explained to Royer-Collard that the only source of strength was to be found either in uniting Thiers and Guizot or in using the one against the other. Salvandy did not think that any government was possible in the Chamber if it did not contain either Thiers or Guizot.[1] Molé was undoubtedly a declining force. In March of 1841 he wrote of his own ministerial career as being finished,[2] and in so far as his only real source of political strength had come from the King, once he had lost royal support then he was a spent force, unable even to take part in the most vital debates since he was a member of the Chamber of Peers and only able to sit in the Deputies when a minister. Molé's activity against the government over the Paris fortifications particularly annoyed the King, who was to be further displeased in 1842 with Molé's intrigue in the diplomatic corps against the customs union with Belgium. In this way, Molé tended to decline as a possible alternative to Guizot, and Thiers became the real leader of the opposition.

This was a situation which suited Guizot. He was always reasonably confident of success against Thiers. This was not because he underestimated him. On the contrary, he was careful to point out his abilities. He saw him as a master of intrigue, 'le grand joueur des marionettes', offering on the one hand a version of Molé's April 15th government, with the other hand offering a reconstitution of Soult's May 12th, promising to support any government from which Guizot was excluded. He saw him as 'a most intelligent leader, extremely active, skilful in upsetting and confusing everything, capable of risking everything'; he described him as 'a man who excels at exploiting and at fomenting the prejudices, passions, stray impulses, memories and instincts which are echoed by this party [the left] and which are still powerful in the country'.[3] He saw the danger of a defeated opposition, uniting itself behind Thiers. But in spite of all this he was able to note that the Chamber did not respond to Thiers and his suggestions, and in particular that the Dufaure and Passy group did not listen to him. He based his confidence on the King's support, on the knowledge that elections were forthcoming, and on his conviction that whilst his opponents could form a powerful opposition, divisions amongst them were such that they would not be able to form an effective government.

[1] Tocqueville: Royer-Collard, September 25th, 1841, ibid., p. 906; Salvandy's letter of February 1842 is quoted by the *Duchesse de Dino*, see below, vol. iii, pp. 162-164.

[2] See the *Duchesse de Dino, Chronique de 1831 à 1862* (edited by Princess Radziwill) Paris, 1909, vol. iii, p. 41.

[3] Guizot: Sainte-Aulaire, December 16th, 1841, June 18th, 1842, Ibid.

It was true that Thiers was not making progress. He was spurred on by Duvergier de Hauranne, who remained in opposition and who added personal spite to his attacks of principle when Duchâtel removed a sub-prefect in the Cher who was a protégé of Duvergier's; but Duvergier did not see much that was encouraging. He regretted Thiers's failure to win over Dufaure, and thought that Thiers had been unjust towards him. He commented on Rémusat's lack of interest in political affairs, and advised Thiers to do something about this if he wanted to have a party which 'looked well'. (It was at this time that Rémusat was writing his drama *Abélard*, from which he used to give readings in various salons.) He also emphasized that Buloz, director of the *Revue des Deux Mondes*, who had published a lot of opposition articles, was becoming less certain in his attitude, and was under pressure from Guizot to drop some of his collaborators and to give the 'Chronique Politique' to Rossi, a friend of Guizot's. All these were details, whilst the great difficulty was to form a party which would be independent both of the monarchy and of democracy; this was a party the elements of which did not seem to exist in France. They therefore had to be created.

But Duvergier's chief worry was his need to stimulate Thiers, to throw him into activity. 'When the leader seems to be withdrawing from the battle, then the soldiers are easily induced to follow his example,' he wrote. He reminded Thiers that in England party leaders were prepared to speak on all subjects, and he pointed out that in this respect Thiers had a great advantage over Guizot. Guizot was accepted as being supreme on the great occasions, when affairs had reached 'a certain diapason'; but in the ordinary everyday discussions Guizot was said to have little understanding of affairs and it was on these matters that Thiers could and should excel. It was necessary that Thiers should speak in debate and speak often, that he should intervene actively and by personal influence keep his party together.[1] But Duvergier was rarely satisfied that Thiers was taking his advice.

Thiers was admittedly in a difficult situation, and one might say that he always remained in the same precarious position that he had occupied in 1840. He wanted to place himself on the popular side; temperamentally he sought the support of the left. But he realized that if he was to be successful in France then he needed the support of the centres and possibly of the right, and he realized too that he should not break with the King: rationally therefore he sought the support of the right-centre. Thus political discussion was for him a

[1] Duvergier de Hauranne: Thiers, June 11th, June 17th, September 23rd, November 13th, November 30th, 1841, together with one undated letter, *Papiers Thiers*, Bibliothèque Nationale, Nouv. acq. 20616.

perpetual 'tour de force'. By resounding and daring language he appealed to instincts and sentiment; by careful and calculated conversation he tried to demonstrate his value to reason and interest. He had to ingratiate himself to those who disliked him; he had to force himself on those who distrusted him. He rarely made debate more thoughtful, he made it more dramatic. He did not seek to popularize ideas, but rather to vulgarize attitudes. He grasped issues as they appeared and treated them on their immediate merits without reference to his earlier opinions. 'Monsieur Thiers is like the earth, he turns round without realizing it,' was Jules Simon's comment. Such versatility had to conceal irresponsibility, and much astuteness was necessary to hide the barrenness of his political thought. In Thiers there were unplumbed depths of shallowness.

He was an actor rather than a statesman, and Guizot once said that with all his talent, Thiers remained a mere imitator. 'At one time he imitates Louis XIV, at another the Jacobins; today the Directory and tomorrow Napoleon. It seems as though, notwithstanding his knowledge of the modern history of France, he has no other way of helping himself out of a difficult case than by asking himself "how would the monarchy, how would the republic, how would the empire have acted under these circumstances?" '[1] But at the same time this dramatic, restless intelligence was quick to tire of such barren activity, and he was anxious to find other fields where he might distinguish himself. In 1841 he visited Holland and Germany in search of material for his book on Napoleon. He was received not as one of many politicians but as a writer whose history of the Consulate and Empire was expected to be a work of European importance. It was noticed that he took great pleasure in wearing his Academician's uniform. 'Thiers the opposition leader' appeared a less attractive rôle than that of 'Thiers the historian of Napoleon'. He had written to Buloz in July, 'I must tell you that as each day I am more attracted to politics on the grand scale, so each day I am less attracted to politics on the small scale, and for me the small scale means what is done from day to day, according to circumstances. This daily bread on which they live in Paris creates in me a disgust which I can hardly overcome. I am a strong supporter of our institutions, since I know of no others which are possible, but they do turn government into a talking-shop. The opposition only speaks in order to embarrass the government this week, whilst the government only acts in order to forestall what somebody will say next week. Everyone is more or less attached to this yoke and whoever tries to see further lacks the sense of relevance which is an indispensable

[1] Guizot made this remark in conversation with Gutzkow. See *Gutzkow, Brief aus Paris (1842); Pariser Endrüche 1846.* Frankfurt 1846.

condition for succeeding in such a changing world! It is a real sacrifice for me to return to such a restricted and agitated present . . .'[1] Naturally there were those who gave less creditable reasons as explanations for Thiers's conduct. Just as it was said that he had continued to support the Paris fortifications, since had they been abandoned questions would have been asked about the money already spent on them and about Thiers's conduct in authorizing the work, so it was rumoured that Thiers had already spent the money which his publishers had advanced on his historical works and that he was being pressed to produce a completed manuscript.

At all events, the course of 1842 saw a further 'volte face' in the position of Thiers, which helped to consolidate Guizot in power, at a time when he might well have anticipated a serious offensive against his government. Guizot had attached great importance to the elections of 1842. Just as the government had survived its first session by basing itself upon the idea of peace, so he thought that he would survive the second session by the idea of imminent elections. The government approached these elections in July 1842 with considerable confidence. Of the 459 elections, Guizot estimated that only 110 would be seriously contested, 70 of these being in circonscriptions held by a member of the opposition, and 40 being held by government supporters (a situation which suggests a similar degree of political choice to that existing in England in 1841, when electoral contests occurred in about 190 constituencies out of 401, or in 1847, when the figure was lower).[2] The government was confident of winning at least some of these doubtful elections, but would have been pleased even had its majority remained unchanged, since all governments since 1830 had seen their majorities reduced in elections. The elections were at first quiet and seemed to be occurring in an atmosphere of calm, even of indifference, which most observers thought would be favourable to the type of reflection which the government was asking the elector to make, comparing the high expenditure of Thiers to their own, more stable, prosperity. It was only at the last moment that the opposition was able to excite feeling against the government, accusing them of being subservient to the English since they had signed a treaty with England which gave British warships the right to search French ships suspected of taking part in the African slave trade. It appeared to the government that this 'right of search' question was the explanation of the opposition's success, in so far as government expectations were disappointed. Duvergier de Hauranne was satisfied with the results, but it was typical of French

[1] Quoted by *Charles de Mazade* in Le Fondateur de la Revue des Deux Mondes—François Buloz. *Revue des Deux Mondes*, June 1st, 1877, p. 499.
[2] Guizot: Sainte-Aulaire, June 18th, 1842, Ibid.

THE SOULT-GUIZOT GOVERNMENT

politics that no one could calculate the relative positions of government and opposition. Duvergier accused the *Journal des Débats* of falsifying the results when it spoke of a government majority of 70; the election of a number of new deputies made the calculation of the all-important floating vote particularly difficult. However, observers had only time to appreciate the uncertainty of the situation and to note how in certain areas, including Paris, the government had suffered a set-back, when on July 13th, 1842, the Duke of Orleans was killed in an accident. The heir to the throne of the ageing King was a little boy, and no one could doubt but that the Orleanist régime was seriously weakened.

Politically, the death of the Duke led to a great deal of discussion. Some provision had to be made for a Regency, and the new Parliament was called to discuss this question in August. Many people felt that as the dynasty had been weakened, it could no longer allow itself to be represented by an unpopular government such as Guizot's, which had so recently demonstrated its failure to hold the country. The name of Molé was relaunched as a probable alternative to Guizot. Other observers believed that Guizot would derive great strength from this situation, since once again danger was apparent and the sentiment of danger would rekindle the loyalty of his most reluctant supporters. Not many people thought that Thiers's chances had improved. Duvergier de Hauranne, always busy and optimistic, spoke of a reconstitution of the government of March 1st, with the left-centre uniting the moderates of the left to a numerous fraction of the conservatives. The chances of such a manœuvre, as he saw it, had been improved by the number of left-centre electoral successes, which he calculated as 12. Had they won as many as 25, then he thought that success would have been absolutely certain.[1] But other observers believed that the situation had been radically altered by the accident to the Duke, and they pointed out that the whole basis of Thiers's political action had disappeared. According to Merruau, of *Le Constitutionnel*, a paper which usually expressed Thiers's views, over the past years Thiers had depended upon 'the reaction of national sentiment against the foreigner'. Ever since the decision had to be taken for or against intervention in Spain (1836), it had been known that Thiers was in constant opposition to the King. Many intelligent people considered that the King was too forgetful of how an opportune and skilfully managed war could make thrones popular and consolidate dynasties. Throughout France there was a growing feeling that sufficient sacrifices had been made to peace, and the anti-English movement which was to be found everywhere in the country showed a growing disposition in favour of some sort of foreign action.

[1] Duvergier de Hauranne: Thiers, July 21st, 1842, *Papiers Thiers*, Ibid.

194

This was a movement which Thiers could regulate and direct, if not under Louis-Philippe, then under his successor. The various oppositions in the country had all used Thiers. The legitimists, those who were opposed to the King's systematic peace policy, the republicans who reproached Thiers with being insufficiently ambitious, and the dynastic left which wanted certain specific reforms. Thiers's position was therefore strong, and in the elections the government saw all its candidates deserting, like rats which foresaw the collapse of a building. Whether they wanted it or not, the legitimists and the radicals were soldiers enrolled in Thiers's army. This, according to Merruau, was the situation which had been completely changed by the death of the Duke of Orleans. If France had lacked the necessary energy to run the risks of war when the dynastic succession was assured, then how could one expect the energy to be forthcoming when the dynasty was once again threatened from within by the republic and by the pretenders? Thiers should therefore concentrate on making the dynasty both popular and secure. In other words, he had to change the whole nature of his policy.[1]

Thiers was very likely influenced by this advice. In his continual 'politique de bascule' it was time to turn more completely to the right, to emphasize Thiers the statesman, Thiers the responsible defender of the monarchy and of the country's institutions. This was the type of action for which Thiers had been impatient. It broke with 'the daily bread' of Chamber politics, and distinguished Thiers from an opposition which opposed systematically and mechanically. It pleased the King, and in the eyes of everyone helped to make Thiers more 'possible' amongst the alternatives to Guizot. Above all, such an action was a skilful remedy. Before July 13th, Thiers was the obvious leader of the opposition; after July 13th, it seemed unlikely that power could be entrusted to anyone so involved with the left; after August 20th, when he supported the government's project for a Regency, according to the principles of male succession, he once again became 'available'.

The result of Thiers's action was not only the government's success, only 94 deputies voted against the Regency law, but a public split in the opposition. Thiers and Odilon Barrot had taken sharply differing attitudes, although on the eve of the debate Thiers believed that he had persuaded Barrot, Tocqueville and others to support the government's law, at least tacitly. Thiers spoke on August 20th in answer to Barrot's unexpected attack on the law, and his action was

[1] Merruau: Thiers, July 15th, 1842, *Papiers Thiers*, Ibid. On Merruau, a former associate of Victor Cousin, see *Véron, Mémoires d'un Bourgeois de Paris*, Paris 1856, vol iii, pp. 292 ff.

therefore more dramatic than he had earlier intended. It was, however, none the less pleasing to Thiers for this reason. At all events, the result was that Duvergier de Hauranne, who had earlier thought of Odilon Barrot as holding an important post in the next Thiers government and who had been thinking in terms of unity, by September and October was stressing the need to divide the left into two, and to create in the left-centre a real 'juste-milieu' party. At times he showed some nostalgia for past ideas. He regretted that Thiers despised the left so much. He reminded him that when people voted they voted either with black or with white balls, there were no grey ones.[1] The result was also the withdrawal of Thiers from political activity. In the course of the session of 1843 he did not speak once. Content with the approbation that his action had received from the King and from many other personalities, including some which were unexpected,[2] he decided to allow these favourable opinions to mature, whilst he devoted himself to the writing of history, and awaited the appropriate moment to reappear.

It is rare for a government's chief opponent to disappear overnight, and Guizot himself wondered whether Thiers supporting the Regency law was not more dangerous to him than Thiers in opposition. But he rightly concluded that the split in the opposition could only be to the government's advantage.[3] The eighteen months' political silence of Thiers was equally to the government's advantage, but one further consequence of all this requires to be shown. With the opposition disunited and its leader absent, there was another volatile and enthusiastic politician who was prepared to offer himself to the Chamber and to the newspapers, Alphonse de Lamartine. The nature of his opposition had a significance of its own.

It is easy for the historian to underestimate Lamartine's importance in 1842, 1843 and the years which follow. It is true that he showed an almost monstrous egotism in any evaluation which he made of his own activity. He had in 1840 considered himself as a serious candidate for office, and in December 1840 he described the Soult-Guizot government as 'trembling between Monsieur Thiers and myself',[4] which was not a very just appreciation of how the government stood. In 1839 he had tried to form a 'social party' amongst the

---

[1] Duvergier de Hauranne: Thiers, September 2nd, October 1st, October 15th, 1842, *Papiers Thiers*, Ibid.

[2] For example the 'Bonapartist' Gustave de Romand: Thiers, October 16th, 1842, *Papiers Thiers*, Ibid.

[3] Guizot: Laure de Gasparin, August 27th, 1842, *Guizot et Madame de Gasparin* (op. cit.), pp. 227-228.

[4] Lamartine: Louis de Pierreclos, December 3rd, 1840, *Correspondance de Lamartine*, edited by Mme Valentine de Lamartine, Paris 1873-1874, 2nd edition, vol. iv, pp. 85-86.

221 who had supported Molé, but he had scarcely got beyond announcing that this party was 'an idea'. In December 1841 he had been a candidate for the presidency of the Chamber, a political act which had pleased Duvergier de Hauranne as a sign of anti-Guizot feeling on the right. He had, however, rallied little support in the centres, and Sauzet, the ministerial candidate, had been elected. It seemed as if there was a great disparity between Lamartine's conception of his own importance and reality, and that his action in 1843 was a desperate attempt to impose himself on the Chamber and to wipe out his earlier failures. 'It is the death of the Duke of Orleans which has turned his head,' commented Sainte-Beuve. Other observers were equally unimpressed. It was pointed out that he had little to offer the opposition in the form of ideas, even in political understanding. Known for his impetuous enthusiasms, it was expected that he would soon tire of political strife, and that his Saturday evening salons in the Rue de l'Université would soon turn to literature, that his political activity in his château of Monceau, near to Mâcon, would soon give way to the more imaginative preoccupations of the traveller and writer. People recalled that when he served on the Commission of the Chamber which examined the legislation concerning railways, he professed to find everything easy, but in reality he never understood the first thing about economics. It was said that in a letter from Lamartine the second page contradicted the first, and that he never made a speech without uttering at least one misconception. 'He changes, too often, his "idée fixe",' was Madame de Girardin's phrase, whilst Béranger remarked 'Lamartine does not realize what ideas he has'. Even in the Chamber, the deputies got tired of his oratory, there were a number of occasions when he failed to get a hearing, and frequently the appearance of Lamartine at the tribune was the signal for newspapers to be opened. He presented a fine target for Guizot, who in 1843 was able to direct a precise and ironic speech against his sonorous but empty phraseology. In 1843, too, Lamartine was in a difficult personal situation. His debts were mounting and by the end of the year they were said to be about one million francs. In July 1843 he had accepted the idea of writing a history of the Girondins, but the exigencies of his publisher made the negotiations which preceded the signing of the contract long and difficult. It did not seem that Lamartine would be able to do more in the political field than make more than a few startling speeches. For all that he had hailed his entry into politics as being his adieu to verse (but not to poetry), it looked as if he would still be obliged to produce verse if only to satisfy his publishers.

It would seem then that Lamartine's intervention, his announcement that he had entered the opposition 'pour toujours', and his speech of January 27th, 1843, attacking the government, was an advantage for the government, and comparable to Thiers's withdrawal. But Lamartine's opposition was not the same as that of Thiers or of Molé. There was something in his grand manner that the others did not have, and that was a refusal to play the political game. Both Thiers and Molé were striving to oust Guizot and either immediately, or at least presently, to replace him. They wanted the system which had been in operation since 1830 to continue and they remained, in their different ways, 'orchestrators' of the parliamentary crises. But to Lamartine such objectives were uninteresting; it was a wretched occupation simply to overthrow a government; he wanted to conquer power, and to impose his ideas. Nothing suggested that he was prepared to work within the same framework as the others. His interpretation of 'democracy', his attacks on despotism, his call to 'another generation of ideas which is not asleep', suggested that it was amongst other institutions that he imagined his success. Nor did there seem to be any likelihood of his collaborating with the other political leaders of the Chamber. 'Guizot, Molé, Thiers, Passy, Dufaure', he once enumerated. 'Five ways of saying the same word. They bore me. . . . Let the devil conjugate them as he will.'[1] It was not surprising, therefore, that Lamartine did not confine himself to attacking one particular government, nor one particular minister; he attacked the whole of the reign, the whole thought and ideology of the régime, the whole system of government.

The government, therefore, was not faced by an opponent in the person of Lamartine. They were faced by a revolutionary, and this was a noticeable distinction between Lamartine and Thiers. And whilst the government had no apparent difficulty in discrediting Lamartine in the Chamber of Deputies, another distinction between the two lay in Lamartine's position in the country. Thiers once told a German visitor that the poor quality of many speeches in the Chamber was to be explained by the desire of certain deputies to have speeches printed in their local papers which their electors could read, and no one, not even themselves, had any other interest in them. But Lamartine's speeches, whilst they failed to impress his colleagues, contained phrases which echoed around France and which still find their way into every textbook which covers this period. The author of *Elvire* had an audience which was ready-made. He is supposed to have said that he would always have the women and the young men on his side and the *Revue des Deux Mondes*, sharply critical of his political rôle, noted his increasing popularity outside the Chamber.[2] He was compared to Daniel O'Connell, he drew vast crowds wherever

[1] October 5th, 1842, quoted in *Thureau-Dangin* (op. cit.), vol. v, p. 146 note 4.
[2] *Revue des Deux Mondes*, April 1st, 1843, p. 167.

he spoke (especially in the Midi), and Michelet claimed that Lamartine had provided France with a political gospel. The table on which he had stood when speaking at Mâcon was sold for 200 francs. That this was for a politician who treated the régime as a 'bloc' which he opposed was certainly significant. Lamartine had intuitively discovered what Tocqueville had rationally seen when he had expressed dissatisfaction that his political choice was limited to Guizot or Thiers, or both together.[1] Lamartine, too, had intuitively dealt with another of Tocqueville's complaints. When the latter had thought of excusing the deputies who considered only their own personal interests, he argued that they had taken themselves for the subjects of their thoughts and actions 'faute de mieux', because there was nothing else which could attract or satisfy them. Lamartine tried to provide an ideal by launching the social question. It recurred in his writings and speeches, and for all that his ideas were vague, they were ardent and generous. This preoccupation linked Lamartine with certain other deputies, notably Billault, the deputy for Nantes, who had made a name for himself by his attacks on England, but whose concern for social reform distinguished him from politicians such as Thiers or Barrot.[2] Lamartine therefore should not be seen as an isolated egocentric. His intervention was both important for the future and symptomatic of the present.

Thus the Soult-Guizot ministry continued in office. Its majority in the 1842-1843 session was normally about 45. In April 1842 the finance minister Humann had died suddenly, and Guizot, having tried to interest Passy in the post, had strengthened his position on the right by making Lacave-Laplagne, a former Molé supporter, the new minister. In January 1843 Molé tried to organize a big intrigue against the minister, in co-operation with Dufaure and Passy, the basis of which was the rumour that the government was considering a customs union with Belgium. Such an association would have presented great political advantages to France, but would have opened an appreciable gap in the system of tariff protection. Hence it was expected that many particular French interests would oppose such a measure, which could prove costly to them, and it was this opposition which Molé hoped to capture. It does seem certain that Guizot did, in the recess of 1842, turn to the left, and that he did ask the newspaper Le Courrier to support his plan; and it was rumoured that the king intended to ask Thiers for his support.[3] But in fact the government was not strong enough to carry out the plan of 'association' and the idea was shelved. This removed the mainspring of

[1] Tocqueville: Royer-Collard, September 25th, 1841, Ibid., p. 906.
[2] See *Theodore Zelden, The Political System of Napoleon III*, 1958, pp. 67-68.
[3] Léon Faucher: Thiers, October 14th, 1842, *Papiers Thiers*, ibid.

Molé's action; he was only able to influence a handful of deputies; Dufaure and Passy, after much hesitation, decided to abandon Molé, and Guizot (who had asked Laure de Gasparin to pray that his throat would last out) spoke to great effect, rallying the waverers. Once again, by March 1843 Molé was convinced that his political career was over and spoke of retiring to a purely private life.[1]

But because the government remained in power, and was breaking all the records for ministerial longevity, was it essentially strong? Its opponents claimed that it had stayed in power only because of the 1840 war-scare and because of the 1842 royal bereavement. Undoubtedly the government had benefited from the division of its opponents, from the temperament of Thiers and from the hesitations of Dufaure and Passy. Guizot had overcome some difficulties by emphasizing national dangers, he had avoided other difficulties by shelving items of policy and withdrawing legislation. Both were the methods of a weak government. It was pointed out that if only twenty deputies changed sides in the Chamber, then the Cabinet would fall. It was claimed that many supported the government without enthusiasm or confidence, only because there was no obvious successor, and it was said that many of those who voted for the government on the question of confidence were its adversaries when it came to legislation. Thus hostile commentators consoled themselves for their failure to oust the government by the thought that Guizot's authority was nominal rather than real, that his majority was only temporary and political, not governmental and administrative, that he was at the mercy of any unpredictable incident.[2] They might have added that the government had met the challenge of Lamartine only in the Chamber; they had not met his challenge in the country.

But the problem remained for the opposition, on what topic would they attack the Cabinet? For the session of 1844, political issues seemed to be dead. Although Thiers broke his long silence, and attacked the government as being unable to govern, unable to deploy a sufficiently large majority with which to direct the country, this argument did not move the Chamber. Such a speech could have been effective had it been made immediately after the elections, before certain deputies had decided upon their attitudes. But it was unlikely that deputies would leave the majority unless Thiers presented them with an issue. The idea of parliamentary reform was not then thought

[1] *Duchesse de Dino*, op. cit., vol. iii, pp. 243-244.
[2] See for example the articles signed 'Un Deputé' published in the *Revue des Deux Mondes* during 1843.

to be opportune. Any change in the law concerning the possibility of being both deputy and government official would have meant new elections, and no one was anxious to have elections so soon after 1842. Hence when this question was raised it did not bring enthusiasm to the opposition, nor did it receive support. There was only one subject on which the opposition was able to criticize the government consistently and regularly, and that was the issue of foreign policy. There was only one form of tactics on which the opposition was able to whip up support, find sympathetic listeners on all sides of the Chamber, and appreciative newspaper readers in all parts of the country, and that was the attack on Guizot personally. There was only one question which arose naturally from the country, and which the opposition was able to utilize, and that was the religious issue, particularly as it concerned education and the Jesuits.

The criticism of the government's foreign policy was given an obvious lead by the reference in the King's speech to the 'entente cordiale' (on December 27th, 1843), and it was relatively easy for speakers such as Billault to show that the interests of the two countries were antagonistic one to another, rather than complementary. It was relatively simple to question the value of this agreement, to recall the events of 1840 and insist on the force of anti-English feeling, to suggest that this was a one-sided understanding, advantageous to the English but not the French. It was always possible to exploit each of the foreign policy questions as they occurred, to press the government for information when negotiations were taking place, to make unfounded allegations. There was no shortage of subject matter. There were the complicated politics of Spain and of Greece; there was the war in Algeria which involved France in war with Morocco, when in 1844 the Algerian rebel leader Abd el Kader withdrew his forces on to Moroccan territory; there was a quarrel with England over French naval action in Tahiti, the alleged mistreatment of the English missionary and consul Pritchard following upon the deposition of the Queen and the annexation of the islands over which France had a protectorate; there were rumours of a commercial treaty between England and France and it was necessary to come to some agreement upon measures to suppress the slave-trade. These were topics which the opposition could exploit. The allegations that the government was behaving as if France were a second-class power found an echo in the newspapers; deputies were worried lest they should be thought unpatriotic, and when the opposition press began to publish the names of government supporters under the heading of 'Pritchardistes', deputies were worried as to the effect of all this on their electoral prospects. In Paris it was always possible to assemble a crowd to shout 'Down with Guizot!' along with 'Down with

Pritchard!',[1] and it seemed that similar sentiments existed in the provinces also.

Yet this instence on foreign affairs had serious weaknesses as a means of overthrowing the government. The opposition was itself at the mercy of events, and when Guizot was able to suggest that the overthrow of Espartero in Spain (1843) and the revolution in Greece (1844) were French successes, when he showed that the Moroccan treaty was based upon French military and naval victories, when the affair of the right of search was terminated by a new agreement in May 1845, then it was the opposition which was discomfited. Even in the most difficult question, Tahiti, Guizot claimed a victory, since the French protectorate which had been established in 1842 was maintained, and since the expelled missionary and ex-consul Pritchard was not allowed to return to the island. The opposition was tempted into gambling on isolated matters. They hoped that when Bugeaud returned from Algeria he would let it be known that in the Moroccan negotiations, terms favourable to France were watered down in deference to England. When Bugeaud failed to say this publicly, the opposition were disappointed. They were disappointed too that Louis-Philippe's visit to England in the autumn of 1844 was apparently successful, the King being enthusiastically received. A number of people, including Lamartine, saw this as a welcome extension of French influence. There can be little doubt that the 'entente cordiale' served Guizot well in his parliamentary difficulties; only occasionally did Sir Robert Peel fail to guard his language, whilst Lord Aberdeen sometimes appeared to be as worried about Guizot's majority as Guizot himself. Thus the opposition did not get as much help from the behaviour of the British government as they could have wished.

It should also be noticed that Guizot defended his foreign policy with a very real talent. His debating technique was never better. When faced with Thiers's appeal to reason in his attempt to demonstrate the uselessness of the 'entente', he answered with reference to Thiers's past policy and to his inefficacious threats of war. When faced with impassioned appeals for action in support of French honour and French interests, he made his own appeals to reason. 'For war to arise out of all this,' he wrote to Lord Brougham, referring to the Moroccan and Tahitian affairs, 'then either the mad will have become masters, or the wise will have become mad.'[2] This appeal to reason was heard in the Chamber, and it was particularly

---

[1] *Flaubert* in *L'Éducation Sentimentale*, however, has them shouting 'À bas Pritchard' before any of the relevant incidents took place.

[2] Guizot: Brougham, August 30th, 1844, *Brougham Papers*, 10, 556, University College Library, London.

well received in one part of the Chamber where the opposition were looking for votes, that is to say in the centre, particularly around Passy and his friends. Passy and a number of other deputies were hostile to the territorial aggrandisement of France, whether in Algeria or in the Pacific, and were decidedly hostile to the idea of an adventurous and expensive foreign policy. They were therefore completely unresponsive to these particular efforts of the opposition.[1] Furthermore, in the country as a whole, as Duvergier de Hauranne noted with regret, people were becoming more attached to the idea of peace.[2] Not all the opposition leaders approved of this whipping-up of anti-English feeling; some, such as Tocqueville, felt that it was dangerous to revive old hatreds in this way.

The policy of Thiers, Barrot, Billault and others therefore made the opposition more dangerous, but it did not better their claim as an alternative government. Much the same could be said of their attack on Guizot personally. It was invariably linked with his foreign policy, and to his supposed subservience to English ideas. He was often called 'Lord Guizot' and 'Sir Guizot' by these critics, and as such he was frequently the subject of their satires and lampoons. This is a fairly typical example:

> Nous avons pour ministre un Englishmann bâtard,
> Très-humble serviteur du révérend Pritchard,
> Qui, de nos ennemis caressant l'insolence,
> De concert avec eux veut avilir la France.[3]

But these personal attacks were not only associated with foreign policy. The most dramatic of all these episodes took place in January 1844, and arose out of the journey to England undertaken by the Duke of Bordeaux, grandson of Charles X and pretender to the throne, towards the end of 1843. Whilst staying in Belgrave Square, London, he received several deputations of French royalists who had crossed the Channel in order to assure him of their loyalty and to toast him as their King. There were probably some 500 'pilgrims' in all, including six deputies (one of whom was Berryer), two peers and Chateaubriand. It was natural that the French government should ask the Chamber to condemn this disloyalty in strong terms. A similar procedure had been followed when a handful of deputies and peers had attended the funeral of Charles X. But the government soon found itself exposed to a dangerous tactical manœuvre. It was suggested that in the address which the Chamber was to vote in reply to the King's speech, the word 'flétrir', or 'brands', should be used,

[1] See a note from Jules Le Chevalier concerning the existence of an 'Anti-English League' in Paris, given to the British ambassador, July 24th, 1844. P.R.O., F.O., 84/586.
[2] Duvergier de Hauranne: Thiers, October 13th, 1843, *Papiers Thiers*, ibid.
[3] *Marcelle, Guizot et Napoléon*, Paris (undated).

and the Chamber was asked to approve the phrase 'this Chamber brands such guilty manifestations'. It seemed that this wording was too strong. But if the government had made other suggestions this could have been represented as showing indifference to the dynasty. Furthermore, a government supporter, Jacqueminot, said that if the government dropped the word, then he would propose using it in an amendment. The government therefore, outmanœuvred, went unwillingly forward with this strong condemnation of legitimist loyalties. All sides of the opposition were thus given a great opportunity to attack Guizot personally.

It had frequently been recalled by Guizot's critics that during the Hundred Days, before Waterloo, he had left France and gone to see Louis XVIII, who was then living in Ghent. He went as the emissary of the constitutional royalists, with the mission of persuading the King to get rid of his extremist advisers and to affirm his confidence in constitutional government. It was argued that if it was a betrayal to visit the Duke of Bordeaux in peace-time, was it not a greater and more shameful betrayal to have made such a journey in war-time, when the enemies of France were invading the country? It was said therefore that no government containing Guizot, 'the man of Ghent', could condemn in such terms the pilgrims to Belgrave Square. Guizot defended himself in detail. He admitted his journey to Ghent and sought, in a most provocative way, to justify it. His speech therefore led to a scene of prolonged violence and clamour which contemporaries compared to certain sessions of the Convention. It was frequently impossible for Guizot to make himself heard; it seemed as if the whole Chamber was on its feet, hurling the insult of traitor and demanding that Guizot should withdraw; he remained at the tribune for nearly two hours, asserting that the interruptions might delay him in his speech, but that they would never prevent him from saying what he had to say. 'You may perhaps exhaust my physical strength but you cannot quell my courage . . . as to the insults, calumnies and theatrical rage directed against me, they may be multiplied and accumulated as you please, but they will never rise above my contempt.' It was with this superb scorn and disdain that Guizot met these attacks; he spoke in all three times in the one day, and retired to the Princess Lieven's in a state of complete exhaustion. The next day, after great uncertainty, the government had a majority of 30.

The opposition jubilation was considerable. They had concerted their scene; what had appeared to be a spontaneous explosion had been carefully prepared. Some 20 or 25 conservatives who owed their election to legitimist support, had voted with the opposition. Many of those who had supported the government considered that Guizot had made a great mistake in defending himself as he had done. He could have ignored the accusations all the more easily since they had frequently been made before; he could have claimed that they were irrelevant to the matter in hand; he could have confined himself to pointing out the anomaly of Royalists accusing him of having betrayed France in the person of Napoleon. Like many great orators he sometimes did not know when it was wiser to remain silent. Perhaps one of the reasons why he had never been popular as a politician was this habit he had of expounding his policy in all its inexorable detail. Prosper de Barante had earlier considered that it was a mistake to proclaim ideas, however reasonable they were, in such a way.[1] Guizot's 'maître d'école' manner, his inflexibility, his conviction that he was right, helped to make him unpopular. Memories of the coalition, his insistence upon a pacific policy, his success in staying in office and in collaborating with the King, were easily translated into accusations concerning his ambition, his lack of patriotism, his subservience to royal influence. His association with the Princess de Lieven was another subject for criticism and calumny. Men who could agree on nothing else could agree on their dislike of Guizot, and in this way the opposition found itself united.[2]

Yet they were no nearer to power. For a time it was rumoured that the King was anxious to dissociate himself from an unpopular minister.[3] But these rumours were not confirmed, indeed the King went out of his way to deny them. And whilst other politicians might have suffered from their unpopularity, Guizot on the contrary seemed to revel in it. Perhaps some Protestant taste for martyrdom, or some Puritan sense that if he was against the world in general then he was in the right, inspired him. At all events the element of struggle was always favourable to his oratory and to his dignity. When he was allowed to rise to the superb heights of his eloquence, then he was successful. When in 1845 illness caused him to absent himself from the Chamber for several weeks, then the deputies had the sentiment that they had lost their principal speaker.[4] Finally, when all is said and done, the opposition can hardly have expected to discredit

[1] Prosper de Barante: Mme Anisson du Perron, May 19th, 1837. *Barante, Souvenirs* (op. cit.), vol. vi, pp. 20-21.

[2] On the Belgrave Square incident and the 'flétrir' debate see Sainte-Beuve: Juste Olivier, February 1st, 1844, *Correspondance* (op. cit.), vol. v, pp. 433-435 and Princess de Lieven: Lord Brougham, January 28th, 1844, *Brougham Papers*, 20, 573, University College Library, London.

[3] This was reported, for example, in the *Revue des Deux Mondes*, February 1st, 1844, p. 138.

[4] He must have been the most frequent speaker. It was estimated that in the parliament 1842-1844 he made no less than 137 speeches. See *Biographie Statistique. Membres de la Chambre des Députés par deux hommes de lettres*, Paris 1846, pp. 65-72.

Guizot permanently. He was no more open to criticism of a personal nature than any other politician. His reputation for personal probity was much higher than that of Thiers, his sense of political principle much higher than that of Molé, his intelligence immeasurably finer than Dupin's. Was he to be ruled out of consideration because he was 'l'homme de Gand'? The president of the Assembly, Sauzet, who had a liking for weak puns, remarked after the 'flétrir' debate, 'Voilà bien du bruit pour un petit ouragan.'

The Catholic question was different. This was a conflict which arose spontaneously in the country, which possessed its own leaders, and which forced itself on the attention of the politicians. Most historians have agreed in noticing the revival of catholicism which began to be important in the late 1830s. The association of the Church with Charles X, and the self-confidence of those who had made the July Revolution, had helped to create a popular form of anti-clericalism, particularly strong in Paris, so that priests were often obliged to disguise themselves before appearing on the streets. Such sentiments did not last for long, and within a few years it was being pointed out that religion was once again fashionable, at least in appearance and certainly in those sections of society which were comfortably off. It was possible for priests to play a more public rôle; Lacordaire in 1833 was delivering religious lectures at the Collège Stanislas which were attracting the general public, and in 1835 and 1836 he repeated this success in his lectures (or 'conférences') at Notre Dame; he was succeeded by the Jesuit Ravignan, and their example was imitated by a great many other preachers. Not only were Guizot and Lamartine and Hugo seen in Notre Dame during these addresses, but so were Thiers, Odilon Barrot and Dupin. Poly-technicians were also seen there, although only a few years previously the finding of a rosary in the corridor of the École Polytechnique had aroused most of the school to derision against its unknown owner. Students at the École Normale admitted that they were converts; specifically Catholic newspapers (particularly after 1833, *L'Univers*) came into existence; books of verse which had been dedicated to Lamartine were now dedicated to the Virgin and the novel of religious sentiment began to have a certain vogue. Most important of all, perhaps, certain politicians began to fear the Church less and the dangers of revolution more, and they began to stress the need for an 'entente' between politics and religion. By 1838 the most prominent of these politicians were Guizot and Montalembert, who published articles almost simultaneously, urging that Catholics should associate themselves with the government that maintained social order.[1]

[1] Guizot's articles are in the *Revue Française* for February, July and October 1838.

But this development was bound to have its corollary. On the one hand the Church, whilst gratified that governments should have become more understanding, wished to play a more direct rôle in society. On the other hand, many Frenchmen, always conscious of the need for national unity and confident of the progress of the modern world, saw in the Church's revival a source of disunity and an impediment to progress. Doubtless these attitudes could have been noticed in 1840; but by the end of 1843 they had hardened considerably. Tocqueville, a conciliator in religious matters, was struck by the distance that separated 'l'esprit libéral' and 'l'esprit de religion'.[1]

The occasion on which the first open disagreement had become evident was that of secondary education. With Cousin in the Thiers government, and later with Villemain in the government of October 29th, the Church had conducted negotiations, using Monseigneur Affre, who had become Archbishop of Paris in 1840, and Montalembert as their representatives. But the project which Villemain presented to the Chamber in March 1841 was very different from that which had been anticipated. Whilst some of the controls of the University, restricting the liberty of teaching, were relaxed, one notable extension of University power was that the 'little seminaries' which had hitherto escaped all control, were henceforth to be treated in the same way as ordinary secondary schools. The bishops of France came together, agreeing that this projected law was unacceptable. The commission of the Chamber, under the presidency of Salvandy, amended it beyond all recognition. Guizot, who in 1836 had passed by in silence the question of the little seminaries, was known to disapprove of the law, and it was hardly surprising that during the parliamentary recess, Villemain announced its withdrawal. But the Catholic offensive against his law had produced its reaction, and the pretentions of the clergy were denounced not only by *Le National* (which believed in compulsory and free state education) but also by *Le Constitutionnel* and *Le Temps*, newspapers of the left centre, and by the *Journal des Débats*, the only real ministerial newspaper. Although Guizot always denied that the *Journal des Débats* was in any way an official publication and although he said that he had no control over its contents,[2] it was known to be in close contact

---

[1] Tocqueville: de Corcelle. November 15th, 1843. *Oeuvres et Correspondance Inédites* (ed. Gustave de Beaumont), Paris 1861, vol. ii, pp. 121-123.

[2] Guizot said this frequently when he feared that foreign governments would be displeased by an article. E.g. Guizot: Sainte-Aulaire, April 14th, 1845, *Archives Nationales*, 42 A.P. 8. Piscatory, ambassador in Athens, claimed that his colleague in Constantinople, Bourqueney, had influence over the *Journal des Débats* and in this way he explained its anti-Greek sentiments. Piscatory: Guizot, October 20th, 1845, Ibid., 42 A.P. 7.

with the government. The fact that the *Journal des Débats* for several years continued to publish articles (usually written by Silvestre de Sacy or by Saint-Marc Girardin) critical of 'the Catholic party' is a sign of a split both in the government and in the majority. In the cabinet, both Guizot and Martin du Nord, the minister responsible for religious affairs, were anxious for conciliation and for co-operation with the Church, whilst Villemain was hostile to clerical claims and determined to defend the power of the University (although his personal relations with Victor Cousin were bad and he rather welcomed attacks upon his predecessor in office). Thus this disagreement was both dangerous and complicated; within a short time it became violent.

Undoubtedly the first movers had been the Catholics, largely led on by Montalembert, one of whose main ideas was to persuade the bishops and the clergy to descend into the political arena.[1] But the counter-offensive came from the University. Part of the revival of the French Church took the form of restoring the Orders to France. The Jesuits had in 1833 returned to a convent in the Rue de Sèvres, the abbé Gueranger had restored the Benedictines, and in 1839 Lacordaire received the Dominican habit with the intention of bringing that Order back to France. It was Lacordaire who probably expressed the aim of all these Orders in supposing that these societies, working and praying together, would find the remedy to the modern scourge of individualism. Naturally, of all these Orders it was the Jesuits who attracted the most attention. They quickly spread from the Rue de Sèvres to the Rue Monsieur and the Rue du Regard, and from there supposedly to the Institut des Hautes Études. Villemain in 1842 gave encouragement to the campaign against them when, discussing the results of a competition organized by the Académie Française, he took the opportunity of criticizing 'this active and imperious society'; in October 1843, when the Court of Cassation reassembled, Dupin made a speech attacking the Order. In April and May 1843 Michelet and Quinet began their lectures at the Collège de France. Michelet claimed that he was performing a great service to the clergy by revealing who were their tyrants; Quinet set out to show that it was amongst the most wretched peoples of Europe that the Society of Jesus had its strongest positions, and said that the society had poisoned the life of Spain and Italy for two centuries. Lacretelle, at the same time, was attacking the Jesuits in his Sorbonne lectures. In mid-1843 Michelet and Quinet published some of their lectures, and their book *Les Jésuites* ran through seven editions in eight months. The *Revue des Deux Mondes* also gave space to this campaign. An Italian

[1] Montalembert: Abbé Delor, April 8th, 1839, *Revue de Paris*, June 1st, 1902, pp. 461-462.

refugee, Libri, then employed by the University, published a series of articles from May 1st, 1843, to April 15th, 1844, and with other writers he showed the increase of Catholic influence in French society.

The attack on the Jesuits became popular. The old rumours that they had a register of family secrets and an unlimited number of agents began to be publicized once again. Alongside the more fantastic stories, and alongside Eugène Sue's *Le Juif Errant* which *Le Constitutionnel* published in instalments, came Michelet's simple statement, that many a man who wondered if there was any truth in the rumours about the Jesuits, did so when his wife was already governed by a confessor who served the Society. 'His wife, his household, his table, his hearth, his bed,' cried Michelet, 'tomorrow they will have his child.'

Parallel to this came the attacks on the University, the attacks on impious schoolmasters, on the scandals of University institutions and on the immorality of the eclectic philosophy. Bishops protested against particular teachers of philosophy within their dioceses, priests became pamphleteers and organized petitions protesting against the University as 'the slave trade of intellect and soul', 'the Algiers of the monopoly'. Sometimes the Catholics claimed their legal rights to teach or to establish schools freely; sometimes they claimed their spiritual right to have themselves the monopoly of teaching; sometimes they sought to frighten the faithful, claiming that parents imperilled the immortal souls of their children by sending them to unreligious schools; sometimes they appealed to faith by accounts of devotion, piety and miracles. It was said that if Eugène Sue sold his tens of thousands, the stories of 'miracle-mongering' sold their hundreds of thousands.

The conflict of the irreligious and of the fanatical did not oblige the government to intervene. But when the leading dignitaries of the Church demanded a change in the education laws, and pointed to the Charter of 1830 as having promised liberty of teaching, and when other prominent personalities demanded the expulsion of the Jesuits, and pointed to the laws which made their presence in France illegal, it became difficult for the government to remain inactive. However, the publication in October 1843 of Montalembert's *Le Devoir des Catholiques dans la question de la liberté de l'enseignement* made it imperative that the government do something. Montalembert, who has been called 'a will o' the wisp on the waste of French politics' and whose devotion to ancient authority conflicted with his desire to display his own ability, was a politician capable of upsetting the political scene. His sincerity, his vanity and his reputation all made him redoubtable. 'Liberty', he wrote, 'is not something which one is given, but something which has to be conquered.' He urged a change of tactics on the part of the Catholics; in public life they should not simply be Catholics, they should be Catholics 'before all else', they should exploit existing institutions, and above all the Catholic party should realize that they would only succeed once they had made themselves 'a serious embarrassment'. In this way Montalembert sought to force the hand of both Archbishop Affre and of Guizot; the two of them would have preferred less open and violent methods of resolving the question.

Guizot himself was favourably disposed to certain parts of the Catholic claims; on friendly terms with Ravignan (who published *De l'existence et de l'Institut des Jésuites* in January 1844, when for the first time since 1764, the monogram of the Society was used and the author's quality 'de la Compagnie de Jésus' given), and to some extent with Montalembert, he nevertheless felt great anxiety at the way in which extremists were becoming dominant in religious, as in political, affairs. Whilst Saint-Chéron, the former director of *L'Univers*, had had doctrinaire sympathies, his successor since 1842, Veuillot, was particularly violent and aggressive. Guizot's main aim, in 1843 as in 1836, was to find some means of effecting a reconciliation. But he was not prepared to sacrifice the University, or to accept the criticisms then being made of its teaching and of its importance. Above all, he was preoccupied by the problem of his majority. When the *Journal des Débats* attacked Montalembert's *Du Devoir*, and even went so far as to associate the author with contemporary events in Belgrave Square, then it seemed that a new majority might be forming; the defence of the University and the attack on the Jesuits could become the long-awaited occasion when the left-centre could draw to it deputies from the right-centre and the conservatives; it could even be the moment when the King, whose dislike of the Catholic agitators was known to equal his inability to understand the Catholic religion, would break with his government. It must be remembered, too, that after the Belgrave Square incidents and the subsequent debate, the legitimists and those of the conservatives who owed their elections to legitimist support were hostile to the government. Therefore when the speech from the throne in December 1843 announced the government's intention to introduce a law on secondary education, and when Villemain presented his project to the Chamber of Peers, on February 2nd, 1844, the affair was of great importance to the cabinet as well as of considerable interest to the public.

Guizot had tried privately to persuade Catholic leaders of his good intentions; he had told Ravignan that the government could not make concessions, but he had held out the promise of greater freedom; he had told Montalembert that he was confident of dealing with attacks on the Jesuits.[1] Other members of the government helped him in this attempt to show conciliation. Neither Duchâtel nor Rambuteau, the Prefect of the Seine, attended the inauguration of Molière's statue in the Rue de Richelieu, in January 1844, since the author of *Tartuffe* had been made into a champion of anti-clericalism. But Guizot was not able to prevent Villemain from prosecuting the abbé Combalot, who in March 1844 was tried for the violence of his *Mémoire adressé aux Evêques de France et aux pères de famille* and sentenced to fifteen days' imprisonment. This was not the only instance that showed that Guizot, whilst appealing for the support of the Catholics and posing as their champion, was also allowing Villemain to appeal to their opponents and pose as their representative. The result was that both parties were disappointed by the projected law. Out of its complicated text there clearly emerged three details. The first was that the 'little seminaries' were this time untouched; the second, that the qualifications necessary to secondary school teachers were retained under the control of the University, and extended to those who only supervised; the third, that teachers had to make a written declaration that they did not belong to any unauthorized congregation, such as the Jesuits. The first was seen as an unacceptable concession to the Catholics; the second and third as unacceptable extensions of administrative tyranny. The government therefore had to face amongst the peers the vehemence both of Montalembert and of Victor Cousin. The former exalted the sons of the Crusaders going forth against the sons of Voltaire, the latter foresaw France divided between those who had been educated by the University and those whose education had come from churchmen whose inspiration was foreign. The result was that the Bill passed by a majority of only 34, which was very low for the Peers; its prospects for the Chamber of Deputies were poor.

It has often been said that Guizot's speech during this debate revealed his embarrassment.[2] However, it is truer to say that he made a carefully worded appeal to calm, suggesting that clerical violence was confined to a small section of the clergy only, claiming that the

---

[1] P. de Ponlevoy, *Vie du Père de Ravignan*, Paris 1862, vol. i, p. 269. Thureau-Dangin, *L'Église et l'État sous la Monarchie de Juillet*, Paris 1880, p. 340.

[2] Louis-Grimaud, *Histoire de la Liberté d'Enseignement* (op. cit.), vol. vi, pp. 655-656. This book is valuable for the whole controversy in so far as it contains many references. However, its summary of debates is sometimes misleading. Both de Broglie and Rossi made better speeches during the debate in the Chamber of Peers than would appear from the account which is given here. Guizot's speech of April 25th, 1844, is in *Histoire Parlementaire*, vol. iv, pp. 318 ff.

necessary collaboration of Church and University would come about in time, and warning his hearers that there were politicians who were seeking to exploit these misunderstandings. But such a speech was quickly forgotten, when in the Chamber of Deputies, Thiers let it be known that he wished to be on the commission examining the Bill. On June 24th he was made the commission's reporter. It was said that the government was very perturbed at this choice, and it was everywhere understood that if Thiers had seized upon this question, it was not because he was particularly interested in it, but because he realized the government's weakness and saw a chance of presenting himself as the upholder of a cause and the leader of a party.[1] It was this, rather than the 'entente cordiale', which was the subject of his most effective return to the political scene.

On July 13th Thiers presented a three-hour report which concluded in favour of Villemain's law. On certain matters of detail he fortified University exigencies; he was hostile to the 'little seminaries'; he stressed the duty of the state in forming citizens, and claimed that whilst the Church could overcome persecution, it would not be able to get the better of reason. It was thus a skilful report, carefully calculated to embarrass the government. If they were to continue with their project, then in order to get it through the Chamber, they would be forced to depend upon Thiers, who had made himself so prominent in this issue.

The Chambers went into recess in August. Soon the developments of the Tahitian and Moroccan affairs caused people to forget, for a time at least, the Education Bill. Guizot tried to encourage the calm. He is supposed to have let it be known that once the law was passed it could not be applied. He also was thought to have applied to Rome in order to get the Vatican to use its influence on the French bishops.[2] But this was only postponing the issue. It was noticed that when the Chambers reassembled at the end of December 1844 the opposition put up as their candidate for the Presidency of the Chamber, Dupin, who had distinguished himself by his intransigeant opposition to the clerical party. He was only defeated by the government candidate, Sauzet, on the second ballot.

This was the situation when on December 30th it was learnt that Villemain had been taken ill. It was widely rumoured that he had gone mad, and that one of the forms of his madness was that he saw Jesuits everywhere. It was certainly true, as his doctor, Poumiès de la Siboutie, reported, that overwork and nervous strain had brought about a collapse, and there was more than an echo of the violent

---

[1] *Revue des Deux Mondes*, July 1st, 1844, pp. 139-140; *Revue de Paris*, June 20th, 1844, and following numbers.

[2] Ch. Guillemant, *Pierre-Louis Parisis*, Paris-Arras 1917, vol. ii, p. 74.

campaign against him in his conviction that his three young daughters (he had married in 1832 Mlle Desmousseaux de Givré) were being menaced by his enemies. At all events, Villemain was transported to a 'maison de santé' at Chaillot, and Guizot proceeded to appoint a successor. He acted with almost undue haste, since Villemain was sufficiently recovered to reappear in public, for Sainte-Beuve's reception at the Academy, by the end of February 1845. There can be little doubt that Villemain's illness gave Guizot the excuse he needed both to drop the projected law and to try for reconciliation once again. He offered the post to Salvandy, who accepted after some hesitation. Salvandy was a minister acceptable to the Catholics; he had also been one of the government's chief adversaries in earlier years, having been closely associated with Molé. His acceptance of the post undoubtedly strengthened the government.

This religious question as Tocqueville described it, represented a real sentiment which was exploited by 'factious passions'.[1] The anti-Jesuit scare had proved very useful to *Le Constitutionnel*, Eugène Sue having rescued its finances. In the same way, the opposition, having failed to oust the government by criticism of foreign affairs, decided in April to return to the safest aspect of the religious issue, the Jesuits. On May 2nd, Thiers went to the tribune, followed by Dupin, to denounce the Jesuits as the fomenters of the recent disturbances. It was almost unanimously that the Chamber voted its confidence in the government to apply the existing laws. It was in expectation of such a move that Guizot had, in February, removed Latour-Maubourg from Rome and replaced him as ambassador by Rossi. It was Rossi's mission to persuade the Pope that it would be wise to withdraw the Jesuits. Only in this way could the government meet opinion in the country and at the same time avoid violence such as would certainly accompany the expulsion of the Society. Helped by the advice of certain French clericals who were present in Rome, such as the abbé de Bonnechose, Rossi wrote to Guizot that he had succeeded in his mission. On July 6th, 1845, the *Moniteur* announced that the Society of Jesus had accepted to withdraw from France. Although this announcement was not altogether exact, since the General of Jesuits had only accepted to disperse his members of the Society resident in certain large towns and in certain large units, the immediate effect was that of a government victory. Once again opposition expectations were disappointed.

Thus over foreign policy, the opposition gained no victory, although a motion relative to the Tahitian affair on January 27th, 1845, reduced the government majority to eight. From their personal

[1] Tocqueville: De Corcelle, September 17th, 1844, *Correspondance* (op. cit.), p. 123.

attacks on Guizot the opposition gained little immediate advantage. Over the religious question the government twice avoided defeat. The truth was that the government was lucky; the illness of Villemain and the vital despatch from Rossi both came at opportune moments. The government had also been very skilful. It had avoided associating itself with violence; it had prevented a delicate situation from becoming worse. The truth was too that the opposition remained divided. Lamartine disliked Thiers far more than he disliked Guizot, and he opposed Thiers's attitude on the education bill. Thiers and his group had no time for Lamartine, 'the postman from Mâcon' as Duvergier called him. Thiers too saw no point in joining in an intrigue with Molé, there was no point in 'swopping' Guizot for Molé. Thiers grew tired of the Tahitian question (which Lamartine had always affected to ignore); Duvergier de Hauranne tried to interest him in it again, claiming it was an excellent string to play.[1] Thiers realized, too, the complexity of the educational question. Just as the bishops looked with mixed feelings on certain of their lay allies, especially Veuillot and Montalembert, so Thiers found himself caught up in various shades of anti-clericalism, together with certain groups amongst the liberal left who traditionally called for freedom of teaching. It is noticeable that after the appointment of Salvandy, Thiers did not press for the educational issue to be taken up again, although he might well have asked for his report to be debated. It is possible that like Guizot he too hoped that the affair could be shelved. Finally, one must notice that he even tired of his attacks on Guizot, and in the spring of 1845 he met Guizot at the Princess de Lieven's, and they had a long and friendly conversation.

At all events, a tendency which had already appeared in the opposition towards the end of 1843 triumphed by 1845. This was the idea that the government should be allowed to continue in office. Various shades of opposition agreed that they would be well advised to await elections, and hope that the government's unpopularity and a general desire for change would favour them. Thus the Soult-Guizot cabinet remained. But the personal attacks on Guizot had their effect. He was never less liked, both by politicians and by the public. Certain of his supporters, such as Saint-Marc Girardin and Mortimer Ternaux, began to drift away from him. Villemain, too, never forgave Guizot for the way in which he had been replaced and he formed a little group which was anything but well disposed to the government. The *Revue des Deux Mondes* returned to its earlier hostility. Even some Protestants affected to criticize Guizot for having supposedly endangered the work of their English co-

[1] Duvergier de Hauranne: Thiers, July 25th, November 23rd, December 25th, 1845, *Papiers Thiers*, ibid.

religionists in Tahiti. But above all, the greatest fault of Guizot was to have kept his position for so long; as Prosper Merimée observed, 'That is something which will never be forgiven him.'[1]

[1] Prosper Merimée: Mme de Montijo, January 18th, 1845, *Correspondance* (op. cit.), vol. iv, p. 224.

5

GUIZOT AND 1848

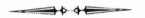

Dans ton hôtel du ministère
Sabre en main, chacun te cherchait,
Tous les yeux brillaient de colère,
Penses-tu ce qu'on te voulait!
Mais déja du beau sol de France
Tu fuyais sans doute au grand trot.
Ton hôtel nous sert d'ambulance,
Qu'en dis-tu, citoyen Guizot?

EUGÈNE BAILLET

I T was on January 27th, 1845, that the Chamber approved the indemnity to Pritchard; it was on May 29th, 1845, that the British and French governments signed an agreement on the suppression of the slave trade; it was on July 6th, 1845, that *Le Moniteur* announced (albeit with some exaggeration) that the Pope had accepted to withdraw the Society of Jesus from France. Thus the French government hoped that it had seen the last of Tahiti, the right of search and the Jesuits, three affairs which had been the principal resource of the opposition. When, in the session of 1845, the opposition had few causes to brandish, it appeared that governmental optimism was justified. The most that the opposition could hope to do was to embarrass the government by raising matters still under negotiation, or about which the government were still hesitant. Only on one occasion did Thiers succeed in arousing public interest, and that was when on March 17th, 1846, he introduced a measure which sought to exclude from Parliament those who received a salary from the civil list. This attack on the King's 'aides-de-camp' was obviously an attack on the King himself and on his allegedly unconstitutional interference in the nation's political life. Thiers and Guizot exchanged their ideas on the rôle of the monarchy, Thiers repeating

216

his phrase of 1830, that the King reigns and does not govern, Guizot some weeks later developing his conception of an active occupant of the throne.[1] Doubtless Thiers was able to strike an attitude, to proclaim his fidelity to revolutionary principles, to look for the admiration of his friends both in France and abroad. But, as had happened before, whenever Thiers demonstrated his radicalism, the left remained unconvinced and the left-centre shivered at the shadow of republicanism. His speech was printed, and a hundred thousand copies were distributed in the country, but Guizot's majority in the Chamber went up.

Guizot was, in January of 1846, undecided about having new elections, but within a few weeks, with his majorities varying between 60 and 80, and with the opposition at a loss, it seemed that the moment could not be more favourable for a dissolution. There did not appear to be any effective cause which the opposition could take up and which would disturb the calm of the 'pays légal', in the way that the right of search treaty had upset the 1842 elections. There was only one question which was pending and which seemed likely to influence the election directly, and that was one which would be to the advantage of the government, or at all events to the advantage of Guizot and to the disadvantage of Thiers. That was the issue of the secondary schools. Montalembert had in 1844 created a *Comité électoral pour la défense de la liberté religieuse*, and in 1845 Montalembert and de Riancey started to organize the Catholic electorate. In September 1845, following in the tradition of the liberal society, *Aide-toi, le ciel t'aidera*, which had explained the laws and processes concerning the right to vote so that no one could be unwittingly disenfranchised by the government of Charles X, they published an electors' guide.[2] In 1846 they issued a series of circulars, culminating in Montalembert's highly successful pamphlet of July, *Du Devoir des Catholiques dans les prochaines élections*. The intention of all this activity was to persuade Catholic electors that they should vote for the candidate who promised to support freedom of teaching and the end of the University monopoly of secondary education. Other considerations, such as party sympathies, personal connections, views on foreign policy or political principles in general were to be considered irrelevant. Like the Anti-Corn Law League, Montalembert's organization had singleness of purpose. These circumstances were more favourable to Guizot than to Thiers. Many Catholics, including most of the episcopate, believed that Guizot was a sincere believer

---

[1] Chambre des Députés, May 28th and 29th. *Histoire Parlementaire* (op. cit.), vol. v, pp. 187 ff.

[2] *Charles de Riancey, Du Droit électoral; de ses conditions et de ses garanties*, Paris 1845.

in their cause. They remembered his own projected law of 1836, his assurances to Montalembert and Ravignan, the speed with which he had replaced Villemain and they had been told that Salvandy was preparing a new law. Above all, when the question of a forthcoming law had been raised in February 1846, Guizot, there being no legislation before the Chamber, had seized the opportunity to make one of the greatest speeches of his career in support of freedom. This was a speech which lost him no immediate support and which aroused Catholic enthusiasm.[1] Thiers, however, was the obstinate champion of the monopoly, from whom Catholics in 1846 apparently had nothing to expect.

Other reasons made an election advisable. Guizot believed that the government derived strength both in the Chamber and in the electorate from the presidency of Marshal Soult. When, during 1845, Soult let it be known that he wished to resign his post as Minister for War, Guizot was anxious to persuade him to stay in office. Soult was insistent, however, that his health obliged him to abandon ministerial functions and in September 1845 he was succeeded as Minister for War by General Moline-Saint-Yon. Soult retained his presidency, but for how long could he remain? By 1846 he was seventy-seven, and whilst Guizot was determined, as he put it, 'to exhaust until the end the Presidency of the Marshal', it was clear that he could not be expected to occupy the position for much longer. Therefore if Guizot was to profit from this presidency, the sooner the elections the better.[2] The state of the conservative party was by 1846 better than it ever had been. Following upon the government's near defeat over Tahiti in January 1845, and inspired by rumours of its impending resignation, some 190 deputies had met, under the presidency of Hartmann, to discuss its organization. These deputies, who also had the support of some 30 others who were unable to be present, had accepted Salvandy's suggestion that a permanent committee should be established to supervise its cohesion and discipline. Only a few weeks later Guizot was able to describe the party as 'very

[1] Chambre des Députés, January 31st, 1846. *Histoire Parlementaire*, ibid., pp. 60 ff. This speech was quoted at length and commented on widely in the Catholic press. See for example *L'Univers*, February 1st, 1846, and succeeding numbers, *Ami de la Religion*, February 5th, 1846, and succeeding numbers.

[2] Guizot: Duchâtel, August 9th and August 13th, 1845, *Papiers Duchâtel*, *Archives Nationales*, 2 A.P. 8. Soult: Louis-Philippe, August 28th, 1845, in *Maréchal Soult, Correspondance Politique et Familière avec Louis-Philippe* (ed. Louis and Antoinette de Saint-Pierre), Paris 1959, pp. 286 ff. Soult's desire to resign the Presidency was popularly attributed to Guizot's refusal to appoint Soult's son, the Duc de Dalmatie, to the embassy at Rome. But as Soult was persuaded to stay until September 1847, this story is obviously an exaggeration.

decided and very compact', but he realised that this unity was very much at the mercy of events.[1] An event which Guizot knew was imminent, and for which he was preparing, was that of the marriage of the Spanish Queen. If this was to be a crisis, then it would be better that elections should precede the crisis rather than follow it.

The session ended in calm, almost in monotony. Before it had ended Soult had retired to Soult-Berg and took no further part in business; it was said that during some of the hot days of June deputies deserted the Chamber for the *École de Natation* which functioned on the Seine near by, and that when a division was announced a 'huissier' was sent to summon the government supporters back to vote. Finally, the royal ordonnance dissolving the Chamber was signed on July 6th and the new elections were to be held on August 1st. On July 7th the Minister of the Interior, Duchâtel, who had been busy for some months preparing the elections and who had been in consultation, directly or indirectly, with the prefects, sub-prefects and legal officials of the departments, let it be known what he expected of the administration. 'As the government is ceaselessly attacked,' he wrote, '. . . those agents which represent it directly, have the duty to win acceptance for the policies which they would not serve if they did not believe them to be good.' He called upon the administration to ensure 'the triumph of those principles of government which are best suited to the needs of our times and of our country'. It was also widely rumoured that the government invited its candidates to give verbal assurances concerning freedom of teaching, and there were undoubtedly occasions when these assurances were given before a number of people and when a record of the discussion was taken.[2]

It is difficult to make generalizations about French elections, and those of 1846 contained the usual confusions. Although the Chamber was apparently well divided into two sections, government and opposition, this was not so in the country. From the declarations and 'professions de foi' of the candidates it is not always possible to tell which are government supporters and which are opponents. They all stress their moderation, their patriotism and their desire for progress. In the administrative correspondence one finds continued uncertainties. Often there is more than one 'ministériel' or 'orléaniste' candidate, and when several men claim the title, they neverthe-

---

[1] Guizot: Sainte-Aulaire, March 18th (almost certainly 1845), *Archives Nationales*, 42 A.P. 8. A favourable description of the conservative party meeting was given in *Le Globe*, January 30th, 1845.

[2] H. de Riancey, *Compte rendu des élections de 1846 avec des pièces justicat-ives . . .*, Paris 1846, p. 53. *Ami de la Religion*, March 5th, 1846.

less make differing declarations. Often a candidate's opposition was reported as being confined to one specific topic. Frequently, too, the election was fought over purely local issues. The looseness of French political organization, particularly in rural areas, and the small number of people who were eligible to stand as candidates, meant that the administration often had little say in the choice of candidates, and sometimes knew little about them. However, one observation which was universally made was that the elections took place in an atmosphere of calm which was quite undisturbed. Even where Montalembert's committees were active, the religious discussions had none of the violence of 1844.

The result was that the elections of 1846 tended to centre around local interests and particular considerations. It is true that most opposition candidates made use of the name of Pritchard; it is true too that many other candidates, even when only vaguely ministerial, contrasted the peace and prosperity of the times to the dangers and uncertainties of 1840. But, in general, the questions which had most excited the Chambers were those which least affected the electoral colleges. The electors of the Manche were concerned with the public works programmes of their ports, such as Barfleur, Cherbourg, Portbail, Carentan and Granville; the electors of the Seine-Maritime were preoccupied with the navigability of the Seine; those of the Nord were anxious about sugar and the attempt to tax home-grown beet-sugar; those of the Eure were most concerned with communications, road, rail and postal, with Paris and with Cherbourg; electors in the south-west were more interested in the international situation, but only because they were dependent upon overseas trade and upon the preservation of peace. Many more examples of regional interests could be given. They, of course, do not include the purely local interests, the real 'politique de clocher' where the election was influenced by the possibility of turning the 'collège communal' into a 'collège royal', by plans for building bridges or locks, by the unwanted zeal of regional tax-collectors or magistrates. In these circumstances, three things were certain. Firstly, that extremist politicians would suffer. Secondly, that there would be a disposition to support the 'conservative' candidate, as one official put it, 'Everyone is convinced by the sound saying, that the wellbeing which one possesses is always preferable to the improvements for which one hopes.'[1] Thirdly, that the influence of the administration was most efficacious in these circumstances. Given that, in the words of another official, 'Justice should never descend into the political arena, but she should give all her collaboration to the

[1] Procureur Général of Bordeaux: Minister of Justice, August 4th, 1846, *Archives Nationales*, BB[17] A 146.

government', then such a principle was only fully practicable when
politics were apparently absent.[1]

Although Thiers and Odilon Barrot had come to an electoral
agreement, and although the left and centre-left thus presented a
united front, alliances between the legitimists and the left were much
rarer in 1846 than in 1842. In places such as Dijon and Metz the
failure of the legitimists and the left to come to an agreement
facilitated the election of governmental candidates, whilst in
Grenoble, in Montpellier and in other places in the south-west,
moderate legitimists tended to rally towards the government. Doubtless it was the absence of any political issue which made alliances
between the left and legitimists more difficult; doubtless it was the
political calm and the emphasis on material prosperity which made
some legitimists ready to rally to the Orleanists.[2] It seems likely that
two attempts on the King's life, in May and in July 1846 might also
have frightened electors away from both radicals and legitimists.

The result of the elections, as Guizot had hardly dared to hope,
was a government victory. Guizot's own interpretation of the returns
were that the legitimists lost 11 seats, the extreme left lost 6 and the
Thiers-Barrot combined left lost 11.[3] Victories in 28 constituencies
meant that the government majority was in the region of 100. To
Duchâtel Guizot described the result as being unique since 1830, if
not since 1814.[4] Xavier Doudan, Albert de Broglie's tutor, wrote
that it was 'raining conservatives in the elections', and described the
ministry as being 'dans une grande joie'.[5] Thiers and Duvergier de
Hauranne were disappointed and perplexed. Duvergier admitted
that they would have to resign themselves once more to four years of
opposition, since although they could conceivably be called to power,
he did not think that, with the new Chamber, they would be able to
hold on to office.[6]

Thus, after staying in power longer than any other ministry of the
July Monarchy, the government of which Guizot was the most
important member gained an electoral victory which was, in French
terms at least, resounding. It appeared therefore as if he could look
forward to parliamentary sessions which would be less unnerving,

---

[1] Procureur-Général of Toulon: Le Garde des Sceaux, ibid.
[2] A useful general survey of the election is *A. Roubaud, Les élections de 1842
et de 1846 sous le Ministère Guizot. Revue d'Histoire Moderne*, 1939, vol. xiv,
pp. 261 ff.
[3] Guizot: Prosper de Barante, August 10th, 1846, *Archives Nationales*,
42 A.P. 8.
[4] Guizot: Duchâtel, August 6th, 1846, Ibid., 2 A.P. 8.
[5] Xavier Doudan: Albert de Broglie, August 5th, 1846, *Doudan, Mélanges et
Lettres*, Paris 1876, vol. ii, pp. 86-87.
[6] Duvergier de Hauranne: Thiers, August 5th, 1846, *Papiers Thiers*, op. cit.

and it was thought that in his greater security he would be able to formulate policy more freely. Yet within a relatively short time this large conservative majority was disintegrating, Guizot was being progressively abandoned and eventually his government was jettisoned. The revival of the opposition and the origin of the Revolution can conveniently be studied in three different sections. Firstly the growth of the parliamentary reform movement, secondly the economic crisis, thirdly the importance of the idea of revolution.

The movement for parliamentary and electoral reform existed long before the elections of 1846. The presence of paid government officials, sitting in the Chamber as elected deputies, had been adversely commented upon under the Restoration, and during the July Monarchy a deputy from the Vosges, Gaugier, used annually to submit a motion which sought to suppress, or reduce, the salaries of these officials for the period of the parliamentary session. The Chamber rarely took Gaugier's proposals seriously, particularly since he had supposedly been affected by a head-wound received in the course of his military career, but the subject was recognized as being important. Rémilly, in 1840, had tried to prevent officials from getting any promotion whilst they remained deputies; in 1842 propositions were made to exclude certain classes of official and to widen the electorate; another unsuccessful attempt at electoral reform was promoted in 1845, by Crémieux, and in the same year, when Thiers and Odilon Barrot drew up an agreed programme of government, they included measures which would increase the numbers of voters and decrease the number of deputies who were also paid government officials. In 1846, as has been seen, Thiers attacked the presence in the Chamber of the King's 'aides-de-camp'. Outside the Chamber a rather ineffective banqueting campaign had been held in 1840 and a number of suggestions for the reform of the electoral law had been made in books and reviews. It had been proposed, for example, that voting should only take place in the main towns of the department, rather than in the small towns of the 'arrondissements'. It had also been suggested that the minimum number of voters in a circonscription, which was 150, should be raised so as to get rid of the small constituency.

It is obvious that this was not an impressive movement. Sometimes electoral reform meant something that was vast, and possibly violent. Rémusat, who as Minister of the Interior had to deal with the 1840 banquets, said that it could mean every possible reform, and that it concealed all the means of agitation used by 'belligerent democracy'.[1] Sometimes electoral reform meant only minor adjust-

[1] *Charles de Rémusat, Mémoires de Ma Vie* (op. cit.), vol. iii, p. 514.

ments, usually supported by people who hoped to get some advantage from them. It is particularly noticeable that in the 1845-46 period, when elections were expected, the opposition made no real attempt to change the law governing elections, although this was the obvious time for such propositions. It is therefore true to say that the campaign for reform, which was organized after 1846, was significantly different from that which had spasmodically existed before the elections. Only in 1847 does Duvergier de Hauranne, followed by a host of speakers, pamphleteers and banqueteers, proclaim that the principle of representative government was in danger, and that France was threatened with the loss of the very liberties which she used gloriously to personify.[1] It seems reasonable to suppose that this development in the political thinking of the opposition was not caused by a reappraisal of political principles but by electoral defeat and by their tactical requirements. Only by changing the law could they hope to defeat a government which seemed firmly entrenched, particularly in the small constituencies. Only by finding a subject which could arouse the political consciousness of the people as a whole could they hope immediately to increase their importance and their effectiveness. Furthermore, as a political commentator was later to remark, the opposition could not distinguish itself from the government in terms of property, industry or commerce. The resistance of opposition to government was founded upon an 'appréciation d'esprit' rather than upon interests.[2] The opposition was therefore, in order to justify its existence, in search of ideas and causes.

The movement for reform, notably the banquet campaign of 1847 and 1848, was not successful since its conclusion was revolution. But it was successful in so far as it created a legend, namely that the Soult-Guizot government existed by means of packed parliaments and bought majorities. The word 'corruption' came to be applied in its widest senses to the French scene. An English review was not content to describe the French electoral scene as one where 'almost every voter was corrupted, either by money, by gifts or by places', but found it necessary to write of Louis-Philippe as 'the huge mercantile monarch, the great chapman and dealer that presided at the Tuileries with the spirit of a Paul Benfield and the family ambition of a Louis XIV. While the father tricked and bartered—cheated and chicaned—cheaped and chaffered about crowns and consciences, the sons revived the morals and rouérie of the Regency

---

[1] *Duvergier de Hauranne, De la Réforme Parlementaire et de la Réforme Électorale*, Paris 1847, pp. vii-viii.

[2] *Gustave Chaudey, De la Formation d'une Véritable Opposition Constitutionnelle*, Paris 1848, p. 49.

and of Dubois.'[1] And even this was not all. Just as an earlier writer had found it a manifestation of 'all the arts of corruption' that scholars and writers such as Guizot, Thiers, Prosper de Barante and so on had moved from literature into politics and official life, thereby revealing his ignorance both of French affairs and of the individuals in question,[2] so another writer attributed the materialism of the age to the government. If Frenchmen thought there was nothing finer in life than 'dinde truffée' or 'suprême de volaille' for dinner and 100,000 francs de rente, no matter how obtained, this was the fault of Guizot, his corrupt ways and management.[3] It would not be worth recalling these judgements if they were not, to some extent, part of a legend which still persists.

Guizot's own defence against these charges was made in a letter he wrote to Lord Aberdeen in 1852, after having been consulted by the British Prime Minister about electoral procedure. He pointed out that of the elections of the July Monarchy, all, except those of 1846, strengthened the opposition rather than the government, which was hardly a sign of corruption; he also drew attention to the fact that what had happened to his government had happened to hardly any other government, namely that all their papers and records had been taken by their enemies and yet the proofs of this alleged corruption had never been found.[4] Historians like to cite as an example of governmental corruption the case of the banker Drouillard, who spent 150,000 francs getting elected at Quimper. Yet his election was invalidated. It is hardly enough to say that doubtless there were others.[5] The case of Charles Laffitte deserves to be as well known as that of Drouillard. Although a nephew of the liberal banker, he was known to have conservative opinions and he had the support of the administration when in 1844 he became a candidate in a by-election at Louviers. He was elected by an overwhelming majority in the first ballot, but it then became widely known that he had undertaken to construct a branch line which would bring Louviers into direct communication with the Paris-Rouen railway, of which he was a shareholder. The government abandoned Laffitte and his election was declared invalidated. On four occasions in all Laffitte was elected, by enormous majorities, and on all four occasions the Chamber invalidated his election. The electors of Louviers invoked the precedent of Wilkes, they attacked the 'puritans' of the Chamber,

[1] *British Quarterly Review*, February 1849, p. 294, p. 275.
[2] *Westminster Review*, October 1837, p. 89.
[3] *British Quarterly Review*, February 1848, p. 134.
[4] Guizot: Lord Aberdeen, April 26th, 1852, *Aberdeen Papers*, published in Douglas Johnson, 'Guizot et Lord Aberdeen en 1852', *Revue d'Histoire Moderne et Contemporaine*, January-March 1958, pp. 57 ff.
[5] *Jean Dautry, 1848 et la IIe République*, Paris 1957, p. 48.

they claimed that it was normal that a deputy should have the interests of his circonscription at heart, but it was of no use. Not until Charles Laffitte had withdrawn his intention to construct the branch line was his fifth election accepted by the Chamber.

Most people who have examined the question are agreed that corrupt practices, the direct buying and selling of votes, the suppression of votes or the falsification of results, must have been extremely rare. All the electors were men of some substance and no serious historian would believe that their votes could be purchased by a meal and a few drinks.[1] The originators of the reform campaign realized that they had not lost the elections of 1846 simply by bribery and corruption. Duvergier admitted that the government had not been able to purchase towns such as Douai, Cambrai or Valenciennes as if they were electoral colleges with only 150 electors.[2] Compared to the England of the 1842 Roebuck Committee, the Anti-Bribery Society and the Kidderminster election, these French elections were unexceptional. One understands Lord Aberdeen's remark that 'for these matters you are certainly a more honest and upright people than we are'.[3]

There remains the question of influence. By this one means three things; that the government controls the votes of its officials within the electoral college, that the government gains support by offering posts and employment, and that the government can win over electors in a specific locality by a carefully contrived railway or road policy, by repairs to the church, scholarships to the schoolchildren and so on. Guizot's defence was that such practices had always existed, that he had employed them in the same way as had all his predecessors, and that he considered them legitimate and necessary. To Lord Brougham he claimed that such administrative action as was being exercised in 1846 was perfectly constitutional and correct, and that it was the French equivalent of the aristocratic privilege

---

[1] A near contemporary historian and a modern historian have both concluded against direct bribery. See *Lanfrey*, 'Le Régime Parlementaire sous Louis-Philippe', *Revue Nationale*, xv, p. 31; *Roubaud, Revue d'Histoire Moderne*, op. cit. It is in the more scurrilous and humorous literature of the time that it is suggested that by feeding the electors one gains their support.

> Ma nappe était toujours ouverte
> Et mon cuisinier était bon,
> En sachant tenir table ouverte
> On s'ouvre le Palais Bourbon.
>
> Il n'est pas d'élécteur si farouche
> Qu'un repas ne gagne parfois,
> En général c'est par la bouche
> Que l'on peut arracher des voix.
>
> *Le Charivari*, November 16th, 1837.

[2] Duvergier de Hauranne: Thiers, August 5th, 1846, *Papiers Thiers*, op. cit.

[3] Aberdeen: Guizot, March 30th, 1852, *Aberdeen Papers*, op. cit.

which existed in England.[1] To his own electors he asked, did they cease to vote freely and conscientiously, because he had helped them to repair their churches and build their schools or because he had helped their children in their careers? Did they feel corrupted?

The essence of this problem is not whether Guizot is to be singled out rather than Casimir Périer or Molé as an example of using governmental influence, but whether the administrative system of France was compatible with an electoral system. This is the question which Duvergier put to Thiers, and he put it as one which he was only, in August 1846, beginning to ask himself.[2] The difficulty of combining an electoral system with a centralized administrative system was one which particularly worried Tocqueville and which has recurred in modern French history. It was one which arose from the very success of the administration and from the fact that in France property and wealth tended to be divided into a great many small sections. Madame de Staël once said that the most popular constitution which could be devised for France would have as its first and only article that all Frenchmen are public functionaries and are paid by the state. Philarète Chasles claimed that there were nearly a million different posts, great and small, which were at the disposal of the government. He believed that there were at least ten applicants for each post, and therefore he imagined an army of some ten million, escorted by their wives, their children and their fathers, and carrying their petitions in their hand.[3] Allowing for the ironical exaggeration of these writers, it is obvious that no government would have wanted to ignore such a tendency, or such an 'army'. The question is, was such action ruinous to the idea of parliamentary government?

A number of comments suggest themselves. In the first place, a great deal depended upon one's conception of representative government. If one believed that representative institutions existed in order to totalize a collection of individual wills, then doubtless it was wrong to try and control these wills. But did Thiers or Duvergier, or for that matter Tocqueville, believe this? On the other hand, if

[1] Guizot: Brougham, July 14th, 1846, *Brougham Papers*, University College Library.
[2] Duvergier de Hauranne: Thiers, August 5th, 1846, *Papiers Thiers*, ibid. For his earlier views see his articles in the *Revue Française*, May and June 1838.
[3] *Philarète Chasles, Étude sur les hommes et les moeurs au XIXe siècle*, Paris 1850, p. 289. The number of salaried officials was calculated as being 667,000. The Prefect of Eure-et-Loire, writing to the Garde des Sceaux on June 26th, 1842, reports that a man who is reputed to dispose of 40 votes at Chateaudun requests a place in the Chancellory for his son. *Archives Nationales*, BB[30] 294. This illustrates the way in which the demand for rewards came from below and could not be easily ignored.

representative institutions existed in order to organize effective
government, and this we know to have been Guizot's belief, then
such influence was a necessary part of the organization. Secondly,
most historians who had studied this have accepted only too easily
the written affirmations of the administrative officials that they had
actively supported a government candidate. Yet much of what was
written was undoubtedly 'protective paper'. The prefects, 'ces
empereurs au petit pied' as Balzac called them, and the sub-prefects
were important personages within their departments and 'arrondissements'. They often had a great deal of practical independence; they
often had influential local connections. It does not seem likely that
they would be so completely docile with regard to a distant and
frequently insecure minister as some historians have assumed.
Prefects, like deputies, had to adapt themselves to the exigencies of
local politics and had to accept the existence of local notabilities.
The administration was sometimes as divided as were other institutions, and instances can be found of officials who supported the
opposition; in 1842, for example, the sub-prefect of Langres was
discovered to have campaigned against the government candidate.
The administration suffered from the confusion of French politics.
How could a prefect be sure that a candidate, once elected, would
support the government? Most candidates made a great point of
their independence. It was not the administration which controlled
the issues of elections; frequently the subjects which had aroused
controversy in the Chamber were ignored in the provinces, and it
sometimes happened that local controversy arose from religious and
scholastic affairs, in which the priests and the municipal councillors
were more important than the prefects. The administration could
often do nothing about local prejudices, as when conservative
candidates fought each other, or when conservatives opposed the
ministerial candidate because he was not a local man. The administration could never silence objections, and observations were
publicly made about the slightest anomaly or confusion in electoral
matters.[1] Thirdly, it was all very well to complain that deputies no
longer represented opinions, but only represented interests and
needs,[2] yet this was a characteristic of a particular society, not a
characteristic of a particular group of politicians. The desire for
continued peace and for increased prosperity represented an ideal
which was relevant to the interests of French society. Indignant

[1] See for example Prefect of the Gironde: Minister of the Interior, April 12th,
1846, *Archives Nationales*, F 1 C III Gironde 4; Protestation des électeurs de
Roanne . . ., August 3rd, 1846, ibid., F 1 C III Loire 4; Prefect of the Eure:
Minister of the Interior, August 15th, 1846, F 1 C III Eure 4.
[2] *Le Charivari*, January 19th, 1844.

refusal to co-operate with England in putting down the slave trade or the desire to go to war with England over Tahiti were opinions which were largely irrelevant to those interests. One should not be surprised that such opinions were in the minority; one is struck by their success over short periods of time.

In short, a degree of administrative influence was inevitable; a degree of materialism was natural. The extent of both depended upon local conditions as well as upon circumstances. There remains the question of the election of public officers to the French Chamber. Here, it was claimed, the government removed a deputy's independence by paying him a salary; a representative became a mere placeman. Before the elections of 1846 it was estimated that there were something like 184 officials in the Chamber (in calculating their number a difficulty arises concerning the members of the Conseil d'État who were 'en service extraordinaire' and who had temporarily lost their salaries); but of these approximately 40 regularly voted with Thiers. It was also said that the rate of appointment and of promotion by the Soult-Guizot administration was much slower than that of other governments, especially when compared to those headed by Laffitte and Thiers.[1] Guizot's own figures for the Chamber elected in 1846 were 185 officials, of whom 39 habitually voted for the opposition.[2] Once again he advanced the argument that he only continued a practice which was widely accepted and used by all his predecessors. Once again, too, one's views on this particular issue depend upon one's ideas on representative government as a whole. It could be said that if one believed, as Guizot did, that representative government was government by discussion, then it would have been folly to have omitted a section of the population who were amongst the best informed and best educated. (This was all the more striking since it had been admitted, in the organization of the National Guard, that there was a shortage of officer material and that 'les capacités pour les grades' were absent from many localities).[3] At the same time, even critics of the system admitted that officials were popular candidates, and it was rare for a paid official to suffer for his position if he offered himself for election.[4] Some deputies found that they became more important and influential as deputies if they became a government officer. Others, who were officials, found it necessary to

[1] *Revue Nouvelle*, April 1st, 1846, pp. 105 ff.

[2] Guizot: Aberdeen, April 26th, 1852, *Aberdeen Papers*, ibid.

[3] *Compte Rendu au Roi par le Ministre du Commerce sur l'exécution des lois relatives aux Gardes Nationales*, Paris 1832.

[4] *Revue des Deux Mondes*, July 15th, 1846, p. 378. A deputy who accepted government employment had to present himself before his constituents for re-election. Between 1830 and 1848, out of 275 deputies affected by this law, only 11 failed to secure re-election.

be deputies if they were to perform their duties. Dubois, for example, who was Director of the École Normale, claimed that if he were not a deputy then any minister could bring pressure upon him, whilst as a deputy it was he who exerted the pressure on the minister in the interests of his functions.[1] The appointment of officials from amongst the deputies was also a double-edged weapon. Louis Blanc wrote in 1839 that for a single 'place' which the minister gave, he armed against him at least ten people who had aspired to it.[2] Finally, those who compared English and French institutions thought that the rôle of the aristocracy in France should be played by the agents of the government and that they would correspond to the aristocratic element of the British House of Commons.[3]

It is clear therefore that the iniquities of the French system were not as simple or as all-embracing as the reformists suggested. However, it was certain that the opposition had found a good tactical weapon, all the more so because the reform movement had different layers of significance. For some it was an end in itself; for others it was a means to better government, and this in itself implied a variety of different reforms, going through many shades of radicalism. The government, taking careful note of the revolutionary nature of some of the movement, chose to refuse all reform.[4] In so doing not only did it lose the initiative in debate and legislation, but also it appeared to identify itself with those parts of France, particularly the small rural area already over-represented by the distribution of seats, which tended to look to the administration for leadership. The government apparently separated itself from the towns which were more ambitious of political rights. In these circumstances it was not possible for the majority to remain united, and the opposition had successfully begun its task of disintegrating the conservative party.

But the opposition was doing more than this. As has been shown the attacks on the Soult-Guizot government have to be seen as attacks on the parliamentary system as a whole. They coincided with, and they encouraged, the anti-parliamentary writers who were active at this time, such as Veuillot, Capefigue, Calixte Bernal and Henri Martin. Since they criticized the King they became confused with republicans. Because they suggested extending the franchise to certain 'capacités' they got caught up in the movement for universal

[1] Dubois: Mellinet, March 13th, 1841. Published in the *Revue de Synthèse*, December 1928, vol. 46, p. 91.
[2] *Revue du progrès social*, March 1st, 1839, p. 219.
[3] Jollivet, *Examen du Système Électoral Anglais Comparé au Système Électoral Français*, Paris 1835. The author, who was a deputy, calculated that in the then House of Commons there sat 102 sons or brothers of Peers, 75 relations of Peers and 82 Baronets.
[4] *Archives Nationales*, BB³⁰ 296.

suffrage. Their refusal to accept certain privileges grew into an attack upon property. Hence the fall of Guizot became the fall of the régime, and a change of ministry became a revolution.

All historians would now agree that there is a close relationship between the political crisis which culminated in the overthrow of the July Monarchy and the economic crisis which marked its final years, from 1846 to 1848. Professor Ernest Labrousse has described the political and economic tensions as together forming an explosive mixture which, on contact with an element of resistance from the government, exploded.[1] It is by means of such a scheme of things that Professor Labrousse has sought to explain not only the events of 1848, but also the Revolutions of 1789 and 1830. There is the same coincidence of economic and political crises; there is the same detonating rôle of the governments' insistence upon their own policies. In 1789 there was the preparation of strong action, in 1830 Charles X issued his ordonnances, in 1848 Guizot and the King refused all reform. Most historians have been greatly influenced by this inter-pretation, and it is rare to find one who does not quote Labrousse with some degree of approval. In the case of 1848, the exact nature of the economic crisis has recently been intensively studied, and whilst there still remains a great deal of uncertainty, one's knowledge of these events has been immensely increased.[2]

Yet there remains a simple question which these historians have neglected to ask themselves, and which is not without interest in understanding the nature of the February Revolution. Why is it that Guizot never attributed his fall, at least in some measure, to the economic crisis? When he was in his English exile, he sought to explain what had happened in letters to many of his friends; when he wrote the final volume of his *Mémoires* he had another opportunity of interpreting events. Yet he does not appear to have attached any importance to the agrarian and industrial difficulties which preceded 1848. He dwells rather on the evil of revolution which persisted in France and which he had mistakenly supposed to be less prevalent than it was. He saw revolutionary ideas and habits as being the cause of the Revolution and he saw them as being part of the malady of the century. He spoke of the necessary disadvantages of parliamentary

[1] E. Labrousse, *Le Mouvement Ouvrier et les Théories Sociales en France au 19e Siècle* (Centre de Documentation Universitaire, Paris, undated), p. 189. See particularly his 'Comment naissent les révolutions' in *Actes du Congrès historique du centenaire de la Révolution de 1848*, Paris 1948.

[2] E. Labrousse (editor), *Aspects de la Crise et de la Depression de l'Économie Française . . . 1846-1851* (Bibliothèque de la Révolution de 1848), Paris 1956. For a bibliographical article see R. *Schnerb* in *L'Information Historique*, 1949, pp. 149 ff.

government, which was obliged to tolerate its worst enemies. He referred frequently to the passions and vanities which had existed, to the bad influence of the newspapers and salons, to the distorted accounts of the government's corruption at home and subservience abroad, and to the weakness of the conservative party which wanted both order and liberty, but which was not prepared to accept either the principle of order or the consequences of liberty. In general terms, he said that the July Monarchy had failed because, like the Empire and the Restoration, it had failed to maintain good relations with the middle classes; in particular terms, he thought that the King had suddenly lost his nerve. But, whatever allusions or implications one wishes to see in these remarks, it is evident that the economic crisis is not considered to have been important.[1]

It has of course been said that Guizot was ignorant of economic affairs, and one could enlarge upon this and suggest that his inability to understand the importance of economic affairs after 1848 was an indication of the same inability existing before 1848, which helps to explain his failure. It is of course true that he was not a great reader of political economy; he did not show in his study of history the detailed interest in the prices of goods which characterized Thiers's work on the Revolution, and in the same way his parliamentary speeches seldom descended to the technical and administrative details of government. Discussion of the economy was left to the ministers concerned and Guizot rarely intervened in these debates. Yet, whilst this is so, it is surely unjustified to assume that he was ignorant of economic affairs and that he was incapable of recognizing a crisis when he saw one. As Minister for Foreign Affairs his correspondence with the Consul-General in London showed both his interest in English economic progress and in the English government's attempts to meet the crisis.[2] As President of the Conseil-Général of Calvados, he had ample opportunity to see the crisis himself. It was the Prefect of Calvados who had, in August 1847, spoken of a crisis 'as violent as it was unexpected, which has troubled all forms of activity'; in the same month, Lisieux, the 'citadelle guizotine' which was the neighbouring town to the Val-Richer, was the scene of violent grain riots, where the National Guard was at first unsuccessfully mobilized and then dissolved.[3] The only ministerial crisis which arose from 1840 to

[1] As an example of this sort of account of events see Guizot: Lenormant, January 11th, 1849, in *Lettres à M. et Mme Lenormant* (op. cit.), pp. 20 ff.

[2] *Archives du Ministère des Affaires Etrangères*, Paris, Correspondance Commerciale, Londres, 31-32.

[3] See *G. Desert*, La région de Caen, and *Michelle Perrot*, 'Les régions textiles de Calvados', in *Labrousse, Aspects de la Crise* (op. cit.), pp. 37 ff. and pp. 164 ff. *Louise Pépin, La Révolution de 1848 en Basse-Normandie*, Paris undated, has used the records of the Conseil-Général of Calvados.

1848 in the sense that a minister had to be dismissed was when, on May 10th, 1847, the Minister of Finance, Lacave-Laplagne, was replaced by the doctrinaire Dumon. It is unthinkable that Guizot, who often dined with Rothschild and who made use of Rothschild's agents in his diplomacy, should have been ignorant of the state and nature of the crisis. The same must be said for his ministers, Duchâtel (a close friend of d'Argout, of the Bank of France), Cunin-Gridaine and Dumon, all of whom were in close touch with business interests.

To blame political failure on economic mishap, and upon the mishap in the first instance of a bad harvest, would have been a satisfying excuse. Businessmen during 1847 had no hesitation in attributing the difficulties then existing to the storms and accidents of 1846, and this providential view of events was also applied to February 1848.[1] Why then did Guizot not make such an excuse? There could be many answers. One would be that it was contrary to his proud nature to look for excuses. Another, that when men are involved in a revolution they tend to explain what has happened to them in terms of conspiracies, plots and enmities, rather than in terms of more general movements and trends. Another, that Guizot saw no reason to look for an explanation; the revolutionaries, the politicians, his own majority, had behaved in 1848 exactly as they had been behaving for years; there was no essential difference between their behaviour in 1840 and their behaviour in 1848, it was only various accidents which had made the result different. However, in addition to these possible explanations, it seems sensible to suggest another. Guizot ignored the economic crisis of 1846 to 1848 because he did not think that it was important in producing the Revolution. In thinking this, of course, he might well have been mistaken. He did not know as much about the crisis as we do, and both as politician and historian he had his blind spots. Yet it is useful to try and explain such an attitude, and it is permissible to make certain suggestions. One is that economic crisis was never far distant from affairs in France, and that the events of 1846 and 1847 appeared less remarkable to the contemporary than they do to those historians who have their eyes fixed to Professor Labrousse's graphs. Another is that the crisis of 1846 and 1847 was, in some respects, over by the time of the Revolution. Still further one might add that some of the worst features of crisis, the agricultural depression, the organization of some form of rural conspiracy, and the flight of capital out of France, occurred after February 1848 and were for many observers associated with the seven weeks of social revolution rather than with the July Monarchy.

Even if we concentrate our attention on the harvest of 1846, this

[1] *Horace Say*, 'La Crise Commerciale', *Journal des Économistes*, March 1st, 1848.

was not such an exceptional year. The growing population had for many years been a strain on the country's food resources. The fear of famine was a traditional part of the French countryside, and even in 1846 there is reason to think that there were some places where fear was more important in creating unrest than an actual shortage of foodstuffs.[1] Agriculture had always been short of capital and improvements were rare; catastrophic years were plentiful in various parts of France (1842, for example, was a particularly bad year in the south-west). Yet, at the same time, there was some reason for a general optimism. With the steady persistence of a numerous agricultural population and the absence of any great wave of emigration abandoning the countryside, with the improving means of transport, with the steady growth of alternative food-crops such as potatoes and maize, and with the possibility of bringing supplies to France from distant parts of Europe, it seemed likely that the country would escape from its dependence upon the cereal harvest. The government was careful to keep the land tax low; it was careful, too, to provide Paris with good supplies.

If one looks at other forms of economic activity, then one finds that, in general, the bad years tend to predominate over the good. Some historians now regard the whole of the period from 1817 to 1850 as a period of depression; another historian records a continuous crisis from 1827 to 1848 (and this year did not of course end the crisis) with only two temporary and brief returns to prosperity, in all, fifteen years of 'crisis and of misery'; the historian of the Lille region finds that of the eighteen years of the July Monarchy, at least ten were years of uncertainty and unemployment, whilst the historian of French banking, more precise in his analysis, records the crisis of 1839 and 1840, the depression which lasts until 1844, and the crisis which begins again in 1846.[2] It is therefore not the crisis which is unusual, it is rather 1845, the year of prosperity, 'l'année des chemins de fer', and if we look more closely at this year even, we find that some observers were pessimistic, and that other sectors of the economy were crying crisis.[3]

[1] P. de Saint-Jacob, 'La situation des paysans de la Côte d'Or en 1848', Études d'histoire moderne et contemporaine, vol. ii, p. 238.

[2] A. Chabert, Essai sur les mouvements des revenus et de l'activité économique en France de 1789 à 1820, Paris 1949; E. Dolléans, Histoire du mouvement ouvrier, 1830-1871, Paris 1948, vol. i, pp. 27-28; A. Lasserre, La situation des ouvriers de l'industrie textile dans la région lilloise sous la Monarchie de Juillet, Lausanne, 1952, pp. 100 and 240; B. Gille, La Banque et le Crédit en France de 1815 à 1848, Paris 1959, pp. 337-369.

[3] Journal des Économistes, November 15th, 1845, p. 380, with reference to investment and railway construction; Lanquetin, De l'Octroi de Paris, de son influence sur la Falsification, la Consommation et les Prix de Vins . . ., Paris 1845, with reference to the crisis in the wine industry.

Whatever Guizot knew or did not know about political economy, he learned a great deal about the economic fragility of France when he was considering the proposed Franco-Belgian Customs Union. His Minister of Commerce explained to him that France had none of the natural advantages of Belgium, resources were not concentrated, transport costs were high, capital was scarce. Union with Belgium would ruin the French woollen industry, spinning and weaving, cutlery, crystal and glass making, as well as saddle and coach making, whilst it would bring crisis to iron production, toolmaking, tanning and the linen industry.[1] At the same time, Guizot must have learnt about the diversity of the French economy and the way in which interests were mutually antagonistic one to another. Guizot was petitioned by wine and spirit producers to go ahead with the treaty; the silk industry too hoped that it would profit from the opening of the Belgian market; the different Conseils-Généraux of the departments constantly expressed contradictory opinions on existing tariffs and commercial agreements, and repeatedly urged the government at once to increase and to modify a variety of duties and charges. Observers used to speak of the war between the North and the South, the conflict between producer and consumer, the rivalry between the ports and the inland towns.[2] Throughout the July Monarchy, politicians and administrators were inundated by protests and petitions from those who were suffering from progress. Everywhere there was a crisis of the artisan; transport by railway threatened transport by waterway; cattle farmers who were used to predominating in a restricted market found themselves threatened by competition from further afield; producers using water-power which dried up in summer and which flooded in winter, but who nevertheless succeeded in making their production pay, found themselves competing with more efficient and better equipped firms. Perhaps the outstanding characteristic of all French industry at this time was the way in which the old-fashioned and antiquated methods persisted, often not far removed from the new[3]; and this variety in

---

[1] Cunin-Gridaine: Guizot, October 11th, 1843, *Archives Nationales*, 42 A.P. 11.

[2] See for example Comité Vinicole de la Gironde: Guizot, September 16th, 1841, *Archives Nationales*, ibid.; for the contradictory requests of the Conseils Généraux see ibid., F^{12} 2490; on the conflict between North and South, the *Journal des Économistes* wrote in 1845, 'La Flandre a executé contre la Provence une de ces incursions ruineuses qui ressemblent beaucoup aux razzias dirigées contre les Arabes', vol. ii, p. 44; on the neglect of the consumer see the Protestant newspaper, *Le Semeur*, 'La consommation est de toutes les faces du sujet celle qu'on a considéré le moins; ce n'est pourtant pas la moins importante', May 24th, 1843; on the conflict between ports and inland towns see *Observations du Comité des Houillères Françaises . . .* in *Archives Nationales*, C 2770.

[3] J. Rollay, 'Structure de l'industrie sidérurgique en France en 1845', *Revue d'Histoire de la Sidérurgie*, 1960, pp. 33-52, for a recent analysis of this. The point

structure meant that for some part of the industry there were always difficulties.

If the agricultural crisis of 1846 was violent, it was not complete. Some Prefects denied that there was a crisis until quite late in the year. Some parts of France were largely spared its worst effects; in the Haute-Garonne, for example, the 1846 harvest was better than the preceding years, whilst in Franche Comté the harvest was also good. In other regions there is no crisis in the production of wheat, although there is a shortage of rye and barley, and although there was often a strain put on the markets by the increased demand which came from departments where wheat supplies were deficitory. If one examines the map of disturbances which has been made by Monsieur Gossez,[1] one is struck by the fact that the areas where shortage of food inspired violent reactions on the part of the populations are localized rather than generalized. Large-scale riots, such as that in Buzançais (Indre), the pillaging of markets, or even simple interference with the free circulation of grain, were totally absent from many parts of France. At all events, just as the crisis was not universal, so it was not prolonged. Although there were further local variations, and although the effects of the crisis were felt for a long time, with dislocated markets, the recollection of violence and a sense of injustice, and with a continued shortage of fodder which affected the small cattle farmer and 'la vache du pauvre' particularly, the harvest of 1847 was a good one and one phase of the crisis was over by autumn.

When one considers the crisis of business affairs and production it is more difficult to generalize. One should more correctly talk of crises rather than of a single crisis. It has been too easily assumed that the agricultural crisis brought about the industrial crisis. This may have been the case in some localities where an eighteenth-century type economy still prevailed. But in general this was not the case. The uncertainties of French industry and commerce were more complicated. One finds a lot of businesses and enterprises which were suffering from the strains and stresses of progress; there was always the danger of a crisis of overproduction in an industry which was being mechanized but which was not developing its overseas markets; in general, linked to much of the industrial crisis and possibly even to the agricultural crisis were difficulties of credit and shortages of

is well made by *David S. Landes*, 'French Entrepreneurship and Industrial Growth in the Nineteenth Century', *Journal of Economic History*, May 1949, pp. 45 ff.

[1] *R. Gossez*, 'Cartes des troubles en 1846-1847' in Labrousse (ed.), *Aspects de la Crise . . .* (op. cit.), pp. 1-3.

capital. It is to the money-market that one must look if one is to find any general explanation of the depression, and here there are indications that contemporaries thought, in 1847, that the crisis was being overcome. By April 1847 there was a lot of talk of the crisis being over, although this was belied by the continued stagnation of affairs and by persistent selling on the market. When in November a government loan was undertaken by Rothschild and when in December the Bank of France reduced its interest rates, then many people believed that the crisis was concluded.[1] The Saint-Simonian Enfantin, whose correspondence with Arlès-Dufour in Lyons is one of the most precise sources of information about this crisis, reported that values on the Bourse were rising in November, and that the government was being encouraging, particularly with regard to the Paris-Marseilles railway project.[2] If one looks at a review particularly concerned with railways, one finds that it hails 1848 as beginning 'under more favourable auspices than 1847'.[3] If one looks at Guizot's correspondence with Cochelet in London, one finds him concerned lest the English crisis will spread to France but pleased that 'the prudence of French commerce has prevented the catastrophes which have afflicted the principal places of Great Britain, the effects of which are at this moment felt as far away as the East Indies'.[4] In some parts of France, of course, industry was suffering from a 'malaise' rather than from a crisis during 1847. It was only well into 1848 in Dauphiné, for example, that production was paralysed, bullion and paper-money particularly scarce, and industrial life at its lowest ebb.[5]

The French businessman has often been accused of being unenter-prising and unimaginative, lacking in courage and in ambition. Yet Frenchmen in general, for all that they might envy or fear the might of British industry, considered that they were in a more secure position than were their English counterparts. Their industrial population was not so large, their dependence upon overseas markets not so extensive, their credit and business organization not so elaborate. If ever government fell before economic crises, then the

[1] A. J. Tudesq, 'La crise de 1847, vue par les milieux d'affaires parisiens', Labrousse (ed.), Aspects de la Crise (op. cit.), pp. 20-26.

[2] Enfantin: Arlès-Dufour, October 28th, November 11th, December 22nd, 1847, Enfantin Papers, Bibliothèque de l'Arsenal, Paris. I must express my gratitude to Monsieur Jacques Grunewald, agrégé de l'Université, for my knowledge of this correspondence.

[3] Journal des chemins de fer, January 1st, 1848.

[4] Guizot: Consul-Général, Londres, January 18th, 1848, Archives du Ministère des Affaires Étrangères, Correspondance Commerciale, Londres, 32.

[5] Pierre Léon, La Naissance de la Grande Industrie en Dauphiné, Paris 1954, vol. ii, pp. 795 ff.

English government was in danger of falling. But the superior political wisdom of the English proved their strength; it was the political mistakes of the French which proved their weakness. In the course of 1847 it was political matters which demonstrated the nervousness of the Paris Bourse. Rumours about the King's health or abdication, uncertainties about the diplomatic situation after the Spanish marriages, the course of the debate in the Chamber, all these received the anxious attention of the financiers. A clear indication of the importance of the political situation to the business world is given by Enfantin, who commented in January 1848 that whilst affairs seemed to be improving in England, in France uneasiness remained, and this he attributed to the fact that 'the King is no longer young, the Chambers and the Government are both somewhat corrupt. . . . It seems to me that if it were not for this uneasiness, then financially and economically we would not be in a dangerous situation.'[1]

One of the constant criticisms levelled at the July Monarchy was that its government was in the hands of speculators. This was an accusation which fitted in very well with the attacks on electoral and political corruption, and it has not lost any of its force because it was subsequently levelled both at the Second Empire and at the Third Republic. Stock-Exchange gambling, jobbery, 'agiotage' of all sorts, were thought of as being the hall-mark of the reign of Louis-Philippe and were considered to have reached their apogee in the years 1845 and 1846. The anti-Semitic Dairnwell wrote of such speculations as being the direct consequence of 1830, the natural effect of a bourgeois triumph.[2] Some writers have claimed that it was because of such speculation, which harmed the country and was essentially unproductive, that French economic progress was slower than that of other countries. However, such accusations and criticisms miss the significance of the financial activity of the 1840s and they omit to appreciate the financial effort which was being made by the government. It has been said, and rightly so, that 'a new France was born under the July Monarchy'; for the first time a French government adopted a public works programme which was meant to endow France with the equipment of a modern state. An immense programme of canal (largely inherited from the laws of 1821 and 1822) and road construction began to swell the obligations of a government which was already spending more than any of its predecessors on items such as Public Instruction, and incurring commitments to

---

[1] Enfantin: Grouin, January 15th, 1848, *Enfantin Papers*, ibid.

[2] *G. M. M. Dairnwell, Guerre aux Fripons* (Chronique sécrète de la Bourse et des Chemins de fer), Paris 1846. The author's name is sometimes spelt Dairnvaell.

which there was no obvious limit in Algeria. To these were added in 1840 the necessity for rearmament, particularly for the fortifications of Paris and for a programme of naval building, and in 1842 the question of railways. It is with regard to this last that the Soult-Guizot government has been most frequently criticized.

By 1842 not only was France well behind England, Belgium and North America in railway construction, but the railway construction that had been projected in France was suffering from discouragement. There was no enthusiasm, no capital available, no certainty as to how development should be organized. The government's law of June 11th, 1842, which laid down a plan of railway construction for many years ahead, and which established the principle that the state should share the expense of construction along with private companies, inaugurated a period of outstanding activity. If one wishes one can call this France's 'railway mania' and disapprove of the excitement which filled the offices of Rothschild and Talabot, the negotiations in the ministerial ante-chambers, the deluge of companies which were formed and dissolved, the coalitions, fusions and emnities which sometimes complicated the actual construction of the lines. But one can also approve of an effort which recognized that economically, militarily and nationally, France both needed and wanted a railway system. It is of course true that many of the companies were clumsy and inefficient; there were many technical mistakes and miscalculations; whilst it was undoubtedly an advantage to bring international capital into France, much of it, especially the English contribution, was speculative, and from September 1845 English banks contributed to the collapse of railway values by a policy of sale and liquidation. But the essential weakness in the situation was that a great reorganization of the capital equipment of France was taking place, the whole of which was based upon a fragile financial structure. The capacity of the bankers has been questioned by Professor Gille; and whilst the Minister of Finance, Dumon, claimed that the state would have been able to meet its commitments, there can be little doubt that existing on a small budget, by a policy of loans and by manipulation of various funds, the state appeared to be living dangerously.[1] Towards the end of 1846 Lord Brougham wrote to the Princess de Lieven, asking why it was that bank reserves were declining, and stating that this movement had aroused discussion as to the solidity of Guizot's government.[2] The totalization of

[1] *Gille, La Banque et le Credit en France* (op. cit.), conclusion; *S. Dumon*, 'De l'Equilibre des budgets sous la Monarchie de 1830', *Revue des Deux Mondes*, September 1849, pp. 885 ff.

[2] Brougham: Princess de Lieven (undated), *Val-Richer MSS*. I have not been able to find any reply to this letter.

the railway share value losses in the course of 1846 seemed to be a barometer of the régime.[1]

Thus it is ironical that the government which was always supposed to have done nothing—'Rien, rien, rien' in the echoing phrase of one of its critics—found itself in difficulties because it was trying to do too much. And it thereby encountered opposition in its own majority and amongst its opponents, of a type which we should now call 'malthusian', and which was analogous to what the economist Bastiat then called 'le Sisyphisme'. The railways were criticized because they reduced the number of man-hours in transporting goods. Thiers wanted there to be only one railway-line constructed, 'la ligne unique' going from north to south. Duvergier de Hauranne wanted the state to abandon the whole of its part in the construction process to the private companies. It became customary to talk of 'les folies de la paix' and to attack any programme of public works, even at a time of unemployment. Conservative members turned to criticizing the government, not always because they were inspired by principles of reform, but because they had promised their electors to have taxation and expenditure reduced. 'Every moment is precious', wrote a paper, which calculated that whilst the Empire spent 1,450 francs a minute, and the Restoration 1,935 francs a minute, the July Monarchy was spending 2,900 francs a minute.[2]

In all these manifestations of opposition one thing is apparent. If historians talk of this period as being 'the golden era of the bourgeoisie', and if cynical commentators such as Alphonse Karr addressed hymns of honour to 'la bourgeoisie', nevertheless this 'bourgeoisie' was rarely unified as a political force, since it suffered from the fragmentation consequent upon the social and historical diversity of France. But a more fundamental dislocation was taking place, which became more apparent as government expenditure increased and as the government relied increasingly upon the resources of big bankers and financiers. Enfantin wrote to Arlès-Dufour, to explain what was happening in the realm of railway finance. '. . . You are, without doubt, the greatest lion of the Lyonnais, but you are decidedly much too provincial to play a part in these affairs . . . only men who cǎrve out enormous portions for themselves can succeed at this game. . . . You must be Bartholony or Talabot, Laffitte or Mackenzie, otherwise you are crushed.'[3] Only in the promotion of

[1] They totalled 24,617,000 francs. *Journal des Chemins de Fer*, December 18th, 1846.

[2] *La Mode*, July 6th, 1847. For an example of the idea that government expenditure should never exceed government income and that the government should not borrow, see *Jules de Lasteyrie*, 'Le Budget et la Situation Financière'. *Revue des Deux Mondes*, October 15th, 1847, pp. 220 ff.

[3] Enfantin: Arlès-Dufour, December 1844. *Enfantin Papers*, ibid.

the secondary lines, like Montpellier-Nîmes or Montereau-Troyes, was it possible for local and regional capital to place itself without being excluded by the Parisians and the English. In these circumstances it is not surprising to see the division between 'petite' and 'moyenne bourgeoisie' on the one side, and 'grande bourgeoisie' on the other, becoming more real. Such a division was all the more important because it rejected one of Guizot's favourite ideas, that the middle classes formed the meeting-ground of all interests and all classes. Although he never developed the idea, it was perhaps of this that he was thinking when he admitted that his government had failed to maintain good relations with the middle classes. In this respect the economic activity of the government, thrown into relief by the economic crises that preceded 1848, was of direct political importance.

During the 1820s it was thought appropriate to the French situation to study the seventeenth-century period of English history, but during the 1840s it was the English eighteenth century which was thought to be relevant. Thus Duvergier de Hauranne, attacking Louis-Philippe, would make mention of George III ('whose sanity was more dangerous than his madness') and government supporters, denigrating the opposition, would compare it to the factious and divided opposition which overthrew Walpole. But a more direct analysis would have suggested that there was only one fundamental division in the French opposition, and that was between those who were prepared to use violence, to consider revolutionary means of overthrowing the government, and those whose aims did not go beyond a parliamentary or an electoral success. The significant feature of the 1840s was that the number of people in the first group appeared to be increasing.

It would be true to say that violence, or the fear of violence, had been part of French life since the Revolution. When the last of the white terrors had been concluded, the idea of violence may have receded, but if this was so, then it was certainly revived by the Revolution of 1830. However much Casimir Périer denied that there had been a revolution, or Guizot proclaimed the legitimacy of the new King, to many people the lesson of 1830 was obvious. The course of history had been changed because the people had taken action.

A number of historians have tried to describe the intellectual developments of this period. Professor Talmon has described the persistence of the passion for rational order, the conviction that some harmony of human interests could be deduced from the nature of man. The late Maxime Leroy has stressed the feeling for unity, the need that was felt to find some single principle which would unite a varied population; he notes the gradual disappearance of what he has called 'l'homme janséniste' and his substitution by 'l'homme masse'. Others have seen the growth of a strong sense of humanity, the dislike of suffering, the desire to remove its cause, the sense of injustice; as Renan recorded, it became normal to regard individual ills as social evils and to consider society as responsible for the misery and degradation of its members.[1] But if one is to explain these ambitions and sentiments, one has to stress the importance of 1830. For some, the revelation of the July Revolution was that history is made by the people. In this sense Croker was right when he wrote to Guizot in 1837, 'Depend upon it, Dear Sir, that your revolution of July and our Reform Bill have made it impossible to stop the democratic machine which they have set in motion.'[2] Professor Labrousse has described the revival of Jacobinism, in the form of a revolutionary cult and a readiness to use new organizations and groups as a means of action. Heine commented on the 'guillotino-manie' of the republicans, and their resuscitation of the language of 1793, whilst in 1847 the Paris correspondent of the London *Economist* noticed that he had heard Robespierre being openly praised.[3]

Republican, socialist and communist organizations were becoming more widespread and more effective as the July Monarchy progressed. The leaders of these societies and their propagandists were rarely workers themselves, but their influence extended into all sections of the population and they were often able to make a satisfactory compromise between the immediate revindication of the workers and their own doctrines. There thus existed a great body of men whose interests made the same demands on society as did the disinterested rationalists who led them. A private source of information told Guizot in 1847 that the political groups which had made the greatest progress over the last ten years were the communists of Lamennais, and the official documents are filled with disturbing reports about the

---

[1] *J. L. Talmon, Political Messianism. The Romantic Phase*, 1960; *Maxime Leroy, Histoires des Idées Sociales en France*, Paris 1950 and 1954, vols. ii and iii; *Armand Cuvillier, Hommes et Idéologies de 1840*, Paris 1956; *Ernest Renan*, 'L'Avenir de la Science' in *Œuvres* (op. cit.), vol. iii, p. 756. Renan added a note saying, 'L'extension plus ou moins grande qu'un peuple donne à la fatalité est la mesure de sa civilisation. Le Cosaque n'en veut à personne des coups de fouet qu'il reçoit: c'est la fatalité; le raïa turc n'en veut à personne des exactions qu'il souffre: c'est la fatalité. L'Anglais pauvre n'en veut à personne s'il meurt de faim: c'est la fatalité. Le Français se révolte s'il peut soupçonner que sa misère est la conséquence d'une organisation sociale réformable.' (Ibid., pp. 1124-1125.)

[2] Croker: Guizot, December 15th, 1837, *Val-Richer MSS.*

[3] *E. Labrousse*, 'Le Mouvement Ouvrier et les Théories Sociales en France' (op. cit.), pp. 98 ff.; *Henri Heine, De La France*, Paris (1873 edition), pp. 57-58; *The Economist*, November 27th, 1847.

state of mind of these groups. Admittedly such reports must be accepted with caution, since they tend to give the impression that a country was always on the brink of revolution, nevertheless they give an impression of violence, suppressed or open, which is very impressive. A colonel of gendarmerie reported in 1841 that communism had fallen on fertile soil in the south, where its progress had been ensured by 'l'exaltation, la vanité et la paresse méridionale'. Communists in Carcassone, for example, had already divided up the property of the Marquis de Penautier, and it was said that throughout the south the movement for electoral reform was only a 'mask' for more violent preparations, the collection of signatures on reform petitions a means of recruitment. It was frequently reported that legitimists were helping communist organizations; in the west it was said that individual legitimists landed by sea, in the south that they were in touch with groups of Spanish refugees. At all times there were reports of violent newspaper articles or of pamphlets which were gratuitously distributed, encouraging movements of violence and attacking the fundamental institutions of society. *Le Charivari* was reported as inciting hatred against one class of society, *Le Représentant du Peuple* was said to be training the people in the making of social revolution.[1]

It is not surprising that Engels should have recorded, when he wrote an introduction to a reprint of Marx's pamphlet on the trial of the Cologne communists, that Paris was regarded as the focal point of early revolutionary action. It has sometimes been thought strange that socialist theory and activity should have been so developed in France, whereas in England where industrialization was much more advanced, both theoretical and practical socialism were less prominent. This is to underestimate the importance of both the historical revolutionary tradition in France, which should not only be thought of as confined to Babeuf and 'Babouvisme', but englobing the traditions of Jacobinism and the 'sans-culotte', and more particularly, the tradition of instability in France, where government was there for the taking. There were, of course, particular conditions which encouraged the spread of revolutionary sentiments. Dr. Talmon has pointed to the conditions of town life as the breaking ground for mental anguish and hopelessness which can cause some men to be 'poisoned by dark morbid impulses'.[2] In the case of France

---

[1] Capefigue: Guizot, June 6th, 1847, *Archives Nationales*, 42 A.P. 22; Rapport du Colonel du 14e légion de la gendarmerie, ibid., BB18 1319-1320; Procureur-Général de Rennes: Garde des Sceaux, October 18th, 1840; Procureur-Général de Dijon, August 24th, 1841, ibid.; Parquet de la Cour Royale de Paris: Garde des Sceaux, September 17th, 1847, ibid., BB18 4463; Minister of Justice: Prefet de Police, October 4th, 1847, ibid., BB18 4829.

[2] *Talmon, Political Messianism* (op. cit.), p. 366.

we must remember in particular the migratory labour which annually made its way from some of the departments into Paris. Groups of men in new surroundings broke away from the traditional controls of their communities (it was said that many of these workers were twenty years in the capital without ever entering a church) and turned to new forms of organization. Martin Nadaud, whose writings have been widely used as a source of information, records that he came to Paris from the Creuse in 1830 and that in 1834 he joined the *Société des Droits de l'homme*.[1] It has been suggested that after 1840 there was a change in the nature of this migrant labour since about that date, whilst the labour continued to come to Paris the return to the provinces became less regular. This meant that the migrants began to break away from the routine of their annual movement; as they became more integrated to the Parisians, they were even more susceptible to the organizations which sought to satisfy their claims and achieve their liberties.[2] There is a natural link between the economic and demographic conditions in which the population of Paris grew and the part which violence played in their lives, their attitude to crime, to their employers or to their leaders. The terrible contradiction that lurked behind economic growth was that whilst a section of the population grew more prosperous, another section grew more conscious of its inferiority. Their resentment was not lessened by any increase of real wages which some of them may have had, or by the availability of cheap cotton clothes. Even those who denied that pauperism was increasing, believed that it had become more obvious as it contrasted with the growing opulence of the middle class and that people were more sensitive to it.[3] The natural leaders of the working populations were to be found amongst the artisans. This section of the population was particularly conscious of hardship as its fear of proletarization was acute both in years of prosperity and in years of recession. The greatest public response to *Les Mystères de Paris* came when Eugène Sue described the misfortunes of the artisan Morel and his family; it was this episode which brought the author the most correspondence.

The existence of misery and suffering, and the presence of a violent or potentially violent population was not, of course, unique to France. England had her armed smugglers until the 1830s and there

[1] *Martin Nadaud, Mémoires de Léonard, ancien garçon maçon*, Bourganeuf 1895; see *A. Chatelain*, 'Les Migrants temporaires et la propagation des idées révolutionnaires en France au XIXᵉ siècle', *Les Révolutions de 1848*, 1951, pp. 6 ff.
[2] *Louis Chevalier, Classes Laborieuses et Classes Dangereuses*, Paris 1958, pp. 545 ff.
[3] *Vée*, 'Du Paupérisme et des Secours Publics dans la ville de Paris', *Journal des Économistes*, 1845, vol. x.

were many countries which can offer examples of brutality and violence. But one has to notice the distinctive behaviour of certain individuals in France whom one would normally have thought of as moderates. It was not merely that the leaders of the republican and socialist groups were not themselves workers and were rather recruited from 'the flower of the young intellectuals',[1] but it was rather that older intellectuals and politicians were sometimes disposed to give an air almost of respectability to violence, even at times to adopt revolutionary attitudes themselves, although they had little real sympathy with such ideas. Thus Barthélémy-Saint-Hilaire, a friend of Cousin and of Thiers, wrote an article in the *Revue des Deux Mondes* for May 1832, devoted to Louvel, the assassin of the Duc de Berry. An even closer friend of Victor Cousin's, Louise Colet, wrote a play about Charlotte Corday (but she did not succeed in finding either a theatre or a publisher until another one of her admirers put up the money). Louis Blanc, who was opposed to the policy of assassination, was unable to keep from his account of the Fieschi incident his sympathy for the assassin, whose 'machine infernale' of 1835 killed a number of by-standers although it failed to kill the King.[2] Lamartine's opposition had always been a total one in its verbal extravagance, in his denunciation of the monarchy and of the régime which had betrayed its principles and which had supposedly sold France to the capitalists. In March 1847 the first two volumes of his *Histoire des Girondins*, together with similar works by Michelet and Louis Blanc, contributed to the cult of the Revolution, and in case the significance of this production had not been realized, Lamartine told a large audience which had gathered to celebrate his literary success, at Mâcon in the following July, 'My book required a conclusion: it is you who are making it.' Thiers did not hesitate to proclaim that he was always on the side of the Revolution, whether in France or in Europe. Duvergier de Hauranne said that he expected nothing from Parliament but everything from the country, and there was hardly an opposition deputy who did not seek to measure his sincerity and his importance by the violence of his language. Capefigue, in his report to Guizot written in 1847, had said that whilst the debates of the Chamber aroused little interest, any politician who accused the government of deceiving the people was sure of an audience. The accusation of corruption spared no detail and would not even recoil before the most ridiculous legends; it was even said that a government candidate had got himself elected by establishing a matrimonial agency.[3] The allegations against the King

---

[1] *Anthime Corbon, Le Secret du Peuple de Paris*, Paris 1863, pp. 76-77.

[2] *Louis Blanc, Histoire de Dix Ans* (op. cit.), vol. v, pp. 443 ff.

[3] *J. Darbaumont, Monsieur Guizot et les Élections de 1846*, Paris 1846. Véron

and his family knew no limit; he was invariably presented as a monstrous figure of cupidity and cunning; on one occasion *Robert Macaire*, the theatrical hero of the boulevards who had robbed the whole of Paris, was played by Frédéric Lemaître made up as Louis-Philippe himself. France ruled by Protestant and Jewish bankers; France subservient to foreign courts and chancelleries; France with its Revolution betrayed and its institutions perverted: this was the picture of France which was presented not so much by extremists as by the official opposition, by the respectable citizens of the dynastic left, the left centre, even by some of the friends of Molé. It was not surprising that the impression was given that things had gone too far for adjustment or repair, and that a break had to be made. In this way even moderate men preached and encouraged violence.

Some of the events of 1847 were given great publicity and confirmed such popular opinions. The conviction of Teste, who had for a time been Minister for Public Works in the Soult-Guizot government, and of General Cubières, Minister for War in Thiers's government of 1840, demonstrated the prevalence of corruption in high places. The sensation of even this case, however, was surpassed by the assassination of the Duchesse de Praslin by her husband. The Duc de Choiseul-Praslin, who had been having an affair with the governess of his children, appeared to have killed the Duchess either to get rid of her, or as vengeance for the governess's dismissal which had taken place shortly before. At all events, although the Duke's guilt seemed obvious, there was some hesitation in arresting a peer, and after he had been arrested the Duke succeeded in committing suicide in mysterious circumstances. It was immediately rumoured that the Duke had, in reality, been allowed to escape to England, and that his suicide was a governmental invention (this was a legend which the peasants of Vaux-Praslin supposedly believed for many years); it was also alleged, with more justification perhaps, that the government had allowed Choiseul-Praslin to escape justice by taking poison. Thus was allowed to grow what Duvergier de Hauranne called 'the most revolutionary of ideas', that there was one justice for the rich and another justice for the poor.[1] At all events popular excitement was unable to distinguish between murderer and murdered, and the Duchess's ageing father, Marshal Sébastiani and his family, were insulted in the streets. The newspapers published all

once said to Thiers, 'Dans l'opposition votre esprit ne s'arrête jamais; le pouvoir, du moins, vous sert de garde-fou'. *Véron* (op. cit.), vol. iii, p. 292.

[1] Duvergier de Hauranne: Thiers, September 2nd, 1847, *Papiers Thiers*, ibid. See also Albert de Broglie on the affair in the *Revue des Deux Mondes*, March 1st, 1925, pp. 156-157.

the relatives of the Duke (which included the de Broglies) in order to show the illustrious names which shared the ignominy of this episode. Such incidents were not isolated. Merruau, of *Le Constitutionnel*, told Thiers that if he was to publish everything that was happening and being said, his newspaper would begin to sound like a policeman.[1]

This turning to violence, the conniving at violence and the growing exasperation with the régime, were all encouraged by some of the characteristics of French life. For one thing, in the closed circle of the French intellectuals, where people who knew each other were continuously writing and talking about each other, there was a great deal of vitality but very little profundity. Such a society tended to reduce its beliefs to the admiration of talent, irrespective of any other consideration. Charles de Rémusat once said that he had such a weakness for talent that he 'could not refuse to vote for that devil of a Veuillot if he became a candidate'. Rémusat was typical of those who had ideas in abundance, who 're-made his web as often as the wind blew it away', but who had little in the way of permanent convictions. Buloz was another of those who searched for talent, whose *Revue des Deux Mondes* claimed a position of authority amongst thinkers, but who himself had few beliefs or ideas. It is little wonder that the young Prévost-Paradol remarked that he had no fear of finding himself in the presence of a real politician, only of finding himself in the presence of a believer.[2] One is reminded of Benjamin Constant's description of 'ce bizarre Paris', when in 1811 he had written of the capital. 'Where everything is said, but where nothing of what is said influences even those who say it, where opinions are on the one side and interests are on the other, but where both live peacefully in a peace which is founded upon their mutual scorn for each other, in this Paris everything is forgiven because no one believes anything, everything is toned down because nothing is valued, there is ill-humour because there is vanity, but there is no revenge because there is no memory, because there is nothing worth remembering, and because what is proved in the evening is disproved the following day.'[3] Since Constant's time the only development had been that these literary circles had developed a taste for the meaningless phrase, the empty but magnificent gesture. Their absence of convictions allowed them to flirt with violence; their expressions of

---

[1] Merruau: Thiers, undated 1847, *Papiers Thiers*, ibid.

[2] *Sainte-Beuve, Nouveaux Lundis* (op. cit.), vol. i, p. 42. On Rémusat see *Hippolyte Castille, Les hommes et les moeurs en France sous Louis Philippe*, Paris 1856, pp. 106-110.

[3] Benjamin Constant: Prosper de Barante, October 11th, 1811. Published in *Revue des Deux Mondes*, July 15th, 1930, p. 547.

5. The Princess Lieven. Lithograph by Gauci from a painting by Lucas.

6. Guizot by Delaroche. In 1847 Guizot sent this portrait to Lord Aberdeen. It still hangs in Haddo House. Lord Aberdeen's portrait still hangs in the Val-Richer.

exaggerated sentiment, and the falsity of this sentiment, in itself constituted a kind of violence.

In France, violence seemed politic. All privileges had been abolished but that of property, and much of this property had been acquired by confiscation or by directed transfers. What had happened once could happen again. Eugène Sue, revealing 'the savages' who lived in the heart of Paris, those whom Proudhon called 'the savages of civilization', had greatly increased the fear of violence, and the conviction grew that once the people went into the streets, then the possessive classes would be obliged to surrender. But above all, in France it began to seem that revolution was inescapable. The bourgeoisie formed a 'bloc'. In government and politics, in law and justice, business and finance, art and literature, there seemed to be a formidable association which had established itself in a position of privilege and profit. To oppose this 'bloc' from within the system appeared increasingly hopeless; there was no alternative but to oppose the system itself.

The artist attacked the bourgeoisie. In 1847, Théophile Thoré, one of the greatest art historians, wrote that a sewerman was more fitted to be painted than a notary or a merchant.[1] The poet's antagonism to society became one of the positive factors of his creation, and Baudelaire's poetry expressed the resistance of the poet to the tendencies of his age. The cultural reaction to a hostile society was a separatist reaction, a rebellion. In much the same way, the worker, suffering what Balzac called 'the poem of his misfortunes', and all those who by their social position, their intellectual ambition or their convictions, felt themselves cut off from the direction of society, were ready to rebel against society itself.

It is tempting to say that the months which followed August 1846 were the months which the locusts ate, and to depict Guizot and Louis-Philippe as doing nothing whilst the situation steadily worsened. Even when at their most myopic both Guizot and the King realized what the situation was in the Chambers. When, in March 1847, a new vice-president of the Chamber of Deputies had to be elected, a number of conservative deputies did not vote for the government candidate and the result was that the opposition candidate, Léon de Malleville, was elected by one vote. When Duvergier de Hauranne tabled his proposal to increase the franchise, the government was unsuccessful in its attempt to have the project ruled out of consideration without discussion. Although on this issue

[1] Quoted in *Philippe Rebeyrol*, 'Art Historians and Art Critics: Théophile Thoré', *Burlington Magazine*, July 1952, p. 197. Thoré had written for the most advanced revolutionary press and in 1840 he had been imprisoned for the violence of his publication *La Verité sur le parti démocratique*.

the government eventually rallied a majority of 98, in April, when Rémusat's motion for the exclusion of paid officials from the Chamber was debated, the government's majority fell to 49. In the same month, a former government supporter, Desmousseaux de Givré, accused the government of breaking up the majority by its own inertia. On every issue, what did the ministers do, what did the ministers say? 'Rien, rien, rien' was his reply to his own question, and this phrase, frequently repeated, was regarded as the epitaph of a government which was as good as dead. In May there were government changes; but although ministerial posts were offered to a number of people (including Dufaure), they were not accepted, and this demonstration of the government's poor standing in the Chambers (since it had to nominate officials rather than politicians to the ministries of Public Works, War and the Marine) was taken by many to be a sign of its imminent collapse. The dissident, or progressive, conservatives became organized, with their leaders, such as de Castellane, Sallandrouze, Hallez-Claparède, de Morny; there were others who were openly critical, such as d'Haussonville; it was thought that there were many more who asked for nothing better than to abandon a failing government. Outside the Chamber there were rumours of violence and discontent. The newspaper with the largest circulation, *La Presse*, derived a large revenue from advertisements and therefore possessed extensive relations in business and commercial circles. It became hostile to the government from the beginning of 1847. Its campaign was intense and incisive, and carrying on its front page for many issues the motto 'Rien, Rien, Rien' it contributed all the more effectively to the government's unpopularity because its director, Émile de Girardin, bitterly disliked the ministers who had refused him certain personal requests.

Yet the government hardly responded to this situation. It behaved as if it was anxious to justify the prophecy of *Le Constitutionnel*, which immediately after the election had asked 'What will the government do?' and had replied 'With a little more confidence, it will start all over again, living from day to day as it has always done, frightened of compromising a majority which has been so painfully acquired, and it will above all put its faith in inertia and immobilism.'[1] Any estimate of Guizot as a statesman requires an explanation of this.

The first reason is not hard to find. There was no reason why Guizot should not have remained relatively optimistic. He was faced by the same type of intrigue as he had known before and he was being successful in dealing with it. Immediately after the elections, the old suggestion was revived that the government should be regrouped so as to derive its strength from all the centre parties; it was the defeat

[1] *Le Constitutionnel*, August 5th, 1846.

of the extremists which supposedly justified this revival, and the name of de Broglie was put forward as the most likely leader of such a reformed ministry. This suggestion soon suffered from a post-election statement by Dufaure, reaffirming his hostility to Thiers, and it had to be completely abandoned when, in April 1847, de Broglie accepted to replace Sainte-Aulaire in London as French ambassador. The diplomatic quarrel between England and France following upon the Spanish marriages awakened hopes in some quarters that the King would think it wise to change his government. Both Victor Cousin and Mignet made the comparison with 1840, when the King had dismissed a government which had brought him international embarrassment. Both thought that the chances of Molé leading a government had improved considerably and Victor Cousin even went so far as to describe Molé as 'the master of the situation'.[1] But the King was loyal to Guizot, and the Chamber approved of the marriages. In this controversy, both Molé and Thiers appeared too anxious to establish friendly relations with the British government. Molé was ostentatiously intimate with Lord Normanby, who had been appointed to the Paris Embassy by Lord Palmerston and who quarrelled with Guizot over a question of etiquette in February 1847. Whilst Molé was inviting Normanby to Champlâtreux, Thiers tried to come to some working arrangement with the British government whereby they could exchange information and co-ordinate their attacks. The insistence of the opposition in co-operating with Normanby whereby, as Guizot put it, 'Le Constitutionnel and Le National have become the Moniteurs of the British Embassy', did not in the long run do them any good. Lord Normanby, as Guizot said, was not a man of great foresight or discretion.[2]

Other rumours surrounded Duchâtel. It was said that after his success in the 1846 elections he thought that the ministry should be re-formed under his own leadership. There is no doubt that he quickly changed from the exuberant minister who in August 1846 gave as his 'mot d'ordre' the phrase 'Comptons-nous'. He did not agree with Guizot's foreign policy. In 1846 he was particularly unenthusiastic about the Spanish marriages and in the course of 1847 he became worried by the government's rapprochement with Metternich and by French support for the Sonderbund. He also had reasons of personal pique since he had asked for his brother to be appointed to the Madrid embassy, once Bresson had left it towards the end of

---

[1] Victor Cousin: Thiers, October 15th, 1846; Mignet: Thiers, October 8th, 1846. Papiers Thiers, ibid.

[2] Guizot: Sainte-Aulaire, February 14th and February 20th, 1846, Archives Nationales, 42 A.P. 8. For Thiers's correspondence with Panizzi, see L. Fagin, The Life of Sir Anthony Panizzi or the Panizzi Papers, B.M. Add. MSS. 36, 716.

1846, and having been led to anticipate that the post was his, he was bitterly disappointed by the nomination of Piscatory. It was for these reasons, and also because he had a breakdown in health in the course of 1847, that Duchâtel was frequently absent from Paris, and when he was present he was often discouraged and weary. However, in spite of all this, and in spite of persistent rumour, he was not a centre of dissidence; nor did he initiate any movement against Guizot, to whom he openly remained loyal.

The Palace was, as always, a great centre of intrigue. The Intendant of the Civil List, Montalivet, a close associate of Molé, has himself described how he endeavoured to persuade the King to break with Guizot.[1] But in spite of his efforts, and in spite of those of the Chancellor, Pasquier, and of the Marshals Sébastiani and Gérard, the King remained more firmly convinced than ever that he should keep Guizot as minister. The Queen's salon, known as 'la bobinette de la reine', and the Pavillon de Marsan, where the Duchess of Orleans lived, were both centres of anti-Guizot activity, but none of the protagonists succeeded in converting the King, or his sister Madame Adelaïde, or any of his sons (with the possible exception of the Prince de Joinville, who was overseas). Nor did the opposition succeed in making the dismissed Minister of Finance, Lacave-Laplagne, into a denunciator of the government.

It is therefore hardly surprising that Guizot could remain relatively optimistic. The opposition was ineffective. Furthermore, as he pointed out in a speech of May 5th, 1847, whilst there could be disagreement between the government and its majority on certain points of detail, this disagreement was in no way fundamental. And this suggestion seemed to be confirmed by one of the conservative critics, d'Haussonville, who wrote an article in July 1847 criticizing the methods of the government rather than its principles. According to d'Haussonville, what was wrong with the government was that it was failing to direct the majority; the co-ordination of ministers was bad, their legislative preparations were inadequate. It was not wrong to reject an extension of the franchise, but it was wrong to refuse to consider such a proposal. It was not wrong that the government should appoint deputies to official posts, but some unworthy appointments had been made. In this way there was objection to details; there was no essential difference over principles, and Guizot could, in July, refer simply to 'a general gust of bad temper and of fantasy'.[2]

---

[1] *Montalivet, Fragments et Souvenirs* (op. cit.), vol. ii, pp. 63 ff.

[2] Chambre des Députés, May 5th, 1847. *Histoire Parlementaire* vol. v, pp. 415-418; *D'Haussonville*, 'De la Situation Actuelle', *Revue des Deux Mondes*, July 1st, 1847, pp. 64 ff.; Guizot: de Broglie, undated (probably July 29th, 1847), *Archives Nationales*, ibid.

Some of the conservative opposition was purely personal. Des-mousseaux de Givré, for example, was greatly influenced by his discontented relative Villemain. In general, Guizot was convinced that the conservative party would remain loyal, and as late as January 1848 the King reaffirmed his determination to support the govern-ment. Whilst Sainte-Beuve once wrote, rather contemptuously, of Guizot having understood that his rôle in politics was 'to stick to the King',[1] it seems that at this time at least, the reverse was true, the King was determined to stick to Guizot, and this alone seemed a reason for ministerial confidence.

Yet the government had much less room for manœuvre than they had had in earlier years. For one thing Guizot was particularly conscious of the delicate state of foreign affairs. 1847, as he saw it, was the year of the greatest change and development in Europe since 1814. With new governments, such as Spain and Greece, trying to establish their institutions; with old governments, such as the Papacy and Prussia, trying to reform their systems, he appealed to the conservatives to be 'more conservative than ever'.[2] He thought that France had to demonstrate the firmness and strength of its govern-ment. Another major preoccupation was financial. Not only had confidence to return to the money-market, but the government needed to demonstrate that return by negotiating a successful loan. Throughout 1847 the government was awaiting a favourable moment and was conscious of the nervousness of the Bourse which could be affected by small details—such as the news of railway accidents. The acceptance of parliamentary reform, or of any other form of experimental action which appeared to endanger the govern-ment, the very idea of change and uncertainty, could have sent the financiers into a further panic. Apart from this financial question, there remained the problem which had always formed the most direct threat to the government, that of secondary education. Having postponed taking any action since Villemain's proposals had been abandoned, the government was nevertheless committed to legislate on this question. With 169 deputies who were reputed to have assured Montalembert's *Comité Electoral* of their support for freedom of teaching, immobilism in this matter was not possible. Yet the dis-sensions amongst ministers and officials were such that the govern-ment's Bill took over eight months to prepare. The minister Salvandy told the Chamber in February 1847 that his proposals would be ready in a few days, but a further two months passed before he tabled his projected law, on April 12th. Salvandy praised the principles of

---

[1] *Sainte-Beuve, Notes et Pensées*, Paris 1926, p. 199, recorded this as said by Victor Cousin in October 1847.

[2] Chambre des Députés, May 5th, 1847, ibid.

freedom, and exalted the rôle of the family and of the clergy in educational matters. He removed some of the restrictions on those wishing to open secondary schools, such as the need to produce a certificate of morality; yet at the same time he retained the general supervision of the University and the need for teachers to be qualified, with certificates and diplomas according to the nature of the school; he even made some of these conditions more severe, by applying them to those who were supervisors as well as to those who were teachers. For what his law maintained, Catholics and some liberals found it tyrannical and irreligious; for what it gave away the 'Universitaires' found it dangerous. Yet all historians have noticed that the controversy which surrounded this law was much less bitter than that of 1844. Most of the bishops kept silent, and some of the politicians were anxious not to become involved. Thiers, for example, was a member of the commission which examined the Bill, and could have continued his earlier work by reporting to the Chamber, as in 1844. But he deliberately stood aside and allowed the reporter to be Liadières (a conservative deputy for the Basses-Pyrénées). Thiers was as uncertain as Guizot about this controversy. The government wanted to avoid complications, and in this affair as in others, was anxious to reduce the political temperature.[1]

It was for these reasons that the government did not find it easy to adopt any clear or decisive policy at home. The government also made a number of mistakes. It was undoubtedly an error to allow the question of Soult's presidency to drag on. From the elections of 1846 until the ordonnance of September 26th, 1847, which gave Guizot the 'présidence du conseil', Soult's resignation had been expected. Such a long wait was contrary to the King's own ideas on the subject, as he had earlier explained them to Duchâtel; delays, 'traînasseries', brought about all sorts of intrigues and rumours, as well as increasing the antipathies which already existed.[2] Yet it is exactly this that was happening in 1847. It was a mistake, too, to reform the government by introducing officials such as Jayr, a prefect who became Minister of Public Works, Montebello, an ambassador who became Minister of the Marine, and Trézel, a general who became Minister for War. Princess de Lieven was

---

[1] Salvandy's projected law was presented on April 12th, Liadières's report was tabled on July 24th. The King's speech of December 28th, 1847, mentioned that the Chambers should debate this matter, but by February 1848 there had been no debate and the project was abandoned with the Revolution. See L. Trénard, 'La Liberté de l'enseignement à la veille de 1848', *Bulletin de la Société d'Histoire Moderne*, Session of October 2nd, 1960; *Louis-Grimaud, Histoire de la Liberté d'Enseignement en France* (op. cit.), vol. 6, pp. 748 ff.

[2] Louis-Philippe: Duchâtel, September 23rd, 1845, *Papiers Duchâtel, Archives Nationales*, 2 A.P. 7.

obviously on the defensive when she told Brougham that the ministers had made a good impression on the Chamber.[1] It would have been wiser to have enlarged the cabinet, creating a special ministry for Algeria, as was already suggested in some quarters, possibly separating Commerce from Agriculture, and Colonies from the Marine. Another mistake undoubtedly lay in Guizot's unhesitating refusal to make any change in the position of deputies who were paid officials. He should have accepted an enquiry in 1847: instead of which he waited until February 12th, 1848, before suggesting 'un examen approfondi'. It is interesting that Peel considered this to have been Guizot's biggest mistake, since the promise of an enquiry had all the evils of a concession without any of the advantages.[2]

Doubtless there were other mistakes. At the same time the government, which had been lucky on a number of occasions in the past such as Thiers's withdrawal from affairs in 1842 or Villemain's illness in 1845, was now unlucky. The surrender of Abd el Kader in Algeria should have been presented as a great victory, associated with the name of the King's son, the Duc d'Aumale, who had become Governor-General in September 1847. But the surrender, which had been negotiated between Abd el Kader and General La Moricière in December, contained the promise that the Arab leader would be allowed to go to Alexandria or to some other place in the Middle East. Once Abd el Kader was a prisoner, such a promise seemed unwise, and it was suggested that to allow the Emir to go free in Egypt would be to rekindle the Algerian war. It was therefore easy for the opposition to criticize the Duc d'Aumale for an error which, strictly speaking, was not his. By stressing his inexperience and unsuitability for such a high post, the opposition was able to exploit the situation and attack the royal family. More damaging to Guizot were the revelations which accompanied another scandal, which became known as the 'affaire Petit'. Monsieur Petit, engaged in a law-suit with one of the owners of the *Journal des Débats*, wrote a memorandum in which he explained how he had secured the resignation of certain officials in return for financial compensation. These resignations were required by the government in order that they could dispose of more posts, and with these places compensate their supporters. The publication of Petit's statement at the beginning of January 1848, and its discussion in the Chamber some weeks later, did not reveal anything new; nor were the incidents complained of recent, as these occurred between 1841 and 1844. But they gave a new impulse to the allegations that everything in the government was

---

[1] Princess de Lieven: Brougham, June 8th, 1847, *Brougham Papers*, 10,425, University College, London.

[2] Aberdeen: Guizot, November 9th, 1848, *Val-Richer MSS.*

corrupt. *Le Constitutionnel* claimed that whether one was talking of laws or roads or railways, pensions, scholarships or decorations, compensation for hail, flood or fire, everything was distributed with a view to electoral or parliamentary votes.[1] Furthermore, for the first time Guizot himself was involved in a scandal. Until then, he had been regarded as above suspicion. At the worst someone like Bugeaud whilst believing in his probity, had thought that anyone who tried to get the support of newspapers was bound to take part in dishonest negotiations.[2] But the Petit memorandum named Génie as the chief negotiator of these transactions; Alphonse Génie was the director of Guizot's private cabinet, and generally known as his factotum. Rémusat afterwards described him as being unscrupulous, and said that because Génie so easily accepted all types of employment, Guizot was led into activities which he would not othe⸱ vise have touched.[3] At all events certain members of the oppositioı Billault, Léon de Malleville, Émile de Girardin, were able to attack 'the Sovereign Pontiff of the conservative party' with particular irony and malevolence. Guizot's personal unpopularity had always been one of the weapons of his adversaries. With the 'affaire Petit' they were able to exploit it effectively.

With the session of 1848 Guizot's career as minister has come full circle. Amongst the closing scenes are a series of violent parliamentary debates, such as those which marked the beginning of the ministry and which opposed him to Thiers over the Eastern Question. But the situation of 1848 differed considerably from that of 1840. In 1840, and in 1841, Guizot was able to elevate the debate into a grand affair, to transform it into a confrontation of diplomacies, a question of peace or war; but in 1848 Guizot was forced into details, so that in the 'affaire Petit' he complained about the 'petits faits', about 'the accessory circumstances', which were being brought forward. He could not be eloquent on these matters, any more than he could reach the heights of his eloquence over the legal and constitutional problems which were raised. When he was able to make a great speech, concerning Switzerland, Italy or the Duc d'Aumale in Algeria, once again the situation had changed. In 1840 and 1841, for all that he had been defending a policy, he had been attacking a predecessor. He had been able to accuse Thiers of being irresponsible, of attaching France to the destinies of a crumbling army, of running up a debt of considerable proportions. But in 1848 it was Thiers who was able to

---

[1] *Le Constitutionnel*, January 29th, 1848.
[2] Bugeaud: Thiers, July 6th, 1847, *Papiers Thiers*, ibid.
[3] *Charles de Rémusat, Mémoires de Ma Vie* (op. cit.), vol. ii, p. 387, pp. 496-497. Génie's action was similar to that of selling and exchanging army commissions, which was quite common in England.

point to the government's defeated ally, the Sonderbund, and it was Thiers who was able to express his concern over the state of the country's finances. In 1840 he was able to suggest that the logical conclusion of Thiers's policies would have been war and revolution. But in January 1848 *Le Constitutionnel* could accuse Guizot of inaugurating the counter-revolution.[1] By 1848 the ministry was on the defensive; it was denying, excusing, promising.

Above all, in 1840, Guizot was not alone. For all that, oratorically, his was a personal confrontation with Thiers, he was supported in debate by Duchâtel, Villemain, Lamartine, Dufaure and others. It was known that there was a vast movement of opinion in favour of peace; it was known that Soult's influence, the influence of the King, and even for a time that of Molé, were in favour of Guizot. But in 1848 Guizot was alone in the Chamber. Only Duchâtel supported him, and although his interventions on the financial question were extremely effective, it was known that his determination had weakened. Montalivet reports that at the beginning of 1848 both Duchâtel and Dumon (the Minister of Finance) believed that it would be better for the government to resign.[2] It would therefore be true to say that Guizot was alone, against all the talents of the Chamber. In the 'affaire Petit', apart from the violent attacks of certain deputies, the speeches of Dufaure, Dupin and Lacave-Laplagne demonstrated the distance which separated him from the centre groups and from moderates in the conservative party. The strain of such a challonge was obviously becoming very great. Guizot, on his bench in the Chamber, looked more frail, more worn, paler; his dignity irritated rather than impressed, and the stiffness of his bearing seemed to make any reconciliation between himself and his critics impossible. Guizot's enemies remained enemies and as a politician one of his greatest weaknesses was his inability to make friends. As a speaker he was at the mercy of accidents, and when on one occasion illness removed from him both the power of gesture and the power of his voice, it was said that he had lost three-fourths of his oratorical talent.[3] It was noticed in January and February that Molé had started attending the debates in the Chamber of Deputies as a spectator; he was anxious to witness the downfall of his old opponent.

Guizot retained one ally, the King. But by 1848 the King was not the same ally as he had been in 1840. Guizot claimed, in his *Mémoires* that he never had difficulty in coming to agreement with the King. The King, he said, was better suited to choose between two lines of

---

[1] *Le Constitutionnel*, January 30th, 1848.
[2] *Montalivet, Fragments et Souvenirs* (op. cit.), vol. ii, pp. 100 ff.
[3] *Le Constitutionnel*, February 4th, 1848.

policy than to inaugurate a policy of his own, and when it came to a choice, the choice of the King was frequently that of Guizot. At times Guizot enforced his policy on the King; for example, it was Guizot's policy to introduce open rather than secret voting in the Chamber in 1845 against the wishes of the King. At times, the King failed to get the policy he wanted; his project, in 1842, of forming a privy council so as to enforce the authority of the throne, was not carried out. But it seems likely that Guizot's picture of easy relations between himself and the King was rather idealized, especially with regard to the closing years of the monarchy. By this time, the King's natural tendency to talk and to reminisce had been greatly exaggerated by old age. This incessant 'bavardage' was not helpful to ministers. Both in the 'conseil des ministres' and in the royal salons, the King's lamentations about the machine of France which was for ever in need of repair, his bitterness about 'Sa Majesté la Majorité' and his threats of abdication were positive embarrassments. In earlier years Louis-Philippe would have known how to handle the dissident conservatives. But in 1847 and 1848 he had little tact or insight, and his ostentatious hostility merely confirmed these deputies in their opposition. Furthermore, it seems certain that the King hampered Guizot in his policies. Guizot had no fundamental objection to slight changes in the electoral or parliamentary systems. For him, as he frequently explained, such changes were a matter of timing and tactics. He might well have been prepared to make some adjustment, but the hesitations which he already had were reinforced by Louis-Philippe's determination to have no reform at all. Guizot's promise, on February 12th, 1848, to look into the question of paid officials was a genuine promise on his part, and there is reason to believe that he was considering a general reform, including changes in the composition of the Chamber of Peers. But the King the next day assured Montalivet that in spite of Guizot's promise there would be no such reform. In his English exile he reaffirmed that he would never have accepted any reform.[1] In all these respects, therefore, Louis-Philippe was a doubtful ally for Guizot.

Yet the fact remains that the government was not defeated in Parliament. In the session of 1848 certain government majorities were clearly expressed, and it was not considered necessary to go through the formality of voting. In divisions where a formal vote was taken the majority was 79 over the 'affaire Petit' and 80 over Swiss affairs. But as the session continued, Desmousseaux de Givré proposed an amendment which would have modified the words with which the government condemned the banqueting campaign, and

---

[1] *Montalivet, Fragment et Souvenirs* (op. cit.), vol. ii, pp. 100 ff.; *Edouard Lemoine, L'Abdication du roi Louis-Philippe*, Paris 1849, pp. 40-44.

this was defeated by only 43. A motion by a dissident conservative Sallandrouze, proposing parliamentary reform, was defeated by only 33, but it was nevertheless defeated. It might well have been that it was the apparent impossibility of overthrowing the government by parliamentary means which caused certain people, both inside and outside the Chamber, to consider the use of violence. It was in order to demonstrate the strength of feeling outside the Chamber, and to display the force of the combined oppositions that the manifestation of a banquet in the Champs Elysées area of Paris was decided upon. Only when hopes of defeating the government in the debate on the address had faded did the official opposition decide to link up with extra-parliamentary groups, and it was for this reason that the banquet became so important. Guizot himself claimed that there were three separate plots in 1848, one to overthrow the government, one to bring about a regency and one to bring about the republic.[1] This is probably so, but in February these plots were confused together. It might well be that like Lamartine, many activists thought of a change of government or of a revolution simply as a means to an end. But the likelihood is that most of the opposition were determined only upon getting rid of the Guizot government. It is certain that their expectations of achieving anything more were far from high.

Since the government was determined to show firmness in the Chamber it was natural that it was equally determined to be resolute in its attitude to the banquet. After some negotiations the Cabinet was unanimous in its decision to prohibit the holding of the banquet. This decision appeared to have been a wise one when on February 21st the organizers of the banquet decided to abandon the whole affair, and the decision appears to have been wise now that historians have shown that in addition to the official opposition, most of the republicans and radicals and most of the secret societies also decided to call off the demonstration.[2] The day of February 22nd was a demonstration of the failure of the opposition. Whilst a disorganized collection of students, artisans and workers were encouraged by a number of political activists to demonstrate in heavy rain and to engage in sporadic violence in which five or six of them were killed, Odilon Barrot and Duvergier de Hauranne decided to revert to a parliamentary offensive. Trying to conceal their retreat over the banquet by the boldness of their words, they tabled a motion accusing the government of having betrayed constitutional liberties. But neither Thiers nor Dufaure would have anything to do with this

[1] Guizot: Léonce de Lavergne, October 11th, 1848. *Correspondance de Guizot avec Léonce de Lavergne* (op. cit.), p. 40.

[2] *Albert Crémieux, La Révolution de Février*, Paris 1912. See *Talmon, Political Messianism* (op. cit.), part v.

motion and it only succeeded in collecting fifty-three signatures. It looked as if the opposition was being humiliated in every respect, and in any case the motion could not have any immediate effect since it was not to be debated for forty-eight hours.

It was the conduct of the National Guard which changed the situation on February 23rd. This part-time military organization, preserving the revolutionary idea that the French people could defend themselves against danger, and maintaining the principle of 'bourgeois democracy' by being officered by men of property, had already been called upon by the demonstrators. In some areas of Paris it appeared to have responded favourably to this call. The government therefore decided that it should itself call out the National Guard. This mark of confidence resulted in members of the Guard appearing not as the guardians of order but as supporters of the demonstration against the government. It has been said that many demonstrators wore uniform but were not, in fact, members of the Guard. It has been claimed that only a small proportion of the Guard appeared and that it was the indifference of the remainder who stayed away which created a false impression. It has also been said that the Guard, in such circumstances, suffered from its essentially dual character, being both popular and governmental. Whatever the explanation, it is clear that the behaviour of the National Guard, as reported to the officials concerned, was quite unexpected. The government had mobilized a demonstration against itself and it was in this circumstance that the King decided upon a change of government.

There is some doubt surrounding the exact nature of Guizot's dismissal. Both Guizot and Duchâtel relate the episode as beginning with Duchâtel's visit to the Tuileries in the early afternoon of February 23rd. There the King, whilst assuring Duchâtel of his determination to maintain the government, explained that he was under pressure to end the crisis by dismissing Guizot. The Queen, Marie-Amélie, was brought into the discussion and she repeatedly expressed her confidence in Guizot's patriotism, meaning that he would be prepared to sacrifice himself by resignation. Duchâtel then expressed the view that he would need to tell Guizot of this conversation. It was agreed that Duchâtel should go to the Chamber and fetch Guizot. This he did, explaining the situation as they travelled from the Palais Bourbon to the Tuileries. Once they were in the Palace, the King began to explain the difficulties of the situation in such a way that, according to Guizot, anyone who was acquainted with him was bound to realize that he had decided to break with the ministry. Guizot insisted on clarifying the situation. If it became known, he said, that the King was even considering such a change, then the government would lose all authority. The King then, without further ado, expressed his regret at having to end their collaboration. Having learned that the King had decided to call upon Molé to form the next government, Guizot returned to the Chamber where he caused a sensation by announcing this news.

However, another account of the incident says that when Guizot was with the King, at about half-past two on the afternoon of February 23rd, as soon as the King mentioned his anxiety and the possibility of changing the government, Guizot abruptly presented his resignation. He maintained this resignation in spite of the King's attempts to dissuade him, and in spite of the King's efforts to persuade him to postpone it for a few days. Thus, according to this version, Guizot, acting partly out of pride and partly out of calculation, abandoned the King at a critical moment when, as Montalivet put it, 'anarchy had but a step to take in order to penetrate into the very heart of public authority'.[1]

To some extent these accounts can be reconciled. When Guizot left the Chamber with Duchâtel he was given a brief explanation of what had happened. It may be that Duchâtel presented the King as having completely made up his mind when this was not altogether the case. It may be that Duchâtel was even relieved at the prospect of leaving his ministry and believed the King to be more decided than he was. Possibly, too, as the journey must have been very short, Guizot got only a garbled version of what had happened and this, together with his knowledge of the sort of intrigues which had been going on in the Palace and the fact that he had been sent for, convinced him that he was about to be dismissed. In these circumstances it was natural that he should resign, and it was natural too that he should regard the King's protestations as insincere.

One should also remember that neither the King nor Guizot believed that the situation was lost. Whilst their strength had been considerable the day before, it had only been disturbed by the incidents with the National Guard, it had not been destroyed. The King's attitude was plain since he sent for Molé exactly as if this were one of the crises of the 1830s. Guizot, in the same way, did not have the impression that the state was being left without government at a moment of acute danger, whilst Molé started upon a round of political consultations as if the conditions were completely normal. Indeed it was not until half-past nine that evening that shooting took place on the Boulevard des Capucines, that a cartload of corpses was

---

[1] *Guizot, Mémoires*, vol. viii, pp. 597 ff.; *Montalivet, Fragments et Souvenirs* (op. cit.), vol. iii, pp. 108 ff. *A. Trognon, La Vie de Marie Amélie*, Paris 1872, makes mention of the Queen's intervention as told by both Guizot and Montalivet. See also *F. de Groiseillez, Histoire de la Chute de Louis-Philippe*, Paris 1851.

trundled around the streets, and that the situation began to appear impossible.

The account of events given by Guizot and Duchâtel has the ring of truth, and it may well be that the king afterwards regretted his action. He certainly showed a great deal of hesitation as to whether he should give Bugeaud the task of suppressing the disturbances and his natural indecision must have been accentuated by the excited visitors to the Tuileries who were profuse with their contradictory councils. Montalivet, who was not an eye-witness, and who repeats in his *Fragments et Souvenirs* the versions of earlier writers, is a doubtful source. He is overanxious to criticize Guizot, and it is ironical that having spent several pages explaining how he urged the King to dismiss Guizot, he then denies that the King did, in fact, dismiss his minister.

It is, of course, noticeable that Guizot made no attempt to persuade the King to keep his ministry. It is true, too, that on returning to the Chamber he had no consultation with the other ministers who were present, but he immediately made his announcement. This could suggest a hurry to be gone. Yet he was probably right when he told the King that once a rumour got about of a possible change of government, then he had lost all his authority. Once certain words had been spoken, discussion was pointless and delay could be dangerous.[1]

The remainder of the story is well known. At midnight Molé gave up his attempt to form a government, and the King accepted the necessity of calling upon Thiers, and of admitting Odilon Barrot, Duvergier de Hauranne and Charles de Rémusat as members of the cabinet. But it was too late; the new government was unable to make any effect upon events, and the army soon gave up any attempt to suppress the popular movement. At midday on February 24th the King abdicated and set off for Normandy, thinking to settle at his château in Eû, but in reality heading for Honfleur and for England. Guizot spent the day of February 24th at the Ministry of the Interior in the Rue de Grenelle. He had thought of going to the Chamber, but

---

[1] There are a great many accounts of Guizot's resignation which introduce slightly different details. One, for instance, suggests that the Duc de Montpensier tried to effect a compromise, proposing that Guizot should immediately table a bill for parliamentary reform. This Guizot refused, thus creating the story that his resignation was against the royal wishes. (*Véron, Histoire d'un Bourgeois de Paris*, op. cit., vol. iv, p. 248.) Thiers has suggested that when the Queen said that Guizot should resign, Duchâtel undertook to persuade Guizot to do so. (*M. Thiers à Mme Thiers et à Mme Dosne, Correspondance, 1841-1865.*) Another legend that has been denied by Guizot is that after his resignation he continued to advise the King in the Tuileries. It is obvious that Guizot cannot have been guilty of all these faults. He cannot have deserted the King and at the same time continued to act as his minister unknown to Molé and Thiers.

was persuaded that to do so would be dangerous. In the afternoon
he was hidden in a near-by house where de Broglie came to inform
him of the King's abdication. In the evening Madame de Mirbel, an
old friend, from the days of the Restoration, fetched him and hid him
in her house for nearly a week. Guizot whiled away the time by
reading Sir Walter Scott. On the afternoon of March 1st, a Wednes-
day, Guizot disguised himself as the servant of the Wurtemburg
ambassador, and took the train to Brussels. From there he went to
Ostend and then on to London, where he arrived on the evening of
March 3rd. His daughters had got there one day earlier, his son
arrived the next day and his mother a fortnight later. Guizot
described his escape as being 'sans incident' and got in touch with
his former colleagues Duchâtel and Dumon, who were also in
London. Louis-Philippe, who was at Claremont, also got in touch
with them. For years he had been sending almost daily notes to his
ministers, addressed 'Mon cher ministre'. He now wrote 'Mon cher
ex-ministre'.

One can look upon this revolution in many different ways. If
one thinks in general terms of French society one thinks of it as a
natural outcome. As a dispirited Molé had written in 1847, in spite
of a display of legality, the government was essentially without
principle, based simply on force and upon individualism. Daniel
Stern (the Countess d'Agoult) later wrote of the revolutionary
ferment being part of the movement which had shaken off all the
beliefs upon which authority relied.[1] But if one thinks in terms of
details, then one concentrates upon the shooting incident of the
Boulevard des Capucines and wonders whether it was not the work
of an 'agent provocateur'. One recalls the allegations of Thiers and
Bugeaud, that there were not enough troops in the capital, and that
those who were there were inadequately supplied. One remembers
that General Bedeau did not succeed in positioning his troops,
perhaps through want of determination. Above all, one is tempted to
echo Louis XIV, who, pointing to James II at Saint-Germain, is
supposed to have said, 'There goes a fool who lost a throne because
of a mass', and one can point to Louis-Philippe at Claremont and say,
'There goes a fool who lost a throne because 140 of his subjects could
not banquet, toast and speechify.' These are not so much differences
of interpretation as different ways of approaching the subject. But
however generally or however minutely one looks at things, there is
one factor which remains constant. Guizot was unpopular. Without

[1] Molé: Prosper de Barante, August 28th, 1847, *Barante, Souvenirs* (op. cit.),
vol. vii, pp. 224-227; *Daniel Stern, Histoire de la Révolution de 1848*, Paris 1850,
vol. i, Introduction.

his unpopularity the opposition might not have been so determined to get rid of him, the conservatives might have been more anxious to preserve his government. How can this unpopularity be explained? Partly by his manner and personality; partly by his intellectual rigidity; partly by the fact that he and his friends seemed to be occupying power to the exclusion of others in a way which seemed excessive. But there are other explanations. For one thing, even if Guizot's government was supposedly the government of the big 'bourgeoisie', Guizot himself was far removed from this world and had little personal sympathy with it. He was not one of the 91 deputies who had interests in railways (of whom Molé was one), he did not have particularly close relations with those deputies who represented the big railway companies, such as Thibeaudeau, Laffitte, Talabot, Koechlin or Libiel. He had few direct interests in business. Another consideration is that the Church, from the beginning of the 1847 crisis, concentrated upon its sacerdotal mission and sought to avoid being otherwise implicated. It was not going to defend a government which had repeatedly disappointed its aspirations in the matter of secondary education. The Catholics had lost hope in Guizot. Finally, and perhaps most important, all classes of Frenchmen had the suspicion that Guizot was not very patriotic in his concept of foreign affairs. The idea persisted that he was timid and pacific, essentially uninterested in the greatness of his country. It is to this subject of foreign policy, therefore, that one must turn.

6

FOREIGN POLICY

La France est assez grande.

ERNEST RENAN

THE private papers of Guizot, like his *Mémoires* and speeches, show that from 1840 to 1848 he devoted the greater part of his time to the examination and discussion of foreign policy and foreign relations. That external questions should apparently assume a greater importance for him than domestic matters is in some ways unexpected, since until his appointment as ambassador in London he had been almost entirely concerned with internal affairs. From time to time it had been suggested that he was unfamiliar with foreign questions[1] and it was generally accepted, especially in the diplomatic corps, that he accepted the embassy to the Court of St. James as a means of breaking the political deadlock in Paris and possibly restoring a damaged political reputation by a carefully timed, and temporary, retirement from the scene.[2] There were occasions when he showed that he was under some misapprehension as to what was happening abroad. In July 1839, for example, he reported that in the Middle East as the Christians were showing themselves to be divided, so the Moslems were becoming united, and he expected Mehemet Ali to be appointed generalissimo of the Turkish Empire, presiding over the new reign in Constantinople.[3] His work as ambassador was highly

---

[1] In 1837, for example, it was rumoured that Guizot was intriguing with Sébastiani in order to form a ministry: there was a report that in this manœuvre Guizot had accepted the Ministry of Foreign Affairs, 'qu'il connait si peu' commented the *Revue des Deux Mondes*, April 15th, 1837, p. 279. Molé had also accused him of being badly informed about foreign affairs.

[2] See Bresson (Berlin): Prosper de Barante, March 28th, 1840. Bresson said that Guizot's nomination to London allowed him to breathe again. *Archives du Ministère des Affaires Etrangères*, Paris [*Archives A.E.*], Mémoires et Documents Allemagne 162.

[3] Guizot: Brougham, July 25th, 1839, *Brougham Papers*, 10, 551.

criticized, both in 1840 and afterwards, and it was a commonplace to say that Guizot had committed some diplomatic blunders. In 1852 Palmerston told Thiers that during his embassy Guizot had shown a great lack of experience, and Rémusat, looking back on the 1840 crisis, thought that Guizot had been too taken up with his social life in London and had not been sufficiently active and forceful in diplomacy.[1]

This type of comment would make it seem that Guizot made a mistake when he chose to dominate the ministry of October 29th from the Ministry of Foreign Affairs. But these comments are only partially true, and to find this continued preoccupation with foreign affairs surprising is to miss the significance of events. For one thing, Guizot was very far from being ignorant about foreign affairs. His historical work and his general intellectual interests had given him a wide knowledge of European countries, especially of England and Germany, and he had been a student of European affairs for many years. Since 1830 he had made a number of speeches on questions of foreign policy and there were few members of either Chamber who were capable of making comparable contributions to the debates. He had learned a lot about the gossip of international diplomacy from his friendship with Princess Lieven, and even after Lord Palmerston had completed the Convention of July 15th, 1840, isolating France in Europe, it was being reported, on Wellington's authority, that Guizot was well-informed and well-advised.[2] Then again, if 1840 was the great crisis of the Orleanist régime, this was in the first instance a crisis of foreign relations, and it was obvious that whoever took office had to face up to this crisis and take over the Ministry of Foreign Affairs. But foreign policy is itself a type of social action. It results from the government's conception of what the national interest is, and it also depends upon the power of the government and the source of that power. Thus when Guizot wrote in his *Mémoires* that the decisive reason why he accepted the invitation to form a government in October 1840 was because he saw in the diplomatic complications then exciting Europe the opportunity to start a new foreign policy, he is really saying that he was able to propose an alternative interpretation of the national interest to that being put forward by Thiers, and he was also suggesting that the source of government power should be different from that implied by Thiers's ministry. Since these interpretations were to confront one another repeatedly over the next few years, it is advisable to spend some time considering them.

It is important to realize that Guizot and his opponents were not simply arguing about this or that detail of diplomacy, as their

[1] Rémusat, *Mémoires de Ma Vie* (op. cit.), vol. iii, p. 439.
[2] Léon Faucher: Thiers, August 7th, 1840, *Papiers Thiers* (op. cit.), 20609.

speeches in the debates of November 1840 would sometimes suggest. They were really arguing about the type of government which France should have, and in this sense Guizot is persisting in the main preoccupation of his political career, which was that of governing France. For some the problems of governing France were so great, the divisions of the country were so considerable, that without the resources of foreign policy neither unity nor effective government was possible. Only in patriotism and in activity could the French forget their internal disagreements and act as one nation. It was Duvergier de Hauranne and Tocqueville who expressed this point of view most clearly and directly, although it was present in some form for most of the deputies who supported the government of Thiers in 1840, or who later opposed the policy of Guizot. It can best be explained in three different ways. Firstly in relation to France as possessing a constitutional government. According to Duvergier de Hauranne, the opponents of parliamentary government in France insisted above all upon the absence of any clear majority or decided national opinion, and it is certainly true that this always was one of the great difficulties of French parliamentary government. It was necessary, then, in order that France should have an effective constitutional government, with the future of France depending upon the will of the nation rather than upon the existence of an individual monarch, that the will and determination of the nation should make itself known and felt. But on what issue could this will and determination show itself to be clear and united? Only the sort of issue which appeared in the summer of 1840, when the other powers of Europe leagued against France in order to defend the integrity of the Ottoman Empire against the attacks of Mehemet Ali, Pasha of Egypt.[1]

Secondly, from the point of view of the dynasty. 'I want this monarchy to endure,' said Tocqueville, in a speech made in 1839, 'but I am convinced that it will not last for long if the idea is allowed to grow that we, once a strong and great nation, accomplishing great things and making the world's affairs our own, now intervene nowhere, no longer take part in anything, and allow everything to go on without us. If ever such an idea took root in the heart of this proud and excitable nation, then let me tell you that such an idea would be more fatal for us than the loss of twenty battles, and that such a belief would necessarily, sooner or later, lead to the burial of the monarchy itself beneath the ruins of our national honour.'[2] The

[1] *Duvergier de Hauranne, De la Politique Extérieure et Intérieure de la France*, Paris 1841. This book consists of three articles originally published in the *Revue des Deux Mondes* with a specially written introduction.

[2] Speech of July 2nd, 1839, quoted in *Rémusat, Mémoires de Ma Vie* (op. cit.), vol. iii, p. 449.

same belief was expressed more directly by Thiers's friend, Merruau, in a letter already quoted in the last chapter. 'Many people', he wrote, 'thought that the King, founder of the dynasty, was forgetting that a little war, carried out aptly and in good conditions, makes thrones solid and popular.'[1]

Thirdly, many observers were struck by an apparent deterioration in the French character. The Frenchman had become self-centred, materialist, unambitious. As Duvergier put it, 'Provided that he can eat, drink, digest, and grumble a bit in his sleep, then he is contented and proud of himself.'[2] What was the remedy for these 'honteux penchants'? Duvergier later suggested the remedy of war. '. . . in these times of gross materialism one is happy to find in the country a patriotic cord which still vibrates a little and a national sentiment which persists. Cut this cord, stifle this sentiment, and there will remain nothing but M. Mimerel, M. Fulchiron and M. de Rothschild. I agree that this is a weapon which is somewhat dangerous and which is rather difficult to handle, but it is one which we cannot completely relinquish without imprudence.'[3] Duvergier, writing in 1841 about the campaign in Algeria, said that it did not matter whether France stayed in Africa, whether France made a settlement or derived any advantage from there. 'Ce qu'il faut, ce sont des combats qui descendent pour un moment comme un rideau brillant sur le triste drame qui se joue, ce sont des bulletins qui fassent battre les coeurs et qui éblouissent les yeux.'[4]

These ideas were expressed in slightly different ways by different thinkers. But essentially this concept of nationalism is the product of a divided, worried country. 'L'orgeuil national est le plus grand sentiment qui nous reste,' wrote Tocqueville to John Stuart Mill.[5] But this was not the way in which Guizot envisaged the matter. Bringing to his study of international relations the same taste for principles and generalizations that characterized his other activities, Guizot sought to elucidate the principles which should govern France's relations with her neighbours. In the past, he considered that the destiny of peoples had been decided arbitrarily by their governments, or putting it in another way, 'l'ancienne routine

---

[1] Merruau: Thiers, July 15th, 1842, *Papiers Thiers*, 20616.

[2] Duvergier de Hauranne: Thiers, October 13th, 1843, Ibid.

[3] Duvergier de Hauranne: Thiers, October 30th, 1845, Ibid. Auguste Mimerel was a rich manufacturer from Roubaix: Jean-Claude Fulchiron was a banker's son who was deputy for Lyons. They were leaders of the movement in favour of tariff protection.

[4] *Duvergier de Hauranne, De la Politique Extérieure et Intérieure* (op. cit.), p. xix.

[5] Tocqueville: John Stuart Mill, December 18th, 1840, *Œuvres et Correspondance Inédites* (ed. Beaumont), vol. ii, p. 110.

européenne' had been guided by considerations of natural frontiers and by alliances which were the outcome of individual ambitions or fanciful inventions. Relations between states, Guizot thought, could no longer be decided in this way. Such considerations were no longer relevant to existing conditions. What counted in modern society was 'the extent and activity of industry and commerce, the necessity of consulting the general good, the habit of frequent, easy, prompt and regular intercourse between peoples, the invincible bias for free association, enquiry, discussion and publicity'. These, according to Guizot, were the features of society which would exercise a preponderating influence on foreign policy. Whereas the old traditional policy made decisions 'par routine et par entraînement', policy in modern times should be made to accord with the needs of the state, with the requirements of dignity, external security and internal conditions. Any policy of adventure or of conquest, any attempt to submit Europe to a system, whether the system was that of Bonaparte, or the Holy Alliance, or the 1830 revolutionaries, was out of date.

In France the old methods and habits of foreign policy came into conflict with the new requirements of civilization. The former, fresh from its recent dramatic achievements, found the principles of peace and respect for law dull and unexciting. 'We are set in the midst of two conflicting currents; one of them is deep and regular and draws us towards the rightful end of our social organization; the other is troubled and superficial and drives us hither and thither in a search for new adventures and uncharted lands'.[1] This was Guizot's way of explaining the dilemma of Frenchmen; in much the same way Prosper Merimée wrote, some years later, 'That devil Napoleon has given us such a reputation as fighters that we cannot rid ourselves of it, even though we are now the greatest friends of tranquillity that are to be found in the world',[2] and later still Xavier Doudan wrote, 'What we have always wanted is to be well fed and well clothed, with a good bed and an early bed, and at the same time to be on the march, barefooted and starving, engaged in the conquest of Europe.'[3]

What in fact Guizot was suggesting was that the rôle of France in Europe as it had supposedly been seen by a Louis XIV or by a Napoleon was no longer a practical or desirable rôle to play. He was proposing an adjustment of French policy. Such a decisive change of

[1] These ideas are expressed in Guizot's *Mémoires*, vol. vi, pp. 7-11, and in a speech made at the beginning of the July Monarchy. Chamber of Deputies, January 27th, 1831, *Histoire Parlementaire*, vol. i, pp. 191-202.

[2] Merimée: Mme de Montijo, July 10th, 1847, *Correspondance* (op. cit.), vol. v, p. 118.

[3] Xavier Doudan: la Baronne de Staël, September 4th, 1850, *Mélanges et Lettres*, vol. iii, p. 263.

policy is never easy to accept and Guizot did not seek to conceal this adjustment behind any trumpery façade of prestige and power, as did some of his successors. Yet his policy was in accordance with the basic conditions of European history as they then existed. The frontiers established in 1815 were a source of strength to France. It was only the idea of imposed frontiers which was thought to be humiliating. If French power and security were to be furthered, then this should be by an increase of economic strength rather than by an extension of these frontiers. It was true that as French economic growth was traditionally seen as taking place within a protectionist system, then there could be complications. It was true, too, that crises could occur which vitally affected France. There could be civil war and English intervention in Spain; there could be national movements and foreign intervention in Belgium or Switzerland, or in the states of Germany or Italy; there could be intervention by the powers in states theoretically controlled by the declining forces of the Ottoman Empire. On all these matters the French were concerned with their frontiers and with any increase of foreign power or influence which could threaten their security, but in these same matters their position was weakened by the apparent hostility of the monarchies of Austria, Prussia and Russia to the France which was the product of the July Revolution, and by the suspicions of Great Britain towards the France which was a possible national and economic rival. It was to the interests of France not to confirm this hostility or to increase this suspicion, but rather to prove that the image of the French as a source of war and revolution was out of date.

Of course, Guizot exaggerated when in his *Mémoires* he claimed that the type of foreign policy which he was advocating was 'très nouvelle'. Many past ministers could have claimed that their policy was realistic and adapted to the needs of France. Nevertheless, Guizot rightly considered that Thiers's handling of the Mehemet Ali crisis was contrary to these principles. The situation was simple. In 1839 war had broken out between the Pasha of Egypt and his overlord the Sultan, in which the first victories went to the Pasha. The powers, thinking that the defeat of the Turks would lead to the invasion of Turkey and that this would end in Russia invoking her rights by the treaty of Unkiar Skelessi and protecting Constantinople by occupying it, sent a collective note to the Sultan urging him to make no separate peace and assuring him that they would make a settlement. This note was dated July 27th, 1839, and for months afterwards no progress was made. This was because the French government, whether headed by Soult or by Thiers, saw no reason why it should compel Mehemet Ali to abandon territory to the Sultan. He had not started the war, nor had he lost the war, and he was an ally of the French. Furthermore, neither the French governments nor their experts could see how Mehemet Ali was to be coerced. They did not believe that an Austrian army either would or could be sent to the area; they did not believe that the British Fleet could attack Mehemet by naval means alone; they could not imagine that a Russian army would be sent to Constantinople, since this was the eventuality which the British government was most eager to avoid.

Guizot, as ambassador, warned his government on several occasions that the practical isolation of France, since all the other powers were agreed on taking action against the Pasha, could take the form of a treaty arrangement from which France would be excluded. These warnings should not have surprised either Thiers or Louis-Philippe; the latter at least had earlier suspected Palmerston of trying to isolate France. It may be that Thiers's informants in Paris, 'Bear' Ellice and Reeve, had spoken too confidently about Palmerston not being strong enough to conclude a treaty without France.[1] But at the same time as he issued these warnings, Guizot was pressing Thiers to make some compromise agreement, or at least to make some suggestion which could be put to the British government. As things turned out, this would have been good diplomacy since it would have weakened Palmerston's contention that there was nothing to be done with the French. Such advice was also in accordance with Guizot's principles of foreign policy since he was obviously asking whether it was altogether in the French interest to be too committed to Mehemet Ali and whether his cause was a good reason for breaking with the rest of Europe.

It is true that Guizot, in spite of his general warnings, was not prepared for the actual conclusion of the Convention on July 15th, which came as a surprise to him, and Palmerston was delighted to see him and the Princess Lieven (especially the Princess) looking 'as cross as the devil'. Guizot tried, by various methods, to undo the Convention. But whilst this absorbed his attention, he was most disturbed by the excitement which was growing in France and which was being encouraged by the press, as well as by the ostentatious preparations for war which Thiers was actively making. Guizot asked the question, what interest had France in risking war in order to maintain the Pasha of Egypt in his conquests? Was not this an example of a policy which was arbitrarily determined? Was not this an example of both government and public opinion acting 'par

[1] See p. 178 (and note 3); Louis-Philippe: Mme Adelaïde, September 26th and 27th, 1839, Unedited Letters of Louis-Philippe, *Fortnightly Review*, 1866, vol. iv, pp. 735-737. Princess Lieven: Lady Palmerston, May 7th, 1840, *The Lieven-Palmerston Correspondence* (ed. Lord Sudley), 1943, p. 188.

routine et par entraînement' in a way which was offensive to reason and logic?

To Duchâtel he explained the situation as he saw it. 'The whole of our conduct, the whole of our diplomatic argument, has been based upon the supposition that the Pasha would resist, that his resistance would be forceful and long, and that this resistance would compromise the peace of Europe. If he makes little or no resistance, then we have made a mistake. It will be an error, a misfortune, an absurdity. But it is not a reason for us to create the resistance which is non-existent, or to start off the blaze which will not catch fire by itself. For us to take this sort of action, then the Syrian question would need to be terribly, immensely important to us. We would need to have such a great, urgent interest in keeping the Pasha in control of Syria that we would be prepared by our own will and action to run the risk of this general conflagration which has been causing us such uneasiness. . . . It is obvious that there is no such interest so far as we are concerned.' Guizot concluded by reminding Duchâtel that France had avoided war when the Polish and Italian questions had been raised. Supposing that the Pasha himself decided to avoid war, was France then going to rush in and do what the French had not been prepared to do over Poland and Italy? 'Beyrouth and Damascus are not worth Warsaw and Bologna,' he concluded.[1] This was for Guizot an example of foreign policy being decided as a result of popular excitement and passion. And this in itself had further implications.

One of Guizot's most decided beliefs was that the essential political and social liberties had been achieved after the Revolution. Those who wished for further change or for further revolution were disarmed by the existence of political liberty and by the growth of prosperity, and they were deprived of the support of the masses. The only remaining hope of the revolutionary therefore lay in war or in some sort of foreign adventure; only in this way could they reopen political and social questions which Guizot wished to consider as closed. Therefore he tended to see the crisis of 1840 as being a revolutionary crisis within France. This interpretation naturally arose from his view of Thiers's government, and his fear that it was becoming increasingly dependent upon the left. He had always regarded the talk of war in the context of the Mehemet Ali question as being a sign of revolutionary danger. Thus as early as June, when explaining (with some confidence) the French position to Duchâtel, he expressed alarm. 'Tell me, please,' he wrote, 'why is it that from Paris come ideas about war, fear of war, a certain rumour that all this will end

[1] Guizot: Duchâtel, September 25th, 1840, *Papiers Duchâtel, Archives Nationales,* 2 A.P. 8.

up in war? Is it possible that amongst the many people who fear war there are some who want it?'[1] After July there was much more reason for alarm. Bulwer's despatches to Palmerston suggested that Thiers had either lost control of the situation, since he was said to be pleading that he was in the hands of the French public and that he could not gainsay the wishes of the nation that he led, or that he was deliberately creating an atmosphere of crisis in order to profit from it.[2] Throughout the crisis one of its features which most worried Guizot was the violence of the French press. Rémusat, who was then Minister of the Interior, dismisses this complaint in his *Mémoires* by asking how this violence could have been prevented. Many people, however, suspected that Thiers was encouraging this aggressive tone, particularly with regard to *Le Constitutionnel*, and Rémusat does not deal satisfactorily with this matter by accusing Guizot of stupidity.[3] At all events, whether Thiers was creating popular excitement or was trying to profit from it, this was not Guizot's conception of government, and he is differing with Thiers over the way in which France should be governed as well as over the interpretation of national interest. In October, when the crisis had developed, Guizot wrote to de Broglie, 'I am disturbed, and more by our internal than by our foreign affairs. We are going back to 1834, towards the revolutionary spirit taking advantage of national enthusiasm and urging on war without legitimate motive or hope of success, with the sole aim and the sole hope being revolution. . . . In France today I believe in the revolutionary tendency of the factions, but I do not believe that the nation has any revolutionary bias.'[4] Guizot did not believe that such a war would be successful in Europe, nor did he believe that it would be supported by the French nation. He had received from Thiers a letter in which the Président du Conseil had dissociated himself from any form of limited action in the Middle East, comparable to Casimir Périer's 1831 occupation of Ancona as a riposte to Austrian troops moving into the Papal States. 'I am not in favour of a naval war . . .,' Thiers had written. 'For my part, I believe only in war in the Alps and on the Rhine.'[5] This confirmed Guizot in his belief that if Thiers stayed in power, then there would be general war. Granville, the British ambassador in Paris, was also convinced that if Thiers continued as minister then he would not be able to pursue a pacific policy and simply wait for action to be taken against the Pasha; nor

[1] Guizot: Duchâtel, June 9th, 1840, Ibid.

[2] Bulwer: Palmerston, July 27th, 1840, *Correspondence Relative to the Affairs of the Levant*, 1841, part 2, pp. 33-35.

[3] *Rémusat, Mémoires de Ma Vie* (op. cit.), vol. iii, p. 452.

[4] Guizot: de Broglie, October 13th, 1840, *Mémoires*, vol. v, pp. 390-391.

[5] Thiers: Guizot, October 9th, 1840, *Archives Nationales*, 42 A.P. 9.

could he ask the Chamber to approve his expenditure on arms if he showed no intention of using those arms.[1] Thus the issue seemed clear. Louis-Philippe's dismissal of Thiers avoided a war. But one must always remember that the possibility of war had been closely allied to the promotion of considerable, if not revolutionary, changes within France. The *Journal des Débats*, expressing the point of view of those who were to approve the King's action in replacing Thiers by Guizot, considered that for some war was only 'a noble pretext'; revolution was the real aim.[2]

The ease with which the ministry of October 29th replaced the ministry of March 1st has already been commented upon; there was no prolonged negotiation amongst the political groups; there was little doubt that the ministry would get a majority when the Middle East question was discussed in the Chamber; the excitement that had been noticeable in the streets of Paris quickly disappeared (thus lending some confirmation to the suggestion that the preceding government had encouraged such exuberance). Apparently, therefore, the foreign policy that was based upon a rational appraisal of the country's interests had prevailed over policy which sought to exploit national sentiment as a means of furthering the country's unity and progress. This triumph would earlier have seemed difficult. Even a doctrinaire, Jouffroy, had insisted upon the political dangers of weak policy. 'France must play a rôle in the Eastern question which is worthy of her. The settlement of these important affairs must not at any price reduce France's rank in Europe. Such a humiliation would not be supported and the internal counter-effects would be perilous.'[3] Even the Princess Lieven had explained to Lord Aberdeen that Louis-Philippe's major interest was to stay united to French national sentiment, and it was for this reason that the King, for all that he was as pacific as ever, had found it necessary to go along with Thiers.[4] What then enabled policy to be changed so efficiently?

One reason was undoubtedly the proofs of Thiers's miscalculations. It was on October 2nd that Paris learned of Napier's operations on the Syrian coast, which showed that both the French belief in the invincibility of the Pasha's armies and their disbelief in the possibility of naval operations were equally without foundation. It was on October 15th that the danger of internal revolution was symbolized by the attempt on the life of the King by Darmès. But before either

[1] Granville: Palmerston, October 15th, 1840, *Correspondence Relative to the Affairs of the Levant* (op. cit.), part 2, p. 207.

[2] *Journal des Débats*, October 6th, 1840. Quoted in *Thureau-Dangin, Histoire de la Monarchie de Juillet* (op. cit.), vol. iv, p. 326.

[3] Quoted in *Rémusat, Mémoires de Ma Vie* (op. cit.), vol. iii, p. 448.

[4] Princess Lieven: Lord Aberdeen, August 19th, 1840, *The Correspondence of Lord Aberdeen and Princess Lieven* (ed. E. Jones Parry), 1938, vol. i, pp. 145-146.

of these dates many observers had noted a cooling of the national enthusiasm, and had in particular noticed that it was amongst the capitalists that this reaction to Thiers's warlike policy was most marked.[1] For Guizot the realization that France's ally was weak and not strong, the discovery that there was a danger of revolution, the calculation that war would cost money and interrupt trade, were signs of a return to reason and sense. But to others the success of the ministry of October 29th was due to the defeat of an ally and to the fears of a certain part of the country's political 'élite'. Therefore, its origins were surrounded in humiliation and in class egoism.

It does not seem that Guizot understood why his policy was unpopular. He thought that the policy of Thiers and his associates had simply been unsuccessful and unreasonable. He never tried to understand why a man as intelligent as Tocqueville should have opposed him over foreign policy, or why men as different as Duvergier de Hauranne, Michelet, Lacordaire or Ernest Renan wanted to see policies of great national success. Guizot never felt any enthusiasm for Mehemet Ali. He supported the Pasha because he thought it was in the nature of things that the Ottoman Empire should become a number of independent states such as Greece and Egypt; he did not share Rémusat's comprehension that Mehemet Ali was popular because he appeared in some sort as a French creation, as an example of the French mission which was to regenerate old governments.[2] In the same way he never felt any enthusiasm for the conquest of Algeria. Privately he regretted this new burden; he saw France being engaged in Algeria for the next fifty years and fighting one or two campaigns each year. At best Algeria was only going to provide France with another naval base, another Toulon; at most Algeria was 'the affair of our leisure time', an activity permissible whilst European affairs were quiet.[3] For Guizot national enthusiasm, for all that he professed to admire it, was inexorably bound up with the spirit of revolution; and he thought that the revolutionary parties, when otherwise defeated, tried to exploit the prejudices and the popular feelings of the country in matters of foreign relations, particularly against England.[4] Patriotism, therefore, began to look to Guizot like a political manœuvre.

---

[1] See for example Bulwer: Palmerston, August 23rd, 1840, *Correspondence Relative to the Affairs of the Levant* (op. cit.), part 2, p. 72.

[2] See Guizot's speech of July 2nd, 1839, *Histoire Parlementaire*, vol. iii, pp. 266 ff.; *Rémusat, Mémoires de Ma Vie* (op. cit.), vol. iii, p. 282.

[3] Guizot: Duchâtel, June 9th, 1840, *Papiers Duchâtel*, ibid.; Guizot: Bugeaud, September 20th, 1842, *Mémoires*, vol. vii, p. 141.

[4] Chambre des Députés, November 26th, 1840, *Histoire Parlementaire*, ibid., p. 339; Guizot: Bresson (Madrid), August 17th, 1844, *Archives Nationales*, 42 A.P. 8.

One of Guizot's contemporaries claimed that in his conduct of foreign affairs he was 'peu capable de détails'.[1] It is true that one of his axioms stressed the necessity of distinguishing between important questions and questions of only secondary importance, and he may occasionally have given the appearance of being disdainful of certain details. However, any close examination of Guizot's methods shows how attentive he was to matters of detail. He belonged to the period when a statesman explained his policy in lengthy despatches which were frequently accompanied by equally lengthy private letters. His correspondence with ambassadors and ministers was voluminous, and he required a regular and informative flow of despatches and letters in return. In 1841 he lamented that it was through a lack of good information that French affairs had been mishandled in the Middle East and in the River Plate.[2] He later wrote to Piscatory that the radical vice of French policy was the vagueness of its knowledge and action. 'Help me to get away from this vice,' he asked.[3] To Rayneval, who was in charge of the embassy in St. Petersburg, he described closely the sort of communication he expected, even from a capital where French policy was not very forward. '. . . It is precisely in those places where the rôle of actor does not exist that the rôle of observer comes first and is most necessary. The rôle of observer means observing everything and repeating everything. Nothing is too small or too insignificant if one is searching the surface for signs of what is going on in the depths, out of sight. The more everything is hidden and silent at the Russian court, then the more valuable are the slightest facts, the smallest indications. However careful a government may be and whatever power it may have for concealment, it is difficult these days for the situation not to be suggested or revealed somewhere, by some incident or detail which attentive observation can seize upon.'[4] He was equally anxious that his agents should be kept informed of what was happening elsewhere. Unless there was a clear and complete understanding of the general situation, then local diplomacy was badly directed, uncertain and incoherent, and it could not be effective.[5] As an additional means of giving and receiving information, he liked to send special missions. He sent Mounier to London in November 1840. Piscatory went on a special mission to Athens in 1841. Pageot went round the capitals of the powers to discuss the marriage of the Queen of Spain in 1842, and after the

---

[1] A. de Brossard, Considérations historiques et politiques sur les Républiques de la Plata dans leurs rapports avec la France et l'Angleterre (Paris 1850), p. 299.
[2] Guizot: Bourqueney (London), January 19th and 28th, 1841, 42 A.P. 10.
[3] Guizot: Piscatory (Athens), July 28th, 1843, 42 A.P. 7.
[4] Guizot: Rayneval (St. Petersburg), November 8th, 1844, 42 A.P. 9.
[5] Guizot: Sainte-Aulaire (London), November 22nd, 1841, 42 A.P. 8.

conclusion of the marriages he sent Edouard Bocher, prefect of his own department of Calvados, on a special mission to Madrid; Klindworth was a special agent, via whom he communicated with Metternich. This was a method which often aroused resentment amongst his permanent representatives, but it shows Guizot's determination to organize information and to avoid misunderstanding.

In his conduct of diplomacy he was always most attentive to the personal side. 'Plus je vais,' he told Prosper de Barante, 'plus je me persuade que ce sont les personnes qui font les choses et qu'on n'en tient jamais assez de compte.'[1] Many of his representatives were close personal friends, and he chose their posts carefully. Sometimes he made diplomatic appointments with an eye to the political situation at home, sometimes he had to consider the wishes of the King, to say nothing of the Princess Lieven, but he usually had men whom he knew and trusted in the vital posts; they were men to whom he could send endless private letters and notes. Such were Sainte-Aulaire and de Broglie in London, Piscatory in Athens, Rossi in Rome. Perhaps the only exception of an ambassador in a vital capital who was not a friend of Guizot's was Bresson, who was moved from Berlin to Madrid in 1843. Bresson's name had been associated with the doctrinaire group during the political confusions of 1834, but this was not important. Bresson was probably chosen for his determination and resourcefulness; possibly too because he had some experience in arranging marriages, as he had arranged the marriage of the Duke of Orleans. But there might have been some sympathy between Guizot and Bresson, for all that their ideas were radically different on some subjects, because they had a similar insistence upon the personal note in diplomacy. Bresson's method was to find one important person over whom he could gain ascendancy; in Berlin this was Wittgenstein, in Madrid it was General Narvaez. Guizot, too, liked to put relations between France and other countries on the basis of personal friendship; this was obviously the basis of his understanding with Aberdeen in the Conservative government of 1841 to 1846. There are indications that he would have liked to establish equally friendly relations with Lord John Russell. After 1844 he gave all his confidence to Colettis, who became Prime Minister of Greece and who had been a neighbour of Guizot's during his long exile in Paris. After 1846 he tried hard to cultivate a personal friendship with Metternich, although he had no illusions about Metternich's conceit, saying of him (what many critics said of Guizot himself) that 'he likes to believe that what he dislikes does not exist'.[2]

[1] Guizot: Barante, March 20th, 1841, *Barante, Souvenirs* (op. cit.), vol. vi, pp. 585-586.
[2] Guizot: de Broglie, July 12th, 1847, 42 A.P. 8.

Whenever he could, Guizot gave detailed advice to his representatives concerning their relations with people and their personal contacts. He told Bourqueney that a good way of communicating with Russell was via Greville, a good way of getting at Peel was via Lord Vesey Fitzgerald, Lansdowne could be influenced by Henry Reeve and MacGregor of the Board of Trade was close both to Lansdowne and Baring. Sir John Bowring was very useful because of his influence in the City, and he advised Bourqueney to see him, but thought he should not confide in him. He suggested that with Lord Palmerston the best method was the direct one. Similarly he advised Sainte-Aulaire not to be put off by Aberdeen's coldness, and suggested that he should complain without hesitation if there were any faults of language or detail in the British conduct of affairs, since he thought that this attitude would be successful with Aberdeen. To Sainte-Aulaire he repeated his advice about Lord Vesey Fitzgerald and Peel, and he said that he should speak French slowly when talking to Peel.[1] To every ambassador he used the device of sending a 'strictly private' letter which could be shown, as if by disobedience on the part of the ambassador, to the relevant foreign government. He used also to quote from 'private' letters which he had himself received whenever this suited him.

This preoccupation with personalities often led him into deep waters, particularly when he disapproved of a minister. The most famous example is Palmerston. It is obvious that Guizot and Palmerston were very different sorts of men; Palmerston was not interested in theories of foreign policy, as was Guizot, he was impatient of abstract generalizations and probably dismissed this side of Guizot as 'bookish', which was the term actually used by Bulwer. His self-confidence, his directness and his unscrupulousness, had shocked the old school of diplomacy, and a sort of clique was organized against him in Europe, in the first instance by Talleyrand, who could not understand, when he became ambassador in London after 1830, that Palmerston should treat him as an ordinary ambassador. The Princess Lieven was part of this clique and doubtless she persuaded Guizot that Palmerston was impossible. But Guizot, as ambassador, soon had cause to discover for himself the difficulties of dealing with Palmerston. It was the British Foreign Secretary whom he saw as the obstacle to a settlement, and he believed that the crisis was being prolonged by Palmerston's obstinacy. Although he had liked Palmerston when he first met him, he quickly found that discussion with him was pointless. Palmerston had a formidable mastery of detail, but it was not this mastery which

[1] Guizot: Bourqueney, November 4th, 1840, Ibid., 42 A.P. 10; Guizot: Sainte-Aulaire, October 26th, 1841, 42 A.P. 8.

overwhelmed Guizot, it was Palmerston's indifference to argument. Guizot could claim to get the better of Palmerston in showing that it was the Sultan, and not the Pasha, who had been the original aggressor in 1839, but this made no difference to Palmerston. He would concede a point, he would change his mind over details, but he stuck to the line of policy he had determined upon. The man who could describe French rearmament as being inadequate for war and incompatible with peace, was not a man to allow logic to stand in the way of his determined policy. It was not surprising then that Guizot should compare Palmerston to a theologian, a man who was so determined to prove that he was right on one particular point, that he could lose sight of all other considerations and was capable of forgetting about the major issue. Palmerston's conclusion of the Convention of July 15th was of course a blow to Guizot's personal vanity, but even supporters of Palmerston had to admit that both the aim of the Convention and the manner of its negotiation were unfriendly towards France.

How could Guizot explain these actions? He could only explain them by supposing that Palmerston was moved by personal hostility towards France and that the British Foreign Secretary cared little for the alliance, or friendship, of France. Such prejudice and apparent readiness to risk war were quite contrary to any rational foreign policy, and therefore it seemed to Guizot that every rational person should agree with him in his condemnation of Palmerston. In 1850, although he was no longer concerned with affairs, and although he had, in 1848, made his public reconciliation with Palmerston by shaking hands with him so vigorously that Greville thought their arms would come off, Guizot still thought the same. He was convinced that everyone in England thought as he and the French did about Lord Palmerston, and the fact that Palmerston remained at the Foreign Office seemed an unparalleled example of short-sightedness and apathy on the part of the English. Palmerston had constantly misunderstood the real interests of England; he had so destroyed and diminished British influence that, according to Guizot, 'every Englishman who is a friend of the consideration and the ascendancy of England in the world must consider Lord Palmerston to be his most fatal enemy'.[1]

This being so, it is not surprising that Guizot should try to meet the menace of Palmerston by personal intrigue. In 1840, as is well known, Guizot was closely involved in an attempt to incite opposition to Palmerston within the Cabinet and the Whig party. His relations with Lord Holland, Greville and others probably went beyond the

---

[1] Guizot: Aberdeen, February 27th, June 21st, 1850, *Aberdeen Papers*, B.M. Add. MSS. 43,134.

bounds of diplomatic etiquette and he was fortunate that one of Palmerston's greatest qualities was his good nature (although Lord Normanby and the British Embassy in 1847 were equally prepared to associate themselves with the opposition to Guizot). But this was not an isolated incident in Guizot's diplomacy. In1846, when Palmerston returned to power, Guizot tried to find an ally against him in the Prime Minister, Lord John Russell,[1] and also in Lord Aberdeen. But the latter was quick to inform Guizot that he was not willing to take part in any anti-Palmerston coalition. He admitted that he had reason to, since 'no one has acted with more hostility or more unfairly than he did towards me during the whole time I was in office . . . I shall take a pride in following a different course and although truth and justice must prevail above all things, it will always be my desire to support and to strengthen the Queen's government.' When Aberdeen had been at the Foreign Office the great object of Palmerston's life had been to replace him, but Aberdeen did not feel the same desire now Palmerston was in office.[2] Undeterred by this, in 1847 Guizot thought that if he were to publish details of the negotiations concerning affairs in the River Plate, when Palmerston separated himself from the French government and called off the blockade of Buenos Aires, then he would place Palmerston in an impossible situation at home. '. . . We would have all the diplomacy of Europe on our side, the whole of the conservative and Peelite party with Lord Aberdeen at their head, and probably five-sixths of the Whig party and the cabinet itself' was Guizot's assessment of the situation.[3]

Guizot was unsuccessful in these attempts to get rid of Palmerston. He underestimated Palmerston's political strength, and he seriously misjudged opinion about his foreign policy. In 1840 Palmerston's policy was criticized until October, when it was shown to be successful; once the Middle East victories were in the air then the opposition faded away and even Melbourne wrote a letter threatening the French.[4] In 1847 Guizot was still less successful. But the question

[1] Guizot: Jarnac (London), October 15th, 1846, 42 A.P. 7.
[2] Aberdeen: Guizot, November 16th, 1846, Ibid.
[3] Memorandum by Guizot, *Archives A.E.*, Correspondance Politique, Argentine 23. *J. F. Cady, Foreign Intervention in the River Plate*, Philadelphia 1929, pp. 233-234, quotes part of this document under its old catalogue number. It is wrongly dated January 1847 and it probably should bear about the same date as a despatch to de Broglie which was dated October 18th, 1847. See also *H. S. Ferns, Britain and Argentina in the Nineteenth Century*, 1960, pp. 277 ff.
[4] Melbourne: King Leopold, October 25th, 1840, *Sir Charles Webster, The Foreign Policy of Palmerston, 1830-1841*, vol. ii, pp. 722-723, suggests that as this letter was forwarded to Louis-Philippe it 'contributed a good deal to the decision which the latter made a few days later', but the actual decision to dismiss the Thiers government had been made long before.

7. Guizot by G. F. Watts (1856).

8. Guizot in Old Age.

remains, whether Guizot was or was not justified in these moves to influence British politicians. Since a country's foreign policy is an attempt to change the policy of other governments, then it was obviously justified. The question then becomes, whether relations between England and France were determined by such considerations as the rivalry of maritime and overseas power and the threat of the Continent being dominated commercially by England, or whether relations between the two countries depended upon the character of the ministers concerned. There can be no doubt that Guizot exaggerated the importance of the latter. This led him to regard the 'entente cordiale' which he established with Aberdeen as an almost idyllic period of friendship, when it was nothing of the kind.

Another mistake which Guizot made about Palmerston was that he failed to understand that the British Foreign Secretary, like himself, was responsible to Parliament. Palmerston had to show that his policy was successful in upholding British interests. Sir Charles Webster has written that 'Palmerston faced combinations of internal and external foes that would have killed most men';[1] this fact made his need for obvious and clear success even more imperative. Sir Robert Peel often complained that whilst Guizot expected English ministers to consider his position in the Chambers, he never seemed to think of the British government's parliamentary position. Guizot was sometimes surprised by the sharpness of Peel's comment on foreign affairs. It did not occur to him that Peel was perhaps closer to Palmerston because they were both House of Commons men, whilst Aberdeen could afford to be more detached because he was in the Lords. Guizot probably exaggerated the rigidity of the English two-party system. He probably too was influenced by his experience in London, when for some time no one seemed interested in foriegn affairs. Before the July 15th Convention, Joseph Hume was the only member who raised the question in the Commons, and even after July 15th, when Guizot was assembling the units of his anti-Palmerston coalition, he was often discomfitted to find London deserted and to come across many individuals who were content to leave foreign affairs entirely to the one man.

Yet in spite of these errors there is something justifiable in Guizot's aversion to Palmerston. Palmerston was a gambler; he was determined to bring pressure on Mehemet Ali at a time when he did not know how he was going to bring the pressure. He believed the reports coming from Colonel Hodges on the Egyptian position in Syria and the Lebanon largely because he wanted to believe them, just as Thiers and Rémusat, anxious to believe that naval operations against

[1] Ibid, p. 784.

Mehemet would not be possible, listened overeagerly to the opinions of Admiral Lalande. This way of conducting business was dangerous. The comparison between Palmerston and Thiers as 'the two most rash and unscrupulous politicians of our time'[1] (which exceeds anything Guizot ever said), cannot be dismissed out of hand as political animosity. Furthermore, Palmerston was prejudiced against the French. He assumed that British interests required the reduction, and if need be the humiliation, of French power; this was not necessarily true. He assumed that all French statesmen were concealing sinister policies and were untrustworthy; this was certainly not true. Although he recognized that there was in France a party that was genuinely attached to peace, he always tried to minimize its importance. By his actions and speeches he provoked reactions of aggrieved nationalism within France and then cited these reactions in order to justify himself. Not only the disreputable criticized Palmerston. Sir James Graham, who was far from being pro-French, told Aberdeen in 1847 that if Palmerston remained Foreign Minister for much longer 'we shall not have a cordial friend in Europe',[2] and before this Brougham had written to Guizot, when the Conservatives seemed to be going out of office, 'If Palmerston becomes your opposite number, then I pity the fate of humanity—for, whilst I know that he is neither an enemy of peace nor of France, he has universally made himself this reputation.'[3] There is reason to think that Palmerston did not always carefully consider the interests of England; on economic matters he sometimes seems to have been surprisingly careless.[4] It is difficult to avoid the conclusion that Palmerston's policy often owed its origins to his egoism, his prejudices and his need for obvious success. In which case Guizot's method was justifiable.

But whilst in European diplomacy Palmerston was quite exceptional, Guizot often instructed French representatives to intervene in the domestic politics of foreign countries, regarding personalities who were thought to be favourably or unfavourably inclined towards France. Guizot's concern with such details is to be seen in his correspondence with Bresson and Glucksberg in Madrid, Piscatory in Athens, and to a lesser extent Rossi in Rome. This was undoubtedly unwise since the influence of France in other countries tended to become associated with, if not dependent on, the internal political evolution of those countries. This form of influence is necessarily fragile.

[1] *The Times*, December 3rd, 1844.
[2] Graham: Aberdeen, August 6th, 1847, *Aberdeen Papers*, 43,190.
[3] Brougham: Guizot, [December] 18th, 1845, *Val-Richer MSS*.
[4] *Lucy Brown, The Board of Trade and the Free Trade Movement*, 1958, pp. 95-96.

Guizot's conduct of foreign policy brought him into contact with two experienced specialists in foreign affairs, Louis-Philippe and Desages, the leading permanent official of the French Ministry. It has always been a matter of speculation as to how far foreign policy was decided by the King. It will never be possible to resolve this matter finally since a great deal must have been settled by the three experts meeting and discussing questions together, without making any written record of their conversations. Certainly Guizot made no attempt to hide the fact that the King took an active part in all deliberations of the government since 'la discussion intérieure entre la couronne et ses conseillers'[1] was for him an essential part of the constitution. It was well known that the King had an almost passionate interest in foreign affairs and that he had endless conversations with ambassadors and foreign visitors. It is not surprising then that many contemporaries believed that it was the King who directed policy, sometimes keeping Guizot ignorant of affairs, sometimes overruling him. It was remembered that he had disliked de Broglie because the Duke had shown a lot of independence in his handling of foreign affairs. Lord Cowley, the British ambassador, wrote in 1842, 'Many things are done at the Tuileries with which Monsieur Guizot has no concern.'[2] It was widely thought that Louis-Philippe had directed all the policy concerning the Spanish marriages, insisting upon a Bourbon, suggesting the Neapolitan prince Trapani as a candidate, fixing up his son Montpensier's marriage with the Infanta, and so on. This was put forward as an example of the way in which the King allowed his dynastic, family interests to overrule the interests of the nation. But the very nature of this argument should warn us against it. Charges of the King's domineering and the minister's subservience were invariably made by political opponents, and some of their allegations are not confirmed by the documents.

For example, Metternich had alleged that the proposed customs union with Belgium, about which there was a great deal of discussion in 1842, was promoted by Guizot only in order to consolidate his position with the King whose personal idea it was: but it seems now that Guizot was genuinely attracted towards such a policy.[3] There is every reason to think that Guizot welcomed the Neapolitan candidate, as fitting in to his general view of policy, and there is direct evidence that Guizot thought it advisable that both the marriages, that of the

[1] Chambre des Députés, May 31st, 1844, *Histoire Parlementaire*, vol. iv, p. 387.
[2] Cowley: Aberdeen, May 9th, 1842, *Aberdeen Papers*, 43,129.
[3] Metternich: Neumann, December 9th, 1842. Quoted in *A. Ridder, Les Projets de l'Union Douanière Franco-Belge et les Puissances Européennes*, Brussels 1933, p. 245 n. 2; *H.-T. Deschamps, La Belgique devant la France de Juillet*, Paris 1956.

Queen and her sister, should take place simultaneously.[1] There are
indications that Guizot sometimes modified the King's instructions.
In July 1846 Guizot reported to Bresson that the King 'qui a toujours
des impressions très vives et des résolutions très soudaines' wanted
General Narvaez to return at once to Madrid. Guizot wanted this
return to take place only if it was considered opportune. In December
Guizot told Bresson that had he had time to see letters sent by Louis-
Philippe to the Spanish king, he would have reworded them. In July
1847 Louis-Philippe spoke to the Austrian and British ambassadors
in Paris of the possibility of having a conference on Swiss affairs;
Guizot warned de Broglie that the King had exaggerated the likelihood of such a conference.[2] It is true that one can find contrary
examples. The King probably influenced Guizot over Swiss affairs,
and in the wording of the protestation over the ending of the Cracow
Republic by the Northern Powers in 1846,[3] but in both cases it seems
that Guizot shared the King's opinions, although perhaps more
hesitantly. By and large it seems that Guizot may have given way on
matters of detail, and that there were some matters about which the
King seems to have been particularly concerned, such as the details of
the Montpensier-Infanta marriage settlement; in his *Mémoires*
Guizot suggests that the King could be very insistent over insignificant
matters; but in general Guizot's ideas were allowed to prevail. Most
contemporary observers were agreed that the King had little in the
way of fixed principles, and Guizot's remark that Louis-Philippe was
better fitted to decide between different counsels rather than to
suggest a course of action was probably correct.[4]

With regard to Desages, 'notre Lord Canning à nous' as Guizot
called him, the question is less complicated. His rôle had always
varied according to whoever was minister. When the minister was
someone like de Rigny or Soult, then most of the work must have
been done by Desages together with the King. The minister he preferred was de Broglie, which is perhaps a suggestion that he liked to
have a minister whom he was seconding rather than a minister who
was a figurehead. Under Guizot his rôle lay in co-operating with the

[1] See the correspondence in the *Revue Rétrospective*, 1848, pp. 180 ff.; see also
the whole treatment of the question in *Silva Mastellone, La Politica Estera del
Guizot*, Florence 1957.
[2] Guizot: Bresson, July 20th, 1846, December 2nd, 1846, 42 A.P. 8; Guizot:
de Broglie, July 5th, 1847, ibid.
[3] See Stratford Canning: Palmerston, December 2nd and 4th, 1847, quoted in
K. Edkinger, *Lord Palmerston und der Schweitzer Sonderbundskrieg*, Berlin 1938,
p. 140 n. 33, p. 142 n. 36; see K. Hillebrand, *Geschichte Frankreichs*, 1879,
vol. ii, p. 164, for the protestation concerning Cracow.
[4] *Mémoires*, vol. iii, p. 39; *Nassau Senior, Conversations with M. Thiers, M.
Guizot and Other Important Persons*, vol. ii, p. 390. See above pp. 255-256.

minister and there was no question of superseding him. Desages had shared with Guizot his opinion of 'ce sot engouement pour Mehemet Ali'[1] and had probably been glad to see the end of the Thiers ministry. Sometimes Guizot and Desages disagreed. Desages seems to have been less tolerant of Piscatory and Colettis than was Guizot, possibly because of his friendship with Bourqueney, who became ambassador to the Porte on leaving London; when the Austrians occupied Ferrara in 1847 Desages was less sanguine of the possibilities of French mediation than was Guizot; nor did Desages share Guizot's determination to associate Palmerston with the collective note to Switzerland in November and December 1847.[2] However, these examples serve to confirm Guizot's personal independence in determining policy rather than the contrary.

Guizot's conduct of foreign affairs can be conveniently divided into three sections. The first from 1840 to 1841, the period when the Eastern Question was settled; the second, 1841-6, the period when he consolidated his ministry, extended French influence abroad and established the 'entente' with England; the third begins in 1846, after the Spanish marriages, when he is concerned essentially with the revolutionary movements in Europe. Without entering into the details of the many complex questions which arose and without going into a year-by-year account of the Ministry, the object of this chapter is to consider what principles guided Guizot and what circumstances affected his actions.

In the first period he attempted to put his situation in France to his profit in Europe. As the statesman who wished to prevent revolution in France and a revolutionary war on the Continent, he claimed special consideration, and in order that he might consolidate his position in the Chamber, he wanted the powers to make concessions to Mehemet Ali. The key to much of Guizot's policy here as elsewhere lies in the need for successes with which to confront the Chambers in Paris. He therefore threatened the European powers with the consequences of his overthrow. He wrote to Bourqueney in London, urging that the treaty of July 15th should not be enforced to the full.

The excitement in the country has not diminished. The formation of the government has given more confidence to friends of peace; but it has redoubled the zeal of those men who are driving, or allowing themselves to be driven, towards war. Those who are ill-intentioned or

[1] Desages: Bourqueney, November 4th, 1840, quoted in *Webster* (op. cit.), vol. ii, p. 900.
[2] Desages: Piscatory, August 7th, 20th and 31st, 1847, 42 A.P. 7; see the correspondence of Guizot and Desages with Rossi in 42 A.P. 9. This has been

who are our rivals, will foment national prejudices and passions. The struggle will be intense and the danger will always be imminent . . .

This is the truth. I shall try to enlighten people and I shall try to restrain their emotions. This is all that I can do and it is not enough. In order that the work of reason can be successful, I must be helped . . . If you are told that this is not possible, that it is intended to respect rigorously the first stipulations of the treaty and that nothing should be granted to France or done for France as proof of a desire to move closer to her or to strengthen the cabinet in its struggle, then the situation will remain violent and uncertain; the cabinet will remain immobile, isolated and expectant. I cannot answer for the future.[1]

It has been pointed out that although Guizot wanted concessions, he was reluctant to make any specific suggestions[2]; this was deliberate on his part, because if a definite proposal was refused, news of such a refusal would affect his position in Paris.

The second policy which Guizot adopted in this period was to try and diminish the smaller question, that of relations between the Porte and the Pasha, by bringing up the bigger question, that of relations in general between the Ottoman Empire and Europe. In the smaller question France was at a disadvantage; in the bigger question France could emerge from her isolation and use her position in Syria, where Guizot believed that France was still the most influential power. Widening the basis of discussion, Guizot made a number of suggestions. He proposed a five-power guarantee of the Ottoman Empire, a guarantee for the Christian population of Syria with particular stipulations for Jerusalem, and a guarantee for communications over the commercial routes between the Mediterranean and the Red Sea, and between the Mediterranean and the Persian Gulf.[3] Although these suggestions were rejected by Palmerston, Guizot had succeeded in taking the initiative (at least apparently) and in turning the discussion towards questions in which France could claim particular interests and which interested Metternich.

To Mehemet Ali Guizot was firm rather than cordial. He wanted no repetition of the situation whereby French diplomacy judged diplomatic proposals by their acceptability in Alexandria. Towards the end of the Middle East crisis Guizot wrote to Rohan-Chabot,

---

published by *Silva Mastellone* in 'Pellogrino Rossi, Ambasciatore Francese à Roma et il problema italiana secondo la corrispondenza particolare', *Rivista Storica Italiana*, vol. lxi, pp. 76-100.

[1] Guizot: Bourqueney, November 4th, 1840, 42 A.P. 10.

[2] *Webster* (op. cit.), vol. ii, p. 728.

[3] Guizot: Barante, December 31st, 1840, 42 A.P. 9. Guizot: Sainte-Aulaire (Vienna), January 13th, 1841, in *Mémoires*, vol. vi, pp. 72-74; and Guizot: Bourqueney, February 15th, 1841, ibid.

then in Egypt, that whilst he understood the Pasha's attempts at modifying the conditions which were being imposed upon him, he did not advise him to hesitate or procrastinate in the hope of being able to recover his lost position. Such action would be fatal to him. So far as France was concerned, Guizot wanted the Pasha to understand that for nearly a year France had accepted a difficult and arduous situation on his behalf. France had done this in order that the Pasha should get the best possible terms in the agreement. 'We now believe that this aim has been achieved. Consequently this is the end of our efforts, we will go no further. If he cannot terminate the affair himself, we will conclude it without him. Do not leave him any illusions about this.'[1] Mehemet seems to have accepted this advice. He bore no grudge against Guizot; indeed he sent him an equestrian portrait of himself which still hangs in the Val-Richer.

After the Convention of July 13th, 1841, Guizot continued to demonstrate the same principles of action in the Eastern Question. He did not believe that France had any hope of playing a lone hand. France had every reason to wish for the maintenance of the European Concert on Turkish affairs. He was all the more anxious for the Concert to continue since he had little belief in the vitality of the Ottoman Empire[2]; he saw the decline of Turkish power and the growth of communities anxious for independence as natural processes; he was not in favour of hastening these developments, he believed that the death agonies of the Empire might be lengthy[3]; he did not think any policy of partition was practicable.[4] If the concert of the powers broke up, then there would only result war or an extension of the power of either England or Russia; the maintenance of the Concert would prevent another Anglo-Russian agreement on Eastern affairs. The disagreement between Russia and Turkey over Servian affairs in 1843 was for Guizot an opportunity for the European powers to meet together and discuss Ottoman affairs in circumstances which would be advantageous to France, since they would demonstrate continued Russian hostility to Turkey, and the inefficiency of Austria as a protector of Turkey.[5] He did not, however, press his suggestion. At the same time Guizot attempted to regain the ground which the French had lost in Syria and the Lebanon by

[1] Guizot: Rohan-Chabot (Alexandria), June 27th, 1841, 42 A.P. 7.

[2] Guizot: Bourqueney (Constantinople), January 7th, 1843, Ibid.

[3] See his speech to the Chambre des Députés, July 2nd, 1839, *Histoire Parlementaire*, vol. iii, p. 269.

[4] 'C'est là de la politique de philosophes ou de badauds, non de la politique de gouvernements.' Guizot: Jarnac (formerly Rohan-Chabot), July 30th, 1844, 42 A.P. 7.

[5] Chambre des Députés, January 22nd, 1844, *Histoire Parlementaire*, vol. iv, pp. 206-8: Guizot: Bresson, September 11th, 1843, 42 A.P. 8.

their past support for Mehemet Ali; France defended the Christian communities and insisted on the necessity for restoring the Shebab family to power.[1]

After July 1841 there is no change in Guizot's essential preoccupation. He had to maintain an uncertain and disunited majority, and he had to align his policy with the humour and interests of the Paris political groups. 'Il faut qu'ici soit toujours ma première pensée',[2] he wrote to Sainte-Aulaire, and this is the basis of his policy. The hope of his diplomacy, as during the 1840 crisis, was that Europe would recognize his virtues, appreciate the delicacy of his position, and foresee the dangers of his fall. One of the most powerful reasons for Guizot's understanding with Lord Aberdeen was that the British Foreign Secretary did all of these things. 'If Guizot stands, all is well,' he wrote to his brother in Vienna, 'Should he fall, "après lui le déluge".'[3]

One of the questions which revealed the sort of problem with which Guizot had to deal was the 'right of search' or 'droit de visite' treaty. England had signed treaties with a great many powers, whereby each power granted to each other's naval squadrons the right to search ships encountered off the coast of Africa; this, it had been claimed, was the only method of stamping out the slave trade. France had signed such a treaty with England, in the agreements of November 30th, 1831, and March 22nd, 1833. Many other countries had similar treaties with Great Britain, but it was not until 1838 that Palmerston, who was one of the most determined opponents of the slave trade, succeeded in persuading the Northern Powers to accept such an agreement. These powers, whilst agreeing in principle, thought that this should form the basis of a Five Power Treaty, establishing reciprocal 'right of search'. Palmerston therefore put in a great deal of work preparing a treaty, which extended the zones where right of search applied and which abolished any limitations which previous agreements may have had on the size of the naval squadrons involved. Then, with rare insensitivity, Palmerston asked Thiers to adhere to this Five Power agreement, ten days after the July 15th Convention had been concluded. Thiers naturally replied that the moment was inappropriate for such an agreement. In July the following year

---

[1] See *Pièces déposées à la Chambre des Députés sur les Affaires du Liban*, 1846. For the reaction of English agents in the area to the increase of French activity in 1841, see Ponsonby: Palmerston, April 21st, 1841, F.O. 78/433 (enclosure); and Werry: Palmerston, May 20th, 1841, F.O. 78/447. Palmerston had been very concerned at the number of men of ability who had been sent to the Balkans and the Levant by the French government. Palmerston: Ponsonby, August 13th, 1841, F.O. 195/183.

[2] Guizot: Sainte-Aulaire, November 13th, 1843, 42 A.P. 8.

[3] Aberdeen: Gordon, December 24th, 1841, *Aberdeen Papers*, 43,211.

Palmerston again asked the French government to sign the agreement. Again his request was refused. This time Guizot's refusal was clearly made a personal matter. Palmerston therefore sent to Bulwer (in Paris) an elaborate explanation of his policy towards the government of October 29th which, whilst not being an apology, was an attempt to assure the French government of his friendly dispositions. Guizot did not accept these explanations, and on August 19th Bourqueney presented Palmerston with the official French refusal to adhere to the Treaty. 'Within English hearts', had written Guizot, 'there is a fair appreciation of the rights and dignity of others, as well as of themselves. But they must realize that we others are just as fair and as proud as they themselves can be.' He later wrote, 'I bear no grudge at all. But I think it right that everybody should know that it is a costly matter when dealing with us to give way to one's humour or fantasy, contrary to justice and decency.'[1]

Bulwer had commented, à propos of this controversy, 'Guizot is a Frenchman and like all Frenchmen vain and susceptible.'[2] Perhaps Guizot was being rather susceptible in one of his reproaches. This was that Palmerston had made no difference in his attitude to the French Cabinet of October 29th and had replied (after a surprising delay) to a despatch from Thiers as if Thiers was still in power. Guizot assumed that his government deserved greater consideration than its predecessor, which must necessarily have been a matter of opinion. The other two complaints throw an interesting sidelight on Palmerston. The one was that having accepted, through the normal diplomatic channels, that Britain and France should co-operate in their policies towards Montevideo and Buenos Aires, then at war with each other, Palmerston proceeded to brutally reject, in the House of Commons, any suggestion that there would be Anglo-French co-operation. The other was that in the election of 1841 Palmerston had chosen to make a bitter (and hypocritical) speech, attacking the French colonization in Algeria on humanitarian grounds and comparing it unfavourably to British action in India. On both occasions one sees Palmerston cultivating a certain type of public personality, and needlessly offending the French whose support of the Treaty he was then requesting. Guizot realized that if he signed an agreement with Lord Palmerston, then he would be open to considerable criticism. Palmerston provided him with reasons for just resentment. But even more than this, he was able to pursue his

---

[1] Guizot: Bourqueney, July 20th, August 11th, 1841, 42 A.P. 10. See *Mémoires*, vol. vi, pp. 131 ff.

[2] He did not include this phrase in his account of the incident in *Bulwer, Life of Palmerston*, 1871, vol. ii, pp. 376-383. It is quoted in *Webster* (op. cit.), vol.ii, p. 776.

campaign against Palmerston. Another letter to Bourqueney suggests that he should see Charles Greville and explain the situation; he was anxious that it would be realized, and via Greville that Russell in particular should realize, that the only reason for the difficulty in adhering to the Treaty was Palmerston.[1]

Therefore Guizot, in refusing to sign with Palmerston, was looking to the opposition at home and looking at his campaign against the English specialist on foreign affairs. He had, it is true, repeated some objections to the wording of the Treaty which Bourqueney had pointed out, but in general he accepted the new version of the 1831 and 1833 agreements, and when Lord Aberdeen, in October, raised the question again, Guizot hastened to accept. Doubtless he was all the more eager to demonstrate how co-operative he was when the Foreign Office was occupied by someone who appreciated the virtues of his government. He did not foresee that the signing of the Treaty in London on December 20th, 1841, would arouse a storm of protest in the Chamber and in the country, so that he would be forced to delay the exchange of ratifications fixed for February 1842.

The opposition to the 'right of search' agreement was led by Billault, deputy for Nantes. He represented shipping interests which claimed to have reason not only to resent, but also to fear, the British naval squadron's interference in the movement of their ships. This opposition then became more general. If the wave of anti-English feeling in 1840 had been checked by the French sense of business, what Mérimée called the 'épicier' side to the French character, which wanted peace in order to sell its 'casseroles', the 'right of search' controversy was actually envenomed by this sense. This was a treaty which was not only offensive to French dignity but possibly harmful to French trade. It is not surprising, therefore, that Guizot began to hesitate and proposed certain modifications concerning the extent of the zones where the reciprocal right of search was possible, and concerning the necessity of revising the Treaty within three years. He had insisted that there was no hurry at all over these negotiations; he was anxious to postpone the issue, since February 1842 was the month when propositions for both electoral and parliamentary reform were being made, and he was fearful of any news which would weaken his position. Within the Cabinet itself there was said to be strong opposition to the 'right of search', led by Duchâtel. It was not surprising, therefore, that Guizot was pleased rather than annoyed when his amendments to the Treaty were refused, and on February 17th Guizot told Sainte-Aulaire that the French government could not ratify and could not say when it would ratify.[2]

[1] Guizot: Bourqueney, September 2nd, 1841, 42 A.P. 10.
[2] Guizot: Sainte-Aulaire, February 8th, February 16th, February 17th, 1842,

But the refusal to ratify did not satisfy the critics of the 'right of search'. They suggested that the government was preparing to ratify when the Chamber was not in session, and these specific accusations, added to the general accusation that the government was neglecting France's national interests, enlivened the electoral campaign of July 1842 and in the eyes of many reduced the expected governmental majority. In preparation for the session of 1843, therefore, Guizot asked that the protocol of the Treaty, which had remained open, should be closed. His attitude towards the British government was typical. He admitted that Aberdeen would have to face up to the 'saints' in Parliament, but this he thought would merely give him embarrassment and trouble for a day, whereas if the protocol remained open, no matter what Aberdeen or the French government said, in France there would be a never-ending series of violent and dangerous debates.[1] This was logical and probably correct; it was nevertheless a particularly restricted way of viewing the matter. He had no doubt at all that his own policy of dropping the 'right of search' and not making an issue of it, was correct. He wrote to his ambassador in Vienna, 'It would have been madness to have compromised, and I am wrong to use the word "compromise", it would have been wrong to have completely lost the majority, the Cabinet, and the whole of conservative policy for a question of this sort.'[2] This attitude aroused disapproval amongst contemporaries and it has caused certain English historians to regard Guizot with disfavour. The first saw the slave trade prospering as a result of Guizot's weakness; the second profess to surprise at finding a states-man who is reluctant to be defeated and who does not regard resigna-tion as being a normal part of a ministerial programme. One such historian has written, 'Resignation does not appear to have suggested itself often enough to him as the right alternative to becoming the tool of a bellicosity of which he is alleged to have disapproved.'[3] It certainly did not occur to him to resign over the 'right of search'. Any Gladstonian gesture of this sort would not have been understood in France; nor can one see what good it would have done either to the anti-slavery movement or to Anglo-French relations; it would have added even further confusion to French politics. If Guizot was some-times ungenerous in his reluctance to see that the English government also had difficulties with Parliament and opinion, this has been more

---

42 A.P. 8; Cowley: Aberdeen, February 14th, February 16th, 1842, *Aberdeen Papers*, 43,129.

[1] Guizot: Sainte-Aulaire, October 4th, 1842, 42 A.P. 8.

[2] Guizot; Flahault, October 29th, 1842, Ibid.

[3] *A. B. Cunningham*, 'Peel, Aberdeen and the Entente-Cordiale', *Bulletin of the Institute of Historical Research*, 1957, vol. xxx, p. 192.

than compensated by the refusal of critics to recognize the conditions of French politics.

But where Guizot can be criticized is in his own failure to appreciate the reasons for the opposition to the 'right of search' within France. He saw this movement as manufactured by his political opponents who were in search of a cause and who were delighted to exploit the passions and prejudices of those who would otherwise have remained politically inert. Guizot was not alone in this belief. Sainte-Beuve, for example, commenting on the way in which this affair had become the rendezvous of all the 'anti-guizotistes', Legitimists, Bonapartists, and followers of both Thiers and Molé, wrote that if they had not been inspired by common hostility to Guizot, the Treaty would soon be forgotten, 'il n'y a pas de quoi fouetter un chat'.[1] But in reality there were some French traders who were genuinely concerned at the possible repercussions of such a treaty. The Rheims Chamber of Commerce, for example, petitioned the government quite early on in the affair. In order to prevent a few speculators from continuing such a revolting trade, supposing that such speculators still existed, they asked if it was necessary to abandon the mastery of the seas to England, who was a rival if not an enemy. Such a treaty would enable English warships to interfere with the shipping of their competitors; they would be able to bring about considerable delays in, say, French commerce going to Brazil. This argument is all the more reasonable when one remembers that long-distance trade, always based on long-term credits and liable to heavy losses, could be adversely affected by delays, especially as the market for European goods was often limited. The Minister of Agriculture and Commerce also commented, in April 1842, on the difficulty of applying the conventions of 1831 and 1833.[2]

Guizot furthermore did not share the suspicions of many Frenchmen concerning the real nature of the British interest in the slave trade and British plans for West Africa. Such suspicions might have been based on simply animosity; they might also have been based on some knowledge of the area and of the policies of some British naval officers. After all, when Fowell Buxton began to publish his remedies for the African slave trade, which implied a more direct intervention by the British government as well as by individuals, there was a move to keep this enterprise secret from other European nations in order to

---

[1] Sainte-Beuve: Juste Olivier, January 18th, 1843, *Correspondance* (op. cit.), vol. v, p. 38.

[2] Chambre de Commerce de Rheims, January 31st, 1842, *Archives Nationales*, F¹² 2648ᴬ. See the letter of the Minister of Agriculture and Commerce in the same carton, concerning a trader from Nantes. It is not clear if this letter was sent to Guizot.

prevent them from 'occupying the ground' before the English.[1] At all events, Guizot did not consider these possibilities. He was more interested in reports that Metternich disapproved of the Treaty, in discussions about the American point of view, and in rumours that the Russian government was seeking to profit from the situation to isolate France once again. He concentrated most upon avoiding defeat in the Chambers. This failure to try and understand an important movement of opposition was a serious weakness in a statesman so concerned with foreign policy.

Nor did the British statesmen try to understand the French opposition to the 'right of search'; but they were ready to accept the French withdrawal, and whilst complaining of the absurdities of the French Chamber, they tried to adapt themselves to the French position. Lord Aberdeen came near to Guizot's position in thinking that although measures against the slave trade were important, perhaps the maintenance of good relations between England and France was more important than the 'right of search', and eventually he allowed himself to be convinced that the 'right of search' was not essential to the suppression of the slave trade.[2] Peel too seemed conscious of the danger of Guizot's overthrow. It was curious that the English ministers should have wished to link the question of the 'right of search' to the Portendic affair. The British government was claiming compensation for losses incurred by British merchants as a result of French warfare against the native peoples of the Portendic region of West Africa. This question had been pending since 1833. Guizot was surprised that the 'right of search' should be linked to Portendic, 'but if we must pass through this door together,' he commented, 'so be it'. The British government accepted the particular conditions on which Guizot insisted before accepting arbitration, the most significant one being that the findings of arbitration should not be made known until the Chamber was in recess.[3]

Considering these affairs, and the way in which Aberdeen and Guizot were handling them, one recalls the remark which Guizot made to Henry Reeve, stating that the usefulness of the understanding with England lay in the way in which the statesmen of each country could estimate the importance of each question, and were thus able to prevent minor questions from becoming bigger.[4] This suggests that Guizot was thinking of his relations with England as

[1] Captain Trotter: Lord John Russell, January 22nd, 1840, *P.R.O.*, C.O. 2/21.
[2] Aberdeen: Cowley, January 9th, 1845, *P.R.O.*, F.O. 84/586.
[3] Guizot: Rohan-Chabot, July 6th, 1842, 42 A.P. 7. Rohan-Chabot, who later became Comte de Jarnac, quoted Peel's conversation over Portendic in his memoir of Aberdeen in the *Revue des Deux Mondes*, July 15th, 1861, pp. 441-443.
[4] *G. P. Gooch* (ed.), *The Later Correspondence of Lord John Russell*, 1925, vol. i, p. 90.

being a method rather than anything else, a means of applying reason to diplomacy. But he went on to give as an example of this method, Aberdeen's submission to French supremacy in Greece and Spain, and the French acceptance of British supremacy in Lisbon and Constantinople. This is no longer a method of applying reason. This rather shows Guizot's constant need to impress the Chambers if he was to remain in power, and to impress the Chambers above all with his conduct of foreign affairs. He had to rebut opposition accusations that French influence in the world was diminishing. But how could he do this? How was French influence to be increased? Guizot was positive that it was not by adventures and aggression. France had lived in Europe as 'un météore enflammé' as a means of making her political and social systems secure. But now this was accomplished France had to take her place as a fixed star in the system of European states, she had to assume a position 'd'astre fixe à cours régulier et prévu'.[1]

Nor could France hope for territorial expansion in any way as immense or as rapid as that of Russia, England or the United States of America. But in face of such expansion Guizot accepted a version of the Balance of Power. He told the Chamber that the Balance of Power had for long been an issue on the Rhine, the Alps and the Pyrenees; then it became an issue on the Vistula and on the Volga, until today, as he said, 'cette question se pose dans le monde entier'.[2] It was to the interests of France that the three expanding states should grow equally in power, that existing states should not be annexed, and that as other powers extended their positions over the oceans and the trading routes of the world, so France should do the same. To Henry Reeve he explained that he was firmly resolved to resist all attempts at colonization or foreign settlement, and he believed that Algeria was 'the only suitable dependency of France'. But at the same time 'he thought that the interests of France and the dignity of the nation rendered it expedient to occupy certain ports or minute positions in various parts of the globe, for the shelter of French merchant vessels'. It was in pursuance of this policy that France occupied the Mayotte Islands (in the Comoras), the Marquesas Islands and Tahiti in the Pacific, and in 1844 planned to occupy some similar position in the Indo-Chinese seas.[3]

This policy was not what many of his critics would have wanted. It made no mention of the 1815 treaties and of the loss of power which

[1] Chambre des Députés, January 21st, 1843, *Histoire Parlementaire*, vol. iv, pp. 13-14.

[2] Ibid., June 10th, 1843, p. 127.

[3] This interview took place on August 27th, 1844. Henry Reeve reported on it to Lord Wharncliffe and his letter is in the *Peel Papers*, B.M. Add. MSS., 40, 550.

they had supposedly inflicted on France; nor was there any mention of France seizing the Rhine, or even of France supervising a revision of the 1815 treaties so as to cancel the various 'usurpations' that had taken place in the name of the balance of power. In fact, Guizot realized that the settlement of 1815 was not unfavourable to France and he was prepared to say so.[1] But any policy which did not profess to achieve the territorial emancipation of France from the treaties of 1815 was easily outbid.

But there were also limitations on Guizot's policy of acquisition. In the first place Guizot was anxious that England should not be alarmed. He wanted Jarnac to assure the British government that he had no intention of occupying Chusan[2]; he was careful to impress upon Lagréné, who was on a special mission to China, and upon Admiral Cecille, that their search for a station in Indo-Chinese waters must be conducted with great reserve and with constant reference to the government at home, since French interests in the Far East were too limited and uncertain to justify complications.[3] Although many naval officers were urging the value to French shipping which would come from the occupation of Madagascar, and although the Governor and Council of Bourbon repeatedly urged the necessity of taking over Madagascar, Guizot constantly refused such a policy.[4] When, however, it seemed that he might be obliged to send a punitive expedition to the coast of Madagascar he immediately suggested that it should be a joint Anglo-French expedition.[5] When in 1845 Captain Bouet put forward a plan for making treaties with the chiefs of the West African coast which would give France possession of territory, Guizot was alarmed at the possible hostility which London might show to such a scheme.[6]

Guizot reveals the same attitude towards England in the Tahitian crisis of 1844. A French naval officer, Dupetit-Thouars, had first intervened in Tahiti in August of 1838 when he had demanded compensation for the harsh treatment which had been inflicted on two French priests. In 1841, now an admiral, he annexed the Marquesas Islands and then, proceeding to Tahiti, he demanded a

[1] Chambre des Députés, January 29th, 1848, *Histoire Parlementaire*, vol. v, p. 543.

[2] Guizot: Jarnac, November 3rd, 1845, 42 A.P. 7.

[3] Guizot: Lagréné, April 9th, 1845, 42 A.P. 9. There was only one French trading house in China of any importance at this time. See *C. de Montigny*, *Manuel du Négociant Français en Chine* (Paris 1846).

[4] See correspondence in 42 A.P. 16 and Note pour le Ministre des Affaires étrangères, November 1845, in 42 A.P. 6.

[5] Guizot: Jarnac, October 24th, 1845, 42 A.P. 7. Guizot's weakness in this matter aroused the scorn of Peel.

[6] Guizot: de Broglie, March 21st, 1845, 42 A.P. 8.

further indemnity for the hostility which, he alleged, had been shown to a number of French traders. In September 1842, in the absence of Queen Pomaré's chief adviser, George Pritchard, an English missionary who was also consul, the Tahitian government asked to be taken under the protection of the French flag. This was accepted by the French admiral and in April 1843 this protectorate was officially recognized by the French government, for whom Tahiti was an excellent marine station, especially well suited to the French whaling industry which was then badly in need of encouragement. But on November 7th Dupetit-Thouars found the island in a state of insurrection and he therefore declared the Queen deposed and the island annexed. On March 2nd, 1844, the supposed author of continuing disturbances, George Pritchard, was arrested by the French, and after spending seven days in prison was put on a ship for England.

The news of the annexation of Tahiti reached Paris in February 1844; after considering the matter for about a fortnight, on February 26th they rejected the annexation and said that they stood by the agreement originally made with Pomaré in 1842. This decision was strongly criticized, and the delay in making the decision was alleged to have been caused by the need to consult England. 'When we examine the march of this affair we are inclined to say that Paris is governed in London', wrote one opposition newspaper.[1] It was certainly true that Guizot's decision to refuse annexation was probably based on the desire to avoid complications with the British government which had accepted the French protectorate with surprising indifference. When the news came of Pritchard's arrest, however, towards the end of July, and when the ex-consul himself arrived in England a few weeks later to tell the story of his ill-treatment, it became more difficult for Guizot to maintain his position. Sir Robert Peel spoke sharply in the House of Commons about 'a gross outrage' having been committed on the person of a British official; the London Missionary Society held a mass meeting of protest, and mention of a possible war with France was greeted with loud cheers; in France the opposition derived great satisfaction from its attacks on England and the supposedly hypocritical and sinister Pritchard. Guizot was prepared to risk English displeasure by refusing to allow Pritchard to return to Tahiti, and by refusing to consider Pritchard as a consul since he had, in November, resigned his office in protest against the French annexation. But he risked considerable opposition from within France by his willingness to pay an indemnity to Pritchard in compensation for the ill-treatment he had received during his imprisonment. Pritchard may have suffered

[1] Quoted in *The Times*, March 1st, 1844.

unjust treatment and he must have had many qualities, but he had been in a very unusual position in Tahiti; as Bulwer put it, he was 'the great man of the Islands and might in reality have been their actual sovereign'; this being so, he was an unsuitable person to have as British consul in the changed condition of the French Protectorate. It was all the bolder for Guizot to have offered compensation when there were a number of unpleasant rumours about Pritchard even in the English press. For example, another English resident in Tahiti claimed that in 1842 Pritchard had been imprisoned for drunkenness, during his visit to England, and in September *The Times* admitted that he was 'a busybody and a disturber'. In these circumstances it was a mark of determined policy for Guizot to have got the Chambers to approve of compensation.[1]

It is this action of Guizot's which is significant. Most historians have stressed the fact that Aberdeen and Guizot had handled the situation so as to avoid war. Actually, as Aberdeen told Peel, there never was any danger of war.[2] The episode illustrates most clearly how Guizot's desire not to offend England limited his policy of expansion. A second limitation was his reluctance to offend the United States. Whilst he wrote to Jarnac of the necessity of recognizing Mexico in order to 'constituer une barrière un peu solide contre le flot des États-Unis', whilst he lectured the Chamber on the advantages of maintaining Texas independent, and whilst he emphasized the fundamental weaknesses of the American organization of states in despatches to his diplomatists, he hesitated to do anything against the American government.[3] He was not prepared to join Aberdeen in any guarantee of Texan independence, nor did he wish to press the United States to allow the 1839 Franco-Texan treaty of commerce to run its full ten years; he was not prepared to follow up Aberdeen's suggestion that France should take some action in California.[4] Whether it was because of the important volume of trade which crossed the Atlantic, or the existence of pro-American sentiment in France, or the realization that American diplomacy could sometimes be useful to France, Guizot stressed the importance

[1] *H. L. Bulwer, Viscount Palmerston* (op. cit.), vol. iii, p. 79; *The Times*, August 17th, September 3rd, 1844; it is not true to say as Cunningham does in the *Bulletin of the Institute of Historical Research*, p. 201, that Guizot dared not ask the Chambers for compensation. See *J. R. Baldwin*, 'England and the French Seizure of the Society Islands', *Journal of Modern History*, vol. x, 1938.

[2] Aberdeen: Peel, December 17th, 1844, *Aberdeen Papers*, 43,064.

[3] Guizot: Jarnac, November 22nd, 1845, 42 A.P. 7; Chambre des Députés, June 10th, 1845, *Histoire Parlementaire*, vol. iv, pp. 562 ff.; Guizot: Bacourt, February 20th, 1841, *Archives A.E.*, États-Unis Correspondance Politique, 97.

[4] See Guizot's correspondence quoted in *M. K. Chase, Les Négociations de la République de Texas en Europe*, Paris 1932; Guizot: Jarnac, October 6th, 1845, 42 A.P. 7.

of France looking to her relations with the United States. He also insisted that France was in a situation different from that of England and had neither the same interests involved nor the same power at her disposal.[1]

The third limitation upon the extension of French influence was a very general one and imposed particular limitations on one of Guizot's most favoured ideas. He thought that one of the most important ways in which French influence could expand and the importance of France in Europe be consolidated was by commercial agreements with neighbouring countries. But these treaties, whilst of obvious political value, were sometimes detrimental to particular French commercial interests. These interests were powerful in the French Chambers, and their opposition to such schemes could not be discounted.

The first example was the commercial treaty with Holland; this had been negotiated by Thiers and his government in the summer of 1840, but Guizot accepted it and presented it to the Chambers in 1841. He was aware of the limitations of this treaty. He believed that it favoured Dutch goods entering into France more than French products entering Holland; he had little confidence in the Dutch King; but he saw a general advantage when France signed a treaty with a country of small production and large consumption, and he believed that local interests should give way to the larger general interest; he thought that the establishment of good relations between France and Holland meant the destruction of an anti-French creation of the 1815 treaties and raised the possibility of the Low Countries passing into the French political sphere.[2]

When, however, he wrote these last passages he was not thinking of Holland alone. He was particularly thinking of French relations with Belgium, and the Belgian desire to get out of their economic difficulties, which were characterized by over-investment and over-production, by some sort of commercial agreement which would open the large French internal market to them. In May 1841, in conversation with the Belgian ambassador Le Hon, Guizot was reported to have said that he attached the greatest importance to the formation of some sort of commercial association between France, Belgium, Holland and Switzerland. This association would then be

[1] A journal which was reputed to be in Guizot's confidence wrote, 'La France peut voir l'expansion américaine sinon avec indifférence du moins avec sécurité.' *Le Portefeuille, Revue Diplomatique*, May 10th, 1846.

[2] Guizot: Boislecomte (The Hague), June 5th, 1841, *Archives A.E.*, Correspondance Commerciale, La Haye 12; Chambre des Députés, May 22nd, 1841, *Histoire Parlementaire*, vol. iii, p. 462; Guizot: Sainte-Aulaire, November 16th, 22nd, 23rd, 1841, 42 A.P. 8. Various observations on the Dutch treaty are collected together in *Archives Nationales*, C 2770.

able to negotiate with the German Zollverein. Guizot thought that the creation of such an association would alone constitute 'pour un ministre un. beau titre de gloire' and the first link in this chain would be the treaty between Belgium and France.[1] Louis-Philippe, who saw a great deal of the Belgian King, who had married his daughter, supported the project of forming some sort of customs union with Belgium and started to try and rally support. But many difficulties occurred. One came from the Belgians themselves, who feared that if there were a customs union between the two countries, then French customs officials would wish to control Belgium's sea frontier, as well as her northern and eastern frontier, and this was thought to be a threat to Belgian sovereignty; in these conditions opposition to the proposal developed within Belgium and this helped to sap the confidence of the French negotiators. Another difficulty came from the powers. Diplomatic protests were made against any arrangement which threatened to affect the practical independence of the Belgian government. But the greatest difficulty came from within France itself.

Lord Aberdeen pointed out, in a despatch which was sent to Vienna, Berlin and St. Petersburg, that few people in France expected any commercial advantages to come from a customs union with Belgium, 'but it is loudly proclaimed that for any commercial sacrifices which France may make, she will be fully indemnified by the political predominance which that Union is likely to confer'.[2] Aberdeen, however, underestimated the resentment which was felt about the commercial sacrifices. All French manufacturers, with the possible exception of those in the silk industry, were alarmed at the prospect of Belgian manufactured products coming untaxed into the country and competing with them. This was not a new French alarm; it was one which had been put forward when Casimir Périer was rumoured to be considering annexation of part of Belgium, and this was in 1831, before the rapid Belgian industrialization of the 1830s. The Minister of Commerce in the government of October 29th became the spokesman of these interests and repeatedly insisted to Guizot that since Belgium had better resources, better communications and greater availability of capital, then such an association would be positively dangerous to France.[3] Guizot realized the

[1] Le Hon: Muelenaere, May 31st, 1841, quoted in Ridder, *Les Projets d'Union Douanière Franco-Belge* (op. cit.), p. 59.
[2] October 28th, 1842. Quoted in *Ridder, Les Projets d'Union Douanière Franco-Belge* (op. cit.), p. 227 n. 2 ff.
[3] For the protestations of several chambers of commerce in 1831 and a reply from Montalivet assuring them that the interests of the localities were not being neglected, see *Archives Nationales*, F¹²2401. For Cunin-Gridaine's communications to Guizot see 42 A.P. 11.

FOREIGN POLICY

importance of this opposition. In some notes he took for a Cabinet meeting, which are undated, one finds he has written that the real objection to a treaty was a matter of internal politics, and he refers to the interests of 'l'aristocratie industrielle et commerciale', which formed the support of the July Monarchy; to the French ambassador in Brussels, Rumigny, he explained that whilst the sacrifices which the French would have to make were obvious and immediate, 'gros comme des maisons' and affecting the government's best friends, the advantages were indirect, distant and not immediately visible to the undiscerning public; to the Belgian ambassador in Paris he explained that his principal aim was to maintain his government and this always remained the dominant consideration.[1]

Guizot did not altogether give up the idea of such a treaty. He persisted in hoping that time would demonstrate its value and that he would be strong enough to conclude it one day; he continued to give what publicity he could to manifestations in favour of the union.[2] Therefore much has been made of the significance of this episode. It has been suggested that Guizot had learned the value of commercial treaties when ambassador in London, and it is certainly true that the general ideas which Guizot expressed concerning the diplomatic relations of states were not so far removed from the arguments put forward by such writers as Léon Faucher, stating that political alliances were incomplete if a customs barrier still existed between the two parties.[3] From this two conclusions have been put forward. The one most critical of Guizot suggests that he abandoned his convictions, and what could well have been a vital step in the evolution of France, to the simple desire to stay in power. The other suggests that this method of extending French influence by means of commercial treaties was the key to the whole of Guizot's foreign policy, and is to be found in his policy towards Spain and the Italian states, as well as in his attitude to Belgium and Holland. Neither of these conclusions are justified.

The first ignores the conditions of French politics. The government had already relied upon its opponents in order to pass one law which was disapproved of by many of its normal supporters, and this

[1] Notes de Guizot (undated), 42 A.P. 11; Guizot: Rumigny, September 29th, 1842, 42 A.P. 9; Le Hon: de Briey, October 22nd, 1841, quoted in *Ridder* (op. cit.), p. 102 n. 2.
[2] See for example *Journal des Débats*, February 24th, 1843.
[3] E. Callet, *Les douanes françaises*, Saint-Nazaire 1882, quoted in *Mastellone, La Politica Estera del Guizot* (op. cit.), p. 42. Mastellone deals with this whole problem in some detail. Faucher's ideas were first expressed in his article 'L'Union du Midi' in the *Revue des Deux Mondes*, March 1st, 1837. It is interesting to see that between 1846 and 1848 a reform of French tariffs was favoured by *Le Portefeuille, Revue Diplomatique*.

precedent of the fortifications of Paris was hardly encouraging. The view taken by one political commentator, who suggested that only if the customs union became the issue between one government and another should the question be posed, was undoubtedly correct.[1] As it happened, there was never a unified and viable government which could propose the union and ask the Chamber or the country to decide. The second conclusion assumes too readily that Guizot's ideas in 1841 and 1842 can be applied indiscriminately to other years, and to other areas of Europe. But the fact is that in 1841 and 1842 Guizot's attention was particularly directed towards these areas not so much by a desire for positive action as by a fear that the Belgian crisis might be so serious as to lead to Belgian absorption by the Zollverein. This fear diminished somewhat after 1842. Furthermore, Guizot was forced to realize, within a short time of 1842, that commercial treaties and conventions brought disappointments. With regard to Holland he was eventually obliged to notice a decline in French trade; with regard to Belgium, the French were soon protesting against the extension of advantages, originally reserved for France, to the Zollverein, and about further changes in the Belgian tariff which were hostile to France.[2]

One must add, too, that Guizot never showed any desire for a commercial agreement with England. If he believed that agreements between nations needed to be strengthened by commercial ties, he showed no sign of wanting to fortify the 'entente cordiale' in this way. It was always the British government which took the initiative in hoping to increase trade between the two countries; Bulwer once even suggested that the British government should try to arouse protests within France against the linen manufacturers and others who were the leading protectionists, by increasing the duties on wines and brandies; Peel sadly commented that he wished the French government 'would give us some encouragement to begin the good work' of bettering trade, and Aberdeen, after the French had revised their linen duties, even more sadly remarked of Guizot, 'I cannot say that we have much reason to boast of his English propensities, whatever they may be, which have made him so unpopular.'[3] Guizot was always adamant. Although at the time of the negotiations with

---

[1] *Revue des Deux Mondes*, October 31st, 1842, p. 119.

[2] Guizot: Boislecomte, June 12th, 1841; Guizot: de Breteuil, April 16th, 1847, *Archives A.E.*, Correspondance Commerciale, La Haye 12; Note pour le ministre sur l'état actuel des nos rapports avec la Belgique, September 16th, 1845, 42 A.P. 2.

[3] Aberdeen: Cowley, August 5th, 1842, *P.R.O.*, F.O. 27/646; Bulwer: Porter, May 25th, 1842, *Ripon Papers*, B.M. Add MSS. 40,863; Peel: Aberdeen, February 9th, 1844, *Aberdeen Papers*, 43,063; Aberdeen: Cowley, July 22nd, 1842, ibid., 43,129.

Belgium he held out the hope that once this agreement was completed he would be able to conclude a commercial treaty with Great Britain, this statement was so isolated that it is difficult not to regard it as an attempt to diminish British hostility to the proposed customs union. Otherwise he stressed his need to have, during commercial negotiations, 'powerful and active interests' which would support him.[1] These interests never appeared, and Guizot made little attempt to mobilize them.

It was much the same with the Zollverein. In 1841 the Commissioners of the Zollverein expressed the opinion that a commercial agreement would be difficult to sign with France because the French Chamber would create too many obstacles. In 1847 we find Guizot himself explaining that the interests of French agriculture and of French industry would not allow tariff concessions to be made.[2] It is clear that the exactions of certain French economic interests imposed considerable limitations upon foreign policy. It was typical of Guizot's method that he was always ready to scrap his plans and start again. He was patient and cautious and he once said that the 'don des miracles' was the 'don de l'à propos'.[3]

If, as has been said, it is convenient to divide Guizot's foreign policy into three phases, the climax of the second period was the episode of the Spanish marriages, which has to be seen as part of his Mediterranean diplomacy. In a speech of 1833 he had drawn attention to the increase of Russian, British and Austrian power in the Mediterranean, and had stated his belief that French power should increase correspondingly.[4] For Guizot the conquest of Algeria was important above all as a means of increasing French power in the Mediterranean; it represented the acquisition of another Toulon rather than the possession of a territory which was to be exploited economically. Furthermore, French interest in the Mediterranean could not be confined to the acquisition of ports or bases; France was interested in the governments of countries which surrounded the Mediterranean. It became one of Guizot's basic beliefs that the French position in Europe would be improved if the governments of Mediterranean countries were favourably inclined to France. Hence the great care which he devoted to Spanish and Greek affairs during the whole of his ministry and, to a lesser extent, the attention

[1] Cowley: Aberdeen, June 27th, 1842, *P.R.O.*, F.O. 27/650; Guizot: Aberdeen, December 14th, 1844, *Aberdeen Papers*, 43,134.

[2] Humann: Guizot, March 23rd, 1841, *Archives A.E.*, Correspondance Commerciale, Berlin 6; Guizot: Dalmatie, October 8th, 1847, biid., Berlin 9.

[3] Guizot: Flahault, February 28th, 1845, 42 A.P. 8.

[4] Chambre des Députés, May 20th, 1833. *Histoire Parlementaire*, vol. ii, p. 160.

which he showed towards the Italian governments at particular moments.

The Spanish and Greek policies represent Guizot's most positive ventures in foreign affairs. In both cases there were serious advantages to be expected. France had every interest in preventing Spain from being a foyer of revolutionary or legitimist activity and in securing her southern frontier. The French position was well put by de Broglie, writing to Brougham in 1833, when he contrasted the English and the French attitudes to Spain. The English, he said, were very much at their ease behind the ocean, professing the principles of non-intervention; they had no neighbours; whatever happened on the Continent, the English could fold their arms and do nothing; their revolution was 150 years old, 'elle a de la barbe au menton'. But none of these things applied to France and this changed things greatly, as he went on to show. 'Had Don Carlos succeeded to the throne in the ordinary way of succession, then he would have been of no more interest to us than his brother. But Don Carlos, succeeding to the throne as the leader of a party, hero of the Counter-Revolution, at the head of an army of monks and royalist volunteers, crying "death to the French liberals" and "long live the Inquisition", offering asylum to all the Vendéens of France, in all probability welcoming the Duchesse de Berry, the Duc de Bordeaux and all the rest, establishing a Vendée on our southern frontier, then, he is a very inconvenient neighbour. It is for this reason that we thought it best to immediately declare our support for the Queen. . . .'[1] Guizot never expressed himself as dramatically as this, but the subsequent developments of Spanish politics, the expulsion of the Queen-Mother Christine and her supporters and the establishment of the Regency of Espartero meant that a government was in Madrid which was reputedly hostile towards France and friendly towards England. For reasons similar to those expressed by de Broglie, Guizot could not ignore this fact. Had he wanted to do so, French representatives in Spain were continually pointing out to him that the Spanish government was doing everything it could to restrict and harm French trade.[2] Or, had he been inclined to forget, the political commentators of Paris repeatedly insisted that the Spanish government in Madrid should cease to be merely an English or Austrian prefecture.[3] Therefore Guizot had little choice. He was obliged to intervene in Spanish affairs, and at first he was very successful. It may be that

[1] de Broglie: Brougham, October 25th, 1833, *Brougham Papers*, 13,706.

[2] Pageot: Guizot, January 19th, February 20th, March 10th, March 26th, October 18th, 1841, *Archives A.E.*, Correspondance Commerciale, Madrid 43; de Lesseps: Guizot, September 18th, 1842, ibid., Barcelone 30.

[3] *Revue des Deux Mondes*, April 30th, 1842, p. 100.

French agents were more active in the peninsula than Guizot officially admitted; but it is certain that the changes which took place in Spain, the overthrow of Espartero, the coming to power of Narvaez and the return to Spain of the Queen-Mother, were not achieved by French intervention, engineered from the Tuileries. Whatever the rôle of French agents and money, these events have to be understood primarily in terms of Spanish politics, and the policy of Guizot was one of appreciating the political scene and of insinuating France into the rôle of protector and adviser. He was much better informed than Aberdeen, and his policy was more supple. He was able to claim that by becoming the patron of constitutional monarchy in Spain he was strengthening constitutional monarchy in France, but he wanted the Spanish government to remain, only broadly speaking, within the vague limits of the constitutional régime, and he did not want the Spaniards to imitate the French constitution too closely.[1]

French statesmen had always been concerned about the future marriage of the Spanish Queen. As early as 1833, in the letter to Brougham already quoted, de Broglie explained that the great disadvantage of Isabella's succession was that some day she would need to get married. By the 1840s Guizot considered that it was time to think seriously about it. Before the expulsion of Espartero in July 1843 Guizot probably insisted that the marriage was a matter of European concern because this was a way of intervening on the Spanish political scene when otherwise he was excluded from it. After the fall of Espartero, it was obvious that the whole régime was somewhat provisional until the Queen's marriage was settled. Thus it was that Guizot devoted all his patience and concentration to this question, which actually ruined his reputation in England, and which became, in Aberdeen's words, 'almost the only Foreign question which has excited any strong feeling, where the great interests of the country have not been concerned'.[2] It was on September 4th, 1846, that the French and Spanish governments announced the forthcoming marriage of Isabella to her cousin, the Duke of Cadiz, and of the Queen's younger sister, the Infanta, to the Duke of Montpensier, youngest son of Louis-Philippe. The marriages took place on October 10th. It was claimed by the British government that the marriages were contrary to the undertaking which had been given by the French in 1845, and repeated by the French King to Queen Victoria at the château d'Eû, that Montpensier would only marry the Infanta after the Queen had married and had children. In this way it had been

[1] Guizot: Sainte-Aulaire, April 30th, 1844, 42 A.P. 8; Guizot: Bresson, May 4th, 1844, ibid.
[2] Aberdeen: Guizot, September 25th, 1849, *Val-Richer MSS.*

hoped that there would never be any succession problem involving a possible union of the French and Spanish Crowns. When this agreement was broken in 1846 the possibility of some future succession problem was made all the more probable by suggestions that the Isabella-Cadiz marriage was not one capable of producing children. Thus although the marriages were made after much arduous diplomacy, nevertheless they produced one of the great diplomatic quarrels of the century. Guizot himself described it as the most considerable event of his ministry. Today it seems that Guizot's insistence upon this subject was out of all proportion to its importance; the more attention he devoted to it, the more important it became and the more attention he was obliged to give to it. Of course, it is true that in the climax of the affair everything was made more dramatic and heavy with consequence by Lord Palmerston. But it is unexpected to find Guizot committing the same mistakes as Palmerston and it is essential therefore to try to understand his actions.

From his earliest comment on this matter, Guizot insisted that the husband of Isabella should be a Bourbon. In many ways this insistence, posed as early as 1841, was the crux of the whole dispute. It meant that a foreign power was imposing a restriction on the Spanish government's choice; it meant that the French government had restricted their own freedom of movement; it both raised and confirmed in English minds, suspicion of French intentions, since the choice of a Bourbon could include one of the sons of Louis-Philippe, and no matter how many denials there were, this suspicion persisted; finally it introduced an unpleasant atmosphere into the whole proceedings, since, as Guizot himself admitted, whilst there were several Bourbon candidates, none of them was particularly attractive.

Why then did Guizot insist upon a Bourbon? There does not seem to be any certain answer to this question. Guizot always stated it as a first principle and never thought it necessary to explain why it should be the first principle. This is all the more surprising since there are indications, particularly in the early stages of the affair, that not all Frenchmen were opposed to a Coburg, and since the Coburg family had connections by marriage with Louis-Philippe, there were many who thought that a Coburg would have been acceptable. Guizot, however, was always anti-Coburg, and this reason can probably be explained. A Coburg marriage might well help to perpetuate the pro-English and anti-French governments of the Espartero period, or, once Espartero had been expelled, such a marriage might well have helped to restore these governments. Whether this was likely or not, undoubtedly there were opponents of Guizot who would say so. Much French wit was expended on the Coburgs. It was said that just as Napoleon always had a chicken on the spit, so that at any time of the day or night he could have something to eat without wasting time, so the Coburgs always had a candidate ready for any possible royal marriage that was going. But a Coburg marriage in Spain would not have been funny for the French government. Before 1843 it would have been proof of the government's exclusion from Spanish affairs; after 1843 it would have been proof that the government's successes had been only superficial; a Coburg marriage concluded while Palmerston was at the Foreign Office would have been completely disastrous.

Much the same could have been said about marriage with an Austrian archduke, with a member of the House of Orange or with any other royal family which could be said to be under the influence of one of the great powers, other than France. Therefore, the only royal house which the French could support was the Bourbons. This policy is less surprising when one remembers that a lot of the governments were thinking dynastically. There can be little question that both Queen Victoria and the Prince-Consort wanted to see their Coburg relative on the Spanish throne. There can be little doubt that the King of Prussia wanted to see Montemolin, the son of Don Carlos, the Prince des Asturias as he called him, marry Isabella and become king. This would have healed the breach in legitimacy which had occurred after the death of Ferdinand VII in 1833, when the succession had gone to his daughter, rather than going in the male line to his brother, Don Carlos. It is not surprising, therefore, that Louis-Philippe and his minister should also think dynastically, and along lines which would enable them to say that if the throne remained in Bourbon hands, amongst the descendants of Philip V, then they were preserving the heritage of Louis XIV.

Guizot chose to work towards a Bourbon marriage by co-operation with England. Before 1843 this was a necessity, since the French government had no influence and no ambassador. After 1843 he thought it advisable because even if he could not persuade Lord Aberdeen to adopt the same candidate as himself, at least he could prevent Aberdeen from having a candidate of his own, and of adopting a positive policy such as Bulwer wanted. In this respect he was successful. But he was not successful in gaining the confidence of Aberdeen or in destroying his suspicions of France. He occasionally lamented that whilst Aberdeen seemed to agree with all his propositions concerning the marriage, he never did anything to help make them a reality; but if he had seen Lord Aberdeen's correspondence with his brother, who was ambassador in Vienna, he would have had more real reasons for complaint. The 'old routine', as Guizot called it, of Anglo-French rivalry in Spain had in no way been abandoned, and Guizot completely exaggerated the significance of the 'entente cordiale' by supposing that it had. Furthermore, the English position was essentially illogical. On the one hand the British government insisted that the Spanish government was free and independent and able to choose whoever they wished; on the other hand the British government was not prepared to allow the choice to fall on a son of the King of France. In other words, whilst protesting indifference, the British government put a ban on the marriage which, from the Spanish point of view, would have been the most popular.

One has to remember, then, when discussing the 'agreements' between Guizot and Aberdeen, that the British government was professing a confidence in French policy which it did not altogether feel, and professing a respect for Spanish freedom of choice which it did not completely respect. It was at Guizot's request that the marriage was discussed between them, and that the question of the marriage became that of the marriages as the possibility of Louis-Philippe's youngest son Montpensier marrying the younger sister of Isabella was brought into the open. As there were doubts concerning Isabella's ability to have children, her development having been retarded, it was thought that her marriage should take place and that she should have children before the Montpensier-Infanta marriage. This conversation was what Guizot wanted. He thought that it implied agreement on having a Bourbon, agreement on the need to hurry on the Queen's marriage and agreement that the two governments should co-operate. But Aberdeen and Peel preferred to let the matter remain vague. They did not want to have any agreement in writing; they were apprehensive of offending the English Court by supporting candidates who were not Coburgs; above all, they were frightened of being tricked by the French. Therefore there was no official sequel to the conversations between Guizot and Aberdeen; the affair was allowed to drift. In exactly the same way, when in 1846 the French ambassador came to Lord Aberdeen and read him Guizot's memorandum of February 27th, whereby Guizot stated that if a candidate was seriously put forward for the Queen's hand who was not a Bourbon, then the French government would resume its liberty of action, again there was no effective response. The British government preferred to remain in vague generalities; it was not prepared to co-operate actively with the French government in finding an acceptable Bourbon.

The question now remaining is whether Guizot's policy ever concealed within it some grand design whereby the marriage would seriously augment French power in the Mediterranean, either by uniting the thrones of France and Spain, or by bringing about some agreement between France, Spain and Naples. The first suggestion can be ruled out. There is no evidence that either Louis-Philippe or Guizot ever thought it desirable or practicable for a son of the French King to marry Isabella. The second suggestion is true, but represents a temporary measure rather than a constant aim of policy. What one has to realize is that although Guizot stated that the claimant to the throne should be a Bourbon, in reality his choice was always even more limited. Amongst the Bourbon candidates Guizot never showed any support for Montemolin, the son of Don Carlos. Whilst Louis-Philippe professed that he was acceptable, Guizot always thought of him as impossible and referred several times to Don Carlos being the centre of legitimist conspiracy, both in France and in Spain. For a long time the two Spanish Bourbons, the Duke of Cadiz and the Duke of Séville, were also impracticable because their mother was on bad terms with her sister, the Queen-Mother. Therefore there remained the Italian Bourbons, and obviously Naples could provide a more attractive match than Lucca. When difficulties arose at the court of Naples, the King being uncertain about letting his brother Trapani become involved in this confusion, and when it was suggested that Metternich was behind this hesitation, then Guizot, in order to support the Trapani candidature, was prepared to challenge Metternich's hold on Italy. But Guizot never lost sight of other candidates and he repeated to Bresson a score of times that the other possible candidates must not be abandoned. When the difficulties in Naples became too great, when the chances of Cadiz and Séville grew better with the death of their mother, then Guizot returned to them. But even when the choice seemed to have become limited to only Cadiz and Séville, the choice was in reality still more restricted since Séville had begun to associate politically with the progressive parties, and by 1846 he was no longer acceptable to the moderates who were then in power. Provided that a Bourbon had to be chosen there only remained Cadiz, and when what was probably the last chance of making this marriage occurred, Guizot took it. It is absurd to suppose that Cadiz was carefully chosen because he was thought, or known, to be impotent, and that in this way the French hoped that the succession would revert to France via the Montpensier-Infanta line. Allegations concerning impotency were not infrequently aimed at members of royal families; they had, for example, already been mentioned with regard to Trapani; it would have been a strange government which based its diplomacy upon such allegations. Furthermore, as Sir James Graham pointed out to Lord Aberdeen, even supposing that the rumours about Cadiz were true, the Queen-Mother knew ways of getting round such deficiencies. Such an idea might well have occurred to French statesmen.

There are three other factors which had a good deal of importance.

The first was that Guizot knew that French influence at Madrid was important, but he also knew that it was not all-powerful. The Spanish royal family and Spanish government wanted a marriage which would consolidate a dynasty that had almost collapsed. Such a marriage would consist either of an alliance with the Coburgs, thus achieving links with the royal families of England and Portugal, or of alliance with the family of Louis-Philippe. The marriage with Cadiz was not a useful marriage in this respect, and therefore, in order to make it acceptable, it had to be intimately associated with the more popular marriage of Montpensier and the Infanta. Had Guizot not accepted this, then the Coburg marriage would undoubtedly have been brought forward.

The second was the rôle played by Bresson. He acquired for himself in this affair the reputation for extreme skill and cunning, mixed up with a certain lack of principle. But his real importance lies in his repeated insistence that for France, in the east and in the west of Europe, there were only rivals or adversaries; in the words of Sieyès, France had no 'voluntary friends', and Bresson believed that whilst America was friendly when it was in her interests to be so, and whilst Prussia had been friendly until the death of the old king in 1840, it was only in Spain that France had a friend. It was essential, then, according to Bresson, that France should not alienate this unique ally, and he was continually pressing Guizot to acknowledge this by allowing a French marriage. Guizot knew how to resist Bresson, but it is likely that when the demand came for the simultaneous marriages, Bresson's continued pressure might have had its effect.

Lastly there was Palmerston. Perhaps Guizot was wrong to be so apprehensive at his return to power in 1846, but he looked forward to a brief honeymoon period with Palmerston, to be followed by a bitter dispute over Spain. Guizot had always believed that Buckingham Palace was behind the movement for a Coburg marriage; when de Broglie had been in London in 1845, he was impressed by the apparent influence of the Crown, and Guizot was convinced that the campaign in favour of the Coburgs had only been held in check by Aberdeen. Thus the return of Palmerston, and the removal of Aberdeen's restraining policy, were viewed with alarm. On July 19th, 1846, Palmerston confirmed all that was feared by his despatch which listed Leopold of Saxe-Coburg first amongst the candidates for the royal marriage, and which, by sharply criticizing the system of government in Spain, irritated the moderate politicians then in power. It was this brusque action, which spurred Guizot on to accepting the double marriage. Whether Palmerston actually intended to conclude a Coburg-Isabella marriage is doubtful. He probably wanted to arrange a marriage between Séville and Isabella, and between Coburg and the Infanta. But there can be no doubt that he intended to reverse the recent trends of affairs. He thought that the influence of France in the Mediterranean had become excessive. Once again the French had to be put in their place. The 'entente' in his eyes had been valuable as a means of restraining France; Guizot had turned it into a means of restraining England. Therefore the 'entente' was useless and Palmerston decided to disregard it. When he realized that his Spanish policy had failed, in part because of the folly of his July 19th despatch which had had such a bad effect in Spain, then he decided to smash the 'entente' entirely. Guizot's action could be publicized as the breaking of a pledge not only to the British government but even, it could be said, to Queen Victoria. The double marriage was an appropriately dramatic issue on which to organize public opinion and rally Europe against France.

When viewed in this light Guizot's policy cannot be accused of being secretive and dishonest; it was rather open and evident, and it was because his policy was so well known that he was forced to arrange the double marriage. Had a Coburg married the Queen, or even the Queen's sister, then London's success would have had serious consequences, as Guizot himself said, serious both in Paris and in Madrid. The double marriage was not the culmination of some ambitious and far-seeing policy: it was rather a hasty expedient to preserve the government from a set-back in Spain which would also become a defeat in the Chamber of Deputies.[1]

Both Guizot and Palmerston admitted subsequently that things might have gone otherwise. Guizot admitted that he might have been caught up in policies which were anachronistic, making national policies dependent upon royal marriages, and Palmerston told Aberdeen that had he been in power, the quarrel might never have come about.[2] Guizot too cannot have been under any illusions about the effects of his triumph. After October 1846 he was anxiously protesting against rumours that Isabella was asking for a divorce, or that Isabella was thinking of abdicating; he was passing on Montpensier's report that the King did not have access to Isabella's bed-

---

[1] This interpretation of Spanish marriages question is based on the private correspondence between Guizot and Bresson in Madrid (42 A.P. 8 and AB XIX 1700-1705), Sainte-Aulaire and Jarnac in London, Flahault in Vienna (42 A.P. 8), Montebello in Naples (42 A.P. 7), Guizot and Aberdeen (Aberdeen Papers in the British Museum and Val-Richer MSS.), Aberdeen and Peel etc.; the correspondence published in the *Revue Rétrospective* 1848 and in the *British and Foreign State Papers* has also been consulted. The fullest treatment of the subject is in E. Jones Parry, *The Spanish Marriages*, 1936, but this book seems to be condemnatory of French policy without making any attempt to understand it.

[2] *Guizot, Sir Robert Peel*, Paris 1856, p. 308; Aberdeen: Guizot, October, 1856, *Val-Richer MSS.*

room. He was continually protesting that the Spanish government was not giving sufficient preference to French trade, or that it was asking for concessions in the French tariff on articles such as wool, wine and oil which would cause France to be inundated with the products of the Zollverein, Portugal, Hungary, Sardinia and elsewhere; he was preoccupied with the activities of Bulwer as he was with the commercial mission of a Mr. Henderson.[1] In fact, what he called 'des nouvelles combinaisons adoptées' brought him very little tranquillity. Perhaps the most revealing document was the letter where Bresson asked to be removed from Madrid. He saw that he had been too involved and that he had become the centre of controversy. 'My presence, and let me say without false modesty, my ascendancy, have become lasting provocations.'[2] So Bresson was appointed ambassador in Naples, where he shortly added the final touch of drama to the Spanish marriages by committing suicide.

Bresson's letter reveals one of the dangers of Guizot's policy. He had become so caught up in the internal politics of the country where he was serving that he could become an embarrassment to his government, and a political change in Madrid could be represented as a national defeat for France. Much the same happened in Greece.

Guizot had always insisted on the importance of 'cette porte de l'Orient', and he had drawn the attention of Europe to the need for European agreement over Greek questions.[3] He had told Lord Aberdeen that England and France should work together; he instructed Piscatory, who was made ambassador in June 1843, to work with his English colleague Sir Edmund Lyons; after the Revolution of September 1843 which forced the lethargic King Otto to grant a constitution, Guizot was suggesting that the main political parties should work together in a coalition government. But with the elections of July 1844 the party of Mavrocordato, reputedly pro-English, was defeated and Colettis became the most important politician. As the personal friend of Guizot, he was soon to be accused of being the creation of Piscatory. In a private letter to de Broglie, Piscatory suggested that he himself was the dominant influence, able to tell Colettis what to do and consulted by the King as to what he should do. 'People swear only by France', reported the jubilant ambassador.[4]

Obviously, in such a position, Guizot's protestation that Piscatory

[1] See the correspondence between Guizot and Glucksberg during 1847, 42 A.P. 7; see the correspondence between Guizot, Bresson, Glucksberg and Dollfus in *Archives A.E.*, Correspondance Commerciale, Madrid 45.

[2] Bresson: Guizot, September 2nd, 1846, AB XIX 1705.

[3] Guizot: Bresson (Berlin), December 16th, 1841, 42 A.P. 8; Despatch of March 11th, 1841, in *Mémoires*, vol. vii, Pièce Historique, xiv, p. 452.

[4] Piscatory: de Broglie, August 28th, 1844, 42 A.P. 4.

was a loyal believer in the 'entente', and that Colettis merely had 'quelque estime pour mon jugement', lacked conviction. Aberdeen could not order Lyons to approve of the Colettis government, 'because I do not approve of it myself', and his remarks concerning Greece, about which he could not think 'with pleasure', became increasingly bitter. He saw the Colettis government placing 'illiterate ruffians . . . men recently in open rebellion . . . at the head of affairs'; he saw the police being entrusted to banditti and highway robbers; he claimed that the elections were being falsified and the Chamber packed, that justice was disappearing and that the finances of the country were disintegrating. Piscatory denied all this. His letters are gay and carefree; he tried to show that brigandage was on the decline, although commenting that Lord Aberdeen would say that this was because all the brigands had been made ministers; if there were rumours of uprisings or of Greek attacks against Turkey, this was because of the attitude of Lyons or other English officials. His descriptions of Greek tranquillity and prosperity were accompanied by references to the newspapers he was financing and to individuals he was supporting (sometimes from funds which were supposedly to support Catholics in the Middle East, but he regarded these Catholics as being so stupid that he had no scruples about robbing them).

Towards the end of 1845 Piscatory's letters show some hesitation. He notes the shortcomings of Colettis; he begins to have doubts as to his majority. By the summer of 1846 he reports that Colettis is thinking of governing the country without the Chamber, and living on what money he could find until he was obliged to hold elections. Piscatory did not think that the French should support such a proposition; he was beginning to feel unduly prominent as the supporter of Colettis against whom a considerable coalition was being formed; along with Guizot he was worried when relations between Greece and Turkey began to deteriorate and when he realised that French policy in Athens was at odds with French policy in Constantinople; several times he asked for an appointment elsewhere. By October 1847 he was telling Desages that he alone was running the government; it was he who controlled King, Cabinet and Chamber and he who had written the address which the Chamber had voted. From all sides therefore he was being attacked; in every action he took he was committing the French government. This was a situation which was bound to remain for as long as he remained in Athens. The French rôle, therefore, had been greatly inflated in Greece. It was bound to collapse; the presence of Piscatory in Athens, like that of Bresson in Madrid, had become a provocation.[1]

[1] See the Guizot-Aberdeen correspondence in *Aberdeen Papers*, 43,134, and

Guizot can be criticized for allowing the activities of his ambassadors to get out of hand in this way. He did not make the same mistake in other Mediterranean countries. The signature of a commercial treaty between France and Piedmont-Sardinia was directly aimed at reinforcing the Austrian antipathies of the Italians, and at the same time of bringing some advantages to French industry. But one has to notice that although the treaty was described as 'un premier pas', the Piedmontese government was not given the concessions in Algeria which it had requested and the treaty was not followed up by any other important overtures.[1] In Morocco the French government was obliged to fight a campaign against the Sultan's armies, as resisting Algerians crossed the uncertain frontier. But Guizot's policy was to avoid conquest. All he wanted was a Moroccan government which would permit the conquest and colonization of Algeria to proceed. The same was true of his attitude to the Bey of Tunis. Yet both in Morocco and in Tunis British representatives sent alarming reports, and the British government and press were suspicious of French intentions. However active or however restrained Guizot's diplomacy may have been, when it came to the Mediterranean the 'entente cordiale' was fraught with suspicion and distrust.

Much has been made of Guizot's turning towards Metternich in 1847, and this has been considered the central feature of his conduct of foreign affairs in the closing years of his ministry. Without going into details of what sort of an arrangement Guizot hoped to conclude with Metternich,[2] it is possible to understand the reasons which led to this 'rapprochement' and Guizot's own interpretation of it. French policy after the conclusion of the Spanish marriages is a reaction to two situations; in the first place, the campaign against France directed by Palmerston; in the second place, the developments in Switzerland, Italy and Germany.

At first Guizot did not anticipate that the double marriages would

---

the Guizot-Piscatory correspondence in 42 A.P. 7. See also *Thouvenel, La Grèce du Roi Othon, Correspondance de M. Thouvenel*, Paris 1890.

[1] See *S. Mastellone*, 'Il trattato di commercio franco-piemontese (1840-1846)', *Rassegna Storica del Risorgimento*, 1952, pp. 143-171, and Guizot's correspondence with Dalmatie (Turin), Soult, Cunin-Gridaine, Lacave-Laplagne, in 42 A.P. 12. For Guizot's view of France as 'la protectrice naturelle de l'Italie' see Guizot: Salvandy (Turin), October 30th, 1843, *Archives A.E.*, Correspondance Politique, Sardaigne 316.

[2] See the correspondence published in Metternich, *Mémoires*, vol. vii, pp. 388 ff., and the interesting article by *Silva*, 'La politica francese in Italia nell' epoca delle riforme, 1846-1848, e l'accordo Metternich-Guizot' in *Revue des études italiennes* (avril-septembre 1936), pp. 276 ff.

311

cause much excitement or resentment in England, and in August
and September he was assuring his ambassadors and colleagues that
although there might be a coolness between France and England, this
would pass.[1] By October he saw a diplomatic offensive being led by
Palmerston against the succession rights of the Montpensier marriage;
he believed that Palmerston was directing an attack on many
fronts. He was attacking the Colettis government in Greece, was
intriguing in the Spanish royal palace, was in touch with revolutionaries in the west and south of Spain, with Montemolin and
other exiled leaders, whilst at the same time circularising the Northern
Powers with legal arguments around the Utrecht stipulation.[2] Guizot
also replied on many fronts. In the first place he replied to Madrid
and Athens, giving instructions to his representatives and asking for
information; in these instructions there is an attention to detail
which is remarkable and which shows very clearly the extent to which
Guizot had linked the future of French influence to particular
personalities. In the second place he answered Palmerston's attacks
on the diplomatic front; this was essentially a defensive policy,
inspired by fear of isolation, and by the knowledge that the only way
in which Palmerston's attack on the Greek government could be met
was by organizing support in Europe.[3] Thirdly, Guizot appealed to
Metternich as he had so frequently appealed to Aberdeen in the past.
Was not a conservative ministry in France worth saving, could not
Metternich distinguish between 'le Ministre Conservateur et le
Ministre brouillon'?[4] Later he more explicitly stated his claim to
Metternich's sympathy. 'If disorder recommences in Spain, will it
not start up in Italy?' he wrote to Flahault. 'Est-ce l'Angleterre qui y
portera remède? N'est-ce pas la France, la France seule qui le peut et
le veut aujourd'hui? Le Prince Metternich mettra-t-il en jeu le repos
de l'Europe pour servir la rancune de Lord Palmerston?'[5] Fourthly,
Guizot pursued a counter-offensive in London; not only an attempt
to justify himself to the public and to find centres of opposition to
Lord Palmerston, but also an attempt to maintain collaboration with
the British Foreign Secretary. His logical mind could not believe that

[1] Guizot: Bresson, August 22nd, 1846, 42 A.P. 8; Guizot: Montebello (Naples),
September 12th, 1846, 42 A.P. 7; Guizot: Duchâtel, September 13th, 1846,
Papiers Duchâtel, 2 A.P. 8.

[2] Piscatory: Guizot, October 30th, 1846, 42 A.P. 7; Guizot: Sainte-Aulaire,
December 10th, 1846, 42 A.P. 8.

[3] Guizot: Piscatory, March 29th, 1847, 42 A.P. 7. Guizot hoped to isolate
Palmerston in Europe over the Greek question but he did not consider that there
was any way of preventing the British government from sending warships to the
Greek coast.

[4] Guizot: Flahault, 14th November, 1846, 42 A.P. 8.

[5] Ibid., February 1st, 1847.

the possibility of distant cousins of the French royal family some day succeeding to the throne of France was sufficient to justify a break in co-operation; he therefore welcomed every opportunity of collaboration, such as the overthrow of the Cracow Republic, the affairs of Portugal, Switzerland and the River Plate; he was anxious to avoid annoying London, and regretted that the Bey of Tunis should visit Paris just when the British government was so preoccupied with French power in the Mediterranean.[1] He wished to avoid any complications with England over Portugal, and later in 1847 he reproached his ambassador in Lisbon, who apparently thought that he had to sustain a 'lutte d'influences' as in Spain.[2] In the summer of 1847 he wrote to de Broglie, the ambassador in London, that his task was to combat the impression that the French were trying to create some exclusive and illegitimate preponderance.[3] By November he is still attempting to bring England into the demonstration of the powers over the Swiss question and assuring them of the advantages of Lord Palmerston's support.[4] It is clear, then, that Guizot never intended to align himself with the continental powers against England; if he had any view of a European system, England was part of it, both as a positive force and as a way of preventing England from embarrassing France.

Whatever the state of relations between France and England, it was inevitable that events in Switzerland, Italy and Germany should cause Guizot to look to his relations with Metternich; in the first two Austria and France were the foreign powers most directly concerned; and in Germany, France and Austria were in a similar position regarding the increasing importance of Prussia in German political and economic life. It was Guizot's policy always to work by agreement rather than by conflict; but he realized that whereas in the Spanish or Greek questions he needed Metternich, in the Swiss and Italian questions Metternich needed him.

He had long expected trouble to come from Switzerland. Within a few weeks of October 29th, 1840, he was writing to Berne that the conflicts between parties in Switzerland could result in civil war, which would raise the whole question of foreign intervention.[5] He

[1] Guizot: Piscatory, October 17th, 1846, 42 A.P. 7. On this journey see the *Revue Tunisienne*, vol. xxv, 1918, pp. 274-284.

[2] Guizot: Varennes (Lisbon), September 5th, 1847, 42 A.P. 3. See *D. M. Greer, L'Angleterre, la France et la Révolution de 1848* (Paris 1926), pp. 101 ff.

[3] Guizot: de Broglie, July 8th, 1847, 42 A.P. 8.

[4] Guizot: Dalmatie (Berlin), November 19th, 1847, *Archives A.E.*, Correspondance Politique, Prusse 301. He had written to de Broglie, 'Je suis bien aise de donner cette preuve de fait que je mets toujours le même prix à l'entente avec l'Angleterre . . .' Guizot: de Broglie, November 18th, 1847, 42 A.P. 8.

[5] Guizot: Mortier (Berne), February 10th, 1841, 42 A.P. 9.

frequently recurred to such warnings. The conflict in Switzerland was essentially of three different sorts: that between radicals and conservatives, which became more serious as Switzerland had become the centre of cosmopolitan radicalism; that between Protestants and Catholics; that over interpretations of the Federal Pact of 1815, both as regards the power of the central government and the power of individual cantons. The situation became difficult when in October 1844 the canton of Lucerne invited the Society of Jesus to take over its theological institutions and opponents of this move sought to prevent it, by use of force if necessary. In December 1845 seven Catholic cantons formed themselves into a defensive league, the Sonderbund; the radical party, which held that the Sonderbund was illegal, being contrary to the Federal Pact, concentrated its efforts on winning power in a number of cantons, so that it would gain the absolute majority in the Federal Diet. By May 1847 the radicals won a victory in the canton of St. Gall and were able to go ahead with their plans for the expulsion of the Jesuits, for the forceful dispersion of Sonderbund forces, and for the reform of the federal constitution.

Guizot's situation was complicated. He was clearly anti-radical. A radical Switzerland was undesirable for the July Monarchy; a radical revision of the constitution, making Switzerland a more unified, stronger state, was also contrary to French interests. But Lucerne's invitation to the Jesuits came at a time when Guizot himself was having considerable trouble with the Society within France, and he did not want to add to his difficulties. Above all, an Austrian intervention into Switzerland in defence of the Sonderbund would be an extension of Austrian power on the French frontiers. Apart from the international complications that it would create, it would certainly lead to a demand within France that French armies should also move into Switzerland, and it would be difficult for them to intervene in co-operation with the Austrians, as their rôle would be to counterbalance the Austrians.

Guizot therefore rejected the idea of intervention, whilst insisting that Europe had the right to advise the cantons and also the right to issue warnings. He hoped that there would not be a temporary victory for one side or the other, but that the spectacle of a united Europe which was not prepared to tolerate any radical change in the federal constitution, and the realization of the suffering which would result from civil war, would act effectively on the great mass of moderate opinion which stood between the two opposing parties.[1] He always believed that a large moderate group existed, even after the civil war, and that the French government, because it was a constitutional government accepted by the other governments of the

[1] Guizot: Jarnac, October 29th, 1846, 42 A.P. 7.

Continent and by 'la portion honnête et sensée des populations',[1] was the natural mediator. In order to maintain this strong position France had to prevent the powers from taking any rash action, and Guizot was able to postpone the calling of a Congress on Switzerland and to postpone taking decisions, by pleading his difficult position in the Chamber.[2] It is probable that this is the nearest Guizot approached to conducting foreign affairs on a grand scale; he could claim that the continental powers modelled their language and their actions on those of France, whilst he defended the immediate interests of French security by opposing radicalism, opposing the creation of a unitary state and preventing Austrian intervention.[3] On 18th January he had quoted, at length, Palmerston's despatch to Percy of June 1832 and claimed that he saw in it the same attitude towards the constitution of Switzerland as the French government had adopted; this speech could well be interpreted as an appeal to England to join in the common front.[4]

But policy on the grand scale can only be really grand when it is successful. There had been general uncertainty about the possibility of the Sonderbund's resistance being successful and Guizot (who had helped to stiffen the Sonderbund's resistance by selling them two thousand rifles at a low price) was not alone in remaining relatively confident. *The Times* of London for a long time expected the Sonderbund soldiers to show great qualities when they were defending their religion and their country, and late in October Palmerston thought that the difficulties of the terrain were such as would favour the Sonderbund. Therefore it is not necessarily true, as many historians have suggested, that Palmerston, postponing negotiations so as to give time for the collapse of the Sonderbund, repeated his triumph of 1840 by being well informed on the military situation. But whatever the reason, Guizot's rather fatalistic belief that a prolonged and bitter conflict would inspire Swiss opinion to turn to the European powers for guidance became irrelevant when the Sonderbund collapsed. Guizot probably overestimated the warmth of Austrian collaboration, and he undoubtedly made a mistake which Palmerston did not make when he failed to distinguish amongst the different strands of radicalism the moderate element which he was so determined to cultivate. He incurred much hostility at home for having apparently supported the Austrians, the Jesuits and the unsuccessful. The most that can be said is that by helping to prevent Austrian

---

[1] Guizot: de Broglie, December 6th, 1847, 42 A.P. 8.

[2] Guizot: Flahault, December 20th, 1847, Ibid.

[3] Chambre des Députés, February 3rd, 1848, *Histoire Parlementaire*, vol. v, pp. 566 ff.

[4] Chambre des Pairs, January 15th, 1848, Ibid., pp. 510 ff.

intervention, he did avoid what could have been a more troublesome crisis.[1]

In Italy the rôle of mediator was even more obvious as Guizot saw it; he was between the revolutionaries and the reactionaries; the policy of the one was territorial and national, the policy of the other was to suppress all reform; both policies could only lead to Austrian intervention, and thus to the necessity of French intervention. For Guizot the solution was to reject both attitudes. 'Il ne s'agit point là de politique, il s'agit d'administration: les gens sages, les populations elles-mêmes ne demandent pas autre chose. Une administration sagement réformée, tel est le besoin du pays. . . .'[2] If the reforming parties in the various states posed the national question, then they inevitably became revolutionary; he urged his ambassador in Rome, Rossi, to persuade the parties that they must work 'fractionnaire-ment' within the limits of their states.[3] France was thus to be the patron of the moderate party and the protector of existing state boundaries; if French policy was successful there would be no Austrian intervention, no revolution in Italy, no general European conflagration, and the influence of France in Italy would triumph with the success of the 'juste milieu' applied by 'les princes, les gouverne-ments, les hommes sages et bien intentionnés de l'Italie'.[4]

It is obvious that Guizot failed completely to understand the importance and force of Italian nationalism, which is all the more striking since he was well aware of the force of German nationalism, and he had some sympathy for Irish nationalism, a subject which he discussed with Gladstone after the latter's resignation from Peel's government. But although he had friends who were partisans of the Italian nationalist movement, such as the Princess Belgioso and Augustin Thierry, he had no belief in Italian nationalism. Even in later years he expressed disbelief in the possibility of Italian unity. Possibly he thought that the Papacy was an obstacle to making Italy one unified country. At all events throughout his ministry he tried to minimize at first the gravity of and then the implications of what was happening in Italy. He made no secret of his hostility towards Sardinian aspirations, telling Mortier in Turin that the Piedmontese government should not underestimate the gravity of a quarrel with

[1] *The Times*, August 10th, October 11th, December 3rd, 1847; Palmerston: Peel, October 29th, 1847, *Correspondence Relative to the Affairs of the Sonderbund*, *House of Commons Sessional Papers*, vol. 65, 1847-1848; see the articles by Louis Burgener and Marc Paschoud in *Zeitschrift für Schweizerische Geschichte*, vol. xxvi, 1947.
[2] Guizot: Flahault, January 12th, 1847, *Rivista Storica Italiana*, vol. lxi, p. 86.
[3] Guizot: Rossi, August 26th, 1847, Ibid., p. 91.
[4] Chambre des Députés, January 29th, 1848, *Histoire Parlementaire*, vol. v, p. 552.

Austria, and that they should not count on getting support from France. He did not see that either the circumstances or the leaders of Piedmont were suitable for the grand rôle which their ambition and their vanity had allotted to them. There can be little doubt that Guizot was apprehensive of an increase in the size of Piedmont, and that he looked on Piedmontese influence in the Middle East as a rival to that of France.[1]

But by the end of Guizot's ministry French influence in Turin and in Naples was nil; in Rome it was declining swiftly. So far as Germany was concerned, he had been quick to see the significance of the Prussian constitutional changes, quicker than most other French politicians. To Flahault he insisted that the independence of the secondary states of Germany was of outstanding importance to France. If Prussia appropriated to herself the ideas of German liberalism and unity, as well as a position of economic preponderance, he feared that Prussian ascendancy would materially alter the sovereignty of these states. These fears were confirmed by certain of his representatives in Germany.[2] But apart from encouraging these states in their refusal to establish a military cordon around the Swiss frontiers, which had been one of Metternich's ideas of meeting the Sonderbund crisis, Guizot does not seem to have done much to consolidate the French position with the lesser German states. Doubtless he was waiting for a favourable moment; undoubtedly he had many other preoccupations. But time was passing and French initiatives were becoming rarer and less successful.

Thureau-Dangin, who has told in some detail the attitude of the French government towards events in Germany, Switzerland and Italy during the years 1847 and 1848, concludes his account by confessing to annoyance that the Revolution of February 24th should provide such a sudden ending to the story; he compares the situation to 'un spectacle qu'un accident ferait cesser brusquement au moment le plus critique du drame'.[3] It is certain that Guizot was overthrown when he was showing the greatest determination and conviction in his conduct of affairs; he was not prepared to compromise with any of the groups in the Chamber over his condemnation of radicals and revolutionaries, nor to heed the promptings of ambassadors who

---

[1] Guizot: Mortier, March 25th, 1847, *Archives A.E.*, Correspondance Politique, Sardaigne 319. See *César Vidal* on the Franco-Piedmontese quarrel over the Christian communities in the Middle East in *Revue des Études Italiennes*, avril-septembre 1936, pp. 268 ff.

[2] Guizot: Flahault, February 25th, 1847, 42 A.P. 8; Bourgoing: Guizot, May 16th, 1847, *Archives A.E.*, Correspondance Politique, Bavière 222; de Fontenay: Guizot, March 20th, 1847, Ibid., Wurtemberg 71.

[3] *Thureau-Dangin, Histoire de la Monarchie de Juillet* (op. cit.), vol. vii, p. 302.

suggested that France would have much to gain by putting herself at the head of liberal parties in various parts of Europe. Once again internal and external affairs were linked, and for those who wished to maintain the existing social and political institutions in France, there was only one policy in Europe.

Nearly eight years of speeches, despatches and letters form a remarkable contribution to the study of European diplomacy: to read them is to see how wrong were those who believed that France was bent upon a policy of territorial aggrandisement similar to that of Louis XIV or Napoleon. To read them is also to see how Guizot tried to fit his policy to the needs of France, and make it appropriate to French requirements and to French power. Although the settlement of 1815 was denounced from every tribune, Guizot realized that modifications in the treaties could be dangerous for France, particularly if they led to an increase in the positions of Prussia or Sardinia, or to a unified Switzerland. He was genuinely annoyed at the Austrian suppression of the Cracow republic since it weakened the strength of the 1815 settlement. He was attached to peace because he believed that a war could endanger France's political settlement at home, as well as compromising gravely the economic activity of the nation. He was confident of the importance of France and believed that France must naturally play a vital part in world affairs; but he believed that this influence was based to a large extent on the institutions consecrated in 1830.

This approach to foreign affairs is in contrast to that of the opposition. When they discussed foreign affairs, they did so not always with an eye to the needs of France but with an eye to their audience both in the Chamber, and 'par la fenêtre', in the country. They rarely discussed questions on their merits; they attitudinized. When one can see their private correspondence, it is often very different from these public utterances; Duvergier de Hauranne, for example, could write in an article that the campaigns in Algeria made the hearts of France beat quicker, but privately he lamented the day when the conquest had begun. Guizot often pointed this out. Sending an expedition to Montevideo, he said, was the sort of folly or 'sottise' which Thiers could suggest at the tribune, but it was something which he would carefully avoid were he in power. Thiers himself told Lord Aberdeen, when he was in London in 1845, that there were only three possible governments in France, that of Guizot, that of Molé or that which he would lead himself, and he claimed that they were all agreed about foreign policy. After 1848, if one looks at principles of foreign policy as practised by Tocqueville, or if one looks at utterances by Thiers, one can see the truth of this. Even Lamartine had said that 'un règne négotiateur' could be as great as 'un règne conquérant'.

Thus to some extent the conflict between Guizot and the opposition over foreign policy was artificial; but it was not completely so. Guizot did not understand the persistence of anti-English sentiments; they were for him anachronisms which would disappear with time and patience; he did not see that they were strengthened by economic competition and by the force of nationalism. He did not understand nationalism either in France or in other countries; he thought that this was a movement which at its best would be satisfied with administrative reforms, which at its worst was determined on resuscitating the Revolution. He did not understand that many Frenchmen were looking for security, that ever since 1815 there had been a longing for some great diplomacy which would give France an ally; he did not understand that his personal understanding with Lord Aberdeen was an ineffective substitute for such a need. Had he adapted his policy to the conditions of society as exactly as he claimed, he would have given more importance to economic considerations. He often thought of financial and commercial matters, such as English participation in the Paris-Rouen railway, as adjuncts to his policy, methods of helping diplomacy rather than the aim of diplomacy. In Europe he did not understand that France was still an object of mistrust, an unstable and divided country. Above all he did not know the dictum that in foreign policy there is no room for gratitude; he should not have expected the other statesmen of Europe to protect him against his critics.

Finally it must be said that he occasionally forgot all about 'une politique extérieure très nouvelle' and became simply a nervous diplomatist, suffering from the complexes of many post-Revolutionary French statesmen, seeing in the journeys of the Czar or in Aberdeen's readiness to listen to Vienna the possibilities of plots and coalitions. He became too preoccupied with details and with personalities, remarking that some person was 'très bon pour nous' or that some diplomatist was showing himself 'très caressant pour nous'. He was overfearful of being duped, overanxious to demonstrate success.

But his greatest weakness was his lack of imagination. A journalist once wrote, 'Ce qui fait qu'en France il faut de l'imagination aux hommes d'état, c'est que le peuple en aura toujours plus qu'eux.'[1] In these circumstances, in Guizot's own words, it is not enough to be right.

[1] C. L. B., 'De l'Amérique du Sud', *Revue des Deux Mondes*, 1838, vol. xxxi, p. 69.

7

HISTORY

> He was the greatest professor of history that we have ever
> had.
> SAINTE-BEUVE

GUIZOT was the first great modern historian of France. He was the founder and most distinguished representative of a school of history which commanded the attention of Europe. Sainte-Beuve called him 'le père de tous nos modernes', and Augustin Thierry wrote that before Guizot there had been no progress in the study of the history of France. From Hotman to Boulainvilliers, from Boulainvilliers to Mably, from Mably to Montlosier, there had only been variations on the same false themes; but with *Essais sur l'Histoire de France* and *l'Histoire de la Civilisation en France*, then as Thierry puts it, 'le progrès éclate de toutes parts'.[1] It is well known that Guizot's lectures on European and French civilization represent perhaps the most successful period of his career, when his work was internationally famous and was admired by Goethe, Mazzini, Thomas Arnold and even by the Francophobe Emerson. His other historical work was also important. The translation and editing of Gibbon was a considerable work of erudition. In addition to correcting many errors and to questioning many interpretations, Guizot took this opportunity of introducing into France the work of the German historical school which was not then widely known, he extended the conventional source material by using numismatic evidence, and he emphasized economic, financial and geographical factors in places where Gibbon appeared to have neglected them. Guizot's Gibbon was published in 1812 and was for many years the

---

[1] Sainte-Beuve: Charles Labitte, July 22nd, 1839, *Correspondance de Sainte-Beuve* (op. cit.), vol. iii, p. 120. *Augustin Thierry*, 'Considérations sur l'Histoire de France' in *Œuvres*, vol. vii, Paris 1878, p. 190.

standard edition. Twenty years after its publication it was still being recommended and it was not until Dean Milman's edition of 1838 that Guizot's edition was superseded. But it was not abandoned, since Milman, like subsequent editions, incorporated Guizot's notes into his own edition.[1]

Guizot's *Histoire de la Révolution d'Angleterre depuis l'Avènement de Charles Ier jusqu'à sa mort* was first published in 1826 and was in the forefront of the serious interest which was arising in this subject. It was between 1825 and 1828 that William Godwin published his *History of the Commonwealth*, Macaulay's essay on Milton was published in 1825 and that on Hampden in 1831. Forster's *Lives of the Statesmen of the Commonwealth* appeared between 1836 and 1839, Carlyle's *Cromwell* was dated 1845, Macaulay's first two volumes of the *History of England* 1849. Guizot's *Discours sur l'Histoire de la Révolution d'Angleterre* (sometimes called *On the Causes of the Success of the English Revolution*) was published in 1850, his study of *Monk*, which had originally appeared as an article in 1837 was revised and published separately in 1851; *Histoire de la République d'Angleterre* appeared in 1854 and *Le Protectorat de Richard Cromwell* in 1856. These, together with the *Portraits Politiques des hommes des différents partis* (studies of Hollis, Ludlow, Lilburne, Edward and Henry Hyde, etc., which were published in book form in 1851), formed the most detailed and most complete history of the period in either English or French. They were unrivalled until S. R. Gardiner began the publication of his many authoritative volumes.

It is therefore strange that certain modern writers should have dismissed Guizot's historical writings as being a mere appendage to his active political life. Guizot has in this way been reduced to the rank either of a politician who happened to write history, or of a politician who wrote political pamphlets disguised as history. Guizot is not alone in being so mistreated. It has been suggested that for the liberals in Restoration France the production of history was nothing more than a political manœuvre, with 'Liberal France' claiming possession of the past. Fustel de Coulanges extended this interpretation to apply to all French historical writing over a wide period; 'For the last fifty years', he wrote in 1872, 'our historians have been men of a party. However sincere they were, or however impartial they thought they were, they followed one or other of the political opinions which divided us. . . . Our writing of history has

---

[1] See *The Quarterly Review*, August 1833, vol. l, pp. 173 ff. In 1924 it was said that whilst even Bury's edition of Gibbon still contained a large number of errors in the text, many of these had been corrected by Guizot in his translation. See the *Times Literary Supplement*, July 24th and 31st, 1924.

been like our legislative assemblies: one can see the right, the left and the centres. . . . Writing the history of France was a way of working for a party and fighting an adversary.'[1]

It is of course true that 'the new school of history' as Chateaubriand called them, or 'the movement for historical reform' which was Sainte-Beuve's more accurate phrase, had close personal links with the liberals. When the writers of the liberal intellectual newspaper *Le Globe* met in a restaurant of the Rue de Serpente, it was not possible to distinguish between those who were politicians and those who were historians. The crowds of young people who applauded Guizot at the Sorbonne or who applauded Amadée Thierry at Besançon, or who were later to applaud Michelet, were enthusiastic for their liberal opinions as much as for their eloquence and erudition. In nineteenth-century France it was never possible to leave politics behind. Every form of thought was charged with politics. A comment on the ambition of Clovis, on the government of Charlemagne or on the usurpations of some aristocracy of the past, appeared to have political significance and was taken to be an allusion to the contemporary scene. The ultras of the right denounced those who were interested in seventeenth-century English history as being revolutionaries who wanted the Bourbons to suffer the same fate as the Stuarts, either in the manner of 1649 or in that of 1688. It was thought that Prosper de Barante's picture of civil agitation, starting with the distracted times of Charles VI and ending with Louis XI, was a warning to the Restoration Monarchy. It was even claimed that Sainte-Aulaire's account of the Fronde was one of a prospective courtier to a prospective king, when he praised the intrigues of the earlier Duke of Orleans. One of Madame de Staël's stories about the Consulate seems applicable to this period of French life. Two men were standing behind Bonaparte at a reception. 'Have you noticed what fine hands the first Consul has?' whispered the one. 'For God's sake,' replied the other, 'don't let's talk politics.'

But because many historians were active in politics and because their works either had, or were attributed, a political significance, it does not mean that history had become a mere province of politics. It is ludicrous to think of Guizot working through Gregory of Tours or Whitelock's *Memorials* in order to further his opposition to Villèle's ministry; and to dismiss the great advance in the conception and technique of historical research which took place in these years

---

[1] *Fustel de Coulanges*, 'Chronique' in the *Revue des Deux Mondes*, September 1st, 1872, p. 243. See also *Stanley Mellon, The Political Uses of History*, Stanford, California 1958, pp. 13-15. The chapter by Professor Pouthas on 'L'Enseignment de Guizot' also, to my mind, overemphasizes the political influence. See *Guizot pendant la Restauration* (op. cit.), pp. 299 ff.

as being incidental to political controversy is seriously to mis-represent an important intellectual movement.

Under the Empire historical studies had been mediocre. Apart from Chateaubriand there were no great names and no great works. Napoleon was interested in history and conscious of its appeal. But the teaching and writing of history had to be organized into one of the supports of his dynasty. His interest in Chateaubriand's *Le Génie de Christianisme*, his desire to use Daunou's edition of Rulhière's *Histoire de l'Anarchie de la Pologne*, his eagerness to see the Papal archives which Chénier brought back from Rome, are illustrations of how he sought historical works which would coincide with the needs of policy. Apart from this his interest in history was purely egotistical. 'Je ne suis pas un homme, je suis un personage historique,' he once said. 'He was interested in history as the great noble whose portrait is being painted is interested in the artist. . .,' is one historian's assessment of Napoleon.[1] The science of history was therefore hardly cultivated and Frenchmen knew little about their past and showed little interest in their archives or monuments. As late as 1821 a writer in the *Quarterly Review* claimed that it was only the English who made any effort to preserve the churches and ruins of Normandy, 'which are doomed to neglect and destruction by the disgraceful sloth and ignorance of the French . . . to whom it was said that all memorials were hateful'.[2]

But with the Restoration, and more particularly after 1820, this situation began to change. Apart from Guizot, many writers became famous through their writings on history. Augustin Thierry began writing historical articles for *Le Censeur Européen* as early as 1817, and in 1820 published the first of his *Lettres sur l'histoire de France*, which were revised and published together in 1827. *L'Histoire de la Conquête d'Angleterre par les Normands* appeared in 1825. His younger brother Amédée Thierry having published a history of La Guyenne, then went on to produce, in 1828, his *Histoire des Gaulois*, a work which Chateaubriand claimed had anticipated much of what he had intended to say in his *Études Historiques* (1831). Prosper de Barante started to publish from 1824 onwards his *Histoire des Ducs de Bourgogne*; two histories of the French Revolution were started in the 1820s, the one by Thiers started to appear in 1823, and that by Mignet came out in 1824. In addition to Villemain's studies of eighteenth-century literature, he had in 1819 produced a *Vie de Cromwell*, and Armand Carrel dealt with the post-Cromwellian period in his *Histoire de la Contre-Révolution en Angleterre* (1822). Michelet's *Précis d'Histoire Moderne* first appeared in 1827; it was

[1] C. Jullian in *Revue de Synthèse Historique*, 1906, p. 131.
[2] *Quarterly Review*, April 1821, vol. 25, p. 147.

in this year too that Michelet completed his translation of Vico, and Edgar Quinet his translation of Herder. Less famous writers produced historical works, sometimes on a large scale, sometimes with great erudition. Daunou, Michaud, Lacretelle and Daru continued to write under the Restoration; Salvandy, Mazure, Capefigue, Monteil, Fauriel, Mazas, Trognon, Saint-Martin, Letronne and Sainte-Aulaire do not exhaust the list of French historians who wrote within this limited period. Abel Rémusat, Champollion, Silvestre de Sacy and Burnouf were orientalists of genius who extended the limits of knowledge and whose work also dates from this time.

With all these historians turning increasingly to the documents and insisting upon erudition, the foundation of the École des Chartes in 1822 was significant. It marks an important stage in the training of archivists, in the realization that archives and libraries needed to be organized and inventoried. At this time, too, local historians and antiquaries began to make their appearance, like the abbé de la Rue in Caen and Le Prévost in Rouen. They began to examine their ancient monuments and enter upon the usual period of uncertainty over their dating, frequently believing that old age and ugliness were synonymous. Publishers began to vie with each other in producing 'Histoires Universelles', 'résumés' and short histories, memoirs and recollections, editions of chronicles, correspondence, translations and histories of foreign countries. All the reviews carried numerous historical articles. There were specialized reviews, such as the *Journal des Savants* (at first edited by Daunou) and the *Bulletin des Sciences Historiques, Antiquités, Philologie*, which were serious and learned; later on there appeared *Le Magasin Pittoresque*, which sought to popularize history. This too was the period of romantic history, 'l'histoire Walter-Scottée', when poets, moralists, painters, decorators, orators, all sought historical subjects and analogies, and concerned themselves, at least apparently, with details of historical accuracy. Religion and philosophy were studied historically, and it is not too much to say that all thought at this time claimed historical knowledge, whether this knowledge was real or affected.

Ernest Renan described this as a revolution which completely changed the face of historical studies, or rather, 'which founded history amongst us'.[1] The explanation of such a change is not hard to find; it is obviously a sign of the cultural crisis brought about by the French Revolution. The age of historical preoccupation was made possible by the age of revolution. During the course of the Revolution individuals had sometimes taken to reading history, as Stendhal's father read Hume on Charles I, in the hope that in history they would

[1] *Ernest Renan*, 'L'Avenir de la Science' in *Œuvres Complètes* (ed. Psichari), Paris 1949, vol. iii, p. 834.

find something that made sense of events around them. In a similar way the generation which followed sought the explanation of the long years of conflict and of division. It had become imperative that they should know where they stood in the course of history, and where that course was taking them. They could no longer accept the answer that human reason or that rational opinion determined events; they could no longer believe that the individual was primary. It therefore was necessary to study the whole organism of which the individual was only part. It was necessary to study the state, the nation, the civilization, society as a whole. Historians were therefore ambitious and moved along an adventurous path.

The Revolution made historians confident. They themselves, or their fathers, had helped to accomplish gigantic transformations. Institutions had collapsed, populations had been freed, boundaries had been changed, rulers had been thrown up and cast down. They were therefore conscious of their knowledge. 'There is not one amongst us children of the nineteenth century', wrote Augustin Thierry, in a passage which has often been quoted, 'who does not know more on the score of rebellion and conquests, of the dismemberment of empires, of the fall and restoration of monarchies, of popular revolution and the consequent reactions, than did Velly or Mably, or even Voltaire himself.'[1] In a later work he was even more explicit, contrasting historians of his day to their predecessors. 'The events of the last fifty years, events hitherto unheard of, have taught us to understand the revolutions of the Middle Ages, to perceive the spirit beneath the letter of the chronicler, to draw from the writings of the Benedictines that which those learned men never saw, or saw only partially, without suspecting its significance. They lacked the comprehension and sentiment of great social transformations. They have studied with curiosity the laws, public acts, judicial formulae, private contracts, etc.; they have discussed, classified, analysed texts . . . with extraordinary sagacity; but the political sense, all that was living beneath the dead letter, the perception of society and its various elements, whether young or old, whether barbarian or civilized, escapes them. Hence the emptiness and the insufficiency of their work. This perception, we have acquired through our experience; we owe it to the prodigious changes of power and of society which have taken place before us.'[2]

The Revolution gave historians a sense of time. Chateaubriand was not alone in posturing between two centuries, between two ages. When Thierry reviewed the *Mémoires historiques sur la vie de*

---

[1] *Augustin Thierry, Lettres sur l'Histoire de France*, Paris 1827, p. 3.

[2] *Augustin Thierry, Considérations sur l'Histoire de France* (op. cit.), pp. 181-182.

Monsieur Suard, he said that the eighteenth century was like another world. The men of those times were nearly his contemporaries, but 'centuries separate them from us'.[1] When Molé read the correspondence of Voltaire he felt that a thousand years had passed since those letters were written.[2] This sense of time gave a sense of relativity. Each age had its own view of the past, its own statement to make. It was realized that the writing of history needed to be renewed incessantly. 'It is impossible', wrote Augustin Thierry, 'whatever the amount of intellectual superiority we possess, to see beyond the horizon of our century, and therefore every new epoch opens for history new points of view and imprints on it a particular form.'[3] The demands of the nineteenth century had to be met, and there grew up a school of middle-class historians writing for middle-class audiences, of French historians writing for French audiences. It is the younger Thierry who expresses this most clearly when he explains how he must correct Montesquieu, not in terms of erudition, but in terms of interpretation. 'By a tendency that was natural to the society of his times,' he wrote, 'Montesquieu made himself a Roman patrician and looked down on the world from the Capitol. I, the son of those whom Caesar conquered, have looked on the Capitol from the depths of a Celtic village.'[4]

The Revolution made historians necessary. The continued uncertainties, the alleged insufficiency of both faiths and scepticism, the absence of any widely accepted doctrines or beliefs, made all thinkers turn to history. Only then could speculation claim a basis. The verification of history was hailed as conclusive because there was no other means of verification. This turning to history was not escapism; it was the only way of understanding. The crisis of their own times gave historians a sense of urgency. They had to dispose of the Revolution which a writer in 1849 was still lamenting as an engine which devoured generation after generation.[5] They had to prepare for fresh upheavals. 'A great revolution is accomplished,' wrote Chateaubriand in 1831, 'an even greater revolution is being prepared. France must recompose her annals, to keep them in touch with the progress of intelligence.'[6]

[1] *Augustin Thierry, Dix Annees d'Études Historiques*, Paris 1883, p. 254.
[2] Molé: Barante, September 1st, 1824, *Barante Souvenirs* (op. cit.), vol. iii, p. 213.
[3] *Augustin Thierry, Histoire de la Conquete de l'Angleterre par les Normands*, Paris 1826, vol. i, pp. xi-xii.
[4] Quoted by *A. Augustin-Thierry* in *Amedée Thierry, Revue des Deux Mondes*, December 1st, 1928, p. 649.
[5] See *Emile Montegut's* study of Carlyle in the *Revue des Deux Mondes*, April 15th, 1849.
[6] *Chateaubriand, Études Historiques*, Paris 1831, Preface, p. 1.

A divided society appeals to history. The individual seeks support in the group, and the group seeks support in the past. It is not surprising that in France there is an identity between those who write history and those who seek to make history. From Chateaubriand to Jaurès this is a characteristic of French society. This does not mean that politics have annexed history. The danger of history annexing politics is equally great, when politico-historians admired something which had lasted simply because it had lasted, or when their admiration of violence in the past implied an acceptance of violence in the present. The historical work of these politico-historians needs to be studied every bit as seriously as their political activities.

The realization that history was part of the philosophy of society meant that the methods of writing history had to be relevant to social science. The historian needed to know the sources; he needed to possess critical acumen; he had to solve the problems of the rise and fall of nations, of the progress of civilization; he needed to be both philosopher and scientist. Most observers were agreed that it was the French historical school rather than the English or the German, which fulfilled these requirements; and most of them were also agreed that the greatest of the French school was Guizot.

It is easy to understand why Guizot appeared so outstanding. Nothing could appear more scientific than his detached and objective style. This is all the more striking when compared to that of many of his contemporaries. In England the personal virulence of Macaulay when he deals with the same subject as Guizot is greatly in contrast to the latter's manner of writing. Guizot has nothing to compare with Macaulay's descriptions of Charles I's 'vices', his 'duplicity', his 'faithlessness', his 'incurable propensity to dark and crooked ways'. Carlyle's Cromwell, with his capital letters and repeated epithets, 'sycophant Mainwaring', 'unreadable Prynne', 'Carrion Heath', seemed immediately to be less objective than Guizot's. When Guizot was compared to his French contemporaries his gravity seemed immeasurably more 'historical' than Michelet's exuberance, with its exaggerated imagery and over-vivid descriptions, perpetually seeking for drama and symbols in plain and ordinary happenings. It also suggested a higher level of historical preoccupation than the more ornamental and picturesque writings of Thierry or Prosper de Barante.

No one would deny that Guizot had prejudices. He appears to be less one-sided than many of his fellow-historians because these prejudices are concerned under an air of dispassionate reason, and are hidden by a screen of erudition. But he simply did not have antipathies on the same scale as Macaulay or Michelet. He has no favourite periods in history. Whilst Voltaire thought that with the fall of

Rome the whole of Europe became degraded and that human nature fell to a sub-bestial level, Guizot saw in the same period chaos and disorder, but he never sought to condemn it as bad. If Guizot never seems surprised by the events he has to recount, one reason is because he does not apparently hope for the victory of any one particular side. If he has particular feelings about periods of history or about individuals, he succeeds in concealing both his dislikes and his attachments. In this last he was more successful than Victor Cousin, who was said to have fallen in love with Madame de Longueville in the course of writing her history, so that when he wrote of La Rochefoucauld he considered him less as an historical character than as a rival.

Guizot avoided controversy more than many of his colleagues, which helped his reputation. One controversy which had been in existence for some time and which was still the centre of discussion was that of the foundations of the French nation. It had been variously claimed that after the fall of Rome, society in France had been governed by an aristocracy, or by a monarchy, by an assembly of the people or by the Church. In this controversy, which is often referred to by the name of three eighteenth-century historians, Boulainvilliers, Dubos and Mably, each of whom put forward one of these theories, Guizot refused to take sides. All the interpretations, he said, were right. Each system had to some extent existed; what was wrong was to make any one of them exclusive.[1] He refused to accept the viewpoint either of those who opposed or of those who supported revolutions, such as the English Revolution or the French Revolution. Whether they were thought of as glorious events or as deplorable calamities, it was wrong, according to Guizot, to consider these episodes as having interrupted the natural course of events. He claimed that these revolutions never said, wished or did anything which had not been said, wished, done or attempted a hundred times before.[2] Thus before Tocqueville, Guizot attempted to re-establish the unity of French history. Nor can Guizot be included amongst those historians whom Fustel de Coulanges (in the article already quoted) decided as loving England, praising Germany and admiring America.[3] Guizot was restrained in his admirations. He rarely admired, he usually tried to explain, and he warned against the German historians, whom he accused of muddling up their sources in their attempt to demonstrate the importance of Germanic influence in France. He refused to interpret a single sentence of Tacitus into a

[1] Guizot, *Histoire de la Civilisation en Europe* (op. cit.), p. 71. *Essais sur l'Histoire de la France* (op. cit.), pp. 294 ff.

[2] *Guizot, Histoire de la Revolution d'Angleterre*, Paris 1825, Preface.

[3] *Fustel de Coulanges* in *Revue des Deux Mondes* (op. cit.), p. 244.

great national achievement for the German nation, and refused to praise the Germans for their domestic virtues and respect for female chastity. On this last question, which had been discussed by Montesquieu, Robertson and Malthus, Guizot was non-committal. He suggests that the customs of the primitive Germans can be understood by reference to the Red Indians, as if they were a characteristic of all primitive people; elsewhere he suggests that respect for women arises from the nature of feudal society not at all from national characteristics.[1]

His preoccupations were entirely modern, and this must have been all the more noticeable at the time, since it was only a relatively short while before that Voltaire himself had been discussing legends and myths as if they were the material of history. Had Romulus really been nursed by a wolf? Was the colouration of the African peoples the result of the mothers' imagination, reproducing in their children the colours with which the African males painted themselves? Such queries were as alien to the work of Guizot as they would be to a twentieth-century historian. Guizot was not any more interested in theories about the origins of society, which had been so prevalent in the eighteenth century as to infuriate Montesquieu. But at the same time Guizot was not too modern. His work was not too scientifically organized, and not attached to any of the prevalent theories which sought to concoct a science of History. The axioms of Vico or Herder, or the theories of Thierry, were often open to question, and writers who attached themselves to them could be accused of wilfully straining facts so as to fit such theories. Guizot could not be accused of such exaggerations.

Guizot too was attractively versatile. Sometimes French historians of this period have been divided into two groups, the narrative and the analytical or philosophical. This distinction is essentially false, but in the case of Guizot it is obviously false. The lectures on civilization were analytical; he seizes the ideas of an epoch, and arranges them; he exhibits European civilization by selecting its characteristics. The books on the English Revolution were narrative; they represent an organized version of many contemporary accounts, with anecdotes, epigrams, personalities and all the other characteristics of the descriptive school of writing. Whilst Guizot frequently praises Montesquieu, the most analytical of historians, he also praises the novels of Scott and Cooper, the imaginative writings of 'mon ami Augustin Thierry', and others.[2] With a taste for detail and for the

[1] See the seventh lecture in *Histoire de la Civilisation en France* (op. cit.), vol. i, and also *Histoire de la Civilisation en Europe* (op. cit.), p. 102.

[2] Although he praised Scott, like Prosper de Barante and Ranke he had reservations about *Quentin Durward*.

picturesque, he avoided the tenacity of the novelist in clinging to everything which seemed piquant or startling.

But these are perhaps secondary reasons why he should have been successful as an historian. A more vital explanation lies in his conception of history.

French historical writing aroused the interest and admiration of English critics. One of them, John Stuart Mill, compared historical studies in England to those in France. 'History with us', he wrote, 'has not passed that stage in which its cultivation is an affair of mere literature or of erudition, not of science. It is studied for the facts, not for the explanation of the facts. It excites an imaginative, or a biographical, or an antiquarian, but not a philosophical interest. Historical facts are hardly yet felt to be, like other natural phenomena, amenable to scientific laws. The characteristic distrust of our countrymen for all ambitious efforts of intellect, of which the success does not admit of being instantly tested by a decisive application to practice, causes all widely extended views on the explanation of history to be looked upon with a suspicion surpassing the bounds of reasonable caution.'[1] What Mill found attractive in the work of French writers, and of Guizot in particular, was the way in which they sought to explain the facts of history. 'A real thinker is shown in nothing more certainly, than in the questions he asked,' he commented,[2] and he was struck by the way in which Guizot took a problem like the fall of the Roman Empire, and endeavoured to give a direct and simple answer. Guizot was, in his own words, seeking for the general and hidden fact which lay enveloped beneath all the external facts.[3] In all his history, and most especially in his works on the history of civilization, he sought to illuminate the past by means of generalizations. This was not simply a habit: it was an obligation. 'Once events have been consummated, when they have become history, what are most important and what man seeks above all, are general facts, are the connexions of causes and effects. These are, so to speak, the immortal part of history, that to which all generations must refer in order to understand the past, and to understand themselves. The necessity for generalisation and rational result is the most powerful and the most glorious of all intellectual needs. . . .'[4]

[1] *Edinburgh Review*, October 1845, vol. 82, p. 382. Other articles which praised French historical writing, and Guizot in particular, are to be found in the *British and Foreign Review*, 1844, No. 31, vol. 16, pp. 72-118 (by G. H. Lewes), and the *Westminster Review*, October 1841, vol. 36, pp. 273-307.

[2] *John Stuart Mill*, Ibid., p. 385.

[3] *Histoire de la Civilisation en Europe* (op. cit.), p. 91.

[4] Ibid., pp. 324-325.

This insistence upon generalization is particularly interesting, since Guizot had shown a tendency to write in this way from the time of his literary beginnings. Whether reviewing or writing himself he invariably sought to put forward general ideas, to generalize principles and to bring the discussion round to general themes. This was a method which he was prepared to recommend, and which he did so early in his career. In his inaugural lecture in the University of Paris, in January 1812, he began by describing the limitations of the historian. He quoted the well-known story of Sir Walter Raleigh who was completing the last part of his *History of the World* whilst in the Tower of London. One day he saw from his windows several people quarrelling. The next day, when telling a visitor about this quarrel, he was surprised to discover that his visitor had not only witnessed the same scene, but also that he had taken part in it. From him, Raleigh then learnt how he had completely misunderstood everything that he had seen, both in the details and in the result. Thus when Raleigh was alone he took up the manuscript of his *History* and destroyed it. If he could be so mistaken about an incident which he had seen himself, then how could he hope to know the subjects which he was writing about? The point of the anecdote was that history could never present a picture of the past; the picture could never be complete, nor could it be reliable. But in spite of all this, Guizot did not think that history should become a forbidden subject; he did not believe that the more people learned about the past, then the more uncertain and confused they would become. The solution lay in distinguishing between the knowledge that was useful and the knowledge that was amassed as the result of curiosity or restlessness. It was of no importance to know what the Emperor Constantine looked like: it was of no importance to know the precise day of his birth; one did not need to know all the particular motives or sentiments which weighed with him in his decisions and conduct, nor did one need to know the details of his victories against Maxentius and Licinius. Such matters only concerned the Emperor, and he had ceased to exist. People still tried to find out these details, because there was a natural interest in great names, but these details were not important. There were, however, matters concerning the Emperor Constantine which were important. His conversion, his administration, the political and religious principles by which he ruled his empire, these were questions which concerned people living in the nineteenth century. The effects of such events and such policies had lasted beyond their own times. Thus there were two sorts of history. There was the history which was dead and without interest, and there was the history of certain dominating ideas and certain great events which determined the character of several generations. Guizot set himself, therefore, the

331

task of studying 'les idées dominantes', and 'les principes généralement adoptes'.[1]

In these early writings Guizot ventured into literary history, always trying to discover and then to examine the general principles around which the history of the period would fit. In his study of Corneille, which was originally written as *La Vie des Poètes Français du Siecle de Louis XIV*, published in 1813, he was trying to find answers to certain problems. Why was it that civil wars in England, France and Italy produced different types of literature? How could one explain the nature of Corneille's genius and success? In his study of Shakespeare, published as an introduction to a new series of translations, he tried to explain the growth of the Elizabethan theatre in terms of the development of Elizabethan political institutions.[2] When he ventured into art criticism in the *Salon de 1810* he took the opportunity of discussing what he considered to be some of the general principles of painting. He claimed that in the seventeenth-century sculptors imitated painters, whilst in his own times this procedure had been reversed and painters modelled their works on the sculptures of antiquity. He believed that for a sculptor the figure should always be in repose but that a painter should show unlimited action. He discussed the evolution in public taste since the Revolution, claiming that people had become more accustomed to dreadful sights, and hence there was a tendency amongst painters to show exaggerated gestures and expressions, and to forget that their true mission lay in painting the beautiful. Guizot took the Salon as an opportunity of determining certain general principles around which he could judge a number of paintings, including some by Girodet, Gros, Prudhon and Gérard.

When he edited Gibbon he recorded his view that most of the historians whose work he had consulted were concerned with facts to the exclusion of general ideas. They neglected those general views which enabled the reader to survey at a single glance a wide extent of country and the progress of humanity. 'These are the views which constitute the philosophy of history, and without which its records are but a heap of incoherent, inconclusive and unconnected facts.'

---

[1] This lecture is published as 'Pièce Historique', no. iii, in the *Mémoires*, vol. i.

[2] See p. xxxix of the 'Notice biographique et littéraire sur Shakespeare' written by Guizot in *Shakespeare*, Paris 1821. Guizot's views on Shakespeare had obviously been influenced by Schlegel, and Professor T. J. B. Spencer has pointed out to me the resemblance between Guizot's essay and Scott's 'Essay on the Drama' in the *Encyclopaedia Britannica*, 1819 edition, reprinted in *Miscellaneous Prose Works of Sir Walter Scott*, 1834, vol. iv. However Guizot seems to have been in advance of much literary appreciation by his admiration for 'Richard II'. Also by his admiration for Ronsard. See *J. A. Hunt* in *French Review*, 1953-1954, vol. 27.

Montesquieu was to be praised for his 'throng of ideas' when dealing with Roman history. Even when mistaken, 'it is the just and happy privilege of genius that its errors are pregnant with truth'.[1]

An historian to whom Guizot was much indebted was the German historian Savigny. Guizot accepted his evidence of the persistence of Roman law and institutions in the Middle Ages, and revised some of the views which he had earlier expressed in the *Essais*. He recommended Savigny to his students and praised his *Geschichte des romischen Rechts in Mittelalter* as a remarkable work. But he also criticized Savigny. History for Guizot had a triple problem to resolve. There was firstly the elucidation and collection of facts; these were the body of history, the members, bones, muscles, organs and material events of the past. They form what Guizot chose to call the anatomy of history. Then, secondly, the historian had to discover how these various facts were concerned together, to determine the laws which governed them and find the forces which engendered them. There was an organization and life of societies as well as of the individual. This organization had its science, 'the science of the secret laws which preside over the course of events'. This second task was the physiology of history. But could the anatomist and the physiologist surmise what man was like if they had never seen him living? The third problem of the historian was to understand how the facts, which were now dead, had lived. He had to reproduce their form and motions, he needed to know 'their external and living physiognomy'. It was possible for the historian to concentrate on any one of these three tasks, but then he would produce a work which would be partial and incomplete. In the case of Savigny, who only studied the anatomy of the past without reference to 'the general and progressive organisation of facts', and without reference to 'their living physiognomy', this incompleteness led him to certain misrepresentations and misunderstandings.[2]

Guizot therefore, more than any other French historian of his time, has an elevated conception of the intellectual mission of the historian. His insistence upon discovering the general principles and ideas links him with some of the writers of the eighteenth century who, as Buckle puts it, 'deplored the backwardness of history' and who claimed for the field of historical enquiry as for others, 'the necessity of generalisation'.[3] Vico, Montesquieu, the Scottish

[1] Guizot's Preface to *Gibbon*. This was translated and published in the *Bohn* edition of 1853. See vol. i, p. viii. Guizot's admiration for Montesquieu was such that he once spoke of him expressing correct views of history even when his basic information was wrong. *Histoire de la Civilisation en France* (op. cit.), vol. iv, pp. 34-35.

[2] *Histoire de la Civilisation en France* (op. cit.), vol. i, pp. 283-288.

[3] H. T. Buckle, *Introduction to the History of Civilisation in England* (ed. J. M. Robertson), 1904, p. 2.

Historical School, Turgot and in many respects Voltaire had all gone beyond the dramatic narrative and the anecdote. But they had frequently limited their comments to observations. They often explained a phenomenon simply by restating it; certain people, they said, had not progressed because they had unprogressive minds. When Gibbon came to discuss the causes of Roman decline, this should have been the climax of his work. Instead he merely indulges in a vague fatalism which is a variation on Montesquieu; it is very far from being a climax. Yet even this seemed out of place to Mably.[1] The Encyclopaedia distrusted all systems of thought.[2] The philosophical framework of the eighteenth century was that of scientific empiricism; genuine knowledge should be based on experience and capable of experimental verification. This standpoint was productive of criticism, but could not become the creator of assertive generalizations, and it hardly offered an explanation of social development.

That Guizot was able to break away from these eighteenth-century limitations is sometimes thought to be the result of German influence. It was with the introduction of Kantian philosophy into France that the philosophical basis of historical enquiry was developed. A Frenchman, writing in 1836, said that since Kant had discovered within the essence of human intelligence certain general forms and certain unchangeable laws, then it became natural to try and discover the same characteristics within collective and social man, and from there developed the philosophy of history.[3] Guizot was friendly with the two men who were most influential in presenting Kant to the French, namely Stapfer and Charles de Villers; he also had certain links with Madame de Staël.[4]

Yet it seems that Guizot had some reservations about Kant's philosophy; in philosophical discussions his manner of reasoning resembles Maine de Biran, whom he of course knew, rather than Kant.[5]

[1] *Mably, De la maniere d'écrire l'histoire*, Paris 1783, pp. 217-218.

[2] See the article 'Système'. On the failure of the eighteenth century to produce systems of thought see *Sainte-Beuve's* article on Diderot, *Premiers Lundis*, Paris 1882, vol. i, p. 373.

[3] Barchou de Penhöen, *Histoire de la Philosophie Allemande*, Paris 1836. The Baron Barchou de Penhöen was the French translator of Fichte, and also the author of a work on the British conquest of India.

[4] See *M. Vallois, La Formation de l'Influence Kantienne en France*, Paris 1924. It was Suard, a close friend of Madame de Staël, who had also known Gibbon, who gave Guizot the task of editing and translating 'The Decline and Fall' after Benjamin Constant had refused to do so. Gibbon as a young man had come near to marrying Suzanne Curchod, who later married the banker Necker. Gibbon used to stay with the Neckers, and when quite elderly is supposed to have received a proposal of marriage from their precocious daughter who was of course the future Madame de Staël.

[5] *Vallois*, op. cit., p. 273 n. 21. See Guizot's article on 'La Pédagogie de Kant'

Perhaps it is reasonable, if one is looking for a direct influence, to find it in Madame de Staël herself. In such a book as *De La Littérature*, published in 1800, Madame de Staël was trying to explain the diversity of national genius and national customs by linking them to the political structure of society, to the nature of religious creeds, or to the accidents of climate and external relations. In the preface to her second edition she reminded her readers that her aim was not to analyse all the distinguished works which made up literature (a task which some of her critics would have said was beyond her since it was rumoured that she judged certain works by hearsay only); she sought to 'characterize' the general spirit of each literature in its relation to religion, morals and politics. This attempt to render the historical sequence understandable makes for a real resemblance between the works of Madame de Staël and Guizot.

Yet rather than consider the influence of one author or another, one must remember that Madame de Staël and Guizot were contemporaries and that together they shared the seriousness of the epoch. 'The traveller whom the storm has washed up on deserted beaches, carves on the cliffs the names of the foods he has found, and indicates the resources which he has used in fighting death, so as to be useful one day to those who undergo the same fate.' So wrote Madame de Staël in 1800. Literature became a message. Those whom chance had cast into the epoch of revolution owed an explanation to future generations. It was no time for idle communication, or for the trivia of learning and sentiment. Hence the positive approach to history and the generalization.

We must remember too that the histories of civilization were originally delivered as lectures. If the relationship between the critic and his audience became closer after 1800, thus allowing the writer to be bolder,[1] the relationship between a lecturer and an enthusiastic audience was bound to lead to the assertive generalization or the dogmatic 'a-priorism'. This was all the more likely since one of the things which constantly worried Guizot was the intellectual isolation of individuals in France. Their wariness with regard to general ideas he saw as one of the signs of this isolation.[3] Thus there is another reason why Guizot insisted upon the generalizing spirit in his treatment of history and gained the reputation of being France's leading historian.

---

in the *Annales de l'Education*, vol. iv, 1812, and his article on a philosophy textbook, Ibid., vol. vi, 1813.

[1] Sainte-Beuve suggests this in 'M. de Feletz et la Critique Littéraire sous l'Empire' in *Causeries du Lundi* (op. cit.), vol. i, pp. 373 ff.

[3] Guizot: Barante, August 30th, 1825, *Barante Souvenirs* (op. cit.), vol. iii, pp. 269-270.

It remains to show and to discuss some of these generalizations. He began his histories of civilization in Europe and in France by trying to describe civilization. He claimed that it was a fact like any other, just as much a fact as is any material and visible event. Civilization therefore was a fact just as a battle was a fact. But it was a particular kind of fact, 'a general hidden complex fact', 'a sort of ocean constituting the wealth of a people', whilst other subjects like a country's institutions, commerce, industry, wars, etc., were like rivers contributing to the growth of this ocean. Civilization was both social and individual, it was both material and moral. It was not sufficient to take one of these aspects if one was to judge a civilization. Thus although seventeenth-century France was probably inferior to England or to Holland from the point of view of material progress, everyone agreed that seventeenth-century France was their superior in intellectual and artistic achievement. It was necessary to consider both the social and the intellectual conquests which made for progress. They were so interwoven that the one form of progress led to the other. An individual who acquires some new idea or some new virtue seeks to communicate it to the community, thus rendering it social; improvement in the organization of society, perhaps the government becoming more benevolent and more just, similarly communicates itself to the individual, who himself becomes more just. Thus social and individual progress, outward and inward reform, are the two connected elements which make up the fact of civilization.[1]

This is a description of civilization; but Guizot needs to define European civilization, and he does so by seizing upon its distinctive characteristic. For him, this is its variety. Other forms of society, outside Europe, have unity and simplicity. These civilizations have come from a single idea, a solitary dominant principle, and once they have passed their earliest phase, they have grown up without there being any opposition to this idea or principle. Their histories have differed in that Greece rose and declined rapidly, whilst India and Egypt remained stationary, but the unity and uniformity of each civilization existed and expressed itself both in politics and in literature. Guizot claimed that tyranny was to be found amongst all the ancient civilizations, society belonged exclusively to one power which would not tolerate any rival. Monotony was the characteristic of Indian literature, and for Guizot, the literature and the arts of Greece had 'a singular uniformity'. But in European civilization there was both diversity and multiplicity; there was a confusion and conflict amongst the different tendencies which were constantly present. All the principles of social organization existed, theocratic, monarchical,

[1] See *Histoire de la Civilisation en Europe* (op. cit.), First Lecture.

aristocratic, democratic. In ideas, there was the same variety of creeds
and beliefs, combating and modifying each other. In sentiment, there
was an insistence upon individuality vying with the fidelity of man to
man, a love of independence existing alongside a great facility of submission. In literature and art there is the same richness. It may be
that any separate element is inferior to its equivalent in the ancient
world, but the very existence of such diversity and conflict, of such
systematic antagonisms, made for the progress and vigour of
European civilization. This, according to Guizot, was its general
principle.[1]

He continuously emphasized variety. In Asia and in Africa
religious society existed in a general and simple form with the clear
preponderance of a single principle. But in Europe all the possible
principles had existed at some time or other, each claiming to be the
true one. It was claimed that the state was subordinate to the Church,
and then it was claimed that it was the state which should establish
the religious organization best suited to society. It was suggested that
the Church should be independent and unnoticed in the state, or that
Church and state should be separate but allied. It was claimed that
the internal government of the Church should be in the hands either
of the clergy or of the whole populace. If it was in the hands of the
clergy it could take the form of a monarchical government, or an
aristocratic government, or a democracy. If the whole populace
governed, then they could form assemblies, or each congregation
could form local independent churches, or there could be no distinct
government at all, all the spiritual functions being organised by the
faithful according to circumstances and inspiration. For Guizot all
these systems played their part in religious history and contributed to
the formation of Christianity.[2]

The rise of the Third Estate was seen by Guizot as a particular
European phenomenon. In no other civilization did one see a class
rise from a low and weak position, to one where it absorbed and
transformed all around it. The Third Estate was varied in its origins;
it contained officers of the crown as well as inhabitants of boroughs
and it achieved power through the persistence of Roman municipal
institutions as well as through insurrection. He criticized those
historians who spoke of the bourgeoisie as if it had always been the
same over a long period. On the contrary, it was necessary to
emphasize its diversity. In the twelfth century, according to Guizot,
it consisted almost entirely of merchants, traders carrying on petty
commerce, small landowners or houseowners who lived in the towns.
But in the sixteenth century it consisted also of lawyers and magis-

[1] Ibid., Second Lecture.
[2] *Histoire de la Civilisation en France* (op. cit.), Third Lecture.

trates, physicians and learned men. If one was to understand the development of the bourgeoisie one had to understand its progressive variety. 'It is perhaps in the diversity of its composition at different epochs of history that we should look for the secret of its destiny,' was Guizot's comment.[1]

This insistence upon variety as a source of progress comes near to becoming a dialectical method. Guizot described in an earlier course of lectures a process which he claimed characterized progress. Various forces, interests and ideas came together to produce the government they wanted. After a certain time, however, new forces, interests and ideas arose which attacked the government. The period of unification was thus followed by a period of dissolution. Once this period was finished then there was a new period of concentration. This was what happened, according to Guizot, between the accession of Clovis in 481 and the accession of Capet in 987. Once feudalism had destroyed both government and society there grew up a movement to reconstitute both. This movement reached its culmination with the monarchy of Louis XIV; a further period of dissolution culminated in the French Revolution. Thus society was impelled onwards.[2]

Later Guizot described these conflicting forces as being 'the struggle of the various classes of society'. This class struggle filled modern history and created modern Europe. But the essence of this class struggle was that it had no ultimate victor. Whereas in Asia one class succeeded, established itself as a caste, and the whole of society was then forced into immobility, yet in Europe this did not happen. No one class was able to subdue the others. The fact that these classes found it necessary successively to fight or to give way, the variety of their interests and ideas, both their hatred and their understanding of each other, has been the cause of European progress.[3]

If one accepts that European civilization possesses this peculiarly complex character, then it must further be asked whether there is any explanation for this. The answer that Guizot gives is historical. The

[1] *Histoire de la Civilisation en France*, Twenty-Third and Twenty-Fourth Lectures. *Histoire de la Civilisation en Europe* (op. cit.), p. 202.

[2] *Histoire des Origines du Gouvernement Representatif* (op. cit.), vol. i, pp. 160-162.

[3] *Histoire de la Civilisation en Europe* (op. cit.), p. 203. Guizot refers to the class struggle in 1849, the year after the publication of *The Communist Manifesto*, when he wrote 'La lutte des diverses classes de notre societe, a rempli notre histoire', *De la Démocratie en France* (op. cit.), p. 35. He believed however, as has been shown, that the achievement of the Revolution was to render a class struggle useless. On this subject see *Robert Fossaert*, 'La Théorie des classes chez Guizot et Thierry', *La Pensée*, Jan.-Feb. 1955, pp. 59-69.

origin of European civilization was threefold, from Rome there came the idea of municipal institutions, the idea of empire and the conception of imperial majesty, a body of written law and the principle of liberty and reason in thought and enquiry. From the Christian Church there came a moral influence, the belief in a law which was divine and which was superior to all human laws, and the idea of liberty of conscience. From the Germanic invaders came the modern spirit of liberty, the claim for individual independence, as well as the idea of voluntary association in war, the bond between a leader and his followers which afterwards, according to Guizot, became feudalism.

Thus the definition of civilization leads Guizot into a series of bold assertions. Although he was writing in the tradition of cultural historians in believing that there was one great civilizing process which was still continuing, he differed from many of his contemporaries in so far as he did not simply equate this process with the growth of Christianity. Bonald, for example, described 'civilization' as being nothing other than the application of the Christian religion to civil society, and the Spaniard Balmès directly accused Guizot of underestimating the rôle of Christianity in the growth of civilization.[1] Guizot's use of the word 'civilization' as meaning intellectual and artistic attainments as well as material progress, was more modern than was the Catholic interpretation. His insistence upon the variety of European civilization as an explanation for its vitality, was an advance on the sort of explanation which Voltaire used to give to this sort of problem,[2] and it has met with the approval of at least one modern philosopher.[3] Modern historians, too, adopt the same ideas as Guizot, when they explain the cultural vitality of the Renaissance period in terms of the variety of social types which created it. However, one must also notice how Guizot, like many of his contemporaries, was unable to understand oriental civilizations.[4]

Guizot's generalizations on European civilization have two implications which one should notice. The first is eclecticism. There is no one element which dominates in this varied civilization, just as there is no single force which impels history onwards. If one believed,

[1] *De Bonald*, 'Recherches Philosophiques' in *Œuvres Complètes*, Paris 1864, vol. iii, p. 84. *J. Balmès, Le Protestantisme comparé au Catholicisme*, Paris 1852, vol. i, pp. 156 ff., p. 191.

[2] See for example Voltaire on the Chinese in 'Essai sur les Moeurs' in *Œuvres Complètes*, Paris 1878, vol. xii, p. 433.

[3] *Ortega y Gasset, Towards a Philosophy of History*, quoted by Sister *Mary Consolata O'Connor, The Historical Thought of François Guizot*, Washington 1955, p. 38 n. 35. Ortega also claims that Ranke was influenced by this theory of Guizot.

[4] See *Ernest Renan, L'Avenir de la Science* (op. cit.), p. 878, p. 1136 n. 89.

with Bonald, that there was one all-important principle, then this belief would lead to certain practical consequences. Movements in the past or in the present which offended against this principle would have to be rejected. Thus Guizot's history is one of conciliation and acceptance, whilst Bonald's is necessarily dogmatic and exclusive. The second implication is that if progress comes from the antagonism of rival elements, then it was necessary that no single power should achieve a complete preponderance in the future. This applied to the Church, to the Crown, and also to the power of numbers. This was an idea which was to be developed at greater length by John Stuart Mill and by Tocqueville.

When Guizot discussed the decline of Rome, he emphasized its bewildering nature. Countries such as Gaul, Italy and Spain were covered with towns, which had been prosperous and well populated. They had many signs of the Roman presence, and in some cases they possessed a rich social existence. Yet when the barbarians came to plunder and conquer, the inhabitants of these territories did not resist. The Roman legions fought the barbarians, but it was as if they were fighting in a desert. Once the legions had been withdrawn then apart from some resistance on the part of bishops and clergy, the populations made no attempt to defend themselves. The problem is intensified for Guizot when he finds that the longer the period of Romanization then the weaker was the resistance. England, for example, was less Romanized than other areas of Roman occupation, and yet was showing resistance to the invasions (Guizot considered that the letter 'The Groans of the Britons' was an exaggeration of helplessness). It was not enough to explain this by reference to the degrading effects of despotism; if an explanation was to be found then the historian would have to search more deeply.

Guizot tries first of all to determine what was the fundamental characteristic of Rome. Like others before him, he decided that it was essentially a municipal civilization. Therefore it was in the condition of the municipalities that the explanation would be found, in the Laws rather than in the Chronicles. The men who were liable to fill the municipal offices were those who possessed a certain landed property. They formed a class, the 'curiales'. But there were certain things to be noticed about the 'curiales' which showed that this rank was not a privilege but a burden. There were many exemptions. Senatorial families, those who had been honoured with the title of 'clarissimi', all the military, all the clergy, were exempted from municipal duties. At the same time there were many laws which reveal how the government was trying to control the 'curiales'; they could not live in the country, they could not serve in the army or enter the Church, they were not allowed to gain exemption until they

340

had filled all the municipal offices, they could not sell their property, their heirs could not marry outside the 'curia' without paying special forfeits, and so on. It is clear, therefore, that men tried to avoid these obligations. The task of the 'curiales' was to collect revenue and to defray the expenses of local administration; they were expected to make up the required amounts from their own property. Hence the position of 'curialis' could lead to impoverishment and ruin, and men would only accept to carry out such functions if compelled. Such a system meant that the 'curiales', or middle class, were sunk beneath a burden of extortion. Whilst certain senatorial families retained their slaves and their lands and continued to live in a privileged situation, the mass of the population was overcome with taxation. Towns became depopulated, large areas of land remained uncultivated. Although documentary evidence was scarce, such evidence as was to be found in the 'album curiae' of Canosa, suggested that the 'curiales' were declining in number. This system of government, according to Guizot, contributed more to the destruction of the Empire than the ravages of the barbarians. The collapse of the 'curiales' was paralleled by the failure of the senators to form an effective aristocracy. Gallo-Roman society did not resist because it was no longer functioning as a society.

Nor was Gallo-Roman society replaced by any clearly organized social system. Guizot did not see the Germanic invasions as the dramatic affair that had often been described. They did not represent a movement of mass destruction. The invading bands were small in numbers, their outrages were limited and quickly forgotten. The very fact of conquest brought about a great change within their own society; landownership created inequalities amongst them which destroyed much of their character as a conquering people. Roman law persisted because there was no other organized form of law; the barbaric royalty tried to imitate the machinery of Rome and to fit the framework of the Empire; the barbaric mind, according to Guizot, was filled with admiration for the Roman world, and all the great men of the conquests, Alaric, Ataulph, Theodoric and others, whilst trampling on Roman society, nevertheless sought to copy it. Thus Roman civilization was at one moment in full decadence, it had no force and no fluidity and it was unable to keep itself alive. But then, after the conquests, it reappears and persists as an influential part of European civilization.[1]

[1] *Essais sur l'Histoire de France* (op. cit.), pp. 1-44. *Histoire de la Civilisation en France* (op. cit.), vol. i, pp. 48 ff., pp. 209 ff., pp. 279 ff. The later treatment of these questions is much less 'catastrophic' than the *Essais*, a fact which has not always been appreciated. See A. Dopsch, *The Economic and Social Foundations of European Civilisation*, 1937, pp. 4-5.

When Fustel de Coulanges came to revise the interpretation of this early period of French history, he corrected Guizot in many points of detail, but it is remarkable how many of Guizot's ideas were developed rather than rejected. This is not a question of erudition only. It is essentially a question of interpretation. Guizot insists that there must be an explanation. It is not enough to speak in general terms about 'despotism'; nor can one explain a great movement by isolated details; nor does Guizot explain events in terms of chance or Providence. Guizot seeks the explanation for the disintegration of a society within that society. 'A society never dissolves itself,' he wrote, 'but because a new society is fermenting and forming in its bosom.' His own conclusions were tentative and his researches limited, but as an approach to history, it proved successful, whether used by Guizot himself, or by Tocqueville, or by Fustel de Coulanges.

The study of Charlemagne presents Guizot with ample opportunity for making judgements and generalizations, all the more so he thought since hitherto Charlemagne had been the subject of both historical and moral commonplaces. People had spoken of his glory without much discrimination, and his failure to establish anything permanent had caused them to speak of the ineffectualness of man's work on earth. Charlemagne appeared as a meteor, suddenly emerging from the darkness of barbarism, and just as suddenly being lost in the darkness of feudalism. But one had to beware of appearances; if one was to understand what had happened, once again one had to look more closely at things, and Guizot had no embarrassment in taking 'the fate and name of Napoleon' as a helpful illustration.

It was necessary to decide the rôle of the great man in history. According to Guizot there were usually two periods in his career. In the first he understood more clearly than other people what were the needs of his time. It was this greater perception which formed the basis for his power. But in the second period he moved away from the region of facts and exigencies towards more personal and more arbitrary undertakings. This is the beginning of egoism and illusion. For a time people continue to follow this man, out of habit, flattery or delusion. But this cannot last long. Eventually the great man is only followed sluggishly and reluctantly; finally he is abandoned and he falls. This dichotomy Guizot finds in both Charlemagne and Napoleon. The first phase is described at some length. Charlemagne realized that the prolonged and desultory warfare should cease. Therefore his wars were neither wars of settlement nor pillage, they were systematic wars aiming at putting an end to the invasion. Charlemagne realized that the insecurity and disorder of government should be replaced by an effective central authority and machinery of administration. Therefore he sought to establish a sovereign unity.

The seventh century was a time of great intellectual decay. Charle-magne attracted distinguished men into his states, protected and encouraged them. The second phase of Charlemagne, his portion of egoism and illusion, lay in his attempt to re-create the Roman Empire. Charlemagne had thus seen clearly the need to restore order and security, and it was his achievement here which allowed local families to prosper, thus forming the basis for feudalism. Charle-magne had not seen the impossibility of creating a great state and a great society at a time when social relations and ideas were limited. Thus Charlemagne's empire declined, not because his successors were less able than him; nor because of the diversity of races, as Thierry suggested; the real explanation, according to Guizot, was because small societies required small governments, and there were formed petty states called fiefs.[1]

Society after Charlemagne was very different from what it had been before. But 'the great man' cannot effect change contrary to the natural tendencies of the times. He cannot create, he can only interpret and reinforce. This is not to say that the personality of rulers is unimportant. Guizot stresses the importance of the character of the kings, from the eleventh to the thirteenth centuries, in the evolution of royalty. He distinguishes between a ruler like Charle-magne, for whom despotism was a means to an end, and a ruler like Philippe le Bel, for whom despotism was an end in itself, and who had no principles or ideas beyond his egoism.[2] But it is the tendencies of society which must be studied. It is they rather than individuals which are the creative forces in history.

Guizot's analysis of feudalism contains many generalizations which seek to reveal its significance. He says that it represents the insulation of one sovereign lord from another; the passing of the social pre-ponderance from town to country; a change in the distribution of the population; a change in the nature of the family. The importance of the feudal lord was centred upon himself; he had no effective superior, no immediate equals around him, his powers and rights came from himself. Hence his pride and insolence, which were important, since at a time when neither the mass of the people nor the kings could defend themselves against the Church, only the feudal nobility were able to resist its domination. Guizot often claimed that the feudal period was one of the most brutal of history, as it was one of the best hated. There was no means of settling issues except by war, it was therefore a time of violence; there was no means of concealing the superiority of one man over his fellows, and there was no means of

---

[1] *Histoire de la Civilisation en France* (op. cit.), Twentieth and Twenty-fourth Lectures.
[2] Ibid., vol. iv, pp. 164-165.

justifying it except by superior force. Feudalism was defined by Guizot as being the fusion of property and sovereignty; 'a prodigious inequality' soon arose amongst the governors of fiefs, inequality of strength led to inequality of rights and hence to the break-up feudalism. Small royalties came to direct the government of various provinces and eventually centralized government ousted the rights of the fief-holders. At the same time the bourgeoisie created centres of urban influence and liberty which could not be absorbed into the feudal structure. Guizot thus depicts feudalism as declining because of the defects inherent in its own position.

One particular problem related to feudalism was the development of English society. An historian such as Guizot, who was writing the history of seventeenth-century England, could not but be aware of the way in which English history followed a path of its own. One explanation of the way in which representative institutions developed in England at the beginning of modern times was to be found in the nature of English feudalism. This differed from continental feudalism because of the circumstances of the conquest. Whereas in Europe the invasion of Goths, Franks and Lombards could not provide any regular civilization with which to replace the Romans, in England the Norman invasion meant the meeting of two similar societies. The similarities between the two societies—he believed for example that something resembling feudalism had evolved amongst the Anglo-Saxons—meant that whilst there was resistance from one society to another, there was eventually a fusion between the two. The Normans did not form wandering bands of warriors, they were organized under an acknowledged leader, and the fact of Saxon resistance only intensified that union. The conquerors did not spread over the country and establish themselves as independent potentates. The Saxon landowners were dispossessed gradually and systematically and it was the Crown which profited most extensively from these confiscations. Thus the Norman chiefs were always more dependent upon the king and upon each other than the equivalent in France. In England if the nobles were to resist the king, then they could only do so by allying together. The very fact of noble confederacy, according to Guizot, led to the frequency of assemblies and of charters; the very fact of rivalry between a powerful monarchy and a powerful nobility led to both sides calling upon the knights and the freeholders, and eventually the burgesses. From William's charter of 1071, promising to maintain the laws of Edward the Confessor, it was customary to try and define the laws and liberties of the kingdom as a whole. Thus whereas in France everything was individual, with a royalty that was nominal, an aristocracy that did not form a united force, and with burgesses who existed in individual towns but not in the state, in England everything was collective. Similar forces and similar situations were compelled to approach one another, to coalesce and to combine.

Before Guizot, various writers had noticed this distinction. De Lolme, for example, had contrasted Hugue Capet who had no real authority over 'the sovereigns, great and small, who swarmed throughout the country', whereas 'William the Acquirer' divided his territory into small fiefs and loaded their possessors with harder conditions of feality. Thus the kingdom of France was divided into parts, each strong enough to be independent and rivals to the throne even, and with each great vassal strong enough to injure his inferiors and make oppression descend in gradation to every order of society. In England, however, the English feudatories had to unite if they were to resist the Crown, and they were compelled by their own weakness to look to the lowest of their vassals for assistance.[1] But Guizot not only examined the historical circumstances of this distinction more closely, he also carried the argument much further. In England, he claimed, different social powers have always developed simultaneously. Civic and spiritual powers, aristocracy, royalty, democracy, local and central institutions have always advanced together, if not with equal rapidity, then very close one to another. The period of the Tudors saw the advance of pure monarchy at the same time as the democratic principle was gaining strength. In the seventeenth century there is revolution which is at once political and religious, but the feudal aristocracy also appears, shows that it still exists and has its part to play. Thus in English history no element perishes completely, and therefore government has always been obliged to reconcile these elements. Hence the English government evolved moderate compromise, and the English nation common sense and practical ability. This was the strength of England. On the Continent, isolated systems or principles had a more exclusive predominance; in this way they were bolder, and political experiments were fuller and more complete. Political ideas and doctrines on the Continent were more fully completed and more intellectually vigorous than in England. This deficiency of general ideas, of doctrine and philosophy, was a weakness of England.[2]

Once again Guizot refers to the importance of diversity in effecting progress. Once again he sees that the significance of an event lies in the meeting of two societies, although he then goes on to see the next three centuries as a political rather than a social struggle. But we must

[1] *Jean Louis de Lolme, The Constitution of England . . .*, London 1775, part 1, chapter 1.
[2] In *Essais sur l'Histoire de France* (op. cit.), pp. 315-436; *Histoire de la Civilisation en Europe* (op. cit.), Fourteenth Lecture.

notice, above all, that once again there is insistence upon an historical explanation. If representative institutions had prospered in England, there had to be a reason for it. If this reason were not historical, then it could only be explained in terms of accident and Providence, or in terms of the character of nations and the greater wisdom of the English. Therefore it had to be historical.

It remains to show how Guizot arrived at this type of generalization.

At the beginning of his course of lectures on French civilization he explained his method, and it is noticeable that this is one of the rare occasions when he departs from his usual clarity. He claimed to continue the school of experimental rationalism. He wanted to apply to the science of the moral world, the method which had been so successful in the science of the material world, namely the observation of facts and, with caution and reserve, the formulation of those generalizations which can be built upon them. No general idea could be of any real value unless it was founded on facts, and Guizot often referred to the scrupulous examination of documents as being the first duty of the critical historian. The making of a generalization was in many ways like a mathematical operation, a mistake in the early stages could lead to the wrong solution.

But there was another side to this rationalism, namely the place that was assigned to ideas, and the belief that the mind could have its effect on the course of the universe. In what Guizot chose to call 'the real order', that is to say in society, in government and administration, and in political economy, it was 'the empire of ideas, of reasoning, of general principles, of what is called theory', which prevailed. This was a reversal of the situation which had existed a hundred years before. Then, in the intellectual world, in both moral and material sciences, facts were hardly considered; one must assume that Guizot is here thinking of the predominance of theological thought. In the political world, on the other hand, facts were dominant, and no one would have claimed any empire for ideas; one must assume that Guizot is here thinking of political despotism which excluded ideas. Since this situation had been changed, it appears that Guizot thought of the historian as having two preoccupations, one with facts and the other with ideas; he directly states that intellectual development could not be regarded as an isolated fact. The discovery of the truth, that is to say of the facts, had to be turned into 'external facts', that is to say knowledge, for the benefit of society.

This conception of historical method is complicated by Guizot's view of facts. In the first place there is an infinitude of facts since history is the study of both social and cultural phenomena; there are therefore all types of facts in the fields of law, and literature, religion

346

and so on, more facts than are usually suspected. In the second place, facts can be examined either in the historical (or chronological) way, in the order in which they appeared, or they could be examined in the reverse order, which was the scientific method. The historical method proceeded from man to society, with facts succeeding one another and reciprocally creating one another. The scientific method proceeded from society to man, and through the study of society arrived at the study of the individual.[1]

It is obvious that such a preoccupation with ideas, with this tendency to work from a given situation of society, obliged Guizot to determine the fundamental characteristics of a particular stage of historical development before he had described that historical development. This does not necessarily mean that an arbitrary scheme, founded upon *a priori* reasoning, was imposed upon historical reality. It may only mean that an hypothesis arose out of observation. However, the danger was that because Guizot started from a phenomenon that needed explaining, then he gave a sense of fatalism to historical growth. Since the Roman Empire had disappeared, and since feudalism had grown up, then the Roman Empire had been bound to collapse and feudalism bound to spread. Since within such a world of inevitability, explanations in terms of individuals or accident are unsatisfactory, and since great events require equally great explanations, then the historian is almost obliged to find such explanations within the society itself. His attention is therefore focused upon the structure of society, and hence it is that he finds that the outstanding feature of Roman civilization was municipal government, whilst other historians thought of Rome as being military rather than administrative, and characterized essentially by conquest. Guizot thought of Western civilization as diverse and varied, whilst many writers both before and after Guizot (such as Gibbon) have singled out the way in which there was a union of 'the Christian republic' producing unity of jurisprudence and 'manners' amongst independent and even hostile nations. Guizot thought of civilization, or of civilizations, as social facts, where other historians thought that one could be civilized in various ways and to various degrees and that 'civilization' therefore was a process rather than a fact. Guizot thought of feudalism as being the dismemberment of people and power into petty nations and petty sovereignties, whereas another historian would define it rather as a means of organizing society in an economy in which land was the main source of wealth.

Undoubtedly this tendency was emphasized by the fact that, in the

---

[1] *Histoire de la Civilisation en France* (op. cit.), First and Second Lectures. See also vol. iv, pp. 34035.

histories of civilization at least, Guizot was lecturing. Apart from the temptation to hold his audience's attention by a striking remark, it was necessary for him to divide his subject into sections and periods. Such divisions necessarily had to possess a conceptual content. Thus he defined modern European civilization as springing from three elements, the Roman, the German and the Christian. Similarly the theological thought of the ninth century could be divided into three intellectual movements: 'l'esprit logique', that of professional theologians, arguing about the deductions derived from certain principles, without doubting the truth of these principles; 'l'esprit politique', that of practical men, concerned with governing the Church; 'l'esprit philosophique', that of men who were simply searching for truth. An instance of the first kind was Gottshalk, of the second Hincmar, and of the third Duns Scotus.

As a lecturer, too, Guizot often sought to illustrate by means of modern comparisons. Thus he compared Charlemagne to Napoleon, Saint Avitus to Milton,[1] or the whole of medieval to the whole of modern society, since a medieval man always knew the extent of his obligations, which was something a modern man could never know. Guizot also sought to illustrate by contrasts and even paradoxes. Thus the communes and republics of Italy were rich and brilliant, but at the same time they were insecure and unprogressive. As the Roman world disappeared, so the Christian world was formed, political unity perished as religious unity came into being. Monasticism in the East was an isolated life and a means to contemplation, monasticism in the West was social, a method of propagating ideas. The thought of antiquity was free, it was disinterested and did not seek directly to influence events, but Christian thought was practical, trying to reform the individual and society, being organized into a Church and thus losing its freedom. Each one of these comparisons implies a clear concept of the subject in question.

Each time that Guizot puts forward a general interpretation of a period or of a position in history, he is working from certain basic assumptions. At times explicitly, and sometimes implicitly, he turns both to historical evidence and to what he calls 'moral probabilities'. This can clearly be seen when he tries to establish the history of territorial property. He lists the ways in which historians such as Montesquieu, Robertson and Mably thought of benefices, as being in the first place completely revocable, in the second place temporary

---

[1] The suggestion that 'Paradise Lost' was inspired by 'De Origine Munde', 'De originali Peccato' and 'De Sententia Dei', the works of Saint Avitus, both impressed and angered a writer in *Blackwoods Edinburgh Magazine*, March 1838, vol. xliii, pp. 303-310. For modern acceptance of this idea see *Watson Kirkonnell, The Celestial Cycle*, Toronto 1952, pp. 3-19, 500-506.

for a fixed period, in the third place for life, and, eventually, hereditary. The first, according to Guizot, was inconceivable, because human nature could not accept the idea of a voluntary association without there being some benefit given in return, and because human nature did not accept that such benefit could be completely and arbitrarily revoked. Therefore, *a priori*, this could not have been the legal and recognized state of the benefices at any time. The historical evidence only confirms this assumption. Montesquieu quotes facts and not laws, he shows what could happen to benefices, not what was their legal condition. The *Book of Fiefs*, which Montesquieu also quoted, is rejected by Guizot as a source, since it was written long after the events, and Guizot found properly contemporary texts which show that people protested against spoliation on the grounds that they had remained faithful to the patron whose beneficiaries they were. Hence this first stage in history of benefices is false.

The second stage, that the concession was used for a fixed time, is equally false. Such an arrangement, according to Guizot, was both delicate and difficult; it could only exist in advanced and well-regulated societies; it required a power which was capable of enforcing decisions. It was therefore unlikely to have been a regular part of barbaric society, and where there is historical evidence that it existed, as in the ecclesiastical 'precaria', Guizot is quite certain that this was only a particular and accidental form of beneficiary property, which in any case was not important. The next stages of property-holdings were that the property was held for life, and then that it should be hereditary. For Guizot the natural form of territorial possession was hereditary, and he claimed that it tended towards such a normal form from its very birth. This is because a man added to the value of land by his own labour and investment; he thus created a capital which was incorporated with the soil and which could not be entirely separated from it. Man also has a natural inclination to fix himself and become the perpetual proprietor of his land. Hence there was a natural tendency for property to become legally hereditary at any time, and this was confirmed by historical evidence of all times and circumstances, and Guizot quotes a treaty of Andelot, concluded in 587, which is an early confirmation of this truth.[1]

One of the subjects to which Guizot gives particular attention is that of Pelagianism, the fifth-century heresy. But before discussing Pelagius, he describes the 'primitive, universal, moral facts' which are inherent in human nature, and then he goes on to describe the particular state of Christianity in the fifth century. His first objective then is 'to distinguish in man in general, independently of all considerations of time, place or particular creed, the natural elements,

[1] Ibid., vol. iii, pp. 236 ff.

349

what one might call the primary material of the Pelagian controversy'. He sets out four 'great moral facts'. The first is that man has a will which is free to decide upon any particular act; the second is that in using this will man feels the need for external support, and this need develops into religious sentiment; the third is that man's judgement may be influenced by circumstances, and the fourth, that moral development and changes can take place, spontaneously and involuntarily, within man. From these four facts it is natural that at all times man should want to discuss the extent to which God directly intervenes in human affairs and the extent to which man's will is important. The Church looked on such discussion from three points of view, from that of philosophy, that of organization and that of theological tradition. Whilst in the first century the Church was concerned with overthrowing paganism, and could therefore have ignored Pelagianism, in the fifth century their concern was essentially one of organization. The ideas of Pelagius and Celestius on the subjects of grace, redemption and salvation weakened some of the weapons with which the Church governed. Therefore Pelagianism, and the semi-Pelagianism of people such as Cassienus, was condemned. But because Pelagianism was a product of the four 'great moral facts' it was a recurrent phenomenon, and in one form or another was to be found 'at all times in European civilization'.

One must note that Guizot proceeds here from the individual, who in certain respects is thought of as unchanging, to society. Had he proceeded from society to the individual, then he might have come to different conclusions. Buckle, for example, thought that the doctrines which insist upon faith rather than works were more suited for the poor, or for democratic countries.[1] One must also note that Guizot proceeds illogically. He takes the Christian doctrine of human insufficiency, and then asks how this fact will be received in the Christian Church; he takes the doctrines of Saint Augustine as an illustration of the principles of the fifth-century Church, which he then finds confirmed in St. Augustine.

The fact that Guizot found it right for the historian to chase the riddle of human life and instincts takes him beyond the normal scope of the rational historian, as has been remarked.[2] But it has not been sufficiently remarked that Guizot is frequently reducing historical conceptions to purely personal ones. He postulates a human being doing something which Guizot finds natural. His inductions come not only from the nature of society but also from the nature of man.

[1] *Buckle* (op. cit.), pp. 480-482.
[2] See *Justus Hashagen*, 'Die Wiedereinsetzung von Religion und kirche unter die Triebkräfte der Geschichtlichen Entwicklung durch François Guizot', *Zeitschrift für Kirchengeschichte*, lxii Band. 1943-1944, p. 305.

Sometimes this leads to wise reflections. A man such as Cromwell was not the same at the end of his life as at the beginning, and a biographer would not make the mistake of overlooking this change. Yet historians find the feudal system, one and entire, when it is still in its cradle, whereas it took several centuries to develop. In a sense Guizot thought that feudal society was the *post hoc* creation of the historian. 'Nothing falsifies history more than logic', was his comment.[1]

But some of the assumptions are more doubtful. He believed that men had a natural tendency to elevate themselves to try to enter 'a sphere superior to their own'. He believed that man naturally tried to extend his relations, 'to animate his social existence' with new acquaintances and activities. Man was naturally shocked by the spectacle of disorder and by the lack of security. He always sought for regular government and for reliable organization. He recognized the natural ascendancy of civilization over barbarism. He refused to accept the superiority of force and only accepted a superior if there was a 'legitimate' reason why this superiority should exist. Because the institution of monarchy had existed at all times and in many different circumstances, then it had to correspond to something in human nature and had to be explained in this way. Within man's nature was the desire for goodness and justice, but the taste for truth and the feeling for beauty could only exist where there was calm. Within man's nature also was the need for novelty and adventure, and when these did not exist in life, then they were sought for in literature and legend. The present was not always enough, it was necessary to go back to the past, and men were naturally attracted to institutions which linked them with the past and gave scope to their imaginations.

These are some of the assumptions upon which Guizot bases much of his historical interpretation. Their existence mean that Guizot was travelling everywhere with his own intellectual etiquette, his own code of social reactions and moral responses. His method of synthesis is to produce an explanation consistent not only with the facts as known but also with the 'moral facts' as assumed. Thus at times Guizot is proceeding from assumption to assumption. This is not an advance upon eighteenth-century history. Voltaire had said that what was not in human nature was not true, and Gibbon had dismissed an opinion by saying that he who would hold it 'would betray a very imperfect knowledge of human nature'. When Guizot works on the historical evidence without reference to his view of individual man, it is then that his conclusions are most valuable. When he seeks to explain the degeneration of the Crusades, he compares the chronicles of the first crusades to those who wrote at the end of the

[1] *Histoire de la Civilisation en Europe* (op. cit.), p. 140.

twelfth century and later. He finds a great intellectual change between these two periods, which helps him to understand the social need and the moral impulse which led to the first crusades and which ceased to apply in the later period. When Guizot discusses the decline of Charlemagne's empire, an examination of the evidence causes him to reject Thierry's explanation that the decline was caused by racial differences, as he rejected the suggestion that it was caused by the personal defects of Charlemagne's successors. His explanation, as has been shown, was that no great empire could exist because there was no great society. Only small states could succeed because there were only small societies.[1]

It is natural to prefer Guizot as an historian when his particular views of humanity and of human nature do not obtrude. However, there are two things which must in fairness be added. First of all, many of those historians or philosophers who chose to criticize Guizot as an historian did so by rejecting his assumptions. But they rejected Guizot's assumptions because they did not agree with their own assumptions. Guizot assumed the necessity for regular and moderate government. Edgar Quinet, in a famous article, assumed the necessity of liberty; Renouvier, writing in 1872, assumed the necessity of political and civil liberty.[2] There is no reason why the one assumption should be preferred to the other. Secondly, if one accepts the view of H. J. Marrou, who says: 'The great historian will be the man who will know how to raise the historical problem in the richest and most fertile way; will understand what question it is important to ask of the past'—then one will forgive Guizot even his unsatisfactory answers, because one appreciates his questions.[3]

One leading English historian has written of Guizot that he 'had some inkling of what revolutions were about; his *Histoire de la République d'Angleterre et de Cromwell* and the succeeding volumes, published in the eighteen-fifties, show more awareness of the class forces at work in the revolution than the writing of most contemporary English historians'.[4] Guizot's own claim was that the French Revolution had thrown a vivid light on the struggle of the

[1] See *Histoire de la Civilisation en Europe* (op. cit.), pp. 225 ff; *Histoire de la Civilisation en France* (op. cit.), vol. ii, pp. 228 ff. For a modern discussion of some aspects of the second of these problems see *F. L. Ganshof*, 'Louis the Pious Reconsidered' in *History*, October 1957, pp. 171-180.

[2] *Edgar Quinet*, 'La Philosophie de l'Histoire en France', *Revue des Deux Mondes*, February 28th, 1855, pp. 925-965; Charles Renouvier in *La Critique Philosophique*, 1872, vol. i, p. 368.

[3] Marrou is quoted by the *Reverend Father M. C. D'Arcy S.J.* in *The Sense of History, Secular and Sacred*, 1959, pp. 57-58.

[4] *Christopher Hill*, 'The English Civil War Interpreted by Marx and Engels', *Science and Society*, Winter 1948, vol. xii, No. 1, p. 132.

seventeenth century, and whilst English historians such as Brodie, Lingard and Malcolm Laing had no natural sympathy for their subjects, a French historian such as Villemain possessed 'a quick and keen comprehension' of revolutions and of revolutionary situations. 'Villemain', he wrote, 'has viewed and judged the English revolution from the midst of that of France . . . he drew life from his own times and infused it into the times he wished to recall.'[1] Guizot thought of himself as describing the Revolution, the Republic and the Restoration from his own understanding of similar events. When his Tory friend J. W. Croker found that he had taken the Civil War too seriously and reminded him of how fox-hunters had passed between the rival sides at Edgehill, Guizot replied that Croker had lived amongst Parliamentary parties, whilst he had lived amongst revolutionary parties. When it was said that he had not fully appreciated the greatness of Monk, Guizot replied simply that he had known men like Monk.[2]

But in addition to the personal experience there was a great deal of erudition. Before publishing his first two volumes on the reign of Charles I, he had published a collection of the original memoirs of the period in twenty-five volumes. He had consulted the archives of Paris and of other European capitals. He published a great many documents *in extenso* (a procedure which Macaulay was careful to avoid), and he considered that these additions to historical knowledge were in themselves justification for his continuation of Hume and Villemain. He readily demonstrated his acquaintance with the documentary sources; he corrected historians such as Brodie or Forster, pointed out an omission in Carlyle, queried a date in Thurloe. He suggested that he was particularly honest in his continuous search for documentary sources, so that when he quoted Hume as saying that in the Parliament of 1628 the House of Commons was three times as rich as the House of Lords, he found it necessary to say that he had not been able to find any precise evaluation of the comparative wealth of the Houses, and that Hume's references were to Sanderson and Walker, historians whom he considered as having little authority.[3]

An almost unique phenomenon in a work of this kind is that there is an interval of twenty-four years between the publication of the Charles I volumes and the 1850 *Discours sur l'Histoire de la Révolu-*

---

[1] *Histoire de la Révolution d'Angleterre* (op. cit.), Preface to the first edition. At least one English reviewer considered, in July 1821, that Villemain's was the most able history of Cromwell that had then been written. *Quarterly Review*, July 1821, p. 326 note.

[2] Croker: Guizot, December 2nd, 1849; Guizot: Croker, January 12th, 1850 (and enclosed notes by Guizot), *Croker Papers*, B.M. Add. MSS., 41, 128.

[3] *Histoire de la Révolution d'Angleterre* (op. cit.), vol. i, p. 130.

tion d'Angleterre, and it was only in 1854 that the Cromwell volumes appeared. The first two volumes were therefore written during the Restoration at a time when Guizot had been put out of official life by right-wing reaction; the remaining volumes appeared after 1848 when Guizot had again been removed from official life, but this time by popular revolution. Yet it cannot be said that there is any great difference in the writing. The later volumes are less dramatic and colourful; the style is more restrained, the general remarks more condensed. One might guess that these later volumes had been written by an older man. It is not likely that a reader could guess that the author had undergone any deep personal transformation in the course of writing his history. The real difference between the first part and the second lies in the nature of the subject. The struggle between King and Parliament is necessarily dramatic. No historian could resist exploiting the suspense which naturally exists in the description of such a conflict. But after 1649, the relevant characters are less picturesque, the nation itself seems less concerned. Once the King has disappeared, the only question to be discussed is that of organizing the government, and these volumes become essays on government and disquisitions on politics. Thus, rather than say that Guizot dominates the subject by reference to his personal position, it would be truer to say that he rather adapts himself to the necessities of his subject.

The change of style between the seventeenth-century histories and the histories of civilization should not be exaggerated. It is true that many of the mannerisms of the lectures are absent from the narrative history. The preliminary discussions, the conclusions, the neatly presented digressions of the lectures are largely absent from the narrative, which is hardly ever interrupted. There is no succinct portrait of either the King or of Cromwell, in spite of the large part that they play in these volumes. Guizot, as narrator, is careful to restrict his vision. He never becomes the observer who sees everything and knows everything. It is rare to find him penetrating into men's secret thoughts, as when he says that with the death of Falkland at Newbury, Charles, in spite of his expressions of regret, was really more at ease in his Council. It is even more rare that Guizot should perceive men's expressions (although he once has Charles 'smiling disdainfully').[1]

But in spite of such obvious differences, the essential method of writing history remained the same. Just as the periodization in the

---

[1] *Histoire de la Révolution d'Angleterre* (op. cit.), vol. i, p. 443; vol. ii, p. 200. It is this apparent refusal of the author to interpose himself into the narrative which caused Taine to compare Guizot to Thucydides. Taine: Cornelis de Witt (Guizot's son-in-law), May 27th, 1854, *Revue des Deux Mondes*, November-December 1902, p. 781.

histories of civilization implied a conceptual content, so the selection of facts for the narrative implied interpretation. The narrative is made to leap forward by a succession of incidents; the course of events is thus made to depend upon a particular choice of episodes, as can be shown by a few examples. In April 1628 the House of Commons unanimously voted a subsidy to the King, and there was an apparent harmony between them; this was marred by the secretary of state Cooke, who 'with the short-sighted meanness of a courtier' reported to the Commons the speech which the hated favourite Buckingham had made in the council, and once again the Commons were both offended and indignant. In May 1640, whilst relations between the King and the newly summoned Parliament were bad, yet the House of Commons had no wish to break with the King, and was willing to consider his requests for twelve subsidies. However, Sir Harry Vane told them that it was not worth their while to deliberate, since the King would never accept less than he had asked for. This declaration, which the King had not authorized, caused astonishment and rage even amongst the most moderate, and in these circumstances the King rather uneasily decided upon dissolution. In October 1641 the King was in Scotland and was producing a good effect with his concessions and apparent complaisance towards the Scottish leaders. This, however, was suddenly ruined by the rumour that he was planning to arrest, or to assassinate, Hamilton and Argyle. It became known that Charles had lent a ready ear to the schemings of Montrose and was seeking to incriminate those English leaders who had supported the invading Covenanters. It therefore seemed that the King was obstinately vindictive; even the moderates in the English Parliament began to think of themselves as being in danger. In September 1643 papers were found on the Earl of Antrim which revealed a royal plan to raise the Highlands, to negotiate a truce with the Irish rebels and to redirect English troops on to Chester and Bristol. The insincerity and untrustworthiness of the King was thus impressed upon many of his loyal supporters. In February 1645, news of Montrose's victory at Inverlochy caused the King to withdraw the concession which he had promised to the Earl of Southampton, including one on the militia which was considered important. Negotiations between the rival parties failed once again. Letters captured at Naseby further demonstrated the bad faith of the King; they silenced the peace party and alienated many supporters. In October 1647 Cromwell and Ireton, waiting disguised in the Blue Boer tavern at Holborn, discovered a letter from Charles to Henrietta Maria, once again revealing the royal tendency to intrigue.

Thus certain episodes are singled out and given importance; they are made into levers by which the narrative can move forward. As certain of them are not in themselves of great importance, they give to the progress of events an impression of inevitability. Both sides are at the mercy of such errors and accidents; no one seems able to arrest the course of development. How is this human insufficiency to be explained? In the *Discours* Guizot says that in seventeenth-century England men had neither the enlightenment nor the political virtues necessary for the establishment of constitutional government. This inadequacy he explains, significantly enough, in terms of human nature. In the heart of man, according to Guizot, there was a combination of both weakness and arrogance, and neither of these tendencies could find satisfaction in the labour and circumspection necessary to the system of constitutional monarchy.[1] As in the histories of civilization, therefore, one quickly unearths a view of humanity as a basic element.

It is interesting to see how Guizot differs from Clarendon, whom he refers to very frequently. It is difficult to understand how anyone can accuse Guizot of following Clarendon blindly.[2] For example, Guizot, like Clarendon, describes the debate on the Remonstrance going far into the night, so that fatigue drove away many members; he quotes Sir Benjamin Rudyard's remark that the verdict would be that of a starved jury; he quotes Cromwell's whisper to Falkland that if the Remonstrance had been rejected then he would have sold all he had the next morning and never have seen England more; he describes the argument over the publication of the Remonstrance, when at one moment the whole House was standing, their hands to their swords, and it seemed that civil war would begin within the walls of Parliament itself. For Clarendon, however, this scene is an illustration of his belief that the rebellion and the war were the work of a minority, deliberately determined to provoke revolution. For him, therefore, the Grand Remonstrance is 'the first visible ground and foundation of that rage and madness in the people of which they could never be cured', and affords an example of how 'a handful of men, much inferior in the beginning, in number and interest, came to give laws to the major part'. For Guizot, however, the Remonstrance debate reveals that the contest between the court and the country has become a struggle between two great parties, each of them claiming to be the upholders of public interests and feelings. Clarendon shows the King's attitude as being entirely passive at this time whereas that of Parliament was aggressive. Guizot, on the other hand, shows how Parliament's 'acerbity' is matched by the organization of the King's friends, the withdrawal of the guard which Essex had established for the safety of the Commons, and how such royalist advances spurred

[1] Ibid., vol. i, pp. 7-8.
[2] E. *Fueter, Histoire de l'historiographic moderne,* Paris 1914, pp. 633-634.

the Commons on to new pretentions. Guizot does not follow Clarendon in believing that the King's principle defect was a lack of
confidence in his own excellent judgement. He rather emphasizes the
King's pride, his haughtiness, recklessness and inconsequence; in
Guizot's narrative he moves irresolutely from despondency to
confidence, from timidity to daring. His acts do not reveal any
coherent design or system. Whereas Macaulay saw the attempt to
seize the five members as a revelation of tyrannical ambition, and
Clarendon saw it as a momentary error of judgement, Guizot simply
sees it as one further link in the long chain of events. He does not
choose to comment on it either in terms of the constitution or in
terms of its wisdom. The King had placed great hopes on this *coup
d'état*; once it had failed he felt to the full the humiliation which
enveloped him in London, and he therefore left Whitehall. Once out
of London, surrounded only by his partisans, without any of the
proofs of his weakness before him, then he gave himself up to the
hope of conquering his enemies by armed force. The episode is
neither a revelation which is to be seized upon nor a passing
folly which is to be excused. It is a stage in a complicated
process.

Guizot's treatment of the King's character is a good example of
how he delighted in complexity, and in the contradictory appearances
which both parties and persons could assume. He never tried to make
a map of the Civil War; one of his constant preoccupations was to
show that even in a county which was decidedly on one side there was
a party which was for the other side, and this conflict of opinion
sometimes led to the neutrality of the county. Amongst the Puritans
there were both ambitious and frivolous men; although they had been
appointed by the King, the monopolists sometimes took the Parliamentary side; men usually followed a day-by-day policy according to
the necessities of the situation, and this situation could not be controlled by mere personalities. However, if this series of events was
complicated, there nevertheless existed an overall explanation, and
Guizot does not allow his insistence on complexity to invalidate his
belief that there were historical causes.

If there were two parties in England it was because two parties
were created by English history. Those who rallied round the King
were often representative of the feudal system, of which deep traces
still persisted. These subjects were little accustomed to reflection or
to debate, they despised the gloom of the Puritan creed, and possessing their own independence they had little interest in doctrines of
public liberty. They had opposed the tyranny of the Crown, as
represented by a Buckingham or a Stafford, but their loyalty was
revived by the innovations of Parliament and by their fear of its

despotism. It was equally possible for an important part of the population to side against the King, since both burgesses and country-gentlemen possessed the means of individual action and of war. The financial, military and judicial affairs of the nation were in the hands of local and virtually independent authorities. Country and town had been represented in the same Parliament for more than three centuries. They could claim a series of privileges going back beyond the Conquest. However, they only became conscious of these rights when they became conscious of their growing economic power. Beneath the political parties Guizot discerned a social question, 'the struggle of the various classes for influence and power'. Although Guizot did not believe that the Civil War was from the first an example of social classification, he suggested that within a short time the nobility had ranged themselves on the one side and the middle classes and people on the other. A great social movement was in that way revealed at the heart of a great political struggle.

The religious question was part of the political, according to Guizot, because in England the Reformation had had a double origin. It had been both royal and popular. The Anglican Church, in separating itself from Rome, became dependent upon the temporal sovereign and thus was linked to despotism. The non-conformists, in attacking their religious adversaries, were obliged to attack the temporal sovereign and to claim political liberties. Religious questions were thus mixed up with political, even in matters of dogma and ritual. Furthermore, Guizot believed that in the course of time, men's minds became increasingly daring; as Protestantism accustomed men's minds to examining the mysteries of divine power, then it seemed natural for them to examine the mysteries of terrestrial power, and the nature of royal government, became a subject of discussion throughout England. The English bourgeois was becoming bolder and more ambitious, whilst the court and the aristocracy, less preoccupied with religious matters, failed to realize this change.

As Guizot describes this religious movement, it is bound to progress. The process of logic impelled it on. Since the monarchy and the aristocracy were to be suppressed in the Church, then why should they not also be suppressed in the state? Since the Roman clergy was unacceptable, and since the episcopal clergy was unacceptable, why should the Presbyterian clergy be tolerated? It was rational to conclude that it was in the congregation of the faithful that religious authority resided, and that it was the Lord alone who chose his saints and revealed to them the means of his triumph. With such a systematic method of thinking it was only a step to talk of equality of rights, to demand the abolition of all abuses and to seek means for the more just distribution of property and wealth. In this way, according to Guizot, emerged the party of the Independents.

The logical and rational process of historical development that exists in the histories of civilization exists here too, in spite of the large complexity of balanced factors. The Duchesse de Broglie found that Guizot's characters were too much the representatives of abstract ideas, and Michelet claimed that Guizot did not appreciate the true significance of the established Church.[1] One might well ask where someone like Lord Falkland would fit in to Guizot's scheme of things, in his royalism, and in his attack upon those who 'have opposed the papacy beyond the seas that they might settle one beyond the water' (he was alluding to Lambeth). But there are four ways in which Guizot's approach appears to be modern. Unlike many English historians, he believed that the cleavage between the two sides was real and violent; he believed that economic motives helped to determine men's actions and that the revolution which began in 1640 was a bourgeois revolution; he believed that the 'untrustworthiness' of the King was important; and finally, since the Revolution became a confusion of projects and ambitions, without any general theory or plan presiding over it, he believed it to be natural that the man who emerged as the figure dominating this confusion should represent a conjunction of rival events, and that he should have as his essential quality, sympathy with other men's ideas.

Many nineteenth-century Frenchmen, historians, dramatists and painters were fascinated by Oliver Cromwell. What fascinated writers such as Lamartine and Charles de Rémusat, or a painter such as Paul Delaroche, was not just the drama of an enterprising military leader but the drama of a man who whilst completely victorious was nevertheless unsuccessful. The situation of Cromwell was thought to be tragic because he was forced into actions which he disliked, pathetic because he was unable to found anything permanent or stable. The conclusion of Guizot's volume has often been quoted and has been thought of as applying to Guizot himself. 'God does not grant to these great men', he wrote, 'who have laid the foundations of their greatness amidst disorder and revolution, the power of regulating at their pleasure and for succeeding ages, the government of nations.' Yet the reflection goes beyond personal reference; it referred to several generations of French experience. What particularly fascinated Guizot was that Cromwell had himself played two rôles, he had tried

---

[1] Duchesse de Broglie: Prosper de Barante, August 23th, 1825, *Barante, Souvenirs* (op. cit.), vol. iii, p. 267. *Michelet, Journal*, vol. i (ed. Paul Viallaneix), Paris 1959, p. 358.

to make and to unmake the Revolution, he had urged on and he had restrained, it was he who had begun, and he who tried to conclude.[1]

When Guizot produced his first two volumes there was no life of Cromwell in existence which had any claim to be complete. Villemain's was probably the best and this was not widely read in England. Cromwell was invariably treated as a hypocrite and usurper, whose beliefs were partly absurd and partly sensible, and whose actions betrayed a mixture of resolution and uncertainty. Hume had dismissed him as 'a fanatical hypocrite' and as late as 1839 Dickens's friend John Forster found it to be 'indisputedly true' that Cromwell had 'lived a hypocrite and died a traitor'.[2] Although Cromwell rarely found a defender, Macaulay remarked in 1829 that he seemed to remain popular with the great body of his fellow-countrymen, but this was a matter of sentiment rather than of knowledge.

Guizot is not very interested in 'Cromwelliana'. He does not discuss a lot of the stories and legends that were being published and republished. He does not, for example, discuss the mutual allegations of cowardice which separated Cromwell from Manchester. He does not go into the 'hypocrisy' of the self-denying ordinance, or into Cromwell's possible exploitation of a preceding fast day as a means of passing his Bill. He gives Cromwell's own account of the New Model Army and refrains from comment (unlike Clarendon who describes these men as being free from any debauchery 'but the wickedness of their hearts'). He does not comment either on Cromwell's letters, such as that written after the battle of Naseby, although he quotes from them quite frequently. He mentions the possibility that Cromwell might have had some foreknowledge of the King's escape to Carisbrooke Castle, he refers to the movement of sentries at Hampton Court and to Cromwell's apparent pleasure at the news, but he does not follow Hollis, Ludlow and others in their speculation as to whether Cromwell had arranged for this escape or not, and what explanation there could be for such a scheme. Guizot, who even avoids the phrase 'cruel necessity', does not require Lord Morley's remark that a 'hunt for conjectural motives for conjectural occurrences is a waste of time'.[3]

Guizot's Cromwell is neither a hypocrite not a fanatic. He is a politician, that is to say a man who desires to govern. As such he

[1] *Histoire de la République d'Angleterre et de Cromwell* (op. cit.), vol. ii, pp. 399-400; Guizot: Léonce de Lavergne, July 11th, 1848, *Correspondance de Guizot avec Léonce de Lavergne* (op. cit.), p. 32.

[2] Quoted in *Maurice Ashley, The Greatness of Oliver Cromwell*, 1957, p. 13. Mr. Ashley makes no mention of Villemain.

[3] Quoted in *Ashley*, op. cit., p. 213.

possessed both great ambition and great skill. He also had religious feelings and convictions which were perfectly genuine; but they did not in any way trouble his political ambition, frequently they only served it. His strength, and this for Guizot was the talent of all great men, lay in his ability to understand events and to appreciate a situation. He could therefore decide what action would command support, and what adjustments to policy were advisable. In this way he could suggest himself as the best resource for a bewildering number of sects and parties.

Nothing is more striking in Guizot's narrative than the way in which the figure of Cromwell is made to vary. There are times when he is positive and commanding. Before the conflict he is described as being little noticed in the Commons, but more deeply engaged than any other in the machinations of the Revolution, active in exciting people and in denouncing the royalists 'out of doors'. His exploits with his troops, his determination to prosecute the war, his dislike of the Scots, his disagreements with Manchester, his knowledge of what was going on, all these are described by Guizot and suggest a considerable personality. But when the situation became more complicated, particularly from 1847 onwards, Cromwell changes. He is shown as being 'devoured by ambition and doubt', when 'the most contrary ambitions and anticipations agitated his mind'. He becomes less positive, less effective. He was closely associated with the visionaries and with the demagogues, the enthusiasts, rationalists, levellers and so on. Everything in Cromwell, according to Guizot, lent itself to such an intimacy. He could easily become the companion of those who were rough; his own language could become mystical and familiar, his imagination had unexpected outbursts, his manner could quickly become exalted. Yet, at the same time, no one was more intimate than Cromwell with the confidants of the King. He frequently saw Berkeley, Ashburnham, Ford and Ashley; Mrs. Cromwell had been received with great honour at Hampton Court; and when Cromwell saw the King amongst his family, he declared that it was the tenderest sight that ever his eyes beheld. It was difficult for Cromwell to remain on such terms with both groups. According to Guizot, he did not believe that republican ideas could produce a well-ordered state, but he was not sure to what extent the King's name was still a power. He tried to put off the obligation to choose between the groups. He visited Lillburne in prison and hinted at imminent release; he asked Berkeley and Ashburnham to visit him less frequently; he called a conference of officers and republicans, and when Ludlow pressed him to reveal his own position, he escaped by throwing a cushion at Ludlow and by leaving the room hurriedly. This period of indecision is not brought to an end by any form of intellectual revelation; it had been brought about by events and it was concluded by events. He discovered further proof of the King's essential untrustworthiness; he was impressed by the growing disorder of the army; he realized that he could only win the support of the soldiers and restore discipline by turning against the King. Once this decision was made, the narrative leaps forward, and Cromwell once again becomes a dramatic, purposeful figure. He might find it necessary to assume a hesitation for reasons of tactics, but he was the decided man who roughly overrode any objections (such as those of Colonel Downes) to the trial and execution of the King.

The conferences between Cromwell and Parliament in April 1657 give Guizot another opportunity of presenting the former in his undecided mood. Cromwell is shown as a man who did not have simple, fixed ideas. He is shown as a man who tends to wander, who sounds the terrain all around him, who moves in all sorts of indirect or contrary directions. His powerful imagination enabled him to see all sides of a question and all the probable and even possible consequences of a decision. When he spoke he was diffuse and obscure, and he spoke in this way both deliberately and naturally. However, this 'comedy', as Guizot called it, had been rendered necessary by the situation as it existed. Cromwell deliberately hesitated in order that the idea that he should become King might have time to circulate and become familiar. He deliberately paused in order to estimate the drift of opinion. Once he had gauged the state of things, then he did not hesitate any more, and he renounced the kingship.

Guizot's Cromwell has many advantages. He is the outstanding man of his time, and was so before the fall of the monarchy. His victories, his administrative ability, his reputation abroad, his ability to win over individuals, all make him considerable, even when Guizot describes this last quality with words like 'seduce' and 'deceive'. Guizot does not try to belittle Cromwell's contemporaries. He avoids criticizing Sir Harry Vane for example, even for his conduct at Strafford's trial, and he refers to his 'high integrity'; he speaks of the ability of others, such as Sidney, Ludlow, Hutchinson; he speaks of the nobility of their cause, and their sense of humanity. But, in general, the other characters as seen by Guizot are like Whitelock and Mayward as seen by Clarendon, 'they have never led but followed and were carried away with the torrent rather than swim with the stream'. Guizot's Cromwell is all the more outstanding since he has none of the vulgarity which others have given him on account of his 'Puritanism'. He was a man of elegant tastes, delighting in pomp and magnificence. He could be gay, excitable, and even at times, 'farceur'.

However, the business of his life was government, and one must notice the qualities with which Guizot chooses to endow him. One must notice particularly that here Cromwell appears as having more fixed and systematic principles. He understands 'the empire of legality', so that when he wishes to act illegally then he surrounds all his actions with the appearance of extreme necessity. He believed that government is naturally situated in the 'superior regions of society'. He perceived, and this for Guizot was the essence of 'Cromwellianism', that the people were not sufficient to create a government. Society was in need of some basis which would be recognized by the people but which was both anterior to and superior to the people. Such a power had existed with the landed aristocracy and with the hereditary monarch. The one had disappeared as property had changed hands, and the other had disappeared with the mistakes of Charles I. It was Cromwell's sagacity that saw the need to fill the gap; it was his ambition that led him to fill it himself; it was his tragedy that he could not do so. For Cromwell's power was a revolutionary power, the product of popular violence. His power could not therefore be anterior and superior to the people, he was debarred from being the accepted and superior force maintaining the general order of society. It is significant that Guizot dated the starting point of Cromwell's decline as being the day when he levied a special tax on royalists, thus emphasizing the partisan nature of his power.[1]

When one examines Guizot's treatment of Cromwell's political ideas one begins to see that the history is not what one thought. What appeared to be a narrative, with a discreet and unobtrusive narrator, with material from which a portrait could be assembled rather than the portrait itself, is in fact a tightly drawn and coherently constructed interpretation. Furthermore, in a work which has ostentatiously sought to demonstrate the documentary justifications for all the statements made, there are a good many assumptions. It is probably reasonable that Guizot should make Cromwell's preoccupation with the aristocracy in both family and state affairs, a matter of policy rather than vanity. It is probably reasonable, too, that Guizot should see Cromwell's instinct for government in his regarding the aristocracy as the force and ornament of his administration, in his trying to gain the adhesion of names consecrated by time. But when Guizot shows Cromwell as seeing the arrogance of the claim to found government on the popular will alone, or when he shows Cromwell as understanding that government is not the affair of men alone, then it is obviously Guizot who is superimposing his own ideas on to

---

[1] *Histoire de la République d'Angleterre et de Cromwell* (op. cit.), vol. i, p. 346; vol. ii, pp. 148, 338. *Histoire du Protectorat de Richard Cromwell et du Rétablissement des Stuarts* (op. cit.), vol. i, pp. 49 ff.

Cromwell. This becomes all the more apparent when he states, quite categorically, that there were three things of outstanding importance in the public conscience. They were hereditary monarchy, government by two chambers and the maintenance of the law. Having claimed that they existed, Guizot then goes on to say that Cromwell recognized their importance and to imply that it was an instance of his greatness that he should do so. This is to make an assumption into a reality, to put it into Cromwell's head, and to be impressed that it should be found there. Guizot offers no evidence either as to the state of the country or as to the state of Cromwell's mind.

In a way, therefore, Cromwell becomes a vehicle, carrying Guizot's own conception of sovereignty and demonstrating that the effective allies of authority are those classes amongst whom conservative interests prevail. Throughout all the volumes devoted to seventeenth-century English history, the 'dramatis personnae' are carrying Guizot's ideas on humanity. If the English are shown as being particularly reverent of law and devoted to monarchy, it is because men always try to attach themselves to principles which appear to be perpetual. Men wish to direct the future in the name of eternal truth. Therefore they are not satisfied with maxims and measures which are exceptional, and which are justifiable in terms of temporary crisis. Men claim them as permanent principles. In 1642 it was this tendency which levered the Revolution forward and made the break with the King one that could not be healed. This is the origin of a Republic which was 'introduced and sustained by pride of spirit and the egoism of faction'.[1] If men were satisfied when their personal interests were satisfied, then those who were in the Parliament of January 1659 would soon have been satisfied and there would have been little disagreement amongst them. The existing régime could have conciliated them all, and Richard Cromwell, for all that Guizot's presentation of him is less flattering than Hume's, was a moderate, equitable man, capable of placating most people. But men are not so easily satisfied. Guizot believed that in their hearts and in their souls there were principles and passions which demanded 'moral satisfactions', and it was these which the government of Richard Cromwell could not provide. History had to move forward once again and the eventual result was the Restoration.[2] Throughout the volumes, where Guizot shows men's fear turning to anger, their zeal turning to obstinacy, their beliefs turning to fanaticism and to hatred, their pity coming too late and remaining ineffective, there remains the belief that in England there was a mass of 'honest people', willing to

[1] *Histoire de Charles I depuis son avènement* (op. cit.), vol. i, pp. 351 ff.; *Histoire du Protectorat de Richard Cromwell* (op. cit.), vol. i, p. 131.

[2] Ibid., vol. i, pp. 46 ff.

be guided by their 'profound instincts' towards a system which was legal and just.

It is because he interprets the accelerations of history in terms of these assumptions that Guizot can be criticized. For Marx, Guizot's *Discours* was a 'banal tale of mere political events'. He had not realized that the fundamental characteristic of English history was the lasting alliance which existed between the English bourgeoisie and the English landowners, and which explains the way in which English development differed from French.[1] It is perfectly true that Guizot did not realize the significance of the fact that English capitalism was both urban and rural since it was connected with the staple woollen industry. His failure to do this was all the more surprising since he was well aware (as has been shown) of extensive social change. The explanation is that Guizot was less concerned with analysing the English bourgeoisie than in attributing to it his own beliefs.

For Sainte-Beuve, Guizot is too certain of things.[2] He complained that whereas with Hume he could argue and contradict, with Guizot he was never allowed to doubt. History, for Sainte-Beuve, was essentially surprising, it could happen in different ways and with different results. Guizot's history was too absolute. Undoubtedly Sainte-Beuve was here showing some 'coquetterie', and one wonders what he really thought of those historians who affect surprise at what they have to record (one thinks of Hallam, unable to understand why Elizabeth could not be tolerant towards the Catholics). Taine took the opposite view to Sainte-Beuve and praised the tightly knit unity of Guizot's work.[3] It is of course true that most historians make the events of history appear at least natural, and that narrative historians allow event to explain event in a way that appears mechanical. But if Guizot's work appears as absolute and unified, one reason at least is that he is necessarily finding the type of political behaviour that he expected to find.

Perhaps the most interesting remark that was made on Guizot's English history was made after the publication of the first two volumes by Theodore Jouffroy, a pupil of Victor Cousin's who had taught philosophy at the École Normale. 'Logic', he wrote, 'is the queen of revolutions; a revolution is only the development of an idea and the development of an idea is nothing other than logic.'[4] Guizot's study

[1] Marx's review of Guizot's *Discours* has recently been republished in *Karl Marx, Neue Rheinische Zeitung*, Berlin 1958.

[2] Sainte-Beuve's review of the *Discours* is in *Causeries du Lundi* (op. cit.), vol. i, pp. 311 ff.

[3] Taine's essay on Guizot was published in the *Revue de l'Instruction Publique*, June 7th, 1856, and is republished in *Essais de Critique de l'Histoire* (Paris Edition of 1920), pp. 130 ff.

[4] *Le Globe*, November 17th, 1827.

of the English Revolution was a study in the logic of revolutions. The first paragraphs of the first volume describe the changes that were taking place; the last paragraph of the last volume indicates the changes that were about to take place. The Revolution advances or recoils; it is never absent. It was this which annoyed J. W. Croker. 'I think . . . that you have too much confounded the *Rebellion* (as *we* always and *you never* call it) with the *Revolution*. I admit that the first helped to produce the other as a dungheap helps to produce asparagus, as filth produces food; but they are not the same thing.'[1] So wrote Croker. But Guizot would not give way. He realized that this was not a trifling disagreement about words, but a criticism which if accepted would imperil a work which sought to demonstrate how England had developed.

One need not spend too much time on the remaining historical works. Guizot's *Washington* first appeared in 1839 as an essay introducing the French edition of Jared Spark's collection of Washington's correspondence. It is interesting in so far as Washington was a man for whom Guizot seems to have had an unlimited admiration, and this essay (which was published as a book in 1851) contributed in a small way to the Washington legend, the picture of a man who had none of the faults but only the virtues of his courage, sagacity and modesty. It would not be too fanciful to suggest that Guizot might have seen some similarities between Washington and himself. Both men presented an austere front to the world; both tried to approach all problems rationally, although surrounded by people who proceeded emotionally; both were given the task of halting a revolution and of bringing order and stability into a democratic society. It is even possible that Guizot saw himself after 1848, in the Val-Richer, like Washington after 1783, at Mount Vernon. But he was too good an historian not to see the differences between their situations. In one way, too, Guizot's essay corrects the legend. When Washington became President, it was the first time that he found himself in complete command. He sought to appear above political or state differences, and to act as a superior, mediating force, lamenting the fact that Jefferson and Hamilton should quarrel, but being careful not to take sides. Guizot does not directly discuss whether this attitude was realistic or not, but he does suggest that Washington's views on government were severely conservative. In this sense his Washington is more than a national shrine where all men can pay their unthinking respects; his Washington stands for certain principles of government on which men have differing ideas. Guizot more than hinted that there were dangers in American society which only a

[1] Croker: Guizot, December 2nd, 1849, *Val-Richer MSS.*

Washington could halt. It would seem that the American Congress-men who voted that Guizot's portrait should be hung in their build-ing, as a tribute to his essay, did not realize that Guizot's praise of Washington implied a criticism of American society.

Guizot's *Sir Robert Peel* appeared in book form in 1856, part of it having been read to the Académie des Sciences Morales et Politiques. Peel represents another personality with whom Guizot felt a particular sympathy. A middle-class, rational and pacific statesman who received unmerited blame and unpopularity could easily appear as the English equivalent to Guizot. It is perhaps for this reason that Guizot emphasizes the differences between English and French politicians. Peel, for example, did not have to choose his political party, he had 'the good fortune' to be born into one. When he discussed the affair of Catholic Emancipation he did not find it necessary to discuss theoretical questions of principle, but only practical issues. The objections to income tax were less important in England than they would have been in France, since in relations between the individual and the state there were better guarantees in England of legality, liberty, publicity and even morality. Peel frequently earned the praise of his political opponents, and when, in 1835 or at other times, he protested that he had no wish for power, his words were heard with respect and were believed. Such protesta-tions would not have been received in the same way by the Chamber of Deputies or by the French newspapers.

This is a study in contemporary history and Guizot is able to add his personal testimony to Peel's speeches and to the *Memoirs* (the first volume only of which had appeared). It was on matters of foreign policy that Guizot had had most to do with Peel and he is at times sharply critical of him. He suggests that Peel shared the prejudices of many of his compatriots and he shows him as being invariably suspicious, whilst on one occasion at least, when the independent republic of Cracow was suppressed by the Eastern Powers in 1847, he chose to misinterpret French policy. On the issue of the Corn Laws Guizot demonstrates his invariable historical technique. Peel, as he understands him, was for several years attracted to the principles of free trade whilst worried by the difficulties involved. The description of Peel following the activities of the Anti-Corn Law League with an eye which is at once benevolent and uneasy is typical of Guizot's love of balanced contradictions.[1] He does not go so far as Lord John Russell, who believed that Peel behaved towards Protection like an advancing general, striking down the minor monopolies and leaving the fortresses of corn and sugar like garrisons in conquered country; but he does suggest that Peel was manœuvring so that the Conser-

[1] *Sir Robert Peel, Étude d'Histoire Contemporaine*, Paris 1856, p. 116.

vative party would be forced to choose between complete and
immediate abolition, as proposed by the opposition, and the more
gentle and delayed abolition which was to be put forward by their
leader. Peel's mistake was to misjudge the temper of his party and the
effect of circumstances, which meant that men had exhausted their
political sagacity. Guizot thus concentrates on the course of events.
But when he comes to consider the charges which were levelled at
Peel, of betraying his party and deceiving his supporters, he does not
choose to defend him on the ground of any particular situation. The
defence which Peel could have made, and it surprised Guizot that he
did not make it, was that change had to be attributed to the times in
which they were all living. Peel could not be the same man as he had
been in earlier years; the conservative party was not the same; the
country itself was transformed. Therefore it was wrong to talk of
desertion or treason. Guizot insisted on seeing a particular event in
terms of a general and comprehensive development. It is interesting
to see how, like Peel, he appeared unaware of the argument that the
exertions of a party imposed obligations on a party chief.[1]

It does not seem that Guizot was being altogether frank when he
wrote in 1869 that he had never had any intention of publishing the
history lessons which he had given to his grandchildren. As early as
August 1848, before he had any grandchildren, he had spoken of
preparing a history of France for the use of children, and he had himself mentioned Scott's *Tales of a Grandfather* as a model.[2] That the
notes made by Guizot himself, and those taken by his daughter,
Madame Cornelis de Witt, were sufficient for several volumes to be
published after his death, suggests that he had considered at least
the possibility of publication.

Each of these volumes contains a great deal that is to be found in
his earlier volumes; many of the opinions and judgements are simply
repeated. He regrets the generous but hasty movements of opinion
which have often led Frenchmen into error; he condemns the
absolutism of opinion which often destroyed the harmony of the
nation; he moralizes on the mysterious ways by which the expectations
of the most skilful statesmen are reversed. He does not simplify this

[1] *Sir Robert Peel, Étude d'Histoire Contemporaine*, Paris 1856, pp. 343, 349.
[2] Guizot: Croker, August 27th, 1878, *Croker Papers*, B.M. Add. MSS. 41,
128; During 1838 also he had spoken about 'une petite histoire de France racontée
à mes enfants', *François Guizot et Madame Laure de Gasparin* (op. cit.), p. 139.
*L'Histoire de France depuis les temps les plus reculés jusqu'en 1789, Racontée
à mes petits-enfants.* Five volumes were published in Paris from 1872 to 1875.
The last volume appeared after the death of Guizot. Further posthumous volumes
were *L'Histoire de France depuis 1789 jusqu'en 1848* . . ., Paris 1878-1879, 2 vols.,
and *L'Histoire d'Angleterre depuis les temps les plus reculés jusqu'à l'avènement de
la Reine Victoria* . . ., Paris, 1877-1878, 2 vols.

history, but because it was for children he renders it more dramatic and personal. From the opening pages, when he asks the children to imagine what it was like to live in Gaul, to the excitements of the States General, the history has life and unity. It has dated less than its illustrations. Unlike most books written at this time, by an old man for young people, these last histories can still be read with pleasure and profit.

These volumes provide a memorial to Guizot and to his family. French Protestants have a great sense of family as well as a cult of history. It was an important moment of the day when the grandchildren would crowd into Guizot's small study in the Val-Richer and together with their mothers would listen to these lessons on the history of France. They also provide a memorial to what was happening in France at the time of their publication. Throughout these pages is a patriotism which had not been necessary in earlier years. Guizot took every opportunity of insisting that he had faith in the power of the French nation. In the past, France had saved herself in many ways; she had known all sorts of rulers and all manner of calamities. The France which had risen superior to invasion and conquest, to the League and to the Fronde, would surely rise superior to whatever enemies presented themselves.

It is easy to point out the errors of an historian writing over a hundred years ago. The abbé Gorini went to some trouble in order to point out some of Guizot's misreadings of documents in so far as they concerned the Church.[1] Later on in the nineteenth century, historians such as Cheruel, Jaroslav Gall, Sir Charles Firth and S. R. Gardiner were able to clear up some of the difficulties surrounding Anglo-French negotiations during the Interregnum, and it was shown that Guizot had accepted the *Ambassades et Négociations de Monsieur le Comte d'Estrades*, published in Amsterdam in 1718, as genuine, when in fact it was apocryphal.[2] More recently it has been shown that Guizot had been given a misreading from the Dutch archives, and that Charles I in his speech from the scaffold did not, as recorded by Guizot, recommend that religion in England should be strengthened by taking the advice of 'Roman Catholic divines', but he had recommended the advice of 'the most pious theologians'.[3] It is easy now to indicate that allodial land was more frequently to be found at the

[1] *Abbé J.-M.-S. Gorini, Défense de l'Église contre les Erreurs Historiques de Mm. Guizot, Aug. et Am. Thierry, Michelet, Ampère, Quinet, Fauriel, Aimé-Martin*, etc., 4 vols., Paris 1869. Although Gorini claims to see many misinterpretations in Guizot, he often quotes him with approval.

[2] See particularly the *Revue Historique*, vol. iv, pp. 315, 321, and the *English Historical Review*, vol. xi, pp. 479-509.

[3] See the *Times Literary Supplement*, February 7th and March 16th, 1951.

time of feudal landholding than Guizot imagined, as it is to show that Guizot was confused about the names of Oliver Cromwell's children.

All historians have to suffer such rectifications. In fact, Guizot is less susceptible to revisions than many others, because of his more analytical approach. Even when his facts have been proved wrong, his conclusions are not necessarily mistaken. We can say of Guizot, as he said of Montesquieu, that often correct judgements were based on erroneous material. It is for this reason that Guizot's historical writings remain more impressive than those of Michelet, and it is surprising that the latter should often have been treated as if he were a more considerable historian. That this is done can probably be explained in political terms, since Michelet was an enthusiastic supporter of the Revolutions of 1830 and 1848 and has therefore been more sympathetically treated than Guizot. It can also be explained by the tendency shown by so many critics of taking writers at their own valuation, and Michelet certainly considered himself to be a better historian than Guizot. He believed that he had given history its real aim and purpose. Whereas Thierry had treated history as 'narrative', and Guizot had treated it as 'analysis', he, Michelet, had given it the name which would stay with it for all time, 'resurrection'.[1] Of the three, it was Michelet's conception which was soonest outmoded.

Although Michelet frequently made references to his own researches into archives and other primary sources, it appears that these were often exaggerated. A careful examination of a certain section of the *Histoire de France* has shown to what extent Michelet relied on secondary works,[2] and it seems likely that he was often in need of a guide. One has only to look at the early volumes of the *Histoire de France* to see how frequently, when he seeks to explain rather than to describe, he has drawn his inspiration from Guizot. His own comments on Guizot were unreliable. Sometimes he was simply jealous, and this jealousy was easily provoked since he was particularly susceptible to journalistic criticism; on one occasion in 1837 he was annoyed because a writer in the *Gazette de France* described Guizot as the prose of French history, and Michelet as the poetry.[3] On other occasions Michelet praised Guizot lavishly, but it is noticeable that he did so when Guizot was minister, and about the

[1] *Michelet, Le Peuple* (op. cit.), Introduction.
[2] See *Gustave Rudler, Michelet Historien de Jeanne d'Arc*, Paris 1925. Michelet made particular use of *L'Averdy, Le Proces de Jeanne*, Paris 1798, and *Lebrun de Charmettes, Histoire de Jeanne d'Arc*, Paris 1817.
[3] See *Sainte-Beuve, Correspondance Générale* (op. cit.), vol. ii, pp. 263-264. Michelet tried to persuade Sainte-Beuve to write an article in his favour, but on this occasion, as on others, Sainte-Beuve did nothing.

time when Guizot appointed him to the Sorbonne.[1] Later, especially after Michelet had been prevented from lecturing in January 1848, he could not find words to express all his dislike of his former colleague. As he despised Guizot's politics and his religion, so he claimed to despise his history, and as late as 1866 he wrote scornfully of the two dominant historical schools which had existed as 'la grisaille', the grey, dull school of Guizot, and 'l'enluminense', the colourful school of Prosper de Barante.[2] However, in another preface, written three years later, he was probably more honest when he recalled that in 1830 he had found only one really valuable work, 'un grand livre fort, systematique (Guizot)'.[3] It seems probable that Michelet, like many of his generation who were called upon to teach history without really knowing it, found Guizot's historical work both valuable and suggestive.

It is of course as a stylist that Michelet has been most appreciated. One could apply to much of his work the judgement that Gabriel Monod made of his 'Tableau de France', when he described it as a literary masterpiece rather than a work of science.[4] One would not make great claims for Guizot's literary style, although it is probably better than has been supposed. Sainte-Beuve had the idea, and as with many of his ideas he persisted with it rather too much, that Guizot only learnt to write as he gained experience in speaking in the Chamber. The fact is that many of the early pamphlets were extremely well written, whilst the early historical works had a clarity and a terseness which many other historians might envy. It is only occasionally that Guizot deliberately strives after effect. In the *Mémoires* there are a series of portraits, incisively drawn and strikingly presented. Lamartine, for example, is described as a problem. He is shown as having been born with all the talents as well as with all the advantages of family and situation. What is surprising is not that he should have experienced the reverses of both private and public fortune—'for who, in our days, is not fallen?' asks Guizot—but that Lamartine should be astonished and angered by this experience. How could a man who looked down upon events from such a great height be so affected by the accidents which happened to him? How could such a sagacious judge of men be so badly acquainted with himself? How could he abandon himself to such bitterness when he had enjoyed so many advantages both from heaven and the world? It seemed to

---

[1] *Oscar Haac, Les Principes Inspirateurs de Michelet*, Paris 1951, p. 175, makes this point. *Gabriel Monod, La Vie et la Pensée de Jules Michelet*, Paris 1923, vol. i, pp. 265-266, remarks on the different ways in which Michelet refers to Guizot, according to whether his statements were public or in private.

[2] See the Preface to the 1866 edition of *L'Histoire Romaine*.

[3] Quoted in *Haac* (op. cit.), p. 173.

[4] *Monod* (op. cit.), vol. i, p. 303.

Guizot that within this nature there must have been much that was missing and a great want of harmony for such things to happen, and Guizot concludes the portrait with these words: '. . . il m'apparaît comme un bel arbre couvert de fleurs, sans fruits qui mûrissent et sans racines qui tiennent; c'est un grand esprit qui passe et repasse incessamment des régions de la lumière dans celles des nuages et qui entrevoit à chaque pas la vérité sans jamais s'y fixer; un coeur ouvert à toutes les sympathies généreuses, et en qui dominent pourtant les préoccupations les plus personnelles'.[1] This is fine writing. It is acute in its perception, malicious in its indulgence and all the more dramatic since the reader is aware of the underlying contrast between Lamartine and Guizot himself. The qualities that Lamartine supposedly lacks are the qualities which Guizot supposedly possesses.

Sometimes Guizot produces sentences which are pointedly direct. Marshal Lobau is described as a worthy representative of the old warriors, 'avec son rude visage, sa gravité brusque, sa parole brève, comme s'il eût été pressé de ne plus parler'.[2] Marshal Soult, without any established political ideas, without a decided party and without permanent adherents, is described as thinking himself entitled to dispense with such possessions, and Guizot remarks on 'cette aptitude volontaire à une sorte de polygamie politique'.[3] Sometimes Guizot writes with sympathy and imagination, as when, in the concluding volume of *Richard Cromwell*, after describing the solemnity and joviality of the Restoration, he goes on to describe some of the apprehensions that certain people felt lest the two sons of Charles I would adopt the ideas and habits of continental royalty. Such fears were not confined to those at court. 'Loin de la cour, dans les villes au sein d'une bourgeoisie laborieuse, dans les campagnes chez des familles de propriétaires, de fermiers, de laboureurs, se réfugièrent le protestantisme ardent et rigide, les moeurs sévères, et ce rude esprit de liberté qui ne s'inquiète ni des obstacles, ni des conséquences, endurcit les hommes pour eux-mêmes comme envers leurs ennemis, et leur fait dédaigner les maux qu'ils subissent ou qu'ils infligent, pourvu qu'ils accomplissent leur devoir et satisfassent leur passion en maintenant leur droit. La restauration laissait à peine entrevoir ses tendances, et déjà les Puritains se raidissaient contre elle, méprisés

[1] *Mémoires*, vol. iv, pp. 289-290: '. . . he appears to me like a fine tree, covered with flowers, which neither bears fruit nor takes root, he is a great mind, moving unceasingly backwards and forwards from the realms of light to the realms of cloud, and who is for ever catching glimpses of the truth without ever accepting it; his heart is open to every generous movement, and yet it is dominated by the most personal preoccupations'.
[2] Ibid., vol. ii, p. 346: '. . . with his rough features, blunt solemnity and laconic speech, as if he were in a hurry to be silent'.
[3] Ibid., p. 359: 'this wilful aptitude for a species of polygamy in politics'.

HISTORY

en attendant qu'ils fussent proscrits, mais passionnément dévoués, n'importe à quels risques et avec quelle issue, au service de leur foi et de leur cause; sectaires farouches et souvent factieux, mais défenseurs et martyrs indomptables de la religion protestante, de l'austérité morale et des libertés de leur pays.'[1]

Thus although Guizot's style is without the enthusiasm and lyricism of Michelet's writing, it should not be neglected. It would be easy to continue contrasting Guizot and Michelet, in their methods and ideas, and weighing up their respective qualities and defects. There were bound to be certain points of contact between two historians who lived contemporaneously and whose activities at times paralleled each other; for example, when Guizot was lecturing on civilization at the Sorbonne, Michelet was lecturing on philosophy and history at the École Normale. But there was necessarily a great difference between the work of a man like Guizot, who pursued his different careers with a placid inflexibility, and a man like Michelet, perpetually under the influence of troubled emotions or bitter uncertainties. Unlike Guizot, Michelet sought in his historical and literary works to resolve his intensely personal problems, some would call them obsessions. However, it is more profitable to confine comparisons to two aspects and to note one important similarity and one revealing difference. Both produced history which was 'engagée'; whereas Michelet was forever seeking after what one conveniently calls a philosophy of history, Guizot, as an historian, had no such preoccupation.

'L'histoire engagée' is not necessarily polemical; it does not have to be the type of history that Macaulay was then writing, partisan history written by a party man. History is 'engagée' when it has a function to perform in contemporary society, when it is presented as something which is vital, rather than as a collection of isolated bits of erudition. Michelet affected to despise those of his colleagues at the

---

[1] *Histoire du Protectorat de Richard Cromwell* (op. cit.), vol. ii, pp. 264-265: 'Far from the court, amongst the industrious bourgeoisie in the towns and amongst the families of landowners, farmers and labourers in the country districts, the zealous and rigid Protestantism of the nation now took refuge. With it went its severe strictness of manners and a stern spirit of liberty which cares neither for obstacles nor consequences, which hardens men towards themselves and towards their enemies, and which leads them to disdain the evils suffered or inflicted provided they can perform their duty and satisfy their zeal by maintaining their rights. Scarcely had the Restoration given but a glimpse of its tendencies, than the Puritans were already preparing to withstand it, despised as they were and proscribed as they were to be, but earnestly devoted, no matter what the risk or what the result, to the service of their faith and of their cause; unyielding and frequently factious sectaries, but indomitable defenders, even to martyrdom, of the Protestant religion, the moral austerity, and the liberties of their country.'

373

Collège de France who thought of their subjects only in terms of criticism or learning. He wanted to draw from history conclusions which he could amplify in his lectures and with which he could influence the minds and actions of younger generations. Guizot believed that a knowledge of history was not only desirable in so far as it gratified man's imagination and his desire for knowledge, but he believed that society which was well instructed in history would have a more wholesome and equitable judgement of its affairs.[1] For both men, the more scientific and accurate the history, then the greater would be its predicant power.

The nineteenth century was a great age for the philosophy of history. Self-assured and speculative, it was never hesitant in producing explanations of humanity and of man's world; many thinkers believed that they could discover various laws governing the universe and that the universe was moving towards an ultimately predictable future. Michelet was one of the more uncertain giants of speculation; although his thought contains much that is contradictory, vague and egotistical, nevertheless he was perpetually trying to find a key which would fit all historical locks. Ordinary analysis (such as practised by Guizot) was inappropriate, because history was concerned with something alive. Philosophy and psychology, intuition and emotion were all part of the historian's attempt to understand mankind in the past and to visualize humanity in the future. Sainte-Beuve criticized the *Introduction à l'Histoire Universelle*, where the influence of Vico was strong, because Michelet was too preoccupied with the struggle of liberty and fatality[2]; although the influence of Vico was to become less, and although Michelet was to conceal his preoccupations behind his literary agility, he remained a philosophical 'littérateur' who once said that the method was everything, the subject only secondary.[3]

Guizot tended to hold aloof from this hankering after grandoise abstractions. Like most professional historians he was more interested in the problem he was studying than in the method used. He philosophized about history rather than produced a philosophy of history, and although his lectures on civilization were considered to be a suitable prelude to such a philosophy, Guizot himself refused to impose metaphysical analysis on to his historical researches.[4] Just as a colleague such as Jouffroy found that thinkers like Vico and Herder

---

[1] *Mémoires*, vol. iii, p. 171.

[2] Sainte-Beuve: Michelet, May 1st, 1831, *Correspondance Générale* (op. cit.), vol. i, p. 232.

[3] *Michelet, Journal*, vol. i (op. cit.), p. 488.

[4] *Amadée Duquesnil, Du Travail Intellectual en France*, vol. ii, p. 232, quoted in *Henri Tronchon, La Fortune Intellectuelle de Herder en France*, Paris 1920, p. 463. Tronchon's book, pp. 430-466, is a discussion of Guizot's refusal to follow Herder in his philosophical approach to history.

were mutually exclusive, the one ignoring the force of nature, the other neglecting the rôle of man,[1] so Guizot refused to be exclusive. He believed in Providence, he believed in the supernatural; he likened man to an artisan working on parts of a vast machine which he did not know or understand. Yet this is not a Providential view of history in the sense of those who believe that God exercises a continual supervision over mankind and intervenes directly in human affairs in ways which are not always comprehensible. There is some-thing in the suggestion that Guizot's reference to Providence in his historical works is little more than a formality.[2] He refused to annex history to a metaphysical system, or to resuscitate the theological historicism that had fallen from favour in the eighteenth century. He believed that essentially it was men who made history. But this did not mean that history was essentially unpredictable or fortuitous. Guizot would never have agreed with those who say that the greatest law of history is its unpredictability. There are moments when individuals can take charge, but these moments are determined by the prevailing conditions. Had William of Orange taken the offensive twenty years earlier, he would simply have perished. Like Sir Edward Grey, Guizot probably thought that in great affairs there is more in the minds of the events than in the minds of the chief actors. But one had to study both the events and the actors in order to understand the one or the other. Different societies, different conditions, different men are the elements which have to be analysed and appreciated. History, for Guizot, is an experimental science.

The only criterion of judgement, outside and beyond the historical process, which Guizot uses is his assumption that there were certain characteristics of human nature which are universally shared. Like Reid, the Scottish philosopher of common sense, whose work was popularized in France by Royer-Collard, he was convinced that in all men's thinking and knowing there were certain general truths which have an unquestionable validity. Some of these have already been discussed. He believed, for example, that men had a natural desire to own property, a natural tendency to look for peace and security, a natural refusal to distinguish the rule of force from the rule of law and so on. The truth of these first principles could not be proved; they were part of the general furniture of the mind, and Guizot accepted them because he thought that everyone believed them. Further than this in philosophical reflection he was not pre-pared to go. In 1827 he wrote to Edgar Quinet about the French edition of Herder, and he said: 'It seems to me that the philosophy of

---

[1] *Le Globe*, May 17th, 1827.
[2] This is suggested in an essay on Guizot's historical works by *Ruth Keiser*, *Guizot als Historiker*, Saint Louis 1925.

history is now in that condition where philosophy itself remained for a long time; men begin dimly to perceive it in its august immensity; they don't yet see it surely and clearly; it is a matter of religion, not yet a matter of science.'[1] Guizot remained convinced of this truth. When he wanted to pursue philosophical questions further he chose to do this as a writer on religious subjects and as a member of an organized Church. Although his religious insight was in many ways socio-historical, it is within the framework of French Protestantism rather than as a French historian that this final phase of his activity should be analysed.

[1] Guizot: Quinet, May 9th, 1827, *Papiers Quinet*. Bibliothèque Nationale, Paris. Nouvelles acquisitions françaises 20789.

8

PROTESTANTISM

Ideas only shall be my enemies.
*Méditations sur l'essence
de la Religion Chrétienne*

G UIZOT's Protestantism cannot be ignored. Whilst there were some French Protestants, such as the Jacobin Joseph Cambon, whose biographers have failed to notice their religion, this could never happen to Guizot. Not only did Church affairs occupy his attention, but a preoccupation with the principles of Christian belief coloured all his thinking. His religion was a private affair, a family cult, but it was also a weapon with which to attack the enemies both of revolution and reaction. Born in Nîmes, yet living for many years in Normandy, he combined the proud defiance of the Cévennes tradition with the adaptability of a bourgeois Norman Protestantism which had little taste for martyrdom. Had Guizot lived a few years longer he would have found himself denounced in the xenophobic mythology of 'le péril Protestant'. As it was, his religious beliefs placed him at the centre of controversy and dispute. This was particularly true during the 1860s and 1870s.

The 1860s saw a great deal of religious and theological d' cussion. If one is to judge by the number of books produced and by the controversy which surrounded many of them, then this was a great religious age in several European countries. In England a book of essays, written mainly by clergymen, was published in 1860. *Essays and Reviews*, as it was called, set out to consider the Bible in the light of new scientific criticism and to emphasize the importance of Christianity as a way of life. The seven authors of this collection soon found that they had provoked a considerable Anglican crisis, and the numerous editions of their book began to reverberate through some of the most respected English institutions, *The Times* and the Bishops' Bench, Convocation, the Court of Arches and the Privy Council. They inspired innumerable replies, such as *Aids to Faith, Replies to 'Essays and Reviews'* and the series *Tracts for Priests and People*, all of which were published in 1861. Yet the 'Septem Contra Christum' were not unique; there were other publications and other controversies. In 1861 Wordsworth published his highly orthodox *New Testament of Our Lord and Saviour Jesus Christ in the Original Greek*, and in 1862 J. W. Colenso, the Bishop of Natal, produced the first part of his critical study of the Pentateuch. In 1863 many of the new interpretations of Biblical scholarship were for the first time put into a form which was certain of widespread circulation in William Smith's three-volume *Dictionary of the Bible*. The following year saw Newman's *Apologia pro Vita Sua*. In 1865 Lecky published his *History of the Rise and Influence of the Spirit of Rationalism in Europe* and Sir John Seeley published anonymously his life of Christ, *Ecce Homo*. Many more examples could be given to explain the remark made by A. P. Stanley, the Dean of Westminster (whose own works greatly increased understanding of the Eastern Church and of the Jewish people), that since the time of the Reformation there had never been so many symptoms of theological change.[1]

In Germany in the 1860s many of the leading exponents of the critical approach to Biblical and religious studies were still writing and teaching. Bruno Bauer was continuing his study of the Pauline Epistles; David Friedrich Strauss, whose *Life of Jesus* had been one of the most important influences of the century, published in 1860 an edition of Ulrich von Hutten's *Dialogues*, and in 1864 he produced a second and revised edition of *Das Leben Jesu* (the first edition was dated 1835). Daniel Schenkel, Weizsäcker, Holtzmann and Theodore Keim all produced, during the 1860s, important work on the Scriptures and on the history of Christ. Döllinger, in 1861, published his study of the Papacy and the temporal power, *The Church and the Churches*, and in 1864, the important Protestant theologian Albert Ritsch began his teaching at Göttingen.

In France, the outstanding religious publication was Ernest Renan's *Vie de Jésus*, which first appeared in June 1863. This sold forty thousand copies within two months and it ran to thirteen editions within four years. Coming after a number of essays and a translation of the Book of Job, and preceding his study of the Acts (*Les Apôtres*), which was published the following year, it might be thought that Renan's attack upon the supernatural and upon the idea of revelation would have exhausted the possibilities of sensation

[1] *Dean Stanley*, 'Theology of the Nineteenth Century', *Fraser's Review*, February 1865, p. 252.

in religious works. But shortly before Christmas 1863 the Abbé Michon produced a novel, *Le Maudit*, to be followed shortly afterwards by a sequel, *La Religieuse*, and then by a series of similar works. It may have been that the anonymity of *Le Maudit* increased the scandal since many distinguished men, including Renan, were rumoured to be the author. At all events, this novel of clerical life, which consisted of a bitter attack on the Jesuits and the allegation that Christianity was being stifled by the swaddling clothes of medieval Catholicism, was denounced from all the pulpits of France. One bishop threatened to suspend any of his clergy who read it and a Cardinal-Archbishop said in the Senate that he regarded it as one of the worst scandals of the age. Other publications were perhaps less sensational but there were many which were thought to be important. Montalembert dealt with the question of Church and state in his *L'Église Libre dans l'État Libre* (1863), and Veuillot was concerned with the same subject in *L'Illusion Libérale* (1865). Michelet's *La Bible de l'Humanité* (1863) was an unimpressive attempt to write about religious (or semi-religious) subjects, whilst Albert Réville's *Études Critiques sur l'Évangile de Saint Matthieu* (1862), Timothée Colani's *Jésus-Christ et les croyances messianiques de son temps* (1864) and Edmond de Pressensé's *Jésus-Christ, Son Temps, Sa Vie, Son Œuvre* (1865) were important and controversial works of scholarship.

This list could be extended to other countries; it could also be extended so as to include writers such as the French Jewish scholar Salvator, or philosophers such as Littré, Vacherot or Taine, scientists such as Claude Bernard or Berthollet (or for that matter, such as Darwin, Huxley or Owen), all of whom produced work which had important effects on religious thought. It was clearly an age of religious preoccupation and it was typical of Guizot that he too should have joined in this spate of publication. He had republished in 1854 some of his earlier articles (*Méditations et Études Morales*), and in the 1860s he published a series of religious works. *L'Église et la Société Chrétiennes en 1861* (1861) was followed by the three volumes of Méditations, *Méditations sur l'Essence de la Religion Chrétienne* (1864), *Méditations sur l'État Actuel de la Religion Chrétienne* (1866), and *Méditations sur la Religion Chrétienne dans ses Rapports avec l'État Actuel des Sociétés et des Esprits* (1868). Finally in 1873 he started the publication of *Les Vie de Quatre Grands Chrétiens*, with his studies of Saint Louis and Calvin, but he never completed this series, as intended, with studies of St. Vincent de Paul and Duplessis-Mornay.

This final venture was of course in the line of Guizot's earlier work as a historian, but in the *Méditations* he is writing about doctrine and belief. That is to say that he is concerned with the study of God and of other things in relation to God. This is theology, and Guizot was therefore obliged to make the transition from theology to history. This is by no means easy, since the theologian's task is to talk about God whilst the historian's is to talk about individual men or about society. The theologian is concerned with something which he probably regards as being perfect and infinite; the historian is concerned with something which is necessarily finite and always imperfect. The theologian thinks of the deeper levels of personal life which demand a particular apprehension, whilst the historian thinks of man's evolution primarily as steps towards the mastery of physical environment. During the nineteenth century, even for those who regarded theology as a science, it was often a very limited science, dredging amongst the folk-lore of Judaism for the residue of revealed religious truth, whilst for others, theology was not at all a science.[1] It is evident then that the task of the theologian is very different from that of the historian, even from the historian of ideas. Lecky compared the two in 1865, writing that the theologian confines his attention to the truth or falsehood of particular doctrines, confining his attention to the arguments upon which they rest, whilst the historian has to try and explain why those doctrines rose or fell. 'The first is restricted to a single department of mental phenomena, and to those logical connexions which determine the opinions of the severe reasoner; the second is obliged to take a wide survey of the intellectual influence of the period he is describing and to trace that connexion of congruity which has a much greater influence upon the sequence of opinions than logical arguments.'[2] It would seem, therefore, that Guizot's move from historical studies to theological implied many difficulties.

One can of course argue that Guizot should no more be called a theologian on the strength of a few religious works than one would attribute this title to Disraeli on the strength of his Oxford speech of November 25th, 1864, when he proclaimed his distrust of the scientists and gave warning of what would happen if religion was abandoned. It is true too that Guizot showed some unfamiliarity with theological weapons and that he possessed few of the particular skills and techniques of the theologian. His original project was to write four volumes of *Méditations*, but he never completed the series, since he omitted the volume of criticism and exegesis. His son Guillaume advised him not to venture on to a terrain where he was at a disadvantage, 'où il n'était pas chez lui', since he knew no

[1] H. L. Mansel, *The Limits of Religious Thought*, 1858, p. 257.
[2] W. E. H. Lecky, *History of the Rise and Influence of the Spirit of Rationalism in Europe*, 1865, vol. i, p. x.

Hebrew and since his Greek was not adequate to the specialized knowledge which he would have required.[1]

However, whilst deprecating the theological knowledge of Guizot, it is necessary to remember that the general standard of theology was not high. Religious controversy was vigorous, but it was not particularly learned or relevant. It used to be said that England had a Church but no theology, whilst Germany had a theology but no Church. The quarrels which surrounded *Essays and Reviews* in England showed how unfamiliar the general public was with many religious questions. Speculation concerning the authorship of the Book of Zachariah or the authorship of the Epistle to the Hebrews was in fact long-standing, but many English clerics and scholars behaved as if these questions had just been invented. Newman knew no German and it has often been noticed that his religious evolution took place entirely within the framework of Anglicanism.[2] There were many doubts about Pusey's scholarship, and Jowett's work on the Epistles of St. Paul was the only English exegetical work to have any continental reputation. Even in Germany, the home of theological rationalism, conservative orthodoxy and pietism made great strides after 1848, so that theology began to lose its boldness and science and started to degenerate into the technical exposition of established systems. Ferdinand Christian Baur, the creator of the Tübingen school of theology who died in 1860, and Strauss both lamented the isolation of their old age, the loss of their early associates, the disappearance of their audiences. Strauss in particular, who said that his *Life of Jesus* had made the path of his life lonely, regretted that the teachers of religion and morality in the 1860s refused to consider the real issues either of their subjects or of their consciences. He believed that from the beginning of their career they had bound themselves to only one principle, the extinction within themselves of any sense of truth.[3]

Yet if this was the state of religious studies in England and in Germany, one must recognize that it was even worse in France. The number of publications and the violence of controversy did not imply any high level of knowledge or understanding. Edouard Reuss, who started to teach theology in Strasbourg from 1828 onwards, described France in 1847 as being without any Biblical science whatsoever.[4]

[1] Guillaume Guizot: Jules Simon, October 21st, 1883, *Papiers Simon, Archives Nationales,* 87 A.P. 3. Guillaume, who had written a book on Menander before his twenty-first birthday, helped his father with textual matters, particularly in the first volume of *Méditations.*

[2] *A. O. J. Cockshutt, Anglican Attitudes,* 1958, p. 9.

[3] See the foreword to *Gespriche von Ulrich von Hutten,* Leipzig 1860.

[4] *A. Causse, La Bible de Reuss et la Renaissance des études d'histoire religieuse en France,* Paris 1928, p. 4, p. 9.

Renan, writing in 1849, said that whilst a mass of learned philologists in Germany had completely transformed Biblical exegesis, in France no one knew the first word of their works. Renan thought that France was the most orthodox country in the world because it was the least religious. The nineteenth century was so far removed from religion that it could not even give birth to a heresy.[1] A modern scholar has said that Strauss's *Life of Jesus*, which was translated into French by Littré, failed to exercise any influence upon French theology or literature and Strauss was one of the German thinkers who remained absolutely foreign and unintelligible to the French mind.[2]

The very nature of Renan's own work and success seems to confirm these judgements. *La Vie de Jésus* and *Les Apôtres* enthralled a public which was ignorant about the subject. A dramatic portrait of Christ, vivid descriptions of the Galilaean scenery and colourful speculations about human behaviour were presented to readers who were very imperfectly acquainted with the New Testament. So far as the author was concerned, in spite of his excursions into the labyrinths of the Talmud and in spite of his long and exhaustive critical surveys, Renan's approach was imaginative and literary rather than scholarly. It was even suggested, in some circles, that Renan was a sort of Rip Van Winkle who had slept through the strife of the preceding thirty years and had reproduced the theories of outmoded scholars such as Paulus (a Heidelberg Professor who had died in 1851). Renan had a most unscholarly appreciation of his own achievement, and to the end of his life he remained convinced that he, and he alone, of all the writers of the nineteenth century had been able to appreciate the real person of Christ.

Before Renan's success, Döllinger had commented on the poor quality of French theological work. He contrasted the existence of a vigorous priesthood and a vigorous laity which was alert to defend the Church with the absence of French theologians and the non-existence of any French school of theology. The seminaries were merely pastoral or educational establishments, and could not be compared to an institute of scientific theology.[3] The more one examines French religious history in this period, the more one finds repeated instances of belief and unbelief being sterile and unthinking, the more examples one finds of Catholic priests without breviaries or of Protestants without Bibles. There was no dictionary of the Bible

[1] *Ernest Renan*, 'L'Avenir de la Science' in *Œuvres* (op. cit.), vol. iii, p. 964, pp. 810-811. Some of these remarks were published in *La Liberté de Penser*, July 15th, 1849.

[2] *Albert Schweitzer, The Quest of the Historical Jesus* (English edition), 1910, p. 108 n. 5.

[3] *Döllinger, The Past and Present of Catholic Theology*, quoted *Quarterly Review*, October 1865, pp. 521-522.

which Frenchmen could use, and works such as the Abbé Migne's *Encyclopédie Théologique*, which spread into many volumes published over many years, revealed little or nothing about the advances in learning. All these considerations suggest that in practice French theology remained amateurish, and therefore the gap between Guizot's historical studies and his religious and theological writings was not so very great.

For Guizot, too, there is a constant connection between aspects of his religious thought and his other intellectual activities. As has been shown, the conception of sovereignty is the key to his political thought, and the starting-point for this theory was the individual's search for truth and justice, that is to say his search for God. As has been shown too, much of his historical thought turned around a conception of personal behaviour, and depended upon an interpretation of human nature, its tendencies and aspirations. These 'moral probabilities', as he called them, can be said to have revealed a self-centredness which is probably a disadvantage to the objective historian. Indeed, Professor Toynbee has described 'self-centredness' as a sin, and he has argued that the historian, by his very nature, is bound to try and overcome it.[1] Yet one can also argue that self-centredness is natural in religious or theological studies, since however one may try to enlarge the nature of religious experience, yet it remains essentially individual. Guizot was brought up in an atmosphere of strict Protestantism, both in France and in Geneva, and although he passed through a period of unbelief during his early years in Paris, when he first became acquainted with Pauline de Meulan and when they edited the *Annales de l'Éducation*, he was never an atheist. He never abandoned the principle that the idea of God completed the nature of man. He wrote in 1864 that he had felt the weight of objections and known the anxieties of doubt concerning both Christianity as a system and each one of its doctrines. But these doubts had passed away and he found his convictions reinforced.[2]

It does not seem that the doubts could have been very persistent. He reconciled Pauline de Meulan to some form of Protestantism rather than remaining attracted to her Deism, and when she died in 1827 she was buried in the cemetery of Père-Lachaise with an address given by Pastor Juillerat. Guizot was always 'un homme du monde' as his Protestant friend and biographer Pédézert pointed out, but he was frequently to be seen in the various Protestant temples of the

---

[1] *Arnold Toynbee, An Historian's Approach to Religion*, 1956.
[2] *Méditations sur l'Essence de la Religion Chrétienne* (op. cit.), p. xviii. For Guizot's short-lived association with Freemasonry in 1805 or 1806, see *H. Dubief*, Le Jeune Guizot et la Franc-Maçonnerie, *Revue d'Histoire Moderne et Contemporaine*, April-June 1962, pp. 139-145.

capital. It seems that he sometimes persuaded the Princess de Lieven to attend Protestant services.[1] When he was minister for foreign affairs, a Protestant pastor used to visit the Ministry each day in order to instruct Guizot's two daughters, and many years later Sainte-Beuve recalled the effect of seeing Guizot's mother in the ministerial salons, 'cette mère du temps des Cévennes', who brought back the memories and the virtues of the persecution and of the desert.[2] It is true that for a long time there was some uncertainty about Guizot's attitude to the 'Réveil', the religious revival of the post-1815 period. But these doubts were removed in 1838 (which was an important year for Guizot's active preoccupation with religious subjects) when he spoke to the *Société Biblique* in Paris. This address caused something of a sensation, and when Guizot said that religion was more than a discipline and was rather a life within man, when he praised enthusiasm and fervour, when he said that faith had not only to enlighten the soul but had to warm it, even to enflame it, then some people compared him to Vinet, the Swiss evangelist and Church leader.[3]

Therefore Guizot had always been conscious of religion and concerned with it, and one can trace a constant interest in religious subjects, from his review of Paley in *Le Publiciste* and his criticisms of Gibbon for not paying enough attention to the *Acts of the Apostles* and to patristic writings, down to his rôle in the Protestant Synod of 1872 and his book on Calvin in 1873.[4] It was a superficial view of his religious opponents to speak of his 'cold impassiveness which reveals none of the Reformed Christian's convictions'.[5]

Guizot liked nothing better than to describe a situation in broad and general terms, seizing the outstanding and distinguishing characteristics of a period. He saw each great epoch in history as being devoted, if not exclusively at least primarily, to one particular problem. The sixteenth century was concerned with the question of religious unity or reformation; the seventeenth century with monarchy and authority; the eighteenth century with philosophical and political liberty. These were, for Guizot, clear and limited questions. But the nineteenth century was plunged into a confusion of problems

---

[1] *Jules Pédézert, Souvenirs et Études*, Paris 1888, p. 231; *Roger-Armand Weigert*, 'Notes du pasteur Rodolphe Cuvier', *Bulletin de la Société d'Histoire du Protestantisme Français* (B.S.H.P.F.), 1948.

[2] *Sainte-Beuve, Nouveaux Lundis* (op. cit.), vol. ix, pp. 96-97.

[3] *Discours de M. Guizot à la Société Biblique Protestante*, Paris 1838; *J. Pédézert, Cinquante ans de Souvenirs Religieux et Ecclésiastiques*, Paris 1896, pp. 50-51.

[4] The review of Paley is reprinted in *Le Temps Passé*, Paris 1887, vol. ii, pp. 211 ff.

[5] *Le Lien*, December 4th, 1841.

and ideas. Wherever he looked, whether to relations between states or relations between peoples, whether to questions of political organizations, social conditions or religious beliefs, out of this labyrinth Guizot distinguished two outstanding characteristics, complexity and uncertainty. Therefore the nineteenth century was unlike any other. But if one looked more closely at France one could see some sort of a pattern emerging. One saw, according to Guizot, that from the beginning of the nineteenth century onwards, France had been impelled forwards by two contradictory forces. On the one hand there were what Guizot called the dangers of modern times, there was violence, revolution, adventure, socialism, materialism and incredulity. At the same time this evil genius in France was matched by a good genius, 'il y a aussi un bon vent qui souffle, un bon courant qui nous pousse', and France possessed a sense of legality, a desire for peace and for a sound economy, a sense of moderation, a sense of spiritual and Christian values which met and contrasted with the contrary dispositions. Modern French history, seen in this way, was simply the story of the struggle between these diverse tendencies. The problem therefore was, what was necessary, what was to be done, to ensure that the good tendency should triumph over the bad? Two things were required, according to Guizot, political liberty and Christianity.[1]

The mention of political liberty by someone writing in the 1860s makes one realize that writing on religious subjects during the reign of Napoleon III had a very particular significance. This in itself should reassure one that Guizot, by writing the *Méditations*, was not completely leaving his usual subjects. Prévost-Paradol, one of the most able writers and journalists of this period, remarked in 1868 that the Second Empire had accepted writing on religious subjects more readily than it had accepted writing on political subjects, and therefore, for a time, theology tended to take the place of politics. This observation was confirmed by the Catholic Falloux, as by the Protestant Pressensé.[2] Guizot undoubtedly joined in this oblique opposition to a government which he described as a mixture of dictatorship and republicanism, and through his consideration of religious and moral problems he was able to make allusions to political liberty. In this sense Guizot's religious writings are a prolongation of his former political activity. But one must not exaggerate this. It would probably be truer to say that there were two problems which preoccupied Guizot genuinely, and which he was anxious to consider for themselves and not as pretexts for political

[1] *Méditations sur la Religion Chrétienne dans ses rapports avec l'état actuel des Sociétés* . . . (op. cit.), Préface.
[2] *Pierre Guiral, Prévost-Paradol, 1829-1870*, Paris 1955, p. 191 and note 220.

insinuations. The first was the general problem of religion and liberty: the second was the particular state of French Protestantism.

The problem of religion and liberty was a problem of the nineteenth century as a whole. 'Religious liberty, that is to say the liberty to believe, to believe variously, or not to believe at all, is perhaps still imperfectly accepted and guaranteed in certain countries; but it is clear that it will become more general, and that before long it will be the common law of the civilized world. One of the causes which render this fact so important is that religious liberty does not stand alone. It is only a unit in the great intellectual and social revolution which after centuries of preparation and fermentation has come about and is accomplishing itself in our days. Science, democracy and freedom, these are the essential characteristics and the inevitable tendencies of this revolution. These new powers may fall into enormous errors and commit enormous faults . . . but they have definitely established themselves in modern society.'[1] In these conditions Christianity had lost its position of privilege and dominance, it had moved to a position of common right. It had therefore to adapt itself to a new situation and it was with this adaptation that Guizot, like Montalembert, was concerned. It was in this sense that he once said that it was the position of the Catholic Church which preoccupied him most.[2]

At first sight it does not seem that there should be a particular problem for Protestantism in France. The nineteenth century was a success story so far as it was concerned. After the persecutions of the Ancien Régime, the revolutionary attacks on religion and the persecution to which many Protestants were subjected immediately after 1815, particularly in Nîmes and in Uzès, there had been a steady Protestant ascension. Protestants, who but a lifetime previously had been unable to worship, became prominent and important members of society. Apart from Guizot himself, there were members of the Chambers such as Jaucourt, Boissy d'Anglas, Pelet de la Lozère, Martel, Elie Gauthier or de la Farelle; there were bankers and businessmen such as Benjamin and François Delessert, Jules Mallet, Bartholdi, Charles Vernes, Hottinguer, Victor de Pressensé; there were writers and intellectuals such as Benjamin Constant, Auguste de Staël, and Guizot's old employer, Stapfer; a distinguished 'retraité' such as the Admiral Ver-Huell, a great scholar like Cuvier, an orientalist like Kieffer, a public figure like Agénor de Gasparin, even a grand aristocrat, the Marquis Henri-Philippe-de Ségur-Bouzely,

[1] *Méditations sur l'Essence de la Religion Chrétienne* (op. cit.), p. iii.
[2] Guizot: Madame Lenormant, November 8th, 1852, *Lettres à M. et Mme. Lenormant* (op. cit.), p. 75.

all these were Protestants. One has to remember, too, the fame in French society of a number of 'grandes dames chrétiennes', such as the Duchesse de Broglie (*née* de Staël), Madame Jules Mallet (*née* Oberkampf), Madame Salvandy (*née* Feray) and Mlle de Chabaud-Latour. A climax in this unhesitating Protestant ascension seemed to be reached under the July Monarchy when the heir to the throne married a Protestant, Helen of Mecklenburg; the new Duchess of Orleans was neither converted to Catholicism nor under the obligation to conceal her religion, she simply took her place in what has often been called 'le Réveil parisien'.

All sorts of Protestant societies were formed. In 1815 the *Société des traités religieux* was founded by the pastor Lissignol in Montpellier. *Sociétés Bibliques* were founded in Strasbourg, Mulhouse, Toulouse, Montauban and then, in 1818, in Paris itself. In 1822 the *Société des Missions Evangéliques* was founded and became the centre of Admiral Ver-Huell's work. In 1829 the *Société pour l'Encouragement de l'Instruction Primaire en France* was formed, in 1833 the *Société Évangelique de France*, in 1847 the *Société Centrale Protestante d'Évangelisation.* There were societies with purely local interests, concerned with the 'Protestants disseminés', Protestants who were scattered through the French countryside; there were organizations concerned with social work and relief amongst the poor, such as the *Société de prévoyance et de secours-mutuels de Paris*, founded by Clémentine Cuvier in 1825; there were associations of learning and erudition such as the *Société pour l'Histoire du Protestantisme Français*, founded in 1852 with Guizot as its first President. Everywhere, in every sort of religious, social or intellectual activity there were Protestant organizations, concerned with Sunday schools, prison reform, child labour, the care of old people, apprentices, holidays by the sea, training of teachers and so on. There was a Protestant press. The *Archives du Christianisme* (founded in 1818 by Juillerat and later directed by Frédéric Monod), *Le Semeur* (founded by Vinet in 1831), *L'Espérance* (financed by Benjamin Delessert, with a distinguished succession of directors, such as Napoléon Roussel, Pédézert and Grandpierre), *Le Lien* (which from 1841 to 1870 represented liberal Protestantism and was closely associated with the Coquerel family) and several others.

Many Protestant churches were built between 1820 and 1848, in Bordeaux, Orléans, Marseilles, Draguignan, Lyons and elsewhere. In the 1850s there were some 35 new Protestant temples opened. The architects of the new churches often constructed them in an austere style which made the work of their English contemporary Rickman seem needlessly ornate. A famous chapel, the 'Chapelle Taitbout', was opened in Paris in 1830, and quickly became one of the centres of Protestant, if not of Paris, society. Although the Duc de Broglie was a Catholic, he used often to attend these services, as did many other non-Protestants. Preachers came from England, Scotland and Germany, and found themselves speaking to densely packed audiences; hymns were written by supporters of the chapel and in 1834 a first collection, 'Chants Chrétiens', was published. There were of course other important Protestant churches and chapels in Paris. In 1844, for example, the Temple of Pentemont was acquired for Protestant worship, mainly thanks to Guizot's influence. French Protestantism in the provinces, particularly in the South, also had its churches and preachers with comparable moments of success. There were centres of the Protestant cult scattered throughout the countryside, in the homes of leading Protestants. The château of Broglie was one such centre. Of the many distinguished Protestants who visited Broglie, one of them, the Scottish divine Thomas Chalmers (who also preached at the Chapelle Taitbout), has told how family prayers were said in the Library, with the Duchess saying prayers and the Duke reading passages from the Bible.[1] In a similar way the Val-Richer, once Guizot was living there, became another Protestant centre. Both Broglie and the Val-Richer were in Lower Normandy, a part of France which had received a lot of attention from Methodists, such as William Mahy from Guernsey, Pierre Du Pontavice and Armand de Kerpezdrou, two converted Breton noblemen, and Pierre Le Sueur. Amongst the scattered and sparse congregations of these regions, the names of Broglie and the Val-Richer were, for a time at least, sources of encouragement and of pride.

This was the 'Réveil', one of the great moments of Protestant history. Protestants such as Pédézert, looking back on this period, recalled it as a movement of exhilaration and of joy; a coachman once remarked that the people whom he drove to the Chapelle Taitbout always seemed very gay. This was not a universal experience. The young Albert de Broglie was taken to the chapel by his mother, and he does not seem to have been conscious of much gaiety, as he recalls sermons which lasted for an hour and a half and hymns in bad verse, all taking place in a chapel which had no paintings, no decorations, no distractions.[2] At all events the 'Réveil' was for some, such as Adolphe Monod, a finer period even than the Reformation, and one of the reasons for its importance was that it revealed the definitive strength of French Protestantism. Estimates of the

---

[1] *The Rev. William Hanna, Memoirs of Dr. Chalmers*, 1849-1852, vol. iv, p. 53. Chalmers noticed that in the school at Broglie there were three pictures, one of Christ, one of Louis-Philippe and one of the Duc de Broglie. Beneath each picture was written 'Vive Jésus-Christ', 'Vive Louis-Philippe', 'Vive le Duc de Broglie'.

[2] See the *Revue des Deux Mondes*, January 1st, 1925, pp. 63-64.

Protestant population varied. Shortly after the Restoration there were said to be about a million Protestants known to the consistories and pastors, with perhaps half a million silent and scattered throughout France, in all between one and a half and two millions. A little later an English review put the figures much lower, referring to about one million (with 600,000 concentrated in 12 departments of the south and south-east). In 1851 Charles Read, who was in charge of the non-Catholic cults, published an estimate of one and a half million Protestants of the 'culte reformé' (Calvinist) and of the Augsburg Confession (Lutheran), distributed in 63 departments. Four of these departments had particularly heavy Protestant representation, the Gard, the Lozère, and the Upper and Lower Rhine departments. A few years later there were Protestants who were suggesting that all official figures were absurdly low, since there were many Protestants who did not declare their religion, either out of timidity or out of principle. They put the Protestant population at just over two millions.[1] However, there could be no doubt that the French Protestant population formed a large and important minority.

When one recalls these events and this history there would hardly seem to be a Protestant problem with which Guizot needed to concern himself. But apart from the success of the 'Réveil' there were other features. The persecution which followed the second Bourbon Restoration in 1815 had been fiercer and more widespread than many historians have supposed, and the bitterness aroused by these events did not easily disappear. Even under the July Monarchy there are many examples of Catholics showing decided hostility towards Protestants, spreading rumours of a Protestant plot, questioning the patriotism of these un-French elements. Guizot himself acquired some of his unpopularity because of his Protestantism. His educational policy was said to be tainted with the religion of the 'Vicaire Savoyard', and the bishop of Chartres wrote in 1836, 'I do not know Monsieur Guizot at all. I know, like everyone else, that he has written a great deal, that he has been a Professor and that he has frequently spoken with great distinction at the legislative tribune. But he is a Protestant, and it is quite natural that his works should be filled with the spirit of his religion.' For the bishop there was a danger that France would move towards Protestantism, which to his mind was the equivalent of atheism.[2] The Duchess of Orleans was also cordially

¯ *Revue Protestante*, vol. ii, p. 252; *Fraser's Magazine*, November 1838, pp. 568-569; *Charles Read, Note de statistique administrative sur les cultes non-catholiques reconnus en France et en Allemagne*, Paris 1851; *Revue de Paris*, January 1st, 1857, pp. 337-355. For the early period one should consult the masterly thesis by Daniel Robert. *Les Églises Réformées en France*, Paris 1961.
² *Archives Nationales*, F¹⁹ 3969.

hated by certain Catholics, doubtless because she appeared openly in the temple at Billettes or in the Église de la Rédemption. It was not at all infrequent for the Catholic hierarchy to attack the Protestant societies, the social work of which might attract non-Protestants. In some regions of France people were so conscious of the differences between the religions that appointments to administrative posts had to be scrutinized from that point of view. On one occasion the Procureur-Général in Montpellier opposed the promotion of a man because he was Protestant. He claimed that in a part of France where the antagonism of the two religions was so pronounced this was sufficient reason for exclusion. A contrary example is to be found, a little later, in Nîmes, when it was pointed out that since the man who had held the post had been a Protestant, then it would be difficult to avoid appointing someone who was not a Protestant.[1] The rivalry of the religions was therefore still very marked.

The legal position of Protestants was not as assured as Article V of the Charter of 1830, stating that everyone had the right to profess his religion, led one to expect. Article 291 of the Code Civil gave discretionary power to the local authorities and to the administration by which they could prevent religious worship or ceremonies if they thought them dangerous or in any way harmful to the community. There grew up a number of 'causes célèbres' around Protestants and Protestant sects. In 1836, a Protestant minister called Oster was forbidden to hold his Sunday meetings in Metz. In 1837 an evangelist, Doine, was prevented from holding meetings in Sceaux. In 1843 an entire commune, Senneville, decided that as all the population was Protestant, then they had no use for their Catholic chapel, and they decided to use it as a Protestant temple. The prefect refused to accept this and used troops in order to drive the Protestants out of the chapel. In 1844 the mayor of another commune refused to allow Protestants to have a religious ceremony in the local cemetery, and he enforced his ruling with the 'gendarmerie'. In 1847 it was the baptists of the Aisne department who were in trouble, their arrests being ordered by the mayor of Servais. These anomalies of the law became more frequent under the Second Empire, when religious gatherings were treated in the same way as political meetings and when they suffered particularly from the campaign against socialism. In the Haute-Vienne the Procureur-Général of Limoges denounced Protestants as socialists, saying that they taught their congregations to hate Catholic priests and to despise all authority.[2] This sort of denunciation was quite common and prominent Protestants, such

---

[1] M. Rousselet, *La Magistrature sous la Monarchie de Juillet*, Paris 1937, pp. 418-419.
[2] *Archives Nationales*, BB[30] 378.

as Guizot, were continually protesting against interference with the liberty of worship, and citing examples of prefects, mayors and other officials who were treating Protestants as if they were political agitators, who were claiming that they had to restrain Protestants 'in the interests of public morality', and who were closing Protestant schools.[1] *The Times* of London reported cases of 'a petty grinding persecution', with closed Protestant churches falling into decay, Catholics making exaggerated protests because a Protestant had 'violated' a Catholic cemetery, Protestant schoolmasters put to considerable hardships, and even, in the Haute-Vienne, of Protestants secretly assembling for worship in the forest, exactly as in the time of Louis XIV and his dragonnades.[2] French Protestants not only protested against these obstacles, by appealing to Imperial justice and by trying to enlist English support, but they also protested that they had no revolutionary or political intention. One group in Besançon protested that the conduct which they followed had been laid down by St. Peter with the words 'Submit yourselves to every ordinance of man for the Lord's sake'.[3]

Many more examples could be given. It is clear that French Protestants faced many difficulties, but the action of those Protestants from Besançon who found it necessary to protest that they were not instigators of political violence clearly indicates one of the major problems of the time, and indicates one of the issues which necessitated Guizot's intervention. Both inside and outside the Reformed religion there was considerable uncertainty as to the nature of Protestantism. Non-Protestants found it difficult to understand what followers of this religion stood for; Protestants found it difficult to agree amongst themselves. Frequently the difficulties with the administration arose over the various sects which accompanied the 'Réveil'. Quakers, Methodists, Baptists, Darbyistes, Mennonites, Moravians, Swedenborgians, Hinschistes and other heterodoxical establishments spread throughout France. Some of them, such as the Swedenborgians, had a very limited success, but others, such as the Methodists, were not only widespread but had a considerable influence, so that the term 'méthodiste' was used very loosely. Most of the large towns had some sort of dissident Church which was often

[1] See, for example, Conseil Central des Églises Réformées: Monsieur le Ministre, May 28th, 1853, *Archives de la Société d'Histoire du Protestantisme Français* (S.H.P.F.); *Rapport de la Société pour l'Encouragement de l'Instruction Primaire*, Paris 1860.
[2] *The Times*, January 2nd, 8th, 9th, 1858.
[3] Quoted in *Pierre Genevray*, 'L'État et le Protestantisme du Réveil . . .', *B.S.H.P.F.*, 1948, p. 137. One should not exaggerate either the extent or the seriousness of these troubles as some French Protestants have tended to do. They cannot be said to represent any consistent or uniform policy of persecution.

highly successful; the 'chapelle Taitbout' was an example of an independent foundation, and some of its congregation (such as the Duchesse de Broglie) used to attend it out of dissatisfaction with the more official services. Furthermore, as many Protestants were scattered through rural France in small groupings, they often practised a form of independence without necessarily declaring their adherence to any particular sect. In this practical independence local influences and rivalries could profit from flexible doctrines and an informal order of service so as to puzzle and alarm the administration. A note for the attention of the minister recalled that Napoléon Roussel, a pastor, had said that 'it is the principles of Protestantism which frighten authority, and this is not surprising since all liberties go together'.[1]

The absence of any agreed body of doctrine arose from the circumstances of Protestantism. It has been pointed out that the period from 1770 to 1820 represents a real break in the history of French Protestantism.[2] For more than a century the Protestants of France had been deprived of their theologians and reduced to the clandestinity of the desert. Their pastors were outlaws and vagabonds with prices on their heads, always on the move, as was Guizot's grandfather, with little opportunity for study. Their theology was almost non-existent. Their knowledge was often little more than a few memorized sermons and an occasional, isolated textbook of doctrine. One of them, Paul Rabaut, is said to have been a pastor for twenty years before he read Calvin's *Institutions*. Such pastors of the heroic period were men of faith and action; they were not scholars. They taught little more than Deism, morality and the cult of their martyrs. Obviously, their congregations were invariably even more ignorant. Sometimes they had no pastor, as they had no place of worship, and the old Huguenot prayer said, 'O Dieu nous sommes sans temple mais remplis ce lieu de ta présence. Nous sommes sans pasteurs mais sois toi-même notre pasteur.' In this way French Protestantism achieved greatness and heroism, but it became intellectually and theologically sterile. It was forced to turn abroad for its culture.

The inspiration that came from abroad was necessarily varied. Geneva, which was one of the areas where contact was easiest, was at the end of the eighteenth century and by the beginning of the nineteenth in a period of theological mediocrity. One of the men who broke away from this state of affairs, Ami Bost, explained that during the four years that he studied at the Academy of Geneva he was never once asked to open the Bible; and César Malan could not

[1] Note de M. Tardif, *Archives Nationales*, F[19] 10926.
[2] *Louis Dallière*, 'Le Protestantisme de nos jours et la doctrine', *Foi et Vie*, November 15th, 1930, pp. 1164 ff.

recall a single instruction concerning the divinity of Christ, the fall of man, or justification by faith.[1] Religion had become a formalism, teaching morality and avoiding devotion. It was in opposition to this, about 1810, that the Genevan 'Réveil' began; and before the Bourbon Restoration in France was more than a few years old, the Genevan dissidents, Bost, Neff, Pyt, Gonthier and their associates, began to appear in France. But at the same time other influences were arriving, notably the influence of two Scotsmen, Robert and James Haldane, and of an English Methodist Wilks. The first two were particularly important in influencing a group of young pastors, and the last named, through his relations with English societies, was able to provide funds which were not available from other sources.[2] Thus it was no unified theology that was brought into France. There were rather a series of controversies, and the only natural resources with which the French Protestants could meet and try to absorb these varied influences was their hatred of Catholicism and their cult of the martyrs. Such emotions served to complicate the issue still further.

There were countries where religious controversy took place within a body of established doctrines or within established ecclesiastical institutions. The authors of *Essays and Reviews*, for example, could complain of the shadows of the twelfth century lying across Protestantism, but they did so from within a broad and powerful organization, the very existence of which put a limit to religious dissidence. Some of these writers held important positions. Jowett and Williams were the ornaments of Oxford and Cambridge. Dr. Temple was Chaplain to the Queen, and others were destined for high office. But in France neither the liberals nor the orthodox enjoyed such security. It was difficult for Protestants to have much sense of coherence and it was difficult to place a limit on disagreement. It was for this reason that one of the constant features of French Protestantism was a move to define and to establish doctrine. And this movement was equally constantly faced by a contrary principle, claiming that Protestantism was by its very nature without doctrine. This was the dialogue into which Guizot intervened.

One of those who rejected a fixed and defined principle of faith was Athanase Coquerel the younger. One can understand the nature of his belief from this passage, which he inserted in his newspaper

[1] A. Bost, *Mémoires pouvant servir à l'histoire du Réveil des Églises Protestantes . . .*, Paris 1854-1855, vol. i, pp. 23-25; César Malan, *La Vie et les travaux de César Malan*, Geneva 1869.

[2] The influence of the Haldanes and of Wilks was stressed by two of Guizot's correspondents who had personal knowledge of this period. See Guillaume de Félice: Guizot, May 29th, 1865; Henri Lutteroth: Guizot, June 2nd, 1865, *Archives S.H.P.F.* For hostility to the Haldanes see the *Revue Protestante* for 1827 and 1828.

Le Lien. 'We believe that to stay immobile when everything around us is moving, and moving under God's impulse, to try in the nineteenth century to live the life of the sixteenth century, we believe that this is the denial of progress; it is to rise up against Providence, to reject its blessings and to misunderstand its teaching. In a word, it is to resist God. We can go further. We believe that the Christian religion, the Christian life, eternal life itself, are nothing but the highest form of progress, by which in this world and in eternity, we move towards God. . . .'[1] This view of Protestantism, as something which was restless and shifting, something which moved with the progress of the world, a series of aspirations rather than a set of beliefs, was offensive of Guizot. It seemed to him that it echoed some of the worst features of his times and reproduced the characteristics of France's evil genius. For Guizot the first condition for the healthy life of Protestantism was healthy doctrine. If the 'Réveil' was an achievement, it was not because a few men had had outstanding personal qualities. It was 'in the intrinsic and permanent values of the doctrines which they preached and not in themselves that they found their strength and their ascendancy'.[2]

Therefore it is doctrine which interests Guizot. In the two questions with which he is concerned, that of religion and liberty and that of the divisions of Protestantism, his writings seek to emphasize the principles of religious belief. It is in this way that he became, at least in some respects, a theologian. Perhaps one of the clearest indications of his attitude can be seen in his commentary on Seeley's *Ecce Homo.* This was a book which he obviously admired and which, because of its use of historical imagination, has some similarity with his own work. He introduced it to French readers and translated several of the passages. But he disapproved of the author's intention of studying the life of Christ without considering him as the creator of religion and of theology. The author had gone so far as to say that one could be a Christian without having any belief in Christ's theology,[3] but for Guizot this seemed to be a mutilation. There were questions concerning the nature of Christ, the nature of his divine and human attributes, the supernatural, the relations of God and nature, which could not be avoided.[4] In other words, whilst others hailed in *Ecce Homo* the moral approach to Christ, as distinct from the rational approach of Strauss or the imaginative approach of Renan, Guizot wanted the doctrinal approach.

[1] *Le Lien*, August 1st, 1853.
[2] *Méditations sur l'État Actuel de la Religion Chrétienne* (op. cit.), p. 144.
[3] *Ecce Homo* (4th edition), 1866, p. 79.
[4] *Méditations sur la Religion Chrétienne dans ses rapports avec l'État Actuel . . .* (op. cit.), pp. 227 ff.

One of the great problems for French Protestants has always been that of deciding upon their position in France. As a minority they could either affirm their position by emphasizing the differences between them and other Frenchmen, or they could hope to strengthen their position by stressing their resemblances to other Frenchmen. French Protestants have always showed considerable self-consciousness in this matter. Some have gone so far as to ask whether there is not a 'Protestant type', whereby one could deduce from a particular Frenchman's behaviour or character whether or not he is a Protestant. Others continually stress that there was never a Protestant political party in France, not even in the sixteenth century. There were some, like Agénor de Gasparin of the *Société des Intérêts du Protestantisme Français*, sometimes thought of as the Montalembert of the Protestants, who wanted to emphasize Protestant particularism in every way. He wanted Protestant schools, hospitals, prisons, and it was said of him that he would have liked to see Protestant regiments and warships. Even de Gasparin, however, must have found that some of the leaflets written by Protestants and circulating under the July Monarchy were too aggressive. 'Why does your Curé prevent you from reading the Bible?' was the title of one, and there were several others which attacked Catholicism, as 'La Religion d'Argent'. But Protestants such as Samuel Vincent, pastor at Nîmes, viewed things differently. He wanted his co-religionists to be mixed with the rest of the population. When they came out of their temples they were Frenchmen like everyone else. He believed that if, in their youth, they were separated into special schools, then two castes would grow up, a sacerdotal spirit would develop on each side, and mutual hatred would lead to further persecution and suffering.[1] It is noticeable that this latter attitude is often presented in an apologetic, even defensive, way. The varied accusations against Protestants have always left their mark, and if in the twentieth century André Siegried could warn his co-religionists that whilst the priest was part of the furniture of France, the pastor was not, then how much greater must have been the sentiment that they were different from other Frenchmen in the nineteenth century, when it was still remembered that during the revolutionary wars there had been some who had prayed:

O Dieu le fort, arbitre de la Guerre,
Fais triompher les armes de l'Angleterre.

It is difficult to decide why, amongst individuals, the one approach is preferred to the other. It may be that those Protestants who were part of the directing spheres of industry or business or of the

[1] *Samuel Vincent*, 'Sur l'état actuel de l'instruction publique parmi les Protestants Français', *Revue Protestante*, vol. i, pp. 97 ff.

administration were those who were most opposed to Protestantism shutting itself off in an autonomous world of its own, building a barrier of faith and human relations against a dynamic and progressive society. It may be that those who were worried at the political implications of a decline in religious and moral beliefs amongst the mass of the population thought that incredulity could only be fought by a united religious front. Or, if one believes that theology is a mere 'monument', a sign of an intellectual operation, explaining religion to possible converts,[1] then it is natural that some intellects wanted to see a large monument, appropriate to a nation rather than to a sect. All these possibilities apply to Guizot. He always tried to minimize the differences between the followers of his religion and other Frenchmen, and this is hardly surprising in a politician who wished to avoid appearing as the spokesman for only a sectarian minority. Furthermore, as a statesman who was above all preoccupied with the unity of France, he was anxious to reduce differences amongst Frenchmen. This probably explains why Guizot as an historian took a very detached view of the Reformation. He describes the Church as going through several different phases of organization from the fall of the Roman Empire onwards. It was imperial, barbarian, feudal, monastic and theocratic. There is no form of organization which is the true one, and the changes of the Reformation are simply the most revolutionary in a long series of changes. The essence of the Reformation for Guizot was the liberation of men's minds, and this only became possible in the sixteenth century because of the accumulation of learning and experience. He does not suggest that there was any doctrinal purity amongst the Reformers; that they were returning to any forgotten truths, or that they showed any reprehensible heresy. Both the Catholic and the Protestant systems corresponded to particular moments in particular societies.

Writing in 1818 Guizot denied that Protestants had been more prominent in the Revolution than had other Frenchmen. He claimed that they had 'liked the Revolution and made the Revolution more or less as France had liked it and France had made it'. They had not achieved any particular preponderance under Bonaparte, and if at the time of the 1814 Restoration one took the Protestants of the Gard department, then they had no characteristics which were particular to them or which could have distinguished them as a separate class of people.[2]

Privately, too, Guizot was for ever urging people not to attach too

---

[1] *Arnold Toynbee, An Historian's Approach to Religion* (op. cit.), p. 282.

[2] *A.P.P.L.*, vol. iv, August 1818, pp. 1 ff. It is not absolutely certain that this article was written by Guizot, but it is very likely that he was the author. At all events he put forward these opinions on a number of different occasions.

much importance to religious differences. To his Catholic friend Lenormant he regretted that men should separate over small matters when they were united over great. 'The day that both Catholics and Protestants mutually recognize each other as Christians, then religious peace, if not religious unity, will be established.' One of his favourite Biblical texts was 'In my father's house are many mansions', and he told his daughter that both the Catholic Church and the sects deformed and rejected the Bible by not recognizing this.[1] One of his stories told of how in the 1830s he had sent money to a convent in the Vosges, and the Mother Superior, writing to thank him, said that she had had a mass said on his behalf, adding, 'People say that you are a Protestant; this does not matter: you only need it all the more.'

Naturally this attitude was criticized by both Catholics and Protestants. For the Spaniard Balmès, Guizot had no sense of the doctrinal unity of the Church; for the Duchesse de Broglie, Guizot was lacking in moral sense, he was too fond of assuming that if something succeeded then it was right, too inclined to believe 'what I ought to feel and what I feel are synonymous'.[2] An article published in the *Revue Française* in 1838, and republished in the *Méditations et Études Morales* of 1852, particularly aroused criticism. This was one of three articles pleading the necessity of religion to society, and it particularly sought to show that of the three systems, Catholicism, Protestantism and Philosophy, no one had been definitively victorious over the others. All three were therefore obliged to live in harmony with each other and were obliged to devise some system whereby mutual adjustments and understanding would be possible. To the Protestants Guizot's message was that the epoch of great conversions was concluded. 'France', he wrote, 'will not become Protestant. Protestantism will not perish in France. There are many reasons for this, but one is decisive. It is not between Catholicism and Protestantism that there is a struggle, a struggle of ideas and of power. Impiety and immorality, there is the enemy which they must both fight. The reawakening of religious life, that is the work to which both are called. . . . Catholics or Protestants, priests or congregations, whoever you are, if you are believers you should not concern yourselves with each other. You should concern yourselves with those who do not believe.'[3] Amongst those who were not believers there were some who were particularly in need of authority; for them Catholicism was

[1] Guizot: Lenormant, February 11th, 1852, *Lettres à M. et Mme Lenormant* (op. cit.), p. 67; Guizot: Mme de Witt, February 25th, 1852, *Monsieur Guizot dans sa famille* (op. cit.), pp. 289-290.

[2] J. Balmès, *Le Protestantisme comparé au Catholicisme* (op. cit.), vol. i, p. 41; Duchesse de Broglie: Prosper de Barante, August 25th, 1828, *Barante, Souvenirs* (op. cit.), vol. iii, p. 463.

[3] *Méditations et Études Morales* (op. cit.), pp. 79-80.

appropriate. There were others who sought for greater intellectual and personal activity; for them, Protestantism was more suitable. In this way Protestantism and Catholicism would be united, their differences would appear to be insignificant, or at least of minor importance. This 'realism' was unacceptable to a Protestant such as Athanase Coquerel the elder. For one thing the disagreements between 'the Catholic principle and our principle' were irreconcilable; for another, he was not prepared to accept lightly the idea that France could not possibly become Protestant. 'Humanity has not said its last word,' he wrote, 'nor has Protestantism, and this is why they can understand each other. But the last word of Catholicism has been said.'[1] For some of the Catholics the alliance suggested by Guizot was not so much impracticable as false. For them there was only one distinction to be made. On the one side was authority, on the other side was free enquiry. Submission to divine authority was either absolute or non-existent. Once the principle of free enquiry had been accepted, then man was chained to his own ignorance and was on the slippery slope that leads to Deism and Rationalism, and from there to Socialism and Communism, to dissolution and chaos. And Guizot's proposal, for one Catholic at least, was not only false, but pointless, since, as he put it, 'a Protestant would swallow an atheist camel but strain at a Catholic gnat'.[2]

However, Guizot persisted in this emphasis on Christian unity. He affirmed this dramatically in 1861 when he made the speech of welcome to Lacordaire, who succeeded Tocqueville at the Academy. To one of the largest audiences that had ever been packed beneath the Coupole, and which included the Empress Eugénie and many other members of the Imperial family, Guizot emphasized the significance of a Protestant receiving a Dominican to the Académie Française. Three months later to the Société pour l'encouragement de l'instruction primaire he said, 'Whatever dissidences or even separations there may be, we are all Christians and we are brothers of all Christians.' The theme that there is such a thing as 'l'église chrétienne', or 'le principe chrétien', and that this Church and this principal were in danger, was the theme which ran through the Méditations. Guizot never proposed or hoped for a fusion of the Churches. This was an allegation put about by his enemies. On a number of occasions he admits that such a fusion would not only be impossible but undesirable. He was rather expressing an idea which was in the minds of many Protestants. Vinet, for example, who was much admired by

---

[1] *Athanase Coquerel, Lettre à Monsieur Guizot*, Paris 1838, p. 30.
[2] *Auguste Nicolas, Du Protestantisme et de toutes les hérésies dans leur rapport avec le Socialisme*, Paris 1854, vol. i, p. 45.

Guizot, once wrote to Béranger saying, 'You are neither Catholic nor Protestant . . . I could almost say that I too am neither the one nor the other. On the question of hierarchy and authority I am Protestant (since I reject Papal authority) but on everything else I am simply Christian.'[1] Edmond de Pressensé, too, in the preface to his *Jésus-Christ*, spoke of Christians uniting in an hour of trouble in order to defend their common standard, and whilst he said that he maintained his particular beliefs, yet he said that he felt himself to be part of 'this great community of the disciples of Christ'. But what distinguished the work of Guizot was that he sought to justify these principles doctrinally. He tried to define a Christianity which would be a mean between the principle Churches; he tried to find a doctrinal minimum, all that was necessary to escape from rationalism and revolution.

In trying to define what this doctrinal minimum was, Guizot was not writing simply in the spirit of disinterested enquiry. He was writing in order to emphasize what united rather than what separated men, believing that at a time of crisis one should say nothing which would shake men's faith. His was much the same attitude as Wilson's when he concluded his Bampton Lectures with the words, 'We should not rob weak wayfarers in this worldy scene of the reeds on which they lean, unless we can strengthen their feeble knees or supply into their right hands stronger staves to lean on.'[2] Therefore trying to see what united believers against unbelievers and what united Christians together, he looked for what was positive. For believers the touchstone was belief in the supernatural; for Christians the important indication was belief in five dogmas, the Creation, Providence, Original Sin, the Incarnation and the Redemption.

To have taken the supernatural as a starting-point was significant. Earlier in the century many Protestants would have taken the Bible as their starting-point. But for Guizot to have done this would have immediately alienated the Catholics, to say nothing of those who were opposed to scriptural sufficiency or 'théopneustie'. 'Bibliolatry' therefore was unsuitable. At the same time Guizot was probably justified in considering that the idea of the supernatural was more fundamental. Both Catholic and Protestant orthodoxy were attacked by those who said that the world was governed by natural laws and that there was no need to suppose that these laws could ever be suspended. It was in this sense that Strauss affirmed that the supernatural element in the recorded life of Jesus was mythical, that Renan

---

[1] Vinet: Béranger, May 25th, 1846, *Lettres d'Alexandre Vinet et de quelques-uns de ses correspondants*, Lausanne 1882, vol. ii, pp. 336-337.

[2] *Henry Bristow Wilson, The Communion of Saints*, 1851, p. 281.

PROTESTANTISM

accepted as a cardinal rule of criticism that there was no place for miracles in any part of the scriptural writings, or that Félix Pécaut asserted that since God was part of the natural order, then any force which was supernatural would be super-divine, exterior and superior to the will of God. The denial of the supernatural was therefore, as Guizot argued, a characteristic of either rationalism or pantheism, both of them opponents to Christianity.

Any mention of 'supernatural' was bound to create some confusion, as was pointed out by critics, since scientists used the word 'nature', in a broad sense, to mean the vast and comprehensive order of existence, whilst theologians used it in a deliberately restricted sense to mean the unreasoning mechanism of the universe, once it was cut off from the divine will. Further confusion was also created by Guizot, because it was not altogether clear whether he thought of the supernatural as a particular form of divine action. He does not define the supernatural except in so far as he refers to a sense of the supernatural being present in every individual. The philosopher Janet wrote to Guizot and queried this presentation of the supernatural. Guizot in his reply tried to clarify his thought by making three propositions. Firstly, he said that whilst the limits of the finite world were the limits of human knowledge, they were not the limits of reality. Secondly, man carries within himself not merely certain ambitions and desires, but also instincts and notions which reveal to him the realities lying beyond the finite world, and whilst man cannot possess a knowledge of these realities at least he is aware of their perspective. Thirdly, even although these realities are unattainable, yet man pursues them, in the same way as he pursues moral perfection, which is also unattainable.[1] Thus it would seem that the supernatural exists because man has a sense of something existing which is beyond the power of his reason. This sense is not only part of man, it is necessary to man.

These arguments have been used by many thinkers both before and after Guizot. Madame de Staël, in the fourth book of De l'Allemagne, wrote about religious emotions awakening in man the sense of the infinite and at the same time satisfying that sense. Ernest Renan was not far removed from this type of thinking when he wrote that it was not reason, it was sentiment which determined the idea of God, and Max Müller once defined faith as being the faculty for apprehending infinity. Some modern thinkers consider the supernatural as being the world which has values which stir the sense of the holy, and which ask to be esteemed as sacred. It is a world with absolute rather than comparative values. Some think of religion as

[1] Quoted in *Paul Janet*, 'Philosophie et Religion', *Revue des Deux Mondes*, May 15th, 1869, pp. 347 ff.

400

being based upon a consciousness of God as a reality lying beyond the world which is normally apprehended.[1] Thus what Guizot says is unexceptional. What is noticeable, however, is that Guizot does not accept this apprehension of the supernatural as creating a form of intuitive insight, even of mystical consciousness in man. He feels obliged to talk of the supernatural in terms of logical reasoning; and he also feels obliged to go further and to list the dogmas of Christianity. Madame de Staël was wiser here. It was impossible to explain the infinite, and she added, 'It is not a few words more which will succeed in explaining what the universe itself has failed to say.' Ernest Renan, too, was more logical. Once man had sensed the existence of God, then all propositions applied to him are impertinent, 'Une seule exceptée: Il est.' Edmond Scherer, a leading critic who was usually thought of as a rationalist Protestant, also noted this inconsequence in Guizot. He pointed out that if the supernatural is Christianity, is God, then religion is the elevation of the soul towards the infinite and the ideal. Religion then does not lie in the acceptance of one or two exceptional facts, and Guizot's dogmas are useless.[2]

Guizot's insistence upon the supernatural leads one to expect a religion of love and sentiment, possibly even of mysticism, but certainly a religion of faith. Yet he continues with a list of dogmas. This is all the more surprising since Guizot was personally attracted towards the religion of faith. He once told Madame Lenormant that one of his favourite pictures was Poussin's painting of a miracle by Saint-François Xavier, where the saint is seen resurrecting the body of a young girl. The saint is praying, and so great is his faith that he does not trouble himself to look and see if the young girl is moving.[3] Guizot also used to say that he never felt the need of any intermediary between himself and God. But the type of religion which he puts forward is arid and unemotional. One can only assume that in accompanying a religion which consists of an individual experience of God with a series of dogmatic beliefs, Guizot was trying not only to make his appeal as wide as possible, but also to strengthen Protestant orthodoxy. In considering religious works it is always important to know for what audience they are intended. Guizot is writing for Christians, for those who believe in 'le principe chrétien'. But he is also writing with an eye on the Protestant Church, and he is careful to avoid doing anything which would weaken orthodoxy

[1] See, for example, *John Oman, The Natural and the Supernatural*, 1950; H. D. Lewis, *Our Experience of God*, 1959.

[2] For *Renan* see 'L'Avenir de la Metaphysique', *Revue des Deux Mondes*, January 15th, 1860, p. 389; for Scherer see *Le Temps*, October 23rd, 1861.

[3] Guizot: Mme Lenormant, February 24th, 1857, *Correspondance de M. et Mme Lenormant* (op. cit.), p. 104.

401

since this would weaken the position of Protestantism in the state. A religion based on belief in the supernatural, in a 'Dieu-Esprit', without any accompanying dogmas, could have been acceptable to some of the rationalists and could have strengthened their position.[1] It had therefore to be avoided.

The first of the dogmas, the Creation, is at first sight strange. During the 1860s there was a conflict between science and theology, if not between science and religion, over this very problem. It therefore seems most unwise to assert the creation of the world as a dogma, supported by references to Cuvier, Flourens, Costes, Quatrefages and 'tous les observateurs sévères de faits' who rejected ideas of evolution and of spontaneous generation.[2] To associate dogma with scientific opinion was doubtful theology; to venture into geological and biological controversy was foolish; to try and find in the past reasons for the existence of God which do not exist in the present was unsound. However, one has to recognize that whilst the creation may not be part of Christian dogma, it has always remained part of Christian argument. Even in the twentieth century and even amongst astronomers there are still some who use the word 'creation'. Furthermore, Guizot's denial that evolution has never applied to man has been echoed by modern scientists who stress the uniqueness of man by asserting that the process of evolution, selection and mutation ceased to apply to man once he had developed as a superior being. Therefore one can say that if Guizot in his search for a minimum set of beliefs was looking for constant beliefs, then he was to some extent successful.

The second dogma was that of Providence. God having created the world did not separate himself from the world. Man saw certain things happening which were the result of his own actions; he saw other happenings which were independent of his actions but which followed certain natural laws which he understood; but there remained further happenings which were not explicable in either of those ways. It was then that the non-believer spoke about 'chance' or 'fatality' whilst the Christian, conceiving Providence, turned to prayer. Some people found it strange that Providence should be made a Christian dogma, since the idea of Providence existed well before Christ. Many Christians would only accept the idea of Providence if accompanied by belief in the efficacy of prayer, but here one must notice that Guizot, whilst insisting on the mystery of Providence, has some uncertainty about prayer. He was questioned about his attitude to prayer by Pédézert, but maintained his attitude, stating that the

[1] This is suggested in a review of *L'Église et la Société Chrétiennes* (op. cit.), in *Le Lien*, November 30th, 1861.
[2] *Méditations sur l'Essence de la Religion Chrétienne* (op. cit.), p. 24.

efficacy of prayer was necessarily uncertain.[1] God, whilst being a hypothesis to explain certain facts, remains the mysterious Godhead about whom man can say little.

The third of the dogmas, that of Original Sin, is perhaps the most important, and probably helps to explain Guizot's thoughts and beliefs on subjects other than religious subjects. Guizot stated the matter simply. Man was born free and he had used this freedom to disobey God's will; the responsibility for this act of violence was hereditary and affected the whole of mankind. Men were now free to act and to take decisions, but they innately possessed the idea that these actions might be wrong and that they were responsible for their wrong actions. They also possessed the idea that there had once existed a state of innocence, a past Utopia which men had lost. Only through the doctrine of Original Sin could such instinct and innate ideas be explained. Only through this doctrine too could the suffering and evil of the world be explained. Otherwise one had to deny the existence of God or one had to attribute evil to God.

The doctrine was to be found in many of the thinkers who had influenced the 'Réveil'. Robert Haldane, for example, published in French a *Commentary on the Epistle to the Romans* in which he insisted that the sin of the first man was transmitted on to others, so that 'Adam's sin is important to his posterity because it is their sin in reality'. Thomas Chalmers was translated in French by Samuel Vincent, amongst others, and was well known to French Protestants. Guizot considered him to be one of the outstanding theologians of the century. He believed that sin was so much a part of man's nature that to put forward the doctrine of original sin was 'no more than to affirm the ferocious nature of the tiger, or the odorous nature of the rose, or the poisonous nature of the fox-glove'.[2] This same doctrine was to be found in orthodox thinkers such as Adolphe Monod and even in the 'modern orthodoxy' of Athanase Coquerel the elder. The implications of this doctrine were wide. They were perhaps put forward in their most famous form by Joseph de Maistre in his *Soirées de Saint-Petersbourg*, when he made this doctrine explain the necessity of suffering and the impossibility of progress through man's reason alone. This belief, not always openly expressed, was one of the principal instruments of those who attacked rationalism and those who attacked the would-be organizers of progress. One has to notice that in the case of Guizot it fits in with his frequent allusions to the insufficiency and inadequacy of man. The great fault of the eighteenth century as he saw it was to believe in man's goodness and in man's right to happiness. Man was justified in being ambitious, but he

[1] See *Pédézert, Souvenirs et Études* (op. cit.), pp. 205-207.
[2] *Thomas Chalmers, Works*, 1836-1842, vol. xxii, pp. 367-370.

PROTESTANTISM

needed to recognize the part of pride and illusion which was included
in this ambition. 'Within our nature there is a vice, within our condition an evil, and this exists in spite of all human effort. Disorder lies
within us, and were it stopped up from all other sources then it would
rise up from ourselves and by our own will. Suffering, suffering that is
unequally divided, is in the providential laws of our destiny. . . .
Arrange institutions as you will; distribute benefits as you please:
neither your wisdom nor your wealth will be enough to fill this abyss.
. . . Always there will be within man more desires than society can
regulate or satisfy, more suffering than society can prevent or cure.'[1]
    In political terms this can simply be a practical warning to limit
ambitions, a hint to keep one's sights low. It is an argument against
the assumption that social evils and social conflicts are simply matters
for social engineering. In religious terms it is also a warning against
rationalism. As Adolphe Monod put it, 'Croire soi, c'est le rational-
isme; croire Dieu, c'est la foi'.[2] It also limits the efficacy of religious
organizations; and more particularly the doctrine of original sin
assumes that the situation and predicaments of mankind will be
extremely varied. It is therefore a dogma which is calculated to
embrace rather than to exclude.
    But it was not popular. Some Catholics suggested that the
Calvinists insisted upon this doctrine because they wanted to show
that man could not co-operate in his own regeneration.[3] Some
Protestants were rejecting the idea of the Fall. Edmond Scherer, in
1853, had suggested that the account of the Fall in Genesis was purely
mythical, and that sin had to be seen as a necessary part of man's
development, as the Revelation offered him knowledge of God's pity
and forgiveness.[4] Albert Réville also held that the idea of the Fall was
purely mythical. He believed, and in some ways Samuel Vincent had
earlier in the century shared this belief, that man had never known
any early state of perfection. On the contrary, man had progressed
out of animalism. Part of this progression had been the realization of
sin. The sentiment of sin, therefore, has to be seen not as a sign of the
insufficiency of mankind, but quite the opposite, as a sign of his
superior development.[5] There were also humanitarians who believed
that the doctrine of original sin was essentially barbaric. Paul Janet,
for example, claimed that this belief reduced the relations between
God and mankind to the level of a vendetta. Philosophically it could

---

[1] 'De la Religion dans les Sociétés Modernes', *Revue Française*, February 1838,
reprinted in *Méditations et Études Morales* (op. cit.), p. 31.
[2] *Adolphe Monod, Discours sur la Doctrine Chrétienne*, Paris 1868, p. 36.
[3] *Abbé Louis Valée, Dictionnaire du Protestantisme*, Paris 1858, col. 1283-1284.
[4] *Revue de Théologie*, 1853, vol. vii, pp. 321 ff.
[5] *Nouvelle Revue de Théologie*, 1863, vol. ix, pp. 134 ff.

be claimed that the doctrine of original sin did not explain how sin came into existence at all, as intellectually it was difficult to believe that a supposed state of innocence could exist for such an infinitesimal space of time. Whilst it was clear that the failure of the individual to rise to the general advance came from outside the individual, and that some term such as 'original sin' might be necessary to explain these human lapses, yet it did not seem necessary to find some definite point at which such individual failure began and call it the Fall. In the 1860s this smacked of historical fiction. There were theologians who pointed out that original sin was intimately connected with baptismal regeneration, or required the corrective of the Immaculate Conception of the Virgin Mary. But Guizot was not prepared to enter into these 'secondary dogmas'. Finally, original sin is a harsh doctrine. Some Protestant theologians who believed in the Fall disliked it. They turned willingly to the belief in the love and forgiveness that was revealed in the divine disclosures. But Guizot's doctrine is austere. He continues to avoid the temptation of the religion of sentiment.

It is again curious to see how Guizot argues in favour of his fourth dogma, that of the Incarnation. First of all he takes the success of Christianity, the extraordinary way in which this religion spread from humble beginnings. This argument was familiar. Strauss had, however, turned it round, saying that he did not know whether any supernatural origins that man may ascribe to Christianity could really do it more honour than was already done by history. Réville was to argue that if Christianity were compared to other religions, he was quite prepared to admit that it was superior to them, he was ready to say that it was the best tree in the forest, but it was a tree, it was not something which had fallen from heaven. Guizot's second argument was based upon certain texts. In making these selections Guizot sought to show that Christ had claimed to be divine, both God and man, and in doing this Guizot was of course running directly contrary to the school of Biblical criticism. Strauss had claimed that the Jesus of the Fourth Gospel who made certain claims for his own divinity could not be given much historical credence. It had also been pointed out that St. Paul's remarks concerning the relations between God and Christ, some of which were difficult to interpret,[1] had no reliable support in the Gospels. The evidence put forward by Guizot on the divinity of Christ was therefore, for some, unhistorical. The third argument was in many ways the most interesting. Having stressed the necessity of staying within generalities in order to understand the sense of the scriptures, rather than

[1] See Guizot's remarks on the Epistle to the Corinthians II 5-8 in *Méditations sur L'Essence* (op. cit.), p. 71 n. 1.

concentrating attention upon supposed interpolations, Guizot asks the direct question, 'What is man himself but an incomplete and imperfect incarnation of God?'[1] That is to say that in all human nature there is a divine element. The implication is that Christ was only a fuller example of incarnation than is found in other men. Christ would therefore not be so much in contrast to other men as analogous to them. But Guizot does not follow up this argument. Had he developed it, it might have been at variance with some of his other beliefs. It would have resembled liberal Protestantism and would have saved him from the accusation of 'Jésulatrie', the Protestant version of the Catholic disease of 'Mariolatrie'.

Thus Guizot uses three arguments to show the truth of his dogma. The final dogma, the Redemption, is described as being the supreme mystery[2] and he says no more about it than that the sins of men are expiated and forgiven by the sacrifice of God who has made himself man. The general nature of this argument makes this section of the book very unimpressive, if not theologically confused. Pédézert remarked on these shortcomings, saying that 'the explanations offered by Guizot finish where the mysteries begin. He accepts dogmas but rejects the dogmatic. He is partisan of the supernatural but wishes to avoid metaphysics. He professes religion but stands a long way away from theology.'[3] In the last volume of the *Méditations* Guizot gives some explanation of this attitude. With the facts of the Scriptures, he says, there arises the desire to understand and to explain them. Hence there grows up, 'plus ou moins légitimement' as he grudgingly puts it, the science of theology. But theologians often misunderstood the limits of their knowledge, they sometimes rendered the divine revelation more obscure, their pride occasionally led them into errors and misconceptions. That is to say, that theology created rather than closed disagreements amongst Christians, and therefore Guizot brought a halt to his speculations.[4] It could be argued that Guizot was not saying any more than many others have said before and since; as Henry Cadbury put it, 'the bitterest controversy is often over the narrowest margin'. But he chose the wrong time in history to try and prevent enquiry. He would have done well to have remembered Jowett's remark that 'Doubt comes in at the window when Inquiry is denied at the door.'

Although Guizot's writings were treated with respect by the

---

[1] See Guizot's remarks on the Epistle to the Corinthians II 5-8 in *Méditations sur L'Essence* (op. cit.), p. 79.

[2] Ibid., p. 84.

[3] *Jules Pédézert, Guizot*, Paris 1874, pp. 20-21.

[4] *Méditations sur la Religion Chrétienne dans ses Rapports avec l'État Actuel* (op. cit.), pp. 454 ff.

PROTESTANTISM

Catholic press ('Monsieur Guizot publishes books which are practically events', wrote Eugène Veuillot[1]), no Catholic writer approved of his attempt to designate the fundamental dogmas of the faith. In so doing he was considered to have demonstrated his fundamental Protestantism. Guizot referred to the disputes of the sixteenth century, saying that the quarrels were about purely secondary dogmas, such as the holy communion, the infallibility of the Pope, the confession, purgatory or the celibacy of priests, whilst on fundamental doctrines all the parties were united in their belief. But one Catholic writer queried this distinction between what was fundamental and what was not. He asked, as many others were to do, what about the dogma of the Trinity? He asked about the dogma of the Real Presence, was this secondary? What of the doctrine of Free Will? Who was to decide what was primary and what was secondary? It was all very well for Guizot to reduce his 'credo' to four points (in 1861 Guizot omitted Providence from his essential dogmas), but how could this be justified? 'The credo of Luther and Calvin was, I think, much longer. On the other hand, how many Protestants have a credo which is still shorter; how many have none at all?'[2] Guizot had invited his readers to embrace Christianity, 'le Christianisme tout entier', yet what he offered Catholics was in their eyes an atrocious mixture of contradictory opinions which had either to be accepted or rejected. If one believed in sin and in redemption, that is if one believed in heaven and hell, then how could one believe that God had come down to earth in order to reveal the doctrine and the laws of salvation, without leaving any aid to men other than a book which could be interpreted in different ways? This meant that the Bible was read at one's risk and peril. Salvation had become a riddle. Only if one guessed rightly did one achieve it, 'the Sphinx of the Greek riddle, there is your redeemer', was the scornful, if well-worn answer of certain Catholics.

A Jesuit commentator drew attention to the principles of Christianity which were conspicuous by their absence. He could not find the Trinity, he could not find anything about the nature of expiation, and he claimed he could find nothing about the divinity of Christ. Such principles were absent, he thought, 'either because M. Guizot himself does not believe in them, or because the opinions of the orthodox leaders on these grave points present considerable difficulties'.[3]

[1] *Revue du Monde Catholique*, October 25th, 1861.
[2] *Du Lac*, ibid., December 10th, 1861, p. 297.
[3] *Le Père Lefévre*, *Études* (Religieuses, historiques et littéraires par les Pères de la Compagnie de Jésus), September 1866, La crise du Protestantisme Français en 1866.

407

For some Protestants, Guizot's insistence upon the supernatural appeared as an eloquent statement of a religious truth. Edmond de Pressensé, for example, approved of it.[1] But others were hesitant about it. Jean Monod was one who thought that 'the supernatural element' was too distinct from 'the human element'; he objected to the supernatural being presented as an apparently arbitrary force, since he preferred to think of it as something which obeyed the laws of the spiritual order.[2] Many Protestants were becoming embarrassed by acceptance of the supernatural. Even moderates amongst them were ridiculing the Catholics for their 'miracle-mongering' in Lourdes and elsewhere[3] and it seemed illogical to pursue this and at the same time to insist upon acceptance of the supernatural being essential to belief.

But as with the Catholics, so with the Protestants, it was the list of dogmas which aroused most hostility. Once these lists were before the Protestant Churches, then it would be clear where the Protestant leaders stood. Guizot was perhaps attracted to clarifying the situation. Perhaps he remembered that he was successful in the Chamber during the 1840s when he could divide it into two, when he could put deputies into those who were in favour of peace and those who were in favour of war. Here he was trying to distinguish between those who were believers and those who were not. He succeeded in making the division. It was clear that the Coquerels and both the liberals and the rationalists reacted to the dogmas, and refused to accept them. They realized the implications of their refusal, Étienne Coquerel asking Guizot if it was possible for people to have the same religious life if they did not share the same religious dogmas.[4] But did they accept that this dogmatic division was one which put them amongst the unbelievers? Were the believers given any greater unity by these arguments? There must have been some who preferred to think of Protestantism as a way of life. There must have been even more, amongst the most religious, who thought with Channing (a religious writer who was well known in France) that Christianity was not a dogma but a spirit, and who would have added, 'You might as well compress the boundless atmosphere, the fire, the all-pervading light, the free winds of the universe, into separate parcels and weigh and label them, as break up Christianity into a few propositions.'[5] Guizot

[1] *Edmond de Pressensé, Jésus-Christ* (op. cit.), p. 14.
[2] Jean Monod: Guizot, November 17th, 1866, *Archives S.H.P.F.*
[3] See *L'Espérance*, July 7th, 1865, for an example of their mocking at Catholic superstition.
[4] *Etienne Coquerel, Monsieur Guizot et l'Orthodoxie Protestante*, Paris 1864.
[5] *William E. Channing, Letter on Creeds*, Liverpool 1837, p. 9.

forgot this 'fides implicita'; at one and the same time he said too little
and too much.

There were few European countries where the liberal humanism
of the nineteenth century did not penetrate into religious studies, and
this is most clearly illustrated in the treatment of the life of Christ.
Many men claimed that the person behind the New Testament was
obviously a purely human non-miraculous figure, for all that he had
a reputation as a prophet. Born in humble and knowable conditions,
this man became a wandering teacher who drifted into conflict with
the authorities in Jerusalem and who was eventually executed by the
occupying power. The quarrel with the religious leaders of his time
probably arose because he had some visionary idea of the end of the
world, and this was wrongly understood to be a sign of messianic
ambition. To this original story the Church later added a resurrection
—along with various miracles which had sometimes entered the often
hysterical imaginations of his followers and which had either become
or were about to become popular legends. The New Testament was in
this way seen as a collection of books which were written after all
real knowledge of Christ had disappeared. The Church itself
developed in ways which had never been envisaged by Christ, and
much of Christian writing was simply Church propaganda. In this
way, nineteenth-century humanism removed the supernatural Christ
and emphasized the social and moral nature of Christianity. Hence a
Benjamin Jowett could say that he believed more and more in
Christianity, meaning by that not miracles, or hell, or verbal
inspiration or atonement, but simply living for others and in going
about doing good. An Albert Réville could say that it was time to
give up faith in Jesus and replace it by the faith of Jesus.

Guizot never wrote a life of Christ, but he devoted a large section
of his *Méditations sur l'Essence de la Religion Chrétienne* to the
Revelation, to the inspiration of the Scriptures, and to the person
and teaching of Christ himself. Yet although this section of the book
is called 'Jésus-Christ selon l'Évangile', the main features of the
synoptic tradition, such as the baptism, the temptation, the ministry
of healing and the crucifixion are absent. Many other questions in the
life of 'the historical Jesus' which were interesting writers at the time
also go unmentioned. For example, the extent to which Christ
regarded himself as the Messiah, the meaning of the Sermon on the
Mount, the significance of Christ's frequenting with sinners, or the
effective division of Christ's life into two periods, the happy period of
Galilee contrasting with the tragic period of Jerusalem, these are all
crucial issues about which Guizot's treatment of Christ is silent. It
can be seen, therefore, that this is a very restrained portrait.

The principal theme is an insistence upon the dual nature of all this history. It was at once divine and human. Guizot believed that theologians quarrelled over Biblical history precisely because they failed to remember this. They had, he thought, descended into the labyrinth of the plain instead of going up into the mountain. Their view was limited and too much detail had blinded them to realization that both God and men were working and acting together. Because of this there were examples of prophecy in the Old Testament, Christ was both divine and human, Christ's teaching was directed both towards God and towards men, and Christianity was composed both of severity and compassion, authority and freedom. In the same way part of the Bible was inspired and was directly the word of God. It is that part of the Bible which is concerned with the infinite which is inspired, but where the Bible is concerned with finite knowledge, then it is human, with errors of calculation and of grammar.

Guizot does not accept the necessity of making a choice from amongst several methods of interpretation. His Christ is both supernatural and historical; his study depends upon both the Synoptic and the Johannine Gospels; he is not distrustful of any texts, he is prepared to quote from anywhere in the Bible to justify a statement, without any of the textual reservations which had become common. He was never prepared to accept the idea that the history of Christ was like any other history; Christianity did not grow and spread for reasons which could be listed; if one tried to consider the history of Christ as based upon documents and upon 'moral probabilities', then one found it incomprehensible if one made Christ an ordinary human being. The choice for Guizot was between 'le roman des hommes' and 'le plan de Dieu', between 'le système' and 'le mystère'.[1] He had no hesitation in his own choice.

All the same, Guizot's account of Christ omits a good many well-attested events which one would have expected to fortify his theme. He has nothing to say about the birth of Christ; he has nothing to say about the baptism, and the 'sign' from the heavens which accompanied it; he does not mention the temptation, which accompanied Christ's retirement into the wilderness and which some scholars thought to be caused by the excitement of mind that followed upon the consciousness of supernatural powers. The only early episode which Guizot mentions is the incident which is said to have occurred when Joseph and Mary visited Jerusalem. Christ was twelve years old at the time and when his parents started back home they discovered that he was not with them. On returning to Jerusalem they found him in the temple, engaged in discussion with the priests. Guizot, recounting this incident briefly, emphasizes two things,

[1] *Méditations sur l'Essence de la Religion Chrétienne* (op. cit.), p. 327.

firstly the answer which Christ gave to Mary, 'Wist ye not that I must be about my Father's business?' and secondly that his mother 'kept all these sayings in her heart'. Other writers emphasized the knowledge which Christ had shown in his discussion with the doctors in the temple, and the wonderment with which his questions and answers were greeted. It seems, therefore, when one considers Guizot's omissions and when one thinks about his treatment of this incident, that whilst emphasizing the supernatural element in Christ, he tries to avoid what is miraculous or magical.

The reason for this is simple. Guizot thought of the miracles as being an essential part of the history. But these miracles differ from those of other religions, where the miracle was an artifice calculated to inspire confidence, or where the miracle was the product of the human imagination which has a natural penchant for fantasy in religious matters. The miraculous actions of Christ were simple and practical. He performed miracles when the occasion arose or when he came across striking examples of faith. He carried out the miracles without ostentation, often commenting sadly upon the indifference with which they were received. Guizot, in this way, saw Christ as a supernatural figure engaged in a supernatural task, for whom the accomplishment of miraculous deeds was part of ordinary activity. Therefore to isolate, or to emphasize, particular incidents would be inappropriate. In the revelation to the first man, in the revelations to Abraham and Moses, in the revelation of Christ and in the success of the Christian religion, Guizot saw the intervention of God in the lives of men. It would not be right to isolate certain miracles and therefore believe in God and in the supernatural. It is because one believes in God and the supernatural that one accepts miracles, with neither greater nor lesser wonderment than one accepts other incidents in the life and teaching of Christ.

Guizot's account of Christ's teaching sought to emphasize its originality. He did not teach like the Pharisees and scribes; he did not propose a system as did Socrates; neither to his disciples nor to those who came to hear him did he speak 'as other men'; he always spoke 'as one having authority'. Guizot saw in the content of Christ's teaching, two elements which were new. Firstly there was to be no privileged race, and the word had to be taught to all 'nations'. Secondly that religious and civil life had to be distinguished one from another. For these essential characteristics of the Christian religion, Guizot could see no filiation and no human origin. Before Christ, religions had been national and they had been part of the ordinary institutions of state, to be suppressed or exalted at will.[1] Guizot's emphasis on these two elements was typical of a statesman's inter-

[1] Ibid., p. 307.

pretation of Christ's teaching, and is comparable to Gladstone's praise for Seeley's idea (in *Ecce Homo*) that Christ had always intended to found and develop a particular society. This passage in Guizot's *Méditations* impressed the Bampton Lecturer of 1866, who quoted him and echoed his words.[1] But to make this the central point of Guizot's treatment would be very wrong. Besides the miracles and teachings of Christ are the dogmas.

Guizot always gives the dogmas precedence, referring to 'the dogmas, the precepts and the teaching of Jesus Christ', and his insistence upon dogmatic beliefs is apparent in his treatment of the idea of charity. Charity was not simply philanthropy. Guizot explained that whereas in other religions it was either nature or men themselves who became God, in Judo-Christianity God was essentially distinct from both nature and mankind. The incarnation of God in the person of Jesus Christ took place in order that man might be saved from original sin; in this sense Christ's crucifixion was God's charity towards men. Therefore the idea of charity is linked to certain dogmas. As Guizot puts it, 'It is the dogma which makes the power of the precept.'[2] This remark makes clear why Guizot introduced the revelations so late in his account of the essence of Christianity; the dogmas had to be explained first.

Guizot is therefore attacking the moralist, humanist version of Christ and Christianity. Human charity, without belief in the Incarnation and without understanding of the reasons for the Incarnation, can be both noble and useful; but it comes from man alone, and for that reason is unsufficient. It cannot relieve the suffering or inspire the welfare of mankind. The teaching of Christ, as Christ himself said, came not from himself but from God who sent him, and to those who thought of the moral teachings of Jesus as being sufficient to form the Christian religion Guizot replied, 'Man is greater and more exacting than these superficial moralists believe. For man, in the deepest instincts of his soul, the law of his life is necessarily linked to the secret of his destiny; only the Christian dogmas can give the Christian morality that sovereign authority which is necessary for the rule and regeneration of humanity.'[3] Even relations between Christ and children have to be seen not as examples of humanism or sentiment but as indications of doctrine. Childhood is for man the image of innocence, the image of mankind before the Fall. Innocence, more than any human science or knowledge, is the surest way of reaching God. When Christ said 'Suffer the little children

---

[1] H. P. Liddon, *The Divinity of Our Lord and Saviour Jesus Christ* (22nd edition, 1908), p. 114 note r.
[2] *Méditations sur l'Essence de la Religion Chrétienne* (op. cit.), p. 283.
[3] Ibid., p. 285.

to come unto me', or when he said 'Thou has hid these things from
the wise and prudent and has revealed them unto babes', he was not
expressing a human emotion; he was rather showing the inadequacy
of man.

Any commentary upon this picture of Christ must point out that
Guizot has made him a more arid figure than have other writers. Not
only has he lost his emotional and humanitarian appeal, but he has
even lost his drama. There is a big difference here between Guizot's
Christ and that of *Ecce Homo*. Seeley explained Christ's success by
his combination of greatness and self-sacrifice; he refused to use on
his own behalf the power which he held for the benefit of others; he
gave up this power and suffered humiliation and death. The Christian
therefore approaches a lovable Christ. But Guizot so avoids anything of this nature that when he added to the 1868 *Méditations*
translated passages from *Ecce Homo*, he omitted the passage where
Seeley, describing the incident of the woman taken in adultery,
imagines Christ's embarrassment and quotes it as an example of his
purity.[1] But Guizot's Christ cannot be approached in this way. He
can only be approached along the more difficult path of the supernatural, and along the more complicated way of doctrine.

There is one doctrine absent from Guizot's religious thought which
one might have expected to find. This is the doctrine of predestination,
the belief that no man could be saved unless God willed that he
should be saved, a doctrine which arose out of Calvin's belief in the
absolute sovereignty of God. One can learn a lot about the Reformed
Church in France, which claimed to be Calvinist (as opposed to the
smaller, more localized Church in the east of France which was
Lutheran) by studying the vicissitudes of this doctrine. At the beginning of the century it was one of the many points of Calvinist
doctrine which was either abandoned or passed over in silence.[2] Then,
of the various foreign influences coming into France there was one,
that of the Wesleyan Methodists, which condemned predestination
and election by grace. Methodists such as Wilks and Cook became
famous in France and the latter translated Wesley's sermon condemning predestination. But another of the foreign influences was
that of the Swiss 'Réveil' and religious leaders such as César Malan
and Alexandre Vinet revived this doctrine. A French orthodox
leader such as Adolphe Monod accepted it, and it was quite widely

[1] *Ecce Homo* (op. cit.), chapter ix. Although *Ecce Homo* is still dismissed by
modern scholars as 'not a very good book' (*Stephen Neill, Anglicanism*, 1960 ed.,
p. 267), and was ignored by Schweizer, it is interesting to see an attempted
rehabilitation of Seeley in *H. G. Wood, Jesus in the Twentieth Century*, 1960,
pp. 111 ff.

[2] Guillaume de Félice: Guizot, May 29th, 1865, *Archives S.H.P.F.*

held, if only in the sense in which it was explained by Monod's friend, the Scotsman Thomas Erskine, who suggested that all men closed their eyes to God, but whilst God allowed some men to continue in their blindness there were others whom he forced to open their eyes. Then in the theological developments of the 1850s, the new theologians were quick to break away from the doctrine of grace and to assert that salvation was the work of men alone.[1]

Guizot was not a Methodist, nor was he one of the scientific theologians of the Strasbourg school. He was an orthodox Protestant, nevertheless he rejected this part of Calvinism. The subject of free will was one which had preoccupied him throughout his life. He had discussed it in his lectures on civilization, especially when dealing with Pelagianism, but it was in 1873, in his study of Calvin, that he dealt most directly with the subject. He described Calvin's religious ideas as containing two errors; firstly the error of believing literally in the Bible, and here Guizot thought that had Calvin known the work of later scholars then he would have modified his system; secondly, the error of thinking that man was not free. For Guizot it was essential to believe that man was free, even although man's moral sense and moral development were to some extent independent of him. What he found unacceptable in the doctrine of Calvin, and in this case of Chalmers too, was that both these thinkers had formed an idea of God's intentions towards and relations with men, when Guizot preferred to think of God as being mysterious. Guizot could not accept that God would not allow any initiative to any will other than his own, that he was an autocratic sovereign 'within his Estates' in precisely this manner. He thought of man as being unique in his liberty, and he thought that this freedom was implied in the doctrine of original sin. Whilst men were denying that they were free, they were actually in possession of their liberty.

One does not therefore need Guillaume Guizot's testimony to see that his father had utterly rejected this side of Calvinism.[2] It is clear that for once Guizot has come down on the side of a form of humanism. Calvin had determined his idea of man from his study of God. Guizot preferred, in this case, to form his idea of God from his study of man. He is no less critical of Calvin in other respects. He saw him as an actor in a revolution rather than a revolutionary. He indulged his love of paradox by describing him as an opponent of liberty who

---

[1] On the subject of predestination see *J. Cadier, La Tradition Calviniste dans le Réveil du XIXe Siècle* (Études Théologiques et Religieuses), Montpellier 1952; *Ernest Rochat, Le Développement de la Théologie Protestante Française au XIXe Siècle*, Geneva 1942.

[2] *La Vie de Quatre Grands Chrétiens Français*, Paris 1873, vol. i, pp. 194-206; Guillaume Guizot: Jules Simon, October 21st, 1883, *Papiers Simon*, ibid.

had helped the cause of freedom, a moralist who mistrusted other men but who had done honour to mankind. One incident in the life of Calvin which has often aroused controversy amongst French Protestants was Calvin's condemnation of Michel Servet, who was burned alive. Guizot had no time for Servet's religion, which he thought of as pantheistic, and he supported Calvin's action.[1] However, it was as a man of action, as an administrator, that Guizot most consistently admired Calvin. It is as an administrator of the Protestant Church in France that Guizot himself must now be considered.

French Protestants had been given their freedom to worship in 1787, but it was not until the Consulate that anything official was done to organize their official existence. After Bonaparte had signed the Concordat with the Papal Legate in July 1801, he turned his attention to the 600,000 Protestants whom an enquiry showed as being on French territory. The law that was eventually proclaimed, the law of the 18th Germinal, Year X (April 7th, 1802), divided the French Protestants into consistories, each of some 6,000 members. Each consistory included, along with the pastors, some half a dozen notables chosen from the wealthiest members of the faithful. With government permission five consistories could meet together, and this could be called a small synod, but Bonaparte did not allow any national synod to exist (contrary to a petition sent him by the pastors of Nîmes in 1802). Pastors were paid by the state; Protestant seminaries were supported by the state in Geneva and Strasbourg (together with one founded at Montauban in 1808); the building and repair of Protestant buildings was also paid for by the state.

At first Protestants were enthusiastic about this law. It was an immense progress on the persecutions which were alive in their memories. For a number of towns the law actually preceded the return to regular worship which the excesses of the Revolution had interrupted. Protestant pastors attended the consecration of Napoleon as Emperor and he addressed certain remarks particularly to them. But it was not long before Protestants began to resent certain of the conditions of this law. The absence of any national synod appeared positively harmful to the Church, particularly as divergences and dissidence within the Reformed Church became more obvious. It was recalled that at the Synod of Loudun Daillé had said that without such assemblies their religion was destined to perish. Not only did the independence of the consistories seem dangerous, but the con-

---

[1] In 1908 a statue to Michel Servet was erected in front of the Mairie of the 14th arrondissement in Paris on which were written three separate inscriptions, all of them hostile to Calvin's actions in this affair. However, these inscriptions were defaced at various times, presumably by those who wished to defend Calvin. See *Albert Mousset*, 'Polémique Lapidaire . . .' in *Le Monde*, July 8th, 1959.

sistory itself was often a practical abstraction. It was the parish which should have been the effective unit. Whilst for many Protestants, including Guizot, one of the best features of Protestantism was the close links between clergy and laity, the law of Germinal brought the pastors under the control of the state rather than of the congregation. Many thought that Protestantism had entered a kind of torpor after the Germinal law, and that this was to be explained by the organization which it had established.

However, in spite of protests, there was no real attempt to change this system. Some historians have expressed surprise that Protestants did not try to profit from the apparently favourable conditions of Louis-Philippe's reign to try and revise the law, but it must be remembered that most of the political leaders of the period were anxious to avoid ecclesiastical questions which could be dangerous for those who raised them. The leading advocate of a complete break between Church and state, was Alexandre Vinet, who collaborated with *Le Semeur*. Some Protestants agreed with Vinet that Protestantism needed above all freedom, and that this could only be established by breaking away from the system of Germinal.[1] The establishment of the free church in the Vaud was a sign of what could be done, but there was no real effort in France to follow suit. It was not until the Revolution of 1848 that the possibility of bringing about change in the system was seriously considered, but then the emphasis was rather on the calling of a national synod. In May 1848 (when Guizot was still in England) a special Protestant assembly in Paris discussed the ways in which a synod could be elected. When it was proposed that only those Protestants who took communion regularly should be elected, then some pastors stated that there were many of their congregations, sometimes the most zealous, who hardly ever communicated. It was decided that those who declared that they belonged to the Reformed Church should have the right to vote, but it was obvious that when the elected delegates of the consistories met in September 1848, the question had to be settled of defining who was a member of the Church.

This question could easily become, what does a member of the Reformed Church believe? It was proposed that an official statement should be made outlining the doctrinal beliefs of the Church. Some thought this wrong, since the outstanding feature of Protestantism was its variety. Others thought it unwise to try and carry out a radical

[1] *L'Église et l'État* (À propos de l'ouvrage de M. Vinet . . .), Paris 1843, puts forward with approval the arguments of Vinet. On Alexandre Vinet (1798-1847), 'the Swiss Chalmers', as a unifying influence in French Protestantism, see E. *Caldesaigues*, Alexandre Vinet d'après son œuvre, *Revue de Théologie d'Aix*, 1947, pp. 178-179.

reform of the Church just then (this group included many of Guizot's friends). For others a statement of doctrine would be misleading. 'Christianity', said Sardinoux, 'is not a rosary of doctrines, it is a life, in fact it is the life.' But there were some delegates, Frédéric Monod, Agénor de Gasparin and Jules Bonnet, who thought that the Church must be based upon a stated doctrine; finding themselves in a minority, they withdrew, and within a short time founded the *Union des Églises Évangeliques de France.*

Another result of this synod, which was unofficial since no government had decreed it, was the new law affecting Protestants made by the Prince-President in March 1852. By this law the parish became a legal unit, electing a Presbyteral Council by universal suffrage. A Central Council of the Churches was set up, with most of its members nominated by the government, which was expected to serve as a link between Church and state and to do the work of a national Synod. It was this Church, organized by the laws of Germinal, Year X, and March 1852, which had to face the doctrinal crises of the 1860s and 1870s.

One of the effects of the law of Germinal had been to give Protestants who were influential in government circles prominence in the Consistoral Councils. The first members of the Paris Consistory under the Empire, for example, included politicians such as Boissy d'Anglas, Jaucourt and Rabaut-Dupui. In this way, and because of his political contacts, Guizot became a member of the Consistoral Council in 1814, and throughout the Restoration he used his influence on behalf of his co-religionists, particularly on behalf of Protestant schools. In 1852 he was elected to the Presbyteral Council of Paris, and in spite of his opposition to the Empire, he was still able to deploy a considerable amount of influence. The Minister concerned with Instruction and the Cults, from 1851 to 1856, Hippolyte Fortoul, had begun his University career under the July Monarchy and Protestants confidently told each other that 'he owed his Legion of Honour to Guizot'. Guizot was also on friendly terms with other ministers, notably Victor Duruy. These friendships, together with his position in the Academy, his reputation abroad (especially in England) and his writings, which made him the first layman since Chateaubriand to have defended Christianity in works of some renown, ensured Guizot's position as an important figure in the Reformed Church.

As early as 1855 Agénor de Gasparin described the crisis into which the Protestants were entering as one of 'pious rationalism'[1]; with the writings of Renan, Colani, Scherer, Pécaut and Réville, it developed into 'les négations extrêmes'. Both for the moderate and

[1] *Archives du Christianisme*, October 27th, 1855.

for the more extreme rationalists Guizot was an enemy. For one thing he used his influence to exclude the rationalists from positions of importance. In 1856, when an appointment had to be made to the seminary of Montauban, both Albert Réville and Bonifas had strong support, but Guizot worked hard to secure the appointment of the orthodox Bonifas, and rumour had it that once the Emperor had accepted to nominate him, Guizot was the first to be informed.[1] But more important perhaps was Guizot's attitude to the Roman Catholic Church. It was quite common for even quite orthodox Protestants to regard Catholicism as Madame de Staël did, as an 'aged lion', or to dismiss it as a form of superstition, comparable to pre-Christian paganism.[2] Guizot was therefore unusual in adopting an attitude favourable towards Catholicism. Both in his 1838 articles (already referred to) and later, when Italian affairs thrust the whole nature of the Catholic Church into prominence, Guizot persisted in this pro-Catholic policy. His reception of Lacordaire in the Academy was deliberately provocative and people who visited him whilst he was preparing this speech saw that he was challenging opinion both in the Protestant and the Catholic worlds. He wanted to underline the significance of those who once had been enemies becoming colleagues. But Étienne Coquerel was only surprised that Lacordaire should be 'si peu catholique' and Guizot 'si peu protestant'.[3] There was even greater indignation amongst Protestants when in a speech to a Protestant society Guizot said that the whole Christian edifice would suffer if one of the great constructions which composed it, meaning the Papacy, was attacked. For some of Guizot's co-religionists it was astonishing that a Protestant could lament the misfortunes of that power which had spilt the blood of Protestants and which for three centuries had fought against the Christian faith and the Bible.[4] Even Guizot's friend Grandpierre found it necessary to disagree and to explain that he saw the blows to the Papal power as being the signs of a great deliverance for the Universal Church[5] L'Église et la Société Chrétiennes en 1861 confirmed many in their hostility to Guizot. Here he expressed his admiration for the French Catholic Church and its response to the dangers of revolution and irreligion.

[1] *Albert Réville* (1826-1906) was the son of a Dieppe pastor who served for a long time in the Walloon church at Rotterdam. A former pupil of Reuss, he collaborated with the leading Biblical scholars of the Continent (including Renan) and published a great many articles and books. In 1880 he was appointed to the Collège de France, and then to the École des Hautes Études.

[2] *Poupot, La Justification Personnelle* (Lettre à Monsieur Guizot), Montauban 1843.

[3] *Le Lien*, February 2nd, 1861.

[4] *Archives du Christianisme*, April 30th, 1861.

[5] *L'Espérance*, May 3rd, 1861.

He believed that Catholicism was a cause which had to be defended by all those who wished to defend religion and liberty. It is not surprising that Guizot was described as an ultramontane Catholic rather than as a Protestant.[1]

But Guizot's supposed 'Catholicism' was not merely a question of policy towards the Papacy. It also affected his attitude to his own Church. In *L'Église et la Société Chrétiennes* he was careful to say that he appreciated the essential diversity of Protestantism, and that he did not consider that it was the right time for any expulsions from the Church, but he also made two things clear. He thought that the Protestant Church should be endowed with its National Synods; he did not believe that people could stay in the Church if they did not share its faith. Supposing Luther and Calvin had tried to remain within the Catholic Church, he wrote; then even supposing that the Catholic Church had admitted religious liberty, would they not have called on them to leave and to take with them all who shared their beliefs?[2] For all Guizot's denials, it looked as if he was thinking of a Synod framing some declaration of doctrine which would be aimed at rationalists.

In 1860 many of these liberals and rationalists had formed themselves into an organization, *L'Union Protestante Libérale*. The Consistory of Paris decided to make a declaration condemning this association and Guizot was given the task of writing it. However, it is noticeable that he was much less vigorous than other laymen who were considering this declaration. Guizot was prepared to speak openly of dissidents with the Church having certain rights, but his collaborators, François Delessert, Chabaud-Latour, Mettetal and others, thought this unwise.[3] Guizot therefore seems genuinely anxious to avoid a break at this time.

This was clearly seen in his relations with Athanase Coquerel the younger. The son of the Athanase Coquerel whose preaching was outstandingly eloquent, so that it was said that after one of his sermons you were more disposed to say 'Bravo' than 'Amen', he was director of *Le Lien* and one of the great champions of liberalism and toleration. He was in the 1860s acting as suffragant preacher in the church of the Rue de Rivoli, and neither his writings nor his sermons were to the taste of the orthodox. The success of his sermons perhaps increased their disapproval (one remembers that Paley once said of a

---

[1] See the many quotations collected together in *Taxile Delord, La Papauté de Monsieur Guizot*, Paris 1865, one of the bitterest attacks ever made on him. Goldwin Smith, who visited Guizot at this time, was surprised at the complacency with which he looked on the Papacy. *Goldwin Smith, Reminiscences*, 1910, p. 94.

[2] *L'Église et la Société Chrétiennes en 1861* (op. cit.), pp. 57-64.

[3] François Delessert: Guizot, June 29th and July 5th, 1861, *Archives S.H.P.F.*

man that he knew nothing against him except that he was a successful preacher); and the fact that he was supported by *L'Union Protestante Libérale* did not make him more acceptable. In 1862 Coquerel preached a sermon on 'Christian minorities', in which he claimed to speak on behalf of one-third of the Church, saying 'God often entrusts the most important rôles to minorities, making them the benefactors of the world'. This was seen as a deliberately provocative address, and his reference to those who were in the majority today finding themselves in the minority tomorrow, was thought to be aggressive. 'This seems to go beyond all limits,' wrote Pelet de la Lozère to Guizot, 'a Consistory which puts up with this abdicates.'[1] But once again Guizot did not join with his colleagues in attacking Coquerel. A year later Coquerel recalled that in circumstances which were painful to him, Guizot alone amongst the majority of the Presbyteral Council showed kindness and fairness to him.[2] Coquerel was writing in 1863 because he was at the centre of yet another controversy. He had tried to put into circulation a new Genevan version of the New Testament, in place of the Ostervald version which was always distributed by the *Société Biblique*. Once again Guizot, after some hesitation, decided to support the distribution of both versions, contrasting with Delessert, who withdrew from the *Société Biblique* and formed an association of his own which would have nothing to do with the new version.

It was in 1864 that Guizot decided he could no longer restrain his friends. The occasion was Coquerel's reaction to Renan's *Vie de Jésus*. It seems that there might have been some misunderstanding here, since Coquerel expressed distaste for the sentimental gloss with which Renan had sought to make his work attractive, but Guizot was moved by Coquerel's reference to Renan as 'cher et savant ami'.[3] The Presbyteral Council decided not to renew Coquerel's suffragance in Paris, and they decided to accompany this decision with a declaration of principles. This declaration was drawn up by Guizot. It stated as the principles of the Church, belief in the supernatural action of God in the world's affairs, belief in the divine and supernatural inspiration of the Scriptures and in their sovereign authority in religious affairs, belief in the miraculous birth and resurrection of Jesus Christ, God-man, Saviour and Redeemer of men. The declaration went on to say that it was incomprehensible that a Church could exist without a common faith, professing 'indifferently' the most

---

[1] Pelet de la Lozère: Guizot, February 5th, 1862, *Archives S.H.P.F.*; *Athanase Coquerel fils, Les Minorités Chrétiennes*, Paris 1862.

[2] Athanase Coquerel fils: Guizot, March 14th, 1863, Ibid.

[3] *Pédézert, Cinquante Ans de Souvenirs Religieux et Ecclésiastiques* (op. cit.), p. 307; *Schweitzer, The Quest of the Historical Jesus* (op. cit.), p. 189.

various and contradictory doctrines; and therefore it seemed inadmissible that those who contested these principles of belief should speak and teach in the name of the Church.[1]
Naturally this decision and this action was bitterly attacked. Newspapers such as *Le Lien* and *Le Temps* claimed that it was contrary to the spirit of Protestantism, contrary even to the law since neither the law of Germinal nor the law of 1852 had recognized any particular doctrine. Taxile Delord referred to 'the encyclical and syllabus of Monsieur Guizot'; another publication accused the Presbyteral Council of having made itself into an intermediary between God and man, and referring to Guizot's declaration, it asked 'What more would a Pope say?'[2] All these questions were raised in the spring of 1865, at a pastoral conference which met in Paris. Guizot spoke in justification of his positive beliefs and dogmas, and reiterated all his customary insistence on faith 'in something which is superhuman'. He was opposed by both the Coquerels, father and son. The younger repeated his frequently stated view that Christ was more than a dogma, or a dogmatiser, he was love itself. It was this Jesus of love that was necessary to mankind; man's hunger and thirst could not be appeased by lists of theories. Athanase Coquerel the elder went even further, for not only did he state that no one any longer believed in the divine Jesus, but he also opposed the whole attitude of the Council. 'If between the Bible and the reader there is any authority whatsoever, then from being Protestants we become Catholics.'[3]

The quarrel went beyond Paris into the consistories and the provincial pastoral conferences. Belief in the supernatural and in the necessity of having some common, determined beliefs within the same Church was sometimes upheld and sometimes refused. The complication was such that the traditional division of French Protestantism into an orthodox north and a radical south was sometimes reversed, as when 121 pastors withdrew from a liberal-controlled conference at Nîmes, and formed the *Conférence Nationale Évangélique du Midi* and subscribed to Guizot's declaration. This became an issue in the elections and in the 1865 elections to the Paris Council great opposition was organized against Guizot. For a time it looked as if

[1] *Pédézert*, ibid., pp. 222-225, 328-329.
[2] *L'Église Réformée. Réponse à la Communication du Conseil Presbytéral de Paris.* Paris 1864, p. 10. This quarrel recalled the controversy earlier in the century when Élie Gasc had been reproved for his views on the Trinity. See *Charles-Louis Frossard, L'Orthodoxie de l'Église Réformée de France*, Paris 1864. See also *Mary, Christianisme et Libre Examen*, Paris 1864. *Monsieur Guizot et la Papauté, Par un Chrétien qui n'a pas été à Gand*, Paris 1864, is an attack on Guizot which resuscitates the old arguments of the 1840s against him, and which suggests that the only principle of authority in religious matters should be a popular vote.
[3] *L'Espérance*, May 5th, 1865.

he would be defeated, and in June 1865 he founded an association, avowedly for the defence of the Christian faith in the Reformed Church of France. This would have made the distinction between the contending parties even sharper, and it was for this reason that he abandoned the idea, although the society was ready to begin its activities. Eventually he was elected, supposedly thanks to the votes of the Protestant workers of Belleville, who joined with the upper bourgeoisie in their defence of the supernatural.

The Consistory of Caen took the controversy a stage further when in November 1866 it decided that every elector was obliged to make a declaration of faith at the moment of voting. Guizot supported this decision and regarded it as well-founded in religious principles and opportune in the state of the Church. The declaration was not being asked from a man who was attending church, it was being asked only from people who wished to vote and to have some influence on Church policy. At a time when the faith was being openly rejected, Guizot thought it a necessity for Protestants to assure themselves that those who actually took part in the presentation of the faith accepted it.[1]

It is interesting to remember that the English controversy on clerical subscription to the Thirty-Nine Articles was taking place at exactly the same time. This controversy had often existed in England. During the eighteenth century the Feathers Tavern petition had claimed the right of every Protestant to interpret scripture for himself without being bound 'by any human explications thereof', but whilst this might be the right of individuals it had always been argued that where there was a clergyman of the established Church, then it was necessary for him to subscribe to the articles and canons. Burke had laid it down that 'if we do not get some security for the doctrines which a man draws from Scriptures, we not only permit but we actually pay for all the dangerous fanaticism which can be produced to corrupt our people and to decry the public worship of the country.' A Member of Parliament, Mr. Buxton, who was trying to get some modifications of University subscription, nevertheless believed that 'those who preach from the pulpits of the Church should be ascertained members of the Church'; and one of the leading theologians of Anglicanism, F. D. Maurice, said that he welcomed the Articles because they checked habits and temper of mind, which interfered with its freedom.[2] If in a Church as well established and as

---

[1] December 30th, 1866. Note by Guizot. *Archives S.H.P.F.*

[2] *Edmund Burke*, Speech on the Act of Uniformity, February 6th, 1772, *Works* (Bohn Edition), op. cit., vol. vi, p. 102. House of Commons, March 16th, 1864, *Hansard*, 3rd series, vol. 174, cols. 146-148. *F. D. Maurice, The Faith of the Liturgy and the Doctrine of the 39 Articles*, 1860.

broadly conceived as the Church of England some form of subscription was thought advisable, it is hardly surprising that it was put
forward in such a disorganized and uncertain Church as the Reformed
Church of France, or to speak the more precise language of Bonaparte, the Reformed Churches of France.

The decision of the Caen Consistory was declared illegal by the
Minister Baroche, but when the Conseil d'État considered the
Consistory's appeal at the end of 1869, then the ministerial decision
was overruled. It was particularly noticed that in the declarations
made by the spokesman of the Conseil d'État, de Belboeuf, it was
clearly held that the Reformed Church did not owe its existence to
the law of Germinal, since it was already in existence, with its own
principles and rules. This declaration was thought to be significant,
not only in terms of the right of consistories, but also in terms of the
Church's right to meet in a National Synod. For some years there
had been a movement in favour of having a Synod, and Guizot was
prominent in this. In 1867 Guillaume de Félice saw the Emperor and
requested a Synod; in 1868 there were a number of attempts to
persuade the authorities that a National Synod was necessary, both
from certain consistories (such as the Consistory of Nancy) and from
individuals, including Guizot.[1] In 1869 Guizot sent a memorandum
to the Minister explaining the attitude of those who wanted a Synod.
'Agreement on the fundamental religious beliefs', he wrote, 'and the
profession, maintenance and propagation of these beliefs, this is the
moral principle of every religious society, this is the character and
condition of every church. It is this principle which the Consistory
of the Reformed Church of Paris is trying to uphold. It is the contrary
principle which its adversaries are trying to assert. The ones claim the
right to associate religiously only with those who share their religious
faith. The others claim the right to remain associated with those
whose religious faith they do not share.' One has to notice that
throughout this memorandum Guizot was particularly anxious to
demonstrate the strength of orthodoxy to the Minister, and to
impress upon him that the Reformed Church was real and
organized.[2]

Not everyone agreed with this. For all that some pastors were just
as opposed to the official Church becoming 'the caravanserai of all
the muddle-heads of all the sects and all the schools', yet they did not
think that a Synod was a good idea. One asked, 'What can be
resolved with forty, or even with a hundred, autocratic consciences,

---

[1] Guillaume de Félice: Guizot, October 23rd, 1867, *Archives S.H.P.F.*;
L'Espérance, October 23rd, 1868.
[2] Guizot: Le Ministre de la Justice et des Cultes, September 1st, 1869, *Archives
S.H.P.F.*

decided to maintain their autocracy against men and against God?'[1] Frédérick de Coninck, from Le Havre, who usually supported Guizot, disagreed with him about the Consistory of Caen, and was rather apprehensive about the effects of a National Synod.[2] But by 1870 it seemed clear that a Synod would be called, and Émile Ollivier formed a commission of lawyers to examine the legality of National Synods. Its chairman, Hamille, who was helped in this work by Guillaume Guizot, decided in favour of their legality.[3]

After the Franco-Prussian War it might well have been felt that at a time when everything in the state was being changed, then it was appropriate to give French Protestants the opportunity of reviewing their institutions. The correspondent of the London *Times* suggested that the discordant nature of Protestantism had been tolerable for as long as French society was forcibly held together by the artificial bond of Imperialism, but once France was obliged to decide upon its future government and society, then French Protestants had to be allowed to reconsider their situation.[4] There were three other considerations, however, which finally persuaded the government to allow a National Synod. Firstly as German occupying troops frequently aroused the indignation of the Catholic hierarchy by taking over Catholic churches, or parts of the churches, for Protestant worship, the Reformed Church was particularly anxious to reassert its position as a national Church.[5] Secondly, the annexation of Alsace-Lorraine removed the greater part of the Lutheran population, and this raised problems concerning co-operation between those Lutherans who remained in France and the Calvinists; before proceeding to this co-operation, the Calvinists needed to clarify their own position. Thirdly, Thiers became head of the government. There can be no doubt that Guizot now had considerable influence. Thiers treated Guizot with friendship and respect; Guizot complied with all Thiers's wishes and kept him fully informed.[6] The Minister concerned with worship was Jules Simon, for long an admirer of Guizot's; the Director of the Non-Catholic section of the Ministry was Guillaume Guizot. People were right when they calculated that it was Guizot who had been most influential in arranging

---

[1] *Maeder*, Rapport sur la situation des partis dans l'église, présenté au Consistoire de Strasbourg, February 4th, 1862, ibid.
[2] De Coninck: Guizot, January 16th, 1867; December 13th, 1871, ibid.
[3] See *Archives Nationales*, F¹⁹ 10177¹.
[4] *The Times*, July 2nd, 1872.
[5] See various documents in *Archives Nationales*, F¹⁹ 5609.
[6] Guizot: Thiers, October 7th, November 11th, 1871, *Papiers Thiers*, op. cit., 20622.

the decree of November 29th, 1871, which called for a National Synod.

To the historian of Guizot not the least dramatic part of the 1872 Synod is the rôle played by both Guizot and Thiers. At the same time as Guizot, now eighty-four years old, was demonstrating to the Protestant world that he was still a masterly orator and skilful debater, Thiers, aged seventy-six, was demonstrating to the National Assembly in Versailles that he too had lost none of his talents, and as the Army Bill was debated, showed that he could still make an assembly dance to the tune of his shrill voice. Both of these men looked back on long lives of activity and importance; both were surrounded by great respect. But it is tempting to say that the differences between them were never so clearly revealed as in this final demonstration. Thiers remained the politician, shuffling and reshuffling the forces of his majority, and such was the longevity of Orleanist politicians, that he was still dealing some of the same names as thirty years earlier, Charles de Rémusat for example. Thiers was still giving evidence of his cleverness; he was still performing the 'tour de force' of uniting a discordant majority, he was still being accused of being a 'dictator', he continued to arouse suspicions about his integrity and honesty of purpose. One understands why Émile Ollivier once said that there was no one so excessive as Thiers in his immobility. But Guizot, always more serious and more profound, had left politics behind; his interests were spiritual and intellectual; he was not negotiating in the tawdry splendour of Versailles, but in the Temple du Saint-Esprit, where the pulpit was decorated by a large, open Bible.

Such a comparison is true, but it is rather unfair to Thiers; it is also misleading so far as the Synod is concerned. The assembly in the Temple was not altogether unlike that in Versailles. It had two parties, a right and a left, which were as distinct as those in the National Assembly; it also possessed a centre which was as indistinct as any in the political world. The differences between parties, the subtleties of manœuvre, the violences of opinion, were all similar. The policy of the right wing, the orthodox or evangelicals as they were called, had been carefully prepared; it had been decided to hold a pre-liminary meeting at the Val-Richer in order to concert orthodox tactics, and it was only for accidental reasons that this preparatory reunion was called off.[1] But in spite of preparation, before the opening of the Synod on June 6th, 1872, there was great apprehension, even anguish, amongst many who had worked hard for the Synod.

[1] Charles Bois (Professor of Theology at Montauban): Guizot, April 28th, May 15th, 1872, *Archives S.H.P.F.*

They foresaw the possible dislocation of their Church, and as one of them wrote to Guizot, 'I need all the faith that God has given me to remove my fears.'[1]

There was essentially only one question before the Synod, and this was the question which had been put forward by Guizot and the Presbyteral Council of Paris in 1864 and 1865. Should the Reformed Church of France be endowed with an official doctrine, an official standard of faith? This question was debated in various forms; there was a discussion over the legality of the Synod, there was a debate on the proposed declaration of faith, and there were animated discussions on the organization of the Church and on the conditions which would be imposed on electors. On all these questions the orthodox or evangelical party rallied a majority which was usually about 16 or 17. *The Times* correspondent was probably justified in commenting that there was something strange about a Church deciding upon its theology by going into divisions on it, and he was undoubtedly correct in wondering whether a Church founded on such divisions could be lasting.[2]

The left wing of the Synod was usually considered to be led by Athanase Coquerel the younger (although he no longer needed that designation since his father had died in 1868, supposedly unhappy in his last years since the Presbyteral Council in Paris had prevented him from having the pastoral assistants of his choice). Coquerel, aided by his brother Étienne, defended the value of diversity, and was so opposed to a declaration of faith that he was reported as saying that he would refuse to sign a declaration saying that two and two made four. There were three men associated with Coquerel who deserve to be noticed. There was Félix Pécaut, who had resigned his pastorship in the Béarn because of difficulties with his Consistory; a pupil of Neander, the Church historian, he had in 1859 published *Le Christ et la Conscience*, a daring and highly controversial book. There was Timothée Colani, a former pastor and teacher of theology who had in 1850 founded the *Revue de Strasbourg*, the meeting-place of the new theology; and Jules Gaufrès, a layman whose contributions to discussions were thought to be amongst the most suggestive and original. One can also notice amongst the laymen of this party Colonel Denfert-Rochereau, the defender of Belfort in the recent war, who had been one of Guizot's rivals in the Protestant elections of Paris. On the right, the most important delegates were the President or Moderator of the Synod, Charles Bastie, from Bergerac, Charles Bois, the Montauban Professor, two deputies Mettetal and Guizot's old friend Chabaud-Latour, and Guizot him-

[1] Ernest Dhombres (a pastor in Paris): Guizot, May 25th, 1872, ibid.
[2] *The Times*, July 12th, 1872.

self. Jalabert, Dean of the Faculty of Law at Nancy, was the acknowledged leader of the third or centre party.

The discussions of the Synod lasted from June 6th until July 10th. The record of the debates shows to what extent they were lively and serious, and no one who reads them can deny that they are to the honour of French Protestantism. Nevertheless, very little that was new emerged from the discussion. The arguments had been gone over many times, in the Pastoral Conferences, in the Protestant press, in the theological reviews, in Guizot's *Méditations* (which Colani referred to as the most important work produced by the orthodox party). The one side argued the necessity of having agreement on the fundamental principles of the Christian faith, and of closing the pulpits and the schoolrooms of the Reformed Church to those who propounded 'négations' rather than these principles of Christian faith and tradition. The other side argued that an obligatory confession of faith was a vice which destroyed the principles of Protestantism and which contracted both conscience and piety. It questioned the articles of faith as put forward by Professor Bois, and in particular it commented upon the absence of the Trinity (which had been absent from Guizot's essential dogmas of 1864) as confirming that the dogma of religion necessarily evolved and changed. It challenged the right of certain individuals to assert that their interpretation of an event such as the resurrection, or their understanding of St. Paul's words, was more valid than that of another scholar. Guizot did not add anything to what he had already said and written, apart from certain remarks of a personal nature. He was able to assure the Synod that he knew Thiers very well, and that it was Thiers's intention to look upon the Synod as a body which had the right to take decisions, not merely as a consultative body. He recalled, too, going in 1807 to visit his great-uncle, who was pastor in Pont-de-Montvert, in the Cévennes. The congregation, of some two or three thousand peasants, met in the open air, high up in the mountains. Guizot read from the Bible before his great-uncle preached. What was it, asked Guizot, that brought those people there and united them together? It was a common faith; it was not any particular knowledge or erudition, it was the common faith which was the natural and necessary link of any religious society. He believed that it was this common faith which the Synod was being asked to confirm.

The Confession of Faith, declared that the Reformed Church remained faithful to its origins; it proclaimed the authority of the Scriptures and salvation through faith in Christ, who was the only begotten Son of God, who had died for man's sins and who had been raised for their 'justification'. On June 20th the declaration was

adopted by 61 votes to 45, with two absentees. On June 26th Guizot
withdrew from the Synod, excusing himself from attending any
further sessions because of extreme fatigue, and giving as a final
message to the Synod, the assurance that he respected the liberty of
his opponents as much as he respected his own liberty. He later wrote
that he had considered that the essential work of the Synod was
accomplished; firstly there had been its convocation and secondly
there had been the declaration of faith.[1] After the break-up of the
Synod, the liberals became active around Thiers, trying to persuade
him that the actions of the orthodox party had been contrary to the
law and that they would necessitate changes in the constitution of the
Church. Once again it was to Guizot that the Moderator, Bois, and
the orthodox party turned. Guizot saw Thiers and persuaded him
that their actions had not been illegal and that no new arrangement
of Church and state was necessary.[2] Although Thiers was sufficiently
nervous to postpone the second session of the Synod which should
have met in November 1872, he allowed it to meet in November
1873; it was then that the liberals did not reply to their convocation
and that the schism of the Church was complete.

It is ironical that Guizot, who began his religious writing by
insisting upon the necessity of all believers uniting, should have
presided over the break-up of the Reformed Church. It was his
opponents who had urged the orthodox to concentrate on the
unbeliever, to look to the enemy; it was his opponents who professed
sadness at the schism. Guizot regarded the Synod of 1872, and the
official sanctioning of the declaration of faith in 1874, as triumphs.
He had in 1866 told Thiers that the religious question was his last
battlefield. He died believing that he had won his last battle.

Guizot's religious thought was sometimes inconsistent and often
incomplete. Many examples of this have already been given. Having
described a religion as instinctive to man, and having expressed his
distrust of theologians and of human science, he goes on to detail a
list of dogmas. Having rejected the total inspiration of the Bible, he
nevertheless goes on to claim the infallibility of those parts which are
inspired, in much the same way as he supported both the Revolution
of 1830 and the legitimacy of Louis-Philippe. His was the austere

[1] Guizot: Andral, November 5th, 1873, *Archives S.H.P.F.* The official dossier
of the Synod is in *Archives Nationales*, F[19] 10177[1]. The most convenient record of
its discussions is *Eugène Bersier, Histoire du Synode Général de l'Église Réformée
de France*, 2 vols., Paris 1872. See also *Edouard de Pressensé*, 'Le Synode Général
du Protestantisme Français et les Divisions des Protestants', *Revue des Deux
Mondes*, August 15th, 1872, pp. 748 ff.
[2] Bois: Guizot, July 20th, August 28th, November 13th, 1873; Guizot:
Bastie, August 5th, 1872, *Archives S.H.P.F.*

religion of the supernatural, the presentation of God as the unfathomable mystery from which all else is derived; but he was humanist enough to reject predestination and to suggest, although tentatively, that every man was the incarnation of God. Although an intellectual, he never believed (as did Döllinger) that the scientific approach to religion could further religious unity. Although a promoter of this unity, he was also a perpetrator of schism.

One can perhaps explain such incompleteness and such inconsistencies by lack of skill. But the true explanation probably lies much deeper. It seems likely that in some ways Guizot was ill at ease in the Protestant Church. This was apparent during the controversies of the 1860s, and in the Synod of 1872 it was clear that certain of Guizot's adversaries were thinking on lines entirely different from himself. There was, for example, their attitude towards the Catholics. Athanase Coquerel described the enemies of Protestantism as being firstly the Catholics, secondly the atheists; Guizot could not agree to this way of putting things. Colani opposed the declaration of faith by saying that a Catholic would be able to sign it; this for Guizot was not a disadvantage. It was frequently said that there could never be collaboration with the Catholics, since besides the cross they placed the figure of the Virgin Mary; but this neither shocked nor perturbed Guizot. It is appropriate to recall that Albert de Broglie once wrote, 'Monsieur Guizot's mind is too French to be entirely Protestant.'[1] Guizot did not see things only from the narrow standpoint of Protestantism, and even the orthodox, such as Charles Bois, did not always agree with his view of Catholicism.

At first sight it is strange that Guizot, who appreciated the value of diversity in rendering European civilization particularly rich, and who explained the vitality of the Church of England by reference to the variety of religious opinions with which it had to contend, should not have agreed with Athanase Coquerel the younger, when he defended the virtues of diversity and variety in Protestantism. But Coquerel's vision was limited to the small world of French Protestantism. Diversity for him was the diversity of those who believed in the resurrection of the spirit being alongside those who believed in the resurrection of the flesh. He did not extend it to the world of Catholicism. But the diversity which Guizot appreciated was the diversity of France.

Coquerel, Colani, Pécaut and their colleagues thought that Protestantism was in danger. But they thought as practising Protestants who were for ever viewing their Church as a collection of people. They wanted this Church to grow; they wanted to convert; they

---

[1] *Albert de Broglie*, 'Le Christianisme et la Société', *Revue des Deux Mondes*, February 1st, 1869, p. 531.

wanted a Church which was active and meaningful, able to resist what Pécaut called 'l'immense flot catholique'; they hoped for a Church which would save the scattered rural communities, where the faithful were drifting away, or were being absorbed by Catholic marriages. For them, the declaration of faith would divide the Church, would sap its energies and reduce its appeal. They feared a Church which would preach only to the converted and would cease to play a vital part in the country. They believed that French Protestants were not conscious of doctrinal dangers; they were moved above all by 'l'instinct de vivre', the desire to live and to grow. Guizot never thought in this way. Like Sainte-Beuve, he did not regret that France had not become Protestant; as a politician he could not think in sectarian or in proselytising terms. Perhaps, too, whilst there were some Protestants who thought in terms of a movement of expansion and conversion, there were others who preferred to be in a restricted, select élite, and Guizot may well have been one of these.

Yet there is something to be said for Guizot's beliefs and for the policy he followed. It is probably true that there are certain claims which Christianity cannot surrender. Most Christians would say that they cannot give up the belief that God is active in history, or that God was incarnate in a particular person, or that the action of God can be perceived. There is a point beyond which one cannot go if what is specific in Christianity is not to disappear. This is all that Guizot, and those who thought like him, were trying to say. Perhaps their mistake was in their manner of stating these essentials. Dogmas are not simply facts: they are value-affirmations, and their significance as such has to be explained. Dogmas may be unchanging; but the commentaries which accompany them are continuously evolving. The Christian religion cannot be only a philosophy of supernatural existence; and religious unity cannot be achieved by asserting a common minimum of doctrine. The focal point of all religion is worship, and one has to note that those who have apparently had most success in promoting union amongst Christians and in divining the real essence of Christianity, have not insisted upon doctrinal formularies, but upon liturgy. And here it must be admitted that Guizot was ill-equipped to discuss such a matter. He had no sense of liturgy, no real sense of worship other than something which was entirely private and natural. Prayer was free and lay; at its most ceremonious it was when three generations kneeled in the study of the Val-Richer; but in the *Méditations* prayer was presented as something uncertain, perhaps even inefficacious. Baptism he never mentions. Pédezert said of him that in this respect he had 'l'âme d'un huguenot'. He never complained about the bare temples, the arid liturgies, the old, boring Psalms, 'the extreme simplicity of our ceremonies'.[1] If he thought of the appearance of the Reformed Church in the state, he thought only of its doctrinal appearance; he thought that it would be judged by the unity and force of its beliefs, the strength of its system. But the position of a French Protestant was always difficult. Often he was made to feel a foreigner; sometimes it seemed that the fate of his religion was being decided in countries outside France. He did not have the confidence to say like Pusey, 'I believe all which the Church believes.' He did not have the sense of security which permitted Dean Stanley to say that less importance was to be attached to belief than to practice. Caught in the shallows of his own history, he could either try to define his position, and this is what Guizot did; or he could simply say, 'Moi, je me tiens pour fils de Huguenot,' and this too Guizot said.

[1] *Pédézert, Souvenirs et Études* (op. cit.), p. 236.

9

CONCLUSION

J'ai eu l'honneur de tomber le premier dans le désastre de
mon pays.   GUIZOT

I T is easy to suggest that Guizot was a complete failure. It could
be said that as a politician he had two main ideas, to maintain a
good understanding with England and to prevent any further
revolution in France; the Spanish marriages as arranged by him and
the uprising in Paris in 1848 meant the ruin of both ideas. As a
political thinker he advocated the sovereignty of reason and the
avoidance of any extremism; but few people adopted this approach
to politics, and violence never disappeared from French political life.
As an educational reformer he hoped for the collaboration of
Church and state and he expected that the 'instituteurs' would play
a moderating and conservative role in French society; but the
hostility of Church and state in educational matters became one of
the worst divisions within the country, and the 'instituteurs' tended
to become an increasingly radical element. As a diplomat he hoped
that the French would adopt an attitude in foreign policy commen-
surate with their resources and interests; but the vision of a grandiose
and elevated mission in the world being reserved to French enterprise
has never ceased to haunt the minds of both statesmen and public.
As an historian he hoped that the study of history would help a
divided and anxious nation towards unity and security; but the
burden of history has often tended to further disagreement and
bitterness. As a Protestant he hoped for reconciliation amongst
Christians and for the anchoring of Protestantism in dogmatic
certitudes; but Protestantism in France has increasingly become a
religion with social rather than doctrinal preoccupations, and in spite
of certain movements, Christian unity has remained distant. In
all these ways Guizot's failure appears evident, and no discussion

432

of his career would be complete without an attempt to explain it.

To some extent this is to return to the subject of his unpopularity which was mentioned in the first chapter, and to the significance of his connections with Nîmes and the Église du Desert, his experience of the Revolution and his unusually cosmopolitan education in Geneva. This background and this upbringing meant that in many respects Guizot was not French, in the sense that he was always rather remote from the French scene, always rather apart from the sentiments and the opinions of his contemporaries. It is significant that when a young man, living in the capital of Imperial France, he is apparently quite unmoved by the 'miracles de bravoure et de génie' of this time, and he never mentioned in letters to his mother the military ceremonies which were then important in the life of Paris. At a time of intense French nationalism, Guizot was preoccupied above all with foreign literature, and when he was contributing to *Le Publiciste*, Pauline de Meulan was justified in reproaching him with knowing nothing about the audience for whom he was writing. Under the Restoration he was a Professor and a journalist, when the University and the press were being attacked; under the July Monarchy he was a minister and an upholder of the established order when it was both facile and modish to be amongst the critics and the opponents of this society. He was a politician who never understood the nature of public enthusiasms. He regretted that July 14th had been chosen as the symbolic date of the Revolution, as he regretted the *Marseillaise*. 'Je ne suis pas un grand soldat comme Thiers', he once wrote to Duchâtel, but for all that his irony was understandable, it is obvious that he never understood that the military allures assumed by Thiers gained him popularity rather than ridicule. He never understood why his foreign policy was unpopular. All he could see was an opposition which was factious or a public which was stupid. And stupidity was something which he could not understand. 'Je comprends les passions, les mauvais intérêts, je dirais presque les vices', he wrote to Bresson, 'Je ne comprends pas les bêtises et je ne m'y résigne pas.' Even as a churchman and historian he did not understand his contemporaries. He was ill at ease in company with many of his co-religionists, and he distinguished himself from them by his respect, if not admiration, for Catholicism. But when he wrote about Catholicism and when he tried to consider the Catholic Church as an institution, it was clear that he had little understanding of either Catholicism or the Church. When Sainte-Beuve wrote of 'cette fibre médiocrement nationale qu'on croit particulière à Monsieur Guizot', he was thinking in 1844 primarily of international relations, but what he said is capable of a wider application. In short, Guizot was frequently at odds with the rest of France.

Yet there were some advantages in being 'un-French'. One has to notice how some of the most skilful political intellects of France have been those of untypical Frenchmen with either an unorthodox preparation for politics or a 'foreign' approach to national affairs. From Napoleon and his nephew, via such men as the Duc de Richelieu and Jules Ferry, to Léon Blum and Mendès-France, there are sufficient examples to suggest that the politician who stands apart from the others benefits from this position at least temporarily, often until his very detachment encourages him to make mistakes which can be final and fatal. Such a politician is often clearer in his judgement and freer in his assessment of a situation than those who are closer to it. Less entangled with the routine of the political game, less subject to irrelevant nostalgia, less dependent upon the inertia of the past, he can more easily become the spokesman and the leader of others. But he remains a lonely figure. If he claims to lead a party, he is nevertheless not of the party. If he claims to be France, he is manifestly not French. If he inspires admiration, he never ceases to arouse distrust.

This was Guizot's position. To this separateness he added the outstanding quality of his career, its continuity. When one form of activity was stopped, then he turned to another. When his political career was brought to a halt in 1814, in 1820 or in 1848, he picked up his pen and continued his writing or lecturing where he had left off, when his university lecturers were stopped, as in 1822, he concentrated on historical and political studies, but when the Sorbonne was re-opened to him, he was ready to resume lecturing and achieved his greatest success; when, for various reasons, matters of international diplomacy appeared to throw the longest shadow in the French political scene, Guizot himself became a diplomat and a specialist of foreign policy; under the Second Empire, when religious writing and discussion assumed a particular importance, he followed the fashion and moved into the world of theology. He was never reduced to idleness and he was never silenced. This was obviously a matter of character; it was proof of his determination, and of his resilience. But it was also much more than this. It represents the fundamental unity of his activities, how he was in fact continuing to play the same rôle although he was playing in different theatres. In a France which was to be distinguished by the confusion of its ideas and by the extent of its uncertainties he sought to present an intellectual framework within which the problems of the day could be understood. In political matters he sought a theory of government; for education, principles of policy; for diplomacy, a rational approach to action; in history a means of understanding; in religion an organization of belief. From his beginnings under the Empire, to his contribution to Protestant affairs under the Third Republic, Guizot's work forms a whole.

It is this that explains his long eminence, his 'strange preponderance'. His intellectual effort, allied to remarkable gifts of oratory and considerable talent as a writer, enabled Guizot to make himself indispensable, one might say unavoidable. For men such as Villèle, Casimir Périer, Thiers or Molé, politics were the day-to-day affairs of an uninspired governing class; Guizot was sufficiently remote to try to place these policies in the movement of world history. Educational matters tended to be part of a sterile quarrel between the Church and the University; Guizot, able to stand apart from the quarrel sufficiently to appreciate the value of both institutions, sought primarily to determine the place of education in modern society. Foreign affairs were surrounded by excitement; Guizot was sufficiently unemotional to insist that French policy should be linked to the real interests of France. He could turn the researches of other scholars into illuminating generalizations and produce a history which made sense. He could elevate the uneasiness of orthodox Protestants into the definition of doctrinal authority. In all these ways he gave direction and justification to affairs. Intellectually he tried to stabilize and clarify at a time of disorder; practically he gave the qualities of distinction and courage to activities which were otherwise without them. This was his major contribution to French life. He can be criticized because he sometimes lost his detachment, and forgetting that his strength lay in his lucidity, became too involved with the intricacies of parliamentary management to be able to distinguish between convenience and necessity. He began to confuse immediate and permanent needs, and between 1840 and 1848 he sometimes took action and sometimes avoided taking any action, in accordance with the prejudices of an unenthusiastic and uncertain majority. On these occasions he became undistinguishable from the host of other politicians who surrounded him. However, if it was his intellectual effort which gave him eminence, it is by this that he must be judged.

When one comes to examine this system closely, one is struck by its inadequacy. Not only does this help to explain Guizot's failures; it also helps to explain why his influence was not lasting. For one thing his thought betrays the strain of being both an intellectual and a practical man of affairs. Too often the principles which he elucidated were those which were convenient. As has been shown in Chapter 2, the sovereignty of reason was a doctrine designed to solve a particular dilemma, an attempt to neutralise two rival groups who believed in the sovereignty of the king or in the sovereignty of the people. It reflected the difficulty of fixing a single point of authority in a complex society. But being subtle rather than profound, being a form of expertize rather than an example of bold logic, it did not take into consideration any theory of individual rights, nor did it consider the purely utilitarian function of government. Furthermore, if the best government was the government which governed most justly, and if government was regarded as a means of attaining the sovereignty of reason, then government is not the product of society, and government is necessarily reserved for a class of experts. There is thus a distinction between government and society. Guizot frequently commented on this as one of the evils of France. On March 7th, 1852, he wrote to Piscatory that there were two Frances, there was the France of the political classes and the France of the popular classes; they knew nothing of each other, and they acted without reference to each other. He realized that this was bad, but he did not apparently see that his political philosophy was inadequate for remedying the situation, even less did he see that the sovereignty of reason positively encouraged such a division. In exactly the same way (as has been shown in Chapter 7) his religious thought was designed to meet a particular situation. In Guizot's attack on rationalism and imperialism he sought to unite all believers in Christianity. He therefore tried to belittle the divisions between Protestants and Catholics, and in his attempt to define what united the faithful he was necessarily obliged to avoid certain topics and to remain silent about particular issues. His theology therefore stopped short, and was of only limited value to Protestants whilst remaining irrelevant to Catholics. It is understandable that Guizot should not have realized the extent to which he was making concessions to particular conditions, and when he wrote to Madame Lenormant 'Les nuances sont à la mode: je suis d'une couleur' he was undoubtedly sincere. But it is strange that he should have maintained his reputation for intellectual absolutism.

Another weakness of Guizot's thought was its eclecticism, or as it was sometimes called, syncretism. The eclectic philosophy is always associated with Victor Cousin, who, in a celebrated preface, explained the problem of philosophy. Philosophy, he believed, could do one of three things. It could abdicate its position and return to the Middle Ages by submitting to 'the ancient authority'; it could continue to adhere to one or more systems which were at war, one with another, and in process of mutually destroying one another; or it could find out what was true in each particular system, and disengaging the truth, construct a system which was superior to all the others. For Cousin the whole of the past had to be accepted, for whilst none of the systems of the past had been completely true, yet none of them had been completely false. The philosophy of eclecticism therefore rejected all exclusive doctrines. It became a philosophy of acceptance and of moderation.

The circumstances of post-revolutionary France encouraged Guizot to take a similar attitude towards politics. As he pointed out, with the restoration of the Bourbons, for the first time since 1792 the France of the Ancien Régime and the France of the Revolution were able to meet in conditions of liberty. Guizot accepted this situation. He accepted the past and the present in order that what was good in the past and the present could be maintained whilst what was bad could be rejected. Thus Guizot accepted that there should be a legitimate monarch, the outstanding characteristic of the Ancien Régime; he accepted that there should be a restricted form of electoral government, as established in the early years of the Revolution; he accepted that there should be a centralized administrative system, as perfected under the Empire. He thought therefore of the system of government established in 1814 as being a drawing together of the achievements of French history, a climax of national development.

In educational matters (as has been shown in Chapter 3) he refused to accept any of the exclusive principles which had existed in the past, by which instruction was the domain of the Church or of the state. He tried to call upon all the resources of society by establishing in primary education supervisory authorities which represented the state, the Church and the local notabilities, and he attempted to establish competition between the Church and the University in secondary education. In his history (as shown in Chapter 6) his view of European civilization was eclectic. In diplomacy (as shown in Chapter 5) he tried to avoid any exclusive alliances; the celebrated 'entente cordiale' with England was never meant to prevent any 'rapprochement' with Austria, and after the Spanish marriages Guizot saw no reason to suppose that his close relations with Metternich would exclude collaboration with England. He never wished to be obliged to choose between Palmerston and Metternich. In religious affairs (as shown in Chapter 7) opponents of his theology pointed out its eclectic nature, its attempted summary of 'the great Christian facts', and Timothée Colani in 1872, attacked the projected declaration of faith as a compilation seeking to take something from the Bible, something from criticism, something from tradition and something from the modern approach.

Pierre Leroux, in a famous attack on eclecticism, claimed that it originated with Napoleon's desire to break up society, so that each part of it could become his instrument. It seems most likely that it arose out of the recognition of French diversity, even perhaps of modern diversity. It is difficult not to believe with Edmond Scherer that there is no error which does not possess some mixture of truth, and that there is no truth which is not partial, narrow, incomplete and 'entâchée d'erreur'. It is certain too that many successful political creeds were essentially eclectic. 'Whiggery', for example, represented for its adherents a well-adjusted mixture of doctrines and ideas, whilst for its opponents such as Froude it had by degrees taken up 'all the filth that has been secreted in the fermentation of human thought'. But however natural eclecticism might have been in the circumstances of the nineteenth century, and however useful a means of procedure it might have provided, no one can doubt that as an intellectual system it was weak and inadequate.

Eclecticism is often the product of weariness; it invariably produces immobilism. Guizot did little or nothing to resolve differences or to revise conditions. Thus although Mallet du Pan before him, and Tocqueville in his own time, believed that there was a fundamental incompatability between a centralized administrative system and a parliamentary system, Guizot preferred to accept both. Although many people believed that there was an inevitable conflict between priest and 'instituteur', he preferred to believe that both had to contribute to the work of education. Although it was said that the system of government installed by the Charter was one of class oligarchy, he preferred to believe that all the elements of society had achieved their representation with the middle classes. Eclecticism led to an enthusiasm for the past rather than to a just appreciation of the present. It presupposed that thought had shot its bolt, that originality was misguided. It made men critics rather than creators, encouraged men to follow events rather than direct them and made it difficult for them to assimilate new developments. But above all the eclectic strain in Guizot's thought meant that he had no ideal and no vision. It was this above all that young men found most dissatisfying with the July Monarchy. Eclecticism is monotonous, it can never be inspiring. It is difficult now to think highly of Victor Cousin, the summarizer of other men's philosophies and the biographer of a string of famous women. Equally it is difficult to appreciate by what 'tour de force' Guizot succeeded in giving to his political eclecticism the appearance of inspiration. Ernest Renan was wiser when, in the preface to *L'Avenir de la Science*, he wrote that without the old dreams one could not rebuild the foundations of a noble and happy life. There were no dreams in eclecticism.

But perhaps the weakest feature of Guizot's thought was the fragility of its basis. In his historical work as well as in his contributions to political theory and to religious discussions, a great deal was based upon assumptions concerning human nature. Behind the generalizations concerning history, civilization, reason and belief, were generalizations concerning the behaviour, the desires and the fears of a hypothetical individual. What appeared to be severely reasoned and carefully constructed arguments were in reality vague and instinctive, proceeding from assumption to assumption. It was as if Guizot remained influenced all his life by his early contact with Maine de Biran and the 'famille des méditatifs intérieurs', but since he never deepened or extended the argument, this early contact seems to have been superficial. At all events, at a time when thought was becoming increasingly social, Guizot persisted in basing his thought upon suppositions concerning the individual.

This was not the only disadvantage. He attributed great importance to the individual man and to his desire for peace and for moral satisfactions; but at the same time he saw the individual man being stirred by ambitions which were necessarily senseless and doomed to failure. Hence he never knew whether to trust or to mistrust men. He could never make up his mind whether within every Frenchman there was a revolutionary trying to get out or an honest citizen looking for order and stability. His insistence upon the reflections and aspirations of the individual also led him to think particularly in terms of those individuals who belonged to that minority in society which was free from the task of keeping life going from day to day. This led him to ignore the labour of the majority, to overlook the importance of man's struggle to conquer his material development. He had an insufficient sense of social development, so that he could not understand how a society could pass from a static to a dynamic condition without prior provocation, or how a 'status quo' could become synonymous with stagnation.

All this meant that for all his detachment and rationalizing, in spite of the advantages of his 'un-French' intellect, he was often unable to understand what was happening in France. On July 28th, 1849, he told Lord Aberdeen that what was happening in France was 'la lutte des vestes contre les habits, les casquettes contre les chapeaux, des mauvais sujets contre les honnêtes gens, de la multitude folle ou perverse contre les classes supérieures'. On July 24th, 1851, he told Croker, 'La France est un malade à la fois impatient et fatigué, qui s'inquiète, surtout du mal qu'il souffre ou de celui qu'il craint, et qui tantôt s'agite à tout risque pour échapper à sa souffrance, tantôt demande qu'on ne le remue pas et qu'on le laisse comme il est de peur de souffrir encore d'avantage. Le combat continuel et le triomphe alternatif de ces deux sentiments, le besoin de la délivrance et le besoin de l'immobilité, c'est là le caractère singulier et dominant de notre situation.' In 1866 he asked Léonce de Lavergne if the decadence of his times would not be brought about by 'la sottise d'une on deux

439

générations'. In all these descriptions and assumptions, in this tendency to see society in terms of an individual, there is an air of profundity rather than any real perception concerning the nature of the divisions in France. In this respect Guizot failed in his mission of understanding and explaining.

But if one can write of Guizot's failure, it is only just to remember that he was not alone in his failure. One recalls how on one occasion he asked: 'Qui de nos jours n'est pas tombé?' and one is inclined to echo the question. The banqueteers of 1847 who campaigned for reform and who succeeded in provoking revolution, the champions of parliamentary government who leapt to the support of Louis Napoleon, and those who thought that the glory of France in the world would be defended by the reluctant dragon of the Second Empire, surely all these must be accounted failures. Nor is their failure surprising. It is difficult to see how any permanent solution to the problems of France could come from such a collection of ambitions and visions. At best it consisted of men who were intensely patriotic but who despised many of their fellow-countrymen, democrats who were authoritarian, socialists who were aristocratic, rebels who were autocrats, sceptics who became dogmatic, and individualists who, seeking after their own salvation, thought and wrote only for 'the happy few'. At worst it represented the myopia of violence, 'les classes dangereuses' and the sort of unthinking convictions that Michel de Bourgnes expressed to Georges Sand as they looked across the Seine to the Tuileries and he said that in order that society should be renewed, the river must flow with blood and the palace must be reduced to ashes. The revolutionaries of the nineteenth century tended to come from an equivocal area between two classes, between the proletariat and the smaller bourgeoisie. Although this 'class' was bitter in its revindications and intransigeant in its principles, it had little sense of progress and no future could be built upon its incoherence.

Guizot was not the last statesman to be baffled by the French public with its long periods of deep indifference interrupted by brusque awakenings. He was not the last to be driven down a cul-de-sac by his conviction that within the French nation there is a community of interest which will harmonize the existing conflicts. Sooner or later all French statesmen put their trust in the apparent stability and tenacious conservatism of the greater part of the population and base their policies on 'cette France sensée, modérée et honnête'. Sooner or later most French statesmen are appealing against 'tout ce qu'il y a de partis pris, d'intérêts particuliers, de passions, de routines ... les claus des rancunes anciennes et nouvelles' and are claiming that such manifestations of opposition are neither typical nor worthy of France, 'tout cela n'est que de l'écume flottant sur les profondeurs', as one of them has said. As in the case of Guizot, such sentiments can be illusions, but it is interesting to see that they are shared by different generations of the French governing classes. It is interesting, too, to note that although there have always been certain Frenchmen who have regarded the government of France as if it were a battle, which could only be successfully fought if entrusted to a particular general, yet sooner or later the institutional void has been filled and the country has reverted to a form of moderate, regular government. France has always rejected her Guizots and has always gone on to rediscover them.

But the qualities of François Guizot have not always been shared by his successors. In a country where, for reasons of history and social structure, public morality has not always been high, Guizot was one of the examples of a statesman untouched by scandal. Not only did he never court popularity, he was never afraid of unpopularity. He was not afraid to face and to explain the facts of power, to point out that France could not envisage an expansion in any way similar to that of America, Russia or England. He realized the importance of education. He rarely yielded to personal prejudices. He did not, like many others, approach the religious question in a narrow, sectarian way; nor did he avoid it altogether, since he believed, in Acton's words, that religious questions were 'the marrow of politics' and he saw how they intensified the division within the country. He understood that the mission of government in France could not be simply utilitarian, he saw that it had also to be intellectual and moral.

Recently certain writers have amused themselves by making a contrast between 'France' and 'Français'. For them, 'France' has a particular meaning, standing for everything that has quality, value and permanence. But 'Français', on the other hand, stands for everything that is unprincipled, unstable and meaningless. Such a contrast need not be taken seriously. It is easy to point out that however many 'Frances' there are, and however diverse the French may be, there have always been Frenchmen who have displayed the most serious and lasting qualities. One thinks of statesmen, confident in the power of reason, of scholars determined to understand and to explain their subjects, of the Protestants, conscious of their ideals. Of all of these it could be said that they represent what is best in France. Of all of these it could be said that they are Guizot's France.

Much has been written about Guizot's unpopularity. In England, however, he always found friends and admiration. He knew this, and shortly before his death he wrote to Henry Reeve, 'Je vis aussi en Angleterre. C'est beaucoup d'avoir deux vies et presque deux patries.'

441

CONCLUSION

N.B. The references for Chapter 9 are: Guizot: Duchâtel undated (possibly written after the military review of September 20th, 1830), *Duchâtel Papers*, Archives Nationales 2 A.P.8; Guizot: Bresson February 28th, 1846, ibid. 42 A.P.8; Sainte-Beuve: Caroline and Juste Olivier, March 4th, 1844, *Correspondance* (op. cit.), vol. v, p. 470; Guizot: Piscatory, March 7th, 1852, *Lettres à sa famille et à ses amis* (op. cit.), pp. 332 ff.; Guizot: Mme Lenormant, October 27th, 1864, *Correspondance de Guizot avec M. et Mme Lenormant* (op. cit.), p. 232; Guizot: Aberdeen, July 28th, 1849, *Aberdeen Papers*, B.M. Add. MSS. 43, 134. Guizot: J. W. Croker, July 24th, 1851, *Croker Papers*, B.M. Add. MSS. 41, 128. Guizot: Léonce de Lavergne, July 26th, 1866, *Correspondance de Guizot avec Leonce de Lavergne* (op. cit.), p. 157; Guizot: Henry Reeve, March 8th, 1874, *Life and Letters of Henry Reeve* (op. cit.), vol. ii, p. 223.

10
BIBLIOGRAPHY

Napoléon disait un jour dans un accès de fatigue: 'Que de
mal pour avoir une demi-page dans l'histoire universelle!'
Je ne prétend qu'à l'histoire de France.

GUIZOT to LAURE DE GASPARIN

THE main source for any study of Guizot is naturally his private
papers and his political works. The private papers are in his
house, the Val-Richer, near to Lisieux in the Calvados department,
in the Archives Nationales, Paris (42 A.P.), and in the Library of the
Société de l'Histoire du Protestantisme Français, Rue des Saints-
Pères, Paris. There is no complete bibliography of his published
works. Bibliographies are to be found in Quérard, *Complément
Périodique de la France Littéraire* (1856); *Polybiblion*, October 1874;
Thième, *Guide Bibliographique de la Littérature Française de 1800 à
1930*, vol. 1, 1933; Talvart et Place, *Bibliographie des Auteurs
Modernes de Langue Française*, vol. 7, 1941. An exhaustive biblio-
graphy covering a limited period is that drawn up by Ch. Pouthas,
Sources et Bibliographie de Guizot pendant la Restauration (1923).

Guizot was a devoted letter writer, and a good method of studying
him is through those letters of his which have been published. His
daughter, Madame Conrad de Witt, edited two publications which
draw very fully on his letters, *Monsieur Guizot dans sa famille et avec
ses amis* (1880), *Lettres de Monsieur Guizot à sa famille et à ses amis*
(1884). Some early letters were included in the collection published
by M. Isler, *Briefe von B. Constant. Görres, Mme de Staël . . .* (1879);
letters to the deputy Mahul in the *Nouvelle Revue Rétrospective*,
October 10th, 1899; to the historian Fauriel (who was later to become
a close friend of Élisa Dillon) are in the archives of the Institut, but
were mostly published in the *Nouvelle Revue*, December 1st, 1901;
*Lettres à M. et Mme Lenormant: Les Années de Retraite de M.
Guizot* (1902); *Correspondance de Guizot avec Léonce de Lavergne*

443

(ed. Cartier, 1910); to the Duchesse Decazes in *Revue Hebdomadaire*, vol. vii, 1912; to his agent in the department of Calvados, André Auzoux, in the *Revue des Études Historiques*, March-April 1912 (these contain references to Guizot's own financial situation in the 1830s when he was looking for 'une petite habitation d'été' in Normandy, as well as demonstrating Guizot's attention to his elector's interests. Letters to de Broglie were sometimes addressed to Auzoux since Guizot was frightened that they would be opened in the post); to Lady Alice Peel in *Revue de France*, vol. iii, 1925; to Madame de Gasparin in André Gayot (ed.), *François Guizot et Madame Laure de Gasparin* (1934); a letter to the 'libraire' Maradan in the *Revue d'Histoire Littéraire de la France* (1936); some of the letters which passed between Guizot and Thiers during the Middle East crisis of 1840 have been published by Ch. Pouthas in *Revue Historique* (1938); E. P. Brush has published correspondence between Guizot and Gladstone in *Journal of Modern History*, June 1939; letters between Guizot and Pauline de Meulan have been published by Edouard Dolléans in *Revue des Deux Mondes* September-October 1954; Douglas Johnson has published letters that passed between Guizot and Lord Aberdeen during 1852, in *Revue d'Histoire Moderne et Contemporaine*, January-March 1958.

Unpublished letters from Guizot are to be found in several collections of private papers, and even without their being letters to or from him, these collections are relevant to the study of Guizot. Thus the papers of Duchâtel and Jules Simon in the Archives Nationales, Paris (the former contain notes which Duchâtel took of Guizot's university lectures); the papers of Thiers and Edgar Quinet in the Bibliothèque Nationale, Paris; the typescript copies in the Société de l'Histoire du Protestantisme Français of the Prévost Papers in Geneva; the papers of Aberdeen, Peel, J. W. Croker, Panizzi, Ripon and Cobden in the British Museum; the papers of Brougham in University College, London. The papers of Casimir Périer, at Pont-sur-Seine, which were consulted by courtesy of Madame Casimir-Périer Sommier, contained no letters from Guizot but were valuable in helping one's understanding of the general situation. Much the same could be said for the papers of Enfantin in the Arsenal.

There are a great many documents to or from Guizot, or directly concerning his actions and policies, in the official archives. It is not intended to list all those consulted; full references have been given in the preceding text whenever necessary. Two things, however, might be stressed. The first is that there are considerable gaps in the material relevant to the July Monarchy, and to the 1840s in particular, in many sections of the Archives Nationales (for example, over electoral and legal matters). The second is that the archives of the Ministry of Foreign Affairs at the Quai d'Orsay (which have been consulted in the sections of Correspondance Politique, Correspondance Commerciale and Mémoires et Documents) are sometimes less valuable for Guizot's administration, since he frequently accompanied the official communication with a private letter.

There is no satisfactory biography of Guizot. The outstanding volumes, fine examples of erudition and judgement, are those by Ch. Pouthas, *La Jeunesse de Guizot* (1936) and *Guizot pendant la Restauration* (1923). Neither of these volumes, however, is concerned with Guizot beyond 1830, and whilst they could claim to study what is in some ways the most attractive period of his life, they necessarily omit the whole of his ministerial experience as well as vital years in his work as a historian and religious thinker. Biographies which try to cover the whole of his life are either rather sketchy, such as that by Jules Pédézert (1874), or rather popular, such as that by J. de Crozals (1893); A. Bardoux published a general sketch of Guizot's life (1894) which contained two papers read to the Académie des Sciences Morales et Politiques on particular aspects of Guizot's work. E. P. Brush, *Guizot in the Early Years of the Orleanist Monarchy* (1929), is a general account of the years following 1830 rather than a biography; it is based mainly on the debates in the two Chambers.

Guizot has been the subject of innumerable books and articles. There is perhaps some value in mentioning a few of the more interesting, beginning with those which were written during Guizot's lifetime and which were invariably hostile to him. Lerminier included Guizot in a series of articles which he wrote for the *Revue des Deux Mondes*, the number of April 15th, 1832, being particularly concerned with him. The same review published an article by Loeve-Weimars on May 15th, 1834, which sought to show Guizot not only as a man of reaction ('toujours la présence de M. Guizot est signalée par des lois de rigueur et d'exception') but also as an egoist ('il a du mépris pour ce qui se constitue sans lui'). Loeve-Weimars, however, did not have a great reputation as a journalist (he was later said to be one of the journalists whose support was 'acquired' by Thiers). The editor of the *Revue Française*, Felix Martin d'Oisy, published a pamphlet, *Coup d'Oeil sur la vie publique de M. Guizot* (1836), which was unusual because it was favourable. Not unnaturally Guizot found this publication 'spirituelle au fond', and the author, who had been a lawyer in Orleans, was appointed to an administrative post in the Ministry of the Interior. Armand Audiganne, the author of a pamphlet *Guizot* (1838), was an intelligent writer. Most of the pamphlets and articles written about Guizot during the 1840s were of course violently hostile. E. Cabet, *L'Émigration du Guizot, est-elle gloire ou infamie?* (1840); Charles Marchal, *Lord Guizot, sa politique et son voyage à Londres* (1844); Ratoudis-de-Biscaras, *Agonie, mort et enterrement de son Excellence Guizot* (1846) are examples among many. In 1843 Guizot was severely treated by Lamennais in *Amschaspands and Darvands* ('il a soutenu toutes les doctrines, flatté toutes les passions, systematisé tous les crimes politiques'). Perhaps the violence of this publication influenced Guizot in his attitude towards Lamennais, 'ce grand esprit égaré dans ses passions', but one has to notice that the portraits of other public men, such as Thiers and Victor Cousin, were neither gentler nor more flattering. Gustave Planche, who had already written a hostile account of Guizot's reception to the Académie Française in the *Revue des Deux Mondes*, vol. 25, 1837, published another article, which was also severe, in the same review for March 15th, 1861. Guizot's co-religionist Guillaume de Félice came to his support with particular reference to the administration of the Protestant Church with *Guizot et sa candidature au conseil presbytérial de l'Église Réformée de Paris* (1865); this was a general defence of Guizot's past career, as well as a defence of his orthodox religious views, and it praised 'un tel homme, avec ses cheveux blancs, sa gloire, son génie, sa piété, ses vertus et ses services'. Taxile Delord, *La Papauté de M. Guizot* (1865), took exactly the opposite point of view. On Guizot's death one should note an article in the *Revue Bleue*, vol. xiv, 1874, and later there are two near-contemporary studies of some importance: Jules Simon, *Thiers, Guizot, Rémusat* (1884), and Émile Faguet's article on Guizot, reprinted in the first volume of *Politiques et Moralistes du Dix-Neuvième Siècle* (1891). Faguet also published an article with the title 'Guizot amoureux' in the *Revue Latine*, March 25th, 1904. With Albert-Émile Sorel's lecture on Guizot, *Conférence sur Guizot* (1914), we reach modern times and have to note a relative shortage of articles. Sometimes a new publication would lead to an attempt to re-assess Guizot in general terms. His correspondence with Laure de Gasparin, for example, caused Émile Henriot in *Le Temps*, October 27th, 1931, to wrote of him, 'Nous croyions avoir affair à un mort, exsangue et figé, momifié dans ses principes comme un pharaon dans ses bandellettes: et quelques pages d'écriture, o merveille! le rendent soudain à la vie et nous permettent d'approcher l'homme, infiniment digne d'estime et de sympathie, malgré ses fautes et son échec. . . .' E. L. Woodward's *Three Studies in European Conservatism* (1929) is devoted to Metternich, Guizot and the Catholic Church in the nineteenth century, the study of Guizot being based mainly on his Memoirs and speeches. There are short articles by Lavondonès in the *Journal de Génève*, July 24th-25th, 1955, by Pierre Poujol in

Évangile et Liberté, February 25th, 1948, and by H. P. Adams in *Festschrift für Walther Maas* (1961).

Guizot's own *Mémoires pour Servir à l'Histoire de Mon Temps* (8 vols., 1856-1864) are the most valuable of the many memoirs available. They were translated into English with a succession of different titles, *History of My Time* (4 vols.), *An Embassy to the Court of St. James*, *Memoirs of a Minister of State*, *France under Louis Philippe*, *The Last Days of Louis Philippe*, and published between 1858 and 1867. All sorts of people, some of considerable importance, others who were hardly on the fringe of importance, wrote their memoirs, or had memoirs constructed for them out of letters and journals, or left correspondence which has been published. The following is a list of those whose memoirs or correspondence is interesting to the student of Guizot:

The Duchesse d'Abrantès, Comtesse d'Agoult (Daniel Stern), d'Alton-Shée, André-Marie and Jean-Jacques Ampère, Apponyi, d'Arçay, Victor de Balabine, Prosper de Barante, Odilon Barrot, Comtesse de Bassanville, Béranger, Béraud, Bersier, Beugnot, Mme de Boigne, Börne, Amy Bost, Albert de Broglie, Victor de Broglie, Maxime de Camp, Lewis Cass, Castellane, Philarète Chasles, Chateaubriand, Constant, Coulmann, Cournot, Cuvillier-Fleury, J. W. Croker, Comtess Dash, Delacroix, Delécluze, the Duchesse de Dino, Mme Dosne, Xavier Doudan, Paul Dubois, Alexandre Dumas, Dupin, Falloux, Frenilly, Saint-Marc Girardin, Gisquet, The Duchesse Gontault-Biron, Greville, Guernon-Ranville, Ludovic Halévy, Haussez, d'Haussonville, d'Hautpoul, Heine, Hyde de Neuville, Victor Jacquemont, Prince de Joinville, Lacordaire, Lafayette, Laffitte, Lamartine, Lambruschini, Lamennais, Martin-Dupont, the Princess Lieven, the Princess de Ligne, Pierre Magne, Mallet du Pan, Mérimée, Metternich, Molé, Adolphe Monod, Montalivet, Montbel, Mme de Montcalm, Mounier, Normanby, Émile Ollivier, The Duc d'Orléans, Pasquier, Pédezért, Perdiguier, Pelet de la Lozère, Pelleport, Pontécoulant, Pontmartin, Puységur, Quinet, Raguse, Raikes, Reeve, Reiset, Mme de Rémusat, Charles de Rémusat, Renan, Rochechouart, de la Rochefoucauld, Roederer, Rozet, Rumigny, the Comtesse de Sainte-Aulaire, Sainte-Aulaire, Sainte-Beuve, Salaberry, Georges Sand, Nassau Senior, Serre, Sers, Sismondi, Soult, Mme de Staël, Stendhal, Taine, Talleyrand, Thibaudeau, Thiébault, Tocqueville, Vaublanc, Véron, Veuillot, Viennet, Villèle, Villemain, Vitrolles.

Guizot's own collections of speeches, *Histoire Parlementaire de France* (5 vols., 1863-1864, do not contain all his speeches to the Chambers) and *Discours Académiques . . .* etc. (1861), can be used along with other collections of speeches by Berryer (1872-1874),

Victor de Broglie (1863), Lamartine (1864-1865), Périer (1839), Serre (1865), Thiers (1879-1889) and Voyer d'Argenson (1845), as well as with extracts from speeches in Duvergier de Hauranne, *Histoire du Gouvernement Parlementaire en France* (10 vols., 1870-1871), or in A. Chabrier, *Les Orateurs Politiques de La France* (1905).

In addition to Pouthas, *Une famille de bourgeoisie française de Louis XIV à Napoléon* (1934), there are a number of studies on Guizot's family and on people who were intimately connected with him. Thus his mother figures in Lescure, *Les Mères Illustres* (1882), and in Véga, *Madame Guizot, la Mère d'un Grand Homme d'État* (1901). Pauline de Meulan was the subject of an article by Sainte-Beuve in the *Revue des Deux Mondes*, May 15th, 1836, which was republished in *Portraits de Femmes*. Her educational ideas are studied by P. Rousselot in *Mémoires de la Société des Sciences Morales de Seine-et-Oise*, vol. 15. For Élisa Dillon see an article by Mme Tastu in the *Revue de Paris*, September 1st, 1836. The Princess Lieven has often been written about. There are biographies of her by Ernest Daudet (1903), H. Montgomery Hyde (1938) and P. Zamoyska (1957), but none of them is altogether satisfactory. Her correspondence with Lord Aberdeen (edited by E. Jones Parry), with Earl Grey (edited by Le Strange), with Metternich (edited by Hanoteau and then by Peter Quennell), with Lady Palmerston (edited by Lord Sudley), as well as a diary and other correspondence which was edited by H. W. V. Temperley, is also available. It is to be noted that Jean Schlumberger and Jacques Naville are publishing Guizot's correspondence with her. For the Duchesse de Broglie see the article by Villemain in the *Revue Française*, October 1838.

Guizot was, of course, associated with many public figures, and their biographies are usually relevant to him. The first important friends he had were P. A. Stapfer, who has been studied by R. Luginbühl (1887), and Suard, who has been written about by Alfred C. Hunter (1925). For Fontanes see Aileen Wilson (1928), for Madame de Staël see Lady Blennerhassett (1887), Pierre Kohler (1916) and J. Christopher Herold (1959), for Georges Cuvier see P. Viénot (1932). It is difficult to find anything on the Abbé de Montesquiou and one has to rely on articles such as that by Jean de Boislisle, in the *Annuaire-Bulletin de la Société de l'Histoire de France* for 1927. Whilst Royer-Collard has attracted many writers, Philippe (1857), Barante (2 vols., 1861), Spuller (1895), Gabriel Rémond (1933), Roger Langeron (1956), other members of the doctrinaire 'canapé' have had few biographers. For Prosper de Barante one has to look at Guizot's essay (1867) and for Victor de Broglie one is again obliged to consult Guizot (1872), although La Varende, *Les Broglies* (1950), has some interesting comments. Camille Jordan can be studied via his friends Gérando, Ballanche, Mounier and Mme de Staël, but there is a good essay on him by Sainte-Beuve in *Nouveaux Lundis*, vol. 12. For Becquey, whose agricultural enquiry of 1814 has aroused little curiosity amongst historians, see Beugnot (1852), for Lainé see Perceval (2 vols., 1926), for Villèle see Fourcassié (1954), for Chateaubriand see Beau de Loménie (2 vols., 1929) and Marie-Jeanne Durry (2 vols., 1933), for Polignac see Robin-Armel (1951), for Decazes see Langeron (1960).

The monarchs of the period from 1814 to 1848 have not been well served. There have been a number of unambitious works, such as Daudet (1899) and Lucas-Dubreton (1925) on Louis XVIII and Lucas-Dubreton (1927) and Garnier (1927) on Charles X. Louis-Philippe failed to find a good biographer in spite of G. N. Wright (2 vols., 1842), Cretineau-Joly (1862), Flers (1891), Cochin (1918), de la Gorce (1931), Bertaut (1936) and Lucas-Dubreton (1938). T. E. B. Howarth, *Citizen King* (1961), has used few original documents, not everyone will agree with his attitude towards the principal politicians, and there are many details which can be queried, but his book is very readable. For the court life of the period there are the memoirs of Theodore Anne (1831), Langeron on Madame Royale (1958), Guichen on Angoulême (1909), Perret on Mme du Cayla (1937), Trognon on Marie-Amélie (1872), Arnaud on Madame Adelaïde (1908), Madame d'Harcourt on the Duchesse d'Orléans (1859).

In the political world of the July Monarchy Thiers has attracted many writers. Laya (2 vols., 1846), Franck (1877), Charles de Mazade (1884), Jules Simon (1885), Paul de Rémusat (1889), Daniel Halévy (1921), Maurice Reclus (1929), Allison (1932), Malo (1932), Pomaret (1948), Lucas-Dubreton (1948), Aubert (1952) and Marquant (1959) inevitably contribute a great deal of information about him. It is interesting to see how emphasis is frequently placed on his patriotism by his admirers (Reclus writes 'Par dessus tout il est national, l'homme par excellence de tout ce qui peut tendre à la grandeur française'), showing with what success Thiers and his associates cultivated this legend at the same time as attacking Guizot as unpatriotic. Events after 1870 emphasized the legend. Perhaps a more revealing publication is Vidalenc, *Lettres de J. A. M. Thomas, Préfet de Bouches-du-Rhône, à Adolphe Thiers, 1831-1836* (1953).

Molé on the other hand has hardly attracted anyone, which is all the more strange since few statesmen with Imperial connections have escaped the historian's grasp. Perhaps this confirms Guizot's remark that 'ce très aimable homme n'avait pas d'amis'. At all events one must turn to the article published by Vitet in the *Revue des Deux Mondes*, December 1st, 1861, or more recently to that by Halda in the *Revue de la pensée française* (1958). Casimir Périer is equally elusive. One has to look mainly at the publications of his contemporaries, such as *La Vie Privée et Politique de Casimir Périer Par EP^XXX* (1832), the article by Loeve-Weimars in the *Revue des Deux Mondes* for January 1st, 1833, or the portraits of him by Charles de Rémusat (1838), Sainte-Vallière (1850) or Hippolyte Castille (1858). Nicoullaud's book on Périer (1894) is concerned with the period prior to 1830 and consists mainly of extracts from his speeches, whilst Lucas-Dubreton (1929) is yet another popular work. Lamartine's political activities can be studied in a number of different books, by Ollivier (1874), Quentin Bauchart (1903), Ethel Harris (1932) or by Guillemin (1940, 1946 and 1948). Duchâtel is the subject of a rather indifferent biography by Vitet (1875), Sébastiani by Mesmay (1948), Odilon Barrot by d'Alméras (1950), Bugeaud by d'Ideville (3 vols., 1881-1882), Berryer by Lacombe (1895), Villemain by Vauthier (1913). Victor Cousin has attracted many interesting writers, notably his friend Barthélemy Sainte Hilaire (3 vols., 1895), Mastellone (1955) and R. R. Bolgar in the *Cambridge Journal*, vol. 2, 1948-1949. Humann is the subject of works by Marsan (1842), Spach (1871), Ponteil (1937) and also by Ponteil in the *Revue d'Histoire Moderne* (1937). A number of articles have been published on Salvandy by Professor Trénard, of the University of Lille, and his book is expected shortly. It is to be regretted that others of Guizot's ministers have not been studied, particularly Cunin-Gridaine, who was responsible for commercial affairs and who was unexpectedly described by Bowring (in a letter to Lord Auckland) as being liberally disposed with regard to protection, and a great friend of Duchâtel. Amongst deputies, Dubois is the subject of an article in the *Revue de Synthèse*, December 1928; amongst civil servants and friends of Guizot, Léonce de Lavagne is described by Cartier in the *Revue des Deux Mondes*, April 15th, 1904, and Ambroise Rendu by Eugène Rendu (1864); amongst the diplomats there is a book on Flahault by Françoise de Bernardy (the French edition of 1954 should be used in preference to the English edition of 1956), an article on Bourqueney by Artonne in the *Revue d'Histoire Diplomatique* (1951), and of course special interest attaches to Jarnac's article on Lord Aberdeen in the *Revue des Deux Mondes* for 1861. For Lamennais see Duine (1922), Le Hir (1948) and Vidler (1954). For Montalembert see Lecanuet (3 vols., 1910-1912) and Trannoy (1942). For general accounts of the Catholic Church and Catholics see Martin, J. P. (1949), Leflon (1949), Duroselle (1951), Philip Spencer (1954) and Father Droulers (1954).

The remainder of this bibliography would become too lengthy were all the books and articles relevant to Guizot to be listed. Full references have been given in the text and need not be repeated. What follows therefore are references to books and articles which will help to fill in the backgrounds to the various chapters. For the chapter on political thought there are several works of a general interest. R. Soltau, *French Political Thought in the Nineteenth Century* (1931), J. P. Mayer, *Political Thought in France from Sieyès to Sorel* (1961 new ed.), Jean Touchard, *Histoire des Idées Politiques*, vol. 2, 1959, Maxime Leroy, *Histoire des Idées Sociales en France*, vols. 2 and 3, 1950, 1954, are all panoramic studies. More detailed with reference to Guizot are Dominique Bagge, *Les Idées Politiques sous la Restauration* (1952), which is witty but at times superficial, J. L. Talmon, *Political Messianism—the Romantic Phase* (1960), and Barbé, *Étude historique des idées sur la souveraineté, 1815-1848* (1904). Relevant as well are two studies of liberalism, the one by J. S. Schapiro (1958), the other by Irene Collins (1957), and amongst many other books mention should be made of Laski's *Authority in the Modern State* (1919) and *Liberty in the Modern State* (1933) as well as D. O. Evans, *Social Romanticism in France* (1952); René Rémond, *La Droite en France de 1815 à nos jours* (1954); A. Cuvillier, *Hommes et Idéologies de 1840* (1956). Amongst many articles two which are particularly suggestive are Raoul Girardet's study of French nationalism in the *Revue Française de Science Politique*, September 1958, and Theodore Zelden's discussion of the influence of English ideals on French political thinking in the *Cambridge Historical Journal* (1959).

The history of primary education up to the passing of Guizot's 1833 Law is well told in Maurice Gontard, *L'Enseignement Primaire en France, 1789-1833* (1959), secondary education can be studied in Georges Weill, *Histoire de l'Enseignement Secondaire en France au XIXe siècle* (1939), whilst university education is discussed by Louis Liard, *L'Enseignement Supérieure en France* (1894), as well as in small studies like that by Pouthas on the University of Paris since the Revolution. A great amount of information is contained in Fernand Buisson, *Dictionnaire de Pédagogie et d'Instruction Primaire* (3 vols., 1882-1883), and the same author has also edited *La Lutte Scolaire en France au XIXe Siècle* (1912). General works which are useful are Compayré, *Histoire Critique des Doctrines de l'Éducation en France depuis le XVIe siècle* (2 vols., 1879); Cournot, *Des Institutions d'Instruction Publique en France* (1864); Duveau's *La Pensée Ouvrière sur l'Éducation pendant la IIe République et le IIe Empire* (1948), and the same author's lively *Les Instituteurs* (1957). For comparison with England one should not only read a classic like Matthew Arnold's *The Popular Education of France* (1861), and an obvious work like Barnard's *The French Tradition in Education*

(1922), but one should read a suggestive and illuminating study of English experience such as Brian Simon, *Studies in the History of Education* (1960). Bibliographies on French education history are to be found in the volumes of Louis-Grimaud, *Histoire de la Liberté d'Énseignement en France*, vols. 5 and 6 (undated), and although the emphasis is away from Guizot's period, the *Education Libraries Bulletin* of the London Institute of Education for Autumn 1960 has a bibliography some of which is relevant.

In the political field the most useful works are still those of Thureau-Dangin, *Royalistes et Républicains* (1874), *Le Parti Libéral sous la Restauration* (1876), *Histoire de la Monarchie de Juillet* (7 vols., 1884-1892), although all of them can be criticized and the last work in particular was said to read as if it were written by a member of Guizot's majority. K. Hillebrand, *Geschichte Frankreichs* ... (2 vols., 1877-1879), is another classic account. The working of institutions can be studied in books by Hello (1848), Deslandres (1933), Sherman Kent (1937), Labès (1938), Hayem (1939), Bastid (1954) and Peter Campbell (1958), whilst a more specialized study by Tudesq on the Chamber of Peers 'au temps de Guizot' in the *Revue d'Histoire Moderne et Contemporaine*, October-December 1956, can usefully be compared to Saint-Marc Girardin's article on the same subject, published in the *Revue des Deux Mondes*, November 1845. There are a great number of articles on allied subjects by Tudesq and one should particularly notice that entitled 'L'attraction parisienne sur le recrutement parlementaire de 1830-1848' in *Politique, Revue Internationale des doctrines et des institutions*, July-September 1958. For a full list of Tudesq's articles one needs to see the *Bibliographie Annuelle de l'Histoire de France*, but his thesis on 'les notabilités' in France during this period is likely to be of outstanding importance and is awaited eagerly. Studies of the 'bourgeoisie' already exist, by Beau de Loménie (vol. 1, 1943), Morazé (1947 and 1957) and Lhomme (1960). The history of the press can be studied in books by Mrs. Irene Collins (1958) and Charles Ledré (1960) and in a lengthy and well-documented article by Jeau-Pierre Aguet in *Schweizerische Zeitschrift für Geschichte*, vol. x, 1960; see also Tudesq, 'Un Journal Gouvernemental du Temps de Guizot', in *Bulletin de la Société d'Histoire Moderne*, November 10th, 1957.

The economic history of the period has to be studied in a number of old-fashioned books by Levasseur (2 vols., 1903-1904, 2 vols., 1911-1912), Ballot (1923), Clapham (4th edition, 1937) and in a rather old-fashioned type of book, nevertheless indispensable, by Sée (1951 edition) and Dunham (1953). More stimulating perhaps are Viallate on economic activity (1937), Gille on banking (1959),

BIBLIOGRAPHY

Cameron on the role of France in the economic development of Europe (1961), and Palmade (1962). Together with the theories of David Landes (as in the *Journal of Economic History*, 1949) and François Perroux (*Income and Wealth*, 1955) these works have considerably advanced our understanding of the period. The same importance must be given to the studies of the French population during this period by Bourgeois-Pichat in *Population* (1951), and by Pouthas (1956). Here too is the place to list Chevalier's *Classes Laborieuses et Classes Dangereuses* (1958).

On questions of French foreign policy Mastellone (1957) is a specialized study so far as Guizot is concerned although he does not consider all his activity. General articles on French foreign policy during Guizot's time include one by Outrey in the *Revue Française de Science Politique* for 1953, one by Jacques Grunewald in *La Politique Étrangère et ses Fondements*, edited by J.-B. Duroselle (1954), a communication by B. Gille published in the *Bulletin de la Société d'Histoire Moderne*, January 1960, and an older but still interesting article by Ch. Pouthas in the *Revue d'Histoire Moderne*, No. 3, 1927. The article by Francesco Sirugo on the 'rivolizione commerciale' in *Studi Storici*, No. 2, 1961, is of wide general interest. Renouvin, *Histoire des Relations Internationales. Le XIXᵉ siècle*, vol. i, 1954, covers the whole period.

On specific questions Hall (1913) and Guyot (1926) discuss relations between France and England, as does Weil in *History* (1921) and Cunningham in the *Bulletin of the Institute of Historical Research*, November 1957. On the Middle East crisis of 1840-1841, one should consult Webster, *The Foreign Policy of Palmerston*, vol. 2, 1951, and perhaps one should look too at an article by Francis Waddington in the *Revue d'Histoire Diplomatique* (1935), in order to see a traditional French view of the treaty of July 15th, 1840. For relations between France and Belgium one should consult Ridder (1933) and Deschamps (1956), as well as looking at the contemporary work by Léon Faucher, *L'Union du Midi* (1842). For the Tahitian affair, see J. R. Baldwin in the *Journal of Modern History* (1938), Jore in the *Revue d'Histoire des Colonies Françaises* (1939), articles in the *Journal de la Société des Océanistes*, vol. 15, 1959, and books by K. L. P. Martin (1924), J. I. Brookes (1941) and J-P. Faivre (1953). For Morocco see F. R. Flournoy, *British Policy Towards Morocco in the Age of Palmerston* (1935), and Emerit's *L'Algérie à l'Epoque d'Abd el Kader* (1951), as well as two articles by Emerit in the *Revue Africaine* (1948 and 1950). For Spain, E. Jones Parry (1936) has examined the beginning of the marriage affair very carefully, although he pays little attention to the 'dénouement' and although he is as suspicious of French motives as was any contemporary English

453

diplomat. On the subject of the Spanish marriages, Mr. J. M. Garcia Lora has drawn my attention to the book by B. Perez Galdós, *Episodios Nacionales (Tercera Serie): Bodas Reales* (1899). This novel particularly shows the reputation which Bresson acquired in Spain ('. . . a gentleman who is perspicacity itself, quicker than lightning and so sharp-witted that if Spain were the eye of a needle he would make himself, King Louis Philippe and the whole of France pass through it with the greatest subtlety and ease. That is the gentleman who, entirely off his own bat, without as much as a thought for the government and only keeping an eye on his rival and opponent the English ambassador—one Mr. Bulwer—pulls all the strings of the Spanish marriages.') So many writers have presented a fictitious account of this affair in the guise of history that one welcomes the chance of recommending a novelist's novel. For relations between France and Switzerland up to 1840 see the thesis by Biaudet (1941); for the Sonderbund see Duffield's article in the *English Historical Review*, vol. x, P. Matter's reply in the *Annales des Sciences Politiques*, vols. x and vol. xi, and a series of articles in the *Schweizerische Zeitschift für Geschichte*, vol. xxvii. For relations between France and Italy see books by Silva (1917), Greer (1925), A. J. P. Taylor (1934) and Moscati (1947), as well as articles by Silva in the *Revue des Études Italiennes* (1936), and Mastellone in *Rivista Storica Italiana* (1949). A good article on French policy towards the west coast of Africa by Bernard Schnapper was published in the *Revue Historique*, January-March 1961. For French relations with America there is the thesis by René Rémond (1960).

On the events of 1830 see the article by David Pinkney in *Review of Politics*, October 1961. For the events of 1848 *Le Livre du Centaire*, edited by C. Moulin (1948), *Aspects de la Crise et de la Depression de l'Économie Française, 1848-1851*, edited by E. Labrousse (1956), and the second edition of Dautry, *1848 et la IIe République* (1957), are essential. More particular aspects of the crisis have been studied in publications of the *Société d'Histoire de la Révolution de 1848*, whose *Tables Analytiques* were published as vol. xvii of the *Bibliothèque de la Révolution de 1848* (1957). One should also consult the article by John J. Baughman on the banquet campaign, 1847-1848, in the *Journal of Modern History* (1959), and Dunham's article on the economic crisis in the *Journal of Economic History* (1948).

Guizot's work as a historian has been studied particularly by Henri de l'Épinois in *Revue des Questions Historiques* (1875), by Ruth Keiser (1925), by Sister Mary Consolata O'Connor (1955) and by D. Gerhard in *Historische Zeitschrift* (1960). More general and recent studies are those by Stanley Mellon, *The Political Uses of History* (1958), a well-informed study of historians during the French Restoration period, and a scholarly work by Peter Stadler, *Geschichterschreibung und Historisches Denken in Frankreich 1789-1871* (1958). Earlier works by Flint (1894), Jullian (1897), Fueter (1914), Gooch (1935) and Thompson (1942) can also be consulted. There have been a number of studies of historians contemporary to Guizot such as that by Engels-Janosi, *Four Studies in French Romantic Historical Writing* (1955), and Augustin Thierry has been particularly studied by Carroll (1951), Prosper de Barante by Teuteberg (1945), Chateaubriand by Tapié (in Levaillant, *Chateaubriand*, 1949), Fustel de Coulanges by Herrick (1954). But the outstanding figure who remains extremely difficult to understand or to study is Michelet, in spite of Monod (1894 and 1923), Refort (1923), Rudler (1925), Carré (1926), Chabaud (1929), Haac (1951), Barthes (1954), Cornuz (1955) and the recent work of Paul Viallaneix and Pommier. It has been pointed out by J. G. Weightman (*Encounter*, June 1961) that the Sorbonne has always had a curious attitude towards Michelet; it is as if his position as a kind of national monument has prevented any persistent critical opinions. See Antoine Adam's article in the *Revue de l'Enseignement Supérieure*, No. 1, 1959. Other works which might well be read as background to a study of Guizot's historical writing are Tronchon, *La Fortune Intellectuelle de Herder en France* (1920); L. Reynaud, *L'Influence Allemande en France* (1922); M. Vallois, *La Formation de l'Influence Kantienne en France* (1924); Eggli, *Schiller et le Romantisme Français* (2 vols., 1927); Henri Sée, 'La philosophie de l'histoire d'Ernest Renan', *Revue Historique* (1932); Pierre Moreau, *L'Histoire en France au 19ᵉ Siècle* (undated); Jacques Barzun, 'Romantic Historiography as a Political Force in France', *Journal of the History of Ideas* (1941). Little has been written about Guizot's art criticism. Anatole de Montaiglon (1852) is not particularly inspiring, but it is interesting to compare Guizot's *Salon de 1810* with the views put forward by Arnold Scheffer in an article in the *Revue Française*, January 1828. For Guizot's Shakespearian criticism see C. M. Haines, *Shakespeare in France* (1925).

The study of Protestantism in nineteenth-century France has recently undergone a significant advance. After Professor B. C. Poland's *French Protestantism and the French Revolution* (1957), which was a pioneering work although it was criticized for writing as if Protestants only existed in the south of France, there have come the specialized works by Daniel Robert, *Les Églises Réformées en France, 1800-1830* (1961) and *Genève et les Églises Réformées de France* (1961) and the useful general survey by Raoul Stephan,

Histoire du Protestantisme Français (1961). Other recent works include G. Lagny, *Le Reveil de 1830 et les Diaconesses de Reuilly* (1958), Pierre Lestringant, *Visage du Protestantisme Français* (1959), and particularly valuable, Émile G. Léonard, *Le Protestant Français* (1955). However, older sources have still to be consulted. An article in *The Spectator*, September 12th, 1863 (probably by Bagehot), and articles in the first two volumes of the *Theological Review* can be picked out of many, whilst vol. ix of the *Theological Review* is particularly interesting since it contains Charles Coquerel's account of the 1872 Synod. Bersier, *Histoire du synode générale de l'Église Réformée de France* (2 vols., 1872); Léon Maury, *Le Réveil Religieux dans l'Église Réformée à Génève et en France* (1892); D. Weil, Le Protestantisme Français au 19 Siècle, *Revue de Synthèse Historique* (1911); Ernest Rochat, *La Revue de Strasbourg et son Influence sur la Théologie Moderne* (1904), and *Le Développement de la Théologie Protestante Française au 19 siècle* (1942), are all important.

For particular studies of Guizot's Protestantism see Pasteur Fr. Martin in the *Revue de la Faculté de Théologie d'Aix* (1941), Justus Hashagen in *Zeitschrift für Kirchengeschichte*, vol. 62, 1943-1944, and Antoine Finet (1957). For other Protestants, see Rambert on Alexandre Vinet (1913) together with *Foi et Vie* (1937), Maurice Blanc on Samuel Vincent (1890), Jules Devèze (1884) and E. Stroehlin (1886) on Athanase Coquerel fils, Octave Gréard on Edmond Schérer (1890), E. Paris, *Libres-Penseurs Religieux* (1905) and Jacques Marty on Timothée Colani (1947). In conclusion, some references for comparative purposes: E. G. Parrinder, 'Present Theological Trends in French Protestantism', *Theology*, vol. 40, 1940; H. D. McDonald, *Ideas of Revelation* (1959); Pierre Bourger, 'Opinions sur le Concile', *Revue Réformée*, No. 45, 1961; Roland de Pury, *Qu'est-ce que le protestantisme?* (1961).

Guizot used often to supply lists of books to his friends and advise them about their reading. He was always ready to help his colleagues, and he gave valuable assistance to historians as different as Henry Hallam (who was a close friend), Agnes Strickland (see her life by Una Pope-Hennessy, 1940), and the American Bancroft, to mention only a few. This bibliography merely seeks to imitate Guizot by being helpful; it does not claim to be exhaustive. Nevertheless mention should be made of the book by Guizot's friend William Vernon, whose *Recollections of Seventy-Two Years* (1917) tells of his visits to the Val-Richer. The author is still referred to by Guizot's descendants as 'Uncle William'.

INDEX

Abd el Kader, 201, 253
Aberdeen, Lord, 202, 272, 276, 288, 289, 291, 295, 297, 299, 302, 310, 318, 319, 439; and Guizot, 9, 10, 11, 275, 286; correspondence with Guizot in 1852, 57, 224-225; and Palmerston, 278; and Thiers, 27; and Spanish affairs, 304-309
Académie Française, 2, 3, 9, 12, 22, 114, 118, 122, 186, 208, 398, 417
Acton, Lord, 42, 52, 441
Adelaïde, Mme, 250, 269
Affre, Monseigneur, 207, 210
Agoult, Comtesse d' (Daniel Stern), 42, 261
Aide-toi, le ciel t'aidera, 6, 62n., 217
Albert, Prince Consort, 49, 304
Alexander I, the Czar, 25, 116
Algeria, 164, 201, 202, 203, 253, 254, 266, 273, 287, 292, 300, 311, 318
Allart, Hortense, 42, 43
Ami de la Religion, 218n.
Ampère, 3, 13
Ancillon, Frederick, 35, 38
Anot, Auguste, 149
Arago, 146
Argout, Comte d', 79, 163, 166, 172, 232
Arlès-Dufour, 236, 239
Arnold, Matthew, 88, 102, 137, 150, 151
Arnold, Thomas, 320
Artois, Comte d', *see* Charles X
Aston, 49
Augier, Émile, 85
Aumale, Duc d', 189, 253, 254
Austin, 41
Austria, 178, 300, 304, 314, 315, 316, 317

Babeuf (and Babouvisme), 242
Baccioli, Mme, 117
Bagehot, 64
Baillet, Eugène, 216
Ballanche, 45
Balmès, 339, 397
Balzac, 17, 66, 135, 138, 227, 247; *Les Secrets de la Princesse de Cadignan*, 17
Banquets, campaign of, in 1840, 222; in 1847-1848, 72, 223, 229, 257, 261

Barante, Prosper de, 10, 30, 31, 33, 155, 157, 179, 224, 275, 322, 323, 327, 371; criticizes Guizot, 205
Barbé-Marbois, 31, 73
Barbès, 165
Baring, 276
Barker, Sir Ernest, 61
Barnave, 75
Baroche, 423
Barrau, Théodore-Henri, 144n.
Barrot, Odilon, 47, 68, 156, 166, 177, 181, 183, 184, 195, 199, 203, 206, 221, 222, 257, 260
Barthe, 79, 125, 132-133, 163, 166, 172
Barthélémy-Saint-Hilaire, 244
Bartholdi, 386
Basedow, 91, 93n.
Bastiat, 86, 239
Bastie, Charles, 426
Baudelaire, 246
Baudrand, General, 176, 178n.
Bauer, Bruno, 378
Baur, F. C., 381
Bausset, Cardinal, 35, 109
Bavoux, 119
Becquey, 4, 30, 31
Belboeuf, 422
Belgioso, Princess, 316
Belgium, proposed customs union with France, 199, 234, 281, 296-299
Bell, 94, 102, 112, 114, 116
Bentham, 41, 54
Béranger, 197, 399
Bernal, Calixte, 229
Bernard, Claude, 379
Berry, Duc de, 6, 35, 119, 120, 244; Duchesse de Berry, 301
Berryer, 10, 156, 166, 203
Berthollet, 379
Beugnot, 33
Bèze, Theodore de, 41
Bibliothèque Britannique, 21
Bignon, 34
Billault, 199, 201, 203, 254, 288
Biot, 117
Blacas, 26, 30
Blackstone, 52
Blanc, Louis, 50, 53, 77, 79, 229, 244
Blanqui, 165
Blum, Léon, 434
Bocher, 275

457

Gonthier, 393
Gorini, abbé, 369
Gossez, R., 235
Gouvion-Saint-Cyr, 32, 33
Graham, Sir James, 23, 70, 280, 306
Grandpierre, 387, 418
Granier de Cassagnac, 77n.
Granville, 271
Greece, 188, 201-202, 250, 300, 309-310
Grégoire, abbé, 27, 34
Greville, 276, 277, 288
Guéneau de Mussy, 103, 107, 127
Gueranger, abbé, 208
Guernon de Ranville, 59
Guizot, André, 2, 19, 20
Guizot (née Élisa Dillon), Madame, 6, 7, 20, 127
Guizot, François, 7, 18, 97, 148
Guizot, François Pierre Guillaume:
life and career, 1-10, 434-435;
early life, 18-22; marriage with
Pauline de Meulan, 3; death of
Pauline de Meulan, 6, 383; marriage
with Élisa Dillon, 6, 7; death of
Élisa Dillon, 127; death of elder son,
François, 148; and mother, 20-21;
and Princess Lieven, 16-18; and
family, 2, 6, 8-9, 19-21, 369, 383-384,
427
his appearance, 22-23; his
character, 4-5, 14-18, 205, 255, 300,
441; his eloquence, 2, 22, 122,
182, 187, 255; his unpopularity,
11-14, 22, 201, 203-205, 224, 261-
262, 389, 433; consistency of
opinions, 51-52, 60-61, 434-435;
and first Restoration, 29-30; and
journey to Ghent during 100 Days,
15n., 30-31, 114, 204-206, 421n.;
and second Restoration, 31-32; and
doctrinaires, 32-37; personal side
to political thought, 41-42; attitude
to monarchs, 48-50, 216-217; view of
social classes, 73-75, 240; and aristocracy, 77-78; and socialism, 80-82;
and electoral system, 73-75, 224-
226; and conservative party, 69-71,
177-178, 183, 218-219
and Belgium, 199, 296-299; and
England, 7-9, 21, 52-53, 57, 64, 73-
74, 78, 176, 177-178, 263, 269, 277-
278, 344-345, 441; and Germany,
7, 21, 94, 316-317; and Italy, 316-
317; and Spain, 301-309
personal qualifications for educational matters, 92-93; his University
lectures in 1812, 118, 331-332; 1820-
1822, 6, 35, 38-39, 51, 119; 1828-
1830, 6, 121-122; and method of
mutual instruction, 114-116; and

Ministry of Public Instruction,
126-127, 148, 150, 155; and primary
education, see Law of June 28 1833
(loi Guizot); and secondary education, 148-150, 207-213; and Catholic
Church, 142-145, 206-208, 210-212,
218, 397-399, 406-408, 418-419, 429;
and schoolteachers, 137, 139-142;
and encouragement of learning,
152; and education of girls, 153
and Coalition, 157, 159, 175n; and
formation of ministry of October 29,
68-69, 155-156, 175-176, 180-181;
and elections of 1842, 188, 193-194;
policy towards the Chamber, 183,
187; danger in these methods, 189;
frequency of speeches, 205; and
elections of 1846, 217-219, 221; and
policy after 1846, 248-252; and
economic crisis, 230-235; and 1848,
254-262; knowledge of foreign
affairs, 263; methods and principles
of foreign affairs, 266-283, 291-300,
318
characteristics as historian, 327-
330, 331-335; methods, 346-352;
and the history of civilization, 336-
337; and the decline of Rome, 340-
341; and Charlemagne, 342-343,
352; and feudalism, 343-345; and
English history, 344-345, 352-366,
369; and American history, 366;
compared to Michelet, 370-374
rôle as theologian, 379-386, 394,
406; and Reformation, 396; and
Calvin, 413-415; and Pelagianism,
349-350, 414; and Christian doctrine,
399-409; and the person and teaching
of Christ, 409-413; and declaration
of faith, 419-422, 426-428; and
Synod, 423-428; nature of his
Protestantism, 429
shortcomings of, 81-83, 85-86, 255,
273, 290-291, 316, 319, 351-352,
363-365, 402, 406, 428-430, 435-440;
eclecticism of, 86, 128, 339-340, 436;
various judgements on, 11-14, 50,
60; conclusion on, 440-441
and Odilon Barrot, 156; and
Lamartine, 197, 200, 371-372; and
Louis-Philippe, 36, 50, 165, 175-176,
225, 231, 281-282; and Molé, 64, 68,
157, 178; and Napoleon, 113, 342,
348; and Napoleon III, 9-10; and
Palmerston, 276-280, 286-288; and
Peel, 279, 367-368; and Lord John
Russell, 22, 275, 278, 288; and
Soult, 68-69, 184-185; and Talleyrand, 51; and Thiers, 6-7, 176-180,
181-182, 186n., 190, 192; and